T0202958

Lecture Notes in Computer Science 14215

The series Lecture Notes in Computer Science (LNCS), including its subseries Lecture Notes in Artificial Intelligence (LNAI) and Lecture Notes in Bioinformatics (LNBI), has established itself as a medium for the publication of new developments in computer science and information technology research, teaching, and education.

LNCS enjoys close cooperation with the computer science R & D community, the series counts many renowned academics among its volume editors and paper authors, and collaborates with prestigious societies. Its mission is to serve this international community by providing an invaluable service, mainly focused on the publication of conference and workshop proceedings and postproceedings. LNCS commenced publication in 1973.

Étienne André · Jun Sun

Editors

Automated Technology for Verification and Analysis

21st International Symposium, ATVA 2023
Singapore, October 24–27, 2023
Proceedings, Part I

 Springer

Editors
Étienne André (ID)
Université Sorbonne Paris Nord
Villetaneuse, France

Jun Sun (ID)
Singapore Management University
Singapore, Singapore

ISSN 0302-9743   ISSN 1611-3349 (electronic)
Lecture Notes in Computer Science
ISBN 978-3-031-45328-1   ISBN 978-3-031-45329-8 (eBook)
https://doi.org/10.1007/978-3-031-45329-8

This Springer imprint is published by the registered company Springer Nature Switzerland AG
The registered company address is: Gewerbestrasse 11, 6330 Cham, Switzerland

Paper in this product is recyclable.

Preface

This volume contains the papers presented at the 21st International Symposium on Automated Technology for Verification and Analysis (ATVA 2023). ATVA intends to promote research in theoretical and practical aspects of automated analysis, verification and synthesis by providing a forum for interaction between regional and international research communities and industry in related areas.

ATVA 2023 was organized during October 24–27, 2023 in Singapore. ATVA 2023 received 115 submissions, of which 30 were accepted as regular papers and 7 as tool papers, while 65 were rejected (another 13 were withdrawn or desk-rejected). All submitted papers went through a rigorous review process with at least 3 reviews per paper, followed by an online discussion among PC members overseen by the TPC chairs. This led to a high-quality and attractive scientific program.

This edition of ATVA was blessed by the presence of three prestigious keynote speakers, who gave talks covering current hot research topics and revealing many new interesting research directions:

- David Basin (ETH Zurich, Switzerland): Correct and Efficient Policy Monitoring, a Retrospective;
- Ewen Denney (NASA Ames Research Center, USA): Dynamic Assurance Cases for Machine-Learning Based Autonomous Systems;
- Reza Shokri (NUS, Singapore): Privacy in Machine Learning.

The conference was preceded by tutorials on important topics given by three renowned experts:

- Jin Xing Lim and Palina Tolmach (Runtime Verification Inc, USA): The K Framework: A Tool Kit for Language Semantics and Verification;
- Ewen Denney (NASA Ames Research Center, USA): Developing Assurance Cases with AdvoCATE.

ATVA 2023 would not have been successful without the contribution and involvement of the Program Committee members and the external reviewers who contributed to the review process (with 311 reviews) and the selection of the best contributions. This event would not exist if authors and contributors did not submit their proposals. We address our thanks to every person, reviewer, author, program committee member and organizing committee member involved in the success of ATVA 2023. The EasyChair system was set up for the management of ATVA 2023 supporting submission, review and volume preparation processes.

The local host and sponsor School of Computing and Information Systems, Singapore Management University provided financial support and tremendous help with registration and online facilities. The other sponsor, Springer LNCS, contributed in different forms to help run the conference smoothly. Many thanks to all the local organizers and sponsors.

We wish to express our special thanks to the General Chair, Jin Song Dong, and to the steering committee members, particularly to Yu-Fang Chen, for their valuable support.

August 2023   Étienne André
Jun Sun

Organization

General Chair

Jin Song Dong   National University of Singapore

Program Co-Chairs

Jun Sun   Singapore Management University
Étienne André   Université Sorbonne Paris Nord

Local Organization Chair

Xiaofei Xie   Singapore Management University

Publicity Chair

Lei Bu   Nanjing University

Program Committee

Étienne André	Université Sorbonne Paris Nord, France
Mohamed Faouzi Atig	Uppsala University, Sweden
Kyungmin Bae	Pohang University of Science and Technology, South Korea
Saddek Bensalem	Université Grenoble Alpes, France
Udi Boker	Reichman University, Israel
Lei Bu	Nanjing University, China
Krishnendu Chatterjee	Institute of Science and Technology, Austria
Yu-Fang Chen	Academia Sinica, Taiwan
Chih-Hong Cheng	Fraunhofer IKS and TU München, Germany
Yunja Choi	Kyungpook National University, South Korea
Thao Dang	CNRS/VERIMAG, France
Susanna Donatelli	Universita' di Torino, Italy
Alexandre Duret-Lutz	EPITA, France

Bernd Finkbeiner	CISPA Helmholtz Center for Information Security, Germany
Stefan Gruner	University of Pretoria, South Africa
Osman Hasan	National University of Sciences and Technology, Pakistan
Ichiro Hasuo	National Institute of Informatics, Japan
Jie-Hong Roland Jiang	National Taiwan University, Taiwan
Ondrej Lengal	Brno University of Technology, Czech Republic
Shang-Wei Lin	Nanyang Technological University, Singapore
Doron Peled	Bar Ilan University, Israel
Jakob Piribauer	TU Dresden, Dresden
Pavithra Prabhakar	Kansas State University, USA
Sasinee Pruekprasert	National Institute of Advanced Industrial Science and Technology, Japan
Kristin Yvonne Rozier	Iowa State University, USA
Indranil Saha	Indian Institute of Technology Kanpur, India
Ocan Sankur	Univ Rennes, CNRS, France
Fu Song	ShanghaiTech University, China
Marielle Stoelinga	University of Twente, The Netherlands
Jun Sun	Singapore Management University, Singapore
Michael Tautschnig	Queen Mary University of London, UK
Tachio Terauchi	Waseda University, Japan
Bow-Yaw Wang	Academia Sinica, Taiwan
Chao Wang	University of Southern California, USA
Jingyi Wang	Zhejiang University, China
Zhilin Wu	Chinese Academy of Sciences, China
Lijun Zhang	Chinese Academy of Sciences, China

Additional Reviewers

Amparore, Elvio Gilberto
Asadian, Hooman
Ashraf, Sobia
Badings, Thom
Beutner, Raven
Bozga, Marius
Caltais, Georgiana
Cetinkaya, Ahmet
Chandshun, Wu
Chang, Yun-Sheng
Chen, Guangke
Chen, Tian-Fu

Chen, Zhenbang
Cheng, Che
Chida, Nariyoshi
Ciardo, Gianfranco
Coenen, Norine
Conrad, Esther
Correnson, Arthur
Dayekh, Hadi
Defourné, Rosalie
Dubut, Jérémy
Dziadek, Sven
Eberhart, Clovis

Fan, Yu-Wei
Fiedor, Jan
Fisman, Dana
Frenkel, Hadar
Gao, Pengfei
Graf, Susanne
Gupta, Aishwarya
Guttenberg, Roland
Hahn, Ernst Moritz
Havlena, Vojtěch
He, Fei
Henry, Léo
Ho, Kuo-Wei
Ho, Son
Holík, Lukáš
Johannsen, Chris
Jéron, Thierry
Karimov, Toghrul
Kempa, Brian
Khoussi, Siham
Ko, Yu-Hao
Kura, Satoshi
Larraz, Daniel
Lawall, Julia
Lefaucheux, Engel
Liu, Depeng
Liu, Wanwei
Lo, Fang-Yi
Luo, Yun-Rong
Mambakam, Akshay
Marinho, Dylan
Meggendorfer, Tobias
Metzger, Niklas
Monat, Raphaël
Nicoletti, Stefano
Pavela, Jiří
Perez, Mateo
Phalakarn, Kittiphon
Pommellet, Adrien

Qin, Qi
Rashid, Adnan
Requeno, Jose Ignacio
Rogalewicz, Adam
Saivasan, Prakash
Sarac, Ege
Schilling, Christian
Schlehuber-Caissier, Philipp
Schmitt, Frederik
Schumi, Richard
Siber, Julian
Soltani, Reza
Srivathsan, B.
Su, Chia-Hsuan
Svoboda, Jakub
Síč, Juraj
Takisaka, Toru
Tsai, Wei-Lun
Turrini, Andrea
van der Wal, Djurre
Waga, Masaki
Wang, Hung-En
Wang, Jiawan
Wang, Limin
Wang, Xizao
Wei, Chun-Yu
Weininger, Maximilian
Widdershoven, Cas
Wienhöft, Patrick
Winkler, Tobias
Yang, Pengfei
Yen, Di-De
Zhang, Hanwei
Zhang, Yedi
Zhao, Qingye
Zhao, Zhe
Zhu, Ziyuan
Ziemek, Robin
Žikelić, Đorđe

Contents – Part I

Synthesis

Neural Networks

Contents – Part II

Tool Papers

Invited Talk

Correct and Efficient Policy Monitoring, a Retrospective

David Basin[1]($\boxtimes$) [iD], Srđan Krstić[1] [iD], Joshua Schneider[1] [iD],
and Dmitriy Traytel[2] [iD]

[1] Institute of Information Security, Department of Computer Science, ETH Zurich,
Zürich, Switzerland
`{basin,srdan.krstic,joshua.schneider}@inf.ethz.ch`
[2] Department of Computer Science, University of Copenhagen,
Copenhagen, Denmark
`traytel@di.ku.dk`

Abstract. The MonPoly project started over a decade ago to build
effective tools for monitoring trace properties, including functional correctness, security, and compliance policies. The original MonPoly tool
supported monitoring specifications given in metric first-order temporal
logic, an expressive specification language. It handled both the online
case, where system events are monitored as they occur, and the offline
case, monitoring logs. Our tool has evolved over time into a family of
tools and supporting infrastructure to make monitoring both scalable
and suitable for high assurance applications. We survey this evolution
which includes: (1) developing more expressive monitors, e.g., adding
aggregation operators, regular expressions, and limited forms of recursion; (2) delimiting efficiently monitorable fragments and designing new
monitoring algorithms for them; (3) supporting parallel and distributed
monitoring; (4) using theorem proving to verify monitoring algorithms
and explore extensions; and (5) carrying out ambitious case studies.

Keywords: runtime verification · monitoring · temporal logic

1 Introduction

Monitoring is a Formal Method for system analysis where one analyzes a system's behavior as system events occur, or afterwards when reading the events
from logs. The objective is to decide whether the system's observed behavior satisfies a given specification and, if not, to report violations. This problem is general
and has wide ranging applications. The events can be at any level of abstraction
(machine instructions, operating system calls, I/O events, etc.) and one can apply
monitoring to hardware, operating systems, software programs and components,
network traffic, etc. Moreover, depending on the problem domain, the specification may state ordering requirements on the events, real-time requirements on
when they occur, or requirements on the relationships between data referenced
by the events. The challenge then is to design monitors that are general enough
to handle many relevant problem domains and to make their decisions efficiently
and effectively, even in the presence of high-velocity event streams.

É. André and J. Sun (Eds.): ATVA 2023, LNCS 14215, pp. 3–30, 2023.
https://doi.org/10.1007/978-3-031-45329-8_1

Tool	Logic	Features	References	Sect.
MonPoly	MFOTL$_{\Omega,\mathrm{def}}^{\mathrm{RANF}}$	online	[20, 26, 28, 31]	4.1
CppMon	MFOTL$_{\Omega,\mathrm{def}}^{\mathrm{RANF}}$	online	[56]	4.1
StaticMon	MFOTL$_{\Omega,\mathrm{def},\mathrm{rec}}^{\mathrm{RANF}}$	online, pre-compiled	[57, 58]	4.1
HashMon	MFOTL$_{\Omega,\mathrm{def}}^{\mathrm{RANF}}$	online, randomized	[91, 92]	4.1
VeriMon	MFODL$_{\Omega,\mathrm{def},\mathrm{rec}}^{\mathrm{RANF}}$	online, verified	[16, 17, 20, 97]	4.1, 6
MFOTL2RANF	MFOTL $\rightarrow$ MFOTL^{RANF}	translation	[82, 85]	4.2
MonPoly-Reg	MFOTL	online	[26, 28]	4.3
Aerial	MDL	equivalence verdicts	[12, 35, 69]	4.4
Hydra	MDL	multi-head	[81, 84, 87]	4.4
Vydra	MDL	multi-head, verified	[81, 87]	4.4, 6
Slicing framework	MFOTL^{RANF}	offline, parallel	[15]	5.1
Slicing framework	MFOTL$_{\Omega,\mathrm{def}}^{\mathrm{RANF}}$, QTL [62]	online, parallel	[43, 94, 96]	5.2
POLIMON	MTL$^{\downarrow}$	unordered input	[32, 34]	5.3
TimelyMon	MFOTL^{RANF}	unordered input	[88]	5.3

Fig. 1. Our monitors and related tools

We have been working for over a decade on different aspects of this problem. Parts of our research were project driven, tackling challenges that arose in applying monitoring to different problem domains and making our monitoring tools scale. Other parts were curiosity driven, exploring different monitoring semantics, algorithms, specification languages, parallelization techniques, and even formal verification applied to monitoring itself. We provide here a retrospective on this work, explaining the tools we have built, summarized in Fig. 1, and highlighting their advances within the context of the larger field of runtime verification. We hope this will be of value both for those researchers interested in understanding our tools and the problems they address and those wishing to understand some of the challenges in bridging theory and practice in this exciting research area.

Our aim has been to develop foundations and tools to cover the largest possible range of applications. Our starting point has been the expressive specification language of metric first-order temporal logic (MFOTL) built on first-order logic with equality and metric temporal logic (MTL) operators. For some applications MFOTL is still not expressive enough. Hence we have systematically explored *extensions* of MFOTL (Sect. 2), such as adding aggregation operators ($-_{\Omega}$ in Fig. 1), regular expressions from dynamic logic ($-$DL), and limited forms of recursion ($-_{\mathrm{rec}}$). Unfortunately, monitoring using expressive specification languages is computationally intractable in the standard monitoring setting (Sect. 3). We have therefore explored ways to mitigate this problem by: delimiting efficiently monitorable *fragments* of MFOTL (Sect. 4), such as those monitorable using relational data structures ($-^{\mathrm{RANF}}$), and designing monitoring algorithms for them; weakening some of the requirements on monitors, such as how they present their output; and providing support for parallel and distributed monitoring (Sect. 5).

As monitoring is often used in critical applications where correctness matters, it is important that monitors themselves are correct. Part of our journey has been

$$
\begin{array}{lll|lll}
\sigma, v, i \models \mathsf{p}(\overline{t}) & \text{if } \mathsf{p}(v(\overline{t})) \in D_i^\sigma & & \sigma, v, i \models \mathsf{tpts}(t_1, t_2) & \text{if } v(t_1) = i \text{ and } v(t_2) = \tau_i^\sigma \\
\sigma, v, i \models t_1 \mathrel{\mathcal{R}} t_2 & \text{if } v(t_1) \mathrel{\mathcal{R}} v(t_2) & & \sigma, v, i \models \exists x.\ \alpha & \text{if } \exists d \in \mathbb{D}.\ \sigma, v[x \mapsto d], i \models \alpha \\
\sigma, v, i \models \neg \alpha & \text{if } \sigma, v, i \not\models \alpha & & \sigma, v, i \models \downarrow^{\mathsf{r}} x.\ \alpha & \text{if } \sigma, v[x \mapsto R_i^\sigma(\mathsf{r})], i \models \alpha
\end{array}
$$

$$
\begin{array}{ll}
\sigma, v, i \models \alpha \vee \beta & \text{if } \sigma, v, i \models \alpha \text{ or } \sigma, v, i \models \beta \\
\sigma, v, i \models \ominus_I \alpha & \text{if } i > 0,\ \tau_i^\sigma - \tau_{i-1}^\sigma \in I, \text{ and } \sigma, v, i-1 \models \alpha \\
\sigma, v, i \models \bigcirc_I \alpha & \text{if } \tau_{i+1}^\sigma - \tau_i^\sigma \in I \text{ and } \sigma, v, i+1 \models \alpha \\
\sigma, v, i \models \alpha \mathbin{\mathsf{S}_I} \beta & \text{if } \exists j \le i.\ \sigma, v, j \models \beta,\ \tau_i^\sigma - \tau_j^\sigma \in I \text{ and } \forall k.\ \text{if } j < k \le i \text{ then } \sigma, v, k \models \alpha \\
\sigma, v, i \models \alpha \mathbin{\mathsf{U}_I} \beta & \text{if } \exists j \ge i.\ \sigma, v, j \models \beta,\ \tau_j^\sigma - \tau_i^\sigma \in I \text{ and } \forall k.\ \text{if } i \le k < j \text{ then } \sigma, v, k \models \alpha \\
\sigma, v, i \models \lhd_I r & \text{if } \exists j \le i.\ (j, i) \in (\!|r|\!)_v^\sigma \text{ and } \tau_i^\sigma - \tau_j^\sigma \in I \\
\sigma, v, i \models \rhd_I r & \text{if } \exists j \ge i.\ (i, j) \in (\!|r|\!)_v^\sigma \text{ and } \tau_j^\sigma - \tau_i^\sigma \in I
\end{array}
$$

$$
\sigma, v, i \models y \leftarrow \Omega(t; \overline{g})\ \alpha \quad \text{if } v(y) = \Omega(M) \text{ and if } M = \{\!|\,|\!\} \text{ then } |\overline{g}| = 0,
$$
$$
\text{where } M = \biguplus_{\overline{d} \in \mathbb{D}^{|\overline{z}|}} \{\!| u(t) \mid \sigma, u, i \models \alpha \text{ where } u = v[\overline{z} \mapsto \overline{d}] |\!\} \text{ and } \overline{z} = \mathcal{V}(\alpha) \setminus \overline{g}
$$

$$
\begin{array}{ll}
\sigma, v, i \models \mathsf{def}\ \mathsf{p}(\overline{x}) := \alpha\ \mathsf{in}\ \beta & \text{if } \sigma[\mathsf{p} \Rrightarrow \lambda j.\ [\![\alpha; \overline{x}]\!]_j^\sigma], v, i \models \beta \\
\sigma, v, i \models \mathsf{rec}\ \mathsf{p}(\overline{x}) := \alpha\ \mathsf{in}\ \beta & \text{if } \sigma[\mathsf{p} \Rrightarrow \lambda j.\ \mathsf{fp}_j(\lambda S\ k.\ [\![\alpha; \overline{x}]\!]_k^{\sigma[\mathsf{p} \Rrightarrow S]})], v, i \models \beta
\end{array}
$$

$$
\begin{array}{lll}
(\!|\star|\!)_v^\sigma = \{(i, i+1) \mid i \in \mathbb{N}\} & (\!|r + s|\!)_v^\sigma = (\!|r|\!)_v^\sigma \cup (\!|s|\!)_v^\sigma & (\!|r^*|\!)_v^\sigma = ((\!|r|\!)_v^\sigma)^* \\
(\!|\alpha?|\!)_v^\sigma = \{(i, i) \mid \sigma, v, i \models \alpha\} & (\!|rs|\!)_v^\sigma = \{(i, k) \mid \exists j.\ (i, j) \in (\!|r|\!)_v^\sigma \text{ and } (j, k) \in (\!|s|\!)_v^\sigma\} & \\
[\![\alpha; \overline{x}]\!]_i^\sigma = \{v(\overline{x}) \mid \sigma, v, i \models \alpha\} & \mathsf{fp}_i(F) = F\ (\lambda j.\ \mathsf{if}\ j < i\ \mathsf{then}\ \mathsf{fp}_j(F)\ \mathsf{else}\ \{\})\ i &
\end{array}
$$

Fig. 2. Semantics of MFOTL (gray background) and its extensions

in using theorem provers to formally verify our monitoring algorithms (Sect. 6). The verified monitors can be run directly, with some performance slowdown compared to their optimized but unverified brethren. Alternatively they can be used to ascertain the correctness of other monitors using differential testing.

We describe our results here as well as substantial case studies that we carried out to learn where bottlenecks and limitations are in practice (Sect. 7).

2 The Logic

We present a logic that unifies our tools' specification languages. Presently, no tool supports all presented features, but all features are supported by some tool (see Fig. 1). We start with metric first-order temporal logic (MFOTL) [28,47] and extend it with regular expressions [17,36], aggregations operators [24], a freeze quantifier [32], and a recursion operator [102]. We refer to the cited publications for detailed explanations and the historical background of each operator.

We fix a set of event names $\mathbb{E}$ and for simplicity assume a single infinite domain of values $\mathbb{D}$. We consider $\mathbb{D}$ to include integers, strings, and floats, as well as POSIX regular expressions to match strings against (not to be confused with the temporal regular expressions occurring in formulas). The event names $\mathsf{p} \in \mathbb{E}$ have associated arities $\iota(\mathsf{p}) \in \mathbb{N}$. An *event* $\mathsf{p}(d_1, \ldots, d_{\iota(\mathsf{p})})$ is an element of $\mathbb{E} \times \mathbb{D}^*$. We further fix infinite sets of variables $\mathbb{V}$ and registers $\mathbb{R}$ such that $\mathbb{V}$, $\mathbb{R}$, $\mathbb{D}$, and $\mathbb{E}$ are all pairwise disjoint. Let $\mathbb{I}$ be the set of nonempty intervals $[a, b) := \{x \in \mathbb{N} \mid a \le x < b\}$, where $a \in \mathbb{N}$, $b \in \mathbb{N} \cup \{\infty\}$, and $a < b$. Terms $\mathbb{T}$ include $\mathbb{V} \cup \mathbb{D}$ and can also be constructed by applying operators defined on $\mathbb{D}$ (e.g., $+$ and $\times$ on integers) to terms. Formulas φ and temporal regular expressions r are defined (mutually) inductively, where t, p, r, x, and I range over $\mathbb{T}$, $\mathbb{E}$, $\mathbb{R}$, $\mathbb{V}$, and $\mathbb{I}$, respectively:

$$\varphi ::= \mathsf{p}(\bar{t}) \mid \mathsf{tpts}(t,t) \mid t\,\mathcal{R}\,t \mid \neg\varphi \mid \varphi \vee \varphi \mid \exists x.\,\varphi \mid \ominus_I\,\varphi \mid \bigcirc_I\,\varphi \mid \varphi\,\mathsf{S}_I\,\varphi \mid \varphi\,\mathsf{U}_I\,\varphi \mid$$
$$\quad\ \ \downarrow^r\!x.\,\varphi \mid x \leftarrow \Omega(t;\bar{x})\,\varphi \mid \mathsf{def}\ \mathsf{p}(\bar{x}) := \varphi\ \mathsf{in}\ \varphi \mid \mathsf{rec}\ \mathsf{p}(\bar{x}) := \varphi\ \mathsf{in}\ \varphi \mid \lhd_I\,r \mid \rhd_I\,r$$
$$r ::= \star \mid \varphi? \mid rr \mid r+r \mid r^*.$$

Here $\mathcal{R} \in \{=, <, \leq, \overset{\text{RE}}{\Leftrightarrow}\}$ is a rigid (i.e., non-changing) relation and $\Omega \in \{\mathsf{CNT}, \mathsf{SUM}, \mathsf{AVG}, \mathsf{MIN}, \mathsf{MAX}, \mathsf{MED}\}$ is an aggregation function on multisets, e.g., $\mathsf{CNT}\,\{\!\{1,1,2\}\!\} = 3$ and $\mathsf{SUM}\,\{\!\{1,1,2\}\!\} = 4$. We write $\bar{a}$ for a list of zero or more a.

MFOTL formulas are built from operators shown in gray background. Formulas $\mathsf{p}(\bar{t})$ are called (*atomic*) *predicates*. The special predicate tpts refers to the current time(-point and time-stamp). Besides logical operators ($\neg$, $\vee$, $\exists$) and rigid relations ($\mathcal{R}$), MFOTL has metric past and future temporal operators $\ominus$ (previous), $\bigcirc$ (next), S (since), and U (until), which may be nested freely. Metric temporal logic (MTL) is a fragment of MFOTL with nullary predicates and no quantification.

The addition of $\lhd$ (past match) and $\rhd$ (future match) operators to MTL and MFOTL results in their dynamic variants MDL and MFODL, respectively. These operators use temporal regular expressions constructed from wildcard ($\star$), test (?), concatenation, alternation ($+$), and star ($*$) operations. We also consider formulas with freeze quantification $\downarrow^r\!x.\,\alpha$. In particular, MTL$^{\downarrow}$ is the extension of MTL with freeze quantifiers. Finally, MFOTL is extended with aggregations $x \leftarrow \Omega(t;\bar{x})\ \alpha$ (called MFOTL$_\Omega$), and with non-recursive (MFOTL$_{\mathsf{def}}$) and recursive (MFOTL$_{\mathsf{rec}}$) definitions. The latter two are given by formulas of the form $\mathsf{def}\ \mathsf{p}(\bar{x}) := \alpha\ \mathsf{in}\ \beta$ and $\mathsf{rec}\ \mathsf{p}(\bar{x}) := \alpha\ \mathsf{in}\ \beta$, respectively. We derive additional operators: truth $\top := 0 = 0$, falsehood $\bot := \neg\top$, inequality $t_1 \neq t_2 := \neg(t_1 = t_2)$, conjunction $\alpha \wedge \beta := \neg(\neg\alpha \vee \neg\beta)$, implication $\alpha \rightarrow \beta := \neg\alpha \vee \beta$, current time-point $\mathsf{tp}(i) := \exists t.\,\mathsf{tpts}(i,t)$ and time-stamp $\mathsf{ts}(t) := \exists i.\,\mathsf{tpts}(i,t)$, universal quantification $\forall x.\,\alpha := \neg(\exists x.\,\neg\alpha)$, eventually $\Diamond_I\,\alpha := \top\,\mathsf{U}_I\,\alpha$, always $\Box_I\,\alpha := \neg\Diamond_I\,\neg\alpha$, once $\blacklozenge_I\,\alpha := \top\,\mathsf{S}_I\,\alpha$, and historically $\blacksquare_I\,\alpha := \neg\blacklozenge_I\,\neg\alpha$. A formula is *future-bounded* iff all subformulas of the form $\alpha\,\mathsf{U}_{[a,b)}\,\beta$ and $\rhd_{[a,b)}\,r$ (including derived operators) satisfy $b < \infty$.

Formulas are interpreted over *temporal structures*, which model executions of a monitored system. A temporal structure σ is an infinite sequence $(\tau_i^\sigma, D_i^\sigma, R_i^\sigma)_{i\in\mathbb{N}}$, where $\tau_i^\sigma \in \mathbb{N}$ is a time-stamp, the *database* $D_i^\sigma \in \mathcal{P}(\mathbb{E} \times \mathbb{D}^*)$ is a finite set of events, and the *register map* R_i^σ assigns each register $\mathsf{r} \in \mathbb{R}$ a single domain value from $\mathbb{D}$. Time-stamps must be *monotone* ($\forall i.\,\tau_i \leq \tau_{i+1}$) and *progressing* ($\forall\tau.\,\exists i.\,\tau < \tau_i$). Note that different time-points $i \neq j$ may have the same time-stamp $\tau_i = \tau_j$.

Figure 2 shows the relation $\sigma, v, i \models \varphi$ defining the satisfaction of the formula φ for a temporal structure σ, a valuation v, and a time-point i. The valuation v assigns domain values to φ's free variables $\mathcal{V}(\varphi)$. Overloading notation, v is also the extension of v to terms $\mathbb{T}$ in the obvious way, e.g., $v(t_1 + t_2) = v(t_1) + v(t_2)$. The valuation $v[x \mapsto d]$ is equal to v except that d is assigned to the variable x. Similarly, trace $\sigma[\mathsf{p} \Rightarrow X]$ is equal to σ except that the set of events for predicate p from D_i^g is replaced by $X(i)$ at each time-point i. The rigid relation $x \overset{\mathsf{RE}}{\Leftarrow} r$ is satisfied by all strings x matched by the POSIX regular expression r. The other rigid relations behave as expected. Aggregations support grouping using variables $\overline{g}$ and their semantics is defined using multiset union $\uplus$. The additional operators are intuitive, e.g., unfolding a non-recursive definition (even under temporal operators) results in an equivalent formula. The semantics of recursive definitions is as expected provided all recursive occurrences of p in φ are evaluated at past time-points.

For $I \in \mathbb{I}$ and $n \in \mathbb{N}$, let $I - n$ denote the interval $\{x - n \mid x \in I\} \cap \mathbb{N}$ and I^- the set of intervals $\{I - m \mid m \in \mathbb{N}\} \setminus \{\varnothing\}$, which is always finite. We write $\mathsf{SF}(\varphi)$ for the set of φ's subformulas and define *interval-skewed subformulas* $\mathsf{ISF}(\varphi)$ as

$$\mathsf{SF}(\varphi) \cup \{\alpha\,\mathsf{S}_J\,\beta \mid \alpha\,\mathsf{S}_I\,\beta \in \mathsf{SF}(\varphi), J \in I^-\} \cup \{\,\triangleleft_J r \mid\, \triangleleft_I r \in \mathsf{SF}(\varphi), J \in I^-\}$$
$$\cup \{\alpha\,\mathsf{U}_J\,\beta \mid \alpha\,\mathsf{U}_I\,\beta \in \mathsf{SF}(\varphi), J \in I^-\} \cup \{\triangleright_J r \mid \triangleright_I r \in \mathsf{SF}(\varphi), J \in I^-\}.$$

3 Monitoring Setting

The central problem in monitoring is, given a policy and a trace from a monitored system, to decide whether the trace satisfies the policy. The monitoring problem has many variants that motivate specialized algorithms. For example, one may grant the monitor random access to the trace for efficiency, or require the timely detection of violations for some applications. Here we sketch the most important problem dimensions as well as the setting in which we position our tools. A more detailed taxonomy for runtime verification tools has been developed by Falcone et al. [52] and extensive introductions to the topic by many others [11,72,90].

Offline monitors run after the monitored system has terminated and therefore read the complete trace, typically stored as a log file. In contrast, *online* monitors run while the monitored system executes and observe a trace's prefix up to the present. They typically receive the trace incrementally, as a stream of events, one event at a time. Equivalently, online monitors read the trace with a single one-way reading head that moves forward only, whereas offline monitors have random access to the entire trace. Every online monitor can be used offline by replaying the log file as a stream, but it may be less efficient than a dedicated offline tool. We primarily develop online monitors, yet we propose a multi-head approach that lies in between offline and online monitoring (Sect. 4.4).

The linear order of events observed by a monitor (be it in a log file or a stream) does not necessarily coincide with the events' temporal order of occurrence in the monitored system. We speak of a *trace* only when they do coincide; otherwise, we call the monitor's input *observations*. For example, most distributed systems do not provide traces in this strict sense because it is difficult to reconstruct the true order of events [98]. Our monitors operate on traces by default. We discuss two approaches that handle more general observations in Sect. 5.3.

All our approaches work with policies of the form $\square\,\varphi$ where φ is future-bounded. Such policies describe *safety properties*,[1] characterized by *bad pre-*

---

[1] Although not every safety property expressible in MFOTL has this form [47].

fixes [5], which are finite traces with all their infinite extensions violating the policy. Our monitors detect all bad prefixes of $\square\,\varphi$ by *evaluating* the formula $\neg\,\varphi$ at every time-point. Their output is monotonic with respect to time-points and consists of exactly those time-points at which $\neg\,\varphi$ is satisfied in all infinite extensions. A non-empty output indicates that $\square\,\varphi$ is violated. Dually, *co-safety* properties [60] of the form $\Diamond\,\varphi'$ can be monitored by evaluating φ' directly.

A monitor's output may range from a single bit to detailed proof trees [73]. As described above, to monitor a policy $\square\,\forall\overline{x}.\ \varphi$, our monitors evaluate $\neg\,\forall\overline{x}.\ \varphi$ at every time-point. After pushing the negation in and dropping the leading existential quantifiers, they can evaluate $\neg\,\varphi$, which has free variables. The computed valuations are output together with the corresponding time-points and provide insight into the policy's violations. The output is never provided for time-points beyond the observed trace prefix. This cannot be avoided in general: a policy $\square\,\varphi$ is violated on all traces (and therefore also on all extensions of the empty prefix) iff φ is unsatisfiable, which is undecidable for MFOTL [22].

4   Restrictions and Algorithms

We describe our algorithms for monitoring fragments of our logic. Restricting the policy language has two advantages. First, without restrictions it may be impossible to build a monitor that satisfies the desired properties. For example, detecting bad prefixes is already undecidable for a much weaker form of quantification than that of MFOTL [37]. Second, algorithms can be tailored to language fragments yielding better performance in exchange for less expressiveness or conciseness.

We focus primarily on fragments that retain MFOTL's first-order aspects and which can be monitored using finite relations (Sect. 4.1). A monitor-independent translation makes these fragments more user-friendly by lifting syntactic restrictions (Sect. 4.2). We also compare the finite relation approach to automatic structures (Sect. 4.3). While less expressive, propositional languages are attractive because they admit better complexity. Notably, we developed two algorithms that achieve (almost) event-rate independence for MDL (Sect. 4.4).

4.1   Relational Algebra Normal Form

In database theory, Codd's theorem [48] states that relational algebra and domain-independent queries expressed using the relational calculus are equally expressive. Relational algebra consists of effectively computable operations on finite relations, whereas the relational calculus is essentially first-order logic. Domain-independence [51] ensures finite query results, independently of the domain that the query's variables range over. *Relational algebra normal form (RANF)* [1,55] is a syntactically defined, domain-independent fragment of the relational calculus with a straightforward translation to the algebra.

The policy language fragment supported by MonPoly [27,31], VeriMon [16, 97], CppMon [56], StaticMon [58], and HashMon [92] is a generalization of RANF

Pattern	Constraint	Relational operation
$r(\bar{t})$	$\forall i.\ t_i \in \mathbb{V} \cup \mathbb{D}$	selection and projection
$\neg\,\alpha$	$\mathcal{V}(\alpha) = \emptyset$	complement relative to $\{()\}$
$\alpha \wedge \beta$	none	natural join
$\alpha \wedge t_1\ \mathcal{R}\ t_2$	$\mathcal{V}(t_1) \cup \mathcal{V}(t_2) \subseteq \mathcal{V}(\alpha)$	selection
$\alpha \wedge x = t$	$\mathcal{V}(t) \subseteq \mathcal{V}(\alpha),\ x \notin \mathcal{V}(\alpha)$	generalized projection
$\alpha \wedge \neg\,\beta$	$\mathcal{V}(\beta) \subseteq \mathcal{V}(\alpha)$	anti-join (generalized difference)
$\alpha \vee \beta$	$\mathcal{V}(\alpha) = \mathcal{V}(\beta)$	union
$\exists x.\ \alpha$	none	projection
$y \leftarrow \Omega(t; \bar{g})\ \alpha$	$\mathcal{V}(t) \cup \bar{g} \subseteq \mathcal{V}(\alpha),\ y \notin \bar{g}$	group-by and aggregation
$\ominus_I\,\alpha,\ \ominus_I\,\alpha$	none	$\left.\rule{0pt}{36pt}\right\}$ monitor-specific
$\alpha\,\mathsf{S}_I\,\beta,\ (\neg\alpha)\,\mathsf{S}_I\,\beta$	$\mathcal{V}(\alpha) \subseteq \mathcal{V}(\beta)$	
$\alpha\,\mathsf{U}_I\,\beta,\ (\neg\alpha)\,\mathsf{U}_I\,\beta$	$\mathcal{V}(\alpha) \subseteq \mathcal{V}(\beta)$, bounded I	

Fig. 3. Relational algebra normal form for a subset of MFOTL

from first-order logic to MFOTL. We sometimes call it the *monitorable fragment* [28] (not to be confused with other notions of monitorability [80]). The motivation is the same as for databases: one can translate this fragment directly to operations acting on (streams of) finite relations. In the following, we first describe aspects common to the aforementioned RANF-based tools, thus speaking of a single abstract monitor, before explaining the main differences between the tools.

General Approach. The basic idea is to view the policy formula as a tree whose nodes correspond to relational operations. The monitor processes the input trace incrementally. Every time-point gives rise to a database that supplies the leaves of the tree with relations. Then, the monitor evaluates the tree, bottom up. The relation obtained at the root, which is appended to the in-order output stream, contains the satisfying valuations of the formula. The main difference to the database setting is that some tree nodes, namely those corresponding to temporal operators, are stateful. Future operators are handled by delaying intermediate computations that depend on those operators. Our monitors over-approximate the required delay using the formula's intervals. Hence they do not detect *minimal* bad prefixes; however, they eventually report a bad prefix when there is one.

Figure 3 defines the RANF fragment for a subset of our logic; we discuss more advanced operators below for those tools that support them. The first column contains patterns: any formula obtained by instantiating a pattern is in RANF if the instantiations of α and β are in RANF, and the constraints in the second column are satisfied. Formulas can often be rewritten to obtain an equivalent RANF formula, e.g., by applying the distributive law to $\mathsf{p}(x, y) \wedge (\mathsf{q}(x) \vee \mathsf{q}(y))$. However, finding suitable rewrite rules becomes difficult once temporal operators are involved. MonPoly implements a simple but incomplete rewriting procedure. We describe a more general translation in Sect. 4.2. The third column in Fig. 3 describes the relational algebra operation that is used to evaluate formulas matching the pattern. Most are standard [1]. The generalized projection evaluates the term t on each tuple in the input relation to compute the value assigned to x in the output relation. The anti-join generalizes set difference such that the "negative" relation may have a subset of the other relation's variables. Aggregation operators are computed by first partitioning the relation into groups (if there are grouping variables) and afterwards, for each group, evaluating the term t on the tuples and combining the results using the appropriate aggregation function (e.g., sum, count, or average).

Temporal Operators. The implementation of the temporal operators is specific to the monitoring setting, although temporal–relational algebras have been studied previously [79,100]. A basic approach, used in MonPoly's original implementation [26,28], employs auxiliary relations that are maintained as part of the monitor's state. For $\ominus_I \alpha$, the auxiliary relation is simply the evaluation result for α at the previous time-point. For $\alpha \, \mathsf{S}_I \, \beta$, the auxiliary relation extends the tuples obtained from β with the corresponding time-stamp, which is used to check the interval constraint I. All tuples must satisfy α since the time-point when they were most recently added to the relation. Several optimizations are possible. For example, the special cases $\diamondsuit$ and $\diamond$ benefit from a sliding-window algorithm [30]. A specialized data structure that improves the evaluation time of S in general was first introduced in VeriMon [17]. The evaluation of future temporal operators is not symmetric to the past operators. Specifically, $\alpha \, \mathsf{U}_I \, \beta$ requires an additional auxiliary relation that stores the time-points at which uninterrupted α sequences start.

Example. We explain how a MonPoly-style algorithm monitors the policy $\Box \forall x. \, \mathsf{p}(x) \rightarrow \diamondsuit_{[0,3]} \, \mathsf{q}(x)$. Specifically, it evaluates $\neg \varphi \equiv \mathsf{p}(x) \wedge \neg \chi$, where $\chi \equiv \diamondsuit_{[0,3]} \, \mathsf{q}(x)$. All subformulas of $\neg \varphi$ have a single free variable x and their evaluation results are thus all unary relations, i.e., sets. The monitor maintains an additional binary relation S_χ in its state, which is used for the $\diamondsuit_{[0,3]}$ operator. This relation stores pairs (τ, x) such that the event $\mathsf{q}(x)$ occurred most 3 time units ago, and τ is the most recent time-stamp for the event. For each input $(\tau_i^\sigma, D_i^\sigma, R_i^\sigma)$, corresponding to the time-point i, the monitor proceeds as follows.

(1) Evaluate $\mathsf{q}(x)$ by computing $E_\mathsf{q} = \{x \mid \mathsf{q}(x) \in D_i^\sigma\}$.
(2) Remove pairs (τ, x) from S_χ where $\tau_i^\sigma - \tau > 3$ or $x \in E_\mathsf{q}$, then add (τ_i^σ, x) for all $x \in E_\mathsf{q}$. This restores S_χ's invariant.
(3) The result of χ is $E_\chi = \{x \mid (\tau, x) \in S_\chi\}$.
(4) Evaluate $\mathsf{p}(x)$ by computing $E_\mathsf{p} = \{x \mid \mathsf{p}(x) \in D_i^\sigma\}$.
(5) Compute $E_{\neg \varphi} = E_\mathsf{p} \backslash E_\chi$ as a special case of anti-join to evaluate $\mathsf{p}(x) \wedge \neg \chi$.
(6) The formula $\neg \varphi$ is satisfied (i.e., the policy is violated) at time-point i iff $E_{\neg \varphi}$ is non-empty. In this case, the monitor outputs $E_{\neg \varphi}$.

Tool-Specific Details and Extensions. The main difference between MonPoly's and VeriMon's algorithms is the scheduling in the presence of delays due to future operators. VeriMon uses buffers attached to every binary operator to "align" the relations computed for the two operands. It evaluates the operator whenever a pair of relations (for the same time-point) is available. The operands are evaluated independently and eagerly. In contrast, MonPoly's scheduling is asymmetric: the second operand is evaluated only once the first has yielded a result, which requires buffering for the atomic predicates. The two strategies differ in their memory usage, which is incomparable because the buffered relations' size depends on the formula.

Extensions compatible with the RANF approach include the "dynamic" operators $\lhd$ and $\rhd$, as well as the def and rec constructs. The operators $\lhd$ and $\rhd$ generalize S and U to regular expressions. We have implemented them in VeriMon using Antimirov's partial derivatives [6]. The syntactic restrictions that guarantee finite relations are subtle, and we refer to the corresponding paper [17] for details. To evaluate def $\mathsf{p}(\overline{x}) := \alpha$ in β, our monitors evaluate α eagerly first and buffer any results to be used in the subsequent evaluation of β. For rec, which is currently supported by VeriMon and StaticMon, we exploit that only the valuations of p at past time-points are relevant when evaluating α. Hence no fixpoint computation is required. The tools syntactically check that every use of p in α is *guarded* by a strict past operator, such as $\ominus$ or $\diamondsuit_I$, where I does not include zero. This guarantees that the monitor can eventually evaluate every time-point [102].

The monitors mentioned so far use immutable tree data structures to represent finite relations. CppMon [56] reimplements VeriMon's algorithm in C++ using mutable hash tables. StaticMon develops this idea further by using C++ template metaprogramming [2] to generate an optimized monitor program tailored for each formula. It outperforms MonPoly, VeriMon, and CppMon on many benchmarks [58]. HashMon [92] reuses MonPoly's evaluation algorithm. In addition, HashMon can automatically replace large domain values, such as long strings, by short, randomized hash values to reduce the monitor's memory usage.

4.2   Translation to RANF

The restrictions imposed by the RANF on negations and the subformula's free variables may hamper concise, intuitive formalizations. While one can often rewrite a formula manually into an equivalent RANF representation, this increases the risk of formalization errors. For example, it is difficult to rewrite the formula $\mathsf{p}(x) \land (\mathsf{q}(x, y) \mathsf{S} \mathsf{r}(y))$, which is not in RANF because of the subformula $\mathsf{q}(x, y) \mathsf{S} \mathsf{r}(y)$. However, this formula is actually domain-independent as $\mathsf{p}(x)$ and $\mathsf{r}(y)$ jointly provide an upper bound on the set of satisfying valuations.

Raszyk proposed an automatic translation for *arbitrary* relational calculus queries [83] and MFOTL formulas [85] into RANF. The translation, implemented in the tool MFOTL2RANF, introduces an additional free variable x_∞. If $x_\infty = 1$ in any satisfying valuation, the set of satisfying valuations for the given trace prefix is infinite and no further guarantees are made. This case cannot occur if the original formula is domain-independent. Otherwise, the satisfying valuations without x_∞ correspond precisely to those of the original formula. For the above example, we get (with minor simplifications)

$$\begin{aligned}
\Big(p(x) \land \big(q(x,y) \mathbin{S} ((\Diamond\, q(x,y)) \land r(y)) \big) \lor \\
p(x) \land \big(q(x,y) \mathbin{S} (q(x,y) \land \ominus ((\bigcirc q(x,y)) \land (\neg \Diamond\, q(x,y)) \land r(y))) \big) \lor \\
p(x) \land r(y) \land \neg \Diamond\, q(x,y) \Big) \land x_\infty = 0 \,.
\end{aligned}$$

The translation detects the domain-independence and it sets x_∞ to zero. The three disjuncts correspond to a case distinction over possible origins of relevant values for x in the evaluation of the subformula $q(x,y) \mathbin{S} r(y)$: either there is a $q(x,y)$ event concurrent with or before $r(y)$, or the earliest occurrence of $q(x,y)$ is strictly within the span of S, or there is no such occurrence and $p(x)$ serves as the bound.

Adding the automatic translation to our monitors is ongoing work. It is an open question whether and how the translation can be extended to cover additional features of MFOTL and our extensions, such as inequalities, aggregations, and rec.

4.3 Automatic Structures

An alternative approach that lifts the restrictions of RANF is to replace finite relations with *automatic structures* [42,68]. These structures represent each relation as a finite-state automaton that recognizes those (suitably encoded) tuples that are in the relation. The main advantage is that automatic structures are closed under all Boolean operations, including negation and projection. Moreover, they can represent and operate on (a subset of the) infinite relations.

Binary decision diagrams (BDDs) are an efficient implementation of automatic structures. They are used in an alternative implementation of MonPoly's algorithm called MonPoly-Reg [26,28], as well as Havelund et al.'s DejaVu tool [61,62]. The two monitors mainly differ in the encoding of tuples representing valuations. MonPoly-Reg, which supports only integer values, uses the MONA library [64], whose automata natively read multiple variables in parallel. DejaVu translates values to bitstrings, which it then concatenates into tuples.

The use of automatic structures has drawbacks. All operators in terms (e.g., $+$) and all rigid relations (e.g., $\leq$), must be expressible as regular languages. This generally limits the scope to Presburger arithmetic and none of the above tools handle aggregations. Moreover, the time and memory used by the BDD operations depend on the internal variable ordering and can be unpredictable [102].

4.4 Propositional Monitoring

A monitor's time and memory performance depends on the sizes of its inputs, i.e., the formula and trace. The latter is typically larger than the former by orders of magnitude. Therefore, one ideally uses *trace-length independent* monitors, whose memory complexity is independent of the trace size. Moreover, for monitors that support real-time constraints, it is desirable that the memory complexity be independent of the trace's event rate, i.e., the number of events per unit of time. Traces arising in practice have a bound on their event rate, although the bound may be unknown in advance. We henceforth focus on such *(event-rate) bounded traces.*

Both event-rate independent (ERI) and trace-length independent (TLI) monitoring algorithms are not attainable for first-order specifications. For example, monitoring $\Diamond\, \mathsf{p}(x)$ requires, in the worst case, memory proportional to the entire trace prefix seen by the monitor. In contrast, TLI monitoring algorithms for the propositional fragments of MFOTL (like MTL) have been proposed in the past. These, however, deviate from our monitoring setting (Sect. 3): they either do not support future operators [29,33,63], only produce a single Boolean verdict for a formula at the trace's first time-point [53,99], or access the trace in an offline manner [89]. The challenge is to develop an online ERI algorithm that supports both future operators and produces verdicts for every time-point. Our monitors achieve this by operating in a slightly modified monitoring setting: they either output out-of-order equivalence verdicts, or use multiple reading heads.

Equivalence Verdicts. Our Aerial tool [12,35] solves the above challenge by outputting verdicts differently. In addition to the standard Boolean verdicts, it outputs equivalence verdicts of the form $j \equiv i$ stating that the verdict at time-point j is identical to the verdict at an earlier time-point $i < j$, although both verdicts are currently unknown. This makes Aerial's output non-monotonic with respect to time-points and requires slightly more effort to understand. To output equivalence verdicts, the algorithm must refer to natural numbers encoding time-points, which requires logarithmic space as time-points increase with the trace length. Aerial refers to time-points using an offset within a block of consecutive time-points labeled with the same time-stamp. It therefore requires logarithmic space in the event rate, since the size of such a block is bounded by the event rate. Due to this logarithmic dependence, Aerial is an *almost* ERI algorithm.

As an example, consider the policy $\square\,(\mathsf{p} \to \Diamond_{[0,3]}\, \mathsf{q})$ similar to the one from Sect. 4.1, only propositional and with a future $\Diamond_{[0,3]}$ operator. The equation

$$\sigma, v, i \models \Diamond_I\, \alpha \quad \text{iff} \quad \sigma, v, i \models \alpha \text{ or } \sigma, v, i+1 \models \Diamond_{I-(\tau_{i+1}-\tau_i)}\, \alpha$$

reduces the satisfaction of $\Diamond_I\, \alpha$ to a disjunction of the satisfaction of α at the same time-point i and the satisfaction of $\Diamond_{I-(\tau_{i+1}-\tau_i)}\, \alpha$ at the next time-point $i+1$. The algorithm can immediately compute the satisfaction at the current time-point i, but it must wait for the one at the next time-point. This also means that after processing time-point i, the algorithm cannot store a Boolean verdict for the formula $\Diamond_I\, \alpha$ in its state. Instead, it stores a dependency in the form of a pointer to the part of its state referring to $\Diamond_{I-(\tau_{i+1}-\tau_i)}\, \alpha$, which becomes available after processing time-point $i + 1$. More generally, for every (interval-skewed) subformula (recall ISF$(\cdot)$ from Sect. 2), the algorithm stores a Boolean combination of such dependencies in the form of symbolic Boolean expressions. By processing the subsequent time-points, the algorithm may resolve some expressions to Boolean values and output them as verdicts. Crucially, if the algorithm detects two semantically equivalent Boolean expressions for the top-level formula at different time-points, it outputs an equivalence verdict and removes one of the two expressions from its state. As the number of semantically different Boolean expressions only depends on the formula, so does the space needed to store them. Aerial extends this idea to MDL operators $\triangleleft$ and $\triangleright$ using partial derivatives [6].

Multi-head Monitoring. Our Hydra tool [84,87] implements an ERI algorithm that supports both past and future operators, but, unlike Aerial, produces *Boolean* verdicts in time-point order. It achieves this by using multiple independent and unidirectional reading heads. If an event is needed for subsequent analysis after it was read, a standard online monitor must keep it in its memory. The idea of using multiple heads is to avoid this memory usage and rely on one of the reading heads to read the event again. The way Hydra reads its input trace makes it neither an online nor an offline monitor. An online monitor does not require the trace to be persistent, whereas Hydra requires this for the part of the trace between its first and last reading head. In contrast, an offline monitor has a reading head without movement constraints, while all of Hydra's reading heads are unidirectional.

Conceptually, a multi-head monitor for an MTL formula φ is built recursively from multi-head (sub-)monitors, one for each direct subformula of φ. The total number of reading heads equals the number of atomic predicates in φ. The algorithm recursively *steps* the monitors in a loop, where a step either advances one reading head or propagates a cached verdict from a sub-monitor to its parent. Once every sub-monitor for φ has produced a verdict, the algorithm computes as many verdicts for φ as possible (which may be none) based on the MTL semantics of φ's top-level operator. For example, Hydra monitors the policy $\square\, (\mathsf{p} \rightarrow \Diamond_{[0,3]}\, \mathsf{q})$ using two reading heads for p and q. The $\Diamond_{[0,3]}$ operator stores a run-length encoded list of integers. In the list, zeros representing time-points are interleaved with the (positive) time-stamp differences between them. The list encodes a sequence of time-points, spanning a time-stamp difference of at most 3, at which q is *not* satisfied. It is updated using the verdicts from the head for q, which runs ahead. Specifically, whenever the head reports a q event, all time-points in the list become positive verdicts for the $\Diamond_{[0,3]}$ operator (after checking the interval constraint). Finally, the $\rightarrow$ operator combines the verdicts returned by its sub-monitors.

Hydra generalizes [86] the idea of multi-head monitoring to MDL operators $\triangleleft$ and $\triangleright$ using a number of heads exponential in the formula's size [87]. Both Aerial and Hydra outperform MonPoly on their specialized fragment.

5   Parallelization

The algorithms described in Sect. 4 all execute sequentially. The only way to make them faster (beyond clever optimizations) is to use a faster processor, which clearly has its limits. It is thus natural to ask how one can parallelize the existing algorithms or develop new parallel ones, which is not straightforward as the linear nature of traces results in a bias towards sequential processing. Theoretical results are promising: Kuhtz and Finkbeiner [70] and later Bundala and Ouaknine [44] showed that LTL and MTL monitoring over finite traces is in the highly parallelizable circuit complexity class NC. However, these results do not generalize to first-order policies, where the complexity rises to PSPACE-complete [37], which likely rules out fast parallel algorithms. We must therefore resort to a best effort strategy.

We discuss task-parallel and data-parallel approaches. With task parallelism, independent operations within the monitor are executed in parallel. Data parallelism partitions the data instead, i.e., the trace. While parallel monitoring, distributed monitoring, and monitoring of distributed systems all have different requirements, there are some connections that we discuss in Sect. 5.3.

5.1   Scalable Offline Monitoring

Offline monitors are more easily parallelized than online ones because all data is available from the start. We summarize results on applying the MapReduce framework [49] to offline monitoring. MapReduce is suitable for computations on large sets of data items. There are two phases. In the first phase, each data item is *mapped* (transformed) individually and the results are each assigned a key, which is used for grouping. In the second phase, each group is independently *reduced* to a result. Clearly, both phases are parallelizable provided the groups are not too large.

Barre et al. [10] evaluate LTL formulas bottom up using one round of MapReduce for each layer of the formula tree. They combine task and data parallelism: the map phase operates on all time-points and operators in the current layer, whereas the reduce phase is organized by operators only. Follow-up work generalized this approach to MTL with aggregations [41] and a more fine-grained partitioning of temporal operators based on their interval constraints [40].

We developed a slicing framework [14,15] based on MapReduce and data parallelism. The map phase applies *slicers* to partition the input trace into a finite collection of slices, which are again traces. Each slice is associated with a *restriction*, a subset of the valuations and time-stamps that the monitor may output for a given policy formula. In the reduce phase, MonPoly is used as a *submonitor* that evaluates the formula on each slice. Its outputs are intersected with the corresponding restriction and combined. For correctness, it is important that the slices are sound and complete with respect to their restrictions. Slices need not be (and, in general, are not) disjoint. However, by choosing the slicers carefully, each slice has significantly fewer events than the input trace, such that each parallel invocation of MonPoly runs for a shorter amount of time and uses less memory.

There are two fundamental types of slicers, which may be composed. A *data slicer* selects events as a function of the events' parameters (domain values). It is parametrized by one of the formula's free variables x and a subset S_x of the domain. Any event that may be involved in a satisfying valuation v of the formula, such that $v(x) \in S_x$, is included in the slice. This is determined using a static over-approximation. For example, for the formula $p(x) \wedge \neg (\exists y.\ q(x, y) \vee q(y, x))$, the slice $S_x = \{3\}$ receives the events $p(3)$, $q(3, c)$, and $q(c, 3)$ for all c.

In contrast, the *time slicer* considers the events' time-stamps. The basic idea is to split the trace into contiguous chunks. However, if the formula uses temporal operators, they cannot be evaluated correctly near the chunk boundaries. Therefore, there must be a sufficient overlap between adjacent chunks. This overlap can again be computed statically in advance based on the formula's *relative intervals*. The relative interval of $p \wedge \Diamond_{[1,2]} (q \vee \Diamond_{[7,7]} r)$ is $[-2, 6]$, for instance, as any relevant event is contained within that interval relative to the current time-stamp.

5.2   Scalable Online Monitoring

MapReduce was designed for offline (batch) processing and it is not directly suitable for low-latency online monitors. In contrast, the *data stream* model of computation is tailored to continuous queries over rapidly changing data [9], which online monitoring can be seen as an instance of. Data stream management systems (DSMS) are generic platforms that provide high-level abstractions, while taking care of common issues in large-scale data stream processing such as scheduling, distributed execution, and fault tolerance [4,46,101].

Our online slicing framework [94,96] transplants the data slicing approach onto the Apache Flink DSMS [4], which parallelizes stream processing using multiprocessing or a distributed cluster. Data slicing is more useful for online monitoring than time slicing as the reduction in the maximum number of events across all slices is often higher over short periods of time. The main criterion for choosing Flink was its support for distributed snapshots [45], which enables fault-tolerance. If a machine in a distributed monitoring cluster fails, for example, the monitor can restart from the latest snapshot, which reduces the latency until it catches up with the event stream. To this end, we implemented a custom operator for Flink's data flow that can extract MonPoly's state.

We improved the slicing framework along several dimensions. The *joint data slicer* takes all free variables of the policy formula into account. Parametrized by a *slicing strategy* (an assignment of valuations over the free variables to slice identifiers), it computes for every event a subset of target slices that the event must be included in. We extended the joint data slicer with support for def and rec and identified a policy fragment for which the submonitors' outputs need not be filtered against the slicing strategy [93], which is otherwise required by (joint) data slicers.

Moreover, we developed an automatic slicing strategy selection for the joint data slicer. It adapts the *hypercube* algorithm for the parallel processing of relational joins [3,38] to our setting. The algorithm is so called because it partitions the domain of every variable separately, such that each slice corresponds to a hypercube of the product space over all variables. The number of splits per variable is optimized to minimize event duplication. This requires specific statistics of the event stream, such as the relative frequency of the different event names. These statistics may change substantially over time in a long-running stream and so may the corresponding optimal strategy. To change the strategy at runtime, we developed a state splitting and merge interface for MonPoly [95], since the submonitors' states must be kept consistent with the current slicing strategy.

Both the offline and the online framework are *black box* approaches because they rely on a standard, non-parallelized monitoring tool. This is convenient because all tool optimizations are readily available and the implementation can be changed relatively easily. For example, we have used not only MonPoly but also DejaVu with our online framework. However, it is known specifically for joins that redistributing data in multiple rounds may improve performance [38]. This corresponds to exchanging data between individual operators in the monitor's execution. We describe such a parallel *white box* monitor in Sect. 5.3.

5.3   Monitoring Distributed Systems

We focus on centralized specifications, which take a holistic view of a distributed system and abstract away from its structure [52]. Many temporal logics for centralized specifications—including MFOTL—assume that a total order is defined over all events. Yet it is often difficult to determine the true order of events generated by different components in an asynchronous distributed systems. The uncertainty about the ordering can be reduced, but not eliminated, using logical clocks such as vector clocks [75]. A global physical (real-time) clock may be approximated by employing synchronization protocols, but it has limits in environments with high event rates [39]. The RV community has developed many approaches that try to circumvent these obstacles [54]. Here we summarize our contributions to this area.

The *interleaving-sufficient fragment* [21,22] is a syntactically defined subset of MFOTL that can be monitored correctly on any interleaving of traces from different sources (e.g., components), meaning that the formula is either satisfied or violated on any interleaving. The only assumption is that a global clock with a possibly low resolution creates the time-stamps across all traces. The *collapse-sufficient fragment* is contained in the interleaving-sufficient fragment and consists of formulas that can be monitored correctly on the collapse, where all events with the same time-stamp are combined into a single time-point. Such fragments are useful because determining whether any (or all) interleavings satisfy a propositional formula is already (co-)NP-complete [22].

We used the collapse-sufficient fragment with the online slicing framework to parallelize slicing itself [19]. In the original framework, the slicer can become a bottleneck if the event rate (number of events per second) is too high. The idea is to slice the streams from each source in parallel and then merge the incoming slices at each submonitor. If the monitored policy is collapse-sufficient, it suffices to sort and group the events by their time-stamp using a (small) buffer. However, this approach still requires a low-resolution global clock. For a propositional fragment, we have shown that monitoring is possible even if the clock has bounded error [23].

When the monitor is operating in a distributed setting, messages sent may get lost or arrive out-of-order and components may even crash. Basin et al. [32, 34] developed a monitoring algorithm that uses a three valued Kleene logic to soundly operate in the presence of knowledge gaps; the third value $\bot$ stands for "unknown". Reasoning is monotonic with respect to a partial order on truth values where t and f are incomparable, and both are greater than $\bot$. Hence verdicts, once emitted, are never retracted, even when knowledge gaps are filled as events come in, out-of-order. The out-of-order monitor (POLIMON) supports the language $MTL^{\downarrow}$, which is MTL augmented with freeze quantifiers, where $\downarrow$ is a quantifier that extracts data values from registers and bind these values to logical variables.

A second, recently developed monitor for the out-of-order-setting is TimelyMon [88]. TimelyMon supports the RANF fragment of MFOTL with proper quantification and is thus more expressive than POLIMON, which is limited to freeze quantification. TimelyMon can receive individual events (not databases) in any order, but expects them to be labeled with the correct time-points and time-stamps (as defined by the temporal structure). It outputs assignments out-of-order, which allows it to signal policy violations much earlier than Mon-Poly and VeriMon, whose verdicts are delayed by the future interval bounds. Technology-wise, TimelyMon is implemented in the Timely Dataflow DSMS [76] and thus constitutes a white box implementation of a data-parallel online monitor (Sect. 5.2). Initial experiments confirm TimelyMon's good scalability with increasing numbers of workers, which is simply a parameter in Timely Dataflow.

6   Verification

Monitors use complex, optimized algorithms to efficiently support expressive specification languages. These algorithms' correctness is rarely obvious. Even worse, pen-and-paper proofs of correctness usually reason about idealized pseudocode. These proofs can be faulty, and so can be the translation from pseudocode to code. Over the years, we have found and fixed various errors in MonPoly's code.

VeriMon [16,17,97,102] was conceived out of our frustration with this build-break-fix cycle. Our original goal was to create a simplified version of MonPoly with strong correctness guarantees, machine-checked using the interactive theorem prover Isabelle/HOL [78]. To this end, we have formalized MFOTL's syntax and semantics, the simplified monitor's specification, and its correctness statement. We then defined invariants on the monitor's state and proved in Isabelle that they are preserved by the monitor's steps and imply the correctness statement. Finally, using Isabelle's code generator [59], we extracted executable OCaml code from our formalization. The resulting functional program, augmented with MonPoly's unverified formula and log parsers and user interface is what we call VeriMon.

Is VeriMon more trustworthy than MonPoly? Isabelle will not accept a vague or incomplete argument: all reasoning passes through Isabelle's kernel, which is a trustworthy guardian. Since Isabelle accepts the proof of VeriMon's correctness statement (expressing that the monitor's output complies with the specified MFOTL semantics), errors can only happen in reused, unverified parts of MonPoly's code or in the formal specification of MFOTL. The actual monitoring algorithm, arguably the most complex part of a monitor, is error-free. To further increase trustworthiness, we are working on verifying the unverified code used by VeriMon and validating MFOTL's specification by manual inspection, asserting that it faithfully represents what we intend to model.

VeriMon proved useful beyond its trustworthiness. Verifying a monitor has significantly improved our own understanding of the matter and provided us with a platform for experimentation and growth. VeriMon has become the incubator for first-order monitoring research. For example, new constructs like temporal regular expressions [17] and recursive definitions [102], previously unseen in any first-order monitor supporting future temporal operators, were introduced in VeriMon. We have also optimized VeriMon's simplified algorithms, sometimes inspired by optimizations used in MonPoly, other times going beyond, e.g., by incorporating multi-way joins from databases [17]. Moreover, we developed entirely new components, such as a type system and a type inference algorithm. In all cases, we took care, with Isabelle's help, to maintain or extend the correctness proof.

Eventually, the new features started migrating to other, unverified monitors, which still outclass VeriMon in efficiency. We have also used VeriMon as a reliable testing oracle. Differential testing on random inputs revealed several previously unknown implementation errors in MonPoly and helped us to localize them [17].

VeriMon is not our only verified monitor. The multi-head monitor Hydra (Sect. 4.4) has a verified counterpart, Vydra, and the online slicing framework's core (Sect. 5.2) is also formally verified. We firmly believe that theorem proving is a must when the goal is to develop and implement complex algorithms one can trust.

7 Applications

Research in monitoring strongly benefits from the plethora of immediate applications and the close interplay between theory and practice. Theoretical advances in monitoring lead to performance improvements in terms of memory use, execution time, parallelism, and even metatheoretic guarantees about what monitoring achieves. Conversely, applications provide insights on which features are useful in practice and whether tools scale in realistic settings. Although the scope of applications for monitoring is wide, our focus has been on problems in security, data protection, and protocols for distributed systems.

7.1 Security and Anomaly Detection

Security policies regulate which actions may and must not happen within a system. The vast majority of these policies constitute safety properties (the exceptions are typically information flow policies, which are hyperproperties). Hence, they are excellent candidates for monitoring since policy violations are detectable on finite traces. Also relevant for security is that monitors can be used to detect anomalous behavior, for example for intrusion detection. Such applications benefit from statistical computations as offered by our logic's aggregations.

A prototypical security policy has the form $\square \, \forall \overline{x}. \; action(\overline{x}) \rightarrow authorized(\overline{x})$. Namely, every occurrence of some *action* must be authorized. The $\overline{x}$ are parameters associated with the action, e.g., attributes of the user responsible for the action, the resource(s) used, or the environment. Moreover, *authorized* specifies that authorization is present or, alternatively, is a formula specifying the conditions for authorization. As a concrete example

$$\square \, \forall u, a, o. \; \mathsf{exec}(u, a, o) \rightarrow \exists r. \; \mathsf{UA}(u, r) \wedge \mathsf{PA}(r, a, o)$$

might formalize access restrictions in a system implementing an access control mechanism based on some variant of Role-based Access Control (RBAC). It states that whenever a user u carries out an action a on an object o, then the user is assigned to the role r under the user assignment relation UA and moreover the role r is granted the privilege to carry out action a on the object o, under the permission assignment relation PA. We provide extensive examples of how security policies can be formalized in MFOTL [25], ranging from simple access control requirements like the above to more complex policies formalizing history-based access control policies like so-called Chinese Wall policies, where access rights change dynamically with each access, and separation-of-duty requirements.

We carried out a large-scale case study with Google, monitoring compliance to access control policies of Google employees using Google's infrastructure [15]. Policies concerned configurations of accessing computers, time limits on the use of authentication tokens, and restrictions on software used during access. We used offline monitoring, taking events from a distributed logging infrastructure recording log data on roughly 35,000 computers accessing sensitive resources over a period of two years. The log data contained roughly 77.2 million time-points and 26 billion events, and required 0.4 TB to store in a compressed form. For each policy, we used 1,000 computers for slicing and monitoring. The original MonPoly system was used together with the offline slicing framework (Sect. 5.1) leveraging Google's MapReduce infrastructure. Namely, we split the log into 10,000 slices whereby each computer processed 10 slices on average. Overall, processing time was on the order of hours (2–12 h), with the vast majority of time being spent on monitoring, and it scaled well with the introduction of more computing resources.

In the context of anomaly detection, we developed policies that aim at identifying fraudulent reviews in an e-commerce setting. The first policy, based on an algorithm by Heydari et al. [65], detects outliers in the number of reviews received by a brand. This required encoding a *tumbling window* [46] by combining aggregations and temporal operators. We applied the policy to a dataset of reviews published on Amazon [77] to evaluate HashMon. Hashing the review texts reduced the memory usage by a third [92]. The other policies detect brands whose products receive identical reviews (as determined by the score and, optionally, the text) from the same user. These policies were designed to be challenging for our monitors as it is difficult or impossible to rewrite them in RANF (Sect. 4.1). The formulas obtained from the MFOTL2RANF tool outperformed other approaches, including MonPoly-Reg, on synthetic data and the Amazon data [85].

7.2 Privacy and Data Protection

We have also carried out case studies on using monitoring to check compliance to privacy and data protection policies. We first used MonPoly in a case study with Nokia [22], which revolved around the use of cell-phone data of participants and ensuring compliance to privacy policies by auditing logs for proper usage of this data. For example, policies required that data would only be propagated to certain systems, that appropriate anonymization steps would be taken prior to sharing, data requested for deletion would actually be deleted from all appropriate systems, etc.

In more recent work [8], we formalized a substantial part of the GDPR in MFOTL. The GDPR has challenges that go beyond traditional access control. For example, once access is granted, data may only be used when there is a legal basis for the usage or users have granted explicit consent. Users may also restrict how their data is processed at any time and have the right to have their data deleted. Our formalization of such rights provided a basis for using MonPoly to determine GDPR compliance. We carried out a case study on the use of sensitive data by a research foundation concerning how they evaluated and awarded grant applications.

Finally, we have used MonPoly as an enforcement component [67] in a data protection framework called *Taint, Track, and Control* (TTC) [66]. Applications developed in TTC natively use dynamic information-flow control to track the provenance information of every value in their memory and persistent storage. This information includes the identifiers of all user whose data affected the value. Users can formulate their data protection policies in MFOTL, and TTC determines if revealing a value conforms to the policies. In particular, the application's execution trace (including the provenance information) is monitored by MonPoly and, based on its output, all attempted violations are prevented.

7.3 Distributed Systems

A significant challenge in the Nokia case study mentioned above was that the data was stored in multiple logs collected from components of a distributed system. Hence, even assuming synchronized clocks, there is only a partial order on time-stamped data rather than a total order assumed by MFOTL's semantics. We tackled this problem by expressing policies with formulas in MFOTL's collapse-sufficient fragment and monitoring the collapse of the trace (Sect. 5.3).

We also used MonPoly in a case study to check properties of the Internet Computer (IC) [18]. The IC is a complex distributed system that facilitates governance and execution of Web3 applications and spans over 1,200 nodes world-

def $\mathsf{NodeAdded}(n, s) := \mathsf{InSubnet}_0(n, s) \vee \mathsf{RegistryAddNodeTo}(n, s)$ in

def $\mathsf{InSubnet}(n, s) := \neg\, \mathsf{RegistryRemoveNodeFrom}(n, s) \mathsf{\ S\ NodeAdded}(n, s)$ in

def $\mathsf{ProperEvent} := \diamondsuit_{[1,\infty)} \top$ in

def $\mathsf{RelevantNode}(n, s) := \mathsf{InSubnet}(n, s) \mathsf{\ S}_{[10\,\min,\infty)} (\mathsf{InSubnet}(n, s) \wedge \mathsf{ProperEvent})$ in

def $\mathsf{RelevantLog}(n, s, lvl, msg, i) := \exists host, comp.$

$\quad \mathsf{Log}(host, n, s, comp, lvl, msg) \wedge comp \overset{\mathsf{RE}}{\Leftarrow} \texttt{"orchestrator"} \wedge n \neq \texttt{""} \wedge \mathsf{tp}(i)$ in

def $\mathsf{MsgCount}(n, s, k) := k \leftarrow \mathsf{SUM}(k'; n, s)$

$\qquad \Big(\big((k' \leftarrow \mathsf{CNT}(i; n, s)\ \diamondsuit_{[0,10\,\min)}\ \mathsf{RelevantLog}(n, s, lvl, msg, i)\big) \wedge$

$\qquad\qquad \mathsf{RelevantNode}(n, s)\big) \vee \big(\mathsf{RelevantNode}(n, s) \wedge k' = 0\big)\Big)$ in

def $\mathsf{TypicalBehavior}(s, m) := \big(m \leftarrow \mathsf{MED}(k; s)\ \mathsf{MsgCount}(n, s, k)\big) \wedge$

$\quad \big(\exists k.\ (k \leftarrow \mathsf{CNT}(n; s)\ \mathsf{RelevantNode}(n, s)) \wedge k \geq 3\big)$ in

def $\mathsf{TypicalBehaviors}(s, m) :=$

$\quad \big(\diamondsuit_{[0,10\,\min)}\ \mathsf{TypicalBehavior}(s, m)\big) \vee \big(\lozenge_{[0,10\,\min)}\ \mathsf{TypicalBehavior}(s, m)\big)$ in

def $\mathsf{BehaviorAndRange}(s, n, k, min, max) := \neg\big(\lozenge_{[0,10\,\min)}\ \mathsf{EndTest}\big) \wedge$

$\quad \big(\exists k'.\ \mathsf{MsgCount}(n, s, k') \wedge k = \mathsf{int2float}(k')\big) \wedge$

$\quad \big(min \leftarrow \mathsf{MIN}(m; s)\ \mathsf{TypicalBehaviors}(s, m)\big) \wedge$

$\quad \big(max \leftarrow \mathsf{MAX}(m; s)\ \mathsf{TypicalBehaviors}(s, m)\big)$ in

def $\mathsf{Exceeds}(s, n, k, min, max) :=$

$\quad (\mathsf{BehaviorAndRange}(s, n, k, min, max) \wedge k > 1.1 \cdot max) \vee$

$\quad (\mathsf{BehaviorAndRange}(s, n, k, min, max) \wedge k < 0.9 \cdot min)$ in

$\mathsf{Exceeds}(s, n, k, min, max) \wedge \neg\,\ominus_{[0,10\,\min)} (\exists a, b, c.\ \mathsf{Exceeds}(s, n, a, b, c))$

Fig. 4. The Internet Computer's `logging-behavior` policy [18]

wide. Web3 applications process data with decentralized ownership (e.g., financial assets). Hence the integrity of their execution must be ensured on devices beyond the asset owner's control. The IC ensures this by combining an efficient consensus protocol and state machine replication [50]. The efficiency of the IC's consensus protocol is achieved by grouping all IC nodes into subnets of manageable size. The configuration of the IC (e.g., the assignment of the nodes to subnets) is highly dynamic and the IC possesses numerous other features that are challenging to monitor, such as a long-lived high event-rate execution, a layered software architecture, and continuous evolution. The policies we have formalized range from common symptoms of the IC's production incidents to properties of the IC's consensus protocol, including malicious behaviors and infrastructure outages that the protocol must tolerate.

For example, Fig. 4 shows our formalization of the `logging-behavior` IC policy. The policy first computes the current assignment of nodes to subnets (predicate InSubnet) based on the IC's initial configuration (InSubnet$_0$) and the nodes that have joined (RegistryAddNodeTo) or left (RegistryRemoveNodeFrom) a subnet. Next, for each subnet the policy compares its nodes' logging frequencies computed over a 10 min sliding window (MsgCount) against the median logging frequency over all nodes in the subnet (TypicalBehavior). Only messages containing `orchestrator` in their component name are relevant for the frequency calculation.

The IC's execution traces were recorded in a detailed JSON format, which required a non-trivial mapping to more abstract events (e.g., RegistryAddNodeTo) with appropriate parameters. This motivated a recent extension of MFOTL and MonPoly with complex data types, like records, variants, and recursive types [74].

8 Conclusions and Open Problems

Monitoring is a fascinating research area given the rich interplay between theory and practice. While the gold standard for system verification is the full verification of implementations using model-checkers and theorem provers, monitoring offers an attractive alternative. Not only is monitoring relatively lightweight and easy to use, it has a larger scope. Namely, one can monitor extremely complex systems, even involving humans and non-technical components, provided one has policies for their behavior. Moveover the verdicts returned are statements about the actual system's behavior, rather than a mathematical model thereof. Below we discuss some research questions and open problems that have arisen from our work.

Whenever monitoring is used in practice, the question arises how to handle policy violations. We learned from our IC case study (Sect. 7.3) that engineers value detailed and precise information about violations, as it helps them identify and fix the root cause more quickly. As a first step towards explainable and certifiable monitor verdicts, we have developed a monitor for MTL that outputs minimal proof objects [13, 73]. Can one go farther and design a feedback loop that aids with fault localization by matching such certificates against the monitored system?

Both a monitor's performance and correctness are critical. VeriMon is frequently outperformed by the unverified tools MonPoly and StaticMon. We believe there are two main reasons for this performance gap: the exclusive use of immutable data structures and the layers of abstractions that were vital for the proofs but cannot be simplified by the compiler. Our long-term goal is to refine VeriMon to a highly efficient, imperative implementation. Despite impressive advances in verified refinement [7, 71], the complex, recursive invariants of VeriMon's state require new ideas to break this effort down into manageable and composable parts.

Complex policies are often built from abstract concepts that must be made precise for monitoring. For example, in the IC case study from Sect. 7.3, the predicate TypicalBehavior was defined as the median logging frequency of nodes in a subnetwork. One could well imagine that what constitutes typical behavior is something that can be learned, using machine learning, rather than specified a priori. Combining monitoring with machine learning is an exciting topic, with many applications, e.g., in security, anomaly detection, and beyond.

Acknowledgments. This paper has four authors, but it reports on a decade of collaboration with numerous other researchers. We would like to explicitly name some of them here. First and foremost, we thank Felix Klaedtke, Martin Raszyk, and Eugen Zălinescu. Felix and Eugen were key contributors during the inception of MonPoly. Martin arrived later but left his mark through his work on Hydra, Vydra, MFOTL2RANF, and VeriMon.

We also thank the past and present monitoring aficionados from our groups at ETH Zürich and the University of Copenhagen: Bhargav Bhatt, Rafael Castro G. Silva, Matúš Harvan, François Hublet, Jonathan Julián Huerta y Munive, Leonardo Lima, Srđan Marinović, Samuel Müller, Lennard Reese. In addition, we are grateful to those B.Sc. and M.Sc. students who contributed to our journey: Berkay Aydogdu, Marc Bolliger, Frederik Brix, Thibault Dardinier, Christian Fania, Artur Gigon Almada e Melo, Matthieu Gras, Emma Pind Hansen, Nico Hauser, Lukas Heimes, Andrei Herasimau, Hróbjartur Höskuldsson, Valeria Jannelli, Nicolas Kaletsch, Jeniffer Lima Graf, Emanuele Marsicano, Galina Peycheva, Sarah Plocher, Jonathan Rappl, Pascal Schärli, Dawit Legesse Tirore, Adrian Wortmann, Simon Yuan, Stefan Zemljic, Sheila Zingg, and Remo Zumsteg. We would also like to thank our external collaborators from the past and present: Emma Arfelt, Daniel Bristot de Oliveira, Germano Caronni, Søren Debois, Daniel Stefan Dietiker, Sarah Ereth, Yliès Falcone, Heiko Mantel, Birgit Pfitzmann, Yvonne-Anne Pignolet, Giles Reger, Arshavir Ter-Gabrielyan, as well as the participants of the ARVI COST Action and many (mostly) anonymous reviewers.

Finally, we acknowledge the generous external funding we have received for research on monitoring from the Swiss National Science Foundation (grant 167162 "Big Data Monitoring" and grant 204796 "Model-driven Security & Privacy"), the US Air Force Research Laborarory (grant FA9550-17-1-0306 "Monitoring at Any Cost"), and the Novo Nordisk Foundation (start package grant NNF20OC0063462).

References

1. Abiteboul, S., Hull, R., Vianu, V.: Foundations of Databases. Addison-Wesley, Boston (1995)
2. Abrahams, D., Gurtovoy, A.: C++ Template Metaprogramming: Concepts, Tools, and Techniques from Boost and Beyond. Addison-Wesley, Boston (2004)
3. Afrati, F.N., Ullman, J.D.: Optimizing multiway joins in a map-reduce environment. IEEE Trans. Knowl. Data Eng. **23**(9), 1282–1298 (2011). https://doi.org/10.1109/TKDE.2011.47
4. Alexandrov, A., et al.: The Stratosphere platform for big data analytics. VLDB J. **23**(6), 939–964 (2014). https://doi.org/10.1007/s00778-014-0357-y
5. Alford, M.W., Lamport, L., Mullery, G.P.: Basic concepts. In: Paul, M., Siegert, H.J. (eds.) Distributed Systems: Methods and Tools for Specification, An Advanced Course. LNCS, vol. 190, pp. 7–43. Springer, Cham (1984). https://doi.org/10.1007/3-540-15216-4_12
6. Antimirov, V.M.: Partial derivatives of regular expressions and finite automaton constructions. Theor. Comput. Sci. **155**(2), 291–319 (1996). https://doi.org/10.1016/0304-3975(95)00182-4
7. Arasu, A., et al.: FastVer2: a provably correct monitor for concurrent, key-value stores. In: Krebbers, R., Traytel, D., Pientka, B., Zdancewic, S. (eds.) 12th ACM SIGPLAN International Conference on Certified Programs and Proofs (CPP 2023), pp. 30–46. ACM (2023). https://doi.org/10.1145/3573105.3575687
8. Arfelt, E., Basin, D., Debois, S.: Monitoring the GDPR. In: Sako, K., Schneider, S., Ryan, P.Y.A. (eds.) ESORICS 2019. LNCS, vol. 11735, pp. 681–699. Springer, Cham (2019). https://doi.org/10.1007/978-3-030-29959-0_33

9. Babcock, B., Babu, S., Datar, M., Motwani, R., Widom, J.: Models and issues in data stream systems. In: Popa, L., Abiteboul, S., Kolaitis, P.G. (eds.) 21st ACM SIGACT-SIGMOD-SIGART Symposium on Principles of Database Systems (PODS 2002), pp. 1–16. ACM (2002). https://doi.org/10.1145/543613.543615

10. Barre, B., Klein, M., Soucy-Boivin, M., Ollivier, P.-A., Hallé, S.: MapReduce for parallel trace validation of LTL properties. In: Qadeer, S., Tasiran, S. (eds.) RV 2012. LNCS, vol. 7687, pp. 184–198. Springer, Heidelberg (2013). https://doi.org/10.1007/978-3-642-35632-2_20

11. Bartocci, E., Falcone, Y. (eds.): Lectures on Runtime Verification: Introductory and Advanced Topics. LNCS, vol. 10457. Springer, Cham (2018). https://doi.org/10.1007/978-3-319-75632-5

12. Basin, D., Bhatt, B.N., Krstić, S., Traytel, D.: Almost event-rate independent monitoring. Formal Methods Syst. Des. **54**(3), 449–478 (2019). https://doi.org/10.1007/s10703-018-00328-3

13. Basin, D., Bhatt, B.N., Traytel, D.: Optimal proofs for linear temporal logic on lasso words. In: Lahiri, S.K., Wang, C. (eds.) ATVA 2018. LNCS, vol. 11138, pp. 37–55. Springer, Cham (2018). https://doi.org/10.1007/978-3-030-01090-4_3

14. Basin, D., Caronni, G., Ereth, S., Harvan, M., Klaedtke, F., Mantel, H.: Scalable offline monitoring. In: Bonakdarpour, B., Smolka, S.A. (eds.) RV 2014. LNCS, vol. 8734, pp. 31–47. Springer, Cham (2014). https://doi.org/10.1007/978-3-319-11164-3_4

15. Basin, D., Caronni, G., Ereth, S., Harvan, M., Klaedtke, F., Mantel, H.: Scalable offline monitoring of temporal specifications. Formal Methods Syst. Des. **49**(1–2), 75–108 (2016). https://doi.org/10.1007/s10703-016-0242-y

16. Basin, D., et al.: VeriMon: a formally verified monitoring tool. In: Seidl, H., Liu, Z., Pasareanu, C.S. (eds.) ICTAC 2022. LNCS, vol. 13572, pp. 1–6. Springer, Cham (2022). https://doi.org/10.1007/978-3-031-17715-6_1

17. Basin, D., et al.: A formally verified, optimized monitor for metric first-order dynamic logic. In: Peltier, N., Sofronie-Stokkermans, V. (eds.) IJCAR 2020. LNCS (LNAI), vol. 12166, pp. 432–453. Springer, Cham (2020). https://doi.org/10.1007/978-3-030-51074-9_25

18. Basin, D., et al.: Monitoring the internet computer. In: Chechik, M., Katoen, J.-P., Leucker, M. (eds.) FM 2023. LNCS, vol. 14000, pp. 383–402. Springer, Cham (2023). https://doi.org/10.1007/978-3-031-27481-7_22

19. Basin, D., Gras, M., Krstić, S., Schneider, J.: Scalable online monitoring of distributed systems. In: Deshmukh, J., Ničković, D. (eds.) RV 2020. LNCS, vol. 12399, pp. 197–220. Springer, Cham (2020). https://doi.org/10.1007/978-3-030-60508-7_11

20. Basin, D., et al.: MonPoly and VeriMon. https://bitbucket.org/jshs/monpoly

21. Basin, D., Harvan, M., Klaedtke, F., Zălinescu, E.: Monitoring usage-control policies in distributed systems. In: Combi, C., Leucker, M., Wolter, F. (eds.) 18th International Symposium on Temporal Representation and Reasoning (TIME 2011), pp. 88–95. IEEE (2011). https://doi.org/10.1109/TIME.2011.14

22. Basin, D., Harvan, M., Klaedtke, F., Zălinescu, E.: Monitoring data usage in distributed systems. IEEE Trans. Softw. Eng. **39**(10), 1403–1426 (2013). https://doi.org/10.1109/TSE.2013.18

23. Basin, D., Klaedtke, F., Marinovic, S., Zălinescu, E.: On real-time monitoring with imprecise timestamps. In: Bonakdarpour, B., Smolka, S.A. (eds.) RV 2014. LNCS, vol. 8734, pp. 193–198. Springer, Cham (2014). https://doi.org/10.1007/978-3-319-11164-3_16

24. Basin, D., Klaedtke, F., Marinovic, S., Zălinescu, E.: Monitoring of temporal first-order properties with aggregations. Formal Methods Syst. Des. **46**(3), 262–285 (2015). https://doi.org/10.1007/s10703-015-0222-7

25. Basin, D., Klaedtke, F., Müller, S.: Monitoring security policies with metric first-order temporal logic. In: Joshi, J.B.D., Carminati, B. (eds.) 15th ACM Symposium on Access Control Models and Technologies (SACMAT 2010), pp. 23–34. ACM (2010). https://doi.org/10.1109/TSE.2013.18

26. Basin, D., Klaedtke, F., Müller, S.: Policy monitoring in first-order temporal logic. In: Touili, T., Cook, B., Jackson, P. (eds.) CAV 2010. LNCS, vol. 6174, pp. 1–18. Springer, Heidelberg (2010). https://doi.org/10.1007/978-3-642-14295-6_1

27. Basin, D., Klaedtke, F., Müller, S., Pfitzmann, B.: Runtime monitoring of metric first-order temporal properties. In: Hariharan, R., Mukund, M., Vinay, V. (eds.) IARCS Annual Conference on Foundations of Software Technology and Theoretical Computer Science (FSTTCS 2008), Volume 2 of LIPIcs, pp. 49–60. Schloss Dagstuhl - Leibniz-Zentrum für Informatik (2008). https://doi.org/10.4230/LIPIcs.FSTTCS.2008.1740

28. Basin, D., Klaedtke, F., Müller, S., Zălinescu, E.: Monitoring metric first-order temporal properties. J. ACM **62**(2), 15:1–15:45 (2015). https://doi.org/10.1145/2699444

29. Basin, D., Klaedtke, F., Zălinescu, E.: Algorithms for monitoring real-time properties. In: Khurshid, S., Sen, K. (eds.) RV 2011. LNCS, vol. 7186, pp. 260–275. Springer, Heidelberg (2012). https://doi.org/10.1007/978-3-642-29860-8_20

30. Basin, D., Klaedtke, F., Zălinescu, E.: Greedily computing associative aggregations on sliding windows. Inf. Process. Lett. **115**(2), 186–192 (2015). https://doi.org/10.1016/j.ipl.2014.09.009

31. Basin, D., Klaedtke, F., Zălinescu, E.: The MonPoly monitoring tool. In: Reger, G., Havelund, K. (eds.) International Workshop on Competitions, Usability, Benchmarks, Evaluation, and Standardisation for Runtime Verification Tools (RV-CuBES 2017), Volume 3 of Kalpa Publications in Computing, pp. 19–28. EasyChair (2017). https://doi.org/10.29007/89hs

32. Basin, D., Klaedtke, F., Zălinescu, E.: Runtime verification of temporal properties over out-of-order data streams. In: Majumdar, R., Kunčak, V. (eds.) CAV 2017. LNCS, vol. 10426, pp. 356–376. Springer, Cham (2017). https://doi.org/10.1007/978-3-319-63387-9_18

33. Basin, D., Klaedtke, F., Zălinescu, E.: Algorithms for monitoring real-time properties. Acta Informatica **55**(4), 309–338 (2018). https://doi.org/10.1007/s00236-017-0295-4

34. Basin, D., Klaedtke, F., Zălinescu, E.: Runtime verification over out-of-order streams. ACM Trans. Comput. Log. **21**(1), 5:1–5:43 (2020). https://doi.org/10.1145/3355609

35. Basin, D., Krstić, S., Traytel, D.: AERIAL: almost event-rate independent algorithms for monitoring metric regular properties. In: Reger, G., Havelund, K. (eds.) International Workshop on Competitions, Usability, Benchmarks, Evaluation, and Standardisation for Runtime Verification Tools (RV-CuBES 2017), Volume 3 of Kalpa Publications in Computing, pp. 29–36. EasyChair (2017). https://doi.org/10.29007/bm4c

36. Basin, D., Krstić, S., Traytel, D.: Almost event-rate independent monitoring of metric dynamic logic. In: Lahiri, S., Reger, G. (eds.) RV 2017. LNCS, vol. 10548, pp. 85–102. Springer, Cham (2017). https://doi.org/10.1007/978-3-319-67531-2_6

37. Bauer, A., Küster, J.-C., Vegliach, G.: From propositional to first-order monitoring. In: Legay, A., Bensalem, S. (eds.) RV 2013. LNCS, vol. 8174, pp. 59–75. Springer, Heidelberg (2013). https://doi.org/10.1007/978-3-642-40787-1_4
38. Beame, P., Koutris, P., Suciu, D.: Communication steps for parallel query processing. J. ACM **64**(6), 40:1–40:58 (2017). https://doi.org/10.1145/3125644
39. Becker, D., Rabenseifner, R., Wolf, F., Linford, J.C.: Scalable timestamp synchronization for event traces of message-passing applications. Parallel Comput. **35**(12), 595–607 (2009). https://doi.org/10.1016/j.parco.2008.12.012
40. Bersani, M.M., Bianculli, D., Ghezzi, C., Krstić, S., San Pietro, P.: Efficient large-scale trace checking using MapReduce. In: Dillon, L.K., Visser, W., Williams, L.A. (eds.) 38th International Conference on Software Engineering (ICSE 2016), pp. 888–898. ACM (2016). https://doi.org/10.1145/2884781.2884832
41. Bianculli, D., Ghezzi, C., Krstić, S.: Trace checking of metric temporal logic with aggregating modalities using MapReduce. In: Giannakopoulou, D., Salaün, G. (eds.) SEFM 2014. LNCS, vol. 8702, pp. 144–158. Springer, Cham (2014). https://doi.org/10.1007/978-3-319-10431-7_11
42. Blumensath, A., Grädel, E.: Automatic structures. In: 15th Annual IEEE Symposium on Logic in Computer Science (LICS 2000), pp. 51–62. IEEE Computer Society (2000). https://doi.org/10.1109/LICS.2000.855755
43. Brix, F., Fania, C., Gras, M., Krstić, S., Schneider, J.: Scalable online monitor. https://bitbucket.org/krle/scalable-online-monitor
44. Bundala, D., Ouaknine, J.: On the complexity of temporal-logic path checking. In: Esparza, J., Fraigniaud, P., Husfeldt, T., Koutsoupias, E. (eds.) ICALP 2014. LNCS, vol. 8573, pp. 86–97. Springer, Heidelberg (2014). https://doi.org/10.1007/978-3-662-43951-7_8
45. Carbone, P., Ewen, S., Fóra, G., Haridi, S., Richter, S., Tzoumas, K.: State management in Apache Flink®: consistent stateful distributed stream processing. Proc. VLDB Endow. **10**(12), 1718–1729 (2017). https://doi.org/10.14778/3137765.3137777
46. Carney, D., et al.: Monitoring streams - a new class of data management applications. In: 28th VLDB Conference (VLDB 2002), pp. 215–226. Morgan Kaufmann (2002). https://doi.org/10.1016/B978-155860869-6/50027-5
47. Chomicki, J., Niwinski, D.: On the feasibility of checking temporal integrity constraints. J. Comput. Syst. Sci. **51**(3), 523–535 (1995). https://doi.org/10.1006/jcss.1995.1088
48. Codd, E.F.: Relational completeness of data base sublanguages. Technical report RJ987, IBM Research Laboratory, San Jose, California (1972)
49. Dean, J., Ghemawat, S.: MapReduce: simplified data processing on large clusters. In: Brewer, E.A., Chen, P. (eds.) 6th Symposium on Operating System Design and Implementation (OSDI 2004), pp. 137–150. USENIX Association (2004). http://www.usenix.org/events/osdi04/tech/dean.html
50. DFINITY Team: The Internet Computer for geeks. Cryptology ePrint Archive, Paper 2022/087 (2022). https://eprint.iacr.org/2022/087
51. Fagin, R.: Horn clauses and database dependencies. J. ACM **29**(4), 952–985 (1982). https://doi.org/10.1145/322344.322347
52. Falcone, Y., Krstić, S., Reger, G., Traytel, D.: A taxonomy for classifying runtime verification tools. Int. J. Softw. Tools Technol. Transfer **23**(2), 255–284 (2021). https://doi.org/10.1007/s10009-021-00609-z
53. Finkbeiner, B., Sipma, H.: Checking finite traces using alternating automata. Formal Methods Syst. Des. **24**(2), 101–127 (2004). https://doi.org/10.1023/B:FORM.0000017718.28096.48

54. Francalanza, A., Pérez, J.A., Sánchez, C.: Runtime verification for decentralised and distributed systems. In: Bartocci, E., Falcone, Y. (eds.) Lectures on Runtime Verification. LNCS, vol. 10457, pp. 176–210. Springer, Cham (2018). https://doi.org/10.1007/978-3-319-75632-5_6

55. Van Gelder, A., Topor, R.W.: Safety and translation of relational calculus queries. ACM Trans. Database Syst. **16**(2), 235–278 (1991)

56. Gras, M.: CPPMon. https://github.com/matthieugras/cppmon

57. Gras, M.: StaticMon. https://github.com/matthieugras/staticmon

58. Gras, M.: Explicit meets implicit monitoring. Master's thesis, ETH Zurich, Switzerland (2022)

59. Haftmann, F.: Code generation from specifications in higher-order logic. Ph.D. thesis, Technical University Munich, Germany (2009). http://mediatum2.ub.tum.de/node?id=886023

60. Havelund, K., Peled, D.: Runtime verification: from propositional to first-order temporal logic. In: Colombo, C., Leucker, M. (eds.) RV 2018. LNCS, vol. 11237, pp. 90–112. Springer, Cham (2018). https://doi.org/10.1007/978-3-030-03769-7_7

61. Havelund, K., Peled, D., Ulus, D.: DejaVu: a monitoring tool for first-order temporal logic. In: 3rd Workshop on Monitoring and Testing of Cyber-Physical Systems (MT@CPSWeek 2018), pp. 12–13. IEEE (2018). https://doi.org/10.1109/MT-CPS.2018.00013

62. Havelund, K., Peled, D., Ulus, D.: First-order temporal logic monitoring with BDDs. Formal Methods Syst. Des. **56**(1), 1–21 (2020). https://doi.org/10.1007/s10703-018-00327-4

63. Havelund, K., Roşu, G.: Synthesizing monitors for safety properties. In: Katoen, J.-P., Stevens, P. (eds.) TACAS 2002. LNCS, vol. 2280, pp. 342–356. Springer, Heidelberg (2002). https://doi.org/10.1007/3-540-46002-0_24

64. Henriksen, J.G., et al.: Mona: monadic second-order logic in practice. In: Brinksma, E., Cleaveland, W.R., Larsen, K.G., Margaria, T., Steffen, B. (eds.) TACAS 1995. LNCS, vol. 1019, pp. 89–110. Springer, Heidelberg (1995). https://doi.org/10.1007/3-540-60630-0_5

65. Heydari, A., Tavakoli, M., Salim, N.: Detection of fake opinions using time series. Expert Syst. Appl. **58**, 83–92 (2016). https://doi.org/10.1016/j.eswa.2016.03.020

66. Hublet, F., Basin, D., Krstić, S.: User-controlled privacy: taint, track, and control. Proc. Priv. Enhancing Technol. **2024**(1) (2024, to appear)

67. Hublet, F., Basin, D., Krstić, S.: Real-time policy enforcement with metric first-order temporal logic. In: Atluri, V., Di Pietro, R., Jensen, C.D., Meng, W. (eds.) ESORICS 2022, Part II. LNCS, vol. 13555, pp. 211–232. Springer, Cham (2022). https://doi.org/10.1007/978-3-031-17146-8_11

68. Khoussainov, B., Nerode, A.: Automatic presentations of structures. In: Leivant, D. (ed.) LCC 1994. LNCS, vol. 960, pp. 367–392. Springer, Heidelberg (1995). https://doi.org/10.1007/3-540-60178-3_93

69. Krstić, S., Traytel, D.: Aerial. https://bitbucket.org/traytel/aerial

70. Kuhtz, L., Finkbeiner, B.: Efficient parallel path checking for linear-time temporal logic with past and bounds. Log. Methods Comput. Sci. **8**(4), 10:1–10:24 (2012). https://doi.org/10.2168/LMCS-8(4:10)2012

71. Lammich, P.: Refinement of parallel algorithms down to LLVM. In: Andronick, J., de Moura, L. (eds.) 13th International Conference on Interactive Theorem Proving (ITP 2022), Volume 237 of LIPIcs, pp. 24:1–24:18. Schloss Dagstuhl - Leibniz-Zentrum für Informatik (2022). https://doi.org/10.4230/LIPIcs.ITP.2022.24

72. Leucker, M., Schallhart, C.: A brief account of runtime verification. J. Log. Algebraic Methods Program. **78**(5), 293–303 (2009). https://doi.org/10.1016/j.jlap.2008.08.004

73. Lima, L., Herasimau, A., Raszyk, M., Traytel, D., Yuan, S.: Explainable online monitoring of metric temporal logic. In: Sankaranarayanan, S., Sharygina, N. (eds.) TACAS 2023, Part II. LNCS, vol. 13994, pp. 473–491. Springer, Cham (2023). https://doi.org/10.1007/978-3-031-30820-8_28

74. Lima Graf, J., Krstić, S., Schneider, J.: Metric first-order temporal logic with complex data types. In: Katsaros, P., Nenzi, L. (eds.) RV 2023, LNCS 14245, pp. 126–147. Springer, Cham (2023). https://doi.org/10.1007/978-3-031-44267-4_7

75. Mostafa, M., Bonakdarpour, B.: Decentralized runtime verification of LTL specifications in distributed systems. In: 29th IEEE International Parallel and Distributed Processing Symposium (IPDPS 2015), pp. 494–503. IEEE (2015). https://doi.org/10.1109/IPDPS.2015.95

76. Murray, D.G., McSherry, F., Isaacs, R., Isard, M., Barham, P., Abadi, M.: Naiad: a timely dataflow system. In: Kaminsky, M., Dahlin, M. (eds.) 24th ACM SIGOPS Symposium on Operating Systems Principles (SOSP 2013), pp. 439–455. ACM (2013). https://doi.org/10.1145/2517349.2522738

77. Ni, J., Li, J., McAuley, J.J.: Justifying recommendations using distantly-labeled reviews and fine-grained aspects. In: Inui, K., Jiang, J., Ng, V., Wan, X. (eds.) Conference on Empirical Methods in Natural Language Processing (EMNLP-IJCNLP 2019), pp. 188–197. Association for Computational Linguistics (2019). https://nijianmo.github.io/amazon/index.html

78. Nipkow, T., Paulson, L.C., Wenzel, M.: Isabelle/HOL: A Proof Assistant for Higher-Order Logic. LNCS, vol. 2283. Springer, Cham (2002). https://doi.org/10.1007/3-540-45949-9

79. Orgun, M.A., Wadge, W.W.: A relational algebra as a query language for temporal DATALOG. In: Tjoa, A., Ramos, I. (eds.) DEXA 1992, pp. 276–281. Springer, Vienna (1992). https://doi.org/10.1007/978-3-7091-7557-6_48

80. Pnueli, A., Zaks, A.: PSL model checking and run-time verification via testers. In: Misra, J., Nipkow, T., Sekerinski, E. (eds.) FM 2006. LNCS, vol. 4085, pp. 573–586. Springer, Heidelberg (2006). https://doi.org/10.1007/11813040_38

81. Raszyk, M.: Hydra and Vydra. https://github.com/mraszyk/hydra

82. Raszyk, M.: MFOTL2RANF. https://github.com/mraszyk/mfotl2ranf

83. Raszyk, M.: Efficient, expressive, and verified temporal query evaluation. Ph.D. thesis, ETH Zurich, Switzerland (2022). https://doi.org/10.3929/ethz-b-000553221

84. Raszyk, M., Basin, D., Krstić, S., Traytel, D.: Multi-head monitoring of metric temporal logic. In: Chen, Y.-F., Cheng, C.-H., Esparza, J. (eds.) ATVA 2019. LNCS, vol. 11781, pp. 151–170. Springer, Cham (2019). https://doi.org/10.1007/978-3-030-31784-3_9

85. Raszyk, M., Basin, D., Krstić, S., Traytel, D.: Practical relational calculus query evaluation. In: Olteanu, D., Vortmeier, N. (eds.) 25th International Conference on Database Theory (ICDT 2022), Volume 220 of LIPIcs, pp. 11:1–11:21. Schloss Dagstuhl - Leibniz-Zentrum für Informatik (2022). https://doi.org/10.4230/LIPIcs.ICDT.2022.11

86. Raszyk, M., Basin, D., Traytel, D.: From nondeterministic to multi-head deterministic finite-state transducers. In: Baier, C., Chatzigiannakis, I., Flocchini, P., Leonardi, S. (eds.) 46th International Colloquium on Automata, Languages, and Programming (ICALP 2019), Volume 132 of LIPIcs, pp. 127:1–127:14.

Schloss Dagstuhl - Leibniz-Zentrum für Informatik (2019). https://doi.org/10.4230/LIPIcs.ICALP.2019.127

87. Raszyk, M., Basin, D., Traytel, D.: Multi-head monitoring of metric dynamic logic. In: Hung, D.V., Sokolsky, O. (eds.) ATVA 2020. LNCS, vol. 12302, pp. 233–250. Springer, Cham (2020). https://doi.org/10.1007/978-3-030-59152-6_13

88. Reese, L., Silva, R.C.G., Traytel, D.: TimelyMon. https://git.ku.dk/kfx532/timelymon

89. Roşu, G., Havelund, K.: Rewriting-based techniques for runtime verification. Autom. Softw. Eng. **12**(2), 151–197 (2005). https://doi.org/10.1007/s10515-005-6205-y

90. Sánchez, C., et al.: A survey of challenges for runtime verification from advanced application domains (beyond software). Formal Methods Syst. Des. **54**(3), 279–335 (2019). https://doi.org/10.1007/s10703-019-00337-w

91. Schneider, J.: HashMon. https://bitbucket.org/jshs/hashmon

92. Schneider, J.: Randomized first-order monitoring with hashing. In: Dang, T., Stolz, V. (eds.) RV 2022. LNCS, vol. 13498, pp. 3–24. Springer, Cham (2022). https://doi.org/10.1007/978-3-031-17196-3_1

93. Schneider, J.: Scalable and trustworthy monitoring. Ph.D. thesis, ETH Zurich, Switzerland (2023). https://doi.org/10.3929/ethz-b-000614295

94. Schneider, J., Basin, D., Brix, F., Krstić, S., Traytel, D.: Scalable online first-order monitoring. In: Colombo, C., Leucker, M. (eds.) RV 2018. LNCS, vol. 11237, pp. 353–371. Springer, Cham (2018). https://doi.org/10.1007/978-3-030-03769-7_20

95. Schneider, J., Basin, D., Brix, F., Krstić, S., Traytel, D.: Adaptive online first-order monitoring. In: Chen, Y.-F., Cheng, C.-H., Esparza, J. (eds.) ATVA 2019. LNCS, vol. 11781, pp. 133–150. Springer, Cham (2019). https://doi.org/10.1007/978-3-030-31784-3_8

96. Schneider, J., Basin, D., Brix, F., Krstić, S., Traytel, D.: Scalable online first-order monitoring. Int. J. Softw. Tools Technol. Transfer **23**(2), 185–208 (2021). https://doi.org/10.1007/s10009-021-00607-1

97. Schneider, J., Basin, D., Krstić, S., Traytel, D.: A formally verified monitor for metric first-order temporal logic. In: Finkbeiner, B., Mariani, L. (eds.) RV 2019. LNCS, vol. 11757, pp. 310–328. Springer, Cham (2019). https://doi.org/10.1007/978-3-030-32079-9_18

98. Stoller, S.D.: Detecting global predicates in distributed systems with clocks. Distrib. Comput. **13**(2), 85–98 (2000). https://doi.org/10.1007/s004460050069

99. Thati, P., Roşu, G.: Monitoring algorithms for metric temporal logic specifications. In: Havelund, K., Roşu, G. (eds.) 4th Workshop on Runtime Verification (RV 2004), Volume 113 of Electronic Notes in Theoretical Computer Science, pp. 145–162. Elsevier (2004)

100. Tuzhilin, A., Clifford, J.: A temporal relational algebra as basis for temporal relational completeness. In: McLeod, D., Sacks-Davis, R., Schek, H.-J. (eds.) 16th International Conference on Very Large Data Bases (VLDB 1990), pp. 13–23. Morgan Kaufmann (1990)

101. Xing, Y., Zdonik, S.B., Hwang, J.-H.: Dynamic load distribution in the Borealis stream processor. In: Aberer, K., Franklin, M.J., Nishio, S. (eds.) 21st International Conference on Data Engineering (ICDE 2005), pp. 791–802. IEEE Computer Society (2005). https://doi.org/10.1109/ICDE.2005.53

102. Zingg, S., Krstić, S., Raszyk, M., Schneider, J., Traytel, D.: Verified first-order monitoring with recursive rules. In: Fisman, D., Rosu, G. (eds.) TACAS 2022. LNCS, vol. 13244, pp. 236–253. Springer, Cham (2022). https://doi.org/10.1007/978-3-030-99527-0_13

Automata

Learning Nonlinear Hybrid Automata from Input–Output Time-Series Data

Amit Gurung$^{(\boxtimes)}$ ⓘ, Masaki Waga ⓘ, and Kohei Suenaga ⓘ

Graduate School of Informatics, Kyoto University, Kyoto, Japan
rajgurung777@gmail.com, {mwaga,ksuenaga}@fos.kuis.kyoto-u.ac.jp

Abstract. Learning an automaton that approximates the behavior of a black-box system is a long-studied problem. Besides its theoretical significance, its application to search-based testing and model understanding is recently recognized. We present an algorithm to learn a nonlinear hybrid automaton (HA) that approximates a black-box hybrid system (HS) from a set of input–output traces generated by the HS. Our method is novel in handling (1) both exogenous and endogenous HS and (2) HA with reset associated with each transition. To our knowledge, ours is the first method that achieves both features. We applied our algorithm to various benchmarks and confirmed its effectiveness.

Keywords: Automata Learning · Inferring Hybrid Systems · Learning Cyber-Physical Systems

1 Introduction

Mathematical modeling of the behavior of a system is one of the main tasks in science and engineering. If a system exhibits only continuous dynamics, it is well modeled by ordinary differential equations (ODE). However, many systems exhibit continuous and discrete dynamics, being instances of *hybrid systems (HS)*. For instance, in modeling an automotive engine, the ODE must be switched following the status of the gear. A similar combination of continuous and discrete dynamics also appears in many other systems, e.g., biological systems [5].

Hybrid automata (HAs) [3] is a formalism for HS. Figure 1 illustrates an HA modeling a bouncing ball. In an HA, a set of locations (represented by a circle in Fig. 1) and transitions between them (represented by an arrow) expresses its discrete dynamics. An ODE associated with each location expresses continuous dynamics. In the HA in Fig. 1, the ODEs at the location show the free-fall behavior of the system, and the transition shows the discrete jump caused by bouncing on the floor (i.e., a change in the ball's velocity).

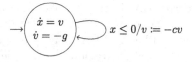

Fig. 1. A bouncing ball model

It is a natural research direction to automatically identify an HA given system's behavior. Not only is it interesting as research, but it is also of a practical

É. André and J. Sun (Eds.): ATVA 2023, LNCS 14215, pp. 33–52, 2023.
https://doi.org/10.1007/978-3-031-45329-8_2

Table 1. Comparison of hybrid automata learning methods

	Non-linear ODEs?	Exo- and Endogenous?	Infer Resets?	Support Inputs?
Ours	Polynomial	Yes	Yes	Yes
[16]	Polynomial	Only Exogenous	No	Yes
[26]	Linear	Yes	No	Yes*
[20, 21]	Linear	Only Endogenous	No	No

* Although this feature is claimed in the paper, the available implementation does not support it.

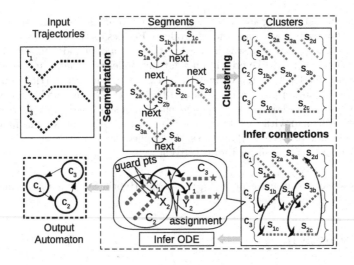

Fig. 2. Overview of our HA learning algorithm. In the below center figure, the circle and the star points stand for each segment's first and last points.

impact since learning a model of a black-box system is recently being applied to automated testing (e.g., black-box checking [15, 19, 24].) There have been various techniques to infer an HA from a set of input–output system trajectories. However, as Table 1 shows, all the existing methods have some limitations in the inferred HA. To the best of our knowledge, there is no existing work that achieves all of the following features: (1) Learned HAs may involve nonlinear ODE as a flow; (2) Learned HAs may be exogenous (i.e., mode changes caused by external events) and endogenous (i.e., mode changes caused by internal events); and (3) Learned HAs may involve resetting of variables at a transition.

This paper proposes an HA-learning algorithm that achieves the three features above. Namely, our algorithm learns an HA that may be exogenous, endogenous or both. A learned HA can reset variables at transitions. These two features make it possible to infer the bouncing ball example in Fig. 1, which is not possible in some of the previous work [16] despite its simplicity. Furthermore, an HA learned by our algorithm may involve ODEs with polynomial flow functions, whereas existing work like [20, 21, 26] can infer only HAs with linear ODEs.

Figure 2 shows the overview of our HA learning algorithm. Our algorithm consists of a *location identification step* and a *transition identification step*. We explain each step below.

Location Identification Step. To identify the locations, our algorithm first splits trajectories into segments so that each segment consists only of continuous dynamics. To this end, the algorithm estimates the derivative of each point on a trajectory with the *linear multistep method (LMM)* [12] and detects the points where the derivative changes discontinuously.

Then, the segments are grouped into clusters so that the segments in each cluster have similar continuous dynamics. For this, we conduct clustering based on the distance determined by *dynamic time warping (DTW)* [4], which takes two segments and computes their similarity in terms of the "shape." We treat each cluster as a location of an HA in the following steps.

After the clustering, our algorithm synthesizes an ODE that best describes the continuous dynamics of the segments in each cluster. Our ODE inference is by a template-based approach. For each location, we fix a polynomial template— a polynomial whose coefficients are symbols for unknowns—for the flow function of the ODE. Then, we obtain coefficients of the polynomial via linear regression of the values in a trajectory and the derivative estimated by LMM.

Transition Identification Step. Once locations are identified, our algorithm next synthesizes the transition relation. It first identifies the pairs of locations (or clusters) between which there is a transition. Concretely, the algorithm identifies a transition from location c_1 to location c_2 if (1) there is a segment s_1 in c_1 and s_2 in c_2 and (2) s_1 immediately precedes s_2 in a trajectory.

The algorithm then synthesizes the guard and the reset on each transition. We synthesize the guard and the reset on each transition in a data-driven manner. Moreover, we introduce type annotation to improve the inference of resets utilizing domain knowledge; we explain the method in detail in Sect. 3.2.

Contributions. Our contributions are summarized as follows.

- We propose an algorithm inferring a general subclass of HAs from a set of input and output trajectories.
- We introduce type annotations to improve the inference of the resets.
- We experimentally show that our algorithm infers HAs fairly close to the original system under learning.

Related Work. Despite the maturity of switched-system identification [9,12], only a few algorithms have been proposed to infer HAs. This scarcity of work in HA learning may be attributed to the additional information that needs to be inferred for HAs (e.g., variable assignments.)

Table 1 summarizes algorithms inferring an HA from a set of trajectories. In [20,21], an HA is learned from a set of trajectories; however, it does not support systems with inputs. Moreover, only linear ODEs can be learned. In [26], an HA with inputs and outputs is learned from trajectories, but the learned ODEs are still limited to linear functions. In [16], an HA with polynomial ODEs is learned from inputs and outputs trajectories. However, the guards in the transitions consist only of the input variables and timing constraints. Due to this limitation, their method cannot infer an endogenous HA such as the bouncing ball model in Fig. 1. Compared with these methods, our algorithm supports the most general class of HAs, to our knowledge.

We remark that most of the technical ingredients used in our algorithm are already presented in the previous papers. For example, using LMM for segmentation and inference of polynomial ODEs is also used by Jin et al. [12] for learning switched dynamical systems and we adapted it for learning HA. The use of DTW for clustering is common in [16]. We argue that our significant technical contribution is the achievement of learning the general class of HAs by an appropriate adaptation and combination of these techniques, e.g., by projecting the output dimensions during segmentation. The use of type annotation to improve the inference of variable assignments is also our novelty, up to our knowledge.

Organization. After reviewing the preliminaries in Sect. 2, we present our HA learning algorithm and an experimental evaluation of it in Sect. 3 and Sect. 4, respectively. Finally, we conclude in Sect. 5.

2   Preliminaries

For a set X, we denote its powerset by $\mathcal{P}(X)$. For a pair $p := (a, b)$, we write $pr_1(p)$ for a and $pr_2(p)$ for b. We denote naturals and reals by $\mathcal{N}$ and $\mathcal{R}$, respectively. For vectors u, and v with the same dimension, the *relative difference* between them is $rd(u, v) := \frac{\|u-v\|}{\|u\|+\|v\|}$ where $\|u\|$ is the Euclidean norm of u. We write $[a, b]$ for the inclusive interval between a and b.

2.1   Trajectories and Hybrid Automata

For a time domain $[0, T] \subseteq \mathcal{R}$ and $n \in \mathcal{N}$, an *n-dimensional (continuous) signal* σ is a function assigning an n-dimensional vector $\sigma(t) \in \mathcal{R}^n$ to each timepoint $t \in [0, T]$. Execution of a system with n_1 dimensional inputs and n_2 dimensional outputs can be modeled by an $(n_1 + n_2)$-dimensional signal.

A *(discrete) trajectory* is a sequence of vectors with timestamps. Concretely, an *n-dimensional trajectory* $(t_1, x_1), (t_2, x_2), \ldots, (t_N, x_N)$ is a finite sequence of pairs of timestamp $t_i \in \mathcal{R}$ and the corresponding value $x_i \in \mathcal{R}^n$ satisfying $t_1 < t_2 < \cdots < t_N$. For a signal $\sigma \colon [0, T] \to \mathcal{R}^n$, a trajectory $(t_1, x_1), (t_2, x_2), \ldots, (t_N, x_N)$ is a *discretization* of σ if for any $i \in \{1, 2, \ldots, N\}$, we have $x_i = \sigma(t_i)$. We call each vector (t_i, x_i) in a trajectory as a *(sampling) point*.

Hybrid automata (HAs) [3,14] is a formalism to model a system exhibiting an interplay between continuous and discrete dynamics. Since we aim to learn an HA from a set of trajectories with inputs and outputs, we employ HAs with input and output variables. To define HAs, we fix a finite set of *(continuous state)* *variables* $\mathcal{X}$, *input variables* $\mathcal{I}$, and *output variables* $\mathcal{O}$ such that $\mathcal{X} = \mathcal{I} \uplus \mathcal{O}$. A *valuation* is a mapping $\delta \in \mathcal{R}^{\mathcal{X}}$ that represents the value of each variable.

Definition 1 (Hybrid automaton). *A hybrid automaton (HA) $\mathcal{H}$, is a tuple $(\mathcal{L}, Inv, Init, Flow, Trans)$ where:*

- *$\mathcal{L}$ is a finite set of locations;*
- *$Inv : \mathcal{L} \rightarrow \mathcal{P}(\mathcal{R}^{\mathcal{X}})$ is a function mapping each location ℓ to the invariant at ℓ;*
- *$Init$, the initial condition, is a pair (ℓ_0, δ_0) such that $\ell_0 \in \mathcal{L}$ and $\delta_0 \in Inv(\ell_0)$;*
- *$Flow$ is a flow function mapping each location $\ell \in \mathcal{L}$ to ODEs of the form $\dot{x} = f(x, u)$, called flow equation, where x is the vector of all the variables in $\mathcal{O}$ and u is the vector of all the variables in $\mathcal{I}$;*
- *$Trans$ is the set of discrete transitions denoted by a tuple $e = (\ell, \mathcal{G}, \mathcal{M}, \ell')$, where $\ell, \ell' \in \mathcal{L}$ are the source and target locations, $\mathcal{G} \subseteq \mathcal{P}(\mathcal{R}^{\mathcal{X}})$ is the guard, and $\mathcal{M} : \mathcal{R}^{\mathcal{X}} \rightarrow \mathcal{R}^{\mathcal{O}}$ is the assignment function.*

For a transition $e \in Trans$, we write $\mathcal{G}(e)$ and $\mathcal{M}(e)$ for the guard and the assignment function of e, respectively.

Intuitively, a guard $\mathcal{G}(e)$ of a transition e is the condition that enables the transition: A transition e can be fired if a valuation δ for the variables satisfies $\delta \in \mathcal{G}(e)$. An assignment $\mathcal{M}(e)$ specifies how a valuation is updated if the transition e fired: A valuation is updated from δ to δ' such that for each $x \in \mathcal{O}$ and $u \in \mathcal{I}$, we have $\delta'(x) = \mathcal{M}(e)(\delta)(x)$ and $\delta'(u) = \delta(u)$ if e is fired.

The semantics of an HA is formalized by the notion of a *run*. A *state* of an HA $\mathcal{H}$ is a pair (ℓ, δ), where ℓ is a location of $\mathcal{H}$ and $\delta \in \mathcal{R}^{\mathcal{X}}$ is a valuation.

Definition 2 (Run). *A run of an HA $(\mathcal{L}, Inv, Init, Flow, Trans)$ is a sequence*

$$(\ell_0, \delta_0) \xrightarrow{\tau_0} (\ell_0, \delta_0') \xrightarrow{e_0} (\ell_1, \delta_1) \xrightarrow{\tau_1} (\ell_1, \delta_1') \xrightarrow{e_1} \dots \xrightarrow{e_{N-1}} (\ell_N, \delta_N) \xrightarrow{\tau_N} (\ell_N, \delta_N')$$

satisfying $(\ell_0, \delta_0) \in Init$ and for each $i \in \{0, 1, \dots, N\}$, there are signals $\sigma_i^x : [0, \tau_i] \rightarrow \mathcal{R}^{\mathcal{O}}$ and $\sigma_i^u : [0, \tau_i] \rightarrow \mathcal{R}^{\mathcal{I}}$ such that (i) for any $x \in \mathcal{O}$ and $u \in \mathcal{I}$, we have $\sigma_i^x(0)(x) = \delta_i(x)$ and $\sigma_i^u(0)(u) = \delta_i(u)$, $\sigma_i^x(\tau_i)(x) = \delta_i'(x)$, and $\sigma_i^x(\tau_i)(u) = \delta_i'(u)$, (ii) for any $t \in [0, \tau_i]$, we have $(\sigma_i^x(t), \sigma_i^u(t)) \in Inv(\ell_i)$ and $\dot{\sigma_i^x}(t) = Flow(\ell_i)(\sigma_i^x(t), \sigma_i^u(t))$, and (iii) we have $\delta_i' \in \mathcal{G}(e_i)$ and δ_{i+1} is such that for each $x \in \mathcal{O}$ and $u \in \mathcal{I}$, we have $\delta_{i+1}(x) = \mathcal{M}(e_i)(\delta_i')(x)$ and $\delta_{i+1}(u) = \delta_i'(u)$. For such a run ρ, a signal $\sigma : [0, T_N] \rightarrow \mathcal{R}^{\mathcal{X}}$ is the signal over ρ if σ is such that $\sigma(t)(x) = \sigma_i^x(t - T_{i-1})(x)$ and $\sigma(t)(u) = \sigma_i^u(t - T_{i-1})(u)$ for each $x \in \mathcal{O}$, $u \in \mathcal{I}$, and $i \in \{0, 1, \dots, N\}$ such that $T_i \leq t < T_{i+1}$, where $T_i = \sum_{j \in 0}^{i} \tau_j$ and $T_{N+1} = \infty$.

2.2 Linear Multistep Method

The *linear multistep method (LMM)* [6] is a technique to numerically solve an initial value problem of an ODE $x(t) = f(x, t)$. Concretely, it approximates the value of $x(t_{n+M})$ by using the values of $x(t_n), \dots, x(t_{n+M-1})$ and

$f(x_n, t_n), \ldots, f(x_{n+M-1}, t_{n+M-1})$—namely, M previous discretized values of x and $f(x,t)$—where $t_{n+i} = t_n + ih$ for some $h > 0$. For this purpose, LMM assumes the following approximation parameterized over $(\alpha_i)_i$ and $(\beta_i)_i$:

$$\sum_{i=0}^{M} \alpha_i x(t_{n-i}) \approx h \sum_{i=0}^{M} \beta_i f(x(t_{n-i}), t_{n-i}).$$

Then, LMM determines the values of $(\alpha_i)_i$ and $(\beta_i)_i$ so that the error of the above approximation, quantified with Taylor's theorem, is minimum; see [6,12,23] for more detail. The approximation with the determined values of $(\alpha_i)_i$ and $(\beta_i)_i$ is used to successively determine the values of $x(t)$ from its initial value.

In the context of our work, we estimate the derivative of a trajectory at each point without knowing the ODE. To this end, we use *backwards differentiation formula (BDF)* [13,23] derived from LMM. The idea is to compute the polynomial passing all the points $(t_n, x(t_n)), \ldots, (t_{n+M-1}, x(t_{n+M-1}))$ using Lagrange interpolation [6,13] and derive the formula to approximate the derivative at $(t_{n+M}, x(t_{n+M}))$ from the polynomial using LMM. Concretely, Lagrange interpolation yields the polynomial: $x(t) \approx \sum_{m=0}^{M} x(t_{n-m}) \prod_{i \neq m} \frac{t - t_{n-m}}{t_{n-i} - t_{n-m}}$. By taking the derivative of both sides and setting t to t_n, we obtain $\dot{x}(t_n) = f(x(t_n), t_n) \approx \sum_{m=0}^{M} x(t_{n-m}) \prod_{i \neq m} (\frac{d}{dt} \frac{t - t_{n-m}}{t_{n-i} - t_{n-m}}) \big|_{t=t_n}$. We use this formula to estimate the derivative at each point in a trajectory. For instance, the formula to estimate the derivatives with $M = 2$ is: $f(x(t_n)) = \frac{1}{h}(\frac{3}{2}x(t_n) - \frac{4}{2}x(t_{n-1}) + \frac{1}{2}x(t_{n-2}))$ [23].

The above formula estimates the derivative at $x(t_n)$ using M previous points—hence called *backward BDF*. Dually, we can derive a formula that estimates the derivative at $x(t_n)$ using M following points called *forward BDF*. We use both in our algorithm.

2.3   Dynamic Time Warping (DTW)

Our algorithm introduced in Sect. 3 first splits given trajectories so that each segment includes only continuous dynamics. Then, it classifies the generated segments based on the "similarity" of the ODE behind. For the classification purpose, we use *dynamic time warping (DTW)* [4]—one of the methods for quantifying the similarity between time-series data in their shapes—as the measure of the similarity inspired by [16]. The previous work [16] applies DTW for HA learning and confirms its effectiveness.

The DTW distance between two time-series data $X := (x_1, x_2, \ldots, x_M)$ and $Y := (y_1, y_2, \ldots, y_N)$, where $M, N \in \mathcal{N}$, is defined as follows. The *alignment path* between X and Y is a finite sequence $P := (p_1, \ldots, p_l)$ where $p_i \in \{1, 2, \ldots, M\} \times \{1, 2, \ldots, N\}$ and P is an alignment between $\{1, \ldots, M\}$ and $\{1, \ldots, N\}$. Concretely, P should satisfy the following conditions: (1) $p_1 = (1,1)$; (2) $p_l = (M, N)$; (3) $(a_{i+1} - a_i, b_{i+1} - b_i)$ is either $(1,0)$, $(0,1)$, or $(1,1)$ for any $(p_i, p_{i+1}) = ((a_i, b_i), (a_{i+1}, b_{i+1}))$. For example, $((1,1), (1,2), (2,3), (3,3), (3,4))$ is an alignment path between $(x_1, \ldots, x_3)$ and $(y_1, \ldots, y_4)$.

An alignment path $P = (p_1, \ldots, p_l)$ between $X := (x_1, x_2, \ldots, x_M)$ and $Y := (y_1, y_2, \ldots, y_N)$ determines the sum $d_P := \sum_{i=1}^{l} \|x_{(pr_1(p_i))} - y_{(pr_2(p_i))}\|$ of the distances between corresponding points in X and Y. Then, the DTW distance $\text{DTW}_{\text{dist}}(X, Y)$ between X and Y is defined by $\min_P d_P$, where P moves all the alignment paths between X and Y. There is an efficient algorithm computing $\text{DTW}_{\text{dist}}(X, Y)$ in $O(MN)$ based on dynamic programming [18].

For X and Y, let P be the alignment that gives the optimal sum of distances between X and Y. We write $\text{DTW}_{\text{correl}}(X, Y)$ for $\text{correl}(P_1, P_2)$, where $P_1 := (pr_1(p_1), \ldots, pr_1(p_l))$, $P_2 := (pr_2(p_1), \ldots, pr_2(p_l))$, and $\text{correl}(P_1, P_2)$ is the Pearson product-moment correlation coefficients between P_1 and P_2. This value becomes larger if P_1 and P_2 increase evenly. Thus, the higher this value is, the more X is similar to Y. The effectiveness of this value in classifying segments is also shown in [16].

3   HA Learning from Input–Output Trajectories

Our proposed algorithm is an offline and passive approach for learning automata, which involves observing input-output behavior from a given dataset without interacting with the system during learning. Here, we present our HA learning algorithm from given trajectories. Our problem setting is formalized as follows.

Passive HA learning problem:
INPUT: trajectories $\{(t_1^i, x_1^i), (t_2^i, x_2^i), \ldots, (t_{N_i}^i, x_{N_i}^i) \mid i \in \{1, 2, \ldots, M\}\}$ that are discretizations of signals over runs of an HA $\overline{\mathcal{H}}$
OUTPUT: an HA $\mathcal{H}$ approximating $\overline{\mathcal{H}}$

Our current algorithm learns an HA such that (i) the invariant of each location is **true**, (ii) each guard is expressed as a polynomial inequality, and (iii) each assignment function is a linear function. We assume that (i) each location of $\mathcal{H}$ has different ODEs and (ii) for each pair (ℓ, ℓ') of locations of $\mathcal{H}$, there is at most one transition from ℓ to ℓ'.

Figure 2 outlines our HA learning algorithm. We first present the identification of the locations and then present that of the transitions.

3.1   Identification of Locations

We identify the locations of an HA by the following three steps: (i) segmentation of the given trajectories, (ii) clustering of the segments, and (iii) inference of ODEs and initial locations.

Segmentation of the Trajectories. The first step in our HA learning algorithm is segmentation. Each trajectory is divided into segments so that the dynamics in each segment are jump-free. We perform segmentation by identifying the change points—the points where the derivative discontinuously changes—along a trajectory. Our approach builds on Jin et al.'s [12] method for learning

---

Algorithm 1. Outline of our segmentation algorithm

Input: A trajectory $\tau = (t_1, x_1), (t_2, x_2), \ldots, (t_N, x_N)$, the step size M in BDF, and the thresholds $\varepsilon_{\text{FwdBwd}}$ and ε_{Bwd}

Output: $cp \subseteq \{1, 2, \ldots, N\}$ is the set of change points

1:   $candidates \leftarrow \emptyset; C \leftarrow \emptyset$
2:   **for all** $i \in \{M + 1, M + 2, \ldots, N - M\}$ **do**
3:      $fwd_i \leftarrow f_{\text{F}}(\tau|_{\mathcal{O}}, i, M)$ ▷ Compute the forward BDF
4:      $bwd_i \leftarrow f_{\text{B}}(\tau|_{\mathcal{O}}, i, M)$ ▷ Compute the backward BDF
5:      **if** $rd(fwd_i, bwd_i) > \varepsilon_{\text{FwdBwd}}$ **then**
6:          **add** i **to** $candidates$
7:   **while** $candidates \neq \emptyset$ **do**
8:      $i \leftarrow \min(candidates)$; **remove** i **from** $candidates$
9:      **if** $i + 1 \notin candidates$ **or** $rd(bwd_i, bwd_{i+1}) \geq \varepsilon_{\text{Bwd}}$ **then**
10:        **add** i **to** cp
11:       **while** $i + 1 \in candidates$ **do**
12:          **remove** $i + 1$ **from** $candidates$; $i \leftarrow i + 1$

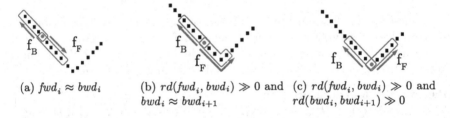

(a) $fwd_i \approx bwd_i$ (b) $rd(fwd_i, bwd_i) \gg 0$ and   (c) $rd(fwd_i, bwd_i) \gg 0$ and
                        $bwd_i \approx bwd_{i+1}$ $rd(bwd_i, bwd_{i+1}) \gg 0$

Fig. 3. Illustration of our segmentation algorithm near a boundary of a segment. The red circle in the right figure is the change point because it is the first point satisfying $rd(fwd_i, bwd_i) > \varepsilon_{\text{FwdBwd}}$ and $rd(bwd_i, bwd_{i+1}) > \varepsilon_{\text{Bwd}}$. (Color figure online)

switched dynamical systems, but we adapted and modified it to extend the approach for learning hybrid systems.

Algorithm 1 outlines our segmentation algorithm. For simplicity, we present an algorithm for a single trajectory; this algorithm is applied to each trajectory obtained from the system. First, for each point in the trajectory, we estimate the derivative using forward and backward BDF (fwd_i and bwd_i, respectively) and deem the point as a candidate of change points if $rd(fwd_i, bwd_i)$ exceeds the threshold. For example, among the three red circles in Fig. 3, we have $fwd_i \approx bwd_i$ for the one in Fig. 3a and $rd(fwd_i, bwd_i) \gg 0$ for the others. Thus, the red circles in Figs. 3b and 3c are the candidates of the change point. We remark that fwd_i and bwd_i are computed with the trajectory $\tau|_{\mathcal{O}}$ projected to the output variables, and our segmentation is not sensitive to the change in the input variables $\mathcal{I}$.

When there are consecutive candidates of the change points, we take the first one satisfying $rd(bwd_i, bwd_{i+1}) \geq \varepsilon_{\text{Bwd}}$ to precisely estimate the change point. Such an optimization is justified under the assumption that there are at least $2M - 1$ points between two consecutive mode changes. For example, in the

Algorithm 2. Outline of the clustering of the segmented trajectories

Input: Set Sg of segments and thresholds ε_{dst} and ε_{cor} for distance and diagonality
Output: $C = \{C_1, C_2, \ldots, C_n\}$ is a set of set of segments such that each C_i is a cluster
1: $C \leftarrow \emptyset$
2: **while** $Sg \neq \emptyset$ **do**
3:     **pick** sg from Sg ▷ We still have $sg \in Sg$ after picking it.
4:     $C' \leftarrow \{sg' \in Sg \mid \text{DTW}_{dist}(sg|_O, sg'|_O) < \varepsilon_{dst} \wedge \text{DTW}_{correl}(sg|_O, sg'|_O) > \varepsilon_{cor}\}$
5:     $Sg \leftarrow Sg \setminus C'$ ▷ C' always includes sg, and sg is removed from Sg.
6:     **add** C' to C

example shown in Fig. 3, the red circle in Fig. 3c is deemed to be the change point because this is the first candidate satisfying $rd(bwd_i, bwd_{i+1}) \geq \varepsilon_{Bwd}$. Note that, in inferring ODEs, we consider only the points within a segment that satisfy $rd(fwd_i, bwd_i) \leq \varepsilon_{FwdBwd}$. This means that candidate points near the boundary of change points are excluded if they do not meet this condition. This is similar to the approach proposed by Jin et al. [12]

The algorithm splits the trajectories at the identified change points into segments; the change points are not included in the segments. Our approach improves upon Jin et al. [12] by adapting their approach for learning switched dynamical systems to the problem of learning hybrid systems. Specifically, we identify change points in a twofold manner. While their approach considers all candidates as change points and drops them from resulting segments, we go a step further and determine the closest change point that precisely separates modes. To achieve this, we search for candidate points until the condition $bwd_i \approx bwd_{i+1}$ is no longer satisfied. This adaptation enables us to include candidate points in the segment actively involved in the transition action, leading to more accurate identification of the transition process.

Clustering of the Segments. Then, we cluster the segmented trajectories so that the segments with similar continuous behaviors are included in the same cluster. For instance, in Fig. 2, the continuous behaviors in S_{1a}, S_{2a}, S_{2d}, and S_{3a} are similar and hence included in a single cluster. We use the identified clusters as the set of locations in the resulting HA. This construction is justified when each location has a different ODE.

Algorithm 2 outlines our clustering algorithm. The overall idea is, the algorithm picks one segment (line 3) and creates a cluster by merging similar segments (line 4). We use both DTW$_{dist}$ and DTW$_{correl}$ to determine the similarity between segments. We remark that we compare the segments $sg|_O$ and $sg'|_O$ projected to the output variables to ignore the similarity in the input variables.

Inference of ODEs and Initial Locations. Our ODE inference is by a template-based linear regression. First, we fix a template $\Phi(x; \theta) = \theta_1 f_1(x) + \theta_2 f_2(x) + \cdots + \theta_N f_N(x)$ of the ODE. In our current implementation, each f_i is a monomial whose degree is less than a value specified by a user, but an arbitrary template can be used. Then, for each cluster C_i and for each output variable $o \in \mathcal{O}$, we construct the set $P_{i,o}$ of points in C_i,[1] and the derivative of o at this point. Formally, $P_{i,o} = \{(x, \dot{x}(o)) \mid \exists sg \in C_i . x \in sg\}$. The derivative $\dot{x}(o)$ is, for example, computed by BDF. Moreover, we can reuse the derivative used in Algorithm 1. Finally, we use linear regression to compute the coefficients θ such that for each $(x, \dot{x}(o)) \in P_{i,o}$, we have $\dot{x}(o) \approx \Phi(x; \theta)$.

In the resulting HA, the initial locations are the locations such that the corresponding cluster contains the first segment for some trajectories. Therefore, we have multiple initial locations if there are trajectories such that their first segments do not satisfy the similarity condition during clustering.

3.2   Identification of Transitions

After identifying the locations of the resulting HA by clustering the segments, we construct transitions. Let $sg_1, sg_2, \ldots, sg_m$ be the segments obtained from a single trajectory by Algorithm 1 and ordered in chronological order; segment sg_i immediately precedes sg_{i+1} in the original trajectory. For each segment sg_g, we denote its initial point, the second last point, and the last point by $sg_g^{\eta_1}$, $sg_g^{\eta_2}$, and $sg_g^{\eta_3}$, respectively.

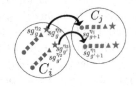

Fig. 4. Illustration of the points connecting clusters C_i and C_j

The idea of the transition identification is to make one transition for each triple $(sg_g^{\eta_2}, sg_g^{\eta_3}, sg_{g+1}^{\eta_1})$—called a *connection triple*—and use these points in a triple to infer its guard and assignment; see Fig. 4 for an illustration. We note that such a triple is always defined since each segment has at least three points.

Formally, for clusters C_i and C_j and a segmented trajectory $sg_1, sg_2, \ldots, sg_m$, the set $T_{i,j}$ of connection triples from C_i to C_j is as follows:

$$T_{i,j} = \{(sg_g^{\eta_2}, sg_g^{\eta_3}, sg_{g+1}^{\eta_1}) \mid g \in \{1, 2, \ldots, m-1\}, sg_g \in C_i, sg_{g+1} \in C_j\}$$

If there are multiple trajectories in HA learning, we construct $T_{i,j}$ for each trajectory and take their union.

We infer guards and assignments using $T_{i,j}$. For each cluster pair (C_i, C_j), the guard of the transition from C_i to C_j is obtained using a support vector machine (SVM) to classify the second last points and the last points. More precisely, for $T_{i,j}^{\perp} = \{sg_g^{\eta_2} \mid \exists (sg_g^{\eta_2}, sg_g^{\eta_3}, sg_{g+1}^{\eta_1}) \in T_{i,j}\}$ and $T_{i,j}^{\top} = \{sg_g^{\eta_3} \mid \exists (sg_g^{\eta_2}, sg_g^{\eta_3}, sg_{g+1}^{\eta_1}) \in T_{i,j}\}$, we compute an equation of hyperplane separating $T_{i,j}^{\perp}$ and $T_{i,j}^{\top}$ using SVM and construct an inequality constraint $\mathcal{G}$ that is satisfied by the points in $T_{i,j}^{\top}$ but not by that in $T_{i,j}^{\perp}$.

For each cluster pair (C_i, C_j), the assignment in the transition from C_i to C_j is obtained using linear regression to approximate the relationship between the valuation before and after the transition. More precisely, we use linear regression

---

[1] Notice that, as mentioned above, we only consider the points within a segment that satisfy $rd(fwd_i, bwd_i) \le \varepsilon_{\mathrm{FwdBwd}}$.

to compute an equation $\mathcal{M}$ such that for each $(sg_g^{\eta_2}, sg_g^{\eta_3}, sg_{g+1}^{\eta_1}) \in T_{i,j}$ and for each $x \in \mathcal{O}$, $sg_{g+1}^{\eta_1}(x)$ is close to $\mathcal{M}(sg_g^{\eta_3})(x)$. Such $\mathcal{M}$ is used as the assignment.

Improving Assignments Inference with Type Annotation. If we have no prior knowledge of the system under learning, we infer assignments using linear regression, as mentioned above. However, even if the exact system dynamics are unknown, we often know how each variable behaves at jumps. For instance, it is reasonable to believe that a variable representing temperature is continuous; hence, it does not change its value at jumps. Such domain knowledge is helpful in inferring precise assignments rather than one using linear regression.

To easily enforce the constraints from domain knowledge on variables, we extend our assignment inference to allow users to annotate each variable with types expressing how a variable is assumed to behave at jumps. We currently support the following types.

No Assignments. If a variable is continuous at a jump (e.g., the variable representing temperature mentioned above), one annotates the variable with "no assignments". For a variable x with this annotation, the procedure above infers an assignment that does not change the value of x.

Constant Assignments. If the value assigned to a variable at a jump is a fixed constant, we annotate the variable with "constant assignments". For instance, in the bouncing ball HA depicted in Fig. 1, the variable x is reset to 0 upon reaching the ground or when the guard condition is satisfied.

Constant Pool. If the value assigned to a variable at a jump is chosen from a finite set, one annotates the variable with "Constant pool" accompanied with the finite set $\{v_1, \ldots, v_n\}$. An example of such a variable is one representing the gear in a model of an automotive. For a variable with this annotation, our algorithm infers the assignment at a jump by majority poll: For a transition from cluster C_i to C_j, it chooses the value most frequently occurring in $T_{i,j}$ as $sg_{g+1}^{\eta_1}$.

3.3   Impact of Parameter Selection on Model Accuracy

We recognize the complexity and potential challenges inherent in ensuring that our proposed hybrid automaton closely emulates the original black-box system, given the intricate and often nonlinear dynamics at play. Nevertheless, our methodology is developed to capture the crucial behaviors of the original system, serving as a foundation for further analysis and understanding. In our method, specific tuning parameters play pivotal roles during the segmentation and clustering processes. To illustrate, the parameter $\varepsilon_{\mathrm{FwdBwd}}$ contributes significantly to effective segmentation, while $\varepsilon_{\mathrm{Bwd}}$ facilitates pinpointing the correct transition point, which in turn allows for the accurate inference of data points for guards and assignments. It is critical to mention that the choice of these thresholds must be well-thought-out. For instance, a large value for $\varepsilon_{\mathrm{FwdBwd}}$ might overlook some change points, while a smaller value could lead to unnecessary redundancy. Therefore, depending on the dynamical class of the system under study, these thresholds may require careful adjustments.

Similarly, during the clustering process, the thresholds DTW_{dist} and DTW_{correl} play instrumental roles in establishing efficient similarity comparisons between segments. While a DTW_{correl} of 0.8 typically works well in deciding segment similarity, the co-adjustment of DTW_{dist} and DTW_{correl} parameters effectively allows the clustering process to manage the number of modes in the learned hybrid automaton, balancing precision in the process. In essence, the judicious selection of these parameters is integral to the success of our method in learning an accurate hybrid automaton.

In addition, it is crucial to emphasize that the accuracy of the learned hybrid automaton heavily depends on the amount of data available. We have adapted our segmentation process and ODE inference from the approach presented by Jin et al. [12], which provides bounds for estimation errors based on sampling time step and a priori knowledge of system dynamics. While perfect replication of the black-box system may not be achievable, the goal is to construct a meaningful and practical model within the framework of a hybrid automaton. See Table 1 for a comparison of these methods.

4   Experiments

We implemented our proposed algorithm using a combination of C++, Python, and MATLAB/Simulink/Stateflow: The HA learning algorithm is written in Python; The learned model is translated into a Simulink/Stateflow model by a C++ program; We use MATLAB to simulate the learned model. We optimized the ODE inference by using only a part of the trajectories when they were sufficiently many. We take $M = 5$ as the step size for BDF. Our implementation is available at https://github.com/rajgurung777/HybridLearner and the artifact at https://doi.org/10.5281/zenodo.7934743.

We conducted experiments (i) to compare the performance of our algorithm against a state-of-the-art method and (ii) to evaluate how the type annotation helps our learning algorithm. For the former evaluation, we compared our algorithm against one of the latest HA learning methods called POSEHAD [16]. Among the recent hybrid-automata learning methodologies, POSEHAD is the closest to ours in that (1) it handles hybrid systems with nonlinear ODEs and (2) it supports input signals to a system; see Table 1. We compared our algorithm with and without a type annotation for the latter evaluation, denoted as "Type" and "W/o Type," respectively. We also compared our method with two other methods (HAutLearn [26] and HySynthParametric [21]); the result is presented in Sect. 4.3.

In the upcoming comparisons in Sects. 4.2 and 4.3, our proposed method is contrasted with several existing approaches, including POSEHAD, HAutLearn, and HySynthParametric. While noteworthy in their respective areas, these methods have certain limitations when it comes to handling the comprehensive features of hybrid automata - a challenge our method is designed to overcome.

Specifically, our approach manages all crucial aspects of hybrid automata, such as guards, nonlinear ODEs, assignments, and support for input signals. It's important to underline that the purpose of these comparisons is not to downplay these existing methods but to highlight the unique scope of functionality and adaptability our method brings to exploring hybrid automata. While this may give an initial impression of an unbalanced comparison, it's essential to emphasize the comprehensive capabilities of our approach, designed to address the gaps left by these other notable methods.

Each benchmark consists of a Simulink/Stateflow model, which we call an *original model*, and two sets of trajectories generated from the original model, which we call *training* and *test* sets. We generated trajectories by feeding random input trajectories and random initial values of the state variables to the original model. The training set is used to learn an HA, which we call a *learned model*, and the test set is used to evaluate the accuracy of the learned model. For each benchmark, the size of the training and test sets are 64 and 32, respectively.

To evaluate the accuracy of the learned model, we feed the same input trajectories and the same initial values to the original and the learned models and compared their output trajectories. The comparison is based on the DTW distance DTW_{dist}. A low DTW distance indicates higher accuracy of the learned model. We denote as δ_{O_1} and δ_{O_2} the DTW distances between trajectories generated from the original and the learned model on the output variable, O_1, and O_2, respectively. We note that, in POSEHAD, the DTW distance is not computed with the entire trajectories but with the segmented trajectories. All the experiments reported in this paper are conducted on a machine with an Intel Core i9 CPU, 2.40GHz, and 32 GiB RAM. We used $\varepsilon_{\text{Bwd}} = 0.01$ in all our experiments.

4.1   Benchmark Description

We briefly describe the benchmarks used in our experiments.

BALL. This is a benchmark modeling a bouncing ball taken from the demo example of Simulink [2]. Figure 1 shows the HA. The acceleration due to the gravity g is taken as input. The range of g is $[-9.9, -9.5]$. We modify the original Simulink model to parameterize the initial values of x and v. We also set the model to operate on a fixed-step solver. We let $x \in [10.2, 10.5]$ and $v = 15$. The reset factor c in Fig. 1 is $c = -0.8$. We execute the model for a time horizon of 13 units with a sampling time of 0.001, i.e., each trajectory consists of 13,000 points. We use $\varepsilon_{\text{FwdBwd}} = 0.1$, $\varepsilon_{\text{dst}} = 9.0$, and $\varepsilon_{\text{cor}} = 0.8$.

TANKS. This benchmark models a two tanks system [11]. Figure 7a shows the HA. The system consists of two tanks with liquid levels x_1 and x_2. The first tank has in/out flow controlled by a valve v_1, whereas, the second tank has outflow controlled by the other valve v_2. Both tanks have external in/out flow controlled by the input signal u. There is also a flow from the first tank to the second tank. In summary, the system has four locations for on and off of v_1 and v_2. The range of the input is $u \in [-0.1, 0.1]$, the initial liquid level of the two tanks are $x_1 = 1.2$ and $x_2 = 1$, and the initial location is *off_ off*. We execute the model for a time

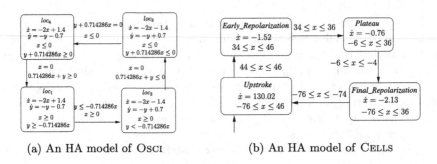

(a) An HA model of Osci   (b) An HA model of Cells

Fig. 5. HA models for Osci and Cells benchmarks

horizon of 9.3 units with a sampling time of 0.001, i.e., each trajectory consists of 9,300 points. We use $\varepsilon_{\text{FwdBwd}} = 0.01$, $\varepsilon_{\text{dst}} = 1.5$ and $\varepsilon_{\text{cor}} = 0.7$.

Osci. This is a benchmark modeling a switched oscillator without filters [8]. Osci is an affine system with two variables, x and y oscillating between two equilibria to maintain a stable oscillation. The HA is shown in Fig. 5a. All the transitions have constant assignments. This system has no inputs. The initial values are $x, y \in [0.01, 0.09]$, and the initial location is loc_1. We execute the model for a time horizon of 10 units with a sampling time of 0.01, i.e., each trajectory consists of 1,000 points. We use $\varepsilon_{\text{FwdBwd}} = 0.1$, $\varepsilon_{\text{dst}} = 1.0$ and $\varepsilon_{\text{cor}} = 0.89$.

Cells. This is a benchmark modeling excitable cells [10, 27], which is a biological system exhibiting hybrid behavior. We use a variant of the excitable cell used in [22]. Our HA model is shown in Fig. 5b. This model has no inputs. We take the initial values for the voltage $x \in [-76, -74]$. The *Upstroke* is the initial location. We execute the model for a time horizon of 500 units with a sampling time of 0.01, i.e., each trajectory consists of 50,000 points. We use $\varepsilon_{\text{FwdBwd}} = 0.01$, $\varepsilon_{\text{dst}} = 1.0$, and $\varepsilon_{\text{cor}} = 0.92$.

Engine. This benchmark models an engine timing system taken from the demo examples in the Simulink automotive category [1]. The model is a complex nonlinear system with two inputs and one output signal. The inputs are the desired speed of the system and the load torque, while the output signal is the engine's speed. We simulate the model for a time horizon of 10 units with a sampling time of 0.01, i.e., each trajectory consists of 1,000 points. We use $\varepsilon_{\text{FwdBwd}} = 0.99$, $\varepsilon_{\text{dst}} = 560$ and $\varepsilon_{\text{cor}} = 0.89$.

4.2 Results and Discussion

Overall Discussion. Table 2 shows the summary of the results. In columns δ_{O_1} and δ_{O_2}, we observe that for all the benchmarks, the HAs learned by our algorithm (both "W/o Type" and "Type") achieved higher accuracy in terms of Avg(δ). This is because of the adequate handling of the input variables and the inference of the resets at transitions. Moreover, type annotation improves model

Table 2. Summary of the results. The columns δ_{O_1} and δ_{O_2} show the minimum (Min), maximum(Max), average (Avg), and standard deviation (Std) of the DTW distance between trajectories generated by the original model and the learned model feeding the test set. The columns Time show the total running time in seconds for learning an HA. Cells with the best results are highlighted.

Model	Measure	W/o Type			Type			POSEHAD		
		δ_{O_1}	δ_{O_2}	Time	δ_{O_1}	δ_{O_2}	Time	δ_{O_1}	δ_{O_2}	Time
BALL	Min(δ)	**0.15**	**0.27**		**0.15**	**0.27**		127.0	1.5e+6	
	Max (δ)	**16.4**	**12.1**	351.2	**16.4**	**12.1**	336.7	39660.7	8.3e+8	41535.9
	Avg (δ)	**1.8**	**2.1**		**1.8**	**2.1**		9566.2	1.7e+8	
	Std (δ)	**3.3**	**3.1**		**3.3**	**3.1**		12695.3	1.8e+8	
TANKS	Min(δ)	0.1	0.3		**0.003**	**0.005**		37.8	7.8e+12	
	Max (δ)	3.9	**2.6**	383.1	**3.2**	**2.6**	383.5	2.3e+4	2.0e+14	13771.5
	Avg (δ)	0.9	1.3		**0.2**	**0.3**		8.1e+3	9.5e+13	
	Std (δ)	1.0	0.68		**0.8**	**0.74**		7.6e+3	5.9e+13	
OSCI	Min(δ)	0.21	0.3		**0.17**	**0.2**		15.8	8.8	
	Max (δ)	0.4	0.7	24.1	**0.3**	**0.6**	24.9	1.5e+3	933.9	404.2
	Avg (δ)	0.3	0.3		**0.2**	**0.2**		1.2e+3	716.0	
	Std (δ)	0.04	0.1		**0.03**	**0.09**		404.0	313.4	
CELLS	Min(δ)	13.2	–		**1.3**	–		2.5e+9	–	
	Max (δ)	155.3	–	2404.2	**150.5**	–	2358.5	5.1e+9	–	191050.0
	Avg (δ)	63.9	–		**58.1**	–		3.1e+9	–	
	Std (δ)	**53.9**	–		57.3	–		8.3e+8	–	
ENGINE	Min(δ)	2.2e+4	–		3.2e+4	–		**2.8e+3**	–	
	Max (δ)	1.7e+5	–	50.6	**5.4e+4**	–	47.9	4.2e+14	–	197.6
	Avg (δ)	6.6e+4	–		**4.2e+4**	–		1.3e+13	–	
	Std (δ)	4.8e+4	–		**5.5e+3**	–		7.4e+13	–	

accuracy, as shown in benchmarks TANKS, OSCI, CELLS, and ENGINE. However, in BALL, both methods perform equally.

We also observe that for the HAs learned by our learning algorithm, the maximum DTW distance Max(δ) tends to be close to the minimum DTW distance Min(δ). This indicates that trajectories generated by our learned model do not have a high deviation from the trajectories generated by the original model. We discuss the detail later in this section. In contrast, in the POSEHAD algorithm, they tend to have a high difference between Min(δ) and Max(δ). We also observe that for the HAs learned by the POSEHAD algorithm, the standard deviation Std(δ) is much larger than that learned from ours. This suggests that our learning algorithm is better at generalization. Moreover, our algorithm takes much less time than POSEHAD. For instance, in the CELLS benchmark, our algorithm takes less than one hour, whereas POSEHAD takes more than 53 h.

Discussion for Each Benchmark. Figure 6 shows the learned HA for BALL produced by our algorithm with a type annotation. We observe that the ODE is precisely learned. Although the guard is far from the expected condition $x \leq 0$, it is close to the expected condition given the range of the state variables; for instance when we have $v \approx -20.55$ and $g \approx -9.8$, the condition is about $x \leq 0.020$, which is reasonably close to $x \leq 0$. Furthermore, our algorithm accurately inferred the assignment of v as $v ::= -0.8v$. In Fig. 8a and 8b, we show plots of the trajectories obtained from the HAs learned by our algorithm (with and without type annotation), the output trajectory predicted by POSEHAD, and the trajectory obtained from the original model. In Fig. 8b, we did not include the predicted trajectory by POSEHAD due to its high error. We observe that the trajectories obtained from our learned models coincide with the original benchmark trajectory, while the trajectory predicted by POSEHAD does not.

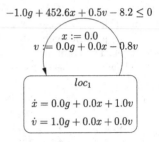

Fig. 6. The HA learned by our algorithm with type annotation on BALL

Figure 7b shows the HA learned by our algorithm with type annotation on the TANKS benchmark. Since the initial value, $x_2 = 1$, is satisfied by the guard at the initial location, the system takes an instant transition to location off_on (see Fig. 7a). Therefore, all trajectories contain data starting from this location, and our algorithm identifies this to be the initial location. Moreover, the trajectories given to the learning algorithm do not include data visiting the location on_on, and this mode is not present in the learned model. We observe that the ODEs are exactly learned, and the guards are close to the original model. In Fig. 8c, we show a plot of the trajectories obtained from the HAs learned by our algorithm (with and without type annotation), the output trajectory predicted by POSEHAD, and the trajectory obtained from the original model. The models learned by our algorithm produced trajectories close to the original model, while several parts predicted by POSEHAD are far from the original one.

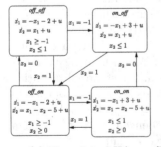

(a) The original HA

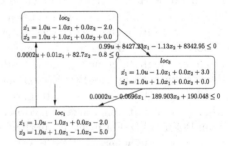

(b) The HA learned by our algorithm with type annotation

Fig. 7. HAs on TANKS benchmark

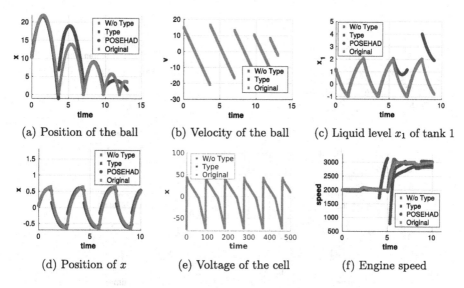

(a) Position of the ball   (b) Velocity of the ball   (c) Liquid level x_1 of tank 1

(d) Position of x (e) Voltage of the cell   (f) Engine speed

Fig. 8. Trajectories on (a–b) BALL (c) TANKS (d) OSCI (e) CELLS and (f) ENGINE

For the ENGINE model, due to the system's complexity, our algorithm produced HAs at most with 37 locations and 137 transitions. In Fig. 8f, we show a plot of the trajectories obtained from the HAs learned by our algorithm (with and without type annotation), the output trajectory predicted by POSEHAD, and the trajectory obtained from the original model. The models learned by our algorithm produced trajectories uniformly close to the original model, while several parts predicted by POSEHAD are far from the original one. Similar observations on accuracy can be drawn from Figs. 8d and 8e on OSCI and CELLS benchmarks, respectively.

4.3   Comparison with Other Methods

We compared our proposed approach with other state-of-the-art methods: HAut-Learn [26] and HySynthParametric [21]. We conducted this experiment using only OSCI, which does not take an input signal, since HAutLearn and HySynthParametric do not support a model taking inputs; see Table 1.

The result is shown in Fig. 9. Figures 9a and 9b (resp., Figs. 9c and 9d) show the plots obtained by the learned models trained with five (resp., 64) trajectories. The training time with five trajectories was as follows: 60.9 s for HAutLearn; 15.6 s for HySynthParametric; 2.2 s for ours. The training time with 64 trajectories was as follows: 1442.3 s for HAutLearn; 1483.6 s for HySynthParametric; 24.9 s for ours.

For the experiment with five training trajectories, the HA learned by HAut-Learn is as precise as our method. However, for the experiment with 64 training trajectories, we observed that the switching guard in the HA learned by HAut-Learn allowed the model to take an early jump from the second jump onwards,

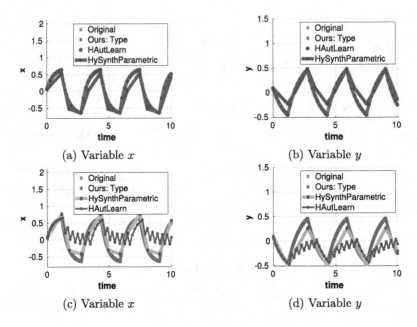

Fig. 9. Trajectories obtained from the learned HAs on the Osci benchmark by the three tools. (a) and (b) are trained using five trajectories, while (c) and (d) show models trained using 64 trajectories.

thus generating plots that do not coincide with the original trajectories. We can observe that the HA learned by HySynthParametric is less precise than ours.

The performance of HAutLearn was largely affected by the values of multiple parameters. The plots in Fig. 9 is obtained by tuning parameters through trials and errors.

5   Conclusion

This paper presents an algorithm to learn an HA with polynomial ODEs from input–output trajectories. We identify the locations by segmenting the given trajectories, clustering the segments, and inferring ODEs. We learn transition guards using SVM with a polynomial kernel and assignment functions using linear regression. Our experimental evaluation suggests that our algorithm produces more accurate HAs than the state-of-the-art algorithms. Moreover, we extended the inference of assignments with type annotations to utilize prior knowledge of a user. In future work, we plan to utilize our learned HA model to perform black-box checking [15,19,24] for falsification, model-bounded monitoring of hybrid systems [25], and controller synthesis [7,17].

Acknowledgements. We are grateful to the anonymous reviewers for their valuable comments. This work was partially supported by JST CREST Grant No. JPMJCR2012, JST PRESTO Grant No. JPMJPR22CA, JST ACT-X Grant No. JPM-JAX200U, and JSPS KAKENHI Grant No. 22K17873 & 19H04084.

References

1. MathWorks: Engine Timing Model with Closed Loop Control. https://in. mathworks.com/help/simulink/slref/engine-timing-model-with-closed-loop-control.html. Accessed 29 Dec 2022
2. MathWorks: Simulation of Bouncing Ball. https://in.mathworks.com/help/simulink/slref/simulation-of-a-bouncing-ball.html. Accessed 29 Dec 2022
3. Alur, R., et al.: The algorithmic analysis of hybrid systems. Theoret. Comput. Sci. **138**(1), 3–34 (1995)
4. Bellman, R., Kalaba, R.: On adaptive control processes. IRE Trans. Autom. Control. **4**(2), 1–9 (1959)
5. Bortolussi, L., Policriti, A.: Hybrid systems and biology. In: Bernardo, M., Degano, P., Zavattaro, G. (eds.) SFM 2008. LNCS, vol. 5016, pp. 424–448. Springer, Heidelberg (2008). https://doi.org/10.1007/978-3-540-68894-5_12
6. Butcher, J.C.: Numerical Methods for Ordinary Differential Equations. Wiley, Hoboken (2016)
7. Filippidis, I., Dathathri, S., Livingston, S.C., Ozay, N., Murray, R.M.: Control design for hybrid systems with tulip: the temporal logic planning toolbox. In: 2016 IEEE Conference on Control Applications (CCA) (2016). https://doi.org/10.1109/cca.2016.7587949
8. Frehse, G., et al.: SpaceEx: scalable verification of hybrid systems. In: Gopalakrishnan, G., Qadeer, S. (eds.) CAV 2011. LNCS, vol. 6806, pp. 379–395. Springer, Heidelberg (2011). https://doi.org/10.1007/978-3-642-22110-1_30, http://spaceex.imag.fr
9. Garulli, A., Paoletti, S., Vicino, A.: A survey on switched and piecewise affine system identification. IFAC Proc. Vol. **45**(16), 344–355 (2012). https://doi.org/10.3182/20120711-3-be-2027.00332
10. Grosu, R., Mitra, S., Ye, P., Entcheva, E., Ramakrishnan, I.V., Smolka, S.A.: Learning cycle-linear hybrid automata for excitable cells. In: Bemporad, A., Bicchi, A., Buttazzo, G. (eds.) HSCC 2007. LNCS, vol. 4416, pp. 245–258. Springer, Heidelberg (2007). https://doi.org/10.1007/978-3-540-71493-4_21
11. Hiskens, I.A.: Stability of limit cycles in hybrid systems. In: Proceedings of the 34th Annual Hawaii International Conference on System Sciences, pp. 6–pp. IEEE (2001)
12. Jin, X., An, J., Zhan, B., Zhan, N., Zhang, M.: Inferring switched nonlinear dynamical systems. Formal Aspects Comput. **33**(3), 385–406 (2021)
13. Keller, R.T., Du, Q.: Discovery of dynamics using linear multistep methods. SIAM J. Numer. Anal. **59**(1), 429–455 (2021)
14. Lygeros, J., Tomlin, C., Sastry, S.: Hybrid systems: modeling, analysis and control. Electronic Research Laboratory, University of California, Berkeley, CA, Technical report. UCB/ERL M, vol. 99, p. 6 (2008)
15. Peled, D.A., Vardi, M.Y., Yannakakis, M.: Black box checking. In: Wu, J., Chanson, S.T., Gao, Q. (eds.) Formal Methods for Protocol Engineering and Distributed Systems, FORTE XII/PSTV XIX 1999, IFIP TC6 WG6.1 Joint International Conference on Formal Description Techniques for Distributed Systems and Communication Protocols (FORTE XII) and Protocol Specification, Testing and Verification (PSTV XIX), 5–8 October 1999, Beijing, China. IFIP Conference Proceedings, vol. 156, pp. 225–240. Kluwer (1999)
16. Saberi, I., Faghih, F., Bavil, F.S.: A passive online technique for learning hybrid automata from input/output traces. ACM Trans. Embed. Comput. Syst. **22**(1), 1–24 (2022). https://doi.org/10.1145/3556543

17. Saoud, A., Jagtap, P., Zamani, M., Girard, A.: Compositional abstraction-based synthesis for cascade discrete-time control systems. In: Abate, A., Girard, A., Heemels, M. (eds.) 6th IFAC Conference on Analysis and Design of Hybrid Systems, ADHS 2018, Oxford, UK, 11–13 July 2018. IFAC-PapersOnLine, vol. 51, pp. 13–18. Elsevier (2018). https://doi.org/10.1016/j.ifacol.2018.08.003
18. Senin, P.: Dynamic time warping algorithm review. Inf. Comput. Sci. Dept. Univ. Hawaii Manoa Honolulu USA **855**(1–23), 40 (2008)
19. Shijubo, J., Waga, M., Suenaga, K.: Efficient black-box checking via model checking with strengthened specifications. In: Feng, L., Fisman, D. (eds.) RV 2021. LNCS, vol. 12974, pp. 100–120. Springer, Cham (2021). https://doi.org/10.1007/978-3-030-88494-9_6
20. Soto, M.G., Henzinger, T.A., Schilling, C.: Synthesis of hybrid automata with affine dynamics from time-series data. In: Bogomolov, S., Jungers, R.M. (eds.) HSCC 2021: 24th ACM International Conference on Hybrid Systems: Computation and Control, Nashville, Tennessee, 19–21 May 2021, pp. 2:1–2:11. ACM (2021). https://doi.org/10.1145/3447928.3456704
21. Soto, M.G., Henzinger, T.A., Schilling, C.: Synthesis of parametric hybrid automata from time series. In: Bouajjani, A., Holík, L., Wu, Z. (eds.) ATVA 2022. LNCS, vol. 13505, pp. 337–353. Springer, Cham (2022). https://doi.org/10.1007/978-3-031-19992-9_22
22. García Soto, M., Henzinger, T.A., Schilling, C., Zeleznik, L.: Membership-based synthesis of linear hybrid automata. In: Dillig, I., Tasiran, S. (eds.) CAV 2019. LNCS, vol. 11561, pp. 297–314. Springer, Cham (2019). https://doi.org/10.1007/978-3-030-25540-4_16
23. Süli, E., Mayers, D.F.: An Introduction to Numerical Analysis. Cambridge University Press, Cambridge (2003)
24. Waga, M.: Falsification of cyber-physical systems with robustness-guided black-box checking. In: Ames, A.D., Seshia, S.A., Deshmukh, J. (eds.) HSCC 2020: 23rd ACM International Conference on Hybrid Systems: Computation and Control, Sydney, New South Wales, Australia, 21–24 April 2020, pp. 11:1–11:13. ACM (2020). https://doi.org/10.1145/3365365.3382193
25. Waga, M., André, E., Hasuo, I.: Model-bounded monitoring of hybrid systems. ACM Trans. Cyber-Phys. Syst. **6**(4), 1–26 (2022). https://doi.org/10.1145/3529095
26. Yang, X., Beg, O.A., Kenigsberg, M., Johnson, T.T.: A framework for identification and validation of affine hybrid automata from input-output traces. ACM Trans. Cyber Phys. Syst. **6**(2), 13:1–13:24 (2022). https://doi.org/10.1145/3470455
27. Ye, P., Entcheva, E., Grosu, R., Smolka, S.A.: Efficient modeling of excitable cells using hybrid automata. In: Proceedings of CMSB, vol. 5, pp. 216–227 (2005)

A Novel Family of Finite Automata for Recognizing and Learning ω-Regular Languages

Yong Li[iD], Sven Schewe[iD], and Qiyi Tang$^{(\boxtimes)}$[iD]

University of Liverpool, Liverpool, UK
qiyitang@liverpool.ac.uk

Abstract. Families of DFAs (FDFAs) have recently been introduced as a new representation of ω-regular languages. They target ultimately periodic words, with acceptors revolving around accepting some representation $u \cdot v^{\omega}$. Three canonical FDFAs have been suggested, called *periodic*, *syntactic*, and *recurrent*. We propose a fourth one, *limit FDFAs*, which can be exponentially coarser than periodic FDFAs and are more succinct than syntactic FDFAs, while they are incomparable (and dual to) recurrent FDFAs. We show that limit FDFAs can be easily used to check not only whether ω-languages are regular, but also whether they are accepted by deterministic Büchi automata. We also show that canonical forms can be left behind in applications: the limit and recurrent FDFAs can complement each other nicely, and it may be a good way forward to use a combination of both. Using this observation as a starting point, we explore making more efficient use of Myhill-Nerode's right congruences in aggressively increasing the number of don't-care cases in order to obtain smaller progress automata. In pursuit of this goal, we gain succinctness, but pay a high price by losing constructiveness.

1 Introduction

The class of ω-regular languages has proven to be an important formalism to model reactive systems and their specifications, and automata over infinite words are the main tool to reason about them. For example, the automata-theoretic approach to verification [24] is the main framework for verifying ω-regular specifications. The first type of automata recognizing ω-regular languages is nondeterministic Büchi automata [6] (NBAs) where an infinite word is accepted if one of its runs meets the accepting condition for infinitely many times. Since then, other types of acceptance conditions, such as Muller, Rabin, Streett and parity automata [25], have been introduced. All the automata mentioned above are finite automata processing *infinite* words, widely known as ω-automata [25].

The theory of ω-regular languages is more involved than that of regular languages. For instance, nondeterministic finite automata (NFAs) can be determinized with a subset construction, while NBAs have to make use of tree structures [21]. This is because of a fundamental difference between these language

© The Author(s), under exclusive license to Springer Nature Switzerland AG 2023
E. André and J. Sun (Eds.): ATVA 2023, LNCS 14215, pp. 53–73, 2023.
https://doi.org/10.1007/978-3-031-45329-8_3

classes: for a given regular language R, the Myhill-Nerode theorem [18,19] defines a right congruence (RC) $\backsim_R$ in which every equivalence class corresponds to a state in the minimal deterministic finite automata (DFA) accepting R. In contrast, there is no similar theorem to define the minimal deterministic ω-automata for the full class of ω-regular languages[1]. Schewe proved in [23] that it is NP-complete to find the minimal deterministic ω-automaton even given a deterministic ω-automaton. Therefore, it seems impossible to easily define a Myhill-Nerode theorem for (minimal) ω-automata.

Recently, Angluin, Boker and Fisman [2] proposed families of DFAs (FDFAs) for recognizing ω-regular languages, in which every DFA can be defined with respect to a RC defined over a given ω-regular language [3]. This tight connection is the theoretical foundation on which the state of the art learning algorithms for ω-regular languages [3,12] using membership and equivalence queries [1] are built. FDFAs are based on well-known properties of ω-regular languages [6,7]: two ω-regular languages are equivalent if, and only if, they have the same set of *ultimately periodic words*. An ultimately periodic word w is an infinite word that consists of first a finite prefix u, followed by an infinite repetition of a finite nonempty word v; it can thus be represented as a decomposition pair (u,v). FDFAs accept infinite words by accepting their decomposition pairs: an FDFA $\mathcal{F} = (\mathcal{M}, \{\mathcal{N}^q\})$ consists of a *leading DFA* $\mathcal{M}$ that processes the finite prefix u, while leaving the acceptance work of v to the *progress DFA* $\mathcal{N}^q$, one for each state of $\mathcal{M}$. To this end, $\mathcal{M}$ intuitively tracks the Myhill-Nerode's RCs, and an ultimately periodic word $u \cdot v^\omega$ is accepted if it has a representation $x \cdot y^\omega$ such that x and $x \cdot y$ are in the same congruence class and y is accepted by the progress DFA $\mathcal{N}^x$. Angluin and Fisman [3] formalized the RCs of three canonical FDFAs, namely periodic [7], syntactic [16] and recurrent [3], and provided a unified learning framework for them.

In this work, we first propose a fourth one, called *limit FDFAs* (cf. Section 3). We show that limit FDFAs are coarser than syntactic FDFAs. Since syntactic FDFAs can be exponentially more succinct than periodic FDFAs [3], so do our limit FDFAs. We show that limit FDFAs are dual (and thus incomparable in the size) to recurrent FDFAs, due to symmetric treatment for don't care words. More precisely, the formalization of such FDFA does not care whether or not a progress automaton $\mathcal{N}^x$ accepts or rejects a word v, unless reading it in $\mathcal{M}$ produces a self-loop. Recurrent progress DFAs reject all those don't care words, while limit progress DFAs accept them.

We show that limit FDFAs (families of DFAs that use limit DFAs) have two interesting properties. The first is on conciseness: we show that this change in the treatment of don't care words not only defines a dual to recurrent FDFAs but also allows us to identify languages accepted by deterministic Büchi automata (DBAs) easily. It is only known that one can identify whether a given ω-language is regular by verifying whether the number of states in the three canonical FDFAs is finite. However, if one wishes to identify DBA-recognizable languages with

---

[1] Simple extension of Myhill-Nerode theorem for ω-regular languages only works on a small subset [4,15].

FDFAs, a straight-forward approach is to first translate the input FDFA to an equivalent deterministic Rabin automaton [2] through an intermediate NBA, and then use the deciding algorithm in [10] by checking the transition structure of Rabin automata. However, this approach is exponential in the size of the input FDFA because of the NBA determinization procedure [8,21,22]. Our limit FDFAs are, to the best of our knowledge, the *first* type of FDFAs able to identify the DBA-recognizable languages in polynomial time (cf. Sect. 4).

We note that limit FDFAs also fit nicely into the learning framework introduced in [3], so that they can be used for learning without extra development.

We then discuss how to make more use of don't care words when defining the RCs of the progress automata, leading to the coarsest congruence relations and therefore the most concise FDFAs, albeit to the expense of losing constructiveness (cf. Sect. 5).

2 Preliminaries

In the whole paper, we fix a finite *alphabet* Σ. A *word* is a finite or infinite sequence of letters in Σ; ϵ denotes the empty word. Let Σ^* and Σ^ω denote the set of all finite and infinite words (or ω-words), respectively. In particular, we let $\Sigma^+ = \Sigma^* \setminus \{\epsilon\}$. A *finitary language* is a subset of Σ^*; an *ω-language* is a subset of Σ^ω. Let ρ be a sequence; we denote by $\rho[i]$ the i-th element of ρ and by $\rho[i..k]$ the subsequence of ρ starting at the i-th element and ending at the k-th element (inclusively) when $i \leq k$, and the empty sequence ϵ when $i > k$. Given a finite word u and a word w, we denote by $u \cdot w$ (uw, for short) the concatenation of u and w. Given a finitary language L_1 and a finitary/ω-language L_2, the concatenation $L_1 \cdot L_2$ ($L_1 L_2$, for short) of L_1 and L_2 is the set $L_1 \cdot L_2 = \{ uw \mid u \in L_1, w \in L_2 \}$ and L_1^ω the infinite concatenation of L_1.

Transition System. A (nondeterministic) transition system (TS) is a tuple $\mathcal{T} = (Q, q_0, \delta)$, where Q is a finite set of states, $q_0 \in Q$ is the initial state, and $\delta : Q \times \Sigma \rightarrow 2^Q$ is a transition function. We also lift δ to sets as $\delta(S, \sigma) := \bigcup_{q \in S} \delta(q, \sigma)$. We also extend δ to words, by letting $\delta(S, \epsilon) = S$ and $\delta(S, a_0 a_1 \cdots a_k) = \delta(\delta(S, a_0), a_1 \cdots a_k)$, where we have $k \geq 1$ and $a_i \in \Sigma$ for $i \in \{0, \cdots, k\}$.

The *underlying graph* $\mathcal{G}_\mathcal{T}$ of a TS $\mathcal{T}$ is a graph $\langle Q, E \rangle$, where the set of vertices is the set Q of states in $\mathcal{T}$ and $(q, q') \in E$ if $q' \in \delta(q, a)$ for some $a \in \Sigma$. We call a set $C \subseteq Q$ a *strongly connected component* (SCC) of $\mathcal{T}$ if, for every pair of states $q, q' \in C$, q and q' can reach each other in $\mathcal{G}_\mathcal{T}$.

Automata. An automaton on finite words is called a *nondeterministic finite automaton* (NFA). An NFA $\mathcal{A}$ is formally defined as a tuple $(\mathcal{T}, F)$, where $\mathcal{T}$ is a TS and $F \subseteq Q$ is a set of *final* states. An automaton on ω-words is called a *nondeterministic Büchi automaton* (NBA). An NBA $\mathcal{B}$ is represented as a tuple $(\mathcal{T}, \Gamma)$ where $\mathcal{T}$ is a TS and $\Gamma \subseteq \{(q, a, q') : q, q' \in Q, a \in \Sigma, q' \in \delta(q, a)\}$ is a set of *accepting* transitions. An NFA $\mathcal{A}$ is said to be a *deterministic* finite automaton (DFA) if, for each $q \in Q$ and $a \in \Sigma$, $|\delta(q, a)| \leq 1$. Deterministic Büchi automata

(DBAs) are defined similarly and thus Γ is a subset of $\{(q, a) : q \in Q, a \in \Sigma\}$, since the successor q' is determined by the source state and the input letter.

A *run* of an NFA $\mathcal{A}$ on a finite word u of length $n \geq 0$ is a sequence of states $\rho = q_0 q_1 \cdots q_n \in Q^+$ such that, for every $0 \leq i < n$, $q_{i+1} \in \delta(q_i, u[i])$. We write $q_0 \xrightarrow{u} q_n$ if there is a run from q_0 to q_n over u. A finite word $u \in \Sigma^*$ is *accepted* by an NFA $\mathcal{A}$ if there is a run $q_0 \cdots q_n$ over u such that $q_n \in F$. Similarly, an ω-*run* of $\mathcal{A}$ on an ω-word w is an infinite sequence of transitions $\rho = (q_0, w[0], q_1)(q_1, w[1], q_2) \cdots$ such that, for every $i \geq 0$, $q_{i+1} \in \delta(q_i, w[i])$. Let $\inf(\rho)$ be the set of transitions that occur infinitely often in the run ρ. An ω-word $w \in \Sigma^\omega$ is *accepted* by an NBA $\mathcal{A}$ if there exists an ω-run ρ of $\mathcal{A}$ over w such that $\inf(\rho) \cap \Gamma \neq \emptyset$. The *finitary language* recognized by an NFA $\mathcal{A}$, denoted by $\mathcal{L}_*(\mathcal{A})$, is defined as the set of finite words accepted by it. Similarly, we denote by $\mathcal{L}(\mathcal{A})$ the ω-*language* recognized by an NBA $\mathcal{A}$, i.e., the set of ω-words accepted by $\mathcal{A}$. NFAs/DFAs accept exactly *regular* languages while NBAs recognize exactly ω-*regular* languages.

Right Congruences. A *right congruence* (RC) relation is an equivalence relation $\backsim$ over Σ^* such that $x \backsim y$ implies $xv \backsim yv$ for all $v \in \Sigma^*$. We denote by $|\backsim|$ the index of $\backsim$, i.e., the number of equivalence classes of $\backsim$. A *finite RC* is a RC with a finite index. We denote by $\Sigma^*/_\backsim$ the set of equivalence classes of Σ^* under $\backsim$. Given $x \in \Sigma^*$, we denote by $[x]_\backsim$ the equivalence class of $\backsim$ that x belongs to.

For a given RC $\backsim$ of a regular language R, the Myhill-Nerode theorem [18,19] defines a unique minimal DFA D of R, in which each state of D corresponds to an equivalence class defined by $\backsim$ over Σ^*. Therefore, we can construct a DFA $\mathcal{D}[\backsim]$ from $\backsim$ in a standard way.

Definition 1 ([18,19]). *Let $\backsim$ be a right congruence of finite index. The TS $\mathcal{T}[\backsim]$ induced by $\backsim$ is a tuple (S, s_0, δ) where $S = \Sigma^*/_\backsim$, $s_0 = [\epsilon]_\backsim$, and for each $u \in \Sigma^*$ and $a \in \Sigma$, $\delta([u]_\backsim, a) = [ua]_\backsim$.*

For a given regular language R, we can define the RC $\backsim_R$ of R as $x \backsim_R y$ if, and only if, $\forall v \in \Sigma^*. xv \in R \iff yv \in R$. Therefore, the minimal DFA for R is the DFA $\mathcal{D}[\backsim_R] = (\mathcal{T}[\backsim_R], F_{\backsim_R})$ by setting final states $F_{\backsim_R}$ to all equivalence classes $[u]_{\backsim_R}$ such that $u \in R$.

Ultimately Periodic (UP) Words. A UP-word w is an ω-word of the form uv^ω, where $u \in \Sigma^*$ and $v \in \Sigma^+$. Thus $w = uv^\omega$ can be represented as a pair of finite words (u, v), called a *decomposition* of w. A UP-word can have multiple decompositions: for instance (u, v), (uv, v), and (u, vv) are all decompositions of uv^ω. For an ω-language L, let $UP(L) = \{ uv^\omega \in L \mid u \in \Sigma^* \wedge v \in \Sigma^+ \}$ denote the set of all UP-words in L. The set of UP-words of an ω-regular language L can be seen as the fingerprint of L, as stated below.

Theorem 1 ([6,7]). *(1) Every non-empty ω-regular language L contains at least one UP-word. (2) Let L and L' be two ω-regular languages. Then $L = L'$ if, and only if, $UP(L) = UP(L')$.*

Families of DFAs (FDFAs). Based on Theorem 1, Angluin, Boker, and Fisman [2] introduced the notion of FDFAs to recognize ω-regular languages.

Definition 2 ([2]). *An FDFA is a pair $\mathcal{F} = (\mathcal{M}, \{\mathcal{N}^q\})$ consisting of a leading DFA $\mathcal{M}$ and of a progress DFA $\mathcal{N}^q$ for each state q in $\mathcal{M}$.*

Intuitively, the leading DFA $\mathcal{M}$ of $\mathcal{F} = (\mathcal{M}, \{\mathcal{N}^q\})$ for L consumes the finite prefix u of a UP-word $uv^\omega \in \mathrm{UP}(L)$, reaching some state q and, for each state q of $\mathcal{M}$, the progress DFA $\mathcal{N}^q$ accepts the period v of uv^ω. Note that the leading DFA $\mathcal{M}$ of every FDFA does not make use of final states—contrary to its name, it is really a leading transition system.

Let A be a deterministic automaton with TS $\mathcal{T} = (Q, q_0, \delta)$ and $x \in \Sigma^*$. We denote by $A(x)$ the state $\delta(q_0, x)$. Each FDFA $\mathcal{F}$ characterizes a set of UP-words $\mathrm{UP}(\mathcal{F})$ by following the acceptance condition.

Definition 3 (Acceptance). *Let $\mathcal{F} = (\mathcal{M}, \{\mathcal{N}^q\})$ be an FDFA and w be a UP-word. A decomposition (u, v) of w is* normalized *with respect to $\mathcal{F}$ if $\mathcal{M}(u) = \mathcal{M}(uv)$. A decomposition (u, v) is* accepted *by $\mathcal{F}$ if (u, v) is normalized and we have $v \in \mathcal{L}_*(\mathcal{N}^q)$ where $q = \mathcal{M}(u)$. The UP-word w is accepted by $\mathcal{F}$ if there exists a decomposition (u, v) of w accepted by $\mathcal{F}$.*

Note that the acceptance condition in [2] is defined with respect to the decompositions, while ours applies to UP-words. So, they require the FDFAs to be saturated for recognizing ω-regular languages.

Definition 4 (Saturation [2]). *Let $\mathcal{F}$ be an FDFA and w be a UP-word in $\mathrm{UP}(\mathcal{F})$. We say $\mathcal{F}$ is* saturated *if, for all normalized decompositions (u, v) and (u', v') of w, either both (u, v) and (u', v') are accepted by $\mathcal{F}$, or both are not.*

We will see in Sect. 4.1 that under our acceptance definition the saturation property can be relaxed while still accepting the same language.

In the remainder of the paper, we fix an ω-language L unless stated otherwise.

3 Limit FDFAs for Recognizing ω-Regular Languages

In this section, we will first recall the definitions of three existing canonical FDFAs for ω-regular languages, and then introduce our limit FDFAs and compare the four types of FDFAs.

3.1 Limit FDFAs and Other Canonical FDFAs

Recall that, for a given regular language R, by Definition 1, the Myhill-Nerode theorem [18,19] associates each equivalence class of $\backsim_R$ with a state of the minimal DFA $\mathcal{D}[\backsim_R]$ of R. The situation in ω-regular languages is, however, more involved [4]. An immediate extension of such RCs for an ω-regular language L is the following.

Definition 5 (Leading RC). *For two $u_1, u_2 \in \Sigma^*$, $u_1 \backsim_L u_2$ if, and only if $\forall w \in \Sigma^\omega$. $u_1 w \in L \Longleftrightarrow u_2 w \in L$.*

Since we fix an ω-language L in the whole paper, we will omit the subscript in $\backsim_L$ and directly use $\backsim$ in the remainder of the paper.

Assume that L is an ω-regular language. Obviously, the index of $\backsim$ is *finite* since it is not larger than the number of states in the minimal deterministic ω-automaton accepting L. However, $\backsim$ is only enough to define the minimal ω-automaton for a small subset of ω-regular languages; see [4,15] for details about such classes of languages. For instance, consider the language $L = (\Sigma^* \cdot aa)^\omega$ over $\Sigma = \{a, b\}$: clearly, $|\backsim| = 1$ because L is a suffix language (for all $u \in \Sigma^*$, $w \in L \Longleftrightarrow u \cdot w \in L$). At the same time, it is easy to see that the minimal deterministic ω-automaton needs at least two states to recognize L. Hence, $\backsim$ alone does not suffice to recognize the full class of ω-regular languages.

Nonetheless, based on Theorem 1, we only need to consider the UP-words when uniquely identifying a given ω-regular language L with RCs. Calbrix *et al.* proposed in [7] the use of the regular language $L_\$ = \{u\$v : u \in \Sigma^*, v \in \Sigma^+, uv^\omega \in L\}$ to represent L, where $\$ \notin \Sigma$ is a fresh letter[2]. Intuitively, $L_\$$ associates a UP-word w in $\mathrm{UP}(L)$ by containing every decomposition (u, v) of w in the form of $u\$v$. The FDFA representing $L_\$$ is formally stated as below.

Definition 6 (Periodic FDFAs [7]). *The $\backsim$ is as defined in Definition 5.*

Let $[u]_\backsim$ be an equivalence class of $\backsim$. For $x, y \in \Sigma^*$, we define periodic RC as: $x \approx_P^u y$ if, and only if, $\forall v \in \Sigma^*$, $u \cdot (x \cdot v)^\omega \in L \Longleftrightarrow u \cdot (y \cdot v)^\omega \in L$.

The periodic FDFA $\mathcal{F}_P = (\mathcal{M}, \{\mathcal{N}_P^u\})$ of L is defined as follows.

The leading DFA $\mathcal{M}$ is the tuple $(\mathcal{T}[\backsim], \emptyset)$. Recall that $\mathcal{T}[\backsim]$ is the TS constructed from $\backsim$ by Definition 1.

The periodic progress DFA $\mathcal{N}_P^u$ of the state $[u]_\backsim \in \Sigma^*/_\backsim$ is the tuple $(\mathcal{T}[\approx_P^u], F_u)$, where $[v]_{\approx_P^u} \in F_u$ if $uv^\omega \in L$.

One can verify that, for all $u, x, y, v \in \Sigma^*$, if $x \approx_P^u y$, then $xv \approx_P^u yv$. Hence, $\approx_P^u$ is a RC. It is also proved in [7] that $L_\$$ is a regular language, so the index of $\approx_P^u$ is also finite.

Angluin and Fisman in [3] showed that, for a variant of the family of languages L_n given by Michel [17], its periodic FDFA has $\Omega(n!)$ states, while the syntactic FDFA obtained in [16] only has $\mathcal{O}(n^2)$ states. The leading DFA of the syntactic FDFAs is exactly the one defined for the periodic FDFA. The two types of FDFAs differ in the definitions of the progress DFAs $\mathcal{N}^u$ for some $[u]_\backsim$. From Definition 6, one can see that $\mathcal{N}_P^u$ accepts the finite words in $V_u = \{v \in \Sigma^+ : u \cdot v^\omega \in L\}$. The progress DFA $\mathcal{N}_S^u$ of the syntactic FDFA is not required to accept all words in V_u, but only a subset $V_{u,v} = \{v \in \Sigma^+ : u \cdot v^\omega \in L, u \backsim u \cdot v\}$, over which the leading DFA $\mathcal{M}$ can take a round trip from $\mathcal{M}(u)$ back to itself. This minor change makes the syntactic FDFAs of the language family L_n exponentially more succinct than their periodic counterparts.

Formally, syntactic FDFAs are defined as follows.

---

[2] This enables to learn L via learning the regular language $L_\$$ [9].

Definition 7 (Syntactic FDFA [16]). *The $\backsim$ is as defined in Definition 5.*

Let $[u]_\backsim$ be an equivalence class of $\backsim$. For $x, y \in \Sigma^*$, we define syntactic RC as: $x \approx_S^u y$ if and only if $u \cdot x \backsim u \cdot y$ and for $\forall v \in \Sigma^*$, if $u \cdot x \cdot v \backsim u$, then $u \cdot (x \cdot v)^\omega \in L \Longleftrightarrow u \cdot (y \cdot v)^\omega \in L$.

The syntactic FDFA $\mathcal{F}_S = (\mathcal{M}, \{\mathcal{N}_S^u\})$ of L is defined as follows.

The leading DFA $\mathcal{M}$ is the tuple $(\mathcal{T}[\backsim], \emptyset)$ as defined in Definition 6.

The syntactic progress DFA $\mathcal{N}_S^u$ of the state $[u]_\backsim \in \Sigma^*/\backsim$ is the tuple $(\mathcal{T}[\approx_S^u], F_u)$ where $[v]_{\approx_S^u} \in F_u$ if $u \cdot v \backsim u$ and $uv^\omega \in L$.

Angluin and Fisman [3] noticed that the syntactic progress RCs are not defined with respect to the regular language $V_{u,v} = \{v \in \Sigma^+ : u \cdot v^\omega \in L, u \backsim u \cdot v\}$ as $\backsim_{V_{u,v}}$ that is similar to $\backsim_R$ for a regular language R. They proposed the recurrent progress RC $\approx_R^u$ that mimics the RC $\backsim_{V_{u,v}}$ to obtain a DFA accepting $V_{u,v}$ as follows.

Definition 8 (Recurrent FDFAs [3]). *The $\backsim$ is as defined in Definition 5.*

Let $[u]_\backsim$ be an equivalence class of $\backsim$. For $x, y \in \Sigma^*$, we define recurrent RC as: $x \approx_R^u y$ if and only if $\forall v \in \Sigma^*$, $(u \cdot x \cdot v \backsim u \wedge u \cdot (xv)^\omega \in L) \Longleftrightarrow (u \cdot yv \backsim u \wedge u \cdot (y \cdot v)^\omega \in L)$.

The recurrent FDFA $\mathcal{F}_R = (\mathcal{M}, \{\mathcal{N}_R^u\})$ of L is defined as follows.

The leading DFA $\mathcal{M}$ is the tuple $(\mathcal{T}[\backsim], \emptyset)$ as defined in Definition 6.

The recurrent progress DFA $\mathcal{N}_R^u$ of the state $[u]_\backsim \in \Sigma^*/\backsim$ is the tuple $(\mathcal{T}[\approx_R^u], F_u)$ where $[v]_{\approx_R^u} \in F_u$ if $u \cdot v \backsim u$ and $uv^\omega \in L$.

As pointed out in [3], the recurrent FDFAs may *not* be minimal because, according to Definition 3, FDFAs only care about the normalized decompositions, i.e, whether a word in $C_u = \{v \in \Sigma^+ : u \cdot v \backsim u\}$ is accepted by the progress DFA $\mathcal{N}_R^u$. However, there are *don't care* words that are not in C_u and recurrent FDFAs treat them all as *rejecting*[3].

Our argument is that the don't care words are *not* necessarily rejecting and can also be regarded as *accepting*. This idea allows the progress DFAs $\mathcal{N}^u$ to accept the regular language $\{v \in \Sigma^+ : u \cdot v \backsim u \implies u \cdot v^\omega \in L\}$, rather than $\{v \in \Sigma^+ : u \cdot v \backsim u \wedge u \cdot v^\omega \in L\}$. This change allows a translation of limit FDFAs to DBAs with a quadratic blow-up when L is DBA-recognizable language, as shown later in Sect. 4. We formalize this idea as below and define a new type of FDFAs called *limit FDFAs*.

Definition 9 (Limit FDFAs). *The $\backsim$ is as defined in Definition 5.*

Let $[u]_\backsim$ be an equivalence class of $\backsim$. For $x, y \in \Sigma^*$, we define limit RC as: $x \approx_L^u y$ if and only if $\forall v \in \Sigma^*$, $(u \cdot x \cdot v \backsim u \implies u \cdot (x \cdot v)^\omega \in L) \Longleftrightarrow (u \cdot y \cdot v \backsim u \implies u \cdot (y \cdot v)^\omega \in L)$.

The limit FDFA $\mathcal{F}_L = (\mathcal{M}, \{\mathcal{N}_L^u\})$ of L is defined as follows.

The leading DFA $\mathcal{M}$ is the tuple $(\mathcal{T}[\backsim], \emptyset)$ as defined in Definition 6.

The progress DFA $\mathcal{N}_L^u$ of the state $[u]_\backsim \in \Sigma^*/\backsim$ is the tuple $(\mathcal{T}[\approx_L^u], F_u)$ where $[v]_{\approx_L^u} \in F_u$ if $u \cdot v \backsim u \implies uv^\omega \in L$.

---

[3] Minimizing DFAs with don't care words is NP-complete [20].

We need to show that $\approx_L^u$ is a RC. For $u, x, y, v' \in \Sigma^*$, if $x \approx_L^u y$, we need to prove that $xv' \approx_L^u yv'$, i.e., for all $e \in \Sigma^*$, $(u \cdot xv' \cdot e \curvearrowright u \implies u \cdot (xv' \cdot e)^\omega \in L) \iff (u \cdot yv' \cdot e \curvearrowright u \implies u \cdot (yv' \cdot e)^\omega \in L)$. This follows immediately from the fact that $x \approx_L^u y$ by setting $v = v' \cdot e$ for all $e \in \Sigma^*$ in Definition 9.

Let $L = a^\omega + ab^\omega$ be a language over $\Sigma = \{a, b\}$. Three types of FDFAs are depicted in Fig. 1, where the leading DFA $\mathcal{M}$ is given in the column labeled with "Leading" and the progress DFAs are in the column labeled with "Syntactic", "Recurrent" and "Limit". We omit the periodic FDFA here since we will focus more on the other three in this work. Consider the progress DFA $\mathcal{N}_L^{aa}$: there are only two equivalence classes, namely $[\epsilon]_{\approx_L^{aa}}$ and $[a]_{\approx_L^{aa}}$. We can use $v = \epsilon$ to distinguish ϵ and a word $x \in \Sigma^+$ since $aa \cdot \epsilon \curvearrowright aa \implies aa \cdot (\epsilon \cdot \epsilon)^\omega \in L$ does not hold, while $aa \cdot x \curvearrowright aa \implies aa \cdot (x \cdot \epsilon)^\omega \in L$ holds. For all $x, y \in \Sigma^+$, $x \approx_L^{aa} y$ since both $aa \cdot x \curvearrowright aa \implies aa \cdot (x \cdot v)^\omega \in L$ and $aa \cdot y \curvearrowright aa \implies aa \cdot (y \cdot v)^\omega \in L$ hold for all $v \in \Sigma^*$. One can also verify the constructions for the syntactic and recurrent progress DFAs. We can see that the don't care word b for the class $[aa]_\curvearrowright$ are rejecting in both $\mathcal{N}_S^{aa}$ and $\mathcal{N}_R^{aa}$, while it is accepted by $\mathcal{N}_L^{aa}$. Even though b is accepted in $\mathcal{N}_L^{aa}$, one can observe that (aa, b) (and thus $aa \cdot b^\omega$) is not accepted by the limit FDFA, according to Definition 3. Indeed, the three types of FDFAs still recognize the same language L.

When the index of $\curvearrowright$ is only one, then $\epsilon \curvearrowright u$ holds for all $u \in \Sigma^*$. Corollary 1 follows immediately.

Corollary 1. *Let L be an ω-regular language with $|\curvearrowright| = 1$. Then, periodic, syntactic, recurrent and limit FDFAs coincide.*

We show in Lemma 1 that the limit FDFAs are a coarser representation of L than the syntactic FDFAs. Moreover, there is a tight connection between the syntactic FDFAs and limit FDFAs.

Lemma 1. *For all $u, x, y \in \Sigma^*$,*

1. $x \approx_S^u y$ *if, and only if $u \cdot x \curvearrowright u \cdot y$ and $x \approx_L^u y$.*
2. $|\approx_L^u| \leq |\approx_S^u| \leq |\curvearrowright| \cdot |\approx_L^u|;\ |\approx_L^u| \leq |\curvearrowright| \cdot |\approx_P^u|.$

Proof. 1.   – Assume that $ux \curvearrowright uy$ and $x \approx_L^u y$. Since $x \approx_L^u y$ holds, then for all $v \in \Sigma^*$, $(uxv \curvearrowright u \implies u \cdot (xv)^\omega \in L) \iff (uyv \curvearrowright u \implies u \cdot (yv)^\omega \in L)$. Since $ux \curvearrowright uy$ holds, then $u \cdot xv \curvearrowright u \iff u \cdot yv \curvearrowright u$ for all $v \in \Sigma^*$. Hence, by Definition 7, if $uxv \not\curvearrowright u$ (and thus $uyv \not\curvearrowright u$), it follows that $x \approx_S^u y$ by definition of $\approx_S^u$; otherwise we have both $uxv \curvearrowright u$ and $uyv \curvearrowright u$ hold, and also $u \cdot (xv)^\omega \in L \iff u \cdot (yv)^\omega \in L$, following the definition of $\approx_L^u$. It thus follows that $x \approx_S^u y$.
   – Assume that $x \approx_S^u y$. First, we have $ux \curvearrowright uy$ by definition of $\approx_S^u$. Since $ux \curvearrowright uy$ holds, then $u \cdot xv \curvearrowright u \iff u \cdot yv \curvearrowright u$ for all $v \in \Sigma^*$. Assume by contradiction that $x \not\approx_L^u y$. Then there must exist some $v \in \Sigma^*$ such that $u \cdot xv \curvearrowright u \cdot yv \curvearrowright u$ holds but $u \cdot (xv)^\omega \in L \iff u \cdot (yv)^\omega \in L$ does not hold. By definition of $\approx_S^u$, it then follows that $x \not\approx_S^u y$, violating our assumption. Hence, both $ux \curvearrowright uy$ and $x \approx_L^u y$ hold.

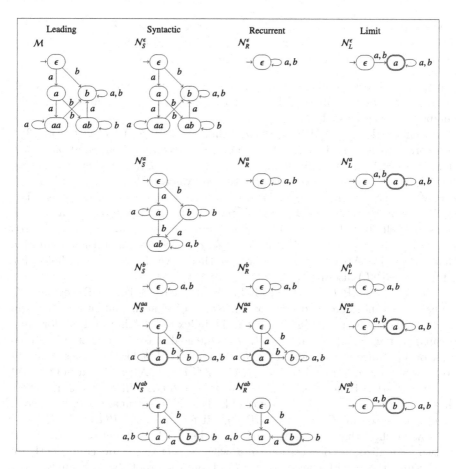

Fig. 1. Three types of FDFAs for $L = a^\omega + ab^\omega$. The final states are marked with double lines.

2. As an immediate result of the Item (1), we have that $| \approx_L^u | \leq | \approx_S^u | \leq | \frown | \cdot | \approx_L^u |$. We prove the second claim by showing that, for all $u, x, y \in \Sigma^*$, if $ux \frown uy$ and $x \approx_P^u y$, then $x \approx_S^u y$ (and thus $x \approx_L^u y$). Fix a word $v \in \Sigma^*$. Since $ux \frown uy$ holds, it follows that $ux \cdot v \frown u \iff uy \cdot v \frown u$. Moreover, we have $u \cdot (xv)^\omega \in L \iff u \cdot (yv)^\omega \in L$ because $x \approx_P^u y$ holds. By definition of $\approx_S^u$, it follows that $x \approx_S^u y$ holds. Hence, $x \approx_L^u y$ holds as well. We then conclude that $| \approx_L^u | \leq | \frown | \cdot | \approx_P^u |$.   □

According to Definition 1, we have $x \frown y$ iff $\mathcal{T}[\frown](x) = \mathcal{T}[\frown](y)$ for all $x, y \in \Sigma^*$. That is, $\mathcal{M} = (\mathcal{T}[\frown], \emptyset)$ is consistent with $\frown$, i.e., $x \frown y$ iff $\mathcal{M}(x) = \mathcal{M}(y)$ for all $x, y \in \Sigma^*$. Hence, $u \cdot v \frown u$ iff $\mathcal{M}(u) = \mathcal{M}(u \cdot v)$. In the remaining part of the paper, we may therefore mix the use of $\frown$ and $\mathcal{M}$ without distinguishing the two notations.

We are now ready to give our main result of this section.

Theorem 2. *Let L be an ω-regular language and $\mathcal{F}_L = (\mathcal{M}[\backsim], \{\mathcal{N}[\approx_u]\}_{[u]_{\backsim} \in \Sigma^*/_{\backsim}})$ be the limit FDFA of L. Then (1) $\mathcal{F}_L$ has a finite number of states, (2) $UP(\mathcal{F}_L) = UP(L)$, and (3) $\mathcal{F}_L$ is saturated.*

Proof. Since the syntactic FDFA $\mathcal{F}_S$ of L has a finite number of states [16] and $\mathcal{F}_L$ is a coarser representation than $\mathcal{F}_S$ (cf. Lemma 1), $\mathcal{F}_L$ must have finite number of states as well.

To show $UP(\mathcal{F}_L) \subseteq UP(L)$, assume that $w \in UP(\mathcal{F}_L)$. By Definition 3, a UP-word w is accepted by $\mathcal{F}_L$ if there exists a decomposition (u, v) of w such that $\mathcal{M}(u) = \mathcal{M}(u \cdot v)$ (equivalently, $u \cdot v \backsim u$) and $v \in \mathcal{L}_*(\mathcal{N}_L^{\tilde{u}})$ where $\tilde{u} = \mathcal{M}(u)$. Here $\tilde{u}$ is the representative word for the equivalence class $[u]_{\backsim}$. Similarly, let $\tilde{v} = \mathcal{N}_L^{\tilde{u}}(v)$. By Definition 9, we have $\tilde{u} \cdot \tilde{v} \backsim \tilde{u} \implies \tilde{u} \cdot \tilde{v}^{\omega} \in L$ holds as $\tilde{v}$ is a final state of $\mathcal{N}_L^{\tilde{u}}$. Since $v \approx_L^{\tilde{u}} \tilde{v}$ (i.e., $\mathcal{N}_L^{\tilde{u}}(v) = \mathcal{N}_L^{\tilde{u}}(\tilde{v})$), $\tilde{u} \cdot v \backsim \tilde{u} \implies \tilde{u} \cdot v^{\omega} \in L$ holds as well. It follows that $u \cdot v \backsim u \implies u \cdot v^{\omega} \in L$ since $u \backsim \tilde{u}$ and $u \cdot v \backsim \tilde{u} \cdot v$ (equivalently, $\mathcal{M}(u \cdot v) = \mathcal{M}(\tilde{u} \cdot v)$). Together with the assumption that $\mathcal{M}(u \cdot v) = \mathcal{M}(u)$ (i.e., $u \backsim u \cdot v$), we then have that $u \cdot v^{\omega} \in L$ holds. So, $UP(\mathcal{F}_L) \subseteq UP(L)$ also holds.

To show that $UP(L) \subseteq UP(\mathcal{F}_L)$ holds, let $w \in UP(L)$. For a UP-word $w \in L$, we can find a normalized decomposition (u, v) of w such that $w = u \cdot v^{\omega}$ and $u \cdot v \backsim u$ (i.e., $\mathcal{M}(u) = \mathcal{M}(u \cdot v)$), since the index of $\backsim$ is finite (cf. [3] for more details). Let $\tilde{u} = \mathcal{M}(u)$ and $\tilde{v} = \mathcal{N}_L^{\tilde{u}}(v)$. Our goal is to prove that $\tilde{v}$ is a final state of $\mathcal{N}_L^{\tilde{u}}$. Since $u \backsim \tilde{u}$ and $u \cdot v^{\omega} \in L$, then $\tilde{u} \cdot v^{\omega} \in L$ holds. Moreover, $\tilde{u} \cdot v \backsim \tilde{u}$ holds as well because $\tilde{u} = \mathcal{M}(\tilde{u}) = \mathcal{M}(u) = \mathcal{M}(\tilde{u} \cdot v) = \mathcal{M}(u \cdot v)$. (Recall that $\mathcal{M}$ is deterministic.) Hence, $\tilde{u} \cdot v \backsim \tilde{u} \implies \tilde{u} \cdot v^{\omega} \in L$ holds. Since $\tilde{v} \approx_L^{\tilde{u}} v$, it follows that $\tilde{u} \cdot \tilde{v} \backsim \tilde{u} \implies \tilde{u} \cdot \tilde{v}^{\omega} \in L$ also holds. Hence, $\tilde{v}$ is a final state. Therefore, (u, v) is accepted by $\mathcal{F}_L$, i.e., $w \in UP(\mathcal{F}_L)$. It follows that $UP(L) \subseteq UP(\mathcal{F}_L)$.

Now we show that $\mathcal{F}_L$ is saturated. Let w be a UP-word. Let (u, v) and (x, y) be two normalized decompositions of w with respect to $\mathcal{M}$ (or, equivalently, to $\backsim$). Assume that (u, v) is accepted by $\mathcal{F}_L$. From the proof above, it follows that both $u \cdot v \backsim u$ and $u \cdot v^{\omega} \in L$ hold. So, we know that $u \cdot v^{\omega} = x \cdot y^{\omega} \in L$. Let $\tilde{x} = \mathcal{M}(x)$ and $\tilde{y} = \mathcal{N}_L^{\tilde{x}}(y)$. Since (x, y) is a normalized decomposition, it follows that $x \cdot y \backsim x$. Again, since $\tilde{x} \backsim x$, $\tilde{x} \cdot y \backsim \tilde{x}$ and $\tilde{x} \cdot y^{\omega} \in L$ also hold. Obviously, $\tilde{x} \cdot y \backsim \tilde{x} \implies \tilde{x} \cdot y^{\omega} \in L$ holds. By the fact that $y \approx_L^{\tilde{x}} \tilde{y}$, $\tilde{x} \cdot \tilde{y} \backsim \tilde{x} \implies \tilde{x} \cdot \tilde{y}^{\omega} \in L$ holds as well. Hence, $\tilde{y}$ is a final state of $\mathcal{N}_L^{\tilde{x}}$. In other words, (x, y) is also accepted by $\mathcal{F}_L$. The proof for the case when (u, v) is not accepted by $\mathcal{F}_L$ is similar. □

3.2 Size Comparison with Other Canonical FDFAs

As aforementioned, Angluin and Fisman in [3] showed that for a variant of the family of languages L_n given by Michel [17], its periodic FDFA has $\Omega(n!)$ states, while the syntactic FDFA only has $\mathcal{O}(n^2)$ states. Since limit FDFAs are smaller than syntactic FDFAs, it immediately follows that:

Corollary 2. *There exists a family of languages L_n such that its periodic FDFA has $\Omega(n!)$ states, while the limit FDFA only has $\mathcal{O}(n^2)$ states.*

Now we consider the size comparison between limit and recurrent FDFAs. Consider again the limit and recurrent FDFAs of the language $L = a^\omega + ab^\omega$ in Fig. 1: one can see that limit FDFA and recurrent FDFA have the same number of states, even though with different progress DFAs. In fact, it is easy to see that limit FDFAs and recurrent FDFAs are incomparable regarding the their number of states, even when only the ω-regular languages recognized by weak DBAs are considered. A *weak* DBA (wDBA) is a DBA in which each SCC contains either all accepting transitions or non-accepting transitions.

Lemma 2. *If L is a wDBA-recognizable language, then its limit FDFA and its recurrent FDFA have incomparable size.*

Proof. We fix $u, x, y \in \Sigma^*$ in the proof. Since L is recognized by a wDBA, the TS $\mathcal{T}[\curvearrowright]$ of the leading DFA $\mathcal{M}$ is isomorphic to the minimal wDBA recognizing L [15]. Therefore, a state $[u]_\curvearrowright$ of $\mathcal{M}$ is either transient, in a rejecting SCC, or in an accepting SCC. We consider these three cases.

- Assume that $[u]_\curvearrowright$ is a transient SCC/state. Then for all $v \in \Sigma^*$, $u \cdot x \cdot v \not\curvearrowright u$ and $u \cdot y \cdot v \not\curvearrowright u$.
  By the definitions of $\approx_R^u$ and $\approx_L^u$, there are a non-final class $[\epsilon]_{\approx_L^u}$ and *possibly* a sink final class $[\sigma]_{\approx_L^u}$ for $\approx_L^u$ where $\sigma \in \Sigma$, while there is a non-final class $[\epsilon]_{\approx_R^u}$ for $\approx_R^u$. Hence, $x \approx_L^u y$ implies $x \approx_R^u y$.
- Assume that $[u]_\curvearrowright$ is in a rejecting SCC. Obviously, for all $v \in \Sigma^*$, we have that $u \cdot x \cdot v \curvearrowright u \implies u \cdot (x \cdot v)^\omega \notin L$ and $u \cdot y \cdot v \curvearrowright u \implies u \cdot (y \cdot v)^\omega \notin L$. Therefore, there is only one equivalence class $[\epsilon]_{\approx_R^u}$ for $\approx_R^u$. It follows that $x \approx_L^u y$ implies $x \approx_R^u y$.
- Assume that $[u]_\curvearrowright$ is in an accepting SCC. Clearly, for all $v \in \Sigma^*$, we have that both $u \cdot x \cdot v \curvearrowright u \implies u \cdot (x \cdot v)^\omega \in L$ and $u \cdot y \cdot v \curvearrowright u \implies u \cdot (y \cdot v)^\omega \in L$ hold. That is, we have either $u \cdot x \cdot v \curvearrowright u \wedge u \cdot (x \cdot v)^\omega \in L$ hold, or $u \cdot x \cdot v \not\curvearrowright u$. If $x \approx_R^u y$ holds, it immediately follows that $(u \cdot x \cdot v \curvearrowright u \implies u \cdot (x \cdot v)^\omega \in L) \iff (u \cdot y \cdot v \curvearrowright u \implies u \cdot (y \cdot v)^\omega \in L)$ holds. Hence, $x \approx_R^u y$ implies $x \approx_L^u y$.

Based on this argument, it is easy to find a language L such that its limit FDFA is more succinct than its recurrent FDFA and vice versa, depending on the size comparison between rejecting SCCs and accepting SCCs. Therefore, the lemma follows. $\square$

Lemma 2 reveals that limit FDFAs and recurrent FDFAs are incomparable in size. Nonetheless, we still provide a family of languages L_n in Lemma 3 such that the recurrent FDFA has $\Theta(n^2)$ states, while its limit FDFA only has $\Theta(n)$ states. One can, of course, obtain the opposite result by complementing L_n. Notably, Lemma 3 also gives a matching lower bound for the size comparison between syntactic FDFAs and limit FDFAs, since syntactic FDFAs can be quadratically larger than their limit FDFA counterparts, as stated in Lemma 1. The language which witnesses this lower bound is given as its DBA $\mathcal{B}$ depicted in Fig. 2. We refer to [13, Appendix A] for detailed proof.

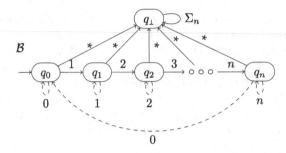

Fig. 2. The ω-regular language L_n represented with a DBA $\mathcal{B}$. The dashed arrows are Γ-transitions and $*$-transitions represent the missing transitions.

Lemma 3. *Let* $\Sigma_n = \{0, 1, \cdots, n\}$. *There exists an ω-regular language L_n over Σ_n such that its limit FDFA has $\Theta(n)$ states, while both its syntactic and recurrent FDFAs have $\Theta(n^2)$ states.*

Finally, it is time to derive yet another "Myhill-Nerode" theorem for ω-regular languages, as stated in Theorem 3. This result follows immediately from Lemma 1 and a similar theorem about syntactic FDFAs [16].

Theorem 3. *Let $\mathcal{F}_L$ be the limit FDFA of an ω-language L. Then L is regular if, and only if, $\mathcal{F}_L$ has finite number of states.*

For identifying whether L is DBA-recognizable with FDFAs, a straight forward way as mentioned in the introduction is to go through determinization, which is, however, exponential in the size of the input FDFA. We show in Sect. 4 that there is a polynomial-time algorithm using our limit FDFAs.

4 Limit FDFAs for Identifying DBA-Recognizable Languages

Given an ω-regular language L, we show in this section how to use the limit FDFA of L to check whether L is DBA-recognizable in polynomial time. To this end, we will first introduce how the limit FDFA of L looks like in Sect. 4.1 and then introduce the deciding algorithm in Sect. 4.2.

4.1 Limit FDFA for DBA-Recognizable Languages

Bohn and Löding [5] construct a type of family of DFAs $\mathcal{F}_{BL}$ from a set S^+ of positive samples and a set S^- of negative samples, where the progress DFA accepts exactly the language $V_u = \{x \in \Sigma^+ : \forall v \in \Sigma^*. \text{ if } u \cdot xv \backsim u, \text{ then } u \cdot (xv)^\omega \in L\}^4$. When the samples S^+ and S^- uniquely characterize a DBA-recognizable language L, $\mathcal{F}_{BL}$ recognizes exactly L.

---

[4] Defining directly a progress RC $\approx^u$ that recognizes V_u is hard since V_u is quantified over all v-extensions.

The progress DFA $\mathcal{N}_L^u$ of our limit FDFA $\mathcal{F}_L$ of L usually accepts *more* words than V_u. Nonetheless, we can still find one final equivalence class that is exactly the set V_u, as stated in Lemma 4.

Lemma 4. *Let L be a DBA-recognizable language and $\mathcal{F}_L=(\mathcal{M},\{\mathcal{N}_L^u\}_{[u]_\backsim \in \Sigma^*/_\backsim})$ be the limit FDFA of L. Then, for each progress DFA $\mathcal{N}_L^u$ with $\mathcal{L}_*(\mathcal{N}_L^u) \neq \emptyset$, there must exist a final state $\tilde{x} \in F_u$ such that $[\tilde{x}]_{\approx_L^u} = \{x \in \Sigma^+ : \forall v \in \Sigma^*.\ u \cdot (x \cdot v) \backsim u \implies u \cdot (x \cdot v)^\omega \in L\}$.*

Proof. In [5], it is shown that for each equivalence class $[u]_\backsim$ of $\backsim$, there exists a regular language $V_u = \{x \in \Sigma^+ : \forall v \in \Sigma^*.\ \text{if } u \cdot xv \backsim u, \text{ then } u \cdot (xv)^\omega \in L\}$. We have also provided the proof of the existence of V_u in [13, Appendix C], adapted to our notations. The intuition of V_u is the following. Let $\mathcal{B} = (\Sigma, Q, \iota, \delta, \Gamma)$ be a DBA accepting L. Then, $[u]_\backsim$ corresponds to a set of states $S = \{q \in Q : q = \delta(\iota, u'), u' \in [u]_\backsim\}$ in $\mathcal{B}$. For each $q \in S$, we can easily create a regular language V_q such that $x \in V_q$ iff over the word x, $\mathcal{B}^q$ (the DBA derived from $\mathcal{B}$ by setting q its initial state) visits an accepting transition, $\mathcal{B}^q$ goes to an SCC that cannot go back to q, or $\mathcal{B}^q$ goes to a state that cannot go back to q unless visiting an accepting transition. Then, $V_u = \cap_{q \in S} V_q$.

Now we show that V_u is an equivalence class of $\approx_L^u$ as follows. On one hand, for every two different words $x_1, x_2 \in V_u$, we have that $x_1 \approx_L^u x_2$, which is obvious by the definition of V_u. On the other hand, it is easy to see that $x' \not\approx_L^u x$ for all $x' \notin V_u$ and $x \in V_u$ because there exists some $v \in \Sigma^*$ such that $u \cdot x' \cdot v \backsim u$ but $u \cdot (x' \cdot v)^\omega \notin L$. Hence, V_u is indeed an equivalence class of $\approx_L^u$. Obviously, $V_u \subseteq \mathcal{L}_*(\mathcal{N}_L^u)$, as we can let $v = \epsilon$, so for every word $x \in V_u$, we have that $u \cdot x \backsim u \implies u \cdot x^\omega \in L$. Let $\tilde{x} = \mathcal{N}_L^u(x)$ for a word $x \in V_u$. It follows that $\tilde{x}$ is a final state of $\mathcal{N}_L^u$ and we have $[\tilde{x}]_{\approx_L^u} = V_u$. This completes the proof. □

By Lemma 4, we can define a variant of limit FDFAs for only DBAs with less number of final states. This helps to reduce the complexity when translating FDFAs to NBAs [2,7,12]. Let n be the number of states in the leading DFA $\mathcal{M}$ and k be the number of states in the largest progress DFA. Then the resultant NBA from an FDFA has $\mathcal{O}(n^2k^3)$ states [2,7,12]. However, if the input FDFA is $\mathcal{F}_B$ as in Definition 10, the complexity of the translation will be $\mathcal{O}(n^2k^2)$, as there is at most one final state, rather than k final states, in each progress DFA.

Definition 10 (Limit FDFAs for DBAs). *The limit FDFA $\mathcal{F}_B=(\mathcal{M},\{\mathcal{N}_B^u\})$ of L is defined as follows.*

The transition systems of $\mathcal{M}$ and $\mathcal{N}_B^u$ for each $[u]_\backsim \in \Sigma^*/_\backsim$ are exactly the same as in Definition 9.

The set of final states F_u contains the equivalence classes $[x]_{\approx_L^u}$ such that, for all $v \in \Sigma^*$, $u \cdot xv \backsim u \implies u \cdot (xv)^\omega \in L$ holds.

The change to the definition of final states would not affect the language that the limit FDFAs recognize, but only their saturation properties. We say an FDFA $\mathcal{F}$ is *almost saturated* if, for all $u, v \in \Sigma^*$, we have that if (u, v) is accepted by $\mathcal{F}$, then (u, v^k) is accepted by $\mathcal{F}$ for all $k \geq 1$. According to [12], if $\mathcal{F}$ is almost saturated, then the translation algorithm from FDFAs to NBAs in [2,7,12] still applies (cf. [13, Appendix B] about details of the NBA construction).

Theorem 4. *Let L be a DBA-recognizable language and $\mathcal{F}_B$ be the limit FDFA induced by Definition 10. Then (1) $UP(\mathcal{F}_B) = UP(L)$ and (2) $\mathcal{F}_B$ is almost saturated but not necessarily saturated.*

Proof. The proof for $UP(\mathcal{F}_B) \subseteq UP(L)$ is trivial, as the final states defined in Definition 10 must also be final in Definition 9. The other direction can be proved based on Lemma 4. Let $w \in UP(L)$ and $\mathcal{B} = (Q, \Sigma, \iota, \delta, \Gamma)$ be a DBA accepting L. Let ρ be the run of $\mathcal{B}$ over w. We can find a decomposition (u, v) of w such that there exists a state q with $q = \delta(\iota, u) = \delta(\iota, u \cdot v)$ and $(q, v[0]) \in \Gamma$. As in the proof of Lemma 4, we are able to construct the regular language $V_u = \{x \in \Sigma^+ : \forall y \in \Sigma^*, u \cdot x \cdot y \backsim u \implies u \cdot (x \cdot y)^\omega \in L\}$. We let $S = \{p \in Q : \mathcal{L}(\mathcal{B}^q) = \mathcal{L}(\mathcal{B}^p)\}$. For every state $p \in S$, we have that $v^\omega \in \mathcal{L}(\mathcal{B}^p)$. For each $p \in S$, we select an integer $k_p > 0$ such that the finite run $p \xrightarrow{v^{k_p}} \delta(p, v^{k_p})$ visits some accepting transition. Then we let $k = \max_{p \in S} k_p$. By definition of V_u, it follows that $v^k \in V_u$. That is, V_u is not empty. According to Lemma 4, we have a final equivalence class $[x]_{\approx_L^u} = V_u$ with $v^k \in [x]_{\approx_L^u}$. Moreover, $u \cdot v^k \backsim u$ since $q = \delta(\iota, u) = \delta(q, v)$. Hence, (u, v^k) is accepted by $\mathcal{F}_B$, i.e., $w \in UP(\mathcal{F}_B)$. It follows that $UP(\mathcal{F}_B) = UP(L)$.

Now we prove that $\mathcal{F}_B = (\mathcal{M}, \{\mathcal{N}_B^u\})$ is *not* necessarily saturated. Let $L = (\Sigma^* \cdot aa)^\omega$. Obviously, L is DBA recognizable, and $\backsim$ has only one equivalence class, $[\epsilon]_\backsim$. Let $w = a^\omega \in UP(L)$. Let $(u = \epsilon, v = a)$ be a normalized decomposition of w with respect to $\backsim$ (thus, $\mathcal{M}$). We can see that there exists a finite word x (e.g., $x = b$ is such a word) such that $\epsilon \cdot a \cdot x \backsim \epsilon$ and $\epsilon \cdot (a \cdot x)^\omega \notin L$. Thus, (ϵ, a) will not be accepted by $\mathcal{F}_B$. Hence $\mathcal{F}_B$ is not saturated. Nonetheless, it is easy to verify that $\mathcal{F}_B$ is almost saturated. Assume that (u, v) is accepted by $\mathcal{F}_B$. Let $\tilde{u} = \mathcal{M}(u)$ and $\tilde{v} = \mathcal{N}_B^{\tilde{u}}(v)$. Since $\tilde{v}$ is the final state, then, according to Definition 10, we have for all $e \in \Sigma^*$ that $\tilde{u} \cdot \tilde{v}e \backsim \tilde{u} \implies \tilde{u} \cdot (\tilde{v}e)^\omega \in L$. Since $v \approx_L^u \tilde{v}$, $\tilde{u} \cdot ve \backsim \tilde{u} \implies \tilde{u} \cdot (ve)^\omega \in L$ also holds for all $e \in \Sigma^*$. Let $e = v^k \cdot e'$ where $e' \in \Sigma^*, k \geq 0$. It follows that $\tilde{u} \cdot v^k e' \backsim \tilde{u} \implies \tilde{u} \cdot (v^k e')^\omega \in L$ holds for $k \geq 1$ as well. Therefore, for all $e' \in \Sigma^*, k \geq 1$, $(\tilde{u} \cdot \tilde{v}e' \backsim \tilde{u} \implies \tilde{u} \cdot (\tilde{v}e')^\omega \in L) \Longleftrightarrow (\tilde{u} \cdot v^k e' \backsim \tilde{u} \implies \tilde{u} \cdot (v^k e')^\omega \in L)$ holds. In other words, $\tilde{v} \approx_L^{\tilde{u}} v^k$ for all $k \geq 1$. Together with that $uv^k \backsim u$, (u, v^k) is accepted by $\mathcal{F}_B$ for all $k \geq 1$. Hence, $\mathcal{F}_B$ is almost saturated. $\square$

4.2 Deciding DBA-Recognizable Languages

We show next how to identify whether a language L is DBA-recognizable with our limit FDFA $\mathcal{F}_L$. Our decision procedure relies on the translation of FDFAs to NBAs/DBAs. In the following, we let n be the number of states in the leading DFA $\mathcal{M}$ and k be the number of states in the largest progress DFA. We first give some previous results below.

Lemma 5 ([12, Lemma 6]). *Let $\mathcal{F}$ be an (almost) saturated FDFA of L. Then one can construct an NBA $\mathcal{A}$ with $\mathcal{O}(n^2 k^3)$ states such that $\mathcal{L}(\mathcal{A}) = L$.*

Now we consider the translation from FDFA to DBAs. By Lemma 4, there is a final equivalence class $[x]_{\approx_L^u}$ that is a *co-safety* language in the limit FDFA of L. Co-safety regular languages are regular languages $R \subseteq \Sigma^*$ such that $R \cdot \Sigma^* = R$. It is easy to verify that if $x' \in [x]_{\approx_L^u}$, then $x'v \in [x]_{\approx_L^u}$ for all $v \in \Sigma^*$, based on the definition of $\approx_L^u$. So, $[x]_{\approx_L^u}$ is a co-safety language. The DFAs accepting co-safety languages usually have a sink final state f (such that f transitions to itself over all letters in Σ). We therefore have the following.

Corollary 3. *If L is DBA-recognizable then every progress DFA $\mathcal{N}_L^u$ of the limit FDFA $\mathcal{F}_L$ of L either has a sink final state, or no final state at all.*

Our limit FDFA $\mathcal{F}_B$ of L, as constructed in Definition 10, accepts the same co-safety languages in the progress DFAs as the FDFA obtained in [5], although they may have different transition systems. Nonetheless, we show that their DBA construction still works on $\mathcal{F}_B$. To make the construction more general, we assume an FDFA $\mathcal{F} = (\mathcal{M}, \{\mathcal{N}^q\}_{q \in Q})$ where $\mathcal{M} = (Q, \Sigma, \iota, \delta)$ and, for each $q \in Q$, we have $\mathcal{N}^q = (Q_q, \Sigma, \iota_q, \delta_q, F_q)$.

Definition 11 ([5]). *Let $\mathcal{F} = (\mathcal{M}, \{\mathcal{N}^q\}_{q \in Q})$ be an FDFA. Let $\mathcal{T}[\mathcal{F}]$ be the TS constructed from $\mathcal{F}$ defined as the tuple $\mathcal{T}[\mathcal{F}] = (Q_T, \Sigma, \iota_T, \delta_T)$ and $\Gamma \subseteq \{(q, \sigma) : q \in Q_T, \sigma \in \Sigma\}$ be a set of transitions where*

- *$Q_T := Q \times \bigcup_{q \in Q} Q_q$;*
- *$\iota_T := (\iota, \iota_\iota)$;*
- *For a state $(m, q) \in Q_T$ and $\sigma \in \Sigma$, let $q' = \delta_{\widetilde{m}}(q, \sigma)$ where $\mathcal{N}^{\widetilde{m}}$ is the progress DFA that q belongs to and let $m' = \delta(m, \sigma)$. Then*

$$\delta((m, q), \sigma) = \begin{cases} (m', q') & \text{if } q' \notin F_{\widetilde{m}} \\ (m', \iota_{m'}) & \text{if } q' \in F_{\widetilde{m}} \end{cases}$$

- *$((m, q), \sigma) \in \Gamma$ if $q' \in F_{\widetilde{m}}$*

Lemma 6. *If $\mathcal{F}$ is an FDFA with only sink final states. Let $\mathcal{B}[\mathcal{F}] = (\mathcal{T}[\mathcal{F}], \Gamma)$ as given in Definition 11. Then, $UP(\mathcal{L}(\mathcal{B}[\mathcal{F}])) \subseteq UP(\mathcal{F})$.*

Proof. Let $w \in UP(\mathcal{L}(\mathcal{B}[\mathcal{F}]))$ and ρ be its corresponding accepting run. Since w is a UP-word and $\mathcal{B}[\mathcal{F}]$ is a DBA of finite states, then we must be able to find a decomposition (u, v) of w such that $(m, \iota_m) = \mathcal{B}[\mathcal{F}](u) = \mathcal{B}[\mathcal{F}](u \cdot v)$, where ρ will visit a Γ-transition whose destination is (m, ι_m) for infinitely many times. It is easy to see that $\mathcal{M}(u \cdot v) = \mathcal{M}(u)$ since $\mathcal{B}[\mathcal{F}](u) = \mathcal{B}[\mathcal{F}](u \cdot v)$. Moreover, we can show there must be a prefix of v, say v', such that $v' \in \mathcal{L}_*(\mathcal{N}^m)$. Since $\mathcal{L}_*(\mathcal{N}^m)$ is co-safety, we have that $v \in \mathcal{L}_*(\mathcal{N}^m)$. Thus, (u, v) is accepted by $\mathcal{F}$. By Definition 3, $w \in UP(\mathcal{F})$. Therefore, $UP(\mathcal{L}(\mathcal{B}[\mathcal{F}])) \subseteq UP(\mathcal{F})$. $\square$

By Corollary 3, $\mathcal{F}_B$ has only sink final states; so, we have that $UP(\mathcal{L}(\mathcal{B}[\mathcal{F}_B])) \subseteq UP(\mathcal{F}_B)$. However, Corollary 3 is only a necessary condition for L being DBA-recognizable, as explained below. Let L be an ω-regular language over $\Sigma = \{1, 2, 3, 4\}$ such that a word $w \in L$ iff the maximal number that

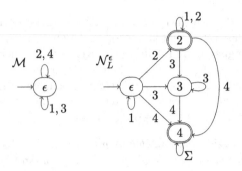

Fig. 3. An example limit FDFA $\mathcal{F} = (\mathcal{M}, \{\mathcal{N}_L^\epsilon\})$

occurs infinitely often in w is even. Clearly, L has one equivalence class $[\epsilon]_\frown$ for $\frown$. The limit FDFA $\mathcal{F} = (\mathcal{M}, \{\mathcal{N}_L^\epsilon\})$ of L is depicted in Fig. 3. We can observe that the equivalence class $[4]_{\approx_L^\epsilon}$ corresponds to a co-safety language. Hence, the progress DFA $\mathcal{N}_L^\epsilon$ has a sink final state. However, L is not DBA-recognizable. If we ignore the final equivalence class $[2]_{\approx_L^\epsilon}$ and obtain the variant limit FDFA $\mathcal{F}_B$ as given in Definition 10, then we have $\mathrm{UP}(\mathcal{F}_B) \neq \mathrm{UP}(L)$ since the ω-word 2^ω is missing. But then, by Theorem 4, this change would not lose words in L if L is DBA-recognisable, leading to contradiction. Therefore, L is shown to be not DBA-recognizable. So the key of the decision algorithm here is to check whether ignoring other final states will retain the language. With Lemma 7, we guarantee that $\mathcal{B}[\mathcal{F}_B]$ accepts exactly L if L is DBA-recognizable.

Lemma 7. *Let L be a DBA-recognizable language. Let $\mathcal{F}_B$ be the limit FDFA L, as constructed in Definition 10. Let $\mathcal{B}[\mathcal{F}_B] = (\mathcal{T}[\mathcal{F}_B], \Gamma)$, where $\mathcal{T}[\mathcal{F}_B]$ and Γ are the TS and set of transitions, respectively, defined in Definition 11 from $\mathcal{F}_B$. Then $\mathrm{UP}(\mathcal{F}_B) = \mathrm{UP}(L) \subseteq \mathrm{UP}(\mathcal{L}(\mathcal{B}[\mathcal{F}_B]))$.*

Proof. We first assume for contradiction that some $w \in L$ is rejected by $\mathcal{B}[\mathcal{F}_B]$. For this, we consider the run $\rho = (q_0, w[0], q_1)(q_1, w[1], q_2)\ldots$ of $\mathcal{B}[\mathcal{F}_B]$ on w. Let $i \in \omega$ be such that $(q_{i-1}, w[i-1], q_i)$ is the last accepting transition in ρ, and $i = 0$ if there is no accepting transition at all in ρ. We also set $u = w[0\cdots i-1]$ and $w' = w[i\cdots]$. By Definition 11, this ensures that $\mathcal{B}[\mathcal{F}_B]$ is in state $([u]_\frown, \iota_{[u]_\frown})$ after reading u and will not see accepting transitions (or leave $\mathcal{N}_B^{[u]_\frown}$) while reading the tail w'.

Let $\mathcal{D} = (Q', \Sigma, \iota', \delta', \Gamma')$ be a DBA that recognizes L and has only reachable states. As $\mathcal{D}$ recognizes L, it has the same right congruences as L; by slight abuse of notation, we refer to the states in Q' that are language equivalent to the state reachable after reading u by $[u]_\frown$ and note that $\mathcal{D}$ is in some state of $[u]_\frown$ after (and only after) reading a word $u' \frown u$.

As $u \cdot w'$, and therefore $u' \cdot w'$ for all $u' \frown u$, are in L, they are accepted by $\mathcal{D}$, which in particular means that, for all $q \in [u]_\frown$, there is an i_q such that there is an accepting transition in the first i_q steps of the run of $\mathcal{D}^q$ (the DBA obtained from $\mathcal{D}$ by setting the initial state to q) on w'. Let i_+ be maximal among them and $v = w[i \cdots i + i_+]$. Then, for $u' \smallfrown u$ and any word $u'vv'$, we either have $u'vv' \not\smallfrown u$, or $u'vv' \smallfrown u$ and $u' \cdot (vv')^{\omega} \in L$. (The latter is because v is constructed such that a run of $\mathcal{D}$ on this word will see an accepting transition while reading each v, and thus infinitely many times.) Thus, $\mathcal{N}_B^{[u]\smallfrown}$ will accept any word that starts with v, and therefore be in a final sink after having read v.

But then $\mathcal{B}[\mathcal{F}_B]$ will see another accepting transition after reading v (at the latest after having read uv), which closes the contradiction and completes the proof. □

So, our decision algorithm works as follows. Assume that we are given the limit FDFA $\mathcal{F}_L = (\mathcal{M}, \{\mathcal{N}_L^q\})$ of L.

1. We first check whether there is a progress DFA $\mathcal{N}_L^q$ such that there are final states but without the sink final state. If it is the case, we terminate and return "NO".
2. Otherwise, we obtain the FDFA $\mathcal{F}_B$ by keeping the sink final state as the sole final state in each progress DFA (cf. Definition 10). Let $\mathcal{A} = \mathtt{NBA}(\mathcal{F}_L)$ be the NBA constructed from $\mathcal{F}_L$ (cf. Lemma 5) and $\mathcal{B} = \mathtt{DBA}(\mathcal{F}_B)$ be the DBA constructed from $\mathcal{F}_B$ (cf. Definition 11). Obviously, we have that $\mathrm{UP}(\mathcal{L}(\mathcal{A})) = \mathrm{UP}(L)$ and $\mathrm{UP}(\mathcal{L}(\mathcal{B})) \subseteq \mathrm{UP}(\mathcal{F}_B) = \mathrm{UP}(L)$.
3. Then we check whether $\mathcal{L}(\mathcal{A}) \subseteq \mathcal{L}(\mathcal{B})$ holds. If so, we return "YES", and otherwise "NO".

Now we are ready to give the main result of this section.

Theorem 5. *Deciding whether L is DBA-recognizable can be done in time polynomial in the size of the limit FDFA of L.*

Proof. We first prove our decision algorithm is correct. If the algorithm returns "YES", clearly, we have $\mathcal{L}(\mathcal{A}) \subseteq \mathcal{L}(\mathcal{B})$. It immediately follows that $\mathrm{UP}(L) = \mathrm{UP}(\mathcal{L}(\mathcal{A})) \subseteq \mathrm{UP}(\mathcal{L}(\mathcal{B})) \subseteq \mathrm{UP}(\mathcal{F}_B) \subseteq \mathrm{UP}(\mathcal{F}_L) = \mathrm{UP}(L)$ according to Lemmas 5 and 6. Hence, $\mathrm{UP}(\mathcal{L}(\mathcal{B})) = \mathrm{UP}(L)$, which implies that L is DBA-recognizable. For the case that the algorithm returns "NO", we analyze two cases:

1. $\mathcal{F}$ has final states but without sink accepting states for some progress DFA. By Corollary 3, L is not DBA-recognizable.
2. $\mathcal{L}(\mathcal{A}) \not\subseteq \mathcal{L}(\mathcal{B})$. It means that $\mathrm{UP}(L) \not\subseteq \mathrm{UP}(\mathcal{L}(\mathcal{B}))$ (by Lemma 5). It follows that L is not DBA-recognizable by Lemma 7.

The algorithm is therefore sound; its completeness follows from Lemmas 6 and 7.

The translations above are all in polynomial time. Moreover, checking the language inclusion between an NBA and a DBA can also be done in polynomial time [11]. Hence, the deciding algorithm is also in polynomial time in the size of the limit FDFA of L. □

Recall that, our limit FDFAs are dual to recurrent FDFAs. One can observe that, for DBA-recognizable languages, recurrent FDFAs do not necessarily have sink final states in progress DFAs. For instance, the ω-regular language $L = a^{\omega} + ab^{\omega}$ is DBA-recognizable, but its recurrent FDFA, depicted in Fig. 1, does not have sink final states. Hence, our deciding algorithm does not work with recurrent FDFAs.

5   Underspecifying Progress Right Congruences

Recall that recurrent and limit progress DFAs $\mathcal{N}^u$ either treat don't care words in $\overline{C_u} = \{v \in \Sigma^+ : uv \not\sim u\}$ as rejecting or accepting, whereas it really does not matter whether or not they are accepted. So why not keep this question open? We do just this in this section; however, we find that treating the progress with maximal flexibility comes at a cost: the resulting right progress relation $\approx_N^u$ is *no* longer an equivalence relation, but only a reflexive and symmetric relation over $\Sigma^* \times \Sigma^*$ such that $x \approx_N^u y$ implies $xv \approx_N^u yv$ for all $u, x, y, v \in \Sigma^*$.

For this, we first introduce *Right Pro-Congruences* (RP) as relations on words that satisfy all requirements of an RC except for transitivity.

Definition 12 (Progress RP). *Let $[u]_\sim$ be an equivalence class of $\sim$. For $x, y \in \Sigma^*$, we define the progress RP $\approx_N^u$ as follows:*

$$x \approx_N^u y \text{ iff } \forall v \in \Sigma^*. \ (uxv \sim u \wedge uyv \sim u) \implies (u \cdot (xv)^\omega \in L \iff u \cdot (yv)^\omega \in L).$$

Obviously, $\approx_N^u$ is a RP, i.e., for $x, y, v' \in \Sigma^\omega$, if $x \approx_N^u y$, then $xv' \approx_N^u yv'$. That is, assume that $x \approx_N^u y$ and we want to prove that, for all $e \in \Sigma^*$, $(u \cdot xv'e \sim u \wedge u \cdot yv'e \sim u) \implies (u \cdot (xv'e)^\omega \in L \iff u \cdot (yv'e)^\omega \in L)$. This follows immediately by setting $v = v'e$ in Definition 12 for all $e \in \Sigma^*$ since $x \approx_N^u y$. As $\approx_N^u$ is not necessarily an equivalence relation[5], so that we cannot argue directly with the size of its index. However, we can start with showing that $\approx_N^u$ is coarser than $\approx_P^u, \approx_S^u, \approx_R^u,$ and $\approx_L^u$.

Lemma 8. *For $u, x, y \in \Sigma^*$, we have that if $x \approx_K^u y$, then $x \approx_N^u y$, where $K \in \{P, S, R, L\}$.*

Proof. First, if $x \approx_P^u y$, $x \approx_N^u y$ holds trivially.

For syntactic, recurrent, and limit RCs, we first argue for fixed $v \in \Sigma^*$ that

- $ux \sim uy \implies uxv \sim uyv$, and therefore
  $ux \sim uy \wedge (u \cdot x \cdot v \sim u \implies (u \cdot (x \cdot v)^\omega \in L \iff u \cdot (y \cdot v)^\omega \in L))$
  $\models (uxv \sim u \wedge uyv \sim u) \implies (u \cdot (xv)^\omega \in L \iff u \cdot (yv)^\omega \in L),$
- $(u \cdot x \cdot v \sim u \wedge u \cdot (xv)^\omega \in L) \iff (u \cdot yv \sim u \wedge u \cdot (y \cdot v)^\omega \in L)$
  $\models (uxv \sim u \wedge uyv \sim u) \implies (u \cdot (xv)^\omega \in L \iff u \cdot (yv)^\omega \in L),$ and
- $(u \cdot x \cdot v \sim u \implies u \cdot (x \cdot v)^\omega \in L) \iff (u \cdot y \cdot v \sim u \implies u \cdot (y \cdot v)^\omega \in L)$
  $\models (uxv \sim u \wedge uyv \sim u) \implies (u \cdot (xv)^\omega \in L \iff u \cdot (yv)^\omega \in L),$

which is simple Boolean reasoning. As this holds for all $v \in \Sigma^*$ individually, it also holds for the intersection over all $v \in \Sigma^*$, so that the claim follows. □

Now, it is easy to see that we can use any RC $\approx$ that refines $\approx_N^u$ and use it to define a progress DFA. It therefore makes sense to define the set of RCs that refine $\approx_N^u$ as $\mathsf{RC}(\approx_N^u) = \{\approx \mid \approx \subset \approx_N^u \text{ is a RC}\}$, and the best index $\mid \approx_N^u \mid$ of our progress RP as $\mid \approx_N^u \mid = \min\{\mid \approx \mid \ \mid \approx \in \mathsf{RC}(\approx_N^u)\}$. With this definition, Corollary 4 follows immediately.

---

[5] In the language $L = a^\omega + ab^\omega$ from the example of Fig. 1, for example, we have $a \approx_N^{ab} \epsilon$ and $a \approx_N^{ab} b$, but $b \not\approx_N^{ab} \epsilon$.

Corollary 4. *For $u \in \Sigma^*$, we have that $|\approx_N^u| \leq |\approx_K^u|$ for all $K \in \{P, S, R, L\}$.*

We note that the restriction of $\approx_N^u$ to $C_u \times C_u$ is still an equivalence relation, where $C_u = \{v \in \Sigma^* : uv \backsim u\}$ are the words the FDFA acceptance conditions really care about. This makes it easy to define a DFA over each $\approx \in \mathsf{RC}(\approx_N^u)$ with finite index: $C_u/\approx_N^u$ is good if it contains a word v s.t. $u \cdot v^\omega \in L$, and a quotient of $\Sigma^*/\approx$ is accepting if it intersects with a good quotient (note that it intersects with at most one quotient of C_u). With this preparation, we now show the following.

Theorem 6. *Let L be an ω-regular language and $\mathcal{F}_L = (\mathcal{M}[\backsim], \{\mathcal{N}[\approx_u]\}_{[u]_\backsim \in \Sigma^*/\backsim})$ be the limit FDFA of L s.t. $\approx_u \in \mathsf{RC}(\approx_N^u)$ with finite index for all u. Then (1) $\mathcal{F}_L$ has a finite number of states, (2) $UP(\mathcal{F}_L) = UP(L)$, and (3) $\mathcal{F}_L$ is saturated.*

The proof is similar to the proof of Theorem 2 and can be found in [13, Appendix D].

6   Discussion and Future Work

Our limit FDFAs fit nicely into the learning framework for FDFAs [3] and are already available for use in the learning library ROLL[6] [14]. Since one can treat an FDFA learner as comprised of a family of DFA learners in which one DFA of the FDFA is learned by a separate DFA learner, we only need to adapt the learning procedure for progress DFAs based on our limit progress RCs, without extra development of the framework; see [13, Appendix E] for details. We leave the empirical evaluation of our limit FDFAs in learning ω-regular languages as future work.

We believe that limit FDFAs are complementing the existing set of canonical FDFAs, in terms of recognizing and learning ω-regular languages. Being able to easily identify DBA-recognizable languages, limit FDFAs might be used in a learning framework for DBAs using membership and equivalence queries. We leave this to future work. Finally, we have looked at retaining maximal flexibility in the construction of FDFA by moving from progress RCs to progress RPs. While this reduces size, it is no longer clear how to construct them efficiently, which we leave as a future challenge.

Acknowledgements. We thank the anonymous reviewers for their valuable feedback. This work has been supported by the EPSRC through grants EP/X021513/1 and EP/X017796/1.

References

1. Angluin, D.: Learning regular sets from queries and counterexamples. Inf. Comput. **75**(2), 87–106 (1987). https://doi.org/10.1016/0890-5401(87)90052-6

---

[6] https://github.com/iscas-tis/roll-library.

2. Angluin, D., Boker, U., Fisman, D.: Families of DFAs as acceptors of ω-regular languages. Log. Methods Comput. Sci. **14**(1), 1–21 (2018)

3. Angluin, D., Fisman, D.: Learning regular omega languages. Theor. Comput. Sci. **650**, 57–72 (2016). https://doi.org/10.1016/j.tcs.2016.07.031

4. Angluin, D., Fisman, D.: Regular ω-languages with an informative right congruence. Inf. Comput. **278**, 104598 (2021). https://doi.org/10.1016/j.ic.2020.104598

5. Bohn, L., Löding, C.: Passive learning of deterministic Büchi automata by combinations of DFAs. In: Bojanczyk, M., Merelli, E., Woodruff, D.P. (eds.) 49th International Colloquium on Automata, Languages, and Programming, ICALP 2022, 4–8 July 2022, Paris, France. LIPIcs, vol. 229, pp. 114:1–114:20. Schloss Dagstuhl - Leibniz-Zentrum für Informatik (2022). https://doi.org/10.4230/LIPIcs.ICALP.2022.114

6. Büchi, J.R.: On a decision method in restricted second order arithmetic. In: 1960 Proceedings of the International Congress on Logic, Method, and Philosophy of Science, pp. 1–12. Stanford University Press (1962)

7. Calbrix, H., Nivat, M., Podelski, A.: Ultimately periodic words of rational ω-languages. In: Brookes, S., Main, M., Melton, A., Mislove, M., Schmidt, D. (eds.) MFPS 1993. LNCS, vol. 802, pp. 554–566. Springer, Heidelberg (1994). https://doi.org/10.1007/3-540-58027-1_27

8. Colcombet, T., Zdanowski, K.: A tight lower bound for determinization of transition labeled Büchi automata. In: Albers, S., Marchetti-Spaccamela, A., Matias, Y., Nikoletseas, S., Thomas, W. (eds.) ICALP 2009, Part II. LNCS, vol. 5556, pp. 151–162. Springer, Heidelberg (2009). https://doi.org/10.1007/978-3-642-02930-1_13

9. Farzan, A., Chen, Y.-F., Clarke, E.M., Tsay, Y.-K., Wang, B.-Y.: Extending automated compositional verification to the full class of omega-regular languages. In: Ramakrishnan, C.R., Rehof, J. (eds.) TACAS 2008. LNCS, vol. 4963, pp. 2–17. Springer, Heidelberg (2008). https://doi.org/10.1007/978-3-540-78800-3_2

10. Krishnan, S.C., Puri, A., Brayton, R.K.: Deterministic ω automata vis-a-vis deterministic Buchi automata. In: Du, D.-Z., Zhang, X.-S. (eds.) ISAAC 1994. LNCS, vol. 834, pp. 378–386. Springer, Heidelberg (1994). https://doi.org/10.1007/3-540-58325-4_202

11. Kurshan, R.P.: Complementing deterministic büchi automata in polynomial time. J. Comput. Syst. Sci. **35**(1), 59–71 (1987). https://doi.org/10.1016/0022-0000(87)90036-5

12. Li, Y., Chen, Y., Zhang, L., Liu, D.: A novel learning algorithm for büchi automata based on family of DFAs and classification trees. Inf. Comput. **281**, 104678 (2021). https://doi.org/10.1016/j.ic.2020.104678

13. Li, Y., Schewe, S., Tang, Q.: A novel family of finite automata for recognizing and learning ω-regular languages (2023)

14. Li, Y., Sun, X., Turrini, A., Chen, Y.-F., Xu, J.: ROLL 1.0: ω-regular language learning library. In: Vojnar, T., Zhang, L. (eds.) TACAS 2019, Part I. LNCS, vol. 11427, pp. 365–371. Springer, Cham (2019). https://doi.org/10.1007/978-3-030-17462-0_23

15. Maler, O., Pnueli, A.: On the learnability of infinitary regular sets. Inf. Comput. **118**(2), 316–326 (1995). https://doi.org/10.1006/inco.1995.1070

16. Maler, O., Staiger, L.: On syntactic congruences for omega-languages. Theor. Comput. Sci. **183**(1), 93–112 (1997). https://doi.org/10.1016/S0304-3975(96)00312-X

17. Michel, M.: Complementation is more difficult with automata on infinite words. CNET, Paris 15 (1988)

18. Myhill, J.: Finite automata and the representation of events. In: Technical Report WADD TR-57-624, pp. 112–137 (1957)
19. Nerode, A.: Linear automaton transformations. In: American Mathematical Society, pp. 541–544 (1958)
20. Pfleeger, C.P.: State reduction in incompletely specified finite-state machines. IEEE Trans. Comput. **22**(12), 1099–1102 (1973). https://doi.org/10.1109/T-C.1973.223655
21. Safra, S.: On the complexity of omega-automata. In: 29th Annual Symposium on Foundations of Computer Science, White Plains, New York, USA, 24–26 October 1988, pp. 319–327. IEEE Computer Society (1988). https://doi.org/10.1109/SFCS.1988.21948
22. Schewe, S.: Tighter bounds for the determinisation of Büchi automata. In: de Alfaro, L. (ed.) FoSSaCS 2009. LNCS, vol. 5504, pp. 167–181. Springer, Heidelberg (2009). https://doi.org/10.1007/978-3-642-00596-1_13
23. Schewe, S.: Beyond hyper-minimisation—minimising dbas and DPAs is NP-complete. In: Lodaya, K., Mahajan, M. (eds.) IARCS Annual Conference on Foundations of Software Technology and Theoretical Computer Science, FSTTCS 2010, 15–18 December 2010, Chennai, India. LIPIcs, vol. 8, pp. 400–411. Schloss Dagstuhl - Leibniz-Zentrum für Informatik (2010). https://doi.org/10.4230/LIPIcs.FSTTCS.2010.400
24. Vardi, M.Y., Wolper, P.: An automata-theoretic approach to automatic program verification (preliminary report). In: Proceedings of the Symposium on Logic in Computer Science (LICS 1986), Cambridge, Massachusetts, USA, 16–18 June 1986, pp. 332–344. IEEE Computer Society (1986)
25. Wilke, T., Schewe, S.: ω-automata. In: Pin, J. (ed.) Handbook of Automata Theory, pp. 189–234. European Mathematical Society Publishing House, Zürich, Switzerland (2021). https://doi.org/10.4171/Automata-1/6

On the Containment Problem for Deterministic Multicounter Machine Models

Oscar H. Ibarra[1] and Ian McQuillan[2(✉)]

[1] Department of Computer Science, University of California,
Santa Barbara, CA 93106, USA
ibarra@cs.ucsb.edu
[2] Department of Computer Science, University of Saskatchewan,
Saskatoon, SK S7N 5A9, Canada
mcquillan@cs.usask.ca

Abstract. A new model of one-way multicounter machines is introduced. In this model, within each transition, testing the counter status of a counter is optional, rather than existing models where they are always either required (traditional multicounter machines) or no status can be checked (partially-blind multicounter machines). If, in every accepting computation, each counter has a bounded number of sections that decrease that counter where its status is tested, then the machine is called *finite-testable*. One-way nondeterministic finite-testable multicounter machines are shown to be equivalent to partially-blind multicounter machines, which, in turn, are known to be equivalent to Petri net languages and languages defined by vector addition systems with states. However, one-way deterministic finite-testable multicounter machines are strictly more general than deterministic partially-blind machines. Moreover, they also properly include deterministic reversal-bounded multicounter machines (unlike deterministic partially-blind multicounter machines). Interestingly, one-way deterministic finite-testable multicounter machines are shown to have a decidable containment problem ("given two machines M_1, M_2, is $L(M_1) \subseteq L(M_2)$?"). This makes it the most general known model where this problem is decidable. We also study properties of their reachability sets.

1 Introduction

One of the most commonly studied decision problems for models of automata is the containment problem (also sometimes called the inclusion problem), which is: "given two machines M_1 and M_2 from the model, is $L(M_1) \subseteq L(M_2)$?". The containment problem is important towards model checking. Indeed, if M_2 contains an automaton-based representation of a specification and M_1 contains a model, then M_1 satisfies the specification if $L(M_1) \subseteq L(M_2)$. This automata-theoretic

The research of I. McQuillan was supported, in part, by Natural Sciences and Engineering Research Council of Canada.

approach was initiated by Vardi and Wolper [28], it enables on-the-fly model checking [8], and it has been studied with different models of automata [23,27]. Furthermore, industrial automated verification tools have implemented and used automata-based methods [11]. Not only is the containment problem undecidable for the context-free languages, it is also undecidable for many restriction of pushdown automata, including deterministic pushdown automata, deterministic one counter automata (the store contains a non-negative integer which can be increased, decreased, and tested for zero), and nondeterministic one counter automata where the counter cannot increase after decreasing [1]. In contrast, one model with a decidable containment problem is one-way deterministic machines with some number of counters, but on every accepting computation, there is a bound in the number of changes in direction between non-decreasing and non-increasing the size of each counter, called *reversal-bounded*, and they are denoted by DRBCM (and the nondeterministic version is denoted by NRBCM).

The emptiness problem, "given machine M, is $L(M) = \emptyset$?", is also important and commonly decidable for more powerful models. Indeed, it is decidable for pushdown automata [12], NRBCM [17], and one-way nondeterministic partially-blind multicounter machines (denoted by NPBLIND) [10]. The latter model contains multicounter machines where each counter contains some non-negative integer, but no differences are allowed in available transitions based on the counter status (whether a counter is empty or not), besides acceptance being defined by final state and all counters being zero in the final configuration. In this sense, counter status checks are not allowed. It is known that NRBCM is properly contained in NPBLIND [10], and also that the following are equivalent: deciding emptiness for partially-blind multicounter machines, deciding the emptiness problem for Petri nets, and deciding reachability of vector addition systems. Later, reachability for Petri nets was shown to be decidable and therefore all three problems are decidable [20,22]. Recently, it was shown that the boundedness problem ("given M, are there words $w_1, \ldots, w_n$ such that $L(M) \subseteq w_1^* \cdots w_n^*$?") is decidable for vector addition systems with states [6], hence for NPBLIND as well.

Some restrictions of NPBLIND (resp. labelled Petri nets, and vector addition systems with states) have also been studied. For example, λ-free deterministic labelled Petri nets have been studied [25,29]. In the latter paper, it was shown that the complement of the language accepted by any λ-free deterministic labelled Petri net could be accepted by a nondeterministic labelled Petri net (equivalent to NPBLIND). From this, and decidability of emptiness for Petri nets, it follows that the containment problem is decidable for λ-free deterministic labelled Petri nets. To note here, this type of Petri net also does not have an explicit label to detect when it has reached the end of the input, which can limit the capacity of the machines. In addition, vector addition systems with states that are boundedly-ambiguous have been studied [5]. When using an acceptance condition defined by an upward-closed set of configurations, the containment problem is decidable.

Here, we study deterministic NPBLIND machines with the input end-marker and also allowing λ transitions, which we denote by DPBLIND. We show that the right input-marker strictly increases the capacity, showing the importance of using this simple construct. Even with λ transitions and the end-marker however, we show the model is still somewhat limited and cannot accept all DRBCM languages.

This inspires a simple and novel restriction of multicounter machines, where the counter status checks are optional. Such a machine is r-testable if, in every accepting computation, each counter has at most r segments where it decreases this counter and checks its status at least once (and it is finite-testable if it is r-testable for some r). This class is denoted by NTCM, and DTCM for the deterministic restriction. While we show that NTCM and NPBLIND are equivalent, DTCM is shown to be strictly more powerful than both DPBLIND and DRBCM. Then we show that the complement of every DTCM (hence DPBLIND) is in NTCM = NPBLIND. From this, it follows that DTCM (and DPBLIND) has a decidable containment problem (hence also equality problem and universe problem). This makes DTCM one of the most general automata model known with a decidable containment problem, as it is significantly more general than DRBCM and allows λ transitions and has an end-marker unlike the model [25].

All omitted proofs appear in the appendix due to space constraints.

2   Preliminaries

Let $\mathbb{N}$ be the set of natural numbers, and $\mathbb{N}_0$ be the set of non-negative integers, and $\mathbb{Z}$ be the set of integers. For $k \in \mathbb{N}$, let $\mathbb{N}(k) = \{1, \ldots, k\}$. For $j \in \mathbb{N}_0$, define $\pi(j)$ to be $\hat{0}$ if $j = 0$ and $\hat{1}$ otherwise. For a set X and $k \in \mathbb{N}$, define X^k to be the set of k-tuples of elements of X. A set $Q \subseteq \mathbb{N}_0^k$ is called a *linear set* if there exists vectors $\vec{v}_0, \vec{v}_1, \ldots, \vec{v}_l \in \mathbb{N}_0^k$ such that $Q = \{\vec{v}_0 + i_1\vec{v}_1 + \cdots + i_l\vec{v}_l \mid i_1, \ldots, i_l \in \mathbb{N}_0\}$. Here, $\vec{v}_0$ is called the *constant*, and $\vec{v}_1, \ldots, \vec{v}_l$ are called the *periods*. The constant and the periods together are called a *representation* of the linear set. A set $Q \subseteq \mathbb{N}_0^k$ is called a *semilinear set* if it is a finite union of linear sets, and a representation of Q is the set of representations of each linear set.

We assume a basic familiarity with automata and formal language theory [12]. Let Σ be a finite alphabet, and let Σ^* be the set of all words over Σ, including the empty word λ, and Σ^+ is the set of all non-empty words. A *language over* Σ is any $L \subseteq \Sigma^*$. Given $L \subseteq \Sigma^*$, the *complement* of L with respect to Σ is, $\overline{L} = \Sigma^* - L$. Given a word $w \in \Sigma^*$, $|w|$ is the length of w; and given $a \in \Sigma$, $|w|_a$ is the number of a's in w.

Given a fixed ordering of an alphabet $\Sigma = \{a_1, \ldots, a_k\}$, then the *Parikh image* of $w \in \Sigma^*$ denoted $\Psi(w) = (|w|_{a_1}, \ldots, |w|_{a_k})$. This is extended to the Parikh image of languages $L \subseteq \Sigma^*$ by $\Psi(L) = \{\Psi(w) \mid w \in L\}$. A language L is said to be *Parikh semilinear* (or simply *semilinear*) if $\Psi(L)$ is a semilinear set. It is known that every regular language (in fact, context-free language) is Parikh semilinear [24]. We say that a set for a given problem is an *effectively determinable semilinear set* if, the set for that problem is a semilinear set, and moreover there is an effective procedure to determine the semilinear representation given inputs to the problem.

A language $L \subseteq \Sigma^*$ is *bounded* if there exists $w_1, \ldots, w_n \in \Sigma^+$ such that $L \subseteq w_1^* \cdots w_n^*$. Given words $w_1, \ldots, w_n \in \Sigma^+$ and $L \subseteq w_1^* \cdots w_n^*$, we define a function ϕ from languages L to subsets of $\mathbb{N}_0^n$ that maps $\phi(L) = \{(i_1, \ldots, i_n) \mid w_1^{i_1} \cdots w_n^{i_n} \in L\}$. We call L a *bounded Ginsburg semilinear* language (or simply Ginsburg semilinear) if $\phi(L)$ is a semilinear set. In the literature, bounded Ginsburg semilinear is often just referred to by bounded semilinear [3]. Note that the Parikh image $\psi(L)$ (which is a subset of $\mathbb{N}_0^k$) may be different than $\phi(L)$ (which is a subset of $\mathbb{N}_0^n$). However, it is known that every bounded Ginsburg semilinear language is also Parikh semilinear [3] but there are Parikh semilinear languages (even bounded ones) that are not Ginsburg semilinear. For example, consider $L = \{a^{2^n} b \mid n > 0\} \cup ba^+$, which is bounded as it is a subset of $a^* b^* a^*$. But given a, b, a, $\phi(L) = \{(2^n, 1, 0) \mid n > 0\} \cup \{(0, 1, n) \mid n > 0\}$, which is not semilinear, and so L is not Ginsburg semilinear. However, $\psi(L) = \{(n, 1) \mid n > 0\}$ (a is first letter, b is second) is semilinear and so L is Parikh semilinear.

We define k-counter machines in a slightly unusual way, where it is possible to either test whether a counter is positive or zero, but also not test the status of a counter. This allows the definition to be used for multiple purposes.

Definition 1. *A one-way nondeterministic k-counter machine is a tuple $M = (Q, \Sigma, \delta, q_0, F)$ with a finite set of states Q, initial state q_0, the final state set $F \subseteq Q$, an input alphabet Σ, and a transition function δ, which is a partial function from $Q \times (\Sigma \cup \{\lambda, \lhd\}) \times \mathbb{N}(k) \times \{\hat{0}, \hat{1}, \hat{\varnothing}\}$ to finite subsets of $Q \times \{0, +1, -1\}$, where $\lhd \notin \Sigma$ is the right input end-marker. Here, we call $\{\hat{0}, \hat{1}, \hat{\varnothing}\}$ the set of tests, with $\hat{0}$ the zero-test, $\hat{1}$ the non-zero-test, $\hat{0}$ and $\hat{1}$ collectively the status tests, and $\hat{\varnothing}$ is the no-test. A transition $(p, e) \in \delta(q, a, i, \tau)$ (which we often write as $\delta(q, a, i, \tau) \to (p, e)$) can be used if q is the current state and $a \in \Sigma \cup \{\lambda, \lhd\}$ is read from the input, and*

- *if $\tau = \hat{\varnothing}$, then it adds e to counter i,*
- *if $\tau = \hat{1}$ and counter i is non-empty, then it adds e to counter i,*
- *if $\tau = \hat{0}$ and counter i is empty, then it adds e to counter i,*

and it switches to state p. Such a machine is deterministic *if,*

1. *for each $q \in Q$ and $a \in \Sigma \cup \{\lhd\}$, there is at most one counter i, denoted $C(q, a)$ if one exists, such that $\delta(q, a, i, \tau) \cup \delta(q, \lambda, i, \tau) \neq \emptyset$, for some $\tau \in \{\hat{0}, \hat{1}, \hat{\varnothing}\}$,*
2. *for all $q \in Q, a \in \Sigma \cup \{\lhd\}, \tau \in \{\hat{0}, \hat{1}\}$, where $i = C(q, a)$,*

$$|\delta(q, a, i, \tau) \cup \delta(q, \lambda, i, \tau) \cup \delta(q, a, i, \hat{\varnothing}) \cup \delta(q, \lambda, i, \hat{\varnothing})| \leq 1.$$

This matches the traditional notion of determinism, except the counter status can influence the deterministic choice of the next transition to apply if and only if a status test is used. If a no-test is used, it must be the only available transition. For example, a deterministic machine could have separate transitions from $\delta(q, a, i, \hat{0})$ and $\delta(q, a, i, \hat{1})$, where the first happens if counter i is zero and the second happens if counter i is positive. But we cannot have separate transitions if either both transitions have the same test, or if one is a no-test as that would lead to multiple possible transitions that could be applied from the same instantaneous description (defined next). It is also required that only one counter can be used from a given state and input letter or empty word, as otherwise multiple instantaneous descriptions could follow a given one.

Definition 2. *An* instantaneous description (ID) *of k-counter machine $M = (Q, \Sigma, \delta, q_0, F)$ is a member of $Q \times (\Sigma^* \lhd \cup \{\lambda\}) \times \mathbb{N}_0^k$. Instantaneous descriptions change via the relation $\vdash_M$ (or $\vdash$ if M is clear) with $(q, aw, y_1, \ldots, y_k) \vdash (q', w, y_1, \ldots, y_{i-1}, y_i + e, y_{i+1}, \ldots, y_k)$, if $\delta(q, a, i, \tau) \to (q', e)$, $y_i + e \geq 0$, and either $\tau = \hat{\varnothing}$ or $\pi(y_i) = \tau$. Then, $\vdash^*$ is the reflexive, transitive closure of $\vdash$. A computation on $w \in \Sigma^*$ is a sequence of IDs,*

$$(p_0, w_0, y_{0,1}, \ldots, y_{0,k}) \vdash \cdots \vdash (p_n, w_n, y_{n,1}, \ldots, y_{n,k}), \tag{1}$$

where $q_0 = p_0, w_0 = w\lhd, y_{0,i} = 0, 1 \leq i \leq k$; and a computation is an accepting computation of w if $y_{n,i} = 0$ for $1 \leq i \leq k$, $w_n = \lambda$, and $p_n \in F$. Thus, accepting computations end at all 0's in the counters and in a final state. Often, we associate labels bijectively from a set Σ_δ to the transitions of M, and write $ID \vdash^t ID'$, $t \in \Sigma_\delta$ if $ID \vdash ID'$ via transition t; and $ID \vdash^x ID'$ for $x = t_1 \cdots t_m, t_i \in \Sigma_\delta$, if $ID = ID_0 \vdash^{t_1} \cdots \vdash^{t_m} ID_m = ID'$. We also define $\text{runs}(M) = \{x \in \Sigma_\delta^* \mid (q_0, w\lhd, 0, \ldots, 0) \vdash^x (q_f, \lambda, 0, \ldots, 0), q_f \in F\}$

Given a computation $ID_0 \vdash^{t_1} \cdots \vdash^{t_n} ID_n, n \geq 0$, for i $1 \leq i \leq k$, we divide it into so-called decreasing i-segments and increasing i-segments as follows: we say $ID_{j-1} \vdash^{t_j} \cdots \vdash^{t_l} ID_l$ is a decreasing i-segment if

- *t_j decreases counter i,*
- *there are no transitions that increase counter i in $t_j, \ldots, t_{l-1}$,*
- *either $l = n$ or t_l increases counter i,*
- *the last transition of $t_1, \ldots, t_{j-1}$ that changes counter i increases it.*

We can naturally order decreasing i-segments. Further, we define the increasing i-segments between the beginning of the computation to the ID at the start of the first decreasing i-segment or the last ID if there are no decreasing i-segments, between the last ID of one decreasing i-segment and the first ID of the next decreasing i-segment, and from the last ID of the last decreasing i-segment to the end if it does not end in a decreasing i-segment or it ends with a transition that increases counter i.

Such a machine M is r-reversal-bounded, if, in every accepting computation, each counter i, $1 \leq i \leq k$, has at most $r + 1$ increasing or decreasing i-segments. It is reversal-bounded if it is r-reversal-bounded for some r. Such a machine is called partially-blind if all transitions have $\hat{\varnothing}$ for tests.

The language accepted by M,

$$L(M) = \{w \in \Sigma^* \mid \text{there is an accepting computation of } w\},$$

and the reachability set of M, $R(M) = \{(q, v_1, \ldots, v_k) \mid (q_0, w\lhd, 0, \ldots, 0) \vdash^* (q, w', v_1, \ldots, v_k) \vdash^* (q_f, \lambda, 0, \ldots, 0), q_f \in F\}$.

As decreasing i-segments are maximal (they start with a decrease, the previous transition that changes that counter is an increase, and they end with either the next increase or the end of the computation), we can split each computation, for each i, uniquely into increasing and decreasing i-segments. The definition of r-reversal-bounded here is equivalent to that of [17] which counts the number of changes in direction in each counter. The definition of partially-blind multi-counter machines is the same to that of [10]. Note these machines do have one implicit test of all zeros in the counters at the end of the computation. With no-tests (and partially-blind machines), the machines "crash" (ie. the computation cannot continue), if any counter tries to go below zero. But the machines cannot detect that the counters are zero (because the transition function does not allow differences based on the contents of the counters). Normally the reachability set is defined without the restriction of appearing within an accepting computation, but we will use this stronger notion here. Also, sometimes it is defined to not include the state as a component. We will usually associate the state component bijectively with a number in $\{1, \ldots, |Q|\}$ so we can, e.g. talk about a reachability set being a semilinear set.

The class of one-way nondeterministic (resp. deterministic) partially-blind k-counter machines is denoted by NPBLIND(k) (resp. DPBLIND(k)), and the class of partially-blind machines is denoted by NPBLIND (resp. DPBLIND). The class of one-way nondeterministic (resp. deterministic) r-reversal-bounded k-counter machines is denoted by NRBCM(k, r) (resp. DRBCM(k, r)), and the family of reversal-bounded multicounter machines is denoted by NRBCM (resp. DRBCM). By a slight abuse of notation, we will use the same notation for a class of machines and the family of languages they accept.

It is also known that one-way deterministic two-counter machines accept all recursively enumerable languages (denoted RE), but there are some recursively enumerable languages that are not in NPBLIND [10]. Deterministic partially-blind machines are a restriction of partially-blind machines, and it is therefore clear that DPBLIND $\subseteq$ NPBLIND $\subsetneq$ RE. Lastly, note DRBCM $\subsetneq$ NRBCM $\subsetneq$ NPBLIND $\subsetneq$ RE, with the latter two shown in [10], and DRBCM is known to be a proper subset of NRBCM [17].

Lastly, we show a simple result in this section which will help throughout the paper. Given a k-counter machine $M = (Q, \Sigma, \delta, q_0, F)$, denote by $M_\delta = (Q_\delta, \Sigma_\delta, \delta', q_0, F')$ the deterministic k-counter machine obtained from M with $Q_\delta = Q \cup Q'$ where Q' is a primed version of the states in Q, F' is the primed versions of the states in F, and δ' is built to read $t \in \Sigma_\delta$ to simulate transition t of M, but it uses states of Q to simulate transitions of M that read letters of $\Sigma \cup \{\lambda\}$, but M' instead reads t, and switches from states in Q to states of Q' if t reads $\triangleleft$ in M, and switches between states in Q' to simulate only λ transitions. Lastly, add $\delta'(q', \triangleleft, 1, \hat{\oslash}) \to (q', 0)$ for all q', where $q \in Q$.

Lemma 3. *Given k-counter $M = (Q, \Sigma, \delta, q_0, F)$, the following are true:*

- *M_δ is deterministic,*
- *runs$(M) = L(M_\delta)$,*
- *$L(M)$ is not Parikh semilinear implies runs(M) is not Parikh semilinear,*
- *$R(M)$ is not semilinear implies $R(M_\delta)$ is not semilinear.*

3   Properties of Deterministic Partially-Blind Machines

We start this section with an example of a DPBLIND machine before analyzing its properties.

Example 4. It is known that NPBLIND contains the so-called one-sided Dyck language on one letter, $D_2 = \{w \in \{a,b\}^* \mid |w|_a = |w|_b$, and if $w = xy$, then $|x|_a \geq |x|_b\}$, which cannot be accepted by any NRBCM [10].
   A NPBLIND(1) machine $M = (Q, \Sigma, \delta, q_0, \{q_1\})$ that accepts this language is as follows,

$$\delta(q_0, a, 1, \hat{\varnothing}) \to (q_0, +1), \ \ \delta(q_0, b, 1, \hat{\varnothing}) \to (q_0, -1), \ \ \delta(q_0, \triangleleft, 1, \hat{\varnothing}) \to (q_1, 0).$$

This machine by definition is deterministic, and therefore $D_2 \in$ DPBLIND(1). Since Dyck languages are Parikh semilinear, this shows that DPBLIND contains Parikh semilinear languages that are not in NRBCM. Furthermore, consider the prefix closure of D_2, $D_2' = \{w \in \{a,b\}^* \mid$ if $w = xy$, then $|x|_a \geq |x|_b\}$. A DPBLIND M' can accept D_2' by adding transition $\delta(q_1, \lambda, 1, \hat{\varnothing}) \to (q_1, -1)$ to M above. Notice that when it reads the end-marker with some value j on the counter, it continually decreases the counter, and as long as it eventually passes over 0 on the counter in state q_1, it accepts.

   The right input end-marker is not necessary for any nondeterministic machine model defined in the previous section, because the machine can guess that it has read the last input symbol, and only accept if it guessed correctly. One could define NRBCM$_{NE}$ (resp. DRBCM$_{NE}$) machines as being NRBCM machines (resp. DRBCM) without containing any transitions on the end-marker, and acceptance is defined as, it reads the entire input w (with no end-marker), and it is in a final state. This notation was used in [7,14] where machines without the end-marker were studied with NRBCM and DRBCM. Hence, NRBCM = NRBCM$_{NE}$. For that reason, when studying nondeterministic machines, we can leave off the end-marker in the machine definition and when examining computations. With deterministic machines though, it is not necessarily so; e.g. it is known that DRBCM$_{NE} \subsetneq$ DRBCM [7,14] (in contrast to say deterministic pushdown automata where they are the same). We do not know of any other one-way input machine model where they are known to be different. Clearly, for any deterministic model defined above, the family of languages accepted without the end-marker is a subset of the entire model as we could simply ignore the marker. So we by default use the more general definition with the end-marker. Deterministic partially-blind multicounter languages have been defined and studied previously, but they were defined without the end-marker [4], and so we are using the more general definition with the end-marker here instead. We use the notation NPBLIND$_{NE}$ (resp. DPBLIND$_{NE}$) to be NPBLIND (resp. DPBLIND) machines and languages without the end-marker, where acceptance occurs by hitting the end of the input in a final state with all counters zero. Then NPBLIND$_{NE}$ = NPBLIND using the same argument as the start of this section.

We next see that in fact the language D_2' from Example 4 requires the end-marker to accept for deterministic machines, leading to the following separation.

Proposition 5. DPBLIND$_{NE}$ $\subsetneq$ DPBLIND.

Therefore, the right end-marker increases the power of DPBLIND, similarly to DRBCM.

Next, we analyze whether DPBLIND and DPBLIND$_{NE}$ contain languages that are not Parikh semilinear, and whether reachability sets can be non-semilinear.

Proposition 6. DPBLIND *and* DPBLIND$_{NE}$ *both contain machines* M *such that* $L(M)$ *is not Parikh semilinear. Furthermore, both contain machines* M *such that* $R(M)$ *and* runs(M) *are not semilinear.*

Proof. It is known that NPBLIND contains languages that are not Parikh semilinear (Theorem 4 of [10]). Let $M \in$ NPBLIND accepting any such language. Considering M_δ, $M_\delta \in$ DPBLIND$_{NE}$ by Lemma 3. Also Lemma 3 indicates that $L(M_\delta) =$ runs(M) is not Parikh semilinear. For the second point, it is known that there are $M \in$ NPBLIND with $R(M)$ not being semilinear (implied by being the case for vector addition systems with states [13]). Using M_δ, Lemma 3 implies $R(M_\delta)$ is not semilinear.   □

Hence, DPBLIND, DPBLIND$_{NE}$, and more general models introduced later in this paper all have languages, 'runs', and reachability sets that are not semilinear. In contrast, languages accepted by NRBCM are all semilinear [17], the 'runs' are semilinear by Lemma 3, and the reachability sets are semilinear, seen as follows: for each $M \in$ NRBCM(k), create $M' \in$ NRBCM($2k$) that nondeterministically guesses and simulates transitions of M but using λ input and by using two identical sets of counters until a nondeterministically guessed spot. Then, it verifies that the input is $1^n c_1^{i_1} \cdots c_k^{i_k}$ where n is a number associated with the current state, and $i_1, \ldots, i_k$ are the same as one copy of the counters. From then, it continues the simulation using the other set of counters. It is evident that $\psi(L(M')) = R(M)$, which is semilinear [17].

Even though DPBLIND contains languages that are not Parikh semilinear, we see next that DPBLIND is still somewhat limited and cannot accept some languages that seem relatively simple and that are Ginsburg semilinear and can even be accepted by a DRBCM(1,1). By contrast DRBCM accepts all Ginsburg semilinear languages [19].

Proposition 7. *The language* $L = \{a^l b^m \mid 0 < l < m\}$ *is in* DRBCM(1,1) *but not in* DPBLIND. *Thus,* DPBLIND *does not contain all Ginsburg semilinear languages.*

Corollary 8. *The families* DPBLIND *(resp.* DPBLIND$_{NE}$*) and* DRBCM *are incomparable.*

The one direction follows from Proposition 7, and the other since DPBLIND and DPBLIND$_{NE}$ contain languages that are not Parikh semilinear by Proposition 6, but DRBCM does not [17].

Proposition 9. DPBLIND *is not closed under complement.*

Proof. Assume otherwise. Consider L from Proposition 7, and let $L' = \{a^n b^m \mid n \geq m\}$. We can see that L' can be accepted by a DPBLIND(1) machine that adds to the counter for each a, then subtracts for each b, and then at the end-marker, switches to final state and continually decreases the counter. Also, DPBLIND is clearly closed under intersection with regular languages. But $\overline{L'} \cap a^+ b^+ = L \in$ DPBLIND, but this is not in DPBLIND by Proposition 7, a contradiction.   □

Despite not being closed under complement, we will see later that the complement of every DPBLIND language is in NPBLIND, which is sufficient to show that DPBLIND has a decidable containment problem; in fact, we will determine a stronger result.

4   Finite-Testable Counter Machines

Next, we introduce a new restriction of counter machines, which will be the focus of the rest of this paper. A k-counter machine $M = (Q, \Sigma, \delta, q_0, F)$ is r-*testable* if, for every acceptable computation and every counter i, $1 \leq i \leq k$, there are at most r decreasing i-segments that contain at least one status test. A machine is *finite-testable* if it is r-testable for some $r \geq 0$. We denote the class of one-way nondeterministic (resp. deterministic) r-testable k-counter machines by NTCM(k, r) (resp. DTCM(k, r)). We use NTCM$(*, r)$ (resp. DTCM$(*, r)$) for r-testable k-counter machines for some k. We also use NTCM (resp. DTCM) to refer to all one-way nondeterministic (resp. deterministic) finite-testable multi-counter machines.

Note, we could have alternatively defined r-testable so that for every accepted word, there is some accepting computation where each counter i has at most r decreasing i-segments; had we done that, given any machine M, another machine M' could be constructed that uses the finite control to count the number of decreasing i-segments in each counter, thereby satisfying the definition we use.

It is immediate that every NRBCM (resp. DRBCM) is a NTCM (resp. DTCM), and therefore NRBCM $\subseteq$ NTCM and DRBCM $\subseteq$ DTCM.

Example 10. It is evident that DPBLIND $\subsetneq$ DTCM since $L = \{a^l b^m \mid 0 < l < m\}$ is in DRBCM(1, 1) but not DPBLIND by Proposition 7. A machine $M \in$ DTCM accepting L contains the following transitions (q_f is a final state):

$$\delta(q_0, a, 1, \hat{0}) \rightarrow (q_1, +1), \qquad \delta(q_2, b, 1, \hat{0}) \rightarrow (q_3, 0),$$
$$\delta(q_1, a, 1, \hat{1}) \rightarrow (q_1, +1), \qquad \delta(q_3, b, 1, \hat{0}) \rightarrow (q_3, 0)$$
$$\delta(q_1, b, 1, \hat{1}) \rightarrow (q_2, -1), \qquad \delta(q_3, \triangleleft, 1, \hat{0}) \rightarrow (q_f, 0),$$
$$\delta(q_2, b, 1, \hat{1}) \rightarrow (q_2, -1)$$

Example 11. Next we provide a more complicated example of a machine accepting a language that cannot be accepted by an NRBCM. Recall $D_2' = \{w \in \{a, b\}^* \mid$ if $w = xy$, then $|x|_a \geq |x|_b\}$ from Example 4 which is not in NRBCM. Let L_1 be D_2' over $\{a_1, b_1\}$ and L_2 be D_2' over $\{a_2, b_2\}$. Let

$$L = \{u_1 v_1 \cdots u_l v_l \$ x_1 y_1 \cdots x_n y_n \mid u_1 \cdots u_l x_1 \cdots x_n \in L_1, v_1 \cdots v_l y_1 \cdots y_n \in L_2,$$
$$\text{and } |u_1 \cdots u_l|_{a_1} = |u_1 \cdots u_l|_{b_1}\}.$$

A DTCM$(2, 2)$ $M = (Q, \Sigma, \delta, q_0, \{q_f\})$ that accepts this language is as follows, for $i \in \{1, 2\}$,

$$\delta(q_0, a_i, i, \hat{\varnothing}) \rightarrow (q_0, +1), \qquad \delta(q_1, \lhd, 1, \hat{\varnothing}) \rightarrow (q_2, 0),$$
$$\delta(q_0, b_i, i, \hat{\varnothing}) \rightarrow (q_0, -1), \qquad \delta(q_2, \lambda, 1, \hat{1}) \rightarrow (q_2, -1)$$
$$\delta(q_0, \$, 1, \hat{0}) \rightarrow (q_1, 0), \qquad \delta(q_2, \lambda, 1, \hat{0}) \rightarrow (q_3, 0),$$
$$\delta(q_1, a_i, i, \hat{\varnothing}) \rightarrow (q_1, +1) \qquad \delta(q_3, \lambda, 2, \hat{1}) \rightarrow (q_3, -1)$$
$$\delta(q_1, b_i, i, \hat{\varnothing}) \rightarrow (q_1, -1) \qquad \delta(q_3, \lambda, 2, \hat{0}) \rightarrow (q_f, 0).$$

This machine is deterministic because from both q_0 and q_1 and on each letter of a_1, b_1, a_2, b_2, only a single no-test transition is possible, and from q_2 and q_3, only one transition on each status test is possible.

It also appears that this language cannot be accepted by a DPBLIND because a DPBLIND cannot test for zero until the very last ID. While it is possible to create two new counters (called the special counters) to count both $|u_1 \cdots u_l|_{a_1}$ and $|u_1 \cdots u_l|_{b_1}$ by counting until $\$$ and then not changing those counters until the end-marker, it seems not possible to deterministically decrease these special counters to zero to test that they are equal in the final instantaneous description while also decreasing the other counters to zero without the ability to test for zero in a subset of the counters before the final instantaneous description. In contrast, the DTCM machine above can detect whether an individual counter is empty unlike NPBLIND, which M does after reading $\$$, and also separately for each counter after reading $\lhd$.

Notice that NTCM$(*, 0)$ corresponds exactly to NPBLIND. Furthermore, we see that with nondeterministic machines, finite-testability and 0-testability are equivalent, although converting to 0-testable increases the number of counters.

Proposition 12. NTCM$(*, 0)$ = NPBLIND = NTCM.

For the rest of this section, we are only concerned with deterministic machines. We start with a normal form that is useful for the next section. We say a DTCM(k, r) $M = (Q, \Sigma, \delta, q_0, F)$ is in *normal form* if, for each $q \in Q, a \in \Sigma \cup \{\lhd\}$, the following are equivalent:

- there is a transition in $\delta(q, b, i, \hat{0})$ with $b \in \{a, \lambda\}$,
- there is a transition in $\delta(q, b, i, \hat{1})$ with $b \in \{a, \lambda\}$,
- there is no transition in $\delta(q, b, i, \hat{\varnothing})$ with $b \in \{a, \lambda\}$.

Furthermore, M is in *strong normal form* if M is in normal form, and

- $Q = Q_1 \cup Q_2, Q_1 \cap Q_2 = \emptyset$, Q_2 only contains λ transitions, and in every computation, M only uses transition from Q_1 before reading $\lhd$, and from Q_2 after reading $\lhd$,
- in every computation, on counter i, at most r successful zero-tests on counter i are possible.

Remark 13. Here, normal form enforces that on each letter of $\Sigma \cup \{\lhd\}$, there is a transition that can be applied with a zero test if and only if there is a transition that can be applied with a non-zero test, and vice versa (which, by determinism would imply that there is not a no-test transition that can be applied). If neither is true, a no-test is available. With strong normal form, as there are only λ transitions from states in Q_2, the normal form rules enforces that for each $q \in Q_2$, there is a transition in $\delta(q, \lambda, i, \hat{0})$ if and only if there is a transition in $\delta(q, \lambda, i, \hat{1})$ if and only if there is no transition in $\delta(q, \lambda, i, \hat{\emptyset})$. Therefore there is always at least one transition that can be applied at each step even after the end-marker, and acceptance purely depends on whether it eventually can hit a final state with all counters zero.

Lemma 14. *Given $M \in$ DTCM, a DTCM M' can be constructed in normal form such that $L(M) = L(M')$, $R(M) = R(M')$, and* runs$(M) =$ runs(M'). *Furthermore, a DTCM M'' can be constructed in strong normal form such that $L(M) = L(M'')$.*

For deterministic machines, we obtain the following more nuanced situation than Proposition 12. As part of that, we see that DTCM is equivalent to 1-testable DTCM (although this increases the number of counters), which in turn in more powerful than 0-testable DTCM which is equal to DPBLIND. The proof largely uses Propositions 7, 6 and Corollary 8.

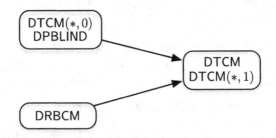

Fig. 1. In the above image, families drawn in the same cell are equal, arrows represent strict containment, and no arrows between cells represents incomparability.

Proposition 15. *The hierarchy diagram in Fig. 1 is correct.*

Despite this, we conjecture that for a fixed number of counters, there is an infinite hierarchy as r increases.

Next, we show DTCM languages are in DLOG (can be accepted in log-space by deterministic Turing machines), and hence can all be accepted by a polynomial time deterministic Turing machine. For the next result, use an encoding of DTCM whereby r is part of the description of M.

Lemma 16. *Let $M = (Q, \Sigma, \delta, q_0, F)$ be a DTCM(k, r). Then the counters are linearly bounded.*

From the lemma, we have:

Proposition 17. DTCM *(hence* DPBLIND*) is in* DLOG.

5 Bounded Languages in **DTCM** and **NTCM**

Next, we demonstrate that despite DTCM containing languages that are not Parikh semilinear, every bounded language in DTCM is both Ginsburg semilinear and Parikh semilinear. This result is interesting on its own, and also useful as a helper towards results in the next section. In parallel, we analyze the reachability sets and the 'runs' of DTCM accepting bounded languages. The connection between the 'runs' and bounded languages has been established in the literature. Vector addition system with states (VASS) have a concept called *flattable*, whereby a VASS is flattable [21] if the set of all runs are included in a bounded language (there, the reachability set and runs just need to be reachable from an initial configuration and not within an accepting computation). It was shown that a VASS is flattable if and only if its reachability set is definable in the Presburger arithmetic.

First we need the following two simple properties which use completely standard constructions, similar to those in [12], and therefore proofs are omitted.

Lemma 18. *For $k, r \geq 0$, DTCM(k, r) is closed under intersection with regular languages and inverse homomorphism.*

Next, we need another intermediate lemma, which uses the regular periodicity of the transitions applied by DTCM when accepting letter-bounded languages.

Lemma 19. *Given $\Sigma = \{a_1, \ldots, a_n\}$ and $M = (Q, \Sigma, \delta, q_0, F) \in$ DTCM(k, r) such that $L(M) \subseteq a_1^* \cdots a_n^*$, both $L(M)$ and* runs(M) *can both be accepted by an NRBCM and are both bounded Ginsburg and Parikh semilinear, and a representation of the semilinear sets can be effectively constructed. Moreover, $R(M) \subseteq \mathbb{N}_0^{k+1}$ is semilinear with an effective procedure.*

From these, we can obtain the following:

Proposition 20. *It is decidable, given $M \in$ DTCM(k, r), whether $L(M)$ is bounded; and if so, we can determine words $u_1, \ldots, u_n \in \Sigma^+$ such that $L(M) \subseteq u_1^* \cdots u_n^*$, and the following are true:*

– $L(M) \in$ NRBCM *is bounded Ginsburg semilinear, $\phi(L(M)) = Q_1 \subseteq \mathbb{N}_0^n$ is effectively semilinear;*

- runs(M) $\in$ NRBCM *is bounded Ginsburg semilinear* $\phi(\text{runs}(M)) = Q_2$ *is effectively semilinear;*
- $R(M) \subseteq \mathbb{N}_0^{k+1}$ *is effectively semilinear;*

Proof. First note that boundedness was recently shown to be decidable for NPBLIND [2,6]. Hence, given $M \in$ DTCM, we can determine whether $L(M)$ is bounded, and if so, we can determine words $u_1, \ldots, u_n \in \Sigma^+$ such that $L(M) \subseteq u_1^* \cdots u_n^*$. Henceforth, we assume $u_1, \ldots, u_n$ are known. Let $a_1, \ldots, a_n$ be new symbols and let h be a homomorphism that maps a_i to u_i for i from 1 to n. As DTCM is closed under inverse homomorphism and intersection with regular languages by Lemma 18, we can construct $M' \in$ DTCM with

$$L(M') = h^{-1}(L(M)) \cap a_1^* \cdots a_n^* = \{a_1^{i_1} \cdots a_n^{i_n} \mid u_1^{i_1} \cdots u_n^{i_n} \in L(M)\} \in \text{DTCM}.$$

By Lemma 19, $L(M)$ is bounded Ginsburg semilinear and we can effectively determine semilinear set Q such that $\phi(L(M)) = Q$. Then given $u_1, \ldots, u_n$, $\phi(L(M)) = Q$, and so $L(M)$ is in NRBCM.

Similarly, it follows that runs(M) $\in$ NRBCM by using M' with the lemma above, and also $R(M)$ is semilinear. $\square$

If one were to examine deterministic vector addition systems with states that either operated with only λ moves, or over bounded languages, the same thing would be true.

Interestingly it was shown in [3] that the bounded Ginsburg semilinear languages are equal to the bounded languages in both NRBCM and in DRBCM. Since DRBCM $\subsetneq$ DTCM by Proposition 15, it follows that the bounded languages in DTCM and DRBCM coincide and are exactly the bounded Ginsburg semilinear languages. It is also known that the bounded languages accepted by multi-head DFAs and multi-head NFAs are also exactly the bounded Ginsburg semilinear languages (this is even the case for 2-head DFAs) [16]. And this is also true for two-way multi-head NPDA where the input heads turn at most a finite number of times. Furthermore, it follows from [3] that the bounded languages in any semilinear trio (a family closed under inverse homomorphism, λ-free homomorphism, and intersection with regular languages) are always a subset of the bounded Ginsburg semilinear languages. Some other examples are given in [3] of families of languages where the bounded languages in the family are exactly the bounded Ginsburg semilinear languages, such as finite-index ET0L, and Turing machines with a one-way input tape and a finite-turn worktape.

Corollary 21. *The bounded languages in the following families are exactly equal to the bounded Ginsburg semilinear languages:*

- DTCM,
- NRBCM,
- *DRBCM,*
- *multi-head* NFA,
- *2-head* DFA.

An interesting question next is whether the bounded languages in NTCM are Ginsburg or Parikh semilinear. We answer that question negatively.

Proposition 22. *The following are true:*

- *there are bounded languages in* NTCM = NPBLIND *that are not Parikh semilinear,*
- *there are bounded languages in* NTCM *that are Parikh semilinear but not Ginsburg semilinear,*
- *there are machines M in* NTCM *where L(M) is bounded but R(M) is not semilinear.*

Certainly though, the bounded Ginsburg semilinear languages in NTCM coincide with the bounded languages in DTCM and those of the families in Corollary 21.

To note, of all the families in Corollary 21 or that are listed above it, the only family we know of that contain languages that are not Parikh semilinear, but where the bounded languages within are only bounded Ginsburg semilinear are the multi-head DFA and NFA families, and now DTCM. It is known however that even 2-head DFA has an undecidable emptiness problem [26]. From this, it follows that it is undecidable whether a 2-head DFA accepts a bounded language (given a 2-head DFA M, construct M' to accept $L(M)\{\$\}\varSigma^*$ where $L(M) \subseteq \varSigma^*$ and $\$$ is a new symbol not in $\varSigma$, which is bounded if and only if $L(M) = \emptyset$). However, DTCM actually can decide if a given machine accepts a bounded language, as DTCM $\subseteq$ NPBLIND where boundedness is decidable [2,6]. Hence, DTCM is the only known class of machines with a decidable boundedness problem (which is needed for Proposition 20) that contains languages that are not Parikh semilinear, but where the bounded languages within are only Ginsburg (or Parikh) semilinear.

We obtain the following interesting property on reachability sets for NTCM. It follows from Proposition 20 that for every bounded DTCM, runs(M) is bounded, and $R(M)$ is semilinear. The following is true even for nondeterministic machines.

Corollary 23. *For each $M \in$ NTCM (and NPBLIND), it is decidable if* runs(M) *is bounded; and if it is, then* runs(M) *is Ginsburg semilinear and can be accepted by a DRBCM, $R(M)$ is a semilinear set, and both semilinear sets can be effectively computed.*

Proof. Given M, build $M_\delta \in$ DTCM. Since it is decidable whether $L(M_\delta)$ is bounded [6], and if so, we can determine $x_1, \ldots, x_d$, where $x_i \in \varSigma_\delta^+$ and $L(M_\delta) \subseteq x_1^* \cdots x_d^*$; this happens if and only if runs(M) is bounded. Using Proposition 20 on $M_\delta \in$ DTCM, it then follows that $R(M_\delta)$ is semilinear, $L(M_\delta)$ is Ginsburg semilinear, and both can be effectively constructed. It is known that all bounded Ginsburg languages are in DRBCM [19]. Lemma 3 says $L(M_\delta) = $ runs(M); and if $R(M)$ were not semilinear then neither is $R(M_\delta)$. Therefore, $R(M)$ is semilinear. □

6   Complement and Containment of Deterministic Finite-Testable Machines

In this section, we show the following interesting and surprising property, that the complement of every DTCM language (hence DPBLIND) is a NTCM = NPBLIND language. Note that the machine constructed in the proof makes extremely heavy use of nondeterminism, using a nondeterministic choice at many moves of the simulation. We also conjecture that DTCM is not closed under complement (as we proved is the case with DPBLIND), but do not have a proof of this.

We require two technical lemmas which are used to decide properties of counter values that can eventually reach zeros on every counter without a zero-test. This will be helpful for constructing the complement. The first will be used after reading the end-marker to help determine if the counter values can eventually pass over a final state with all counters being zero, which is required for acceptance. This proof essentially follows from the proof in the previous section that all bounded DTCM languages are Parikh semilinear.

Lemma 24. *Given a* DTCM(k, r) $M = (Q, \Sigma, \delta, q_0, F)$ *in strong normal form with Q partitioned into Q_1 and Q_2, and $q \in Q_2$, where $t_1, t_2, \ldots$ is the sequence of transitions from q on λ transitions with only non-zero tests or no-tests. Then*

$$S_q = \{\vec{v}_0 \mid (p_0, \lambda, \vec{v}_0) \vdash^{t_1} \cdots \vdash^{t_l} (p_l, \lambda, \vec{v}_l), p_0 = q, \vec{v}_l = \vec{0}, p_l \in F\},$$

is an effectively determinable semilinear set.

Proof. Sequence $t_1, t_2, \ldots$ is infinite by strong normal form. S_q can be seen to be semilinear as follows: Create $M' \in$ DTCM(k, r) over $\{a_1, \ldots, a_k\}$ that on input $a_1^{j_1} \cdots a_k^{j_k} \lhd$, puts j_i on counter i and then after reading $\lhd$, simulates M. Since $L(M') \subseteq a_1^* \cdots a_k^*$, then $\psi(L(M')) = S_q$. The result is true by Lemma 19.   □

We also require another technical lemma, with a proof akin to Lemma 19.

Lemma 25. *Given a* DTCM $M = (Q, \Sigma, \delta, q_0, F)$ *in strong normal form with Q partitioned into Q_1 and Q_2, and $q \in Q_2$ where $t_1, t_2, \ldots$ is the sequence of transitions from q on λ-transitions with only non-zero-tests or no-tests. Then*

$$R_q = \{\vec{v}_0 \mid (p_0, \lambda, \vec{v}_0) \vdash^{t_1} \cdots \vdash^{t_l} (p_l, \lambda, \vec{v}_l), p_0 = q, (t_{l+1} \text{ has non-zero-test on} \\ \text{some counter } i \text{ and } \vec{v}_l(i) = 0) \text{ and } l \text{ is minimal where this is true}\},$$

is an effectively semilinear set.

Now we will show the main result.

Proposition 26. *For all $L \in$ DTCM, $\overline{L} \in$ NTCM = NPBLIND.*

Proof. Let $M = (Q, \Sigma, \delta, q_0, F)$ be a DTCM(k, r) in strong normal form with Q partitioned into Q_1 and Q_2. Let $q \in Q$. As in the proof of the previous lemmas, there is a unique sequence of λ transitions that can be applied starting in state q without a zero-test,

$$t_1, t_2, \ldots \tag{2}$$

This sequence could be infinite if and only if some transition t occurs in this list at least twice since M is deterministic. We can precompute whether this sequence for each $q \in Q$ is finite or infinite. Moreover, for $q \in Q_2$ the sequence must be infinite by strong normal form (see Remark 13), and we can compute the semilinear representation of

$$S_q = \{\vec{v}_0 \mid (p_0, \lambda, \vec{v}_0) \vdash^{t_1} \cdots \vdash^{t_l} (p_l, \lambda, \vec{v}_l), p_0 = q, \vec{v}_l = \vec{0}, p_l \in F, l \geq 0\}.$$

This set contains all counter values $\vec{v}_0$, such that starting in state q with $\vec{v}_0$ on the counters, it can eventually hit some ID with 0 in all counters, and in a final state. Also, we can precompute for each $q \in Q_2$ a semilinear representation of

$$R_q = \{\vec{v}_0 \mid (p_0, \lambda, \vec{v}_0) \vdash^{t_1} \cdots \vdash^{t_l} (p_l, \lambda, \vec{v}_l), p_0 = q, (t_{l+1} \text{ has a non-zero-test on}$$
$$\text{counter } i \text{ and } \vec{v}_l(i) = 0) \text{ and } l \text{ is minimal where this is true}\}.$$

It is known that given two semilinear sets P_1, P_2, that $P_1 - P_2$ is also effectively semilinear [9]. As $\mathbb{N}_0^k$ is semilinear (where there is a period with a single 1 in one component and zeros in the other components), therefore $\mathbb{N}_0^k - S_q$ is effectively semilinear, which we denote by $\overline{S_q}$, and similarly for R_q producing $\overline{R_q}$.

Now we will build a NTCM $\overline{M}$ with $(2r + 3)k^2$ counters accepting $\overline{L(M)}$. The machine has only a single new final state q_f. We describe $\overline{M}$ as follows. In $\overline{M}$, it operates differently before, and after the end-marker $\triangleleft$. Before the end-marker in M, the only way to not accept some input w would be if the machine crashes (a no-test transition to be applied would cause a counter to go below 0), or it enters an infinite loop on λ-transitions (note that there is always at least one transition that can be applied by strong normal form). Therefore before the end-marker (including the transition that reads $\triangleleft$ but no transition after) $\overline{M}$ simulates M faithfully using counters that we call $C_1^0, \ldots, C_k^0$, except for the following: first, before simulating each transition t of M that decreases some counter, i say, $\overline{M}$ instead makes a nondeterministic choice (we call this the *crashing strategy simulation*):

1. $\overline{M}$ guesses that the simulation can continue, and simulates t;
2. $\overline{M}$ guesses that the transition t that decreases counter i will cause counter i to go below 0. In this case, $\overline{M}$ subtracts all counters other than i by some nondeterministically guessed amount greater than or equal to 0 (but does not change counter i), and then it reads the rest of the input including $\triangleleft$, and switches to q_f (which will then accept if and only if all counters are zero). Note that here, $\overline{M}$ accepts in this way exactly when M would have crashed on t because it would have decreased counter i below zero, but in $\overline{M}$, counter i does not decrease counter i so must be zero in order for $\overline{M}$ to accept.

Second, we want $\overline{M}$ to accept if M would have entered an infinite loop on λ before hitting $\triangleleft$. After simulating each transition that reads an input symbol $a \in \Sigma$ and ending in state q, we check if the sequence (2) is infinite which was predetermined. If it is finite, we continue the simulation using the crashing strategy simulation until either it reads the next letter, or there is a zero-test in some counter i with zero on the counter, from which $\overline{M}$ can continue to simulate. To note, if there is a successful zero-test, taking to state q', then there may be additional transitions on λ, but this will happen at most r times across an entire accepting computation for each counter.

Assume sequence (2) is infinite. Let $\alpha < \beta$ be such that $t_\alpha = t_\beta$ and they are the smallest values where this is the case and therefore the sequence is $t_1, \ldots, t_{\alpha-1}$ followed by $t_\alpha, \ldots, t_{\beta-1}$ repeated indefinitely by the determinism of M. Considering the cycle $t_\alpha, \ldots, t_{\beta-1}$, let $\vec{u} \in \mathbb{Z}^k$ be the sum of the counter values changed in this sequence. If there is some position i of this vector that is negative, then when simulating this sequence from any counter ID, it will eventually stop either by crashing, or detecting a zero with a zero-test. Then we can continue this simulation using the crashing strategy simulation. If all values in $\vec{u}$ are at least 0, then this will enter an infinite loop from a given ID if it is defined on $t_1, \ldots, t_{\beta-1}$ without a successful zero-test (if there is a successful zero-test, this cycle ends and $\overline{M}$ continues the simulation). Thus it executes this initial sequence of length $\beta - 1$ (detecting crashes with the crashing strategy simulation), and then after this sequence, M is in an infinite loop. So, $\overline{M}$ instead switches to q_f, reads the rest of the input, and reduces all counters by some nondeterministically guessed amount in order to accept.

Next, we will consider the case after reading the end-marker $\lhd$. Let $q_{(0)}$ be the state after reading $\lhd$, and let $\vec{v}_0$ be the counter values.

First, $\overline{M}$ guesses a number $m \geq 0$ such that there are m successful tests of 0 that can occur in any computation starting from $q_{(0)}$ and $\vec{v}_0$. By strong normal form $0 \leq m \leq rk$. This guessed m will later be verified. If guessed correctly, then the only way for M to not accept is after the mth successful test for zero, either M crashes, or enters an infinite loop (it does not stop by strong normal form as there is always at least one transition that can be applied), and M does not pass over any IDs with all counters 0 in a final state at any point after reading the end-marker. We will build $\overline{M}$ to guess and verify m while at the same time accepting if and only if M would not accept.

Construct $\overline{M}$ as follows: first $\overline{M}$ guesses and remembers m in the state. Then for each j one at a time from 0 to $m - 1$, $\overline{M}$ makes copies of the values currently stored in counters $C_1^j, \ldots, C_k^j$ into counters named $D_1^j, \ldots, D_k^j$ and $C_1^{j+1}, \ldots, C_k^{j+1}$ respectively. Then using $D_1^j, \ldots, D_k^j$, $\overline{M}$ verifies that $\vec{v}_j \in \overline{S_{q_{(j)}}}$, thereby verifying that it will not pass over a final state with all counters zero before the next successful zero-test. To do so, it guesses a linear set in the semilinear set, then subtracts the constant, and subtracts each period a nondeterministically guessed number of times, and these counters are then verified to be 0. Then it continues to simulate M using $C_1^{j+1}, \ldots, C_k^{j+1}$ until a successful zero-test in some counter ending in some state $q_{(j+1)}$ say with counter values $\vec{v}_{j+1}$, thereby verifying that at least $j + 1$ zero-tests were successful. Then it continues at the beginning of this paragraph for $j + 1$ until it hits m.

When in $q_{(m)}$ with counter values $\vec{v}_m$, then it copies counters $C_1^m, \ldots, C_k^m$ into both $D_1^m, \ldots, D_k^m$ and $E_1, \ldots, E_k$. Using $E_1, \ldots, E_k$, it verifies that $\vec{v}_m \in \overline{R_{q_{(m)}}}$ (using the same technique as above where it guesses a linear set, subtracts the constant, and each period a guessed number of times), thereby verifying that another zero-test will not be successful, and then verifies that $\vec{v}_m \in \overline{S_{q_{(m)}}}$ using $D_1^m, \ldots, D_k^m$ thereby verifying that it will not pass over a final state with all counters 0. If so, then $\overline{M}$ accepts, otherwise $\overline{M}$ will never enter a final state and cannot accept.

Next, we will verify that $\overline{L(M)} = L(\overline{M})$.

Let $w \in \overline{L(M)}$. There are several ways for M to not accept w. First, before the end-marker, M could crash by trying to subtract from a 0 counter, or it could enter an infinite loop. After the end-marker, it could not pass over all zeros in a final state, which could be the result of crashing, or entering an infinite loop without hitting all 0's in a final state.

If M crashes before the end-marker, then $\overline{M}$ would accept by guessing the exact ID before simulating the next transition causing the crash, which would therefore have to be zero before the crash. Then $\overline{M}$ can nondeterministically reduce all other counters by some amount, read the rest of the input and accept. Similarly if M gets in an infinite loop on λ before the end-marker, then in $\overline{M}$, after reading each letter of Σ or successfully simulating a zero-test, it then knows the state, and if no counter decreases in the cycle part, it can detect whether M would enter an infinite loop by executing one cycle of the loop, and so $\overline{M}$ reads the rest of the input and accepts. After reading the end-marker resulting in state $\vec{v}_0$ in state $q_{(0)}$, say that M has $0 \le m$ successful zero-tests, where m must be less than or equal to kr (this m exists whether or not M accepts w). Then, M either crashes, or goes into an infinite loop (as mentioned earlier, it cannot stop). In any case, as w is not accepted, M will not pass over a final state with all counters being 0. If M has m successful zero-tests and does not pass over all 0 in a final state before that, then $\overline{M}$ will guess m. Indeed, after hitting each successful zero-test up to m, it is verified that from the current state $q_{(j)}$ and counter values $\vec{v}_j$, that it will not pass over a final state with all 0's in the counters by verifying that $\vec{v}_j \in \overline{S_{q_j}}$, and indeed Lemma 24 implies that it cannot pass over all 0's in a final state. If M either crashes or enters an infinite loop after the mth successful zero-test (without passing over 0's in a final state beforehand), then another successful zero-test will not occur and it will not pass over all 0's in a final state, and so $\vec{v}_m$ will be in both $\overline{S_{q_m}}$ and $\overline{R_{q_m}}$ which is enough for $\overline{M}$ to accept w. Thus, $w \in L(\overline{M})$.

Let $w \in L(\overline{M})$. Before the end-marker, $\overline{M}$ could guess that the next simulation transition that decreases some counter i would cause M to go below 0, and instead nondeterministically reduce all other counters by some amount and accept. Thus, in this situation, $w \in \overline{L(M)}$. The next way that $\overline{M}$ can accept is if there is an infinite sequence of transitions that can be applied on a non-zero-test or a no-test, and no counter value applied in a cycle can decrease, and applying this cycle at least once without a successful zero-test, which causes $\overline{M}$ to accept; in this scenario, M would then be in an infinite loop, and $w \in \overline{L(M)}$.

After the end-marker, the only way for $\overline{M}$ to accept is if it guesses a number $m \ge 0$ such that there are m successful zero-test, it can simulate M up until that mth zero-test, for each j from 0 to m, the counter values $\vec{v}_j$ and state $q_{(j)}$

right after the jth successful zero-test all have $\vec{v}_j \in \overline{S_{q_{(j)}}}$, which means that M would not pass over all counters being 0 in a final state after the jth section; and $\vec{v}_m \in \overline{R_{q_{(m)}}}$ which means that another zero-test would not be successful. Hence, M cannot accept w, and $w \in \overline{L(M)}$.   □

This can be used to show the following interesting decidability property.

Theorem 27. *The containment problem is decidable for* DTCM *(and* DPBLIND*). Furthermore, the problem, "given a* NTCM M_1 *and a* DTCM M_2, *is* $L(M_1) \subseteq L(M_2)$?" *is decidable.*

Proof. Given a nondeterministic machine M_1 and a deterministic machine M_2, first construct $\overline{L(M_2)} \in$ NPBLIND = NTCM by Proposition 26. Then construct $L(M_1) \cap \overline{L(M_2)} \in$ NPBLIND, as NPBLIND is closed under intersection [10], and then test emptiness [20,22], which is empty if and only if $L(M_1) \subseteq L(M_2)$.   □

This result generalizes the known decidability of the containment problem for DRBCM [17] as DRBCM $\subsetneq$ DTCM.

However, it is also known that finite-crossing 2DRBCM (these are two-way DRBCMs where the input is finite-crossing (a machine is finite-crossing if every accepted word has an accepting computation where there is a bound on the number of times the boundary between each two adjacent input cells is crossed) [17], and also 2DRBCM(1) (these are two-way DRBCM machines with a single reversal-bounded counter) [15,18] have a decidable containment problem, which could be more general or incomparable to DTCM. The latter family, 2DRBCM(1) is also powerful enough to accept languages that are not Parikh semilinear like DTCM. Then, DPBLIND and DTCM join these families as having a decidable containment problem, and joins 2DRBCM(1) as one which contains languages that are not Parikh semilinear. This is quite strong as even NRBCM(1, 1) has an undecidable containment problem [1].

7 Future Directions

Below are some interesting problems that deserve further investigation. Although we determined here that DPBLIND is not closed under complement, it is open whether or not DTCM closed under complement. Also, is DTCM with no end-marker weaker than with the end-marker, as was the case with DPBLIND? Next, although we showed that DTCM coincides with 1-testable DTCM, is there a hierarchy in terms of DTCM(k, r) for fixed k or r? Lastly, although we showed that the complement of every DTCM is in NTCM = NPBLIND, is it also true that the complement of every unambiguous NTCM (or unambiguous NPBLIND) is in NTCM?

References

1. Baker, B.S., Book, R.V.: Reversal-bounded multipushdown machines. J. Comput. Syst. Sci. **8**(3), 315–332 (1974)
2. Baumann, P., et al.: Unboundedness problems for machines with reversal-bounded counters. In: 25th International Conference on Foundations of Software Science and Computation Structures (FoSSaCS) (2023)
3. Carpi, A., D'Alessandro, F., Ibarra, O.H., McQuillan, I.: Relationships between bounded languages, counter machines, finite-index grammars, ambiguity, and commutative regularity. Theoret. Comput. Sci. **862**, 97–118 (2021)
4. Crespi-Reghizzi, S., Pietro, P.S.: Deterministic counter machines and parallel matching computations. In: Proceedings of the 18th International Conference on Implementation and Application of Automata, CIAA 2013, vol. 7982, pp. 280–291 (2013)
5. Czerwiński, W., Hofman, P.: Language inclusion for boundedly-ambiguous vector addition systems is decidable. In: Klin, B., Lasota, S., Muscholl, A. (eds.) Proceedings of the 33rd International Conference on Concurrency Theory (CONCUR 2022), pp. 16:1–16:22 (2022)
6. Czerwinski, W., Hofman, P., Zetzsche, G.: Unboundedness problems for languages of vector addition systems. In: Chatzigiannakis, I., Kaklamanis, C., Marx, D., Sannella, D. (eds.) 45th International Colloquium on Automata, Languages, and Programming (ICALP 2018). Leibniz International Proceedings in Informatics (LIPIcs), vol. 107, p. 119. Schloss Dagstuhl-Leibniz-Zentrum fuer Informatik, Dagstuhl, Germany (2018)
7. Eremondi, J., Ibarra, O.H., McQuillan, I.: Insertion operations on deterministic reversal-bounded counter machines. J. Comput. Syst. Sci. **104**, 244–257 (2019)
8. Gerth, R., Peled, D., Vardi, M.Y., Wolper, P.: Simple on-the-fly automatic verification of linear temporal logic. In: PSTV 1995. IAICT, pp. 3–18. Springer, Boston, MA (1996). https://doi.org/10.1007/978-0-387-34892-6_1
9. Ginsburg, S.: The Mathematical Theory of Context-Free Languages. McGraw-Hill Inc, New York (1966)
10. Greibach, S.: Remarks on blind and partially blind one-way multicounter machines. Theoret. Comput. Sci. **7**, 311–324 (1978)
11. Holzmann, G.J.: The SPIN Model Checker: Primer and Reference Manual. Addison-Wesley, Boston (2003)
12. Hopcroft, J.E., Ullman, J.D.: Introduction to Automata Theory, Languages, and Computation. Addison-Wesley, MA (1979)
13. Hopcroft, J.E., Pansiot, J.J.: On the reachability problem for 5-dimensional vector addition systems. Theoret. Comput. Sci. **8**(2), 135–159 (1979)
14. Ibarra, O., McQuillan, I.: The effect of end-markers on counter machines and commutativity. Theoret. Comput. Sci. **627**, 71–81 (2016)
15. Ibarra, O., Yen, H.: On the containment and equivalence problems for two-way transducers. Theoret. Comput. Sci. **429**, 155–163 (2012)
16. Ibarra, O.H.: A note on semilinear sets and bounded-reversal multihead pushdown automata. Inf. Process. Lett. **3**(1), 25–28 (1974)
17. Ibarra, O.H.: Reversal-bounded multicounter machines and their decision problems. J. ACM **25**(1), 116–133 (1978)
18. Ibarra, O.H., Jiang, T., Tran, N., Wang, H.: New decidability results concerning two-way counter machines. SIAM J. Comput. **23**(1), 123–137 (1995)

19. Ibarra, O.H., Seki, S.: Characterizations of bounded semilinear languages by one-way and two-way deterministic machines. Int. J. Found. Comput. Sci. **23**(6), 1291–1306 (2012)
20. Kosaraju, S.R.: Decidability of reachability in vector addition systems. In: Proceedings of the Fourteenth Annual ACM Symposium on Theory of Computing, STOC 1982, pp. 267–281 (1982)
21. Leroux, J.: Presburger vector addition systems. In: Proceedings of the 28th Annual ACM/IEEE Symposium on Logic in Computer Science, pp. 23–32 (2013)
22. Mayr, E.W.: An algorithm for the general Petri net reachability problem. SIAM J. Comput. **13**(3), 441–460 (1984)
23. Mottet, A., Quaas, K.: The containment problem for unambiguous register automata and unambiguous timed automata. Theory Comput. Syst. **65**, 706–735 (2021)
24. Parikh, R.: On context-free languages. J. ACM **13**(4), 570–581 (1966)
25. Pelz, E.: Closure properties of deterministic Petri nets. In: Brandenburg, F.J., Vidal-Naquet, G., Wirsing, M. (eds.) STACS 1987. LNCS, vol. 247, pp. 371–382. Springer, Heidelberg (1987). https://doi.org/10.1007/BFb0039620
26. Rosenberg, A.L.: On multi-head finite automata. In: 6th Annual Symposium on Switching Circuit Theory and Logical Design (SWCT 1965), pp. 221–228 (1965)
27. Tang, N.V.: Pushdown Automata and Inclusion Problems. Ph.D. thesis, Japan Advanced Institute of Science and Technology, Japan (2007)
28. Vardi, M.Y., Wolper, P.: An automata-theoretic approach to automatic program verification. In: Chatterjee, K., Sgall, J. (eds.) Proceedings of the 1st IEEE Symposium Logic in Computer Science (LICS 1986), pp. 332–344. IEEE Computer Society (1986)
29. Vidal-Naquet, G.: Deterministic languages of Petri nets. In: Girault, C., Reisig, W. (eds.) Application and Theory of Petri Nets. Informatik-Fachberichte, vol. 52, pp. 198–202. Springer, Berlin (1981). https://doi.org/10.1007/978-3-642-68353-4_34

Parallel and Incremental Verification
of Hybrid Automata with Ray and Verse

Haoqing Zhu[✉️] , Yangge Li , Keyi Shen , and Sayan Mitra

Coordinated Science Laboratory, University of Illinois at Urbana-Champaign,
Champaign, USA
{haoqing3,li213,keyis2,mitras}@illinois.edu

Abstract. Parallel and distributed computing holds a promise of scaling verification to hard multi-agent scenarios such as the ones involving autonomous interacting vehicles. Exploiting parallelism, however, typically requires handcrafting solutions using knowledge of verification algorithms, the available hardware, and the specific models. The Ray framework made parallel programming hardware agnostic for large-scale Python workloads in machine learning. Extending the recently developed Verse Python library for multi-agent hybrid systems, in this paper we show how Ray's fork-join parallelization can help gain up to 6× speedup in multi-agent hybrid model verification. We propose a parallel algorithm that addresses the key bottleneck of computing the discrete transitions and exploits concurrent construction of reachability trees, without locks, using dynamic Ray processes. We find that the performance gains of our new reachset and simulation algorithms increase with the availability of larger number of cores and the nondeterminism in the model. In one experiment with 20 agents and 399 transitions, reachability analysis using the parallel algorithm takes 35 min on a 8 core CPU, which is a 6.28× speedup over the sequential algorithm. We also present an incremental verification algorithm that reuses previously cached computations and compare its performance.

1 Introduction

The hybrid automaton framework is useful for precisely describing and simulating scenarios involving interacting autonomous vehicles and other types of intelligent agents [1,4,8,9,11,15,20,23]. Parallel computing holds promise in scaling the verification of such hybrid models to scenarios with many agents, which in turn, multiply the number of expensive mode transitions that have to be computed. Despite several recent efforts [3,7,12] that we discuss in Sect. 2, building effective parallel verification algorithms remains a difficult art. It requires detailed knowledge of the computing hardware, the parallelism in the target models and how parallelism could be exploited in the verification algorithm.

This research was funded in part by NASA University Leadership Initiative grant (80NSSC22M0070) and a research grant from the NSF (SHF 2008883).

Parallelization is particularly important for multi-agent hybrid scenarios. As the agents interact, they make decisions that are modeled as discrete transitions and the number of transitions to be computed usually blows up over the analysis time horizon. For *reachability analysis* algorithms—a mainstay for verification—the set of reachable states is computed using two functions: (a) a *postCont* function computes the set of states that can be reached over a fixed time, while the agents follow a given dynamics (or mode). And, (b) a *postDisc* function computes the change in state when an agent makes a decision or a transition. For nondeterministic decisions (e.g., brake *or* steer to avoid collision), multiple postDisc computations have to be performed. A reachability algorithm thus builds a tree, the *reachtree*, where each branch corresponds to the unique choices made by all the relevant agents. Even with deterministic models, as a set of states is propagated forward in reachability analysis, this set can trigger multiple transitions. All of this contributes to an explosion of the reachtree, which often grows exponentially with longer analysis horizons and larger numbers of agents.

The Ray framework from RISELab has made it easier for application developers to scale-up their data science and machine learning algorithms through parallel computing, without having them worry about compute infrastructure details [19,21]. Ray supports the fork-join style of parallelization with remote function calls that run on other cores on the same machine or other machines. This style of parallelization is hardware agnostic and is easier to use as it does not involve the explicit use of synchronization primitives like locks.

In this paper, we propose and implement a Ray-based parallel reachability algorithm that utilizes the fact that different branches in the reachtree can be computed independently. This approach allows us to compute multiple branches of the tree simultaneously, which improves analysis performance. We use the recently developed Python Verse library [18] for multi-agent hybrid systems, as the underlying framework within which we develop our parallelized algorithm. In our experiments, we see that the parallel reachability algorithm can be effective in improving performance, especially in more complex hybrid automata models where more nondeterministic branching can occur. In an experiment involving several vehicles in a 4-way intersection (called isect(4,20) in Sect. 5), we get a $6.28\times$ performance boost over the original sequential version of the reachability algorithm in Verse.

In industrial applications, verification procedures can be integrated in the CI/CD pipelines [6,22]. For engineers to use the verification results, it has been observed that the algorithms should run in 15–20 min and not over hours [5, 22,24]. One of the ways in which this level of performance is achieved in the above studies is by performing *incremental verification*. That is, the verification algorithm only runs on the relevant part of the codebase that changes in each developer commit, and the algorithm *reuses* proofs from in previous verification runs. Inspired by these observations, our second contribution in this paper is the development of an incremental verification algorithm for hybrid scenarios.

This algorithm maintains a cache which contains information on previously computed trajectories and discrete transitions. These results are indexed with the state of the system. If the system reaches a state similar to one in the cache, then its result can be reused. Instead of caching the result of every timestep, the incremental verification algorithm uses the same task unit as the parallel algorithm, making it possible to use both algorithms at the same time and have the best of both worlds. In the experiments we see that the incremental verification algorithm is able to reuse some computations and significantly speed up analysis in some situations, while in others it provides no benefits.

The rest of the paper is organized as follows: In Sect. 2 we discuss related work on parallel verification of hybrid systems. Section 3 introduces hybrid multi-agent scenarios and how they translate into hybrid automata. We will present the design and the correctness of our parallel and incremental verification algorithms in Sect. 4. Finally, in Sect. 5 we will present the experimental evaluation of these algorithms.

2 Related Work

A number of software tools have been developed for creating, simulating, and analyzing hybrid system models. Table 1 summarizes the actively maintained tools and those that have incorporated some form of parallelization.

Table 1. Parallelization methods used in hybrid verification tools.

Tool name	Parallelization target	Supported dynamics	Language/library
C2E2 [8]	None	nonlinear	C++
SpaceEx [11]	None	linear	Java
Flow* [4]	None	nonlinear	C++
DryVR [10]	None	nonlinear	Python
XSpeed [12]	CPU & GPU	linear	C++
JuliaReach [3]	CPU	nonlinear	Julia
CORA [1]	None	nonlinear	Matlab
dreach [17]	None	nonlinear	C++
HyLAA [2]	None	linear	Python
PIRK [7]	CPU & GPU	nonlinear	C++, pFaces
this paper	CPU	nonlinear	Python, Ray

Both CPUs and GPUs can be used to parallelize computation, but they differ in the type of tasks suitable for parallelization on each. The complex cores of CPUs today make them good at computing complex algorithms serially, but common desktop-grade CPUs only have 8 to 32 cores. On the other hand, GPUs have much simpler cores but many of them, from hundreds to thousands. This makes them efficient at performing many numerical calculations at the same time, but unsuitable for any algorithm involving complex logic.

JuliaReach [3] utilizes CPU-based parallelization for boosting the performance of reachability computation. PIRK [7] uses the pFaces [16] runtime to parallelize reachability of continuous states using both CPUs and GPUs. XSpeed [12] besides CPU also support using GPUs for accelerating the computation of continuous and discrete state evolutions. The Ray framework [21] was developed at RISELab at UC Berkeley with the aim to make parallel and distributed computing easier for researchers by helping them focus on application development work, regardless of the specifics of their compute cluster. The Ray framework has been used in several successful projects, including Uber using it for performing large-scale deep learning training for autonomous vehicles. To the best of our knowledge, our work is the first to parallelize hybrid system reachability analysis with Ray.

One approach to parallelize reachability analysis algorithms is to spawn a collection of threads, each of which explores a part of the reachable state space. The downside of this approach is that resources, such as memory, are shared between different threads, which in turn, implies the need for locking. We have chosen to use Ray [21], a popular parallelization framework for Python, for implementing parallel verification algorithms. The use of Ray allows us to implement algorithms without using locks.

XSpeed is a hybrid automaton verification tool that incorporated several parallelization algorithms [12]. We have adapted the *AsyncBFS* algorithm implemented in XSpeed to Verse. However, there are several differences in the designs. First, XSpeed is only able to handle linear systems, more specifically, invertible linear systems, while our algorithm is able to handle non-linear systems. Second, explicit locking is no longer necessary due to Ray's design. Last but not least, we have chosen a different granularity of parallelization in Verse that is coarser than the algorithm presented in XSpeed. XSpeed's algorithm assigns one pair of postCont and postDisc as the task for a single thread. However, we have chosen to use a batch of several post operations as a task. This is mainly due to one of Python's limitations. The Python interpreter uses a Global Interpreter Lock (GIL) which prevents Python code from utilizing multi-threading capabilities, and multiple processes have to be used instead to achieve parallelism. In this case, all the resources, including the input hybrid automaton and computed reachable sets, have to be copied back and forth between different processes and the overhead for this can be high. Therefore, we choose to use the batch operation to reduce the number of copying needed.

3   Preliminaries: Hybrid Multi-agent Scenarios

In this paper, we are basing our algorithms on hybrid multi-agent scenarios. Each of these scenarios contains a collection of agents interacting in an environment. We will describe the agents and scenario in this section and in Sect. 3.2 we will discuss how a scenario formally defines a hybrid system.

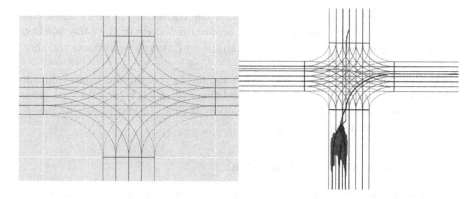

Fig. 1. *Left:* A 4-way intersection scenario with 2 lanes in each direction, showing the lane boundaries. Each lane extends very far outside of the picture. *Right:* Computed reachsets with 3 agents (represented with 3 different colors) on the intersection scenario with 3 lanes in each direction. The red car goes from north to south, the green car goes from east to west, and the blue car goes from east to south. (Color figure online)

3.1 Agents in Hybrid Scenarios

An *agent* is a hybrid automaton that reacts based on the states of all agents in the scenario. An $\mathcal{A}$ in a scenario with $k - 1$ other agents is defined by a tuple $\mathcal{A} = \langle X, D, X^0, d^0, G, R, F \rangle$, where

1. X and D are the *continuous state space* and *discrete mode space* respectively, X^0 is the set of initial continuous states and d^0 is the initial mode;
2. G and R are the guards and resets functions for the agent, which jointly define the discrete transitions for the agent;
3. F is the *flow* function, which defines the evolution of the continuous states.

We will describe each of these components briefly.

X is the agent's continuous state space. In Fig. 1 we show the environment of an intersection example. The continuous state variables can be x, y, θ, v for the position, heading, and speed for the vehicle agents in this example. D is the agent's discrete mode space. In the intersection example, some of the modes can correspond to the internal state of the agent, while others can correspond to its location in the environment. One possible discrete mode could be $\langle \text{SW-0}, \text{Normal} \rangle$, where SW-0 means the agent is tracking the leftmost lane going from south to west, and Normal means the agent is cruising along the road.

The guard G and reset R functions jointly define the discrete transitions. For a pair of modes $d, d' \in D$, $G(d, d') \subseteq X^k$ defines the condition under which a transition from d to d' is enabled, and $R(d, d') : X^k \rightarrow X$ defines how the continuous states of the agent are updated when the mode switch happens. Both of these functions take as input the full continuous states of all the other

$k - 1$ agents in the scenario. This means that the transitions of every agent can depend on its own state that also on the observable[1] state of the other agents. For a single agent, we refer to the combination of guards and resets for that agent as a *decision logic*.

The *flow* function $F : X \times D \times \mathbb{R}^{\geq 0} \to X$ defines the continuous time evolution of the continuous state. For any initial condition $\langle x^0, d^0 \rangle \in Y$, $F(x^0, d^0)(\cdot)$ gives the continuous state of the agent as a function of time. In this paper, we use F as a black-box function (see footnote[2]).

3.2   Scenario to Hybrid Verification

A scenario SC is defined by a collection of k agent instances $\{\mathcal{A}_1...\mathcal{A}_k\}$. We assume agents have identical state spaces, i.e., $\forall i, j \in \{0, ..., k - 1\}, X_i = X_j, D_i = D_j$, but they can have different decision logics and different continuous dynamics. We make this assumption to simplify the implementation of the handling of the decision logic. This does not affect the expressive power of Verse as different state variable and mode types could be unioned into a single type.

Next, we define how a scenario SC specifies a hybrid automaton $H(SC)$. We will use a hybrid automaton close to that in Definition 5 of [10]. As usual, the automaton has discrete and continuous states and discrete transitions defined by guards and resets.

Given a scenario with k agents, $SC = \{\mathcal{A}_1, ...\mathcal{A}_k\}$, the corresponding hybrid automaton $H(SC) = \langle \mathbf{X}, \mathbf{X}^0, \mathbf{D}, \mathbf{D}^0, \mathbf{G}, \mathbf{R}, \mathbf{TL} \rangle$, where

1. $\mathbf{X} := \prod_i X_i$ is the *continuous state space*. An element $\mathbf{x} \in \mathbf{X}$ is called a *state*. $\mathbf{X}^0 := \prod_i X_i^0 \subseteq \mathbf{X}$ is the set of *initial continuous states*.
2. $\mathbf{D} := \prod_i D_i$ is the *mode space*. An element $\mathbf{d} \in \mathbf{D}$ is called a *mode*. $\mathbf{d}^0 := \prod_i d_i^0 \subseteq \mathbf{D}$ is the *initial mode*.
3. For a pair of modes $\mathbf{d}, \mathbf{d}' \in \mathbf{D}$, $\mathbf{G}(\mathbf{d}, \mathbf{d}') \subseteq \mathbf{X}$ defines the continuous states from which a transition from $\mathbf{d}$ to $\mathbf{d}'$ is enabled. A state $\mathbf{x} \in \mathbf{G}(\mathbf{d}, \mathbf{d}')$ iff there exists an agent $i \in \{1, ..., k\}$, such that $\mathbf{x}_i \in G_i(\mathbf{d}_i, \mathbf{d}_i')$ and $\mathbf{d}_j = \mathbf{d}_j'$ for $j \neq i$.
4. For a pair of modes $\mathbf{d}, \mathbf{d}' \in \mathbf{D}$, $\mathbf{R}(\mathbf{d}, \mathbf{d}') : \mathbf{X} \to \mathbf{X}$ defines the change of continuous states after a transition from $\mathbf{d}$ to $\mathbf{d}'$. For a continuous state $\mathbf{x} \in \mathbf{X}$, $\mathbf{R}(\mathbf{d}, \mathbf{d}')(\mathbf{x}) = R_i(\mathbf{d}_i, \mathbf{d}_i')(\mathbf{x})$ if $\mathbf{x} \in G_i(\mathbf{d}_i, \mathbf{d}_i')$, otherwise $= \mathbf{x}_i$.
5. $\mathbf{TL}$ is a set of pairs $\langle \xi, \mathbf{d} \rangle$, where the *trajectory* $\xi : [0, T] \to \mathbf{X}$ describes the evolution of continuous states in mode $\mathbf{d} \in \mathbf{D}$. Given $\mathbf{d} \in \mathbf{D}, \mathbf{x}^0 \in \mathbf{X}$, ξ should satisfy $\forall t \in \mathbb{R}^{\geq 0}, \xi_i(t) = F_i(\mathbf{x}_i^0, \mathbf{d}_i)(t)$.

---

[1] The observable state is defined by a *sensor* function; here we assume that the full state is observable.

[2] This design decision is relatively independent. For reachability analysis, we currently uses black-box statistical approaches implemented in DryVR [10] and NeuReach [25]. If the simulator is available as a white-box model, such as differential equations, then the algorithm could use model-based reachability analysis.

In [18] it is shown that $H(SC)$ is indeed a valid hybrid automaton for a scenario with k agents $SC = \{\mathcal{A}_1, ..., \mathcal{A}_k\}$ provided that all agents have identical sets of states and modes, $Y_i = Y_j, \forall i, j \in \{0, ..., k-1\}$.

For some trajectory ξ we denote by $\xi.fstate$, $\xi.lstate$, and $\xi.ltime$ the initial state $\xi(0)$, the last state $\xi(T)$, and $\xi.ltime = T$. For a sampling parameter $\delta > 0$ and a length m, a δ-execution of a hybrid automaton $H = H(SC)$ is a sequence of m labeled trajectories $\alpha(\mathbf{x}^0, \mathbf{d}^0; m) := \langle \xi^0, \mathbf{d}^0 \rangle, ..., \langle \xi^{m-1}, \mathbf{d}^{m-1} \rangle$, such that

(1) $\xi^0.fstate = \mathbf{x}^0 \in \mathbf{X}^0, \mathbf{d}^0 \in \mathbf{D}^0$;
(2) $\forall i \in \{1, ..., m-1\}, \xi^i.lstate \in \mathbf{G}(\mathbf{d}^i, \mathbf{d}^{i+1})$ and
    $\xi^{i+1}.fstate = \mathbf{R}(\mathbf{d}^i, \mathbf{d}^{i+1})(\xi^i.lstate)$;
(3) $\forall i \in \{1, ..., m-1\}, \xi^i.ltime = \delta$ for $i \neq m-1$ and
    $\xi^i.ltime \leq \delta$ for $i = m-1$.

We define the first and last state of an execution $\beta = \alpha(\mathbf{x}^0, \mathbf{d}^0; m) = \langle \xi^0, \mathbf{d}^0 \rangle, ..., \langle \xi^{m-1}, \mathbf{d}^{m-1} \rangle$ as $\beta.fstate = \xi^0.fstate = \mathbf{x}^0$, $\beta.lstate = \xi^{m-1}.lstate$ and the first and last mode as $\beta.fmode = \mathbf{d}^0$ and $\beta.lmode = \mathbf{d}^{m-1}$.

3.3 Bounded Reach Sets

We will define a pair of *post* operators, that will be useful in the computation of executions. Consider a scenario SC with k agents and the corresponding hybrid automaton $H(SC)$. For any $\delta > 0$, continuous state $\mathbf{x} \in \mathbf{X}$ and a pair of modes $\mathbf{d}, \mathbf{d}'$, the discrete $post_{\mathbf{d},\mathbf{d}'} : \mathbf{X} \to \mathbf{X}$ and continuous $post_{\mathbf{d},\delta} : \mathbf{X} \to \mathbf{X}$ operators are defined as follows:

$$post_{\mathbf{d},\mathbf{d}'}(\mathbf{x}) = \mathbf{x}' \iff \mathbf{x} \in \mathbf{G}(\mathbf{d}, \mathbf{d}') \text{ and } \mathbf{x}' = \mathbf{R}(\mathbf{d}, \mathbf{d}')(\mathbf{x})$$

$$post_{\mathbf{d},\delta}(\mathbf{x}) = \bigcup_{t \in [0,\delta)} \prod_{i \in \{1,...,k\}} F_i(\mathbf{x}_i, \mathbf{d}_i, t)$$

These operators are also lifted to sets of states in the usual way. If part of the input states are not contained within the guard conditions, they will be ignored in the returned result by $post_{\mathbf{d},\mathbf{d}'}$.

In addition, we define $post_{\mathbf{d},\delta}(\mathbf{x}).lstate = \prod_{i \in \{1,...,k\}} F_i(\mathbf{x}_i, \mathbf{d}_i, \delta)$, in other words $post_{\mathbf{d},\delta}(\mathbf{x}).lstate$ represents the frontier of the continuous states after δ-time. We conclude this section with the definition of the bounded reachable states of $H(SC)$.

Definition 1. *The bounded reachable states of $H(SC)$ is*

$$Reach(\mathbf{X}^0, \mathbf{d}^0, \delta, T_{\max}) = \bigcup_{\mathbf{x}^0 \in \mathbf{X}^0} \alpha(\mathbf{x}^0, \mathbf{d}^0; m)$$

where: (1) $\boldsymbol{X}^0 \subseteq \boldsymbol{X}$ and $\boldsymbol{d}^0 \in \boldsymbol{D}$ are the initial states of the hybrid automaton; (2) $T_{\max}$ is the time horizon; (3) $\alpha(\boldsymbol{x}^0, \boldsymbol{d}^0; m)$ is a valid execution; (4) $m = \lceil \frac{T_{\max}}{\delta} \rceil$ is the length of execution.

4   Parallel and Incremental Verification Algorithms

In this section, we will describe the parallel and incremental algorithms for computing reachable states that we have implemented in Verse. We will also discuss their correctness. For the sake of a self-contained presentation, we will first introduce several important notations and subroutines in the context of the sequential reachability algorithm. Then in Sect. 4.2 and 4.3, we will add in optimizations before getting to the final version of the algorithm.

4.1   Reachability Analysis

Recall that for a scenario SC and its hybrid system model $H(SC)$, $\mathbf{X}$ and $\mathbf{D}$ are respectively the continuous state space and discrete mode space. The building blocks for all reachability algorithms are two functions $\texttt{postCont}(\mathbf{d}^0, \delta, \mathbf{X}^0)$ and $\texttt{postDisc}(\mathbf{d}^0, \mathbf{d}^1, \mathbf{X}^0)$ that compute (or over-approximate) $post_{\mathbf{d}^0, \delta}(\mathbf{X}^0)$ and $post_{\mathbf{d}^0, \mathbf{d}^1}(\mathbf{X}^0)$, respectively. Similar to Sect. 3.3, we will use $\texttt{postCont}(\mathbf{d}^0, \delta, \mathbf{X}^0)$. $lstate$ to denote the frontier of $\texttt{postCont}(\mathbf{d}^0, \delta, \mathbf{X}^0)$. In Verse, $\texttt{postCont}$ is implemented using algorithms in [10,25].

The sequential $\texttt{verify}$ function implements a reachability analysis algorithm using these post operators (Algorithm 1). This algorithm constructs an execution tree $Tree = V$ up to depth $T_{\max}$ in breadth-first order. Each node $N = \langle \mathbf{X}, \mathbf{d}, t, stride, children \rangle \in V$ is a tuple of a set of states, a mode, the start time, the stride, which can be computed by $\texttt{postCont}$, and children of the current node. The root is $\langle \mathbf{X}^0, \mathbf{d}^0, 0, stride, children \rangle$ given a initial set of states $\mathbf{X}^0$ and mode $\mathbf{d}^0$. The $children$ field of each node provides the edge relations for the tree. There is an edge from $\langle \mathbf{X}, \mathbf{d}, t, stride, children \rangle$ to $\langle \mathbf{X}', \mathbf{d}', t', stride', children' \rangle$ if and only if $\mathbf{X}' = post_{\mathbf{d}, \delta}(post_{\mathbf{d}, \mathbf{d}'}(\mathbf{X})).lstate$ and $t' = t + \delta$. We will use the dot field access notation to refer to fields of a node. For example for a node N, $N.stride$ and $N.\mathbf{X}$ refers to the stride and the set of initial states in N.

Note that one of the arguments to the $\texttt{verify\_step}$ function is a node with only the $\mathbf{X}$, $\mathbf{d}$ and t fields populated. After this function executes, it populates the $stride$ and $children$ fields of the node N and returns a completed node.

To show the correctness of the $\texttt{verify}$ algorithm, we will first show some key properties of the $\texttt{verify\_step}$ function in Proposition 1. Throughout this section, we fix a scenario SC and the corresponding hybrid automaton $H(SC)$. Let $\mathbf{X}$ and $\mathbf{D}$ be the continuous and discrete state spaces of $H(SC)$.

Algorithm 1

1: **function** verify_step(N, δ) **where** $N.stride = \varnothing$, $N.children = \varnothing$
2:    $N.stride \leftarrow$ postCont($N.\mathbf{X}, N.\mathbf{d}, \delta$)
3:    **for** $\mathbf{d}' \in \mathbf{D}$ s.t. $\mathbf{G}(N.\mathbf{d}, \mathbf{d}') \cap N.stride.lstate \neq \varnothing$ **do**
4:       $\mathbf{X}' \leftarrow$ postDisc ($N.stride.lstate$, $N.\mathbf{d}$, $\mathbf{d}'$)
5:       $N.children \leftarrow N.children \cup \langle \mathbf{X}', \mathbf{d}', N.t + \delta, \varnothing, \varnothing \rangle$
6:    **return** N

7: **function** verify($H, \mathbf{X}^0, \mathbf{d}^0, \delta, T_{\max}$)
8:    $queue \leftarrow [\langle \mathbf{X}^0, \mathbf{d}^0, 0, \varnothing, \varnothing \rangle]$
9:    $reachset \leftarrow \varnothing$
10:   **while** $queue \neq \varnothing$ **do**
11:      $N \leftarrow queue.\text{dequeue}()$
12:      $N \leftarrow$ verify_step(N, δ)
13:      $reachset \leftarrow reachset \cup N.stride$
14:      **for** $N' \in children$ s.t. $N'.t < T_{\max}$ **do**
15:         $queue.\text{add}(N')$
16:   **return** $reachset$

Proposition 1. *For any set of states $\mathbf{X}^0 \subseteq \mathbf{X}$, mode $\mathbf{d}^0 \in \mathbf{D}$ and time t, the node $N =$ verify_step($\langle \mathbf{X}^0, \mathbf{d}^0, t, \varnothing, \varnothing \rangle, \delta$) satisfies the following:*

$$post_{\mathbf{d}, \delta}(\mathbf{X}) \subseteq N.stride \tag{1}$$

$$\forall N' \in N.children, \mathbf{G}(N.\mathbf{d}, N'.\mathbf{d}) \cap N.stride.lstate \neq \varnothing \tag{2}$$

$$\forall N' \in N.children, post_{N.\mathbf{d}, N'.\mathbf{d}}(post_{N.\mathbf{d}, \delta}(N.\mathbf{X}).lstate) \subseteq N'.\mathbf{X}. \tag{3}$$

Proof. For (1), from line 2 in Algorithm 1, $N.stride =$ postCont($N.\mathbf{X}, N.\mathbf{d}, \delta$). As we assumed about postCont in the start of Sect. 4.1, $post_{N.\mathbf{d}, \delta}(N.\mathbf{X}) \subseteq N.stride$ and $post_{N.\mathbf{d}, \delta}(N.\mathbf{X}).lstate \subseteq N.stride.lstate$.

For (2), from the loop condition at line 3, for every children $N' \in N.children$:
$\mathbf{G}(\mathbf{d}^0, N'.\mathbf{d}) \cap N.stride.lstate \neq \varnothing$

For (3), for every children $N' \in N.children$:

$$post_{N.\mathbf{d}, N'.\mathbf{d}}(post_{N.\mathbf{d}, \delta}(N.\mathbf{X}).lstate) \subseteq post_{N.\mathbf{d}, N'.\mathbf{d}}(N.stride.lstate)$$
$$\subseteq \text{postDisc}(N.stride.lstate, N.\mathbf{d}, N'.\mathbf{d})$$
$$= N'.\mathbf{X}$$

$\square$

Proposition 2. *Given initial states $\mathbf{X}^0 \subseteq \mathbf{X}$ and $\mathbf{d}^0 \in \mathbf{D}$, time step δ and time horizon $T_{\max}$,*

$$Reach(\mathbf{X}^0, \mathbf{d}^0, \delta, T_{\max}) \subseteq \text{verify}(\mathbf{X}^0, \mathbf{d}^0, \delta, T_{\max}).$$

Proof. Let $m = \lceil \frac{T_{\max}}{\delta} \rceil$ be the height of the reachset tree, and $\epsilon = T_{\max} - (m-1) \times \delta$. According to the Definition 1 of bounded reachable states, we have $Reach(\mathbf{X}^0, \mathbf{d}^0, \delta, (m-1) \times \delta + \epsilon) = \bigcup_{\mathbf{x}^0 \in \mathbf{X}^0} \alpha(\mathbf{x}^0, \mathbf{d}^0; m)$.

We will prove by induction on the height of the reachset tree $Reach(\mathbf{X}^0, \mathbf{d}^0, \delta, (m-1) \times \delta + \epsilon)$. For the base case, $Reach(\mathbf{X}^0, \mathbf{d}^0, \delta, \epsilon) \subseteq$ verify$(\mathbf{X}^0, \mathbf{d}^0, \delta, \delta)$. Let $N = \langle \mathbf{X}^0, \mathbf{d}^0, 0, \varnothing, \varnothing \rangle$, then it follows immediately that $Reach(\mathbf{X}^0, \mathbf{d}^0, \delta, \epsilon) = post_{\mathbf{d}^0, \epsilon}(\mathbf{X}^0) \subseteq$ postCont$(\mathbf{X}^0, \mathbf{d}^0, \delta) =$ verify_step$(N, \delta).stride =$ verify$(\mathbf{X}^0, \mathbf{d}^0, \delta, \delta)$.

Induction hypothesis: Given $Reach(\mathbf{X}^0, \mathbf{d}^0, \delta, k \times \delta + \epsilon) \subseteq$ verify$(\mathbf{X}^0, \mathbf{d}^0, \delta, (1+k) \times \delta)$ where $k \in [1, m-1)$, show $Reach(\mathbf{X}^0, \mathbf{d}^0, \delta, (k+1) \times \delta + \epsilon) \subseteq$ verify$(\mathbf{X}^0, \mathbf{d}^0, \delta, (k+2) \times \delta)$.

Induction step:

$$\text{verify}(\mathbf{X}^0, \mathbf{d}^0, \delta, (k+2) \times \delta) = \text{verify}(\mathbf{X}^0, \mathbf{d}^0, \delta, (k+1) \times \delta)$$
$$\cup \bigcup_{\mathbf{X}^k, \mathbf{d}^k} \text{verify\_step}(\mathbf{X}^k, \mathbf{d}^k, \delta).stride$$
$$Reach(\mathbf{X}^0, \mathbf{d}^0, \delta, (k+1) \times \delta + \epsilon) = \bigcup_{\mathbf{x}^0 \in \mathbf{X}^0} \alpha(\mathbf{x}^0, \mathbf{d}^0; k+1)$$
$$= \bigcup_{\mathbf{x}^0 \in \mathbf{X}^0} \alpha(\mathbf{x}^0, \mathbf{d}^0; k) \cup \bigcup_{\mathbf{x}', \mathbf{d}'} \alpha(\mathbf{x}', \mathbf{d}'; 1)$$

where $\mathbf{d}' \in \mathbf{D}$ s.t. $\alpha(\mathbf{x}^0, \mathbf{d}^0; k).lstate \in \mathbf{G}(\alpha(\mathbf{x}^0, \mathbf{d}^0; k).lmode, \mathbf{d}')$ and $\mathbf{x}' = \mathbf{R}(\alpha(\mathbf{x}^0, \mathbf{d}^0; k).lmode, \mathbf{d}')(\alpha(\mathbf{x}^0, \mathbf{d}^0; k).lstate)$.

$\mathbf{X}^k$ and $\mathbf{d}^k$ come from the nodes in the queue. Since the verify algorithm uses BFS, these nodes will be all the *children* from the last layer in verify$(\mathbf{X}^0, \mathbf{d}^0, \delta, (k+1) \times \delta)$, thus $\bigcup_{\mathbf{X}^k, \mathbf{d}^k}$ verify_step$(\mathbf{X}^k, \mathbf{d}^k, \delta) \supseteq \bigcup_{\mathbf{x}', \mathbf{d}'} \alpha(\mathbf{x}', \mathbf{d}', \epsilon)$.

Combining this with the induction hypothesis:

$$Reach(\mathbf{X}^0, \mathbf{d}^0, \delta, k \times \delta + \epsilon) = \bigcup_{\mathbf{x}^0 \in \mathbf{X}^0} \alpha(\mathbf{x}^0, \mathbf{d}^0, k+1) \subseteq \text{verify}(\mathbf{X}^0, \mathbf{d}^0, \delta, (1+k) \times \delta)$$

we get $Reach(\mathbf{X}^0, \mathbf{d}^0, \delta, (k+1) \times \delta + \epsilon) \subseteq$ verify$(\mathbf{X}^0, \mathbf{d}^0, \delta, (k+2) \times \delta)$, which completes the proof. □

4.2 Parallel Reachability with Ray

In this section, we show how we parallelize the verification algorithm shown above using Ray [21]. Ray uses remote functions as an abstraction for performing parallelization. Remote functions in Ray can be called on one process but will be executed in another process. These processes can be on different cores of the same machine, or cores on other network-connected machines. Throughout this paper, we will assume that the remote functions execute on other cores within the same machine. However, we note that thanks to Ray's abstraction, our implementation can as easily take advantage of networked clusters.

For a Python function with arguments `f(args)`, the function `f` can be turned into a remote function by decorating the definition of the function with the `ray.remote` decorator. Such remote functions can be called via `f.remote(args)`. In order to simplify the pseudocode, we will simply use a **remote** keyword instead.

In Ray, two processes communicate through a distributed database. For a remote function, both the arguments and the return value will be stored in the database. From the caller's side, when a remote function is called, the arguments to the function will be sent automatically to the database, and a reference to the return value of the function is returned immediately. For the remote process, the arguments are first fetched from the database, then the function will run, and lastly, the return value is sent back to the database. The caller can poll and fetch the value back by using the `ray.wait()` function. For an array of value references `refs`, `ray.wait(refs)` blocks until one of the references in `refs` is available, fetches and returns that value along with the rest of the references.

The basic parallel algorithm is shown in Algorithm 2. The `verify_parallel` algorithm uses a queue to explore the tree just like `verify`, however there are two branches in the loop. One of them pops nodes from the queue and calls `verify_step` on the node as a remote function, while the other waits for the results to come back, processes the result, and adds new nodes to the queue. The algorithm prioritizes sending out computations, which means there can be multiple remote computations inflight at the same time, increasing parallelism and thus speedup. As more branching in the scenario benefits the algorithm more, we can use the number of leaves in the reachtree as a simple metric to measure this potential benefit. In other words, the more leaves there are in a scenario's reachtree, the more speedup we expect to see. Note that as several nodes can happen in parallel, they may be computed in a different order compared to `verify`.

Proposition 3. *For any set of states $X^0 \subseteq X$ and mode $d^0 \in D$,*

$$\texttt{verify\_parallel}(X^0, d^0, \delta, T_{\max}) = \texttt{verify}(X^0, d^0, \delta, T_{\max})$$

Proof. To prove the equality, we can show that the set of calls to `verify_step` in `verify` and `verify_parallel` are the same. In `verify`, `verify_step` is called at line 12; in `verify_parallel`, `verify_step` is called at line 8 as a remote function call. We assume that remote calls in Ray will always return and that given the same arguments, remote function calls to `verify_step` will return the same values as non-remote calls. We can then compare the tree generated

Algorithm 2

1: **function** verify_parallel($H, \mathbf{X}^0, \mathbf{d}^0, \delta, T_{\max}$)
2:    $queue \leftarrow [\langle \mathbf{X}^0, \mathbf{d}^0, 0, \varnothing, \varnothing \rangle]$
3:    $refs \leftarrow \varnothing$
4:    $reachset \leftarrow \varnothing$
5:    **while** $queue \neq \varnothing \vee refs \neq \varnothing$ **do**
6:       **if** $queue \neq \varnothing$ **then**
7:          $N \leftarrow queue.\text{dequeue}()$
8:          $refs.\text{add}(\text{remote verify\_step } (N, \delta))$
9:       **else**   ▷ wait only when $queue$ is empty
10:          $\langle N, refs \rangle \leftarrow \text{ray.wait}(refs)$
11:          $reachset \leftarrow reachset \cup N.stride$
12:          **for** $N' \in N.children$ **do**
13:             **if** $N'.t < T_{\max}$ **then**
14:                $queue.\text{add}(N')$
15:    **return** $reachset$

by both verify and verify_parallel and prove by induction on the height of the tree currently computed. Note that due to the nondeterministic ordering of node traversal, the verify_parallel can begin computing nodes that have $k + 1$ depth before finishing nodes at depth k.

Base Case: Given a set of initial states $\mathbf{X}^0 \subseteq \mathbf{X}$ and initial mode $\mathbf{d}^0 \subseteq \mathbf{D}$, we want to show that

$$\text{verify}(\mathbf{X}^0, \mathbf{d}^0, \delta, 1 \times \delta) = \text{verify\_parallel}(\mathbf{X}^0, \mathbf{d}^0, \delta, 1 \times \delta)$$

and the children of both trees are the same.
   Let $N = \text{verify\_step}(\langle \mathbf{X}^0, \mathbf{d}^0, 0, \varnothing, \varnothing \rangle, \delta)$, then:

$$\text{verify}(\mathbf{X}^0, \mathbf{d}^0, \delta, 1 \times \delta) = N.stride$$
$$= \text{verify\_parallel}(\mathbf{X}^0, \mathbf{d}^0, \delta, 1 \times \delta)$$

Thus, the two trees are equal. The children for both are $N.children$, and they are equal.

Induction Step: Given $\text{verify}(\mathbf{X}^0, \mathbf{d}^0, \delta, k \times \delta) = \text{verify\_parallel}(\mathbf{X}^0, \mathbf{d}^0, \delta, k \times \delta)$ where $k \in [1, m)$, and their children are equal, show

$$\text{verify}(\mathbf{X}^0, \mathbf{d}^0, \delta, (k+1) \times \delta) = \text{verify\_parallel}(\mathbf{X}^0, \mathbf{d}^0, \delta, (k+1) \times \delta)$$

Since the children of all nodes at depth k for verify and verify_parallel are the same, they must generate the same set of nodes at depth $k + 1$, which gives the same set of reachable states.   □

Note that in practice, computing `verify_step` is cheap. Calling small remote functions like this will incur a lot of overhead due to the cost of communication and serialization/deserialization of data. When implementing the algorithm `verify_parallel`, we have chosen to batch together these computations, so that each remote function call computes as many timesteps as possible until a discrete mode transition is hit.

4.3   Incremental Verification

In this section, we show how we implement an incremental verification algorithm on top of `verify_parallel`.

Consider two hybrid automata $H_i = H(SC_i)$, $i \in \{1,2\}$ that only differ in the discrete transitions. That is, (1) $\mathbf{X}_2 = \mathbf{X}_1$, (2) $\mathbf{D}_2 = \mathbf{D}_1$, and (3) $\mathbf{TL}_2 = \mathbf{TL}_1$, while the initial conditions, the guards, and the resets are slightly different[3]. SC_1 and SC_2 have the same sensors, maps, and agent flow functions. Let $Tree_1 = V_1$ and $Tree_2 = V_2$ be the execution trees for H_1 and H_2. Our idea of incremental verification is to reuse some of the computations in constructing the tree for H_1 in computing the same for H_2.

Recall that in `verify`, expanding each vertex N_1 of $Tree_1$ with a possible mode involves a guard check, a computation of $post_{\mathbf{d},\delta}$ and $post_{\mathbf{d},\mathbf{d}'}$. The algorithm `verify_incremental` avoids performing these computations while constructing $Tree_2$ by reusing those computations from $Tree_1$, if possible. To this end, `verify_incremental` uses a *cache (C)* that stores the result of a batch of `verify_step`. This is the same as that in Sect. 4.2, which simply batches together all the adjacent `verify_step` that have the same discrete modes. We'll call this batch operation `verify_batch`. The pseudocode for `verify_batch` is described in Algorithm 3. Formally, here are the properties of `verify_batch`:

Proposition 4. *For any set of states* $\mathbf{X}^0 \subseteq \mathbf{X}$, *mode* $\mathbf{d}^0 \in \mathbf{D}$, *time step* δ *and time horizon* $T_{\max}$, *let* $\langle reachset, branches, N^0 \rangle = $ `verify_batch`$(\langle \mathbf{X}^0, \mathbf{d}^0, 0, \varnothing, \varnothing \rangle, \delta, T_{\max})$. *Then for the* i^{th} *node explored in* `verify_batch`, *we have:*

$$N^i \in \texttt{verify\_step}(N^{i-1}, \delta).children$$
$$N^i.\mathbf{d} = N^{i-1}.\mathbf{d}$$

we further have:

$$branches = \bigcup_{i \in [0,k)} \{N' \mid N' \in N^i.children \ s.t. \ N'.\mathbf{d} \neq N^i.\mathbf{d}\}$$

$$reachset = \bigcup_{i \in [0,k)} N^i.stride$$

$$N^0 = \langle \mathbf{X}^0, \mathbf{d}^0, 0, \varnothing, \varnothing \rangle; \forall N \in branches, N.\mathbf{d} \neq \mathbf{d}^0; k \leq \lceil \tfrac{T_{\max}}{\delta} \rceil$$

where k *is the number of nodes in the batch.*

---

[3] Note that in this section subscripts index different hybrid automata, instead of agents within the same automaton (as we did in Sects. 3 and 3.2).

For $\texttt{verify\_batch}(\mathbf{X}^0, \mathbf{d}^0, \delta, T_{\max})$, the cache C will be indexed by $\langle \mathbf{X}^0,$ $\mathbf{d}^0 \rangle$, and the value will be the same as that of $\texttt{verify\_batch}$. Unlike normal caches, a cache hit can happen for C when the incoming key $\langle \mathbf{X}', \mathbf{d}' \rangle$ satisfies $\mathbf{X}' \subseteq \mathbf{X}^0 \wedge \mathbf{d}' = \mathbf{d}^0$.

The incremental verification algorithm is presented in Algorithm 3. The function $\texttt{verify\_incremental}$ checks C before every *post* computation to retrieve and reuse computations when possible. The cache can save information from any number of previous executions, so $\texttt{verify\_incremental}$ can be even more efficient than $\texttt{verify\_parallel}$ when running many consecutive verification runs.

The correctness property of $\texttt{verify\_incremental}$ is the same as that of algorithm $\texttt{verify\_parallel}$ in Sect. 4.2, i.e. the reachset computed by algorithm $\texttt{verify\_incremental}$ for SC_2, when given a cache populated with data from SC_1, is an overapproximation of the reachset computed by $\texttt{verify}$. More formally:

Proposition 5. *Given scenarios SC_1 and SC_2 with the same sensors, map, and agent flow functions, for cache $C = \varnothing$, any initial conditions $\mathbf{X}_1^0, \mathbf{X}_2^0 \subseteq \mathbf{X}$, $\mathbf{d}_1^0, \mathbf{d}_2^0 \in \mathbf{D}$, timestep δ and time horizon $T_{\max}$, after $\texttt{verify\_incremental}(H_1, \mathbf{X}_1^0, \mathbf{d}_1^0, \delta, T_{\max}, C)$ is executed,*

$$\texttt{verify}(H_2, \mathbf{X}_2^0, \mathbf{d}_2^0, \delta, T_{\max}) \subseteq \texttt{verify\_incremental}(H_2, \mathbf{X}_2^0, \mathbf{d}_2^0, \delta, T_{\max}, C)$$

Proof. For any initial conditions $\mathbf{X}_1^0, \mathbf{X}_2^0 \subseteq \mathbf{X}$, $\mathbf{d}^0 \in \mathbf{D}$, timestep δ, time horizon $T_{\max}$ and time t, let:

$$\langle reachset_1, branches_1 \rangle = \texttt{verify\_batch}(\mathbf{X}_1^0, \mathbf{d}^0, \delta, T_{\max}, t)$$
$$\langle reachset_2, branches_2 \rangle = \texttt{verify\_batch}(\mathbf{X}_2^0, \mathbf{d}^0, \delta, T_{\max}, t)$$

Given that $\texttt{verify\_batch}$ simply batches together $\texttt{postCont}$ and $\texttt{postDisc}$ operations, $\mathbf{X}_1^0 \subseteq \mathbf{X}_2^0 \implies reachset_1 \subseteq reachset_2$. As the cache C just stores the result of $\texttt{verify\_batch}$, $\mathbf{X}_1^0 \subseteq \mathbf{X}_2^0 \implies reachset_1 \subseteq C(\mathbf{X}_2^0, \mathbf{d}^0)$. That is, $\texttt{verify\_incremental}(H_2, \mathbf{X}_2^0, \mathbf{d}^0, \delta, T_{\max}, \varnothing) \subseteq \texttt{verify\_incremental}(H_2,$ $\mathbf{X}_2^0, \mathbf{d}^0, \delta, T_{\max}, C)$. That is, the reachset returned from a $\texttt{verify\_incremental}$ with caches would be an overapproximation of a version that doesn't have caches.

From Proposition 4, a $\texttt{verify\_batch}$ call can simply be decomposed into multiple $\texttt{verify\_step}$ calls. With the two conditions stated above, the algorithm for $\texttt{verify\_incremental}$ can be simplified to be the same as the algorithm of $\texttt{verify\_parallel}$, which we have proven to be equivalent to $\texttt{verify}$. Thus, it follows that $\texttt{verify}(H_2, \mathbf{X}_2^0, \mathbf{d}_2^0, \delta, T_{\max}) = \texttt{verify\_parallel}(H_2, \mathbf{X}_2^0, \mathbf{d}_2^0, \delta, T_{\max})$ $\subseteq \texttt{verify\_incremental}(H_2, \mathbf{X}_2^0, \mathbf{d}_2^0, \delta, T_{\max})$. $\qquad \square$

Algorithm 3

1: **function** VERIFY_BATCH($N^0, \delta, T_{\max}$) **where** $N^0.stride = \varnothing, N^0.children = \varnothing$
2:     $branches \leftarrow \varnothing$
3:     $reachset \leftarrow \varnothing$
4:     $N \leftarrow N^0$
5:     **while** $t < T_{\max}$ **do**
6:         $N \leftarrow \text{verify\_step}(N, \delta)$
7:         $reachset \leftarrow reachset \cup N.stride$
8:         **if** $\exists N' \in N.children$ s.t. $N'.d = N.d$ **then**
9:             $branches \leftarrow branches \cup (N.children \setminus N')$
10:            $N \leftarrow N'$
11:            $t \leftarrow t + \delta$
12:        **else**
13:            **return** $reachset, branches \cup N.children, N^0$

14: **function** verify_incremental($H, \mathbf{X}^0, \mathbf{d}^0, \delta, T_{\max}, C$)
15:     $queue \leftarrow [\langle \mathbf{X}^0, \mathbf{d}^0, 0, \varnothing, \varnothing \rangle]$
16:     $refs \leftarrow []$
17:     $reachset \leftarrow \varnothing$
18:     **while** $queue \neq \varnothing \vee refs \neq \varnothing$ **do**
19:         **if** $queue \neq \varnothing$ **then**
20:             $N \leftarrow queue.\text{dequeue}()$
21:             **if** $C(N.\mathbf{X}, N.\mathbf{d}) \neq \varnothing$ **then**   ▷ queries the cache
22:                 $\langle subreachset, branches \rangle \leftarrow C(N.\mathbf{X}, N.\mathbf{d})$
23:                 $reachset \leftarrow reachset \cup subreachset$
24:                 **for** $N' \in branches$ s.t. $N'.t < T_{\max}$ **do**
25:                     $queue.\text{add}(N')$
26:             **else**
27:                 $refs.\text{add}(\textbf{remote verify\_batch } (N, \delta, T_{\max}))$
28:         **else**   ▷ wait only when $queue$ is empty
29:             $\langle \langle subreachset, branches, N \rangle, refs \rangle \leftarrow \textbf{ray.wait}(refs)$
30:             $C(N.\mathbf{X}, N.\mathbf{d}) \leftarrow \langle subreachset, branches \rangle$ ▷ update the cache with results
31:             $reachset \leftarrow reachset \cup subreachset$
32:             **for** $N' \in branches$ s.t. $N'.t < T_{\max}$ **do**
33:                 $queue.\text{add}(N')$
34:     **return** $reachset$

---

5 Experimental Evaluation

We have implemented parallel and incremental verification algorithms in the Verse library [18], and in this section we will evaluate their performance against Verse's original sequential algorithm. Our goal is to glean qualitative lessons. We are not comparing against parallel tools mentioned in Sect. 2 because (a) it is not straightforward to implement multi-agent models in these other tools and (b) it is hard to draw fair conclusions comparing running time and memory usage across C++ and Python tools.

We perform these experiments on scenarios described in Table 2. Besides the intersection scenario, we also adopt some examples from [18]. Types of agents include: (1) 4-d vehicle with bicycle dynamics and Stanley controller [13], and (2) 6-d drone with a NN-controller [14]. Some of the agents have collision avoidance logics (CA) for switching tracks. All experiments were performed on a desktop PC with 8 core (16 thread) Intel Xeon E5-2630.

Table 2. Name and description of scenarios.

Scenario	Description
isect(l,n)	4-way intersection of Fig. 1 with l lanes and n vehicles, all having CA
drone	3 straight parallel tracks in 3D space with 3 drones, one having CA
drone8	3 Figure-8 tracks in 3D space with 2 drones, both having CA
curve	3-lane curved road with 3 vehicles, one having CA
wide(n,a)	5-lane straight road with n vehicles, a of which having CA
race	3-lane circular race track with 3 vehicles, one having CA

5.1   Parallel Reachability Speeds up with Cores and Branching

Table 3 shows the experimental results on running `verify_parallel` on these scenarios on using 2, 4, and 8 CPU cores. The data is sorted according to the number of leaves of the reachtree, which we use as a metric to measure the potential parallelism in a scenario, as we discussed in Sect. 4.2.

Table 3. Runtime for verifying the examples in Table 2. Columns are: name of the scenario (name), number of timesteps simulated (length), number of mode transitions (#Tr), the width of the execution tree (#leaves), the run time of the `verify` (serial), the run time of `verify_parallel` using 2, 4, or 8 cores and the corresponding speedup in parentheses. All running times are in seconds.

name	length	#Tr	#leaves	serial	2 cores	4 cores	8 cores
curve	400	4	2	50	56 (0.89)	55 (0.91)	56 (0.89)
drone	450	7	2	29	37 (0.78)	30 (0.97)	29 (1)
race	600	7	2	220	162 (1.36)	156 (1.41)	157 (1.4)
drone8	400	8	4	31	36 (0.86)	36 (0.86)	37 (0.84)
wide(7,2)	1600	37	7	188	135 (1.39)	136 (1.38)	137 (1.37)
isect(4,9)	1000	37	11	342	349 (0.98)	190 (1.8)	130 (2.63)
isect(4,10)	800	59	15	587	606 (0.97)	318 (1.85)	197 (2.98)
wide(8,3)	600	105	20	311	313 (0.99)	172 (1.81)	104 (2.99)
isect(4,15)	1000	102	37	2115	2085 (1.01)	1081 (1.96)	653 (3.24)
isect(4,20)	1060	399	140	13100	8416 (1.56)	4477 (2.93)	2085 (6.28)
isect(4,12)	800	589	225	7136	4445 (1.65)	2214 (3.3)	1302 (5.62)

First, we observe that for scenarios with more than 37 transitions, parallelization speeds up reachability analysis with at least 4 cores. Secondly, the number of leaves in a scenario roughly correlates to the speedup gained. This is illustrated in the experiments as we move down the table, we can see that the speedup ramp-up. Lastly, for each scenario the speedup generally increases with the number of cores. Maximum gains are made with the isect(4,20) scenario, which has a wide execution tree with many transitions. The verify_parallel algorithm reduces the running time from over 3 and a half hours to a little over 30 min. This performance gain can make a tool usable, where previously it was not [22, 24].

Because of the overhead of parallelism, some scenarios can be slower while using verify_parallel than verify. The overhead mainly comes from 2 areas: process creation and communication costs. As the number of parallel tasks increase, Ray creates more processes dynamically to handle those work, and the time caused by creating and initializing those processes can be larger than the benefit provided by parallelism. In addition, it takes time to send the inputs to and receive the results from the remote processes. This overhead gets larger with more agents in the scenario, larger state and/or mode spaces, longer time horizon, and more complex decision logics. However, from our results, this overhead does not overshadow the savings the verify_parallel algorithm introduce.

5.2 Incremental Verification Can Speed up Reachability Across Model Updates

To test our incremental verification algorithm, we apply it to several scenarios undergoing changes and edits. In this section we will report on the drone8, wide(8,3), and isect(4,15) scenarios. We will modify the initial condition or behavior of agents in the scenario. We measure the similarity across the models using the earliest time (T_{change}) when the automaton's behavior changes: for two identical scenarios T_{change} would be ∞, when the initial conditions of one of the agents is changed then $T_{change} = 0\%$, and when the decision logic code of one of the agents is changed T_{change} indicates the time where the change affects runtime behavior. We run each of the experiments with the verify, serialized verify_incremental, verify_parallel, and parallelized verify_incremental algorithms. The results are shown in Table 4.

From the table we can observe that when compared to the non-incremental versions of the algorithms, the incremental versions provide more speedup when the behavior of the automata are closer. We can see from the table that as T_{change} goes higher, the speedups provided by incremental verification trend upwards. In the ideal case, where the same scenario is verified again, the verification time is reduced from 575 s to 20 s for isect(4,15). For a case when the scenario is changed, the maximum gain we observe is from 404 s to 82 s for isect(4,15).

Secondly, we observe that combination of incremental verification and parallelization can sometimes give us more savings. For example, in row 5 of Table 4, we can observe that the parallelized verify_incremental algorithm, which

Table 4. Runtime for verifying the examples in Table 2. Columns are: name of the scenario (name), number of timesteps simulated (T), single or repeated runs (single), number of mode transitions (#Tr), the width of the execution tree (#leaves), the time for the first change in automaton behavior (T_{change}), the run time of `verify` (ser), the run time and hit rate of `verify_incremental` without parallelization (inc ser, hit rate), the run time of `verify_parallel` (par), the run time and hit rate of `verify_incremental` with parallelization (inc par, hit rate). The unit of run time is in seconds.

name	T	#Tr	#leaves	T_{change}	ser	inc ser	hit rate	par	inc par	hit rate
drone	450	9	3	75%	53	29	90%	51	30	90%
wide(8,3)	600	51	10	15.67%	173	20	100%	80	51	96.74%
wide(8,3)	600	105	20	∞	335	17	100%	104	16	100%
wide(8,3)	600	49	8	0%	182	129	95.31%	72	53	87.95%
isect(4,15)	400	5	2	0%	116	98	59.57%	100	83	29.79%
isect(4,15)	400	37	12	∞	575	36	100%	189	20	100%
isect(4,15)	400	24	9	82.25%	404	35	100%	159	82	39.7%

takes 83 s to finish, out performs both the serialized `verify_incremental` algorithm and the `verify_parallel` algorithm alone, which takes 98 s and 100 s respectively. However, in some situations the serial `verify_incremental` algorithm can be much faster than the parallel `verify_incremental` algorithm. This typically happened when the number of leaves is small as shown in row 7 of the table. The situation is caused by the overhead introduced from parallelization. Even though the cache provides run time savings, the trajectories will need to be copied to the remote processes when they are in the cache, which causes more overhead.

6   Conclusions and Future Directions

In this paper, we presented parallel and incremental verification algorithms for hybrid multi-agent scenarios using Ray and Verse. For large scenarios with more than 10 agents, and large number of branches, the speedup can be 3 or 6 times. The incremental verification algorithm `verify_incremental` makes it faster to iterate on models. When the states and decision logics do not change much, the algorithm can give significant speedups.

This work suggests several directions for future research. Currently the algorithms parallelize the computation on a per-branch basis. Agent-level parallelization could be useful for large scenarios with clusters of non-interacting agents. Being able to divide up tasks at a finer scale would mean more opportunities for parallelization, but we would also need to be careful of too small task sizes and develop batching algorithms that both take advantage of the parallelization and minimizing the overhead induced. In incremental verification, the algorithm currently redoes the computation as soon as any of the agents reaches states or exhibits behaviors never seen before. This is fairly evident from the experiments, where the caching is not able to provide runtime improvements when the initial conditions change. Finer-grained analysis of agent interactions can be done so that changes in agents' states or behaviors will only trigger recomputation of agents that will be affected. Moreover, in some situations the verify_incremental algorithm can become slower due to enabling parallelization. We can improve this by avoiding using remote functions when the result is already in the cache.

References

1. Althoff, M.: An introduction to CORA 2015. In: Proceedings of the Workshop on Applied Verification for Continuous and Hybrid Systems (2015)
2. Bak, S., Duggirala, P.S.: HyLAA: a tool for computing simulation-equivalent reachability for linear systems. In: Proceedings of the 20th International Conference on Hybrid Systems: Computation and Control, pp. 173–178. ACM (2017)
3. Bogomolov, S., Forets, M., Frehse, G., Potomkin, K., Schilling, C.: JuliaReach: a toolbox for set-based reachability. In: Proceedings of the 22nd ACM International Conference on Hybrid Systems: Computation and Control, pp. 39–44 (2019)
4. Chen, X., Ábrahám, E., Sankaranarayanan, S.: Flow*: an analyzer for non-linear hybrid systems. In: Sharygina, N., Veith, H. (eds.) CAV 2013. LNCS, vol. 8044, pp. 258–263. Springer, Heidelberg (2013). https://doi.org/10.1007/978-3-642-39799-8_18
5. Chong, N., et al.: Code-level model checking in the software development workflow. In: Proceedings of the ACM/IEEE 42nd International Conference on Software Engineering: Software Engineering in Practice, ICSE-SEIP 2020, pp. 11–20. Association for Computing Machinery, New York (2020). https://doi.org/10.1145/3377813.3381347
6. Chudnov, A., et al.: Continuous formal verification of Amazon s2n. In: Chockler, H., Weissenbacher, G. (eds.) CAV 2018. LNCS, vol. 10982, pp. 430–446. Springer, Cham (2018). https://doi.org/10.1007/978-3-319-96142-2_26
7. Devonport, A., Khaled, M., Arcak, M., Zamani, M.: PIRK: scalable interval reachability analysis for high-dimensional nonlinear systems. In: Lahiri, S.K., Wang, C. (eds.) CAV 2020. LNCS, vol. 12224, pp. 556–568. Springer, Cham (2020). https://doi.org/10.1007/978-3-030-53288-8_27
8. Duggirala, P.S., Mitra, S., Viswanathan, M., Potok, M.: C2E2: a verification tool for stateflow models. In: Baier, C., Tinelli, C. (eds.) TACAS 2015. LNCS, vol. 9035, pp. 68–82. Springer, Heidelberg (2015). https://doi.org/10.1007/978-3-662-46681-0_5
9. Fan, C., Qi, B., Mitra, S., Viswanathan, M.: DRYVR: data-driven verification and compositional reasoning for automotive systems. In: Majumdar, R., Kunčak, V. (eds.) CAV 2017, Part I. LNCS, vol. 10426, pp. 441–461. Springer, Cham (2017). https://doi.org/10.1007/978-3-319-63387-9_22
10. Fan, C., Qi, B., Mitra, S., Viswanathan, M.: DRYVR: data-driven verification and compositional reasoning for automotive systems. In: Majumdar, R., Kunčak, V. (eds.) CAV 2017. LNCS, vol. 10426, pp. 441–461. Springer, Cham (2017). https://doi.org/10.1007/978-3-319-63387-9_22

11. Frehse, G., et al.: SpaceEx: scalable verification of hybrid systems. In: Gopalakrishnan, G., Qadeer, S. (eds.) CAV 2011. LNCS, vol. 6806, pp. 379–395. Springer, Heidelberg (2011). https://doi.org/10.1007/978-3-642-22110-1_30

12. Gurung, A., Ray, R., Bartocci, E., Bogomolov, S., Grosu, R.: Parallel reachability analysis of hybrid systems in XSpeed. Int. J. Softw. Tools Technol. Transf. **21**(4), 401–423 (2018). https://doi.org/10.1007/s10009-018-0485-6

13. Hoffmann, G.M., Tomlin, C.J., Montemerlo, M., Thrun, S.: Autonomous automobile trajectory tracking for off-road driving: controller design, experimental validation and racing. In: 2007 American Control Conference, pp. 2296–2301 (2007)

14. Ivanov, R., Weimer, J., Alur, R., Pappas, G.J., Lee, I.: Verisig: verifying safety properties of hybrid systems with neural network controllers. In: Proceedings of the 22nd ACM International Conference on Hybrid Systems: Computation and Control, pp. 169–178 (2019)

15. Kaynar, D.K., Lynch, N., Segala, R., Vaandrager, F.: The Theory of Timed I/O Automata. Synthesis Lectures on Computer Science. Morgan Claypool (2005). Also available as Technical Report MIT-LCS-TR-917

16. Khaled, M., Zamani, M.: PFaces: an acceleration ecosystem for symbolic control. In: Proceedings of the 22nd ACM International Conference on Hybrid Systems: Computation and Control, HSCC 2019, pp. 252–257. Association for Computing Machinery, New York (2019). https://doi.org/10.1145/3302504.3311798

17. Kong, S., Gao, S., Chen, W., Clarke, E.: dReach: δ-reachability analysis for hybrid systems. In: Baier, C., Tinelli, C. (eds.) TACAS 2015. LNCS, vol. 9035, pp. 200–205. Springer, Heidelberg (2015). https://doi.org/10.1007/978-3-662-46681-0_15

18. Li, Y., Zhu, H., Braught, K., Shen, K., Mitra, S.: Verse: a python library for reasoning about multi-agent hybrid system scenarios. In: Enea, C., Lal, A. (eds.) CAV 2023. LNCS, vol. 13964, pp. 351–364. Springer, Cham (2023). https://doi.org/10.1007/978-3-031-37706-8_18

19. Liang, E., et al.: RLlib: abstractions for distributed reinforcement learning. In: International Conference on Machine Learning, pp. 3053–3062. PMLR (2018)

20. Mitra, S.: Verifying Cyber-Physical Systems: A Path to Safe Autonomy. MIT Press, Cambridge (2021)

21. Moritz, P., et al.: Ray: a distributed framework for emerging {AI} applications. In: 13th {USENIX} Symposium on Operating Systems Design and Implementation ({OSDI} 2018), pp. 561–577 (2018)

22. O'Hearn, P.W.: Continuous reasoning: scaling the impact of formal methods. In: Proceedings of the 33rd Annual ACM/IEEE Symposium on Logic in Computer Science, LICS 2018, pp. 13–25. Association for Computing Machinery, New York (2018). https://doi.org/10.1145/3209108.3209109

23. Platzer, A.: Differential logic for reasoning about hybrid systems. In: Bemporad, A., Bicchi, A., Buttazzo, G. (eds.) HSCC 2007. LNCS, vol. 4416, pp. 746–749. Springer, Heidelberg (2007). https://doi.org/10.1007/978-3-540-71493-4_75

24. Sadowski, C., Aftandilian, E., Eagle, A., Miller-Cushon, L., Jaspan, C.: Lessons from building static analysis tools at google. Commun. ACM **61**(4), 58–66 (2018)

25. Sun, D., Mitra, S.: NeuReach: learning reachability functions from simulations. In: Fisman, D., Rosu, G. (eds.) TACAS 2022, Part I. LNCS, vol. 13243, pp. 322–337. Springer, Cham (2022). https://doi.org/10.1007/978-3-030-99524-9_17

An Automata Theoretic Characterization of Weighted First-Order Logic

Dhruv Nevatia[1] and Benjamin Monmege[2(✉)]

[1] ETH Zurich, Zurich, Switzerland
dhruv.nevatia@inf.ethz.ch
[2] Aix Marseille Univ, LIS, CNRS, Marseille, France
benjamin.monmege@univ-amu.fr

Abstract. Since the 1970s with the work of McNaughton, Papert and Schützenberger [21,23], a regular language is known to be definable in the first-order logic if and only if its syntactic monoid is aperiodic. This algebraic characterisation of a fundamental logical fragment has been extended in the quantitative case by Droste and Gastin [10], dealing with polynomially ambiguous weighted automata and a restricted fragment of weighted first-order logic. In the quantitative setting, the full weighted first-order logic (without the restriction that Droste and Gastin use, about the quantifier alternation) is more powerful than weighted automata, and extensions of the automata with two-way navigation, and pebbles or nested capabilities have been introduced to deal with it [5,19]. In this work, we characterise the fragment of these extended weighted automata that recognise exactly the full weighted first-order logic, under the condition that automata are polynomially ambiguous.

Keywords: Weighted logics · weighted automata · aperiodic monoids

1 Introduction

Early works by McNaughton, Papert and Schützenberger [21,23] have enabled an automata-theoretic characterisation of first-order logic over finite words: a regular language is definable in the first-order logic if and only if its syntactic monoid is aperiodic. From the minimal automaton recognising the language, we can compute its syntactic monoid and check aperiodicity to conclude. Moreover, from the aperiodic minimal automaton, we can deduce a first-order formula equivalent to it.

More recently, Droste and Gastin [10] have extended this result to deal with quantitative extensions of the first-order logic and automata. These quantitative extensions find their origin in the works of Schützenberger [22] that investigated *weighted automata*, and their expressive power in terms of *(formal power) series*

We thank the reviewers that helped greatly improving the readability of this article. The work was partially done during an internship of the first author at Aix-Marseille Université, partially funded by CNRS IRL 2000 ReLaX.

É. André and J. Sun (Eds.): ATVA 2023, LNCS 14215, pp. 115–133, 2023.
https://doi.org/10.1007/978-3-031-45329-8_6

that are mappings from finite words to weights of a *semiring*. Weighted automata were originally thought as finite state automata where each transition (as well as initial and final states) are equipped with weights of a semiring. Along a run, weights are combined by the multiplication of the semiring, while non-determinism is resolved by considering the sum of the weights of all accepting runs over a word. By changing the semiring we consider, weights can model cost, rewards, energy or probabilities in a unified way: see [12]. Many extensions have then been considered, by allowing for more structures than words (infinite words [15], trees [16], nested words [3,14]) and more weights than semirings (valuation monoids [13], multioperator monoids [18]).

In order to describe the series describable by weighted automata in a more readable way, it might be useful to have more high-level ways of description, like weighted logics based on monadic second order (MSO) features, introduced by Droste and Gastin [9]. Based on the seminal result by Büchi, Elgot, and Trakht-enbrot [6,17,24], they have explored a weighted extension of MSO logic on finite words and semirings: the semantics of disjunction and existential quantification are based on the sum of the semiring, while the ones of conjunction and universal quantification are based on the product. The appropriate restriction on the logic was found in order to obtain the exact same expressivity as weighted automata: a restriction is needed for combinatorial reasons, certain operators of the logic being able to generate series growing too quickly with respect to the length of the input word. In particular, universal quantifications must be used only once over very basic formulas, and conjunction is not allowed. Once again, this seminal result relating weighted automata and weighted logics has been extended in many ways: on trees [16], on nested words [3,14], with weights valuation monoids [13], to cite only a very few.

In [20], the semantics of weighted automata and weighted MSO logic has been revisited in a uniform way allowing one to obtain many previous results in a simplified way. First, an *abstract semantics* is defined, mapping each word to a multiset of sequences of weights (one sequence per accepting run): this abstract semantics does not depend on the weight structure, since no actual computation is made. The abstract semantics can then be aggregated into a single output weight by an ad-hoc operator: we call this the *concrete semantics*. Methodologically speaking, showing that two models have equal abstract semantics is sufficient (but not necessary in general) to show that they have equivalent concrete semantics.

In [10], Droste and Gastin consider the first-order fragment WFO of the weighted MSO logic, with the same kind of restrictions as the one explored for weighted MSO logic to recover the same expressive power as weighted automata. Under this restriction, they show that the logic WFO is expressively equivalent to weighted automata that are *aperiodic* (defined similarly as in the unweighted setting) and *polynomially ambiguous*. Moreover, the proof is constructive and works for the abstract semantics (and thus for any concrete semantics).

In order to express more properties than the restricted logics (WFO and weighted MSO), weighted automata with two-way navigation and pebbles or nested capabilities have been introduced [5,19], with an equivalent logic based on an extension of WFO with some limited transitive closure operators. As noted in [10] by Droste and Gastin, this is thus natural to ask what the models of two-way nested/pebble weighted automata are that recognise exactly the full WFO logic. In this work, we answer this question: the series recognised by WFO logic can be obtained from two-way nested/pebble weighted automata that are aperiodic and polynomially unambiguous. This generalises the results of [10] only working for a small fragment of WFO, and one-way (non-nested) weighted automata, but the condition has a similar flavour. The aperiodicity condition on two-way automata models has been explored in [7]. Our proof is constructive and goes through a special case of two-way automata that are called *sweeping* where every change of direction happens on the border of the input word (and not in the middle). This allows us to more easily reuse the work by Droste and Gastin, which only works for one-way models.

After defining the weighted first-order logic we study in Sect. 2, and the nested two-way weighted automata in Sect. 3, we prove the equivalence between the various formalisms in subsequent sections: the translation from the logic to sweeping nested weighted automata is done in Sect. 4; sweeping nested weighted automata are translated back in the logic in Sect. 5. The most difficult part of the proof is the translation from two-way nested weighted automata to sweeping nested weighted automata: this does not hold if we do not have nesting mechanisms, and this translation thus raises the number of nesting necessary in the model.

2   Weighted First-Order Logic

In this section, we introduce the weighted first-order logic whose power we will characterise in the following with respect to some automata model. The logic used in [10] is a fragment of this logic where nesting of operations is limited to be as expressive as weighted automata.

Definition 1. *For a set* K *of weights and an alphabet* A, *we let* $\mathsf{WFO}(\mathsf{K}, A)$ *be the logic defined by the following grammar:*

$$\varphi ::= \top \mid P_a(x) \mid x \leq y \mid \neg \varphi \mid \varphi \wedge \varphi \mid \forall x \, \varphi \qquad \text{(FO)}$$

$$\Phi ::= 0 \mid 1 \mid k \mid \varphi ? \Phi : \Phi \mid \Phi + \Phi \mid \Phi \cdot \Phi \mid \Sigma_x \Phi \mid \Pi_x \Phi \mid \Pi_x^{-1} \Phi \qquad \text{(WFO)}$$

where $a \in A$, $k \in \mathsf{K}$ *and* x, y *are first order variables.*

Formulas φ stand for the classical (Boolean) first-order logic over words on the alphabet A. Their semantics is defined classically over words $u = u_1 u_2 \cdots u_n \in A^*$ and valuations $\sigma \colon \mathcal{V} \to \{1, 2, \ldots, n\}$ of the free variables $\mathcal{V}$ of the formula, letting $u, \sigma \models \varphi$ when the formula is satisfied by the word and the valuation.

Formulas Φ are weighted formulas that intuitively associate a weight with each word and valuation of free variables. As described in [19], the semantics is defined in two steps: first we give an *abstract* semantics associating with each word and valuation a multiset of sequences of weights in K; then we may define a *concrete* semantics by describing how to fuse the multiset of sequences into a single weight. This differs from the classical semantics that directly compute the concrete semantics, but for our later proofs the other equivalent definition is much easier to manipulate.

Let $u \in A^*$ be a word and $\sigma \colon \mathcal{V} \to \{1, 2, \ldots, n\}$ be a valuation where $\mathcal{V}$ is a set of variables. The abstract semantics of a WFO formula ϕ, with $\mathcal{V}$ as free variables, is denoted by $\{\!|\phi|\!\}_{\mathcal{V}}(u, \sigma)$: it is a multiset of sequences of weights, i.e. a series of $\mathbb{N}\langle K^* \rangle$ mapping each sequence to its multiplicity in the multiset. As usual, we denote multisets via the symbols $\{\!| . |\!\}$. The disjoint union of two multisets is obtained as the sum of the associated series, it is denoted by $S_1 \cup S_2$. The product of two multisets is obtained as the Cauchy product of the associated series, it is denoted by $S_1 \cdot S_2 = \{\!| s_1 s_2 \mid s_1 \in S_1, s_2 \in S_2 |\!\}$. This defines a structure of semiring on multisets where neutral elements are the empty multiset (i.e. the series mapping all sequences to 0), denoted by $\emptyset$, and the singleton $\{\!|\varepsilon|\!\}$ that only contains the empty sequence. The constants $\mathbf{0}$ and $\mathbf{1}$ of the logic represent those constants.

The semantics of WFO is defined inductively as follows:

$$\{\!|\mathbf{0}|\!\}_{\mathcal{V}}(u, \sigma) = \emptyset \qquad \{\!|\mathbf{1}|\!\}_{\mathcal{V}}(u, \sigma) = \{\!|\varepsilon|\!\} \qquad \{\!|k|\!\}_{\mathcal{V}}(u, \sigma) = \{\!|k|\!\}$$

$$\{\!|\varphi? \Phi_1 : \Phi_2|\!\}_{\mathcal{V}}(u, \sigma) = \begin{cases} \{\!|\Phi_1|\!\}_{\mathcal{V}}(u, \sigma) & \text{if } u, \sigma \models \varphi \\ \{\!|\Phi_2|\!\}_{\mathcal{V}}(u, \sigma) & \text{otherwise} \end{cases}$$

$$\{\!|\Phi_1 + \Phi_2|\!\}_{\mathcal{V}}(u, \sigma) = \{\!|\Phi_1|\!\}_{\mathcal{V}}(u, \sigma) \cup \{\!|\Phi_2|\!\}_{\mathcal{V}}(u, \sigma)$$

$$\{\!|\Phi_1 \cdot \Phi_2|\!\}_{\mathcal{V}}(u, \sigma) = \{\!|\Phi_1|\!\}_{\mathcal{V}}(u, \sigma) \cdot \{\!|\Phi_2|\!\}_{\mathcal{V}}(u, \sigma)$$

$$\{\!|\Sigma_x \Phi|\!\}_{\mathcal{V}}(u, \sigma) = \bigcup_{i \in \{1, 2, \ldots, |u|\}} \{\!|\Phi|\!\}_{\mathcal{V} \cup \{x\}}(u, \sigma[x \mapsto i])$$

$$\{\!|\Pi_x \Phi|\!\}_{\mathcal{V}}(u, \sigma) = \{\!|\Phi|\!\}_{\mathcal{V} \cup \{x\}}(u, \sigma[x \mapsto 1]) \cdots \{\!|\Phi|\!\}_{\mathcal{V} \cup \{x\}}(u, \sigma[x \mapsto |u|])$$

$$\{\!|\Pi_x^{-1} \Phi|\!\}_{\mathcal{V}}(u, \sigma) = \{\!|\Phi|\!\}_{\mathcal{V} \cup \{x\}}(u, \sigma[x \mapsto |u|]) \cdots \{\!|\Phi|\!\}_{\mathcal{V} \cup \{x\}}(u, \sigma[x \mapsto 1])$$

For sentences (formulas without free variables), we remove the set $\mathcal{V}$ of variables as well as the valuation σ from the notation. Given a series $f \in (\mathbb{N}\langle K^* \rangle)\langle A^* \rangle$ we say that f is WFO-*definable* if there exists a sentence Φ_f such that for all words $u \in A^*$, $f(u) = \{\!|\Phi_f|\!\}(u)$.

We also define the 1-way fragments WFO$^{\to}$ and WFO$^{\leftarrow}$ by discarding binary product $(\cdot)$, as well as Π_x^{-1} and Π_x, respectively.

The fragment rWFO$^{\to}$ of logic studied in [10] is obtained by the following grammar:

$$\Psi ::= k \mid \varphi? \Psi : \Psi \qquad \qquad \text{(step-wFO)}$$
$$\Phi ::= \mathbf{0} \mid \varphi? \Phi : \Phi \mid \Phi + \Phi \mid \Sigma_x \Phi \mid \Pi_x \Psi \qquad \text{(rWFO}^{\to})$$

where $k \in K$, φ is a formula of FO, and x is a first order variable.

Notice that the abstract semantics of a formula from step-wFO maps every word to a singleton multiset. Since $\mathbf{1}$ is removed, as well as the binary product, and Π_x is restricted to step-wFO formulas, it is easy to check inductively that the abstract semantics of a formula from $\mathsf{rWFO}^{\rightarrow}$ maps every word u to a multiset of sequences of weights all of the length of u.

To interpret the abstract semantics in terms of a single quantity, we moreover provide an aggregation operator $\mathsf{aggr} \colon \mathbb{N}\langle \mathsf{K}^* \rangle \to S$ to a set S of weights. The concrete semantics of a formula Φ is then obtained by applying aggr over the multiset obtained via the abstract semantics. The set S can be equipped of various algebraic structures, like semirings or valuation monoids [11], as explained in [19]. In the case of a semiring, we for instance let $\mathsf{aggr}(f)$ be the sum over all sequences $k_1 k_2 \cdots k_n$ of $f(k_1 k_2 \cdots k_n) \times k_1 \times k_2 \times \cdots \times k_n$.

Example 1. As a first example, consider as a set of weights the languages over the alphabet A. It is naturally equipped with a structure of semiring, where the addition is the union of languages and the multiplication is the concatenation of languages. This semiring is non-commutative which validates our introduction of two product quantification operators, one from left to right and one from right to left. For instance, suppose we want to compute the mapping $f \colon A^* \to 2^{A^*}$ that associates to a word u all the words of the form $\tilde{w}w\tilde{w}$ with w all factors of u (i.e. consecutive letters taken inside u), where $\tilde{w}$ denotes the mirror image of the word w. For instance, $f(abb) = \{aa, bb, baba, bbbb, bbabba\}$. We can describe this function via a formula of WFO as follows. We suppose that $A = \{a, b\}$ to simplify, and we let $\mathsf{K} = \{\mathbf{a}, \mathbf{b}\}$ be the weights that represent the singleton languages $\{a\}$ and $\{b\}$. Then, we describe a formula $\mathsf{mirror\text{-}factor}(x, y)$ that computes the mirror image of the factor in-between positions pointed by x and y:

$$\mathsf{mirror\text{-}factor}(x, y) = \Pi_z^{-1} \, (x \leq z \wedge z \leq y)?(P_a(z)?\mathbf{a} : \mathbf{b}) : \mathbf{1}$$

Then, the mapping f can be described with the formula Φ:

$$\Sigma_x \Sigma_y \, (x \leq y)?[\mathsf{mirror\text{-}factor}(x, y) \cdot \mathsf{mirror\text{-}factor}(x, y)] : \mathbf{0}$$

The abstract semantics of the formula associates a multiset of words $\tilde{w}w\tilde{w}$ with w all factors of u. For instance, $\{\![\Phi]\!\}(aa) = \{\!\{aa, aa, aaaa\}\!\}$. To provide a concrete semantics, we simply consider the aggregation operator that computes the product of sets of weights and removes duplicates in multisets.   □

Example 2. As a second example, consider the alphabet $A = \{a, b\}$, and the natural semiring $(\mathbb{N}, +, \times, 0, 1)$, i.e. the aggregation operator that naturally comes with a semiring. It is a commutative semiring, thus the operator Π^{-1} becomes semantically equivalent (with respect to the concrete semantics, but not to the abstract one) to Π. Consider the series $f \colon A^* \to \mathbb{N}$ defined for all words $u \in A^*$ by $f(u) = |u|_a^{|u|_b}$, where $|u|_c$ denotes the number of a given letter c in the word u. This series can be defined by the following formula, where we intentionally reuse the same variable name twice (but the semantics would be unchanged if the internal variable x was renamed y): $\Pi_x \, (P_b(x)?\Sigma_x \, (P_a(x)?1 : 0) : 1)$. The abstract semantics maps a word with m letters a and n letters b to the multiset containing m^n copies of the sequence 1. For instance, for the word $abbaa$, the abstract semantics computes $\{\!\{\varepsilon\}\!\} \cdot \{\!\{1, 1, 1\}\!\} \cdot \{\!\{1, 1, 1\}\!\} \cdot \{\!\{\varepsilon\}\!\} \cdot \{\!\{\varepsilon\}\!\}$, where we have decomposed it with respect to the outermost Π_x operator. Once aggregated, all sequences map to 1, and we thus count m^n as expected.   □

3   Nested Two-Way Weighted Automata

Weighted automata are a well-studied model of automata equipped with weights, introduced by Schützenberger [22]. They have been extended to several weight structures (semirings, valuation monoids), once again with a unified abstract semantics introduced in [19]. They also have been extended with two-way navigation, and pebbles or nested capabilities, in order to get more power [5, 20]. In order to simplify our later proofs, we first redefine the semantics of the nested two-way weighted automata with the abstract semantics seen above for the logic.

Since we consider two-way navigation in a word, it is classical to frame the finite word by markers, both on the left and on the right, so that the automaton knows the boundary of the domain. We denote by $\triangleright, \triangleleft$ the left and right markers of the input word, respectively, that are supposed to be symbols not already present in the alphabet A we consider.

Definition 2. *First, by convention, we let (-1)-nested two-way weighted automata to be constants of K. Then, for $r \geq 0$, we let r-NWA(K, A) (or, r-NWA if K and A are clear from the context) be the class of r-nested two-way weighted automata over a finite set K of constants and alphabet A, that are all tuples $\mathcal{A} = \langle Q, \mathsf{Tr}, I, F \rangle$ where*

- *Q is a finite set of states;*
- *Tr is the transition relation split into two subsets.*
  1. *For $a \in A$, there are transitions of the form $(q, a, \mathcal{B}, d, q') \in Q \times A \times (r-1)$-NWA$(\mathsf{K}, A \times \{0,1\}) \times \{\leftarrow, \rightarrow\} \times Q$, meaning that the automaton is in state q, reads the letter a, calls the $(r-1)$-nested two-way weighted automaton $\mathcal{B}$ over the same set K of weights and alphabet $A \times \{0,1\}$ (used to mark the current position), decides to move in the d-direction, and changes its state to q'.*
  2. *For $a \in A \cup \{\triangleright, \triangleleft\}$, there are some other transitions where the automaton $\mathcal{B}$ is replaced by a weight from K, or by the special constant $\mathbf{1}$ (that we used in the logic WFO) to forbid the call of a nested automaton (especially on the markers): these transitions are thus of the form*

$$(q, a, k, d, q') \in \quad (Q \times A \times (\mathsf{K} \cup \{\mathbf{1}\}) \times \{\leftarrow, \rightarrow\} \times Q)$$
$$\cup \, (Q \times \{\triangleright\} \times (\mathsf{K} \cup \{\mathbf{1}\}) \times \{\rightarrow\} \times Q)$$
$$\cup \, (Q \times \{\triangleleft\} \times (\mathsf{K} \cup \{\mathbf{1}\}) \times \{\leftarrow\} \times Q)$$

where we have chosen to remove the possibility to move right on a right marker, and left on a left marker (to avoid exiting the possible positions in the input word);
- *$I \subseteq Q$ is the set of initial states;*
- *$F \subseteq Q$ is the set of final states.*

An automaton $\mathcal{B}$ that appears in the transitions of an automaton $\mathcal{A}$ is called a *child* of $\mathcal{A}$, and reciprocally $\mathcal{A}$ is a *parent* of $\mathcal{B}$ (notice that an automaton could have several parents, since it can appear in the transitions of several automata). This describes a directed acyclic relationship of dependency between automata: we thus say that an automaton is a *descendant* of another one if they are related by a sequence of parent-child relationship. The unique automaton with no ancestors shall be called the *root*.

In the following a transition of the form (q, a, x, d, q') is said to go from state q to state q', reading letter a, having weight x, and is called a d-transition.

We now define the abstract semantics of an r-NWA(K, A) $\mathcal{A}$, mapping each word $u \in A^*$ to a multiset of sequences of weights $\{\!\|\mathcal{A}\|\!\}(u) \in \mathbb{N}\langle K^* \rangle$. Configurations of such an automaton are tuples (u, i, q) where $u = u_1 \cdots u_n$ is the word in $\{\varepsilon, \triangleright\} A^* \{\varepsilon, \triangleleft\}$ (that could start and end with the markers, or not, in order to be able to define subruns on an unmarked word, that we will use later), $i \in \{1, \dots, n\}$ is a position in the word, and $q \in Q$ is the current state. We call run a sequence $\rho = (u, i_0, q_0) \xrightarrow{\delta_0, f_0} (u, i_1, q_1) \xrightarrow{\delta_1, f_1} \cdots \xrightarrow{\delta_m, f_m} (u, i_m, q_m)$, where $i_0, \dots, i_{m-1} \in \{1, \dots, n\}$, $i_m \in \{0, 1, \dots, n, n+1\}$ is the final position (that could *exit* the word on left or right) $\delta_0, \dots, \delta_m \in \mathsf{Tr}$ and $f_0, \dots, f_m$ are multisets in $\mathbb{N}\langle K^* \rangle$ such that for all $j \in \{0, \dots, m-1\}$:

- δ_j is a transition from state q_j to state q_{j+1} reading letter u_{i_j};
- if δ_j is a $\rightarrow$-transition then $i_{j+1} = i_j + 1$, otherwise $i_{j+1} = i_j - 1$;
- if $u_{i_j} \in A$ and the transition has weight $\mathcal{B}$ that is a $(r-1)$-NWA(K, $A \times \{0, 1\}$), then $f_j = \{\!\|\mathcal{B}\|\!\}(u')$ where u' is the word over alphabet $A \times \{0, 1\}$, that will later be denoted by (u, i_j), whose left component is u and whose right component is the constant 0 except at position i_j where it is 1;
- if the transition has weight $k \in K$, then $f_j = \{\!\| k \|\!\}$,
- if the transition has weight $\mathbf{1}$, then $f_j = \{\!\| \varepsilon \|\!\}$.

The *initial position* of the run is i_0, and its *final position* is i_m. The run is *accepting* if $q_0 \in I$, $q_m \in F$. Notice that we do not require runs to start on the left marker and stop at the right marker. The weight $\mathsf{wt}(\rho)$ of this run is given as the product of multisets $f_0 \cdot f_1 \cdots f_m$.

A run is called *simple* if it never goes twice through the same configuration. Not all runs are simple, but we restrict ourselves to using only those in the semantics: otherwise, an infinite number of runs should be summed, which would produce an infinite multiset (and then the aggregator function should be extended to add this possible behaviour). This restriction was also considered in [5,20].

We then let $\{\!\|\mathcal{A}\|\!\}(u)$ be the union (as multiset) of the weights of accepting simple runs (whatever their initial and final positions). As for the logics above, we may then use an aggregation operator to obtain a *concrete semantics* $[\![\mathcal{A}]\!]$ mapping each word u to a weight structure S.

Given a series $f \in (\mathbb{N}\langle K^* \rangle)\langle A^* \rangle$ we say that f is NWA-*definable* if there exists $r \geq 0$ and an r-NWA(K, A) $\mathcal{A}$ such that for all words $u \in A^*$, $f(u) = \{\!\|\mathcal{A}\|\!\}(u)$.

Example 3. We describe in Fig. 1 a 2-NWA $\mathcal{A}$ that recognises the series described in Example 1. Two levels of nesting are used to mark non-deterministically the positions x and y, such that $x \leq y$ (or only one of them if $x = y$). Then, the last

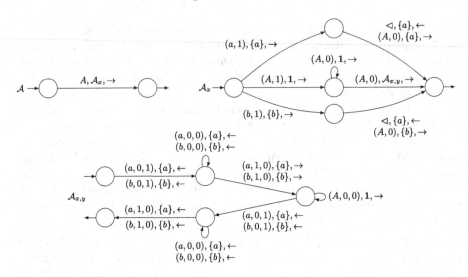

Fig. 1. An 2-NWA that recognises the series described in Example 1. The letter A is used in transitions to denote the presence of all possible letters from A. Notice that the runs of all the automata may start and stop at any position of the word, as described in the semantics.

level of nesting is used to compute the value of the formula mirror-factor(x, y) · mirror-factor(x, y) by two passes from right to left.   □

A run over a word u is called *left-to-right* (resp. *left-to-left*, *right-to-right*, *right-to-left*) if its initial position is 1 (resp. 1, $|u|$, $|u|$) and its final position is $|u| + 1$ (resp. 0, $|u| + 1$, 0). Intuitively, we thus use this terminology to detect if a run starts on the first or last position of the word, and if it exits the word either on the left or on the right.

Navigational Restrictions. An r-NWA$^{\rightarrow}$ (respectively, r-NWA$^{\leftarrow}$) is an r-NWA where all transitions appearing in the automaton or its descendants are $\rightarrow$-transitions (resp. $\leftarrow$-transitions). Those models are called *one-way* in the following, since the head movement is fixed during the whole run.

An r-nested *sweeping* weighted automaton (r-swNWA) is an r-NWA where changes of directions are only allowed (in this automaton or its descendants) at markers. More formally, states of the automaton and each of its descendants are separated in two sets $Q^{\rightarrow}$ and $Q^{\leftarrow}$ such that for all transitions $(q, a, \mathcal{B}, d, q')$ or (q, a, k, d, q'),

- if $q, q' \in Q^{\rightarrow}$, then $d = \rightarrow$;
- if $q, q' \in Q^{\leftarrow}$, then $d = \leftarrow$;
- if $q \in Q^{\rightarrow}$ and $q' \in Q^{\leftarrow}$, then $d = \leftarrow$ and $a = \triangleleft$;
- if $q \in Q^{\leftarrow}$ and $q' \in Q^{\rightarrow}$, then $d = \rightarrow$ and $a = \triangleright$.

Ambiguity. An r-NWA $\mathcal{A}$ is called *polynomially ambiguous* if there is a polynomial p such that over every word u on its alphabet the number of accepting runs of $\mathcal{A}$, as well as the number of accepting runs of any of its descendants, is at most $p(|u|)$. If the polynomial p is linear, $\mathcal{A}$ is said to be *linearly ambiguous*. If the polynomial p is the constant 1, $\mathcal{A}$ is said to be *unambiguous*. Notice that the condition deals with all runs, and not only the simple ones.

Polynomial ambiguity (indeed even *finite* ambiguity, where the number of accepting runs must be finite for all words) implies that all accepting runs are simple: otherwise, there would be an infinite number of accepting runs, by allowing the loops to happen as many times as possible.

The 2-NWA of Fig. 1 is linearly ambiguous since the toplevel automaton $\mathcal{A}$ has only to choose the position where to start the run, the automaton $\mathcal{A}_x$ has then only to choose the position where to call the next automaton, and the automaton $\mathcal{A}_{x,y}$ is unambiguous.

Aperiodicity. In order to define a notion of aperiodicity for NWA, we need to enhance the usual notion of aperiodicity for automata to incorporate weights, two-way navigations, and nesting. As in [10], we simply do not care about weights and thus require that the unweighted version of the automata are aperiodic. For two-way navigations, we rely on existing extensions of the notion of *transition monoid* for two-way automata and transducers [1,2,7]. Finally, for nesting, we simply require that each automaton appearing in an NWA is aperiodic.

More formally, given a NWA $\mathcal{A}$ over the alphabet A, its transition monoid is the quotient of the free monoid A^* by a congruence relation capturing the equivalence of two *behaviours* of the automaton. As for runs, we distinguish four types of behaviours: left-to-left, left-to-right, right-to-left and right-to-right. The left-to-left behaviour $\mathsf{bh}_{ll}^{\mathcal{A}}(w)$ of $w \in \{\varepsilon, \triangleright\}A^*\{\varepsilon, \triangleleft\}$ in $\mathcal{A}$ is the set of pairs of states (p, q) such that there exists a left-to-left run over w from state p to state q (notice that we do not care if the descendant automata that are called along this run are indeed "accepting" the word). The other behaviours can be defined analogously.

Definition 3. *Let* $\mathcal{A} = \langle Q, \mathsf{Tr}, I, F \rangle$ *be a* NWA(K, A). *The transition monoid of* $\mathcal{A}$ *is* $A^* \backslash \sim_{\mathcal{A}}$ *where* $\sim_{\mathcal{A}}$ *is the conjunction of the following congruence relations, defined for* $w, w' \in A^*$ *by:*

- $w \sim_{ll}^{\mathcal{A}} w'$ *iff* $\mathsf{bh}_{ll}^{\mathcal{A}}(w) = \mathsf{bh}_{ll}^{\mathcal{A}}(w')$
- $w \sim_{lr}^{\mathcal{A}} w'$ *iff* $\mathsf{bh}_{lr}^{\mathcal{A}}(w) = \mathsf{bh}_{lr}^{\mathcal{A}}(w')$
- $w \sim_{rl}^{\mathcal{A}} w'$ *iff* $\mathsf{bh}_{rl}^{\mathcal{A}}(w) = \mathsf{bh}_{rl}^{\mathcal{A}}(w')$
- $w \sim_{rr}^{\mathcal{A}} w'$ *iff* $\mathsf{bh}_{rr}^{\mathcal{A}}(w) = \mathsf{bh}_{rr}^{\mathcal{A}}(w')$

Notice that in the previous definition, we only focus on words not containing markers. This is because we only use this monoid in order to define aperiodicity of the automata where we focus on powers of elements of the monoid, which correspond to runs on iterates of a word in which it makes no sense to duplicate some markers.

An r-NWA is *aperiodic* if its transition monoid, as well as the ones of all its descendants, are aperiodic (i.e. for all elements x of the monoid, there is a natural number n such that $x^n = x^{n+1}$).

Given an NWA $\mathcal{A}$, its *left-to-right* (resp. *right-to-left*) projection is the NWA $\overrightarrow{\mathcal{A}}$ (resp. $\overleftarrow{\mathcal{A}}$) obtained by only keeping $\rightarrow$-transitions (resp. $\leftarrow$-transitions) in the root automaton. Interestingly, when starting from sweeping automata, aperiodicity is preserved when taking such projections.

Lemma 1. *If a* swNWA $\mathcal{A}$ *is aperiodic then* $\overrightarrow{\mathcal{A}}$ *and* $\overleftarrow{\mathcal{A}}$ *are aperiodic.*

Proof. Let $\mathcal{A} = \langle Q, \mathsf{Tr}, I, F \rangle$ be a swNWA(K, A). We prove the result for $\overrightarrow{\mathcal{A}}$. The proof for $\overleftarrow{\mathcal{A}}$ follows analogously.

Consider the word $u \in A^*$. Then there exists a natural number k such that $\mathsf{bh}_e^{\mathcal{A}}(u^k) = \mathsf{bh}_e^{\mathcal{A}}(u^{k+1})$ for $e \in \{ll, lr, rl, rr\}$. If $u = \varepsilon$, then $\mathsf{bh}_e^{\overrightarrow{\mathcal{A}}}(u) = \{(p, p) \mid p \in Q\} = \mathsf{bh}_e^{\overrightarrow{\mathcal{A}}}(u^2)$ for $e \in \{ll, lr, rl, rr\}$. It remains to prove the lemma when u is not empty. Immediately, we have $\mathsf{bh}_{ll}^{\overrightarrow{\mathcal{A}}}(u) = \mathsf{bh}_{ll}^{\overrightarrow{\mathcal{A}}}(u^2) = \mathsf{bh}_{rl}^{\overrightarrow{\mathcal{A}}}(u) = \mathsf{bh}_{rl}^{\overrightarrow{\mathcal{A}}}(u^2) = \emptyset$. Since no run of the sweeping automaton $\mathcal{A}$ over u can change the direction of its head movement over w that does not contain end markers, we have $\mathsf{bh}_{lr}^{\overrightarrow{\mathcal{A}}}(u^k) = \mathsf{bh}_{lr}^{\mathcal{A}}(u^k) = \mathsf{bh}_{lr}^{\mathcal{A}}(u^{k+1}) = \mathsf{bh}_{lr}^{\overrightarrow{\mathcal{A}}}(u^{k+1})$. Finally, $\mathsf{bh}_{rr}^{\overrightarrow{\mathcal{A}}}(u) = \{(p, q) \mid (p, u_{|u|}, x, \rightarrow, q) \in \mathsf{Tr}\} = \mathsf{bh}_{rr}^{\overrightarrow{\mathcal{A}}}(u^2)$.

For every word $u \in A^*$, we thus have $\mathsf{bh}_e^{\overrightarrow{\mathcal{A}}}(u^{k'}) = \mathsf{bh}_e^{\overrightarrow{\mathcal{A}}}(u^{k'+1})$ for $e \in \{ll, lr, rl, rr\}$, where $k' = \max(1, k)$. Hence, $\overrightarrow{\mathcal{A}}$ is aperiodic.   □

Results. The goal is to find an adequate characterisation of the automata models that recognise exactly the series WFO-definable or the fragments introduced before. Droste and Gastin [10] paved the way of this study by characterising rWFO$^{\rightarrow}$ with a fragment of the classical one-way weighted automata, that are 0-NWA$^{\rightarrow}$ where the semantics is computed by only considering accepting runs that start on the first letter of the word, and end on the last letter of the word: this is because of the specific type of multiset produced by formulas of rWFO$^{\rightarrow}$, all elements being of the same length (the length of the input word). In particular, markers are useless in this context.

Theorem 1 ([10]). *For all series* $f \in (\mathbb{N}\langle K^* \rangle)\langle A^* \rangle$, *the following conditions are equivalent:*

1. f *is definable by a polynomially ambiguous aperiodic* 0-NWA$^{\rightarrow}$
2. f *is* rWFO$^{\rightarrow}$-*definable.*

Here, and in the following, classes $\mathcal{C}_1$ and $\mathcal{C}_2$ of models are said to be equivalent if for all models $\mathcal{M}_1 \in \mathcal{C}_1$ and $\mathcal{M}_2 \in \mathcal{C}_2$ working on the same alphabet and the same sets of weights, and for all words u, the abstract semantics $\{\!|\mathcal{M}_1|\!\}(u)$ is equal to the abstract semantics $\{\!|\mathcal{M}_2|\!\}(u)$. This then implies that, for every aggregation function, the concrete semantics are also the same.

The proof of this theorem is constructive in both directions, and we will revisit it in the next sections, providing generalisations of it in order to get our main contribution:

Theorem 2. *For all series $f \in (\mathbb{N}\langle\mathsf{K}^*\rangle)\langle A^*\rangle$, the following conditions are equivalent:*

1. *f is definable by a linearly ambiguous aperiodic NWA;*
2. *f is definable by a polynomially ambiguous aperiodic NWA;*
3. *f is WFO-definable;*
4. *f is definable by a linearly ambiguous aperiodic swNWA*
5. *f is definable by a polynomially ambiguous aperiodic swNWA.*

The rest of the article is devoted to a sketch of the proofs of Theorem 2. We provide in Sect. 4 the sketch of proof of $3 \Rightarrow 4$, in Sect. 5 the sketch of proof of $5 \Rightarrow 3$, and in Sect. 6 the sketch of proof of $2 \Rightarrow 5$. We can then conclude by the trivial implications $4 \Rightarrow 1 \Rightarrow 2$.

As a side result, we also obtain a characterisation for one-way models:

Theorem 3. *For all series $f \in (\mathbb{N}\langle\mathsf{K}^*\rangle)\langle A^*\rangle$, the following conditions are equivalent:*

1. *f is definable by a linearly ambiguous aperiodic NWA$^{\rightarrow}$;*
2. *f is definable by a polynomially ambiguous aperiodic NWA$^{\rightarrow}$;*
3. *f is WFO$^{\rightarrow}$-definable.*

These theorems complete the picture initiated in [5, Theorem 5.11] where it is shown that, in commutative semirings, NWA (called *pebble two-way weighted automata*, with a more operational view of dropping/lifting pebbles, but the expressive power is identical) are equivalent to an extension of the logic WFO with a bounded weighted transitive closure operator. It is also noted that, even in non commutative semirings, the whole logic WFO$^{\rightarrow}$ with the bounded transitive closure operator can be translated into equivalent NWA.

4   From the Logic to Automata

In this section, we prove the implication $3 \Rightarrow 4$ of Theorem 2. This is obtained by a generalisation of the proof given by Droste and Gastin in [10, Theorem 16], where they only deal with restricted one-way logic and non-nested one-way automata. The proof is indeed simpler since we can rely on the use of nesting, contrary to them where they need a careful construction for formulas $\Pi_x \Psi$ of rWFO$^{\rightarrow}$.

The construction is performed by induction on the formula of WFO, making use of nesting in automata, as originally demonstrated in [5, Proposition 5.13] to transform every formula of a logic containing WFO (as well as a bounded weighted transitive closure operator) into NWA.

As known since [21,23], from every formula φ of FO, we can obtain an equivalent classical deterministic finite state automaton that is aperiodic, starts on the marker $\triangleright$ and ends on the marker $\triangleleft$. By putting on every transition the weight $\mathbf{1}$, this results in a 1-NWA$^{\rightarrow}$ $\mathcal{A}_\varphi$ that is unambiguous and aperiodic, whose abstract semantics is equal to the formula $\varphi ? \mathbf{1} : \mathbf{0}$.

Consider then a formula $\Phi = \varphi?\Phi_1 : \Phi_2$, where, by induction, we already have two r-NWA $\mathcal{A}_1$ and $\mathcal{A}_2$ for Φ_1 and Φ_2 (without loss of generality we adapt the maximal level r of nesting by adding useless levels). We can use the 1-NWA$^{\rightarrow}$ $\mathcal{A}_\varphi$ in order to produce an r-NWA equivalent to Φ: the first level consists in $\mathcal{A}_\varphi$, and once it unambiguously reach the marker $\lhd$, we continue the run by going back to the left marker, and continue either to $\mathcal{A}_1$ or to $\mathcal{A}_2$, whether the formula φ was concluded to be satisfied or not, respectively.[1]

The sum and product of two formulas can be computed by taking the disjoint union of two automata, or by starting the computation of the second after the computation of the first one (either by going back to the beginning of the word, or using a level of nesting).

For the quantification operators, we use one more level of nesting. Suppose that we have an r-NWA$(\mathsf{K}, A \times \{0,1\})$ $\mathcal{A}$ equivalent to a formula Φ with a free variable x. Then, the formula $\Sigma_x \Phi$ can be defined by the following $(r+1)$-NWA(K, A), making use of the fact that we can non-deterministically start and end a run wherever we want: the automaton thus has a single transition that calls $\mathcal{A}$. For the Π_x operator, the toplevel automaton scans the whole word from left to right, and calls $\mathcal{A}$ on each position (that is not a marker). For the Π_x^{-1} operator, we do the same but starting from the right marker and scanning the whole word from right to left. In both the cases, the root of the resulting automaton is aperiodic.

To conclude that the constructed NWA is linearly ambiguous and aperiodic, we make use of the fact that linearly ambiguous aperiodic automata are closed under disjoint union, nesting and concatenation with unambiguous (even finitely ambiguous) automata. It is indeed true for the case of disjoint unions, the individual automata still preserve the aperiodicity in their simulations and any run in the new automaton must be restricted to one of the automata. In the case of nesting, every transition of the *soon-to-be-child* automaton is replaced by all its extensions with respect to the input letter. Since the transitions are now oblivious to the marking of an input, the aperiodicity of the new child automaton is once again ensured under the extended alphabet. To understand the closure of linear ambiguity of automata under concatenation with unambiguous automata, one must just observe that the concatenation of automata essentially multiples the ambiguities of the factor automata, since every run in the concatenation is the sequence of a run in the first factor and one in the second.

5 From Nested Sweeping Weighted Automata to the Logic

This section aims at proving the implication $5 \Rightarrow 3$ of Theorem 2. We shall first prove it in the 1-way case.

---

[1] In the proof of Theorem 3, we replace this construction by the use of nesting that allows one to restart from the first position of the word in order to compute the behaviour of either $\mathcal{A}_1$ or $\mathcal{A}_2$.

Lemma 2. *For all polynomially ambiguous aperiodic* r-NWA$^\rightarrow$ *(resp.* r-NWA$^\leftarrow$), *there exists an equivalent formula of* WFO$^\rightarrow$ *(resp.* WFO$^\leftarrow$).

Proof. Once again, we only deal with the left-to-right result, the other one being obtained symmetrically. Let $\mathcal{A}_{p,q}$ denote the r-NWA$^\rightarrow$ obtained from $\mathcal{A}$ where the initial and final states are p and q respectively. We prove by induction on r, that for all r-NWA$^\rightarrow$ $\mathcal{A}$ and each pair of states p and q, we can construct a WFO$^\rightarrow$ sentence $\Phi_{p,q}$ such that $\{\!|\mathcal{A}_{p,q}|\!\} = \{\!|\Phi_{p,q}|\!\}$. We then conclude by considering all initial states p and final states q.

If $r = 0$, the result follows, after trimming the root of $\mathcal{A}$ so that all states can be reached from an initial state and reach a final state (no matter if the descendant automata called on the transition indeed accept the word), directly from the construction of Droste and Gastin [10, Proposition 9 and Theorem 10]. Note that trimming the automaton does not alter its semantics. The main difference in our case is the fact that our automata can non-deterministically start and end in the middle of the word. We may however start by modifying them to force them to start on the left marker and end on the right marker: it suffices to add self-loop transitions at the beginning and the end of weight 1 (so that these additional transitions do not modify the abstract semantics).

We now suppose that $r > 0$, and assume that the result holds for $r - 1$. Consider an r-NWA$^\rightarrow$(K, A) $\mathcal{A}$ that we suppose trimmed. As in the previous case, we can produce a formula Φ for $\mathcal{A}$, abstracting away for now the weight $k_\mathcal{B}$ on the transitions that stands for a $(r-1)$-NWA$^\rightarrow$(K, $A \times \{0,1\}$) $\mathcal{B}$.

We use the induction hypothesis to produce a formula $\Phi_\mathcal{B}$ of WFO for every $(r-1)$-NWA$^\rightarrow$(K, $A \times \{0,1\}$) $\mathcal{B}$ that appears in the transitions of $\mathcal{A}$. We modify this formula so that we incorporate a fresh first order variable x standing for the position on which $\mathcal{B}$ is called. Then, we replace every subformula $P_{(a,i)}(y)$ with $(a,i) \in A \times \{0,1\}$ by $P_a(y) \wedge y = x$ if $i = 1$, $P_a(y) \wedge y \neq x$ if $i = 0$.

In the formula Φ produced by Droste and Gastin, each weight $k_\mathcal{B}$ appears in a subformula with a distinguished first order variable x encoding the position of the letter read by the transition that should compute the weight $k_\mathcal{B}$. Thus, we simply replace every such weight $k_\mathcal{B}$ by the modified formula $\Phi_\mathcal{B}$ above. □

We then turn to the case of sweeping automata.

Lemma 3. *For every polynomially ambiguous aperiodic* swNWA, *there exists an equivalent formula of* WFO.

Proof. The proof also goes by induction on the level of nesting, and follows the same construction as the previous lemma. The only novelty is the treatment of change of directions in the runs. We thus only consider the case of 0-swNWA below.

For a 0-swNWA $\mathcal{A} = \langle Q, \mathsf{Tr}, I, F \rangle$, we show that for each pair of states p and q, we can construct a formula of WFO $\Phi_{p,q}$ equivalent to $\mathcal{A}_{p,q}$. As before, without loss of generality, we can suppose that every accepting run starts on the left marker, and stops on the right marker.

Given a word $w = w_1 \cdots w_m$, every run from p to q on $\triangleright w \triangleleft$ can then be decomposed as

$$(p, \triangleright, k_0, \rightarrow, p_0)\rho_1(p_1, \triangleleft, k_2, \leftarrow, p_2)\rho_2(p_3, \triangleright, k_4, \rightarrow, p_4) \cdots$$
$$(p_{2n-1}, \triangleright, k_{2n}, \rightarrow, p_{2n})\rho_{2n+1}(p_{2n+1}, \triangleleft, k_{2n+2}, \leftarrow, q)$$

where ρ_{2i+1} only contains $\rightarrow$-transitions (for $i \in \{0, \ldots, n\}$), and ρ_{2i} only contains $\leftarrow$-transitions (for $i \in \{1, \ldots, n\}$). Since we assume polynomial ambiguity of $\mathcal{A}$, we must have $n \leq |Q|$. Otherwise, there exists a position which is visited twice in the same state, thus allowing infinitely many runs over the input word by pumping this looping fragment of the run. We then immediately obtain that, for every word w, the multiset $\{\!|\mathcal{A}_{p,q}|\!\}(w)$ can be decomposed as

$$\sum_{\substack{n \leq |Q| \\ (p,\triangleright,k_0,\rightarrow,p_0),\ldots, \\ (p_{2n+1},\triangleleft,k_{2n+2},\leftarrow,q) \in \mathsf{Tr}}} \{\!|k_0|\!\}\{\!|\overrightarrow{\mathcal{A}}_{p_0,p_1}|\!\}(w)\{\!|k_2|\!\}\{\!|\overleftarrow{\mathcal{A}}_{p_2,p_3}|\!\}(w) \cdots \{\!|\overrightarrow{\mathcal{A}}_{p_{2n},p_{2n+1}}|\!\}(w)\{\!|k_{2n+2}|\!\}$$

It remains to show that the above decomposition can be translated into an equivalent WFO sentence. Since trimming preserves aperiodicity, using Lemma 1, we know that for every $p, q \in Q$, both $\overrightarrow{\mathcal{A}}_{p,q}$ and $\overleftarrow{\mathcal{A}}_{p,q}$ are aperiodic. By Lemma 2, we can thus construct equivalent WFO sentences $\overleftarrow{\Phi}_{p,q}$ and $\overrightarrow{\Phi}_{p,q}$, respectively. We now define,

$$\Phi_{p,q} = \sum_{\substack{n \leq |Q| \\ (p,\triangleright,k_0,\rightarrow,p_0),\ldots, \\ (p_{2n+1},\triangleleft,k_{2n+2},\leftarrow,q) \in \mathsf{Tr}}} k_0 \cdot \overrightarrow{\Phi}_{p_0,p_1} \cdot k_2 \cdot \overleftarrow{\Phi}_{p_2,p_3} \cdots \overrightarrow{\Phi}_{p_{2n},p_{2n+1}} \cdot k_{2n+2}$$

It can be proved that $\{\!|\mathcal{A}_{p,q}|\!\} = \{\!|\Phi_{p,q}|\!\}$. Finally, we set $\Phi = \sum_{p \in I, q \in F} \Phi_{p,q}$ and we can check that this formula is equivalent to $\mathcal{A}$. $\square$

6   From Nested Two-Way Weighted Automata to Nested Sweeping Weighted Automata

In this section we finally provide a sketch of the proof of $2 \Rightarrow 5$ in Theorem 2. This is the most novel and challenging part of the proof. In particular, notice that such an implication requires the use of nesting: the following example of 0-NWA does not have an equivalent 0-swNWA, even under the restriction of polynomial ambiguity and aperiodicity.

Example 4. Consider the 0-NWA(K, A) $\mathcal{A}_{ex}$ depicted in Fig. 2, over the alphabet $A = \{a, b\}$ and with weights $K = \{f, g\}$. Its semantics maps every word of A^* of the form $u = a^{m_1}b \cdots a^{m_n}b$ to the multiset $\{\!|f^{m_1}g^{m_1} \cdots f^{m_n}g^{m_n}|\!\}$, and every word of the form $u = a^{m_1}b \cdots a^{m_n}$ to the multiset $\{\!|f^{m_1}g^{m_1} \cdots f^{m_n}|\!\}$. The automaton $\mathcal{A}_{ex}$ is unambiguous (even deterministic). By a computation of its transition monoid, it can also be shown to be aperiodic. We can prove (see the long version [8]) that it has no equivalent 0-swNWA, since it is crucial that the automaton switches direction several times in the middle of the word. $\square$

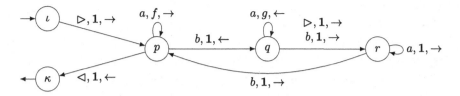

Fig. 2. A 0-NWA $\mathcal{A}_{ex}$.

Consider now a 0-NWA $\mathcal{A}$ (we will explain at the very end how to do this for an r-NWA). We build an swNWA $\overline{\mathcal{A}}$ equivalent to it, that will moreover be aperiodic and polynomially ambiguous if $\mathcal{A}$ is.

To understand our construction of $\overline{\mathcal{A}}$, consider an accepting simple run of $\mathcal{A}$ over a word u. In order to get closer to a sweeping automaton, we first split the run into subruns that go from the beginning of the run of the left marker to the right marker or the end of the run (possibly hitting in the mean time the left marker), and then to the left marker again (possibly hitting in the mean time the right marker), and so on. We get at most $|Q|$ subruns by doing so, since the run is simple (and thus cannot visit more than $|Q|$ times each marker).

For each subrun, we further decompose them as follows. We only present here the decomposition for the left-to-right case, the other one being symmetrical.

For a left-to-right run over the word $w = w_1 \cdots w_n$ (with w_1 possibly being equal to $\triangleright$, but $w_n \neq \triangleleft$), we decompose it into the interleaving of subruns with only $\rightarrow$-transitions, ending in an increasing sequence of positions $(i_j)_{1 \leq j \leq m}$, and some right-to-right subruns on the prefix words $w_1 \cdots w_{i_j}$. Formally, every left-to-right run can be written as $\rho_1 \lambda_1 \rho_2 \lambda_2 \cdots \lambda_{m-1} \rho_m$ where we have a sequence of positions $0 = i_0 < i_1 < \cdots < i_{m-1} < i_m = n+1$ such that

- for all $j \in \{1,\ldots,m\}$, ρ_j is a run over $w_{i_{j-1}+1} \cdots w_{i_j-1}$ with only $\rightarrow$-transitions: notice that this run can be empty if $i_j = i_{j-1} + 1$;
- for all $j \in \{1,\ldots,m-1\}$, λ_j is a right-to-right run over $w_1 \cdots w_{i_j}$ that starts with a $\leftarrow$-transition.

We exemplify the decomposition on the left of Fig. 3. We thus build an NWA $\overline{\mathcal{A}}$ whose root automaton is a sweeping automaton that emulates the black ρ-parts, interleaved with some new $\rightarrow$-transitions from state p (in a position i_j) to state q (in the corresponding position $i_j + 1$): the weight of this transition is a (non-sweeping) NWA(K, $A \times \{0,1\}$) $\mathcal{A}_{(p,q)}$ that is in charge of emulating the blue subrun λ_j from state p to state q of $\mathcal{A}$, keeping marked the position i_j in the second component of the alphabet $A \times \{0,1\}$.

We treat the various new automata $\mathcal{A}_{(p,q)}$ recursively to transform them to sweeping automata too. We thus similarly decompose the λ-subruns as before, by adapting the previous decomposition working only for left-to-right runs. In the decomposition of a right-to-right run over the word $w = w_1 \cdots w_n$ (with w_1 possibly being equal to $\triangleright$, but $w_n \neq \triangleleft$), the ρ-parts will be right-to-left, and we will add a special left-to-right additional run τ at the end to come back

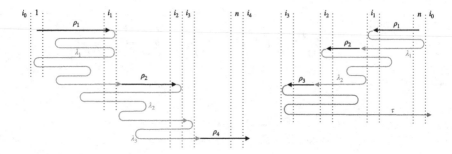

Fig. 3. On the left, the decomposition of a left-to-right run as a sequence $\rho_1\lambda_1\rho_2\lambda_2\rho_3\lambda_3\rho_4$ with ρ_3 being empty. On the right, the decomposition of a right-to-right run as a sequence $\rho_1\lambda_1\rho_2\lambda_2\rho_3\tau$.

to the right of the word. Formally, every right-to-right run can be written as $\rho_1\lambda_1\rho_2\lambda_2\cdots\lambda_{m-1}\rho_m\tau$ where we have a sequence of positions $1 \le i_m < \cdots < i_1 < i_0 = n + 1$ such that

- for all $j \in \{1,\ldots,m\}$, ρ_j is a left-to-right run over $w_{i_j+1}\cdots w_{i_{j-1}-1}$ with only $\rightarrow$-transitions: notice that this run can be empty if $i_{j-1} = i_j + 1$;
- for all $j \in \{1,\ldots,m-1\}$, λ_j is a left-to-left run over $w_{i_j}\cdots w_n$ that starts with a $\rightarrow$-transition;
- τ is a left-to-right run over $w_{i_m}\cdots w_n$.

We exemplify the decomposition on the right of Fig. 3. Once again, the automaton $\mathcal{A}_{(p,q)}$ is transformed into a NWA where the root automaton is a sweeping automaton that emulates the black ρ-parts, interleaved with some new $\leftarrow$-transitions with a weight being a NWA that computes the λ-subruns as well as the τ one. We once again treat these NWA recursively similarly as before (new cases occur in terms of directions).

This recursive decomposition of the runs, and thus the associated construction of sweeping automata, can be terminated after a bounded number of iterations. Indeed, in all simple runs of $\mathcal{A}$, no more than $|Q|$ configurations are visited for a particular position of the word. Since each recursive step in the decomposition consumes each position in the black runs, this implies that after $|Q|$ steps, there are no remaining blue subruns to consider. At level $|Q|$ of nesting, we thus do not allow anymore the addition of new transitions that would simulate further blue λ-subruns. The previous argument is the core of the correctness proof showing that the sweeping automaton produced is equivalent to $\mathcal{A}$.

In case $\mathcal{A}$ is an r-NWA, we use the black ρ-subruns to compute the children automata of $\mathcal{A}$ with nested calls. In contrast the added transitions that are supposed to launch the emulation of the blue λ-subruns call another sweeping automaton below.

Example 5. We apply the construction on the 0-NWA of Example 4. This will produce the 2-swNWA $\overline{\mathcal{A}}$ in Fig. 4. We also depict the actual decomposition of

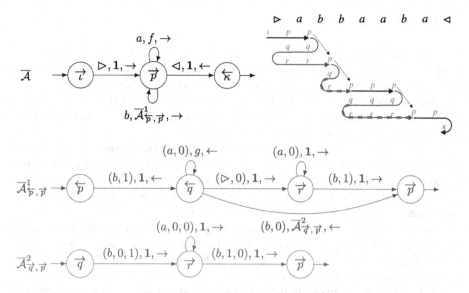

Fig. 4. 2-swNWA $\overline{\mathcal{A}}$ obtained by our construction, starting from the automaton of Example 4, and the decomposition of a run of this automaton showing which sweeping automaton computes each subrun.

a run over the word $\triangleright abbaaba \triangleleft$. The black subruns are the ρ-parts that are computed by the sweeping root automaton (it is sweeping, and not one way, just because of the final transition). The automaton $\overline{\mathcal{A}}^1_{\overleftarrow{p}, \overrightarrow{p}}$ is in charge of computing the blue λ-subruns. Notice that the subscript tells the automaton that it should start (at the marked position, which is checked by the first transition of the automaton) in state p going left, and should stop (once again at the marked position) in state p going right. There are two cases. For the leftmost λ-subrun, the sweeping automaton can entirely compute it. For the other ones, it cannot since there is a change of direction in the middle of the word. The red dotted part is thus the τ-final piece of the decomposition in the second step of the recursion, that is taken care of by automaton $\overline{\mathcal{A}}^2_{\overrightarrow{q}, \overrightarrow{p}}$.

The above construction preserves the ambiguity of the automata. However, we are not able to directly show that it preserves aperiodicity. We must encode more information in the state space of the various sweeping automata in order to allow for the proof of aperiodicity. In particular, we encode some pieces of information on the behaviours allowed in the current position, allowing us to better understand the structure of the transition monoid of the built automaton. The full construction and proof is given in the long version [8], which concludes the proof of the last implication of Theorem 2.

7   Conclusion

We have extended the results of Droste and Gastin [10] relating restricted weighted first-order logic and aperiodic weighted automata with some restrictions about ambiguity. We thus have closed open questions raised by them, introducing an abstract semantics for a full fragment of weighted first-order logic, and showing the equivalence between this logic and aperiodic nested weighted automaton with linear or polynomial ambiguity.

We have only studied linear and polynomial ambiguity, contrary to Droste and Gastin that have also characterised finitely-ambiguous and unambiguous aperiodic weighted automata with fragments of the logic. We leave as future work similar study for nested weighted automata, but we do hope that similar restrictions may apply also in our more general case.

However, dropping the condition on polynomial ambiguity would certainly lead to a logical fragment beyond weighted first-order logic. In particular, the main difficulty is that the logic is not easily able to check the simplicity condition of the accepting runs in this case.

Having introduced two-way navigations (and also nesting) makes possible to ask similar questions to other input structures than words, like finite ranked or unranked trees [16], nested words [3,14], or even graphs [4]. Nested weighted automata and weighted logics have already been studied in this setting, without any characterisation of the power of first-order fragments.

Last but not least, contrary to the unweighted setting, our characterization (as well as the one by Droste and Gastin) does not yet lead to a procedure deciding if the series recognised by a given (nested two-way) weighted automaton is indeed recognisable by an aperiodic one, i.e. in the convenient first-order fragment of the logic. We still lack the algebraic tools allowing for such decision procedures.

References

1. Birget, J.C.: Concatenation of inputs in a two-way automaton. Theoret. Comput. Sci. **63**(2), 141–156 (1989)
2. Birget, J.C.: Two-way automaton computations. RAIRO-Theor. Inform. Appl. **24**(1), 47–66 (1990)
3. Bollig, B., Gastin, P., Monmege, B.: Weighted specifications over nested words. In: Pfenning, F. (ed.) FoSSaCS 2013. LNCS, vol. 7794, pp. 385–400. Springer, Heidelberg (2013). https://doi.org/10.1007/978-3-642-37075-5_25
4. Bollig, B., Gastin, P., Monmege, B., Zeitoun, M.: Logical characterization of weighted pebble walking automata. In: CSL-LICS 2014. ACM (2014). https://doi.org/10.1145/2603088.2603118
5. Bollig, B., Gastin, P., Monmege, B., Zeitoun, M.: Pebble weighted automata and weighted logics. ACM Trans. Comput. Log. **15**(2:15) (2014). https://doi.org/10.1145/2579819
6. Büchi, J.R.: Weak second-order arithmetic and finite automata. Zeitschrift Math. Log. Grundlagen Math. **6**, 66–92 (1960)

7. Carton, O., Dartois, L.: Aperiodic two-way transducers and FO-transductions. Research Report 2103.15651, arXiv (2021)
8. Dhruv, N., Monmege, B.: An automata theoretic characterization of weighted first-order logic. Research Report 2307.14707, arXiv (2023). https://arxiv.org/abs/2307.14707
9. Droste, M., Gastin, P.: Weighted automata and weighted logics. Theoret. Comput. Sci. **380**(1–2), 69–86 (2007)
10. Droste, M., Gastin, P.: Aperiodic weighted automata and weighted first-order logic. In: MFCS 2019. No. 76 in LIPIcs, Schloss Dagstuhl-Leibniz-Zentrum für Informatik (2019). https://doi.org/10.4230/LIPIcs.MFCS.2019.76
11. Droste, M., Götze, D., Märcker, S., Meinecke, I.: Weighted tree automata over valuation monoids and their characterization by weighted logics. In: Kuich, W., Rahonis, G. (eds.) Algebraic Foundations in Computer Science. LNCS, vol. 7020, pp. 30–55. Springer, Heidelberg (2011). https://doi.org/10.1007/978-3-642-24897-9_2
12. Droste, M., Kuich, W., Vogler, H.: Handbook of Weighted Automata. EATCS Monographs in Theoretical Computer Science, Springer, Heidelberg (2009). https://doi.org/10.1007/978-3-642-01492-5
13. Droste, M., Meinecke, I.: Weighted automata and weighted MSO logics for average and long-time behaviors. Inf. Comput. **220–221**, 44–59 (2012)
14. Droste, M., Pibaljommee, B.: Weighted nested word automata and logics over strong bimonoids. In: Moreira, N., Reis, R. (eds.) CIAA 2012. LNCS, vol. 7381, pp. 138–148. Springer, Heidelberg (2012). https://doi.org/10.1007/978-3-642-31606-7_12
15. Droste, M., Rahonis, G.: Weighted automata and weighted logics on infinite words. In: Ibarra, O.H., Dang, Z. (eds.) DLT 2006. LNCS, vol. 4036, pp. 49–58. Springer, Heidelberg (2006). https://doi.org/10.1007/11779148_6
16. Droste, M., Vogler, H.: Weighted logics for unranked tree automata. Theory Comput. Syst. **48**, 23–47 (2011)
17. Elgot, C.C.: Decision problems of finite automata design and related arithmetics. Trans. Am. Math. Soc. **98**, 21–52 (1961)
18. Fülöp, Z., Stüber, T., Vogler, H.: A Büchi-like theorem for weighted tree automata over multioperator monoids. Theory Comput. Syst. **50**, 241–278 (2012)
19. Gastin, P., Monmege, B.: Adding pebbles to weighted automata: easy specification and efficient evaluation. Theoret. Comput. Sci. **534**, 24–44 (2014). https://doi.org/10.1016/j.tcs.2014.02.034
20. Gastin, P., Monmege, B.: A unifying survey on weighted logics and weighted automata. Soft. Comput. **22**(4), 1047–1065 (2015). https://doi.org/10.1007/s00500-015-1952-6
21. McNaughton, R.F., Papert, S.A.: Counter-Free Automata, vol. 65. MIT Press, Cambridge (1971)
22. Schützenberger, M.P.: On the definition of a family of automata. Inf. Control **4**, 245–270 (1961)
23. Schützenberger, M.P.: On finite monoids having only trivial subgroups. Inf. Control **8**, 190–194 (1965)
24. Trakhtenbrot, B.A.: Finite automata and logic of monadic predicates. Dokl. Akad. Nauk SSSR **149**, 326–329 (1961)

Probabilistic Systems

Graph-Based Reductions for Parametric and Weighted MDPs

Kasper Engelen◉, Guillermo A. Pérez◉, and Shrisha Rao(✉)◉

University of Antwerp – Flanders Make, Antwerp, Belgium
{kasper.engelen,guillermo.perez,shrisha.rao}@uantwerpen.be

Abstract. We study the complexity of reductions for weighted reachability in parametric Markov decision processes. That is, we say a state p is never worse than q if for all valuations of the polynomial indeterminates it is the case that the maximal expected weight that can be reached from p is greater than the same value from q. In terms of computational complexity, we establish that determining whether p is never worse than q is **coETR**-complete. On the positive side, we give a polynomial-time algorithm to compute the equivalence classes of the order we study for Markov chains. Additionally, we describe and implement two inference rules to under-approximate the never-worse relation and empirically show that it can be used as an efficient preprocessing step for the analysis of large Markov decision processes.

Keywords: Markov decision process · sensitivity analysis · model reduction

1 Introduction

Markov decision processes (MDPs, for short) are useful mathematical models to capture the behaviour of systems involving some random components and discrete (non-deterministic) choices. In the field of verification, they are studied as formal models of randomised algorithms, protocols, etc. [1,6] In artificial intelligence, MDPs provide the theoretical foundations upon which reinforcement learning algorithms are based [17,20].

From the verification side, efficient tools have been implemented for the analysis of MDPs. These include, for instance, PRISM [15], Storm [12], and Modest [9]. While those tools can handle ever larger and complexer MDPs, as confirmed by the most recent Comparison of Tools for the Analysis of Quantitative Formal Models [4], they still suffer from the state-explosion problem. While most tools can check the MDP against a rich class of specifications (linear temporal logic, probabilistic computation-tree logic, etc.), they often reduce the task to reachability analysis and solve the latter using some version of value iteration [10] which has an exponential worst-case complexity. When implementing

This work was supported by the Belgian FWO "SAILor" (G030020N) and Flemish inter-university (iBOF) "DESCARTES" projects.
© The Author(s), under exclusive license to Springer Nature Switzerland AG 2023
É. André and J. Sun (Eds.): ATVA 2023, LNCS 14215, pp. 137–157, 2023.
https://doi.org/10.1007/978-3-031-45329-8_7

model checkers, it is usual for a pre-processing step to remove as many states and transitions as possible while preserving the maximal reachability probability.

In this work we focus on reduction techniques to improve the runtime of MDP analysis algorithms as implemented in the aforementioned verification tools. We are particularly interested in reductions based on the graph underlying the MDP which do not make use of the concrete probability distributions. Such reductions can also be applied to partially known MDPs that arise in the context of reinforcement learning [2]. Several graph and automata-theoretic reduction techniques with these properties already exist. They focus on the computation of states with specific properties, for instance: extremal-value states (i.e. states whose probability of reaching the target set of states is 0 or 1), maximal end components (i.e. sets of states which can almost-surely reach each other), and essential states [5,7] (i.e. sets of states which form a graph-theoretic separator between some given state and the target set), to name a few. In [16], Le Roux and Pérez have introduced a partial order among states, called the *never-worse relation* (NWR, for short), that subsumes all of the notions listed above. Their main results in that work were establishing that the NWR the natural decision problem of comparing two states is **coNP**-complete, and giving a few inference rules to under-approximate the full NWR.

In this paper, we extend the NWR to weighted reachability in parametric MDPs. Formally, we have assign weights to the target set of states and allow for transitions to be labelled with polynomials instead of just concrete probability values. Then, we say a state p is never worse than q if for all valuations of the indeterminates, it is the case that the maximal expected weight that can be reached from p is at least the same value from q. Beyond the fact that weighted reachability is a natural extension of reachability, it is well-known that optimizing the expected mean-payoff can be reduced to optimizing expected weighted reachability (see, e.g., [14]).

We show that determining whether p is NWR than q is **coETR**-complete, so it is polynomial-time interreducible with determining the truth value of a statement in the existential theory of the reals. Along the way, we prove that the NWR for weighted reachability reduces in polynomial time to the NWR for (Boolean) reachability. Regarding theoretical results, we further establish that the equivalence classes of the NWR can be computed in polynomial time for a special class of parametric Markov chains. In contrast, for parametric MDPs, deciding equivalence is just as hard as the corresponding NWR decision problem. Finally, we improve (and corrected small errors in) the inference rules from Le Roux and Pérez and give a concrete algorithm to use them to reduce the size of a given MDP. We then evaluate the an implementation of our algorithm on a number of benchmarks from the Quantitative Verification Benchmark Set [11].

2   Preliminaries

For a directed graph $\mathcal{G} = (V, E)$ and a vertex $u \in V$, we write $uE = \{v \in V \mid (u, v) \in E\}$ to denote the set of *(immediate) successors* of u. A *sink* is a vertex

u such that $uE = \emptyset$. For a finite alphabet Σ, Σ^* is the set of all finite words over Σ including the empty word ε, and Σ^+ is the set of all non-empty words.

Let $X = \{x_1, \ldots, x_k\}$ be a finite set of variables and $p(x_1, \ldots, x_k)$ be a polynomial with rational coefficients on X. For a valuation $\mathsf{val} : X \to \mathbb{R}$ of the variables, we write $p[\mathsf{val}]$ for the image of p given $\mathsf{val}(X)$, i.e. $p(\mathsf{val}(x_1), \ldots, \mathsf{val}(x_k))$. We write $p \equiv 0$ to denote the fact that p is syntactically equal to 0 and $p = 0$ to denote that its image is 0 for all valuations. Finally, we write $\mathbb{Q}[X]$ to denote the set of all polynomials with rational coefficients on X.

2.1 Stochastic Models

A distribution on a finite set S is a function $f : S \to \mathbb{R}_{\geq 0}$, with $\sum_{s \in S} f(s) = 1$.

Definition 1 (Markov chains). *A (weighted) Markov chain is a tuple $\mathcal{C} = (S, \mu, T, \rho)$ with a finite set of states S, a set of target states $T \subseteq S$, a probabilistic transition function $\mu : (S \setminus T) \times S \to \mathbb{R}_{\geq 0}$ with $\forall s \in S \setminus T : \sum_{s' \in S} \mu(s, s') = 1$ (i.e. μ maps non-target states onto probability distributions over states), and a weight function $\rho : T \to \mathbb{Q}$ that assigns weights to the target states.*

Note that all states in T are sinks: $\mu(t, s)$ is undefined for all $t \in T, s \in S$.

A *run* of $\mathcal{C}$ is a finite non-empty word $\pi = s_0 \ldots s_n$ over S such that $0 < \mu(s_i, s_{i+1})$ for all $0 \leq i < n$. The run π *reaches* $s' \in S$ if $s' = s_n$. The probability associated with a run is defined as $\mathbb{P}_\mu(\pi) = \prod_{0 \leq i < n} \mu(s_i, s_{i+1})$.

We also define the probability of reaching a set of states.

Definition 2 (Reachability). *Given a Markov chain $\mathcal{C} = (S, \mu, T, \rho)$, an initial state $s_0 \in S$ and a set of states $B \subseteq S$, we denote by $\mathbb{P}_{\mathcal{C}}^{s_0}[\lozenge B]$ the probability of reaching B from s_0. If $s_0 \in B$ then $\mathbb{P}_{\mathcal{C}}^{s_0}[\lozenge B] = 1$, otherwise:*

$$\mathbb{P}_{\mathcal{C}}^{s_0}[\lozenge B] = \sum_{\pi = s_0 \ldots s_n \in (S \setminus B)^+ B} \mathbb{P}_\mu(\pi).$$

For brevity, when $B = \{a\}$, we write $\mathbb{P}_{\mathcal{C}}^{s_0}[\lozenge a]$ instead of $\mathbb{P}_{\mathcal{C}}^{s_0}[\lozenge \{a\}]$.

Now, we use the weights of targets states to define a weighted reachability value.

Definition 3 (Value of a state). *Given a Markov chain $\mathcal{C} = (S, \mu, T, \rho)$ and a state $s_0 \in S$, the (expected reward) value of s_0 is $\mathrm{Rew}_{\mathcal{C}}^{s_0} = \sum_{t \in T} \mathbb{P}_{\mathcal{C}}^{s_0}[\lozenge t] \cdot \rho(t)$.*

Finally, we recall a definition of parametric Markov decision processes.

Definition 4 (Markov decision processes). *A weighted and parametric Markov decision process (wpMDP) is a tuple $\mathcal{M} = (S, A, X, \delta, T, \rho)$ with finite sets S of states; A of actions; X of parameters; and $T \subseteq S$ of target states. $\delta : (S \setminus T) \times A \times S \to \mathbb{Q}[X]$ is a probabilistic transition function that maps transitions onto polynomials and $\rho : T \to \mathbb{Q}$ is a weight function.*

We assume, without loss of generality, that there is an extra state *fail* $\in T$, with $\rho(fail) = 0$. Intuitively, this is a "bad" target state that we want to avoid. Throughout the paper, we sometimes only specify partial probabilistic transition functions. This slight abuse of notation is no loss of generality as (for all of our purposes) we can have all unspecified transitions lead to *fail* with probability 1. We also assume that all states with no path to a target state can be replaced with a state with a transition to *fail*. It is known that all such states can be computed in polynomial time [1, Algorithm 45].

In this paper, we will work with the following subclasses of wpMDPs.

pMDPs or (non-weighted) parametric MDPs are the subclass of wpMDPs which have only two states in T, namely, $T = \{fin, fail\}$ where $\rho(fin) = 1$ and $\rho(fail) = 0$. For pMDPs, we omit ρ from the tuple defining them since we already know the weights of the targets.

w$\tilde{p}$MDPs or weighted *trivially parametric* MDPs have, for each transition, a unique variable as polynomial. That is, the probabilistic transition function is such that $\delta(s, a, s') \equiv 0$ or $\delta(s, a, s') = x_{s,a,s'} \in X$, for all $(s, a, s') \in (S \backslash T) \times A \times S$. Since all parameters are trivial in such wpMDPs, we omit their use. Instead, an w$\tilde{p}$MDPs is a tuple (S, A, Δ, T, ρ) where $\Delta \subseteq (S \backslash T) \times A \times S$ represents all transitions that do not have probability 0.

$\tilde{p}$MDPs or (non-weighted) trivially parametric MDPs are both non-weighted and trivially parametric. We thus omit ρ and X from their tuple representation (S, A, Δ, T) where Δ is as defined for w$\tilde{p}$MDPs.

For the rest of this section, let us fix a wpMDP $\mathcal{M} = (S, A, X, \delta, T, \rho)$.

Definition 5 (Graph preserving valuation, from [13]). *A valuation* val : $X \rightarrow \mathbb{R}$ *is graph preserving if the following hold for all* $s \in (S \backslash T), s' \in S, a \in A$:

- *probabilities are non-negative:* $\delta(s, a, s')[\mathsf{val}] \geq 0$,
- *outgoing probabilities induce a distribution:* $\sum_{s'' \in S} \delta(s, a, s'')[\mathsf{val}] = 1$,
- $\delta(s, a, s') \not\equiv 0 \implies \delta(s, a, s')[\mathsf{val}] \neq 0$.

The set of all such graph-preserving valuations is written as $\mathsf{Val}_{\mathcal{M}}^{\mathrm{gp}}$.

A graph-preserving valuation of any wpMDP $\mathcal{M}$ gives an MDP (with real probabilities) that we call $\mathcal{M}[\mathsf{val}]$ by substituting each parameter with the corresponding real number and computing the value of the polynomials on each transition. Such an MDP is equivalent to the ones that appear in the literature [1,13,16].

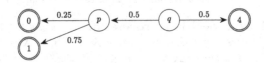

Fig. 1. Example of a Markov chain $\mathcal{C}$ with $\mathrm{Rew}_{\mathcal{C}}^{p} = 0.75$ and $\mathrm{Rew}_{\mathcal{C}}^{q} = 2.375$. Circles depict states; arrows, transitions; double circles, target states with their integer labels being their weights.

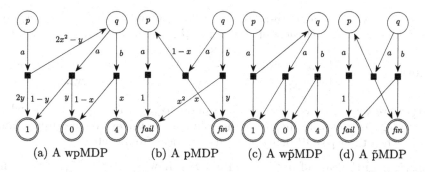

(a) A wpMDP   (b) A pMDP   (c) A wp̄MDP   (d) A p̄MDP

Fig. 2. Examples of all wpMDP subclasses we consider. Solid squares represent state-action pairs (see Sect. 2.2).

Definition 6 (Strategies). *A (memoryless deterministic) strategy σ is a function $\sigma : (S \backslash T) \rightarrow A$ that maps states to actions. The set of all such deterministic memoryless strategies is written as $\Sigma^{\mathcal{M}}$.*

The wpMDP $\mathcal{M}$ with a valuation val and strategy σ induce a Markov chain $\mathcal{M}_{\text{val}}^{\sigma} = (S, \mu, T, \rho)$ where $\mu(s, s') = \delta(s, \sigma(s), s')[\text{val}]$ for all $s \in (S \setminus T), s' \in S$.

Remark 1. Note that we only consider memoryless deterministic strategies. This is because we are interested in strategies that maximise the expected reward value for a given valuation. Since all targets are trapping, one can prove, e.g., by reduction to quantitative reachability or expected mean payoff [1], that for all valuations, there is an optimal memoryless and deterministic strategy.

2.2 The Graph of a WpMDP

It is convenient to work with a graph representation of a wpMDP. In that regard, we consider states s (depicted as circles $\bigcirc$) and state-action pairs (s, a) (depicted as squares $\square$) to be vertices. We call the vertices in $S_N = (S \setminus T) \times A$ *nature vertices* and we will use these to denote state-action pairs throughout the paper. We use $V = S \cup S_N$ to denote the set of vertices of a wpMDP. The graph $\mathcal{G}(\mathcal{M}) = (V, E)$ of a wpMDP is thus a bipartite graph with S and S_N being the two partitions. We define the set of edges as follows.

$$E = \{(s, (s, a)) \in S \times S_N \mid \exists s' \in S \setminus \{fail\} : \delta(s, a, s') \not\equiv 0\}$$
$$\cup \{((s, a), s') \in S_N \times S \mid \delta(s, a, s') \not\equiv 0\}$$

That is, there is an edge from a state to a nature vertex if the nature vertex has that state as the first component of the tuple and if it can reach some state other than *fail* with non-zero probability; there is one from a nature vertex to a state if the polynomial on the corresponding transition is not syntactically zero.

Let val $\in$ Val$_{\mathcal{M}}^{\text{gp}}$ be a graph-preserving valuation and $\sigma \in \Sigma^{\mathcal{M}}$ a strategy. We now define the *(reward) value* of a vertex in $\mathcal{G}(\mathcal{M})$ with respect to val and σ.

$$\text{Rew}^{\sigma}_{\mathcal{M}[\text{val}]}(v) = \begin{cases} \sum_{s' \in vE} \delta(s, a, s')[\text{val}] \cdot \text{Rew}^{\sigma}_{\mathcal{M}[\text{val}]}(s') & \text{if } v = (s, a) \in S_N \\ \text{Rew}^{v}_{\mathcal{M}^{\sigma}_{\text{val}}} & \text{otherwise} \end{cases}$$

Further, we write $\text{Rew}^{\sigma}_{\mathcal{M}[\text{val}]}(v)$ for the value $\max_{\sigma \in \Sigma^{\mathcal{M}}} \text{Rew}^{\sigma}_{\mathcal{M}[\text{val}]}(v)$, i.e. when the strategy is chosen to maximise the value of the vertex. We use $\text{Rew}^{\sigma}_{\text{val}}$ and $\text{Rew}^{*}_{\text{val}}$ when the wpMDP being referred to is clear from context.

Remark 2. In the case of pMDPs and p̃MDPs, $\text{Rew}^{\sigma}_{\mathcal{M}[\text{val}]}(v) = \mathbb{P}^{v}_{\mathcal{M}^{\sigma}_{\text{val}}}[\lozenge \text{fin}]$. The reader can easily verify this by looking at the definition of reward.

Example 1. In Fig. 2a, the valuation val $= \{x = 0.6, y = 0.28\}$ is a graph-preserving one. We then get $\text{Rew}^{*}_{\text{val}}(q, a) = 1 - 0.28 = 0.72$ and $\text{Rew}^{*}_{\text{val}}(q, b) = 0.6(4) = 2.4$. Hence, the optimal strategy for state q will be to choose action b and $\text{Rew}^{*}_{\text{val}}(q) = 2.4$. Now, we get that $\text{Rew}^{*}_{\text{val}}(p) = \text{Rew}^{*}_{\text{val}}(p, a) = 2(0.28) + (2(0.6)^2 - 0.28)\text{Rew}^{*}_{\text{val}}(q) = 1.616$.

2.3   The Never-Worse Relation

Let $\mathcal{M} = (S, A, X, \delta, T, \rho)$ be a wpMDP and $\mathcal{G}(\mathcal{M}) = (V, E)$. We will now take the never-worse relation (NWR) [16] and generalise it to take into account polynomials on transitions and weighted target states.

Definition 7 (Never-worse relation for wpMDPs). *A subset $W \subseteq V$ of vertices is* never worse *than a vertex $v \in V$, written $v \trianglelefteq W$, if and only if:*

$$\forall \text{val} \in \text{Val}_{\mathcal{M}}^{\text{gp}}, \exists w \in W : \text{Rew}^{*}_{\text{val}}(v) \leq \text{Rew}^{*}_{\text{val}}(w).$$

We write $v \sim w$ if $v \trianglelefteq \{w\}$ and $w \trianglelefteq \{v\}$, and $\tilde{v}$ for the equivalence class of v.

For brevity, we write $v \trianglelefteq w$ instead of $v \trianglelefteq \{w\}$. For two subsets $U, W \subseteq V$, we write $U \trianglelefteq W$ if and only if $U \neq \emptyset$ and $u \trianglelefteq W$ for all $u \in U$.

Example 2. In Fig. 2a, we have $p \trianglelefteq q$. This is because the constraints $2x^2 - y + 2y = 1$ and $0 < 2y < 1$ on any graph preserving valuation ensure that $\frac{1}{2} < x$. Thus, $\text{Rew}^{*}_{\text{val}}(q) = \text{Rew}^{*}_{\text{val}}(q, a) > 2$. Now, the value of p will be a convex combination of 1 and $\text{Rew}^{*}_{\text{val}}(q)$. Hence, it's value will be at most the value of q.

3   From Weighted to Non-Weighted MDPs

In this section, we show that we can efficiently transform any wpMDP into a non-weighted one with a superset of states and such that the NWR is preserved. Technically, we have two reductions: one to transform wpMDPs into pMDPs and one to transform wp̃MDPs into p̃MDPs. The former is easier but makes use of the non-trivial polynomials labelling transitions while the latter is more involved. It follows that algorithms and complexity upper-bounds for the NWR as studied in [16] can be applied to the trivially parametric weighted case.

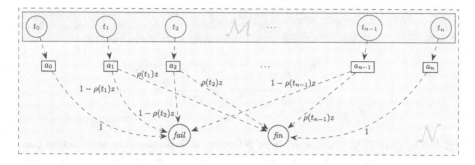

Fig. 3. The pMDP $\mathcal{N}$ constructed from $\mathcal{M}$, where $z = 1/\rho(t_n)$ and a_i represents the state-action pair (t_i, a). The ratio of the reward values in $\mathcal{N}$ of all the target states in $\mathcal{M}$ is the same as in $\mathcal{N}$.

Remark 3. Below, we will make the assumption that the target states all have distinct non-negative weights. That is $T = \{t_0, \ldots, t_n\}$ with $0 = \rho(t_0) < \rho(t_1) < \cdots < \rho(t_n)$. This is no loss of generality. If we have negative weights, we can subtract the smallest negative weight $(-k)$ from all the weights. This will make all the weights non-negative and the never-worse relations will be preserved since the reward value of each state will increase by k. If t_i and t_j have $\rho(t_i) = \rho(t_j)$ then, because all target states are trapping, we can add (on any action $a \in A$) a transition such that $\delta(t_i, a, t_j) = 1$ and remove remove t_i from T. This can be realised using logarithmic space, does not add states, and it preserves the NWR.

3.1 Removing Weights from Parametric MDPs

Let $\mathcal{M}$ be a wpMDP. We construct a pMDP $\mathcal{N}$ equivalent to $\mathcal{M}$ as described in Fig. 3. The idea is to add transitions from the target states to freshly added *fail* and *fin* states to preserve the ratio between the values of the original target states. That is, for all states $p, q \in T \setminus \{t_0\}$, our construction guarantees the following: $\mathrm{Rew}^p_{\mathcal{M}^\sigma_{\mathrm{val}}}/\mathrm{Rew}^q_{\mathcal{M}^\sigma_{\mathrm{val}}} = \mathrm{Rew}^p_{\mathcal{N}^\sigma_{\mathrm{val}}}/\mathrm{Rew}^q_{\mathcal{N}^\sigma_{\mathrm{val}}}$, for all parameter valuations $\mathrm{val} \in \mathrm{Val}^{\mathrm{gp}}_{\mathcal{M}}$ and all strategies $\sigma \in \Sigma^{\mathcal{M}}$. It is then easy to see, by the definition of values, that all other pairs of vertices in $\mathcal{G}(\mathcal{M})$ — excluding t_0, which preserves its exact value — also have the ratio between their values preserved.

Theorem 1. *Given a wpMDP $\mathcal{M}$, let $\mathcal{G}(\mathcal{M}) = (V, E)$ and $\mathcal{N}$ be the pMDP obtained by the above construction. If $v \in V$ and $W \subseteq V$, we have $v \trianglelefteq W$ in $\mathcal{M}$ if and only if $v \trianglelefteq W$ in $\mathcal{N}$.*

In the next section, we give an alternative reduction which preserves the property of being trivially parametric. That is, it does not add transitions with non-trivial probabilities.

3.2 Removing Weights from Trivially Parametric MDPs

From a given wp̃MDP $\mathcal{M}$, we construct a p̃MDP $\mathcal{N}$ by adding to it $n+3$ vertices and $3n+2$ edges as depicted in Fig. 4. To simplify things, we make the assumption

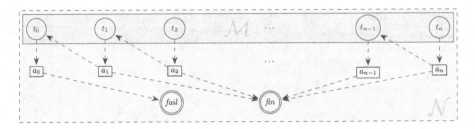

Fig. 4. The p̃MDP $\mathcal{N}$ constructed from $\mathcal{M}$ where a_i represents the state-action pair (t_i, a). The ordering of the reward values of the vertices is preserved but not the ratio.

that any nature vertex $v \in S_N$ which does not have a path to *fin* has an edge to t_0. This is no loss of generality as such vertices can be detected in polynomial time (see, e.g. [1, Algorithm 46]) and this preserves their value.

Unlike in the parametric case, the ratio of the reward values of the target vertices is not preserved but their ordering is: $\rho(t_i) < \rho(t_j)$ in $\mathcal{G}(\mathcal{M})$ if and only if $\mathbb{P}^{t_i}_{\mathcal{N}^\sigma_{\text{val}}}[\Diamond \textit{fin}] < \mathbb{P}^{t_j}_{\mathcal{N}^\sigma_{\text{val}}}[\Diamond \textit{fin}]$ for all valuations val $\in$ Val$^{\text{gp}}_{\mathcal{N}}$ and all strategies $\sigma \in \Sigma^{\mathcal{N}}$.

Lemma 1. *In the non-weighted p̃MDP $\mathcal{N}$, for all valuations* val $\in$ Val$^{\text{gp}}_{\mathcal{N}}$ *and all strategies* $\sigma \in \Sigma^{\mathcal{N}}$, *we have* $0 = \mathbb{P}^{t_0}_{\mathcal{N}^\sigma_{\text{val}}}[\Diamond \textit{fin}] < \mathbb{P}^{t_1}_{\mathcal{N}^\sigma_{\text{val}}}[\Diamond \textit{fin}] < \cdots < \mathbb{P}^{t_n}_{\mathcal{N}^\sigma_{\text{val}}}[\Diamond \textit{fin}]$.

We show that this property, although it may not seem intuitive, is sufficient to preserve all the never-worse relations.

Theorem 2. *Given a wp̃MDP $\mathcal{M}$, let $\mathcal{G}(\mathcal{M}) = (V, E)$ and $\mathcal{N}$ be the p̃MDP obtained by the above construction. If $v \in V$ and $W \subseteq V$, we have $v \trianglelefteq W$ in $\mathcal{M}$ if and only if $v \trianglelefteq W$ in $\mathcal{N}$.*

Proof (Sketch). We first prove the contrapositive of the "if" direction: Suppose $v \ntrianglelefteq W$ in the wp̃MDP $\mathcal{M}$, then there is a valuation val $\in$ Val$^{\text{gp}}_{\mathcal{M}}$ for which Rew$^*_{\mathcal{M}[\text{val}]}(v) >$ Rew$^*_{\mathcal{M}[\text{val}]}(w)$ for all $w \in W$. We can now construct a valuation val$' \in$ Val$^{\text{gp}}_{\mathcal{N}}$ so that Rew$^*_{\mathcal{N}[\text{val}']}(v) >$ Rew$^*_{\mathcal{N}[\text{val}']}(w)$ for all $w \in W$. The existence of such a val$'$ will show that $v \ntrianglelefteq W$ in $\mathcal{N}$, thus concluding the proof in this direction. More concretely, val$'$ is obtained from val by adding probabilities to the dashed edges in $\mathcal{G}(\mathcal{N})$ so that the ratio of the reward values of states in T in $\mathcal{N}$ is the same as the ratio of their weights in $\mathcal{M}$.

Second, we prove the contrapositive of the "only if" direction: Suppose $v \ntrianglelefteq W$ in the non-weighted p̃MDP $\mathcal{N}$. This means that there exists a valuation val $\in$ Val$^{\text{gp}}_{\mathcal{M}}$ such that Rew$^*_{\mathcal{N}[\text{val}]}(v) >$ Rew$^*_{\mathcal{N}[\text{val}]}(w)$ for all $w \in W$. We can then use the reward values of vertices in $\mathcal{G}(\mathcal{N})$ (for this fixed val) to partition the vertices so that all vertices in a same partition have the same reward value. This partition reveals some nice properties about the structure of $\mathcal{G}(\mathcal{N})$, and hence $\mathcal{G}(\mathcal{M})$. We use this to construct a new valuation val$' \in$ Val$^{\text{gp}}_{\mathcal{M}}$ for the original wp̃MDP $\mathcal{M}$ and show that Rew$^*_{\mathcal{M}[\text{val}']}(v) >$ Rew$^*_{\mathcal{M}[\text{val}']}(w)$ for all $w \in W$.   □

4   The Complexity of Deciding the NWR

It has been shown in [16] that deciding the NWR for trivially parametric MDPs[1] is **coNP**-complete and remains **coNP**-hard even if the set of actions is a singleton (i.e. the MDP is essentially a Markov chain) and even when comparing singletons only (i.e. $v \trianglelefteq w$). We have shown, in the previous section, that any w$\tilde{\mathrm{p}}$MDP can be reduced (in polynomial time) to a $\tilde{\mathrm{p}}$MDP while preserving all the never-worse relations. Observe that the reduction does not require adding new actions. These imply **coNP**-completeness for deciding the NWR in w$\tilde{\mathrm{p}}$MDPs.

Theorem 3. *Given a w$\tilde{\mathrm{p}}$MDP $\mathcal{M}$ with $\mathcal{G}(\mathcal{M}) = (V, E)$ and $v \in V, W \subseteq V$, determining whether $v \trianglelefteq W$ is **coNP**-complete. Moreover, the problem is **coNP**-hard even if both W and the set A of actions from $\mathcal{M}$ are singletons.*

Regarding general wpMDPs, known results [13,19] imply that deciding the NWR is **coETR**-hard. The *existential theory of the reals* (ETR) is the set of all true sentences of the form:

$$\exists x_1 \ldots \exists x_n \varphi(x_1, \ldots, x_n) \tag{1}$$

where φ is a quantifier-free (first-order) formula with inequalities and equalities as predicates and real polynomials as terms. The complexity class **ETR** [18] is the set of problems that reduce in polynomial time to determining the truth value of a sentence like in (1) and **coETR** is the set of problems whose complement is in **ETR**. It is known that $\mathbf{NP} \subseteq \mathbf{ETR} \subseteq \mathbf{PSPACE}$.

For completeness, we provide a self-contained proof of the NWR problem being **coETR**-hard even for pMDPs. To do so, we reduce from the bounded-conjunction-of-inequalities problem, BCON4INEQ for short. It asks, given polynomials $f_1, \ldots, f_m$ of degree 4, whether there is some valuation val : $X \rightarrow (0,1)$ such that $\bigwedge_{i=0}^{m} f_i[\mathsf{val}] < 0$? This problem is **ETR**-hard [13, Lemma 5].

Theorem 4. *Given a pMDP $\mathcal{M}$ with $\mathcal{G}(\mathcal{M}) = (V, E)$ and $v \in V, W \subseteq V$, determining whether $v \trianglelefteq W$ is **coETR**-complete. Moreover, the problem is **coETR**-hard even if both W and the set A of actions from $\mathcal{M}$ are singletons.*

Proof (Sketch). To show **coETR**-hardness, we first reduce BCON4INEQ to the problem of deciding whether there exists a graph-preserving valuation for a given pMDP $\mathcal{M}$. Let $f_1, \cdots, f_m$ be the polynomials. Let $k > k_i$ for all i where k_i is the sum of the absolute values of the coefficients of the polynomial f_i. We define new polynomials $f'_1, \ldots, f'_m$ where $f'_i = \frac{f_i}{k}$. Note that for any val : $X \rightarrow (0,1)$, we have $\bigwedge_{i=0}^{m} f_i[\mathsf{val}] < 0$ if and only if $\bigwedge_{i=0}^{m} f'_i[\mathsf{val}] < 0$ and we have $-1 < f'_i[\mathsf{val}] < 1$ for any such val. We now define a pMDP including the states and distributions shown in Fig. 5. All the edges from the set $\{n_1, \ldots, n_m\}$ to $\{fail, fin\}$ ensure that $0 < -f_i < 1$ for all $1 \leq i \leq m$ and the edges from the set $\{v_1, \ldots, v_n\}$ to $\{fail, fin\}$ ensure that the variables can only take values from the open set $(0,1)$.

---

[1] Technically, Le Roux and Pérez show that the problem is hard for *target arenas*. In appendix, we give reductions between target arenas and $\tilde{\mathrm{p}}$MDPs.

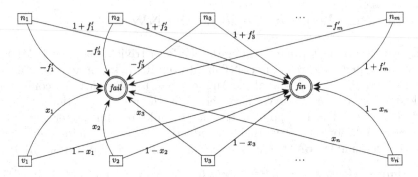

Fig. 5. The pMDP used to show **coETR**-hardness of determining whether there exists a graph-preserving valuation for a pMDP.

Thus, this pMDP has a graph-preserving valuation if and only if there is some val : $X \to (0,1)$ for which $-1 < f'_i < 0$. To conclude, we note that $\textit{fin} \not\trianglelefteq \textit{fail}$ if and only if there is a graph-preserving valuation for the pMDP we constructed. Observe that to obtain the full pMDP we can add states $\{s_1, \ldots, s_m\}$ and edges from s_i to n_i, for all i. Hence, the set of actions A can be a singleton.

To show that deciding the NWR is in **coETR**, we simply encode the negation of the NWR into a formula as in (1) that is in ETR if and only if the negation of the NWR holds. The encoding is quite natural and can be seen as a "symbolic" version of the classical linear programs used to encode MDP values. □

We conclude this section with a discussion on the NWR equivalence relation.

4.1   The Complexity of Deciding NWR Equivalences

Unfortunately, deciding NWR equivalences is just as hard as deciding the NWR in general. To prove this, we give a small gadget which ensures that $v \sim w$ if and only if some NWR holds.

Theorem 5. *Given a pMDP* $\mathcal{M}$ *with* $\mathcal{G}(\mathcal{M}) = (V, E)$ *and* $v, w \in V$, *determining whether* $v \sim w$ *is* **coETR**-*hard. If* $\mathcal{M}$ *is a* $\tilde{p}$*MDP then the problem is* **coNP**-*hard in general and in* **P** *if its set of actions* A *is a singleton.*

To show that NWR equivalences are decidable in polynomial time for $\tilde{p}$MDPs with one action, we argue that $u \sim w$ holds if and only if there exists a unique $z \in V$ such that $\mathbb{P}^u_C[\Diamond z] = \mathbb{P}^w_C[\Diamond z] = 1$. This characterisation allows us to compute all equivalence classes based on where every state is almost-surely reachable from. The latter can be done in polynomial time [1, Algorithm 45].

5   Action Pruning via the NWR

In this section, we show various ways to efficiently under-approximate the NWR — that is, obtain subsets of the relation — and use these under-approximations to reduce the size of the wpMDP by pruning actions and by collapsing equivalent states of a wpMDP. As we have shown in Sect. 3, any weighted w̃pMDP can be efficiently converted into a (non-weighted) p̃MDP while preserving all the never-worse relations from the original weighted model. Hence, we present under-approximations for non-weighted models only (i.e., $T = \{fin, fail\}$). We will also focus on trivially parametric MDPs only. Note that if $U \trianglelefteq W$ in a p̃MDP, then $U \trianglelefteq W$ in any pMDP having the same underlying graph as the first p̃MDP. (That is, as long as it admits a graph-preserving valuation.)

Henceforth, let $\mathcal{M} = (S, A, \Delta, T)$ be a non-weighted trivially parametric MDP and write $\mathcal{G}(\mathcal{M}) = (V, E)$. We make the assumption that all *extremal-value vertices* [16] have been contracted: An extremal-value vertex $v \in V$ is such that either $\mathrm{Rew}^*_{\mathsf{val}}(v) = 0$ or $\mathrm{Rew}^*_{\mathsf{val}}(v) = 1$ holds for all $\mathsf{val} \in \mathrm{Val}^{\mathrm{gp}}_{\mathcal{M}}$. The set of all such vertices can be computed in polynomial time [1, Algorithm 45]. One can then contract all value-1 vertices with *fin* and all value-0 with *fail*, without changing the values of the other vertices.

5.1   The Under-Approximation Graph

We will represent our current approximation of the NWR by means of a (directed) *under-approximation graph* $\mathcal{U} = (N, R)$ such that $N \subseteq 2^V$. For $U, W \in N$, let $U \xrightarrow{\mathcal{U}} W$ denote the fact that there is a path in $\mathcal{U}$ from U to W. Throughout our algorithm we will observe the following invariant.

$$\forall U, W \in N : U \xrightarrow{\mathcal{U}} W \implies U \trianglelefteq W \tag{2}$$

Initializing the Graph. For our initial under-approximation of the NWR, we construct $\mathcal{U}$ with vertex set $N = \{\{v\}, vE \mid v \in V\}$. That is, it contains all states, all state-action pairs, and all sets of immediate successors of states or state-action pairs. For the edges, we add them so that the following hold.

1. $R \ni (\{fail\}, n)$ for all $n \in N$
2. $R \ni (n, \{fin\})$ for all $n \in N$
3. $R \ni (\{v\}, vE)$ for all $v \in V$
4. $R \ni (vE, \{v\})$ for all $v \in S$

Recall that V and S are the set of all vertices and the set of all states of the MDP respectively. This initialization yields a correct under-approximation.

Lemma 2. *Let $\mathcal{U}$ be the initial under-approximation graph as defined above. Then, invariant (2) holds true.*

Below, we describe how the under-approximation graph can be updated to get ever tighter under-approximations of the NWR.

Updating and Querying the Graph. Whenever we add a vertex U to some under-approximation graph $\mathcal{U}$, we also add:

- an edge from $\{fail\}$ and each $U' \in N$ such that $U' \subset U$ to U,
- an edge from U to $\{fin\}$ and each $U'' \in N$ such that $U \subset U''$, and
- an edge from U to W if $\{u\} \xrightarrow{\mathcal{U}} W$ holds for all $u \in U$.

When we add an edge (U, W) to $\mathcal{U}$, we first add the vertices U and W as previously explained, if they are not yet in the graph. Finally, to query the graph and determine whether $U \xrightarrow{\mathcal{U}} W$, we simply search the graph for W from U as suggested by the definitions.

Lemma 3. *Let $\mathcal{U}'$ be an under-approximation graph satisfying invariant (2) and $\mathcal{U}$ the under-approximation graph obtained after adding an edge $(U, W) \in 2^V \times 2^V$ as described above. If $U \trianglelefteq W$ then $\mathcal{U}$ satisfies invariant (2).*

Before we delve into how to infer pairs from the NWR to improve our approximation graph, we need to recall the notion of *end component*.

5.2   End Components and Quotienting

Say (P, B) is a sub-MDP of $\mathcal{M}$, for $P \subseteq S$ and $B \subseteq \{(p, a) \mid (p, (p, a)) \in E\}$, if:

- for all $p \in P$ there is at least one $a \in A$ such that $(p, a) \in B$, and
- for all $p' \in S$ and $(p, a) \in B$ with $((p, a), p') \in E$ we have $p, p' \in P$.

One can think of sub-MDPs as a collection of connected components of the original MDP obtained by removing some actions from some states.

A sub-MDP (P, B) of $\mathcal{M}$ is an *end component* if the subgraph of $\mathcal{G}(\mathcal{M})$ induced by $P \cup B$ is strongly connected. The end component (P, B) is maximal (a MEC) if there is no other end component $(P', B') \neq (P, B)$ such that $B \subseteq B'$. The set of MECs can be computed in polynomial time [1, Algorithm 47].

It is known that end components are a special case of the NWR. In fact, all vertices in a same end component are NWR-equivalent [16, Lemma 3]. Hence, as we have done for extremal-value states, we can assume they have been contracted. It will be useful, in later discussions, for us to make explicit the *quotienting* construction realizing this contraction.

MEC Quotient. Let $s \in S$. We use the notation $[\![s]\!]_{\mathrm{MEC}}$ to denote the unique MEC (P, B) containing s. That is, $[\![s]\!]_{\mathrm{MEC}} = \{s\}$ if s is not part of any MEC; and $[\![s]\!]_{\mathrm{MEC}} = P$ otherwise. Now, we denote by $\mathcal{M}_{/\mathrm{MEC}}$ the *MEC-quotient* of $\mathcal{M}$. That is, $\mathcal{M}_{/\mathrm{MEC}}$ is the p̃MDP $\mathcal{M}_{/\mathrm{MEC}} = (S', A, \Delta', T')$ where:

- $T' = \{[\![t]\!]_{\mathrm{MEC}} \mid \exists t \in T\}$,
- $S' = \{[\![s]\!]_{\mathrm{MEC}} \mid \exists s \in S\}$, and
- $\Delta' = \{([\![s]\!]_{\mathrm{MEC}}, a, [\![s']\!]_{\mathrm{MEC}}) \mid \exists (s, a, s'') \in \Delta, [\![s]\!]_{\mathrm{MEC}} \neq [\![s'']\!]_{\mathrm{MEC}}\}$.

The construction does preserve the never-worse relations amongst all states.

Proposition 1. *For all $U, W \subseteq S$ we have that $U \trianglelefteq W$ in $\mathcal{G}(\mathcal{M})$ if and only if $\{[\![u]\!]_{\mathrm{MEC}} \mid \exists u \in U\} \trianglelefteq \{[\![w]\!]_{\mathrm{MEC}} \mid \exists w \in W\}$ in $\mathcal{G}(\mathcal{M}_{/\mathrm{MEC}})$.*

We now describe how to prune sub-optimal actions while updating the approximation graph via inference rules for the NWR.

5.3   Pruning Actions and Inferring the NWR

The next theorem states that we can prune actions that lead to sub-optimal vertices with respect to the NWR once we have taken the MEC-quotient.

Theorem 6. *Let $\mathcal{M}$ be a $\tilde{p}MDP$ such that $\mathcal{M}$ is isomorphic with $\mathcal{M}_{/\mathrm{MEC}}$. Then, for all valuations* val $\in \mathsf{Val}_{\mathcal{M}}^{\mathrm{gp}}$ *and all $(s,a) \in S \times A$ with $(s,a) \trianglelefteq (sE \setminus \{(s,a)\})$:*

$$\max_{\sigma} \mathbb{P}^s_{\mathcal{M}_\sigma^{\mathsf{val}}}[\Diamond \mathit{fin}] = \max_{\sigma'} \mathbb{P}^s_{\mathcal{N}_{\sigma'}^{\mathsf{val}}}[\Diamond \mathit{fin}],$$

where $\mathcal{N} = (S, A, \Delta \setminus \{(s,a,s') \in \Delta \mid \exists s' \in S\}, T)$.

It remains for us to introduce inference rules to derive new NWR pairs based on our approximation graph $\mathcal{U}$. The following definitions will be useful.

Essential States and Almost-sure Reachability. We say the set $W \subseteq V$ is *essential for*[2] $U \subseteq V$, written $U \sqsubseteq W$, if each path starting from any vertex in U and ending in *fin* contains a vertex from W. (Intuitively, removing W disconnects U from *fin*.) We say that $U \subseteq V$ *almost-surely reaches* $W \subseteq V$, written $U \xrightarrow{\mathrm{a.s.}} W$, if all states $u \in U$ become value-1 states after replacing T with $W \cup \{\mathit{fail}\}$ and making all $w \in W$ have weight 1. Recall that value-1 states are so for all graph-preserving valuations and that they can be computed in polynomial time. Similarly, whether W is essential for U can be determined in polynomial time by searching in the subgraph of $\mathcal{G}(\mathcal{M})$ obtained by removing W. We also define, for $W \subseteq V$, a function $f_W : 2^S \to 2^S$:

$$f_W(D) = D \cup \left\{ z \in V \; \middle| \; \{z\} \xrightarrow{\mathcal{U}} W \cup D \right\}$$

and write $\mu D.f_W(D)$ for its least fixed point with respect to the subset lattice.

Inference Rules. For all $U, W \subseteq V$, the following rules hold true. It is worth mentioning that these are strict generalisations of [16, Propositions 1, 2].

$$\frac{U \sqsubseteq \mu D.f_W(D)}{U \trianglelefteq W} \qquad \frac{\exists w \in W : \{w\} \xrightarrow{\mathrm{a.s}} \{s \in S \mid U \xrightarrow{\mathcal{U}} \{s\}\}}{U \trianglelefteq W} \tag{3}$$

Example 3. Fig. 6 depicts two $\tilde{p}$MDPs for the two inference rules. In Fig. 6a, we see that the set $\{v, \mathit{fin}\}$, a set of vertices better than v, can almost-surely be reached by u. Hence, $v \trianglelefteq u$ by the second inference rule. In Fig. 6b, we use the first inference rule: D is initialized as empty. Then, we see that u is never worse than w and x from the initialization and thus get $D = \{u, w, x\}$. We can continue this to add the two actions of v to D, however, we can already see that $\{u, w, x\}$ is essential for v. Hence, we get that $v \trianglelefteq u$.

---

[2] This definition is inspired by [7] but it is not exactly the same as in that paper.

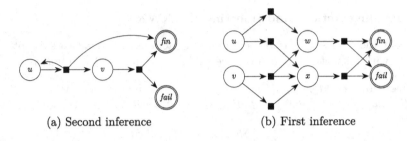

(a) Second inference   (b) First inference

Fig. 6. Examples showing how the two inference rules are used

Lemma 4. *Let $\mathcal{U}$ be an approximation graph satisfying (2). Then, the inference rules from (3) are correct.*

Our proposed action-pruning method is given as Algorithm 1. Note that in line 15 we do a final contraction of NWR equivalences. These are the equivalences that can be derived between any two singletons $\{x\}$ and $\{y\}$ that lie on a same cycle in $\mathcal{U}$. The algorithm clearly terminates because the NWR is finite, there is no unbounded recursion, and there are no unbounded loops. Finally, correctness follows from the results in this section and, for the aforementioned contraction of NWR equivalence classes, from [16, Theorem 1].

Algorithm 1: Reduction using the under-approximation

    Inputs : A p̃MDP $\mathcal{M} = (S, A, \Delta, T)$
    Output : A (hopefully) smaller p̃MDP
1   Initialize $\mathcal{U}$;
2   **repeat**
3   **for** $s \in S$ **do**
4   **for** $(s, a) \in sE$ **do**
5         $W \leftarrow sE \setminus \{(s, a)\}$;
6   **if** $\{(s, a)\} \xrightarrow{\mathcal{U}} W$ **then**
7   Prune all $\{(s, a, s') \in \Delta \mid \exists s' \in S\}$;
8   **else if** $\{(s, a)\} \sqsubseteq \mu D.f_W(D)$ **then**
9   Add edge $((s, a), W)$ to $\mathcal{U}$;
10   Prune all $\{(s, a, s') \in \Delta \mid \exists s' \in S\}$;
11   **else if** $\exists w \in W : \{w\} \xrightarrow{\text{a.s.}} \{s' \in S \mid \{(s, a)\} \xrightarrow{\mathcal{U}} \{s'\}\}$ **then**
12   Add edge $((s, a), W)$ to $\mathcal{U}$;
13   Prune all $\{(s, a, s') \in \Delta \mid \exists s' \in S\}$;
14 **until** $\mathcal{U}$ *is unchanged*;
15 Contract NWR equivalences from cycles in $\mathcal{G}$;
16 Return the new p̃MDP;

---

6   Experiments

In this section, we show the results of the experiments that we have conducted to assess the effectiveness of the techniques described in the previous sections. We first motivate the research questions that we wish to answer using the experiments. Then, we describe the models that we have used during the experiments, including the pre-processing steps that were performed. Next, we describe the different setups in which our techniques have been applied to the selected and pre-processed models. Finally, we discuss the results that we have obtained during the experiments. Everything needed to re-run our experiments is in [8].

We approach our experiments with the following research questions in mind.

Q1. Is the NWR really useful in practice?
Q2. Does our under-approximation give us significant reductions in the size of some models? How do these reductions compare to the known reductions?
Q3. Does the under-approximation yield reductions in early iterations?

Note that the first question is (intentionally) vague. To approach it, we thus focus on the more concrete two that follow. Namely, for the under-approximation, we want to know whether we can reduce the size of common benchmarks and, moreover, whether such reduction in size is obtained through a small number of applications of our inference rules. On the one hand, a positive answer to Q2 would mean the NWR is indeed useful as a preprocessing step to reduce the size of an MDP. On the other hand, a positive answer to Q3 would imply that a small number of applications of our inference rules is always worth trying.

6.1   Benchmarks and Protocol

For the experiments, we have considered all discrete-time MDPs encoded as PRISM models [15] from the Quantitative Verification Benchmark set [4], provided that they have at least one maximal reachability property. From these, we have filtered out those that have an unknown number of states, or more than 64.000 states, as specified on the QComp website, in order to limit the runtime of the experiments.

We have added every maximal reachability property from the `props` files as labels in the model files. In some cases, either out of curiosity, or to compare with other known reductions, we have introduced new labels to the models as final states. For example, in the `wlan_dl` benchmark, instead of checking the minimum probability of both stations sending correctly within deadline, we check the maximum probability of doing so. In the `consensus` benchmarks, we add new labels `fin_and_all_1` and `fin_and_not_all_1` to compare our reductions to the ones used by Bharadwaj et al. [2]. Some of these labels used in the tables and graphs later are listed below:

1. Model: `consensus`. Labels: `disagree`, `fin_and_all_1`, `fin_and_not_all_1`.
   The label `disagree` is one of the properties in the property file and the other two labels are meant for comparisons with past results [2].

2. Model: `zeroconf_dl`. Label: `deadline_min`. The minimum probability of not finishing within the deadline does not look like a maximum reachability probability question, but it turns out to be the same as the maximum probability of reaching a new IP address within the deadline.
3. Model: `zeroconf`. Label: `correct_max`.
4. Model: `crowds`. Label: `obs_send_all`.
5. Model: `brp`. Labels: `no_succ_trans`, `rep_uncertainty`, `not_rec_but_sent`.

The PRISM files, with the added labels, have then converted into an explicit JSON format using STORM [12]. This format was chosen since it explicitly specifies all states and state-action pairs in an easy to manipulate file format.

We have then applied two pre-processing techniques. Namely, we have collapsed all extremal states and state-action pairs and collapsed all MECs. These two techniques, and the way they relate to the never-worse relation, are described in the previous sections. Some models were completely reduced after collapsing all extremal states, with only the *fin* and *fail* states remaining. We have not included such MDPs in the discussion here onward, but they are listed in [8]. Collapsing the MECs does not prove to be as effective, providing no additional reductions for the models under consideration.

6.2   Different Setups

In each experiment, we repeatedly apply Algorithm 1 on each model. If for two consecutive iterations, the collapse of equivalent states (see line 15) has no effect then we terminate the experiment. Each iteration, we start with an empty under-approximation graph, to avoid states removed during the collapse being included in the under-approximation. This is described in Algorithm 2.

Algorithm 2: The experimental setup

Inputs : A p̃MDP $\mathcal{M} = (S, A, \Delta, T)$
Output : A p̃MDP that can be analysed
1 Contract extremal-value states;
2 Contract MECs;
3 **repeat**
4 | Start with an empty under-approximation $\mathcal{U}$;
5 | Apply Algorithm 1;
6 **until** *collapsing NWR equivalences has no effect*;

In order to reduce the runtime of the experiments, we consider a maximal number of iterations for the loops specified on line 2 of Algorithm 1 and line 3 of Algorithm 2. We refer to the loop of Algorithm 1 as the "inner loop", and to the loop of Algorithm 2 as the "outer loop". During the experiments, we found that running the inner loop during the first iteration of the outer loop was too time-consuming. We therefore decide to skip the inner loop during the first iteration of the outer loop. Even then, running the inner loop turns out to be impractical for some models, resulting in the following two experimental setups:

1. For some models, we allow the outer loop to run for a maximum of 17 times. In our experiments, no benchmark required more than 7 iterations. The inner loop is limited to 3 iterations.
2. For others, we ran the outer loop 3 times without running the inner loop.

The Markov chains considered in our experiments are always used in the second experimental setup because Markov chains are MDPs with a single action for each state, making the action-pruning inner loop redundant.

Remark 4. Every time we add a node U to the under-approximation graph, we skip the step "an edge from U to W if $\{u\} \xrightarrow{u} W$ holds for all $u \in U$" since we found that this step is not efficient.

6.3   Results, Tables and Graphs

Remark 5. We use the term *choice* to denote a state-action pair in the MDP.

Table 1 shows the state-space reduction in some of the benchmarks we ran. After preprocessing, we obtain a 61% reduction on average in all the brp benchmarks with "no_succ_trans" and "rep_uncertainty" as final states and a 40% reduction on average with "not_res_but_sent" as final states. In the zeroconf_dl benchmarks, we obtain a further 50% reduction on average and around 69% reduction in all zeroconf benchmarks. In consensus benchmarks with "disagree" final states, we get around 37% further reduction after the preprocessing only removed less than 16% of the states. The rest of the data (including further benchmarks) can be found in [8]. All of these observations[3] point to Q2 having a positive answer.

Among all the benchmarks we tested, only zeroconf and some instances of consensus and zeroconf_dl see any improvements after the first iteration of the algorithm [8]. Even then, the majority of the improvement is seen in the first iteration, the improvement in the later iterations is minimal, as depicted in Fig. 7, and no benchmark runs for more than 7 iterations. The consensus benchmark with "disagree" final states runs with the second setup for $(N = 2, K = 8), (N = 2, K = 16)$ and with the first setup for $(N = 2, K = 2), (N = 2, K = 4)$. As seen in Table 1, all the instances gave us around a 36% further reduction after preprocessing, although the ones where the algorithm ran only for one iteration are significantly faster. This gives us a positive answer for Q3.

---

[3] We were not able to properly compare our results to the ones in [2]. The sizes reported therein do not match those from the QComp models. The authors confirmed theirs are based on modified models of which the data and code have been misplaced.

Table 1. Table with the number of states and choices during each step of running the benchmarks. The last column has the running time after preprocessing. The experiments with (gray) colored running time were run with the first experimental setup.

benchmark	instance	original size		preprocessing		under-approx		
		#st	#ch	#st	#ch	#st	#ch	time
consensus "disagree" (N,K)	(2,2)	274	400	232	344	148	260	78.17s
	(2,4)	530	784	488	728	308	548	383.13s
	(2,8)	1042	1552	1000	1496	628	1124	19.38s
	(2,16)	2066	3088	2024	3032	1268	2276	78.47s
consensus "fin_and_all_1" (N,K)	(2,2)	274	400	173	280	127	232	124.33s
	(2,4)	530	784	365	600	271	504	674.17s
	(2,8)	1042	1552	749	1240	561	1052	14.14s
	(2,16)	2066	3088	1517	2520	1137	2140	57.78s
consensus "fin_and_not_all_1" (N,K)	(2,2)	274	400	165	268	123	226	61.15s
	(2,4)	530	784	357	588	267	498	317.95s
	(2,8)	1042	1552	741	1228	555	1042	14.00s
	(2,16)	2066	3088	1509	2508	1131	2130	58.24s
zeroconf_dl "deadline_min" (N,K,reset,deadline)	(1000,1,true,10)	3837	4790	460	552	242	333	98.47s
	(1000,1,true,20)	7672	9775	2709	3351	1313	1945	79.49s
	(1000,1,true,30)	11607	14860	4999	6211	2413	3605	266.00s
	(1000,1,true,40)	15642	20045	7289	9071	3513	5265	560.82s
	(1000,1,true,50)	19777	25330	9579	11931	4613	6925	1013.18s
	(1000,1,false,10)	12242	18200	460	552	242	333	95.69s
zeroconf "correct_max" (N,K,reset)	(1000,2,true)	672	814	388	481	118	150	29.13s
	(1000,4,true)	1090	1342	674	855	206	260	76.06s
	(1000,6,true)	1508	1870	960	1229	294	370	161.01s
	(1000,8,true)	1926	2398	1246	1603	382	480	237.69s
crowds "obs_send_all" (TotalRuns,CrowdSize)	(3,5)	1200	1198	268	266	182	180	1.03s
	(4,5)	3517	3515	1030	1028	632	630	11.93s
	(5,5)	8655	8653	2930	2928	1682	1680	87.76s
	(6,5)	18819	18817	6905	6903	3782	3780	467.08s
	(3,10)	6565	6563	833	831	662	660	13.12s
	(4,10)	30072	30070	5430	5428	3962	3960	481.47s
	(3,15)	19230	19228	1698	1696	1442	1440	69.90s
brp "no_succ_trans" (N,MAX)	(64,2)	2695	2693	1982	1980	768	766	26.76s
	(64,3)	3528	3526	2812	2810	1087	1085	53.80s
	(64,4)	4361	4359	3642	3640	1406	1404	89.44s
	(64,5)	5194	5192	4472	4470	1725	1723	134.57s
brp "rep_uncertainty" (N,MAX)	(64,2)	2695	2693	1982	1980	768	766	25.74s
	(64,3)	3528	3526	2812	2810	1087	1085	52.20s
	(64,4)	4361	4359	3642	3640	1406	1404	87.62s
	(64,5)	5194	5192	4472	4470	1725	1723	133.96s
brp "not_rec_but_sent" (N,MAX)	(64,2)	2695	2693	8	6	5	3	0.004s
	(64,3)	3528	3526	10	8	6	4	0.01s
	(64,4)	4361	4359	12	10	7	5	0.01s
	(64,5)	5194	5192	14	12	8	6	0.01s

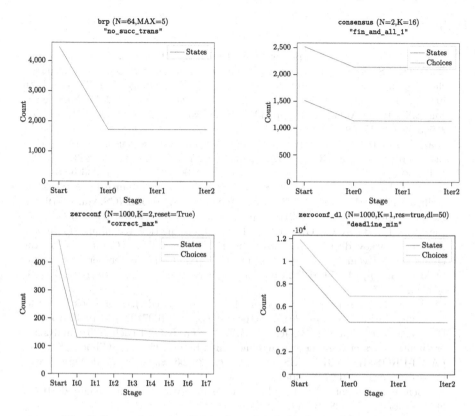

Fig. 7. Some plots visualizing the reductions obtained per iteration.

7   Conclusions

We have extended the never-worse relation to the quantitative reachability setting on parametric Markov decision processes. While the complexity of deciding the relation is relatively high (**coETR**-complete), efficient under-approximations seem promising. We believe that the relation could be made more applicable by exploring the computation of such under-approximations in an on-the-fly fashion such as, for instance, on-the-fly MEC algorithms [3]. The following questions also warrant futher (empirical) study: What kind of MDPs have large reductions under the NWR? What do the reduced MDPs look like? What kinds of states are detected and removed by the NWR under-approximations?

As additional future work, we think it is worthwhile to study approximations that are (more) efficient when the MDP is encoded as a reduced ordered binary decision diagram (BDD) or in a particular modelling language such as the PRISM language. For the latter, an initial work in this direction is [21].

References

1. Baier, C., Katoen, J.: Principles of Model Checking. MIT Press, Cambridge (2008)
2. Bharadwaj, S., Roux, S.L., Pérez, G.A., Topcu, U.: Reduction techniques for model checking and learning in MDPs. In: Sierra, C. (ed.) Proceedings of the Twenty-Sixth International Joint Conference on Artificial Intelligence, IJCAI 2017, Melbourne, Australia, 19–25 August 2017, pp. 4273–4279. ijcai.org (2017). https://doi.org/10.24963/ijcai.2017/597
3. Brázdil, T., et al.: Verification of Markov decision processes using learning algorithms. In: Cassez, F., Raskin, J.-F. (eds.) ATVA 2014. LNCS, vol. 8837, pp. 98–114. Springer, Cham (2014). https://doi.org/10.1007/978-3-319-11936-6_8
4. Budde, C.E., et al.: On correctness, precision, and performance in quantitative verification. In: Margaria, T., Steffen, B. (eds.) ISoLA 2020. LNCS, vol. 12479, pp. 216–241. Springer, Cham (2021). https://doi.org/10.1007/978-3-030-83723-5_15
5. Ciesinski, F., Baier, C., Größer, M., Klein, J.: Reduction techniques for model checking Markov decision processes. In: Fifth International Conference on the Quantitative Evaluaiton of Systems (QEST 2008), 14–17 September 2008, Saint-Malo, France, pp. 45–54. IEEE Computer Society (2008). https://doi.org/10.1109/QEST.2008.45
6. Clarke, E.M., Henzinger, T.A., Veith, H., Bloem, R. (eds.): Handbook of Model Checking. Springer, Cham (2018). https://doi.org/10.1007/978-3-319-10575-8
7. D'Argenio, P.R., Jeannet, B., Jensen, H.E., Larsen, K.G.: Reachability analysis of probabilistic systems by successive refinements. In: de Alfaro, L., Gilmore, S. (eds.) PAPM-PROBMIV 2001. LNCS, vol. 2165, pp. 39–56. Springer, Heidelberg (2001). https://doi.org/10.1007/3-540-44804-7_3
8. Engelen, K.: Code for graph-based reductions for parametric and weighted MDPs. https://doi.org/10.5281/zenodo.7915828
9. Hartmanns, A., Hermanns, H.: The modest toolset: an integrated environment for quantitative modelling and verification. In: Ábrahám, E., Havelund, K. (eds.) TACAS 2014. LNCS, vol. 8413, pp. 593–598. Springer, Heidelberg (2014). https://doi.org/10.1007/978-3-642-54862-8_51
10. Hartmanns, A., Junges, S., Quatmann, T., Weininger, M.: A practitioner's guide to MDP model checking algorithms. In: Sankaranarayanan, S., Sharygina, N. (eds.) Tools and Algorithms for the Construction and Analysis of Systems - 29th International Conference, TACAS 2023, Held as Part of the European Joint Conferences on Theory and Practice of Software, ETAPS 2022, Paris, France, 22–27 April 2023, Proceedings, Part I. LNCS, vol. 13993, pp. 469–488. Springer, Cham (2023). https://doi.org/10.1007/978-3-031-30823-9_24
11. Hartmanns, A., Klauck, M., Parker, D., Quatmann, T., Ruijters, E.: The quantitative verification benchmark set. In: Vojnar, T., Zhang, L. (eds.) TACAS 2019. LNCS, vol. 11427, pp. 344–350. Springer, Cham (2019). https://doi.org/10.1007/978-3-030-17462-0_20
12. Hensel, C., Junges, S., Katoen, J., Quatmann, T., Volk, M.: The probabilistic model checker storm. Int. J. Softw. Tools Technol. Transf. 24(4), 589–610 (2022). https://doi.org/10.1007/s10009-021-00633-z
13. Junges, S., Katoen, J., Pérez, G.A., Winkler, T.: The complexity of reachability in parametric Markov decision processes. J. Comput. Syst. Sci. 119, 183–210 (2021). https://doi.org/10.1016/j.jcss.2021.02.006
14. Křetínský, J., Meggendorfer, T.: Efficient strategy iteration for mean payoff in Markov decision processes. In: D'Souza, D., Narayan Kumar, K. (eds.) ATVA 2017.

LNCS, vol. 10482, pp. 380–399. Springer, Cham (2017). https://doi.org/10.1007/978-3-319-68167-2_25

15. Kwiatkowska, M., Norman, G., Parker, D.: PRISM 4.0: verification of probabilistic real-time systems. In: Gopalakrishnan, G., Qadeer, S. (eds.) CAV 2011. LNCS, vol. 6806, pp. 585–591. Springer, Heidelberg (2011). https://doi.org/10.1007/978-3-642-22110-1_47

16. Le Roux, S., Pérez, G.A.: The complexity of graph-based reductions for reachability in Markov decision processes. In: Baier, C., Dal Lago, U. (eds.) FoSSaCS 2018. LNCS, vol. 10803, pp. 367–383. Springer, Cham (2018). https://doi.org/10.1007/978-3-319-89366-2_20

17. Russell, S., Norvig, P.: Artificial Intelligence: A Modern Approach, 4th ed. Pearson, Hoboken (2020). http://aima.cs.berkeley.edu/

18. Schaefer, M.: Complexity of some geometric and topological problems. In: Eppstein, D., Gansner, E.R. (eds.) GD 2009. LNCS, vol. 5849, pp. 334–344. Springer, Heidelberg (2010). https://doi.org/10.1007/978-3-642-11805-0_32

19. Spel, J., Junges, S., Katoen, J.-P.: Are parametric Markov chains monotonic? In: Chen, Y.-F., Cheng, C.-H., Esparza, J. (eds.) ATVA 2019. LNCS, vol. 11781, pp. 479–496. Springer, Cham (2019). https://doi.org/10.1007/978-3-030-31784-3_28

20. Sutton, R.S., Barto, A.G.: Reinforcement Learning - An Introduction. Adaptive Computation and Machine Learning, MIT Press, Cambridge (1998). https://www.worldcat.org/oclc/37293240

21. Winkler, T., Lehmann, J., Katoen, J.-P.: Out of control: reducing probabilistic models by control-state elimination. In: Finkbeiner, B., Wies, T. (eds.) VMCAI 2022. LNCS, vol. 13182, pp. 450–472. Springer, Cham (2022). https://doi.org/10.1007/978-3-030-94583-1_22

Scenario Approach for Parametric Markov Models

Ying Liu[1,2], Andrea Turrini[1,3], Ernst Moritz Hahn[4], Bai Xue[1(✉)],
and Lijun Zhang[1,2,3(✉)]

[1] State Key Laboratory of Computer Science, Institute of Software,
Chinese Academy of Sciences, Beijing, China
{xuebai,zhanglj}@ios.ac.cn
[2] University of Chinese Academy of Sciences, Beijing, China
[3] Institute of Intelligent Software Guangzhou, Guangzhou, China
[4] Formal Methods and Tools, University of Twente, Enschede, The Netherlands

Abstract. In this paper, we propose an approximating framework for
analyzing parametric Markov models. Instead of computing complex
rational functions encoding the reachability probability and the reward
values of the parametric model, we exploit the scenario approach to synthesize a relatively simple polynomial approximation. The approximation is probably approximately correct (PAC), meaning that with high
confidence, the approximating function is close to the actual function
with an allowable error. With the PAC approximations, one can check
properties of the parametric Markov models. We show that the scenario
approach can also be used to check PRCTL properties directly – without synthesizing the polynomial at first hand. We have implemented our
algorithm in a prototype tool and conducted thorough experiments. The
experimental results demonstrate that our tool is able to compute polynomials for more benchmarks than state-of-the-art tools such as PRISM
and STORM, confirming the efficacy of our PAC-based synthesis.

1   Introduction

Markov models (see, e.g., [52]) have been widely applied to reason about quantitative properties in numerous domains, such as networked, distributed systems,
biological systems [37], and reinforcement learning [4,59]. Properties analyzed on
Markov models can either be simple, such as determining the value of the probability that a certain set of unsafe states is reached and how an expected reward
value compares with a specified threshold, or complex, involving employing temporal logics such as PCTL [10,35] and PRCTL [1]. To verify these properties, various advanced tools have been developed, such as PRISM [44], STORM [24,36],
MRMC [42], CADP 2011 [28], PROPhESY [23] and IScASMc [33].

In this paper we consider *parametric* discrete time Markov chains (pDTMCs),
whose transition probabilities are not required to be constants, but can depend

---

A. Turrini—Co-first author.

© The Author(s), under exclusive license to Springer Nature Switzerland AG 2023
É. André and J. Sun (Eds.): ATVA 2023, LNCS 14215, pp. 158–180, 2023.
https://doi.org/10.1007/978-3-031-45329-8_8

on a set of parameters. For this type of model, the value of the analyzed property can be described as a *function* of the parameters, mapping either to truth values or to numbers. In many cases, these functions are *rational functions*, that is, fractions of co-prime polynomials. The exact rational function is commonly challenging to compute as it often involves polynomials with very high degree [5,41]. Moreover, the Markov models applied in real life may be very large, with thousands of states, so it is very complicated to compute the rational functions accurately. However, to analyze the properties of such Markov models in practical applications, we often allow for a certain acceptable level of error, without guaranteeing that the given property holds absolutely.

Contribution of the Paper. In this work, we propose an alternative approach to replace the exact solution of function f_φ that describes the value of the analyzed property φ in the given pDTMC and pDTMRM. The main idea is exploiting the scenario approach [16,18] to learn an *approximating function* – polynomial $\tilde{f}_\varphi$ with low degree to approximate the actual function f_φ with probably approximately correct (PAC) guarantee, i.e., with high confidence $1 - \eta$, the probability that the approximation error is within an error margin λ is at least $1 - \varepsilon$.

We demonstrate how to use PAC approximation $\tilde{f}_\varphi$ to synthesize parameters and analyze the properties of original functions f_φ. We use PAC approximation to check the safe region of the parameter space and some global probability properties. We also extend to reward properties: we show how to use PAC approximation to estimate the lower bound of the expectation of f_φ over the domain of the parameters. Extending our approach to parametric MDPs is also feasible, as long as we treat the MDP strategy as in [2], we allow the strategy to change for the different MDP instances.

Experimental results show that our prototype PACPMA can solve more properties under the same conditions than the state-of-the-art verification tools STORM and PRISM, and provide PAC approximations with a statistical guarantee. We demonstrate that as the degree of the polynomial approximation increases, the computed error margin λ approaches zero, indicating that the polynomial with higher degree provides a more accurate approximation of the original function. As for the accuracy of the approximation, we show that PAC approximation $\tilde{f}_\varphi$ can approximate f_φ two to three orders of magnitude more accurately than the Taylor expansion of the actual function f_φ. We also demonstrate that the PAC approximation can approximately capture the lower bound of the expected reward of pDTMRM with high confidence, thus can help to verify the reward properties.

Related Work. Model checking of parametric Markov models is not a new area and a number of related works exist, each with different strengths and weaknesses. In the following, we demarcate our work from the existing ones.

Daws has devised a language-theoretic approach to solve the reachability problem of parametric Markov chains [22], where the model is viewed as a finite automaton. Based on the state elimination approach [38], the regular expression describing the language of such an automaton is computed, which is transformed into a rational function over the parameters of the model in a postprocessing step. The method has been improved by intertwining the state elimination and the computation of the rational function [32], this improved algorithm has been implemented in the tool PARAM [31]. PARAM also supports bounded reachability, relying on matrix-vector multiplication with rational function entries, and reachability rewards [11, 25]. All these works [31, 32] compute the precise rational function that describes the property of interest. Unfortunately, it is challenging to evaluate it, due to the large coefficients and high exponents. Moreover, the works discussed above do not consider properties specified by a temporal logic.

Several improvements have been proposed in later works. Jansen et al. [39] perform the state elimination in a more systematic order, often leading to better performance in practice. The work [53] provides the first sound and feasible technique for parameter synthesis of Markov decision processes, Spel et al. [57] achieved efficient parameter optimization by combining monotonicity checking and parameter lifting, allowing for further evaluation of the safety of parameter space. The work [27] uses arithmetic circuits, which are DAG-like structures, to represent such rational functions. A further work [30] follows a related approach to solve (potentially nested) PRCTL formulas for Markov decision processes: the state space is divided into hyperrectangles, and one has to show that a particular decision is optimal for a whole region. The work [5] improves the computation of the rational function by means of a fraction-free Gaussian elimination; the experimental evaluation confirms its effectiveness. There are also methods for checking parametric continuous time Markov chains [34], by using a scenario approach [3] or by being based on Gaussian processes [13, 14]. A recent work [26] proposes a fast parametric model checking method named fPMC, which extends the current parametric model checking approaches to systems with complex behaviors and multiple parameters. A recent survey [40] provides an overview of parameter synthesis for Markov models. In the above Markov model checking methods, the accurate algorithm is computationally complex, while the approximate algorithms rarely provide a probability guarantee. However, our proposed method for verifying parametric Markov models based on scenario approach provides both efficiency and probabilistic guarantee.

The scenario approach was first introduced in [15], based on constraint sampling to deal with uncertainty in optimization. The works [16, 18, 19] study a probabilistic solution framework for robust properties, the work [50] proposes a method to solve chance constrained optimization problems lying between robust optimization and scenario approach, which does not require prior knowledge of the probability distribution of the parameters. Based on [15, 16], the work [17] allows violating some of the sampled constraints in order to improve the optimization value, and the work [58] expands the scenario optimization problem to multi-stage problems. Recently, the scenario approach has been applied to verify safety properties of black-box continuous time dynamical systems [60] and the robustness of neural networks [48].

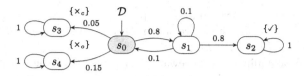

Fig. 1. An example of discrete time Markov chain

The most related to our work is [2], which also applies the scenario approach for analyzing parametric Markov chains and Markov decision processes. The main difference with our work is that in [2], the authors compute the probability that the instances of the parametric MDP satisfy a given property φ, by sampling the parameter values according to some assumed distribution. Instead, our work targets at computing an approximation of the complicated function f_φ depending on the parameters – such as the one corresponding to the reachability probability φ. Our framework can bound the error between the actual function and the approximation we compute. Moreover, as a side result, our PAC approximations can be used for visualizing the reachability probability, finding counterexamples, and analyzing the properties of the original functions with a certain confidence.

Organization of the Paper. After giving in Sect. 2 some preliminaries, models, and logic we use in this paper, in Sect. 3 we present our PAC-based model checking approach; we evaluate it empirically in Sect. 4 before concluding the paper in Sect. 5 with some final remarks.

Due to space constraints, the proofs are provided in the technical report [49].

2 Preliminaries

In this section, we first recall DTMCs, a well-known probabilistic model (see, e.g., [6]), reward structures, the probabilistic logic PRCTL we adopt to express properties on them, and then consider their extension with parameters.

2.1 Probabilistic Models

Definition 1. *Given a finite set of atomic propositions AP, a (labelled) discrete time Markov chain (DTMC) $\mathcal{D}$ is a tuple $\mathcal{D} = (S, \bar{s}, \mathbf{P}, L)$ where S is a finite set of states; $\bar{s} \in S$ is the initial state; $\mathbf{P} \colon S \times S \to [0,1]$ is a transition function such that for each $s \in S$, we have $\sum_{s' \in S} \mathbf{P}(s, s') = 1$; and $L \colon S \to 2^{AP}$ is a labelling function.*

The *underlying graph* of a DTMC $\mathcal{D} = (S, \bar{s}, \mathbf{P}, L)$ is a directed graph $\langle V, E \rangle$ with $V = S$ as vertices and $E = \{ (s, s') \in S \times S \mid \mathbf{P}(s, s') > 0 \}$ as edges.

As an example of DTMC, consider the DTMC $\mathcal{D}$ shown in Fig. 1. $\mathcal{D}$ has 5 states (from s_0 to s_4), with s_0 being the initial one (marked with the gray background and the small incoming arrow); transitions with probability larger than 0 are depicted as arrows, so for example we have $\mathbf{P}(s_0, s_1) = 0.8 > 0$, while the labels assigned to each state are shown on the top-right corner of the state itself, e.g., $L(s_2) = \{\checkmark\}$ while $L(s_0) = \emptyset$.

DTMCs can be equipped with reward structures that assign values to states and transitions; such reward structures can be used to count the number of transitions taken so far or to attach "costs" or "gains" to the DTMC.

Definition 2. *A discrete time Markov reward model (DTMRM) $\mathcal{R}$ is a pair $\mathcal{R} = (\mathcal{D}, \mathfrak{r})$ where $\mathcal{D}$ is a DTMC and $\mathfrak{r} \colon S \cup (S \times S) \to \mathbb{R}_{\geq 0}$ is a reward function.*

For example, the reward function $\mathfrak{c}$ defined as $\mathfrak{c}(s) = 0$ and $\mathfrak{c}(s, s') = 1$ for each $s, s' \in S$ allows us to "count" the number of steps taken by the DTMC.

Let $\mathcal{D}$ be a DTMC; a *path* π of $\mathcal{D}$ is a (possibly infinite) sequence of states $\pi = s_0 s_1 s_2 \cdots$ such that for each meaningful $i \in \mathbb{N}$, we have $\mathbf{P}(s_i, s_{i+1}) > 0$; we write π_i to indicate the state s_i. We let $Paths^*(\mathcal{D})$ ($Paths(\mathcal{D})$, resp.) denote the sets of all finite (infinite, resp.) paths of $\mathcal{D}$. Given a finite path $\pi = s_0 s_1 s_2 \cdots s_n$, we denote by $|\pi|$ the number of states $n + 1$ of π.

Given a DTMRM $\mathcal{R} = (\mathcal{D}, \mathfrak{r})$, we can define the *expected cumulative reward* $ExpRew_s^{\mathcal{R}}$ as follows (cf. [6,32,43]): given set $T \subseteq S$ of states, $ExpRew_s^{\mathcal{R}}(T)$ is the expectation of the random variable $X^T \colon Paths(\mathcal{D}) \to \mathbb{R}_{\geq 0}$ with respect to the X^T defined as follows:

$$X^T(\pi) = \begin{cases} 0 & \text{if } \pi_0 \in T, \\ \infty & \text{if } \pi_i \notin T \text{ for each } i \in \mathbb{N}, \\ \sum_{i=0}^{\min\{n \in \mathbb{N} \mid \pi_n \in T\}-1} \mathfrak{r}(\pi_i) + \mathfrak{r}(\pi_i, \pi_{i+1}) & \text{otherwise.} \end{cases}$$

2.2   Probabilistic Reward Logic PRCTL

To express properties about probabilistic models with rewards, we use formulas from PRCTL, the Probabilistic Reward CTL logic [1], that extends PCTL [10,35] with rewards. Such formulas are constructed according to the following grammar, where φ is a *state formula* and ψ is a *path formula*:

$$\varphi ::= a \mid \neg\varphi \mid \varphi \wedge \varphi \mid \mathsf{P}_{\bowtie p}(\psi) \mid \mathsf{R}_{\bowtie r}(\mathbf{F}\varphi)$$

$$\psi ::= \mathbf{X}\varphi \mid \varphi \, \mathbf{U} \, \varphi \mid \varphi \, \mathbf{U}^{\leq k} \, \varphi$$

where $a \in AP$, $\bowtie \in \{<, \leq, \geq, >\}$, $p \in [0, 1]$, $r \in \mathbb{R}_{\geq 0}$, and $k \in \mathbb{N}$. We use freely the usually derived operators, like $\varphi_1 \vee \varphi_2 = \neg(\neg\varphi_1 \wedge \neg\varphi_2)$, $\mathsf{tt} = a \vee \neg a$, and $\mathbf{F}\varphi = \mathsf{tt} \, \mathbf{U} \, \varphi$. The PCTL logic is just PRCTL without the $\mathsf{R}_{\bowtie r}(\mathbf{F}\varphi)$ operator.

The semantics of a state formula φ and of a path formula ψ is given with respect to a state s and a path π of a DTMRM $\mathcal{R} = (\mathcal{D}, \mathfrak{r})$, respectively. The semantics is standard for all Boolean and temporal operators (see, e.g., [6,20]); for the $\mathsf{P}_{\bowtie p}$ operator, it is defined as $s \models \mathsf{P}_{\bowtie p}(\psi)$ iff $Pr_s(\{\pi \in Paths(\mathcal{D}) \mid \pi \models \psi\}) \bowtie p$ and, similarly, $s \models \mathsf{R}_{\bowtie r}(\psi)$ iff $ExpRew_s(\{\pi \in Paths(\mathcal{D}) \mid \pi \models \psi\}) \bowtie r$.

With some abuse of notation, we write $\mathcal{R} \models \varphi$ if $\bar{s} \models \varphi$; we also consider $\mathsf{P}_{=?}(\psi)$ and $\mathsf{R}_{=?}(\psi)$ as PRCTL formulas, asking to compute the probability (resp.

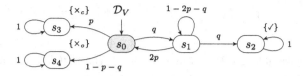

Fig. 2. An example of parametric discrete time Markov chain

expected reward) of satisfying ψ in the initial state $\bar{s}$ of $\mathcal{R}$, i.e., to compute the value $Pr_{\bar{s}}(\{\pi \in Paths(\mathcal{D}) \mid \pi \models \psi\})$ (resp. $ExpRew_{\bar{s}}(\{\pi \in Paths(\mathcal{D}) \mid \pi \models \psi\}))$.

Consider the DTMC $\mathcal{D}$ shown in Fig. 1. As an example of PRCTL formula, there is $\mathrm{P}_{=?}(\mathbf{F}\checkmark)$ that asks to compute the probability of eventually reaching a state labelled with $\checkmark$, for which we have $\mathrm{P}_{=?}(\mathbf{F}\checkmark) \approx 0.78$.

2.3 Parametric Models

We now recall the definition of parametric models from [30,32]. Given a finite set of *variables*, or *parameters*, $\mathrm{V} = \{v_1, \ldots, v_n\}$, let $\mathbf{v} = (v_1, \ldots, v_n)$ denote the vector of parameters and range: $\mathrm{V} \to \mathbb{R}$ be the function assigning to each parameter $v \in \mathrm{V}$ its closed interval $range(v) = [L_v, U_v] \subseteq \mathbb{R}$ of valid values. Given the ring $\mathcal{P}_\mathrm{V}$ of the polynomials with variables V over the field $\mathbb{R}$ of real numbers, a *rational function* f is a fraction $f(\mathbf{v}) = \frac{g_1(\mathbf{v})}{g_2(\mathbf{v})}$ where $g_1, g_2 \in \mathcal{P}_\mathrm{V}$; let $\mathcal{F}_\mathrm{V}$ denote the set of rational functions. An *evaluation* ν is a function $\nu \colon \mathrm{V} \to \mathbb{R}$ such that for each $v \in \mathrm{V}$, $\nu(v) \in range(v)$. Given $f = \frac{g_1}{g_2} \in \mathcal{F}_\mathrm{V}$ and an evaluation ν, we denote by $f\langle\nu\rangle$ the rational number $f(\nu(\mathbf{v})) = f(\nu(v_1), \ldots, \nu(v_n))$; we assume that $f\langle\nu\rangle$ is well defined for each evaluation ν, that is, we assume that $g_2\langle\nu\rangle \neq 0$ for each evaluation ν.

Definition 3. *Given a finite set of parameters* V, *a parametric discrete time Markov chain (pDTMC)* $\mathcal{D}_\mathrm{V}$ *with parameters* V *is a tuple* $\mathcal{D}_\mathrm{V} = (S, \bar{s}, \mathbf{P}, L)$ *where* S, $\bar{s}$, *and* L *are as in Definition 1, while* $\mathbf{P} \colon S \times S \to \mathcal{F}_\mathrm{V}$.

Definition 4. *Given a pDTMC* $\mathcal{D}_\mathrm{V} = (S, \bar{s}, \mathbf{P}, L)$, *an evaluation* ν *induces the DTMC* $\mathcal{D}\langle\nu\rangle = (S, \bar{s}, \mathbf{P}_\nu, L)$, *provided that* $\mathbf{P}_\nu(s, s') = \mathbf{P}(s, s')\langle\nu\rangle$ *for each* $s, s' \in S$ *satisfies the conditions given in Definition 1.*

The extension to parametric DTMRMs (pDTMRMs) is trivial: a pDTMRM $\mathcal{R}_\mathrm{V}$ is just a pair $\mathcal{R}_\mathrm{V} = (\mathcal{D}_\mathrm{V}, \mathfrak{r})$ where $\mathcal{D}_\mathrm{V}$ is a pDTMC and $\mathfrak{r}$ is a reward function.

To simplify the presentation and ensure that the underlying graph of $\mathcal{D}_\mathrm{V}$ does not depend on the actual evaluation, we make the following assumption:

Assumption 1 (cf. [30]). *Given a pDTMC* $\mathcal{D}_\mathrm{V}$, *for each pair of evaluations* ν_1 *and* ν_2, *for the induced DTMCs* $\mathcal{D}_\mathrm{V}\langle\nu_1\rangle$ *and* $\mathcal{D}_\mathrm{V}\langle\nu_2\rangle$ *we have that for each* $s, s' \in S$, *it holds that* $\mathbf{P}_{\nu_1}(s, s') = 0$ *if and only if* $\mathbf{P}_{\nu_2}(s, s') = 0$.

By this assumption, either a state s' has probability 0 to be reached from s (i.e., it is not reachable) independently of the evaluation, or it is always reachable, with possibly different probability values.

As an example of pDTMC, consider the model shown in Fig. 2: now, p and q are the parameters, with e.g. range$(p) = [0.01, 0.09]$ and range$(q) = [0.25, 0.8]$. One evaluation is $\nu(p) = 0.05$ and $\nu(q) = 0.8$, which gives us the DTMC shown in Fig. 1. The rational function corresponding to the PRCTL formula $P_{=?}(\mathbf{F}\checkmark)$ is $\frac{q^2}{q+2p-2pq} \approx 0.78$ when evaluated on ν, as one would expect.

3 Probably Approximately Correct Function Synthesis

In this section, we show how to approximate the exact functions for the properties of Markov models such as reachability probability with low-degree polynomials, while providing a statistical PAC guarantee on the closeness of the approximating polynomial with the approximated function.

3.1 Probably Approximately Correct Models

Our method provides a PAC approximation, with respect to the given significance level η and error rate ε. First, we define the PAC approximation of a generic function f as follows.

Definition 5. *Given a set of n variables $V = \{v_1, \ldots, v_n\}$, their domain $X = \prod_{i=1}^{n} \text{range}(v_i)$, and a function $f \colon X \to \mathbb{R}$, let P be a probability measure over X, $\lambda \in \mathbb{R}_{\geq 0}$ be a margin to measure the approximation error, and $\varepsilon, \eta \in (0, 1]$ be an error rate and a significance level, respectively.*

We say that the polynomial $\tilde{f} \in \mathcal{P}_V$ is a PAC approximation of f with (ε, η)-guarantee if, with confidence $1 - \eta$, the following condition holds:

$$P(|\tilde{f}(\mathbf{v}) - f(\mathbf{v})| \leq \lambda) \geq 1 - \varepsilon.$$

In this work, we assume that P is the uniform distribution on the domain $X = \prod_{i=1}^{n} \text{range}(v_i)$ unless otherwise specified. Intuitively, our aim is to make the PAC approximation $\tilde{f}$ as close as possible to f, so we introduce the margin λ to describe how close the two functions are. The two statistical parameters η and ε are the significance level and error rate, respectively; they are used to measure how often the difference between $\tilde{f}$ and f respects the threshold λ. Specifically, the significance level η is a threshold set to describe the degree of risk of accepting an error while the error rate ε is used to describe the probability that the difference between the value $f(\mathbf{v})$ and $\tilde{f}(\mathbf{v})$ obtained by randomly sampled $\mathbf{v}$ in the domain X exceeds λ, so we can adjust these parameters to change the quality of the approximation.

3.2 The Scenario Approach

PAC approximation is inspired by the scenario approach proposed in [16,18], where the scenario approach was originally applied to robust convex programming problems [7,8,29]. Robust convex programming problems are a type of uncertain convex optimization problem, which has a general form as follows:

$$\min_{\theta \in \Theta \subseteq \mathbb{R}^m} \quad \mathbf{a}^T \theta$$
$$\text{s.t.} \quad f_\omega(\theta) \leq 0 \qquad \forall \omega \in \Omega \tag{1}$$

under the assumption that $f_\omega \colon \Theta \to \mathbb{R}$ is a convex function of $\theta \in \Theta$ for every uncertain parameter $\omega \in \Omega$. We also assume that the set Θ is convex and closed.

The set Ω has an infinite number of elements in general, the main obstacle on solving the optimization problem (1) is that it has infinitely many constraints. In most cases, robust convex optimization problems are NP-hard [7,8]. Instead of solving the problem (1), based on the famous Helly theorem in convex analysis [54], the work [16] transform problem (1) to scenario optimization problem as formalized in Definition 6 by using finitely many constraints, while providing statistical guarantee on the error rate made with respect to the exact solution of (1).

Definition 6. *Let P be a probability measure over set Ω and $\omega_1, \ldots, \omega_l$ be l independent identically distributed samples taken from Ω according to P. The scenario optimization problem corresponding to the problem (1) is defined as*

$$\min_{\theta \in \Theta \subseteq \mathbb{R}^m} \quad \mathbf{a}^T \theta$$
$$\text{s.t.} \quad \bigwedge_{i=1}^{l} f_{\omega_i}(\theta) \leq 0 \qquad \omega_i \in \Omega \tag{2}$$

The optimization problem (2) can be seen as the relaxation of the problem (1), since we do not require that the optimal solution θ_l^* of the problem (2) satisfies all constraints $f_\omega(\theta_l^*) \leq 0$ for each $\omega \in \Omega$, but only the constraints corresponding to the l samples from Ω according to P. The issue now is how to provide a strong enough guarantee that the optimal solution θ_l^* of (2) also satisfies the other constraints $f_\omega(\theta) \leq 0$ with $\omega \in \Omega \backslash \{\omega_i\}_{i=1}^l$ we have not considered.

To answer this question, an *error rate* ε is introduced to bound the probability that the solution θ_l^* violates the constraints of problem (1); we denote by η the *significance level* with respect to the random sampling solution algorithm. Statistics theory ensures that as the number of samples l increases, the probability that the optimal solution of the optimization problem (2) violates the other unseen constraints will tend to zero rapidly. The minimal number of sampled points l is related to the error rate $\varepsilon \in (0, 1]$ and significance level $\eta \in (0, 1]$ by:

Theorem 1 ([18]). *If the optimization problem (2) is feasible and has a unique optimal solution θ_l^*, then $P(f_\omega(\theta_l^*) > 0) < \varepsilon$, with confidence at least $1 - \eta$, provided that the number of constraints l satisfies*

$$l \geq \frac{2}{\varepsilon} \cdot \left(\ln \frac{1}{\eta} + m \right),$$

where m is the dimension of θ, that is, $\theta \in \Theta \subseteq \mathbb{R}^m$, ε and η are the given error rate and significance level, respectively.

Theorem 1 indicates that the number of sampling points can be flexibly changed according to the error rate, confidence level, and the number of parameters. We can observe that when the error rate ε is fixed, the number of sampling points l is linearly related to the number of parameters m. In Theorem 1, we assume that the optimization problem (2) has a unique optimal solution θ_l^*. This is not a restriction in general, since for multiple optimal solutions we can just use the Tie-break rule [16] to get a unique optimal solution.

3.3   Synthesizing Parametric Functions

We now apply the above scenario approach to the synthesis of the parametric functions for pDTMRMs. Given a pDTMRM $\mathcal{R}_V = (\mathcal{D}_V, \mathbf{r})$ with $\mathcal{D}_V = (S, \bar{s}, \mathbf{P}, L)$, let $\mathbf{v}$ denote the vector of parameters $(v_1, \ldots, v_n)$ of $\mathcal{D}_V$. For a PRCTL state formula φ, the analytic function $f_\varphi(\mathbf{v})$, representing the probability or the expected reward of the paths satisfying φ in the pDTMRM $\mathcal{R}_V$, can be a rational function with a very complicated form [31,32] since the polynomials in these rational functions may have exponentially many terms. Our aim is to approximate the function $f_\varphi(\mathbf{v})$ with some low degree polynomial $\tilde{f}_\varphi(\mathbf{v})$.

The reason why we choose a polynomial $\tilde{f}_\varphi(\mathbf{v})$ with low degree to fit the rational function $f_\varphi(\mathbf{v})$ is that the graph of polynomials $\tilde{f}_\varphi(\mathbf{v})$ and original functions $f_\varphi(\mathbf{v})$ are both surfaces and the polynomial $\tilde{f}_\varphi(\mathbf{v})$ can approximate the rational function $f_\varphi(\mathbf{v})$ well if we synthesize appropriately the coefficients $\mathbf{c} = (\mathbf{c}_0, \mathbf{c}_1, \mathbf{c}_2)$ of the polynomial by learning them.

It is worth mentioning that no matter how complicated the function $f_\varphi(\mathbf{v})$ is (it could also be any kind of function other than rational functions), we can still obtain an approximating polynomial $\tilde{f}_\varphi(\mathbf{v})$ of $f_\varphi(\mathbf{v})$ by solving an optimization problem, and utilize it to analyze various properties the original function $f_\varphi(\mathbf{v})$ may satisfy. In the remainder of this section, we show how we synthesize such coefficients $\mathbf{c}$, and thus the polynomial; we first introduce some notations.

Given the vector of parameters $\mathbf{v}$ and a degree $d \in \mathbb{N}$, we denote by $\mathbf{v}^d$ the vector of monomials $\mathbf{v}^d = (\mathbf{v}^\alpha)_{\|\alpha\|_1 = d}$, where each monomial $\mathbf{v}^\alpha$ is defined as $\mathbf{v}^\alpha = v_1^{\alpha_1} v_2^{\alpha_2} \cdots v_n^{\alpha_n}$, with $\alpha = (\alpha_1, \ldots, \alpha_n) \in \mathbb{N}^n$ and $\|\alpha\|_1 = \sum_{i=1}^n \alpha_i$. Then, we associate a vector $\mathbf{c}_i$ of coefficients to each of the monomials in the vector $(\mathbf{v}^i)_{i=0}^d$, obtaining the PAC approximation $\tilde{f}(\mathbf{v}) = \sum_{i=0}^d \mathbf{c}_i \cdot \mathbf{v}^i$. For example, if the pDTMC $\mathcal{D}_V$ has two parameters v_1 and v_2, then for $d = 2$ we get the quadratic polynomial $\tilde{f}(\mathbf{v}) = \mathbf{c}_0 + \mathbf{c}_1 \cdot \mathbf{v} + \mathbf{c}_2 \cdot \mathbf{v}^2 = c_0 + (c_{11} \cdot v_1 + c_{12} \cdot v_2) + (c_{21} \cdot v_1^2 + c_{22} \cdot v_1 \cdot v_2 + c_{23} \cdot v_2^2)$. In general, for n parameters and a polynomial of degree d, we need $\binom{n+d}{n}$ coefficients.

Given a PAC approximation schema $\tilde{f}(\mathbf{v}) = \sum_{i=0}^d \mathbf{c}_i \cdot \mathbf{v}^i = \mathbf{c} \cdot (1, \mathbf{v}, \cdots, \mathbf{v}^d)^T$, we solve the following Linear Programming (LP) problem with infinitely many constraints to learn the coefficients $\mathbf{c} = (\mathbf{c}_i)_1^d$ of the polynomial $\tilde{f}(\mathbf{v})$:

$$\min_{\mathbf{c}, \lambda} \quad \lambda$$

$$\text{s.t.} \quad -\lambda \leq f(\mathbf{v}) - \mathbf{c} \cdot (1, \mathbf{v}, \ldots, \mathbf{v}^d)^T \leq \lambda, \qquad \forall \mathbf{v} \in X, \qquad (3)$$

$$\mathbf{c} \in \mathbb{R}^{\binom{n+d}{n}}, \lambda \geq 0$$

where $f(\mathbf{v})$ is the analytic function on the domain $X = \prod_{i=1}^n \text{range}(v_i)$, the domain $\mathbb{R}^{\binom{n+d}{n}}$ of vectors $\mathbf{c}$ is convex and closed, and the constraints of (3) are continuous convex functions with respect to the variable $\mathbf{c}$ for any $\mathbf{v}$, which satisfies the condition of Theorem 1. Note that for pDTMRMs we do not need to compute the rational function f_φ used as f in problem (3) to get its value on $\mathbf{v}$, since we can first instantiate the pDTMRM with $\mathbf{v}$ and then compute the value of φ in the instantiated DTMRM.

Given the error rate ε and the significance level η, by Theorem 1 we need only to independently and identically sample at least $l \geq \frac{2}{\varepsilon}\left(\ln\frac{1}{\eta} + \binom{n+d}{n} + 1\right)$ points $\tilde{X} = \{\mathbf{v}_i\}_{i=1}^l$ to form the constraints used in the relaxed LP problem, as done in the problem (2). Concretely, we get the following LP problem:

$$
\begin{aligned}
&\min_{\mathbf{c},\lambda} \quad \lambda \\
&\text{s.t.} \quad \bigwedge_{i=1}^{l} -\lambda \leq f(\mathbf{v}_i) - \mathbf{c}\cdot(1,\mathbf{v}_i,\cdots,\mathbf{v}_i^d)^T \leq \lambda, \qquad \forall \mathbf{v}_i \in \tilde{X}, \quad (4) \\
&\qquad \mathbf{c} \in \mathbb{R}^{\binom{n+d}{d}}, \lambda \geq 0.
\end{aligned}
$$

We solve the optimization problem (4) to get the coefficients $\mathbf{c}$, hence the PAC approximation $\tilde{f}$ of the original function f, with the statistical guarantees given by Definition 5; in the context of a pDTMRM $\mathcal{R}_V$ and a PRCTL state formula φ, we get the PAC approximation $\tilde{f}_\varphi$ of the original function f_φ.

3.4 PRCTL Property Analysis

Given the probabilistic formula $\varphi = \mathsf{P}_{=?}(\psi)$ with path formula ψ, we can obviously use the PAC approximation $\tilde{f}_\varphi$ to check whether the domain of parameters X is safe, with PAC guarantee. In this section, we introduce a direct PAC based approach for checking domain's safety, without having to learn the approximations first. Then, we consider linear approximations and discuss how counterexamples can be generated in this case before showing how the polynomial PAC approximation $\tilde{f}_\varphi$ can be used to analyze global properties of f_φ over the whole parameter space X. Lastly, we present how to extend the approach to the reward formula $\varphi = \mathsf{R}_{=?}(\mathbf{F}\varphi')$.

Definition 7 (Safe Region). *Let $X = \prod_{i=1}^{n} \mathrm{range}(v_i)$ be the domain of a set of n parameters V. Given a function $f: X \to \mathbb{R}_{\geq 0}$ and a safety level $\zeta \in \mathbb{R}_{\geq 0}$, we say that the point $\mathbf{v} \in V$ is safe if and only if $f(\mathbf{v}) < \zeta$; we call X safe if and only if each $\mathbf{v} \in V$ is safe.*

Intuitively, we hope that the probability of the pDTMRM $\mathcal{R}_V$ to reach an unsafe state under any choice of the parameters will be less than the given safety level, to check whether the domain X of the parameters is safe, we can resort to solve the following optimization problem with respect to the given error rate ε and significance level η, and compare the obtained optimal solution λ^* with ζ:

$$
\begin{aligned}
&\min \quad \lambda \\
&\text{s.t.} \quad f(\mathbf{v}) \leq \lambda \qquad \forall \mathbf{v} \in \tilde{X},
\end{aligned}
\qquad (5)
$$

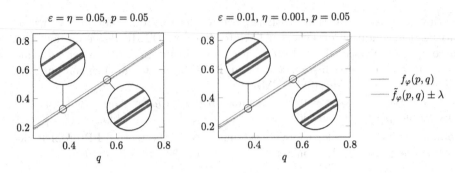

Fig. 3. The rational function $f_\varphi(p,q) = \frac{q^2}{q+2p-2pq}$ and its linear approximations $\tilde{f}_\varphi(p,q)$ with different choices of ε and η

where $\tilde{X} \subseteq X$ is a set of samples such that $|\tilde{X}| \geq \left\lceil \frac{2}{\varepsilon} \cdot (\ln \frac{1}{\eta} + 1) \right\rceil$. The optimization problem (5) can be solved in time $\mathcal{O}(|\tilde{X}|)$, since it only needs to compute the maximum value of $f_\varphi(\mathbf{v})$ for $\mathbf{v} \in \tilde{X}$ as the optimal solution λ^*. Although the calculation is very simple, polynomials with degree 0, i.e., constants, also have good probability and statistical meaning, so we have the following result as a direct consequence of the definitions:

Lemma 1. *Given the safety level ζ, if the optimal solution λ^* of the problem (5) satisfies $\lambda^* < \zeta$, then the domain X is safe with (ε, η)-guarantee. Otherwise, if $\lambda^* \geq \zeta$, then the parameter point $\mathbf{v}^* \in \tilde{X}$ corresponding to λ^* is unsafe.*

By Lemma 1, we can analyze with (ε, η)-guarantee whether the parameter space is safe or not. For example, consider the pDTMC $\mathcal{D}_V$ shown in Fig. 2 and the safety property $\mathsf{P}_{<0.8}(\mathbf{F}(\times_c \vee \times_o))$. If we set $\varepsilon = \eta = 0.05$, by sampling in the region $X = [0.01, 0.09] \times [0.25, 0.8]$ at least 160 points and solving the resulting optimization problem (5), we get the optimal value $\lambda^* = 0.747$ by rounding to three decimals. Since $\lambda^* = 0.747 < 0.8$, by Lemma 1, the region X is safe with $(0.05, 0.05)$-guarantee.

Linear PAC Approximation and Counterexamples. Since constants can approximate the maximum value of the function f with the given (ε, η)-PAC guarantee, linear functions can also be used to approximate f, which are more precise than constants. Also, we can check whether there is an unsafe region in the domain of parameters X with a given confidence, by the following Lemma 2, and further search counterexamples by linear PAC approximations.

Lemma 2. *Given the domain of parameters X, a function $f : X \to \mathbb{R}_{\geq 0}$, and a probability measure P over X, let $\tilde{f}$ be a PAC approximation of f with (ε, η)-guarantee. Given the safety level $\zeta \in \mathbb{R}_{\geq 0}$, if for each $\mathbf{v} \in X$ we have $\tilde{f}(\mathbf{v}) + \lambda < \zeta$, then $P(f(\mathbf{v}) < \zeta) \geq 1 - \varepsilon$ holds with confidence $1 - \eta$. In turn, if $P(\tilde{f}(\mathbf{v}) - \lambda > \zeta) > \varepsilon$, then there exist $\mathbf{v} \in X$ such that $f(\mathbf{v}) > \zeta$ holds with confidence $1 - \eta$.*

The plots in Fig. 3 show the results of applying linear PAC approximation on the function $f_\varphi(p,q)$, with $\varphi = P_{=?}(\mathbf{F}\checkmark)$, for the pDTMC $\mathcal{D}_V$ shown in Fig. 2. We sampled 280 points for $\varepsilon = \eta = 0.05$ and 2182 points for $\varepsilon = 0.01$ and $\eta = 0.001$, respectively, according to Thm. 1. The plot on the left, where we fix the parameter $p = 0.05$, shows that even if we sample just 280 points, $f_\varphi(p,q)$ and $\tilde{f}_\varphi(p,q)$ are closer than the computed margin λ. For the case $\varepsilon = \eta = 0.05$, the linear approximation is $\tilde{f}_\varphi(p,q) = -0.035 + 1.063q - 0.718p$ with $\lambda = 0.011$ by rounding the coefficients to three decimals. We can easily check that for each $(p,q) \in X$ we have $\tilde{f}_\varphi(p,q) + \lambda < 0.85$ by linear programming, so $X = [0.01, 0.09] \times [0.25, 0.8]$ is a 0.85-safe region with respect to $f_\varphi(p,q)$ with $(0.05, 0.05)$-guarantee. However, if we set $\zeta = 0.6$, we can prove $P(\tilde{f}_\varphi - \lambda > \zeta) = 0.288 > \varepsilon = 0.05$, so by Lemma 2 we get that there exist an unsafe region such that $f(p,q) > \zeta$, with confidence 95%.

We can take advantage of the easy computation of linear programming with linear functions to further search for potential counterexamples that may exist. The maximum value of $\tilde{f}_\varphi$ can be found at $(0.01, 0.8)$, according to the linearity of $\tilde{f}_\varphi$, so we can instantiate the pDTMC $\mathcal{D}_V$ in Fig. 2 with the parameter point $(0.01, 0.8)$ to get that $f_\varphi(p,q) = 0.796$. Since $f_\varphi(p,q) > 0.6$ for the safety level $\zeta = 0.6$, we can claim that the *real counterexample* $(0.01, 0.8)$ is found. In the case that the parameter point $\mathbf{v}_0 = (p,q)$ corresponding to maximum value of $\tilde{f}_\varphi$ is a spurious counterexample for the pDTMC with respect to φ, we can learn a more precise approximation by adding $\mathbf{v}_0$ to $\tilde{X}$. One may also divide the domain X into several subdomains and analyze each of them separately.

As for the computational complexity, it is easy to find the maximum value of a linear function by linear programming; on the other hand, computing the maximum value of polynomials and rational functions is rather difficult if their degree is very high or the dimension of the parameter space is too large. So a linear function is a good alternative to compute the maximum value of f with PAC guarantee, while polynomials are suitable for analyzing more complicated properties, such as the global ones considered below.

Polynomial PAC Approximation. One advantage of polynomials over rational functions is that they make it easy to compute complex operations such as inner product and integral [55], as needed to evaluate e.g. the L_p norm $\|g\|_p = \sqrt[p]{\int_Z |g(z)|^p \, dz}$ of a function $g \colon Z \to \mathbb{R}$, with $p \geq 1$. This means that we can adopt polynomials to check some more complicated properties of a pDTMRM $\mathcal{R}_V$, such as whether the function f_φ is close to a given number β on the whole parameter space X. This is useful, for instance, to evaluate how much the behavior of $\mathcal{R}_V$ with respect to the property φ is affected by the variations of the parameters. We can model this situation as follows:

Definition 8. *Given the domain X of a set of parameters, a function $f \colon X \to \mathbb{R}_{\geq 0}$, a safety level ζ, and $\beta \in \mathbb{R}_{\geq 0}$, we say that f is near β within the safety level ζ on X with respect to the L_p norm, if $\|f - \beta\|_p < \zeta$.*

To verify the above property, we can rely on the following result:

Lemma 3. *Given X, f, ζ, and β as in Definition 8, let M be an upper bound of $f(X)$ and $\tilde{f}$ be a PAC approximation of f with (ε, η)-guarantee and margin λ; let $|X| = \int_X 1 \, d\mathbf{v}$. For each $p \geq 1$, if $\tilde{f}$ satisfies the condition*

$$\sqrt[p]{\left(\lambda \sqrt[p]{(1-\varepsilon) \cdot |X|} + \|\tilde{f} - \beta\|_p\right)^p} + \varepsilon \cdot |X| \cdot \max(|M - \beta|^p, \beta^p) < \zeta \quad (6)$$

then $\|f - \beta\|_p < \zeta$ holds with confidence $1 - \eta$.

Consider again the pDTMC $\mathcal{D}_V$ shown in Fig. 2 and $\varphi = \mathrm{P}_{=?}(\mathbf{F}\checkmark)$; since f_φ represents probabilities, we have the well-known upper bound $M = 1$. Here we consider the L_2 norm, which is widely used in describing the error between functions in the signal processing field (see, e.g., [12, 21]), as it can reflect the global approximation properties and is easy to compute. To simplify the notation, let UB denote the complex expression occurring in the formula (6), that is:

$$UB(\tilde{f}_\varphi, X, \beta) = \sqrt{\left(\lambda \sqrt{(1-\varepsilon) \cdot |X|} + \|\tilde{f}_\varphi - \beta\|_2\right)^2 + \varepsilon \cdot |X| \cdot \max(|1 - \beta|^2, \beta^2)}.$$

We want to know whether $f_\varphi(p, q) = \frac{q^2}{q + 2p - 2pq}$ is near 0.5 within 0.05, i.e., given the safety level $\zeta = 0.05$, we want to check $\|f_\varphi - 0.5\|_2 < 0.05$. According to Lemma 3, we first compute a PAC approximation $\tilde{f}_\varphi$ of f_φ. By setting $\varepsilon = \eta = 0.05$, we get the quadratic polynomial $\tilde{f}_\varphi(p, q) = 0.013 + 0.925q - 1.442p + 0.953pq + 2.072p^2 + 0.085q^2$, by rounding to three decimals. In this case, we get $UB(\tilde{f}_\varphi, X, \beta) = 0.0432 < \zeta = 0.05$, so Lemma 3 applies. If, instead, we would have chosen $\zeta' = 0.04$, then we cannot prove $\|f_\varphi - 0.5\|_2 < 0.04$ by relying on Lemma 3. To do so, we need to consider the more conservative values $\varepsilon = 0.01$ and $\eta = 0.001$, which give us $UB(\tilde{f}_\varphi, X, \beta) = 0.0379 < \zeta' = 0.04$, so we can derive that $\|f_\varphi - 0.5\|_2 < 0.04$ holds with confidence 99.9%.

Extension to Reward Models. The extension of the constructions given above to reward properties is rather easy: for instance, we can approximate the rational function representing the state property $\varphi = \mathrm{R}_{=?}(\mathbf{F}\varphi')$, the reward counterpart of $\mathrm{P}_{=?}(\psi')$, by instantiating $f_\varphi(\mathbf{v}_i)$ in Problem (4) with the expected reward value computed on the pDTMC instantiated with $\mathbf{v}_i$. Similarly, we can compute linear and polynomial PAC approximations for safe regions, with the latter defined in terms of the value of the reward instead of the probability.

We can consider also the following case: given a pDTMRM $\mathcal{R}_V$, we want to verify whether the expected value of $\varphi = \mathrm{R}_{=?}(\mathbf{F}\varphi')$ over the parameters $\mathbf{v}$, denoted $f_\varphi(\mathbf{v})$, can reach a given reward level ρ. This model the scenarios where, to make a decision, we need to know whether the expectation of the rewards for a certain decision satisfies the given conditions. We formalize this case as follows:

Definition 9. *Given the domain X of a set of parameters, a function $f \colon X \to \mathbb{R}_{\geq 0}$, a reward level ρ, and a probability measure P over X, we say that the expectation of f on X with respect to P can reach the reward level ρ, if*

$$\int_X f(\mathbf{v}) \, dP(\mathbf{v}) > \rho. \quad (7)$$

We can resort to the following lemma to check condition (7):

Lemma 4. *Given X, f, P, and ρ as in Definition 9, let $\tilde{f}$ be a PAC approximation of f with (ε, η)-guarantee and margin λ. If $\tilde{f}$ satisfies the condition*

$$\int_X (\tilde{f}(\mathbf{v}) - \lambda)\, dP(\mathbf{v}) - \varepsilon \cdot |X| \cdot \max_{\mathbf{v} \in X}(\tilde{f}(\mathbf{v}) - \lambda) > \rho, \qquad (8)$$

then Condition (7) holds with confidence $1 - \eta$.

4 Experimental Evaluation

We have implemented the PAC-based analysis approach proposed in Sect. 3 in a prototype tool named PacPMA[1], the PAC-based Parametric Model Analyzer, and evaluated it on several benchmarks: we considered the DTMCs from the PRISM benchmark suite [45], some of the resulting models are also available as examples in the STORM [36] repository[2]. We replaced the probabilistic choices in them with parameters. The probabilistic choices in most of the models correspond to the flip of a fair coin, so we considered three possibles ranges for the parameters, namely $[0.01, 0.33]$, $[0.33, 0.66]$, and $[0.66, 0.99]$, to represent the fact that the coin is strongly unfair to head, rather fair, and strongly unfair to tail, respectively. For the remaining models, where the choice is managed by the uniform distribution over several outcomes, we split the outcomes into two groups (e.g., odd and even outcomes) and then used a parametric coin and five intervals to choose the group. By considering the reachability properties available for each DTMC and the choice of the constants controlling the size of the DTMCs, we get a total of 936 benchmarks for our evaluation for probabilistic properties and 620 benchmarks for expected rewards. We performed our experiments on a desktop machine with an i7-4790 CPU and 16 GB of memory running Ubuntu Server 20.04.4; we used BENCHEXEC [9] to trace and constrain the tools' executions: we allowed each benchmark to use 15 GB of memory and imposed a time limit of 10 min of wall-clock time.

PacPMA is written in JAVA and uses STORM [36] and MATLAB to get the value of the analyzed property and the solution of the LP problem, respectively. We also used STORM v1.7.0 and PRISM [44] v4.7 to compute the actual rational functions for the benchmarks, to check how well our PAC approximation works in practice. We were unable to compare with the fraction-free approach proposed in [5] since it is implemented as an extension of STORM v1.2.1 that fails to build on our system. To avoid to call repeatedly STORM for each sample as an external process, we wrote a C wrapper for STORM that parses the input model and formula and sets the model constants only once, and then repeatedly instantiates the obtained parametric model with the samples and computes the corresponding values of the property, similarly to the batch mode used in [3]. We

---

[1] https://github.com/iscas-tis/PacPMA/.

[2] https://github.com/moves-rwth/storm/.

Table 1. Overview of the outcomes of the experiments

	Outcome	PRISM	STORM	PACPMA^d (1 thread/8 threads)				
				$d=1$	$d=2$	$d=3$	$d=4$	$d=5$
$P_{=?}[\psi]$	Success	522	576	594/629	585/621	576/621	576/621	576/603
	Memoryout	18	63	0/306	0/306	0/306	0/306	0/306
	Timeout	396	297	342/1	351/9	360/9	360/9	360/27
$R_{=?}[\psi]$	Success	153	224	302/302	302/302	302/302	302/302	302/302
	Memoryout	0	0	0/282	0/282	0/282	0/282	0/282
	Timeout	467	396	318/36	318/36	318/36	318/36	318/36

also implemented a multi-threaded evaluation of the sampled points, by calling multiple instances of the wrapper in parallel on a partition of the samples.

4.1   Overall Evaluation

In Table 1 we show the outcome of the different tools on the 936 probabilistic (marked with $P_{=?}[\psi]$) and 620 reward (marked with $R_{=?}[\psi]$) benchmarks, namely whether they successfully produced a rational function or whether they failed by timeout or by running out of memory. Besides the results for PRISM and STORM computing the actual rational function, we report two values for each outcome of PACPMA^d, where the superscript d indicates the degree of the polynomial used as template: in e.g. the pair 594/629, the first value 594 is relative to the single-threaded PACPMA^1, while the value 629 is for the 8-threaded PACPMA^1, i.e., PACPMA with 8 instances of the STORM wrapper running in parallel. As parameters for PACPMA, we set $\varepsilon = \eta = 0.05$; for the benchmarks with two parameters, this results in sampling between 280 and 1000 points, for $d=1$ to $d=5$, respectively. To make the comparison between the different templates fairer, we set the same random seed for each run of PACPMA; this ensures that all samples used by e.g. PACPMA^2 are also used by PACPMA^5.

As we can see from Table 1, PACPMA is able to compute polynomials with different degrees for more benchmarks than STORM and PRISM. By inspecting the single experiments, for the probabilistic properties we have that PRISM $\subseteq$ STORM $\subseteq$ PACPMA^d_n $\subseteq$ PACPMA$^{d'}_n$ for each $d' < d$ degrees and n threads, as sets of successfully solved cases; we also have that PACPMA$^d_1$ $\subseteq$ PACPMA$^d_8$ for each d. For the reward properties we have that PACPMA^d_n = PACPMA$^{d'}_{n'}$ for each combination of $d, d' \in \{1, \cdots, 5\}$ and $n, n' \in \{1, 8\}$ and that STORM, PRISM $\subseteq$ PACPMA^d_n; however STORM and PRISM are incomparable, with cases solved by STORM but not by PRISM, and vice-versa. In the next section we will evaluate how the margin λ changes depending on the degree d and the statistical parameters ε and η through the induced number of samples.

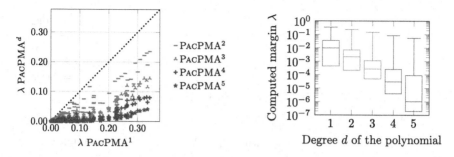

Fig. 4. Scatter plot for the margin λ for different PACPMA^d and box plots for the margin λ

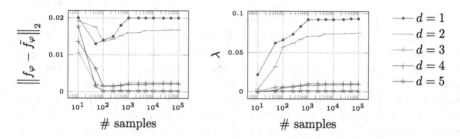

Fig. 5. Value of $\|f_\varphi - \tilde{f}_\varphi\|_2$ and of λ vs. degree of polynomials and number of samples

4.2 Relation of the Polynomial Degree d and the Number of Samples with the Margin λ and the Distance $\|f_\varphi - \tilde{f}_\varphi\|_2$

In Fig. 4 we present plots for PACPMA using polynomial templates with different degrees and how the computed λ changes. As we can see from the plots, by using a higher degree we get a lower value for the margin λ, as one would expect given that polynomials with higher degree can approximate better the shape of the actual rational function: from the box plots on the right side of the figure, we can see that using higher degree polynomials allows us to get values for λ that are much closer to 0. Note that in these box plots we removed the lower whiskers since they are 0 for all degrees, and we use a logarithmic y-axis. The scatter plot shown on the left side of Fig. 4, where we compare the values of λ produced by PACPMA^1 with those by PACPMA^d, for $d = 2, 3, 4, 5$, confirms that the higher the degree is, the closer to 0 the corresponding mark is, since the points for the same benchmark share the same x-axis value.

In Fig. 5 we show the value of $\|f_\varphi - \tilde{f}_\varphi\|_2$ for different degrees of the polynomial and the number of samples, as well as the corresponding values of the computed λ. The plots are relative to one benchmark such that the corresponding rational function (a polynomial having degree 96) computed by STORM can be managed by MATLAB without incurring obvious numerical errors while having the margin λ computed by PACPMA^2 reasonably large ($\lambda \approx 0.063$).

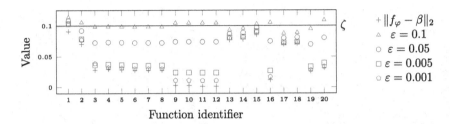

Fig. 6. Comparison of $\|f_\varphi - \beta\|_2$ with $UB(\tilde{f}_\varphi, X, \beta)$ for $\eta = 0.05$ and different ε

From the plots, we can see that we need at least 100 samples to get a rather stable value for $\|f_\varphi - \tilde{f}_\varphi\|_2$, so that the value of $\|f_\varphi - \tilde{f}_\varphi\|_2$ is smaller for higher degrees, which reflects the more accurate polynomial approximation of the original function, in line with the plots in Fig. 4. However, for the same degree, increasing the number of samples does not always lead to a decrease in $\|f_\varphi - \tilde{f}_\varphi\|_2$ value. This happens because with few points, the polynomial can fit them well, as indicated by the low value of λ; however, such few points are likely to be not enough to represent accurately the shape of f_φ. By increasing the number of samples, the shape of f_φ can be known better, in particular where it changes more; this makes it more difficult for the polynomials to approximate f_φ, as indicated by the larger λ; on the other hand, they get closer to f_φ, so $\|f_\varphi - \tilde{f}_\varphi\|_2$ stabilizes.

4.3 Relation of the Statistical Parameters ε and η with the Distances $\|f_\varphi - \beta\|_2$ and $UB(\tilde{f}_\varphi, X, \beta)$

We now consider the behavior of f_φ and whether it remains close to some number β within ζ, that is, we want to check whether $\|f_\varphi - \beta\|_2 < \zeta$ holds. Here we set the safety level ζ to be 0.1 and consider different β's values for different functions f_φ. We consider 20 rational functions computed by STORM that MATLAB can work without incurring in obvious numerical errors, such as those outside the probability interval $[0, 1]$. For each of the function, we computed the corresponding value of β by sampling 20 points for the parameters and taking the average value, rounded to the first decimal, of the function on them. We rely on Lemma 3 to perform the analysis; the results are shown in Fig. 6.

In the figure, we plot the actual value of $\|f_\varphi - \beta\|_2$, the boundary ζ, and the value of $UB(\tilde{f}_\varphi, X, \beta)$ computed with respect to $\eta = 0.05$ and different choices of ε for the 20 functions. As we can see, the smaller ε, the higher the number of cases on which Lemma 3 ensures $\|f_\varphi - \beta\|_2 < \zeta$; this is expected, since a smaller ε increases the number of samples, so the approximating polynomial $\tilde{f}_\varphi$ gets closer to the real shape of f_φ. Moreover, when $\|f_\varphi - \beta\|_2$ is already close to ζ, there is little space for $\tilde{f}_\varphi$ to differ from f_φ, as happens for the e.g. the function 1. Thus it is more difficult for us to be able to rely on Lemma 3 to check whether $\|f_\varphi - \beta\|_2 < \zeta$ holds, even if this actually the case.

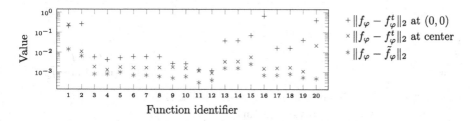

Fig. 7. Distance from f_φ of the Taylor expansion vs. the approximating polynomial

4.4   Comparison with the Taylor Expansion

We compare the accuracy of PAC approximation against that of the Taylor expansion on the same cases used for Fig. 6; the comparison is shown in Fig. 7. For the comparison with f_φ, we consider the degree 2 for both the Taylor expansion f_φ^t and the approximating polynomial $\tilde{f}_\varphi$ computed with $\varepsilon = \eta = 0.05$. For the Taylor expansion f_φ^t, we considered two versions: the expansion at the origin, i.e., $(0,0)$ for two parameters (marked as "$\|f_\varphi - f_\varphi^t\|_2$ at $(0,0)$" in Fig. 7), that is commonly used since it is cheaper to compute than the expansions at other points; and the expansion at the barycenter of the space of the parameters (marked as "$\|f_\varphi - f_\varphi^t\|_2$ at center" in Fig. 7).

As we can see from the plot, that uses a logarithmic scale on the y-axis, the distance $\|f_\varphi - \tilde{f}_\varphi\|_2$ is between one and three orders of magnitude smaller than $\|f_\varphi - f_\varphi^t\|_2$ at the origin. If we consider $\|f_\varphi - f_\varphi^t\|_2$ at the barycenter, we get values much closer to $\|f_\varphi - \tilde{f}_\varphi\|_2$, but still larger up to one order of magnitude. One of the reasons for this is that the Taylor expansion reflects local properties of f_φ at the expansion point, while the PAC approximation provides a global approximation of f_φ, thus reducing the overall distance. Compared with the Taylor expansion, the PAC approximation has also other advantages: the PAC approximation can handle both white-box and black-box problems, i.e., we do not need to get the analytical form of f_φ; this means that we can treat it as a black box and get a good approximation of it while the Taylor expansion can only be applied after computing the actual function f_φ. Moreover, the PAC approximation is able to generate polynomials with any given error rate and provide probabilistic guarantee, while Taylor expansion cannot.

4.5   Extension to Reward Models

In Fig. 8 we show how Eq. (8) applies to $\int_X f_\varphi(\mathbf{v}) \, dP(\mathbf{v})$ for a selection of 30 reward properties f_φ computed by STORM; as usual, we compute $\tilde{f}_\varphi$ with $\varepsilon = \eta = 0.05$. In the figure, we report the actual value of $\int_X f_\varphi(\mathbf{v}) \, dP(\mathbf{v})$ as well as that of the expression in Eq. (8) computed for the polynomial PAC approximations $\tilde{f}_\varphi$ at different degrees. As we can see from Fig. 8, the higher the degree of $\tilde{f}_\varphi$, the more accurate the estimation of the $\int_X f_\varphi(\mathbf{v}) \, dP(\mathbf{v})$'s lower bound is. In particular, the quadratic $\tilde{f}_\varphi$ provides a very close lower bound for $\int_X f_\varphi(\mathbf{v}) \, dP(\mathbf{v})$; this

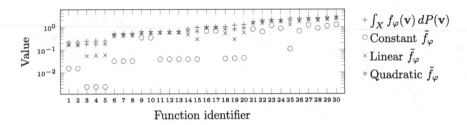

Fig. 8. Lower bound for Eq. (7) by PAC approximation with different degrees

is remarkable, since evaluating $\max(\tilde{f}(\mathbf{v}) - \lambda)$ in Eq. (8) is often an NP-hard non-convex optimization problem [51,56] and, for cubic or higher polynomials, it requires specialized theories and tools to solve [46,47,61].

5   Conclusion

In this paper, we presented a PAC-based approximation framework for studying several properties of parametric discrete time Markov chains. Within the framework, we can analyze the safety regions of the domain of the parameters, check whether the actual probability fluctuates around a reference value within a certain bound, and get a polynomial approximating the actual probability rational function with given (ε, η)-PAC guarantee. An extended experimental evaluation confirmed the efficacy of our framework in analyzing parametric models.

As future work, we plan to investigate the applicability of the scenario approach to other Markov models and properties, such as continuous time Markov chains and Markov decision processes with and without rewards, where parameters can also control the rewards structures. Moreover, we plan to explore the combination of the scenario approach with statistical model checking and black-box verification and model learning.

Acknowledgements. We thank the anonymous reviewers for their useful remarks that helped us improve the quality of the paper. Work supported in part by the CAS Project for Young Scientists in Basic Research under grant No. YSBR-040, NSFC under grant No. 61836005, the CAS Pioneer Hundred Talents Program, the ISCAS New Cultivation Project ISCAS-PYFX-202201, and the ERC Consolidator Grant 864075 (*CAESAR*).

◼ This project is part of the European Union's Horizon 2020 research and innovation programme under the Marie Skłodowska-Curie grant no. 101008233.

Data Availibility Statement. An environment with the tools and data used for the experimental evaluation presented in this work is available in the following Zenodo repository: https://doi.org/10.5281/zenodo.8181117.

References

1. Andova, S., Hermanns, H., Katoen, J.-P.: Discrete-time rewards model-checked. In: Larsen, K.G., Niebert, P. (eds.) FORMATS 2003. LNCS, vol. 2791, pp. 88–104. Springer, Heidelberg (2004). https://doi.org/10.1007/978-3-540-40903-8_8
2. Badings, T.S., Cubuktepe, M., Jansen, N., Junges, S., Katoen, J., Topcu, U.: Scenario-based verification of uncertain parametric MDPs. Int. J. Softw. Tools Technol. Transf. **24**(5), 803–819 (2022). https://doi.org/10.1007/s10009-022-00673-z
3. Badings, T.S., Jansen, N., Junges, S., Stoelinga, M., Volk, M.: Sampling-based verification of CTMCs with uncertain rates. In: Shoham, S., Vizel, Y. (eds.) CAV 2022 Part II. LNCS, vol. 13372, pp. 26–47. Springer, Cham (2022). https://doi.org/10.1007/978-3-031-13188-2_2
4. Bai, H., Cai, S., Ye, N., Hsu, D., Lee, W.S.: Intention-aware online POMDP planning for autonomous driving in a crowd. In: IEEE International Conference on Robotics and Automation, ICRA 2015, Seattle, WA, USA, 26–30 May, 2015, pp. 454–460. IEEE (2015). https://doi.org/10.1109/ICRA.2015.7139219
5. Baier, C., Hensel, C., Hutschenreiter, L., Junges, S., Katoen, J., Klein, J.: Parametric Markov chains: PCTL complexity and fraction-free Gaussian elimination. Inf. Comput. **272**, 104504 (2020). https://doi.org/10.1016/j.ic.2019.104504
6. Baier, C., Katoen, J.: Principles of Model Checking. MIT Press, Cambridge (2008)
7. Ben-Tal, A., Nemirovski, A.: Robust convex optimization. Math. Oper. Res. **23**(4), 769–805 (1998). https://doi.org/10.1287/moor.23.4.769
8. Ben-Tal, A., Nemirovski, A.: Robust solutions of uncertain linear programs. Oper. Res. Lett. **25**(1), 1–13 (1999). https://doi.org/10.1016/S0167-6377(99)00016-4
9. Beyer, D., Löwe, S., Wendler, P.: Reliable benchmarking: requirements and solutions. Int. J. Softw. Tools Technol. Transfer **21**(1), 1–29 (2017). https://doi.org/10.1007/s10009-017-0469-y
10. Bianco, A., de Alfaro, L.: Model checking of probabilistic and nondeterministic systems. In: Thiagarajan, P.S. (ed.) FSTTCS 1995. LNCS, vol. 1026, pp. 499–513. Springer, Heidelberg (1995). https://doi.org/10.1007/3-540-60692-0_70
11. Blackwell, D.: On the functional equation of dynamic programming. J. Math. Anal. Appl. **2**(2), 273–276 (1961)
12. Boggess, A., Narcowich, F.J.: A First Course in Wavelets with Fourier Analysis. Wiley, Hoboken (2015)
13. Bortolussi, L., Milios, D., Sanguinetti, G.: Smoothed model checking for uncertain continuous-time Markov chains. Inf. Comput. **247**, 235–253 (2016). https://doi.org/10.1016/j.ic.2016.01.004
14. Bortolussi, L., Silvetti, S.: Bayesian statistical parameter synthesis for linear temporal properties of stochastic models. In: Beyer, D., Huisman, M. (eds.) TACAS 2018. LNCS, vol. 10806, pp. 396–413. Springer, Cham (2018). https://doi.org/10.1007/978-3-319-89963-3_23
15. Calafiore, G.C., Campi, M.C.: Uncertain convex programs: randomized solutions and confidence levels. Math. Program. **102**(1), 25–46 (2005). https://doi.org/10.1007/s10107-003-0499-y
16. Calafiore, G.C., Campi, M.C.: The scenario approach to robust control design. IEEE Trans. Autom. Control. **51**(5), 742–753 (2006). https://doi.org/10.1109/TAC.2006.875041
17. Campi, M.C., Garatti, S.: A sampling-and-discarding approach to chance-constrained optimization: feasibility and optimality. J. Optim. Theory Appl. **148**(2), 257–280 (2011). https://doi.org/10.1007/s10957-010-9754-6

178   Y. Liu et al.

18. Campi, M.C., Garatti, S., Prandini, M.: The scenario approach for systems and control design. Annu. Rev. Control. **33**(2), 149–157 (2009). https://doi.org/10.1016/j.arcontrol.2009.07.001
19. Carè, A., Garatti, S., Campi, M.C.: Scenario min-max optimization and the risk of empirical costs. SIAM J. Optim. **25**(4), 2061–2080 (2015). https://doi.org/10.1137/130928546
20. Clarke, E.M., Henzinger, T.A., Veith, H., Bloem, R. (eds.): Handbook of Model Checking. Springer, Cham (2018). https://doi.org/10.1007/978-3-319-10575-8
21. Conway, J.B.: A Course in Functional Analysis, vol. 96. Springer, Cham (2019)
22. Daws, C.: Symbolic and parametric model checking of discrete-time Markov chains. In: Liu, Z., Araki, K. (eds.) ICTAC 2004. LNCS, vol. 3407, pp. 280–294. Springer, Heidelberg (2005). https://doi.org/10.1007/978-3-540-31862-0_21
23. Dehnert, C., et al.: PROPhESY: A PRObabilistic ParamEter SYnthesis Tool. In: Kroening, D., Păsăreanu, C.S. (eds.) CAV 2015. LNCS, vol. 9206, pp. 214–231. Springer, Cham (2015). https://doi.org/10.1007/978-3-319-21690-4_13
24. Dehnert, C., Junges, S., Katoen, J., Volk, M.: A storm is coming: A modern probabilistic model checker. In: Majumdar, R., Kuncak, V. (eds.) Computer Aided Verification. CAV 2017. LNCS vol. 10427, pp. 592–600. Springer, Cham (2017). https://doi.org/10.1007/978-3-319-63390-9_31
25. Dubins, L.E., Savage, L.: How to Gamble If You Must. McGraw-Hill (1965)
26. Fang, X., Calinescu, R., Gerasimou, S., Alhwikem, F.: Fast parametric model checking through model fragmentation. In: 43rd IEEE/ACM International Conference on Software Engineering, ICSE 2021, Madrid, Spain, 22–30 May 2021, pp. 835–846. IEEE (2021). https://doi.org/10.1109/ICSE43902.2021.00081
27. Gainer, P., Hahn, E.M., Schewe, S.: Accelerated model checking of parametric Markov chains. In: Lahiri, S.K., Wang, C. (eds.) ATVA 2018. LNCS, vol. 11138, pp. 300–316. Springer, Cham (2018). https://doi.org/10.1007/978-3-030-01090-4_18
28. Garavel, H., Lang, F., Mateescu, R., Serwe, W.: CADP 2011: a toolbox for the construction and analysis of distributed processes. Int. J. Softw. Tools Technol. Transf. **15**(2), 89–107 (2013). https://doi.org/10.1007/s10009-012-0244-z
29. Ghaoui, L.E., Oustry, F., Lebret, H.: Robust solutions to uncertain semidefinite programs. SIAM J. Optim. **9**(1), 33–52 (1998). https://doi.org/10.1137/S1052623496305717
30. Hahn, E.M., Han, T., Zhang, L.: Synthesis for PCTL in parametric Markov decision processes. In: Bobaru, M., Havelund, K., Holzmann, G.J., Joshi, R. (eds.) NFM 2011. LNCS, vol. 6617, pp. 146–161. Springer, Heidelberg (2011). https://doi.org/10.1007/978-3-642-20398-5_12
31. Hahn, E.M., Hermanns, H., Wachter, B., Zhang, L.: PARAM: a model checker for parametric Markov models. In: Touili, T., Cook, B., Jackson, P. (eds.) CAV 2010. LNCS, vol. 6174, pp. 660–664. Springer, Heidelberg (2010). https://doi.org/10.1007/978-3-642-14295-6_56
32. Hahn, E.M., Hermanns, H., Zhang, L.: Probabilistic reachability for parametric Markov models. Int. J. Softw. Tools Technol. Transf. **13**(1), 3–19 (2011). https://doi.org/10.1007/s10009-010-0146-x
33. Hahn, E.M., Li, Y., Schewe, S., Turrini, A., Zhang, L.: ISCASMC: a web-based probabilistic model checker. In: Jones, C., Pihlajasaari, P., Sun, J. (eds.) FM 2014. LNCS, vol. 8442, pp. 312–317. Springer, Cham (2014). https://doi.org/10.1007/978-3-319-06410-9_22
34. Han, T.: Diagnosis, synthesis and analysis of probabilistic models. In: Bernstein, A., et al. (eds.) Ausgezeichnete Informatikdissertationen 2009, LNI, vol. D-10, pp. 81–90. GI (2009). https://dl.gi.de/handle/20.500.12116/33657

35. Hansson, H., Jonsson, B.: A logic for reasoning about time and reliability. Formal Aspects Comput. **6**(5), 512–535 (1994). https://doi.org/10.1007/BF01211866
36. Hensel, C., Junges, S., Katoen, J., Quatmann, T., Volk, M.: The probabilistic model checker storm. Int. J. Softw. Tools Technol. Transf. **24**(4), 589–610 (2022). https://doi.org/10.1007/s10009-021-00633-z
37. von Hilgers, P., Langville, A.N.: The five greatest applications of Markov chains. In: Proceedings of the Markov Anniversary Meeting, pp. 155–168 (2006)
38. Hopcroft, J.E., Motwani, R., Ullman, J.D.: Introduction to Automata Theory, Languages, and Computation, 3rd edn. Addison-Wesley, Pearson international edition (2007)
39. Jansen, N., et al.: Accelerating parametric probabilistic verification. In: Norman, G., Sanders, W. (eds.) QEST 2014. LNCS, vol. 8657, pp. 404–420. Springer, Cham (2014). https://doi.org/10.1007/978-3-319-10696-0_31
40. Jansen, N., Junges, S., Katoen, J.: Parameter synthesis in Markov models: a gentle survey. In: Raskin, J., Chatterjee, K., Doyen, L., Majumdar, R. (eds.) Principles of Systems Design. LNCS, vol. 13660, pp. 407–437. Springer, Cham (2022). https://doi.org/10.1007/978-3-031-22337-2_20
41. Junges, S., Katoen, J., Pérez, G.A., Winkler, T.: The complexity of reachability in parametric Markov decision processes. J. Comput. Syst. Sci. **119**, 183–210 (2021). https://doi.org/10.1016/j.jcss.2021.02.006
42. Katoen, J., Zapreev, I.S., Hahn, E.M., Hermanns, H., Jansen, D.N.: The ins and outs of the probabilistic model checker MRMC. Perform. Evaluation **68**(2), 90–104 (2011). https://doi.org/10.1016/j.peva.2010.04.001
43. Kwiatkowska, M., Norman, G., Parker, D.: Stochastic model checking. In: Bernardo, M., Hillston, J. (eds.) SFM 2007. LNCS, vol. 4486, pp. 220–270. Springer, Heidelberg (2007). https://doi.org/10.1007/978-3-540-72522-0_6
44. Kwiatkowska, M., Norman, G., Parker, D.: PRISM 4.0: verification of probabilistic real-time systems. In: Gopalakrishnan, G., Qadeer, S. (eds.) CAV 2011. LNCS, vol. 6806, pp. 585–591. Springer, Heidelberg (2011). https://doi.org/10.1007/978-3-642-22110-1_47
45. Kwiatkowska, M.Z., Norman, G., Parker, D.: The PRISM benchmark suite. In: Ninth International Conference on Quantitative Evaluation of Systems, QEST 2012, London, United Kingdom, September 17–20, 2012, pp. 203–204. IEEE Computer Society (2012). https://doi.org/10.1109/QEST.2012.14
46. Lasserre, J.B.: A semidefinite programming approach to the generalized problem of moments. Math. Program. **112**(1), 65–92 (2008). https://doi.org/10.1007/s10107-006-0085-1
47. Lasserre, J.B.: Moments, Positive Polynomials and their Applications, vol. 1. World Scientific, Singapore (2009)
48. Li, R., Yang, P., Huang, C., Sun, Y., Xue, B., Zhang, L.: Towards practical robustness analysis for DNNs based on PAC-model learning. In: 44th IEEE/ACM 44th International Conference on Software Engineering, ICSE 2022, Pittsburgh, PA, USA, May 25–27, 2022, pp. 2189–2201. ACM (2022). https://doi.org/10.1145/3510003.3510143
49. Liu, Y., Turrini, A., Hahn, E.M., Xue, B., Zhang, L.: Scenario approach for parametric Markov models. CoRR abs/2304.08330 (2023). https://doi.org/10.48550/arXiv.2304.08330
50. Margellos, K., Goulart, P., Lygeros, J.: On the road between robust optimization and the scenario approach for chance constrained optimization problems. IEEE Trans. Autom. Control. **59**(8), 2258–2263 (2014). https://doi.org/10.1109/TAC.2014.2303232

51. Pardalos, P.M., Ye, Y., Han, C.G.: Algorithms for the solution of quadratic knapsack problems. Linear Algebra Appl. **152**, 69–91 (1991)

52. Puterman, M.L.: Markov Decision Processes: Discrete Stochastic Dynamic Programming. Wiley Series in Probability and Statistics, Wiley, Hoboken (1994). https://doi.org/10.1002/9780470316887

53. Quatmann, T., Dehnert, C., Jansen, N., Junges, S., Katoen, J.-P.: Parameter synthesis for markov models: faster than ever. In: Artho, C., Legay, A., Peled, D. (eds.) ATVA 2016. LNCS, vol. 9938, pp. 50–67. Springer, Cham (2016). https://doi.org/10.1007/978-3-319-46520-3_4

54. Rockafellar, R.T.: Convex Analysis, vol. 11. Princeton University Press, Princeton (1997)

55. Rudin, W.: Principles of Mathematical Analysis, vol. 3. McGraw-Hill, New York (1976)

56. Sahni, S.: Computationally related problems. SIAM J. Comput. **3**(4), 262–279 (1974). https://doi.org/10.1137/0203021

57. Spel, J., Junges, S., Katoen, J.-P.: Finding provably optimal Markov chains. In: TACAS 2021. LNCS, vol. 12651, pp. 173–190. Springer, Cham (2021). https://doi.org/10.1007/978-3-030-72016-2_10

58. Vayanos, P., Kuhn, D., Rustem, B.: A constraint sampling approach for multi-stage robust optimization. Automatica **48**(3), 459–471 (2012). https://doi.org/10.1016/j.automatica.2011.12.002

59. Watkins, C.J.C.H., Dayan, P.: Q-learning. Mach. Learn. **8**, 279–292 (1992). https://doi.org/10.1007/BF00992698

60. Xue, B., Zhang, M., Easwaran, A., Li, Q.: PAC model checking of black-box continuous-time dynamical systems. IEEE Trans. Comput. Aided Des. Integr. Circuits Syst. **39**(11), 3944–3955 (2020). https://doi.org/10.1109/TCAD.2020.3012251

61. Yang, J., Ye, K., Zhi, L.: Computing sparse Fourier sum of squares on finite Abelian groups in quasi-linear time. CoRR abs/2201.03912 (2022)

Fast Verified SCCs
for Probabilistic Model Checking

Arnd Hartmanns🆔, Bram Kohlen$^{(\boxtimes)}$🆔, and Peter Lammich🆔

University of Twente, Enschede, The Netherlands
b.kohlen@utwente.nl

Abstract. High-performance probabilistic model checkers like the Modest Toolset's mcsta follow the topological ordering of an MDP's strongly connected components (SCCs) to speed up the numerical analysis. They use hand-coded and -optimised implementations of SCC-finding algorithms. Verified SCC-finding implementations so far were orders of magnitudes slower than their unverified counterparts. In this paper, we show how to use a refinement approach with the Isabelle theorem prover to formally verify an imperative SCC-finding implementation that can be swapped in for mcsta's current unverified one. It uses the same state space representation as mcsta, avoiding costly conversions of the representation. We evaluate the verified implementation's performance using an extensive benchmark, and show that its use does not significantly influence mcsta's overall performance. Our work exemplifies a practical approach to incrementally increase the trustworthiness of existing model checking software by replacing unverified components with verified versions of comparable performance.

1 Introduction

Probabilistic model checking [2] is an automated verification technique for system models with randomness, such as Markov decision processes (MDPs). Today's probabilistic model checkers like PRISM [26], STORM [22], or the MODEST TOOLSET [17] check MDPs of tens to hundreds of millions of states on common desktop hardware in minutes. This performance is in part achieved by using the "topological approach" [8, 18] where the analysis treats every sub-MDP corresponding to a strongly connected component (SCC) in the MDP's state-transition graph separately, solving them in their reverse topological order. The most well-known such method is topological value iteration [8], but the same idea applies to other approaches like using linear programming (LP) solvers, with one linear program generated for each SCC.

As verification tools, probabilistic model checkers are critical software: we use them in the design and evaluation of safety- and performance-critical systems, and rely on them delivering correct results. Yet, they are *not* thoroughly verified

Authors are listed in alphabetical order. This work was funded by NWO grant OCENW.KLEIN.311, the EU's Horizon 2020 research and innovation programme under MSCA grant no. 101008233 (MISSION), and NWO VENI grant 639.021.754.

É. André and J. Sun (Eds.): ATVA 2023, LNCS 14215, pp. 181–202, 2023.
https://doi.org/10.1007/978-3-031-45329-8_9

themselves: they constitute large trusted code bases (the MODEST TOOLSET, for example, consists of approx. 150 k lines of C# code as of the writing of this paper) developed ad-hoc in academic contexts. In addition to the danger of implementation bugs, unsound algorithms have been used in probabilistic model checking in the past [14], and published pseudocode contains mistakes (e.g. that of the sound value iteration algorithm given in [41]). This calls for the application of verification technology to the probabilistic model checkers themselves.

Replacing a complete model checker's code base by a fully verified one, keeping the original tool's capabilities and performance, is a gigantic task. For this reason, we today only see inefficient fully verified (non-probabilistic) model checkers [6,44], and fully verified certifiers [43,45] that a posteriori establish the correctness of an unverified model checker's result. The latter, however, require cooperation from the unverified tool to produce an additional compact certificate, and the existence of an efficient certificate verification procedure.

In this paper, we exemplify a third, practical approach with an emphasis on performance: to incrementally replace an existing tool's unverified code by verified implementations of verified algorithms, component-by-component. In order to avoid performance regressions, the new components must use the original data structures and interfaces, and the verifier must work with or generate efficient imperative implementations. With every step, the trusted code base shrinks, and the trustworthiness of the larger tool increases. At every step, the new verified code can be thoroughly benchmarked and optimised.

We apply this approach to the mcsta probabilistic model checker of the MODEST TOOLSET. It consists of components with well-defined interfaces, ranging from input language semantics over state space exploration, graph-based precomputations [12], finding SCCs, end component elimination, and essential states reduction [9] to the actual numeric solution methods like variants of value iteration or linear programming. Of these components, we chose to replace the step of finding SCCs that enables the topological solution methods. This is because (i) it is a critical step for both the performance of the solution method and the correctness of the final result, and (ii) we can reuse parts of an existing formalization [30] of Gabow's SCC-finding algorithm [13], allowing us to focus on the performance and tool integration challenges.

To produce a verified algorithm that works directly on the imperative data structures of mcsta, we use the Isabelle LLVM tool [32,34] that produces verified LLVM code using the Isabelle theorem prover [38]. To keep the abstract algorithmic ideas separate from the actual implementations and data structures, we use a stepwise refinement approach supported by the Isabelle Refinement Framework [35], consisting of four conceptual steps: A correctness proof for general path-based SCC algorithms (Sect. 3), the use of Gabow's particular data structures (Sect. 4), the imperative implementation (Sect. 5), and the generation of LLVM code (Sect. 6). The first two steps are an adaptation of the ideas of the existing verified but slow functional implementation of Gabow's algorithm [30] to prepare for the imperative refinement. The last two steps are entirely new, using new imperative data structures both internally and on the interface to mcsta. In particular, the algorithm needs to work with mcsta's representation of the graph (in terms of an MDP) and return the information about the found SCCs to mcsta.

To assess the impact of replacing an unverified component of a probabilistic model checker by a correct-by-construction version, we performed an extensive experimental comparison using benchmarks from the Quantitative Verification Benchmark Set [20] (Sect. 7). We found that, by using an imperative implementation and avoiding costly glue code and transformations or copies of the data (e.g. of mcsta's MDP data structures into a more generic graph representation), our verified implementation outperforms the existing implementation of Tarjan's algorithm in mcsta (being around twice as fast) and achieves performance comparable to a manually-optimised unverified C implementation of Gabow's algorithm that we newly built as a comparison baseline (which on average is only a bit faster). This means that we have replaced a unverified algorithm with a faster, provably correct one.

Related Work. Only a few verified model checker implementations exist that can be applied to significant problem sizes: CAVA [6,10] is a fully verified LTL model checker, featuring a fragment of Promela [37] as input language. While able to check medium-size examples in reasonable time, it is much slower than highly optimized unverified tools such as SPIN [25]. Similarly, the fully verified MUNTA model checker [44] for timed automata is still significantly slower than the highly optimized unverified counterpart UPPAAL [5], and the verified IsaSAT solver [11] placed last in the SAT2022 competition [4].

On the other hand, the results of model checking can be certified by a formally verified certifier. This requires the existence of a practical certification mechanism, and the support of the unverified model checker. Formally verified certification tools that work on significant problem sizes exist for e.g. timed automata model checking [43,45] and SAT solving [23,33].

There are some formalizations of Markov decision processes and value iteration in Isabelle/HOL [24] and Coq [42]. However, there is no documentation on extracting executable code from these proofs. Additionally, there is a formalization of value iteration for discounted expected rewards [36] which extracts Standard ML code from the proof. Strongly connected component finding algorithms have been formally verified with various tools, including Isabelle/HOL [30], Coq [39], and Why3 [7]. However, [39] and [7] do not report on extracting executable code from their verification at all, and the code extracted from [30] is roughly one order of magnitude slower than a textbook reference implementation of the same algorithm in Java.

Our replacement of mcsta's unverified SCC-finding implementation by a verified one is part of a larger effort to improve the trustworthiness of the tool, in which we already developed an efficient sound variant of value iteration [19] and proposed a way to avoid floating-point rounding errors with limited performance impact [16], but did not yet apply verification to the tool itself.

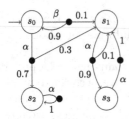

Fig. 1. MDP $\mathcal{M}_{ex}$

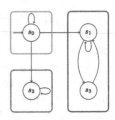

Fig. 2. Graph $G_{ex} := (S, E_{\mathcal{M}_{ex}})$ with its SCCs

2 Preliminaries

$\mathbb{R}$ is the set of real numbers; $[0, 1] \subseteq \mathbb{R}$ denotes the real numbers from 0 to 1. For a set X, 2^X is its power set. A *(discrete) probability distribution* over a set X is a function $\mu \colon X \to [0, 1]$ where $support(\mu) \stackrel{\text{def}}{=} \{ x \in X \mid \mu(x) > 0 \}$ is finite and $\sum_{x \in support(\mu)} \mu(x) = 1$. $Dist(X)$ is the set of probability distributions over X.

2.1 Markov Decision Processes

Our work is implemented in the context of the probabilistic model checker mcsta. One of the core problems in probabilistic model checking are *reachability properties*, where an optimal solution regarding some metric towards reaching a set of target states is computed in a *Markov decision process (MDP)* [40].

Definition 1. *An MDP is a triple* $\mathcal{M} = (S, s_0, prob)$ *of a finite set of states S with initial state $s_0 \in S$ and a transition function* $prob \colon S \to 2^{Dist(S)}$.

An MDP moves in discrete time steps. In each step, from current state s, one distribution $\mu \in prob(s)$ is chosen non-deterministically and sampled to obtain the next state. A *policy* resolves the non-determinism in an MDP by choosing one probability distribution for each state. The goal is to find a policy that maximizes/minimizes the probability or expected reward to reach a target state.

Example 1. Figure 1 shows an MDP with states s_0 to s_3 where s_0 is the initial state. Using distribution α, we go to state s_1 with probability 0.3 and to s_2 with probability 0.7. Using distribution β, we go to state s_0 and s_1 with probability 0.9 and 0.1 respectively. The maximal probability to reach state s_1 is 1, achieved by the policy that chooses β until we reach s_1, where it chooses α indefinitely.

A *graph* is a pair $G = (V, E)$ of a set of vertices V connected by edges $E \subseteq V \times V$. E^* is the reflexive transitive closure of E.

Definition 2. *A strongly connected component (SCC) of G is a set $U \subseteq V$ such that $U \times U \subseteq E^*$ (it is strongly connected) and $\forall U' \supsetneq U \colon \neg(U' \times U' \subseteq E^*)$ (it is maximal).*

Given $\mathcal{M} = (S, s_0, prob)$, let $E_{\mathcal{M}} \stackrel{\text{def}}{=} \{ (s, s') \mid \exists \mu \in prob(s) \colon s' \in support(\mu) \}$. Then $(S, E_{\mathcal{M}})$ is the graph of $\mathcal{M}$. U is an SCC of $\mathcal{M}$ iff U is an SCC of $(S, E_{\mathcal{M}})$.

Example 2. Figure 2 shows the graph G_{ex} of MDP $\mathcal{M}_{ex}$ from Fig. 1. It also shows the three SCCs of G_{ex} outlined in green, blue, and red.

The optimal value (probability or expected reward) of a state (and consequently the decision of the optimal policy) only depends on the optimal values of its successors. Decomposing the MDP into its SCCs and solving the SCCs in reverse topological order guarantees that each state's successors have either been solved to (ϵ-)optimality before, or are being considered in the current SCC. This approach breaks down the MDP into smaller subproblems; if the MDP consists of many similarly sized SCCs, the computation uses much less time and memory than naive methods [8,18]. mcsta currently implements topological LP solving.

2.2 Program Verification Based on Refinement in Isabelle/HOL

To comprehend (and verify) the optimized implementation of an algorithm, we use a stepwise refinement approach. We start with the abstract algorithmic idea describing the essence of the algorithm on the level of manipulating mathematical objects like maps and sets. We then use a series of refinement steps to gradually replace the abstract mathematical objects by actual data structures until we arrive at the executable implementation. In the process, we prove that each refinement step preserves correctness. The steps are typically independent, which helps to keep the overall proof structured and manageable. Different components can be refined independently (e.g. separating data and program refinement), to be assembled at a later stage or used in other algorithms, without re-playing the intermediate steps. A good refinement design is key to a manageable proof, and, as all design choices, requires experience and involves trade-offs.

The Isabelle Refinement Framework (IRF) [35] implements stepwise refinement on top of Isabelle/HOL. It provides a formal notion of programs and refinement, tools like a verification condition generator that facilitate proving, and a library of reusable verified data structures. Its recent LLVM backend [32] supports the generation of LLVM bytecode. In the following, we give a brief overview of the IRF. For an in-depth description, we refer the reader to [32,35].

Programs are modelled by shallow embedding into a nondeterminism error monad $'a\ nres \equiv \textbf{fail}\ |\ \textbf{spec}\ ('a \Rightarrow bool)$. Intuitively, a program fails (**fail**) or nondeterministically returns a result that satisfies P (**spec** P). The **return** x combinator returns the only result x, and the bind combinator $\textbf{do}\ \{x{\leftarrow}m;\ f\ x\}$ selects a result x of m, and then executes $f\ x$. A program fails if there is at least one nondeterministic possibility to fail. Thus, $\textbf{do}\ \{x{\leftarrow}m;\ f\ x\}$ fails if m fails, or if f fails for at least one possible result of m. The **assert** P combinator does nothing (i.e. returns a unit value) if P holds, and fails otherwise. The IRF provides further combinators and syntax for control flow.

A (concrete) program m' *refines* an (abstract) program m (written $m' \leq m$) if every possible result of m' is a result of m. Also, $m' \leq \textbf{fail}$ and $\textbf{fail} \not\leq \textbf{spec}\ P$: the intuition is to assume that the abstract program does not fail, i.e. the concrete program can do anything in case the abstract program fails. We lift a refinement relation R between concrete and abstract data to program m using $\Downarrow\! R\ m$, which returns all concrete results that are related to some abstract result of m.

Example 3. We use the IRF to refine a pop operation of a stack:

(*1*)
$ssel :: {}'a\ set \Rightarrow ({}'a \times {}'a\ set)\ nres;\ lpop :: {}'a\ list \Rightarrow ({}'a \times {}'a\ list)\ nres$
$ssel\ s \equiv \textbf{do}\ \{\ \textbf{assert}\ s{\neq}\{\};\ \textbf{spec}\ \lambda\ (x,s').\ x{\in}s \wedge s'{=}s{-}x\ \}$
$lpop\ l \equiv \textbf{do}\ \{\ \textbf{assert}\ l{\neq}[];\ \textbf{return}\ (last\ l,\ butlast\ l)\}$
$'a\ da = 64\ word \times 64\ word \times {}'a\ ptr$ (* *length, capacity, pointer to array* *)
$apop :: {}'c\ da \Rightarrow ({}'c \times {}'c\ da)\ llM$
$apop\ (l,c,a) \equiv \textbf{do}\ \{\ l{\leftarrow}ll\_sub\ l\ 1;\ p{\leftarrow}ll\_ofs\_ptr\ a\ l;\ r{\leftarrow}ll\_load\ p;\ \textbf{return}\ (r,(l,c,a))\ \}$

(*2*)
$R_{ls} :: {}'a\ list \times {}'a\ set;\ R_{ls} \equiv \{\ (xs, set\ xs)\ |\ xs.\ distinct\ xs\ \}$
$(l,s) \in R_{ls} \implies lpop\ l\ \leq{\Downarrow}(Id \times R_{ls})\ (ssel\ s)$ (*short:* $lpop,ssel : R_{ls} \rightarrow Id \times R_{ls}$)
$A_{da} :: ({}'a \Rightarrow {}'c \Rightarrow assn) \Rightarrow {}'a\ list \Rightarrow {}'c\ da \Rightarrow assn;$ (* *definition elided* *)
$apop,\ lpop : (A_{da}\ e)^d \rightarrow e \times A_{da}\ e$

(*3*)
$A_{set} :: ({}'a \Rightarrow {}'c \Rightarrow assn) \Rightarrow {}'a\ set \Rightarrow {}'c\ da \Rightarrow assn;\ A_{set}\ e \equiv A_{da}\ e\ O\ R_{ls}$
$apop,\ ssel : (A_{set}\ e)^d \rightarrow e \times A_{set}\ e$

First (1) we define functions to remove an arbitrary element from a non-empty set (*ssel*) and to pop the last entry of a non-empty list and dynamic array (*lpop/apop*). Then (2) we define the refinement relation R_{ls} between distinct lists and sets. We show for related arguments $(l,s){\in}R_{ls}$ that all possible outputs of *lpop l* and *ssel s* are related through $Id \times R_{ls}$, i.e. the first elements of the pair are equal, and the second elements are related by R_{ls}. We also introduce a shortcut notation that elides the parameter names. We then define a refinement between dynamic arrays and lists: $A_{da}\ e\ l\ d$ is a separation logic assertion that states that the dynamic array *d* contains the elements from list *l*, where the elements themselves are refined by e[1]. The annotation ^{d} on a parameter refinement indicates that this refinement is no longer valid after execution of the concrete program (typically the data has been destructively updated). Finally (3) we compose (*O*) our assertion with a relation to show that *apop* refines *ssel*.

2.3   Existing Formalisation of Gabow's Algorithm

Our work builds on an existing formalisation [30] of Gabow's algorithm [13]. That formalisation uses an early version of the IRF [29], targeting purely functional SML code; it is an order of magnitude slower than a reference implementation in Java. While incompatible with our goal of creating a fast drop-in replacement to be used directly on the mcsta data structures, we can reuse parts of the existing abstract formalisation. In the following sections, we indicate the parts we reused, referring to the existing work as the *original formalization*.

---

[1] Note that the order of the refinement relations $(({}'a \times {}'c)\ set)$ is different from the assertions $({}'c{\Rightarrow}'a{\Rightarrow}assn)$.

3   Abstract Path-Based Algorithm

Gabow's SCC-finding algorithm is a *path-based* algorithm: It maintains a path
from the start node that is extended in each iteration via an edge from the path's
tail. When the edge leads back onto the path, the resulting cycle is collapsed
into a single node. When there are no more outgoing edges left, the last node
corresponds to an SCC and is removed from the path. We follow a similar design
approach as the original formalization: We first define a *skeleton* algorithm that
performs the DFS, but discards the found SCCs. We then reuse parts of the skeleton to define an actual SCC-finding algorithm. This technique makes the proof
more modular, factoring out general properties of Gabow-style algorithms [30].

3.1   The Skeleton Algorithm

```
1   skeleton ≡ do {
2     let D0 = {};
3     r ← foreach outer_invar V0 (λv0 D0. do {
4       if v0∉D0 then do {
5         s ← initial v0 D0;
6         (p,D,pE,vE) ← while (invar v0 D0) (λ(p,_). p ≠ []) (λ(p,D,pE,vE). do {
7           (vo,(p,D,pE,vE)) ← select_edge (p,D,pE,vE);
8           case vo of
9             None ⇒ do { return (pop (p,D,pE,vE)) }
10            | Some v ⇒ do {
11              if v ∈ ⋃(set p) then do { return (collapse v (p,D,pE,vE)) }
12              else if v∉D then do { push v (p,D,pE,vE) }
13              else do { return (p,D,pE,vE) }
14            }
15          }) s;
16          return D
17        } else return D0
18      }) D0;
19    return r}
```

The outer loop of the skeleton (l. 3) iterates over all nodes $V0$. The inner loop
performs a DFS, maintaining a program state consisting of a segmented path
$p :: 'v\ set\ list$, the "done" nodes $D :: 'v\ set$, pending edges $pE :: 'v\ multiset$, and
visited edges $vE :: 'v\ set$. The operations perform changes to that state, e.g.

definition *collapse* v $(p,D,pE,vE) \equiv$
let $i=idx\_of\ p\ v; p = take\ i\ p\ @\ [⋃(set\ (drop\ i\ p))]$ **in** (p,D,pE,vE)

where @ appends two lists, $idx\_of\ p\ v$ returns the index of v in p (which we
prove to exist) and $take\ i\ p / drop\ i\ p$ yields/discards the first i elements of p. In
essence this operation combines all segments from index i onwards. For the other
operations we refer to the supplementary material.

   In each step, the skeleton selects a pending edge from the last segment of
the path (l. 7). If no such edge exists (l. 9), the last segment is an SCC. In the

Fig. 3. The state of the path based SCC algorithm before and after a collapse step. The dotted nodes and edges are not yet visited by the algorithm.

skeleton, we pop the last segment from the path. Later, we will perform some extra work to mark the found SCC. Otherwise (l. 10), if the selected edge goes back into the path (l. 11), we have found a cycle, and collapse all its nodes into a single segment. If the edge leads to a new node (l. 12), we add this node to the current path. Otherwise (l. 13), the edge leads to a done node and we ignore it.

Example 4. Figure 3 visualizes a step in the program where $p = [\{0\}, \{1,3\}, \{2\}]$, $D = \{\}$, $pE = \{(1,4),(2,3)\}$ and $vE = \{(0,3),(3,1),(1,3),(1,2)\}$. Then, exploring e.g. back edge $(2,3)$ collapses all segments in that cycle. Now $p = [\{0\}, \{1,3,2\}]$, $D = \{\}$, $pE = \{(1,4)\}$ and $vE = \{(0,3),(3,1),(1,3),(1,2),(2,3)\}$.

The original formalization only supports successor functions that return a set of nodes. However, the successor function on the graph data structure of mcsta is more efficient if we allow duplicates in the list of successors. This can cause the same edge to be explored multiple times, which, however, does not matter as the target node is marked as done on successive explorations. To later allow this implementation, we had to change pE to be a multiset of pending edges in the abstract algorithm. This revealed a problem in the original formalization: the set of visited edges was defined implicitly, but a multiset of pending edges does not allow for such implicit representation. We solved this by explicitly introducing vE into the abstract state, which even simplified the existing proofs. Note that vE is a *ghost variable*, i.e. no other parts of the state depend on it. Thus, we can easily eliminate it in the next refinement step (Sect. 4.1).

Invariants. To define the invariants, we use Isabelle's locale mechanism [3] that allows us to define named hierarchical contexts with fixed variables and assumptions. First, we define a set of initial nodes $V0$. Then, we define finite graphs as an adjacency function E_succ that maps each node to a list of adjacent nodes and an according abstraction E_α that returns the set of edges induced by E_succ:

locale fr_graph = **fixes** $V0 :: \text{'}v\ set$ **and** $E\_succ :: (\text{'}v \Rightarrow \text{'}v\ list)$
  assumes *1: finite* $(E\_\alpha^* \text{ `` } V0)$

The invariant of the outer loop extends fr_graph, adding the loop's state (it,D):

locale $outer\_invar\_loc$ = $fr\_graph\ V0\ E\_succ$
  for $V0$ **and** $E\_succ :: (\text{'}v \Rightarrow \text{'}v\ list)$ + **fixes** $it :: \text{'}v\ set$ **and** $D :: \text{'}v\ set$
  assumes *1: $it \subseteq V0$* **and** *2: $V0 - it \subseteq D$*
  and *3: $D \subseteq E\_\alpha^* \text{ `` } V0$* **and** *4: $E\_\alpha \text{ `` } D \subseteq D$*

The invariant guarantees that (1) the nodes we still have to iterate over (*it*) are in $V0$, (2) the nodes we already have iterated over ($V0 - it$) are done, (3) done nodes are reachable, and (4) done nodes can only reach other done nodes. The invariant *invar_loc* of the inner loop is defined using the same locale construct, but with more extensions. The invariant states that: all nodes within a segment of path p are mutually reachable and segments are topologically ordered; done nodes remain done, are reachable, and only reach other done nodes; edges in pE start in p; and visited edges lead to segments that are topological successors of the source segment. Furthermore, we added restrictions to the new set of visited edges. These state that: edges from done nodes are visited; visited edges only exist between done and path nodes; and unvisited edges from p are pending.

The termination proof of the original formalization was more involved. But using vE we were able to simplify it significantly: Each iteration of the inner loop decreases the lexicographic ordering of the number of unvisited edges, pending edges, and length of the path. Using the IRF's verification condition generator (VCG), we prove that every operation preserves the invariant and decreases the termination ordering. Equipped with these lemmas, the VCG can automatically show that the skeleton terminates and preserves the invariant.

3.2 Abstract SCC-Finding Algorithm

We can then refine the algorithm to also compute a list $l::'v$ *set list* of the SCCs in topological order. Formally:

$$scc\_set \equiv \{\, scc.\ is\_scc\ E\_\alpha\ scc \wedge scc \subseteq E\_\alpha^*\ ``\ V0\}$$
$$ordered\ l \equiv (\forall i\ j.\ i < j \longrightarrow j < length\ l \longrightarrow l!i \times l!j \cap E\_\alpha^* = \{\})$$
$$compute\_SCC\_spec \equiv \mathbf{spec}\ (\lambda l.\ set\ l = scc\_set \wedge ordered\ l)$$

For this, we add a list l of discovered SCCs to the algorithm's state and amend the pop function to add the identified SCC to that list. We call that new algorithm *compute_SCC*. To prove it correct, we extend the invariant of both the outer and inner loop by the statement that l contains exactly the SCCs of the done part of the graph, in topological order (definition elided). With this extension, and reusing the lemmas we have already proved for the skeleton, it is straightforward to show:

theorem *compute_SCC_correct: compute_SCC* $\leq$ *compute_SCC_spec*

4 Formalizing Gabow's Algorithm

The main challenge of path-based approaches is finding efficient data structures to capture the segments. Gabow's data structure exploits the behaviour of the DFS: it stores the path as a stack of nodes, in the order they are visited. Adjacent nodes in the path are in the same SCC or in a topological successor/predecessor, such that a list of boundary indices can be used to encode the segmentation.

4.1   The Skeleton of Gabow's Algorithm

To refine our algorithm to use Gabow's data structure, we again work in two steps: We first refine the skeleton, then reuse this refinement for an actual SCC-finding algorithm. Gabow's data structure uses three stacks and a map to represent the state: The *sequence* stack $S :: {}'v\ list$ contains the states on the path in the order they were first visited. The *boundaries* stack $B :: nat\ list$ contains natural numbers representing indices (or bounds) on stack S: all nodes on S between subsequent entries in B form a segment, the last entry of B being the start index of the last segment. The *working list* $P :: ({}'v \times {}'v\ list)\ list$ contains a tuple of nodes on the path and a nonempty list of pending successors. Finally, the node state map $I :: {}'v \Rightarrow node\_state\ option$ maps nodes to *node states*:

datatype $node\_state = STACK\ nat\ |\ DONE\ nat$

$I\ v = None$ indicates that node v has not yet been discovered, *Some* $(STACK\ i)$ indicates that v is on the sequence stack S at index i, and *Some* $(DONE\ j)$ indicates that v is done and belongs to SCC number j. Note that we do not use j in the skeleton, but already add it to *node_state* for convenience.

Similarly to the abstract algorithm, the operations perform changes to the concrete program state, e.g.

definition *collapse_impl_fr* $(S,B,I,P)\ v \equiv$ **do** {
  $i \leftarrow idx\_of\_impl\ (S,B,I,P)\ v;$ **assert** $(i+1 \le length\ B);$
  let $B = take\ (i+1)\ B;$ **return** (S,B,I,P) }

where *idx_of_impl* implements *idx_of* through a lookup using I and B. For the other implementations we refer to the supplementary material.

Data Structure Invariants. The invariant *oGS_invar* makes sure that the stack is empty on the outer loop. *GS_invar* for Gabow's data structure remained largely unchanged w.r.t. the original formalization: it ensures that B is sorted, distinct, and points to a node on S; as long as there are nodes in S, there are bounds in B starting at 0; I specifies that node v lies at index j in S; parent nodes in P are also in S and have unprocessed successors; parent nodes in P are distinct and sorted by their index in S. We added that S consists only of reachable nodes (*set* $S \subseteq (E\_\alpha^*\ ``V0))$. While this is not required to show the correctness of the data structure at this abstraction level, it comes in handy to show that the length of the stack is bounded when we refine the indexes to 64-bit machine words in the next step. This is a recurring design pattern: some assertions that are only required for a concrete refinement step are most easily proved already on the abstract level.

Example 5. A possible encoding of Fig. 3 in Gabow's data structure is $S = [0,3,1,2]$, $B = [0,1,3]$, $I: [0 \mapsto Some\ (STACK\ 0), 1 \mapsto Some\ (STACK\ 2), 2 \mapsto Some\ (STACK\ 3), 3 \mapsto Some\ (STACK\ 1), 4 \mapsto None]$, $P = [(1,[4]),(2,[3])]$. Then, back edge $(2,3)$ is explored. We pop that entry in P, i.e. $P = [(1,[4])]$. $I(3) = Some\ (STACK\ 1)$ so we pop B until we reach $v \le 1$; B becomes $[0,1]$.

Iterators. We implement P as a stack containing pairs of a node of the graph and an iterator over its successors. We also considered implementing P as a stack of stacks, where the inner stacks contain the unvisited successors. This was slower in practice as it requires more memory allocations and deallocations. While the iterator is an implementation detail of the data structure that we consider in Sect. 5, we reason about iterators here because we expect that reasoning about the link between the iterators and the graph in separation logic in the next refinement layer would be more complex. We define an iterator as a tuple of a node u and an index ci representing the ci-th index of $E\_succ\ u$. We let $succ\_count\ u \equiv length\ (E\_succ\ u)$ and define five operations for the iterator:

$$index\_begin\ u = (u,0) \quad get\_state = \lambda\ (u,ci).\ u$$
$$successor\_at = \lambda\ (u,ci).\ (E\_succ\ u)\ !\ ci$$
$$has\_next \equiv \lambda\ (u,ci).\ Suc\ ci < succ\_count\ u \quad next\_index = \lambda\ (u,ci).\ (u,ci+1)$$

$index\_begin$ creates an iterator pointing to the start of the iteration sequence; get_state returns the source node of the iterator (in other words the state whose successors we iterate over); $successor\_at$ returns the element that the iterator points to; has_next checks if there exists a next element in the sequence (in our case it checks there are unprocessed successors left); and $next\_index$ updates the iterator to point to the next element in the sequence.

Refinement Relation. We connect Gabow's data structure to the abstract program state via an abstraction function:

$$seg\_start\ i \equiv B!i \quad seg\_end\ i \equiv \textbf{if}\ i+1 = length\ B\ \textbf{then}\ length\ S\ \textbf{else}\ B!(i+1)$$
$$seg\ i \equiv \{S!j \mid j.\ seg\_start\ i \leq j \wedge j < seg\_end\ i\ \} \quad remaining\_successors$$
$$= (\lambda\ (u,ci).\ map\ (\lambda\ ci'.\ successor\_at\ (u,ci'))\ [ci..{<}succ\_count\ u])$$
$$edges\_of\_succs = (\lambda\ (u,ci).\ map\ (\lambda v.\ (u,v))\ (remaining\_successors\ (u,ci)))$$
$$p\_\alpha \equiv map\ seg\ [0..{<}length\ B] \quad D\_\alpha \equiv \{v.\ \exists\ i.\ I\ v = Some\ (DONE\ i)\}$$
$$pE\_\alpha = mset\ (concat\ (map\ edges\_of\_succs\ P))$$
$$GS\_\alpha \equiv (p\_\alpha,D\_\alpha,pE\_\alpha) \quad oGS\_\alpha\ I \equiv \{v.\ \exists\ i.\ I\ v = Some\ (DONE\ i)\}$$

Here, $map\ f\ xs$ returns a list in which each element in xs is mapped using f, $mset$ turns a list into a multiset and $concat$ concatenates a list of lists into a single list. This reconstructs the p, D, and pE parts of the abstract state from the concrete state. The vE part is a ghost variable and remains unconstrained in the refinement relation. We define:

$$GS\_rel \equiv \{\ (c,(p,D,pE,vE))\ .\ (c,(p,D,pE)) \in br\ GS\_\alpha\ (GS\_invar\ V0\ E\_succ)\ \}$$
$$oGS\_rel \equiv br\ oGS\_\alpha\ (oGS\_invar\ V0\ E\_succ)$$

Here, $br\ \alpha\ Inv \equiv \{(c,\ \alpha\ c) \mid c.\ Inv\ c\}$ builds a relation from an abstraction function and invariant.

Refinement Proof. We first show that the concrete operations refine the corresponding abstract ones, e.g.

lemma *collapse_refine:* $(s, (p, D, pE, vE)) \in GS\_rel \land (v, v') \in Id \land v' \in \bigcup(set\ p)$
$\implies collapse\_impl\_fr\ v\ s \leq \Downarrow GS\_rel\ (RETURN\ (collapse\ v'\ (p, D, pE, vE)))$

We proceed analogously for the other operations. This allows us to show that the concrete inner loop refines the abstract inner loop. This works similarly for the outer loop. Finally, we get the following theorem:

theorem *skeleton_impl_refine:* $skeleton\_impl \leq \Downarrow o GS\_rel\ skeleton$

4.2 Gabow's SCC-Finding Algorithm

We implement the list l of SCCs in the abstract algorithm by the length i of the list and the node state map: the nodes of the SCC $l!j$ have state $Some\ (DONE\ j)$:

$SCC\_at\ I\ j \equiv \{v.\ I\ v = Some\ (DONE\ j)\}$
$SCC\_\alpha\ (i, I) \equiv map\ (SCC\_at\ I)\ [0..<i]$

locale $GSS\_invar\_ext = \ldots\ +$
  assumes *1:* $j < i \implies SCC\_at\ I\ j \neq \{\}$ **and** *2:* $j \geq i \implies SCC\_at\ I\ j = \{\}$
  assumes *3:* $finite\ (SCC\_at\ I\ j)$ **and** *4:* $I\ v \neq None \implies v \in E\_\alpha^*\ ``V0$

locale $SCC_invar = GSS_invar_ext + $ **assumes** *5:* $I\ v \neq Some\ (STACK\ i)$
$SCC\_rel \equiv br\ SCC\_\alpha\ SCC\_invar$

The invariant ensures that (1) every index $j < i$ is assigned to a non-empty SCC, and (2) no indices $j \geq i$ have been assigned. Moreover, (3) SCCs are finite and (4) only assigned to reachable nodes. During the outer loop, and for the representation of the returned result (SCC_rel), we additionally know (5) that the stack is empty.

The algorithm *compute_SCC_impl* adds the counter i to the skeleton algorithm. Reusing the lemmas from refining the skeleton algorithm, it is straightforward to show

theorem *compute_SCC_impl_refine:*
  $compute\_SCC\_impl \leq \Downarrow SCC\_rel\ compute\_SCC$

That is, our new algorithm returns a pair (i, I) that represents the topologically ordered list of SCCs returned by the abstract algorithm *compute_SCC*.

5 Refinement to LLVM

We now make the step from our model of Gabow's algorithm with abstract data types (*compute_SCC_impl*) to a model of an LLVM implementation with concrete LLVM data types along mcsta's interface (*Modest_compute_SCC_impl*). At this point, we depart from the path taken by the original formalisation.

Some of the data structures we refine to are standard and well-supported by the IRF library: we represent nodes and indices as 64-bit words, use dynamic arrays for the stacks S, B, and P in the algorithm state, and represent I by an *array map*: an array of node states indexed by the nodes. In this section, we highlight the two most interesting refinements.

5.1 Node State

Recall (cf. Sect. 4.1) that the node state is either *None*, *STACK j*, or *DONE k*, where j is an index into the stack S, and k is the number of the SCC that the node belongs to. For a graph with N nodes, we have $j, k < N$. This gives us a straightforward encoding of node states into 64-bit words: *None* becomes -1, *STACK j* becomes j, and *DONE k* becomes $k + N$. While certainly not optimal, this encoding is easy to realise with the IRF standard library. We consider the incurred graph size bound of $N < 2^{62}$ to be sufficient.

5.2 MDP Graph Data Structure

Performance-wise, it is crucial that our algorithm works on the state space (MDP) data structure provided by mcsta, rather than copying to its own data structure. mcsta encodes a state (node) as a 64-bit word $< N$, where N is the number of states in the MDP. It represents the graph structure of the MDP by three arrays St, Tr, and Br. Each element of St indicates an interval in the Tr array, describing the outgoing transitions (i.e. distributions) of a state. Similarly, Tr represents intervals in the Br array, describing the outgoing branches (i.e. elements of the distribution's support) of the transition. Finally, the Br array contains the target nodes of the branches. The intervals in St and Tr are encoded as a 20-bit length and 44-bit start index, packed into a single 64 bit word.

The iterator on the graph is independent of mcsta. We use a structure for the iterator consisting of five 64-bit words (v, tc, te, bc, be). v represents the state, tc and te represent the current and last index of the iteration sequence to Tr and bc and be represent the current and last index to Br.

Example 6. By representing the bit-packing as a tuple of natural numbers we have that $St = [(2,0),(1,2),(1,3),(1,4)]$, $Tr = [(2,0),(2,2),(2,4),(1,6),(1,7)]$ and $Br = [1,2,0,1,1,3,2,1]$ encodes G_{ex} from Fig. 2. State s_1 (at index 1) has 1 transition at index 2 (derived from $St[1] = (1,2)$). This transition has 2 branches starting at index 4 (derived from $Tr[2] = (2,4)$). The successors of s_1 are thus s_1 (as $Br[4] = 1$) and s_3 (as $Br[5] = 3$). The iterator $(v, tc, te, bc, be) = (1,0,1,1,2)$ points to s_3. We observe $v = 1$ which means we consider a successor of state s_1. We also observe that $tc = 0$ which means that the iterator points to transition index 0. We also remember that the transition sequence for this state starts at index 2 ($St[1] = (1,2)$) which we add to tc. So the index points to transition 2. Lastly, we observe that $bc = 1$, which is also relative. The branch sequence for transition 2 starts at 4 ($Tr[2] = (2,4)$) which we add to bc. So the iterator points to branch 5. Since $Br[5] = 3$ the iterator points to state s_3.

We have to implement the graph and the iterator with its operations from Sect. 4. We choose a two-step approach, following a similar structure as in Example 3. We model the graph as $mg_1 :: (nat \times nat)\ list \times (nat \times nat)\ list \times nat\ list$ and the iterator as $it_1 :: (nat \times nat \times nat \times nat \times nat)$:

$$R_{mg_1}\ N :: (mg_1 \times ('v \Rightarrow 'v\ list))\ set;\ R_{mg_1}\ N \equiv br\ mg\_\alpha\ (mg\_invar\ N)$$

$R_{it1} :: (it_1 \times ('v \Rightarrow 'v\ list))\ set;\ R_{it1} \equiv br\ it\_\alpha\ (it\_invar)$
$succ\_at_1 :: mg_1 \Rightarrow it_1 \Rightarrow nat\ nres;\ (definition\ elided)$
$succ\_at_1,\ successor\_at : R_{mg1}\ N \to R_{it1} \to Id$

Refinement relation R_{mg1} N uses abstraction functions mg_α and mg_invar (definitions elided) that encode that we have N states, indices are in bounds, and intervals do not overlap, which ensures that the numbers of successors are bounded by N. Refinement relation R_{it1} uses abstraction functions it_α and it_invar (definitions elided) which encode that the iterator is valid for the given graph structure and is within bounds. Function $succ\_at_1$ refines $successor\_at$ w.r.t.R_{mg1} and R_{it1}, which we prove using the IRF's VCG. The representation of the result does not change (as indicated by the Id relation).

In the next step, we do the bit-packing (A_{bp}), represent nodes by 64-bit words (A_{snat}), and use arrays for the lists (A_{arr}). The output list is refined by

$A_{bp} :: nat \times nat \Rightarrow 64\ word \Rightarrow assn$ $\qquad$ $A_{snat} :: nat \Rightarrow 64\ word$
$A_{arr} :: ('a \Rightarrow 'c \Rightarrow assn) \Rightarrow 'a\ list \Rightarrow 'c\ ptr \Rightarrow assn$

$mg_2 \equiv 64\ word\ ptr \times 64\ word\ ptr \times 64\ word\ ptr$
$A_{mg2} :: mg_1 \Rightarrow mg_2 \Rightarrow assn;\ A_{mg2} \equiv A_{arr}\ A_{bp} \times A_{arr}\ A_{bp} \times A_{arr}\ A_{snat}$

$it_2 \equiv 64\ word \times 64\ word \times 64\ word \times 64\ word \times 64\ word$
$A_{it2} :: it_1 \Rightarrow it_2 \Rightarrow assn;\ A_{it2} \equiv A_{snat} \times A_{snat} \times A_{snat} \times A_{snat} \times A_{snat}$

$succ\_at_2 :: mg_2 \Rightarrow it_2 \Rightarrow 64\ word\ da\ llM\ (def.\ elided,\ generated\ by\ Sepref)$
$succ\_at_2,\ succ\_at_1 : A_{mg2} \to A_{it2} \to A_{snat}$

The definition of $succ\_at_2$ and the refinement lemma are synthesised by Sepref, which implements a heuristics to apply data refinements automatically [31].

Finally, we combine the two steps to get the desired refinement from abstract graphs to mcsta's concrete MDP data structure, which we can then use to refine our main algorithm:

$A_{mg}\ N :: ('v \Rightarrow 'v\ list) \Rightarrow mg_2 \Rightarrow assn$
$A_{mg} \equiv A_{mg2}\ O\ R_{mg1}\ N \qquad A_{it} \equiv A_{it2}\ O\ R_{it1}$
$succ\_at_2,\ successors\_at :: A_{mg}\ N \to A_{it} \to A_{snat}$

We have omitted similar steps for the other iterator operations. For those, we refer to the supplementary material.

5.3   Main Algorithm

We again use Sepref to synthesise an implementation of $compute\_SCC\_impl$ which we call $Modest\_compute\_SCC\_impl$. We use the aforementioned refinements to achieve this. We combine all refinements to relate it with the specification $compute\_SCC\_spec$ (cf. Sect. 3.2). The resulting theorem states that our implementation is correct. As this is part of the trusted code base, we invested some effort into making the theorem readable and eliminate unnecessary dependencies on internal IRF concepts. At the end, we obtain a Hoare triple using separation logic and refinement assertions for the input and output data types:

theorem *Modest_graph_SCC_impl_correct_htriple: llvm_htriple*
(*1*) $(A_{snat} \ N \ ni * A_{mg} \ N \ E\_succ \ Ei * N < 2^{62})$
(*2*) (*Modest_compute_SCC_impl ni Ei*)
(*3*) $(\lambda ri. \ EXS \ r. \ A_{snat} \ N \ ni * A_{mg} \ N \ E\_succ \ Ei * N < 2^{62} * A_{out} \ r \ ri *$
(*4*)   *set* $r = scc\_set \wedge ordered \ r$)

The precondition (1) requires a signed 64-bit integer ni with value $N :: nat$, and an MDP graph data structure Ei representing an abstract successor function E_succ with N nodes. We also assume that N is within the bounds incurred by our encoding of node states (cf. Sect. 5.1). Then (2) running our LLVM program *Modest_compute_SCC_impl ni Ei* yields that (3) ni and the graph remain unaltered, and (4) the result ri encodes a list r of SCCs in topological order.

Here, $ri = (ii, Ii)$ contains the number of SCCs and an array that contains the SCC number for each node. The assertion A_{out} first maps ri to a natural number and an actual map (A_{am}), and then uses SCC_rel (cf. Sect. 4.2) to map that to a list of SCCs:

$$A_{out} \equiv (A_{snat} \times A_{am}) \ O \ SCC\_rel$$

6   Implementation in the Modest Toolset

We have now refined our specification into a model of LLVM in Isabelle/HOL. As the last step in our approach, we extract executable LLVM code. We generate a C header with type definitions to encapsulate our data so that it can be used by LLVM as well as from C. This allows us to easily align the header with the format that mcsta supports. The **export_llvm** command generates the LLVM code of our SCC finding algorithm as well as the corresponding C header file:

export_llvm *Modest_compute_SCC_impl* **is**
*void compute_SCC(my_size_t, modest_graph_t *, scc_result_t *)* **defines** ‹
    typedef *uint64_t my_size_t;* **typedef** *my_size_t node_t;*
    typedef *uint64_t shared_nat_t;* **typedef** *uint64_t *bitset_t;*
    typedef *struct { shared_nat_t *states; struct*
        *{ shared_nat_t *transitions; node_t *branches; }; } modest_graph_t;*
    typedef *struct { my_size_t num_sccs; node_t *scc_map;*
    } scc_result_t;
› **file** *modest_gabow.ll*

The nested anonymous **struct** in *modest_graph_t* reflects Isabelle/HOL's modelling of tuples as right-nested pairs. We compile the LLVM code into a shared library and invoke the functions in this library from mcsta via C#'s "P/Invoke" mechanism to use libraries following the C ABI. In mcsta, we added a command-line option to choose the SCC algorithm to use for its topological LP implementation: the previous unverified C# implementation of Tarjan's algorithm; a new, manually implemented and optimized version of Gabow's algorithm in C that we added for a fairer performance comparison; and the new verified Isabelle LLVM implementation. This allows us to easily run tests and performance benchmarks on the three algorithms.

The topological LP implementation in mcsta requires not only that the SCCs are topologically sorted—which is a postcondition of our LLVM program—but also that the states are sorted by SCC. The latter is done on-the-fly by mcsta's Tarjan implementation, and currently by unverified "glue code" integrating the new algorithms. We aim to either remove this requirement from mcsta, or adapt the verified implementation to include the on-the-fly sorting of states as well.

7   Benchmarks

We benchmark our new SCC implementation to show that unverified and verified code have similar performance. We do so by comparing the runtime of all three algorithms now available in mcsta on a set of benchmark instances (combinations of a parametrised system model, parameter values, and a property to check) from the Quantitative Verification Benchmark Set (QVBS) [20].

7.1   Benchmark Selection

We consider three types of models from the QVBS for our benchmark set: DTMC, MDP, and probabilistic timed automata (PTA) [28]. mcsta syntactically converts the latter to MDP via the digital clocks approach [27]. As SCC algorithms have linear complexity, we need large state spaces to stress-test the implementations. This means that memory is our main bottleneck. We thus selected all DTMC, MDP, and PTA benchmark instances from the QVBS that have between 1 and 100 million states. We found that models with fewer states finish too quickly for reliable runtime measurements, while larger models lead to out-of-memory situations on the machine we use.

A benchmark instance includes a property (e.g. a query for a maximum reachability probability) to check. Since our focus is not on the actual numeric algorithms computing the value of the property, but the SCC-finding preprocessing step, we limit ourselves to one property per applicable model-parameters combination, and instruct mcsta via its --exhaustive option to explore the full state space. This leaves us with 39 different instances to benchmark.

7.2   Benchmarking Setup

All our benchmarks were performed on an Intel Core i7-12700H system with 32 GB of RAM running 64-bit Ubuntu Linux 22.04. We use the mobench utility of the MODEST TOOLSET to run the benchmarks in an automated fashion based on a JSON file specifying the benchmark instances to use and tools to execute. For the latter, we specify three command line invocations for mcsta: one for our new verified implementation of Gabow's algorithm ("Isabelle Gabow"), one for the manual C implementation of the same algorithm ("C Gabow"), and one for the pre-existing C# implementation of Tarjan's algorithm ("Tarjan"). Running

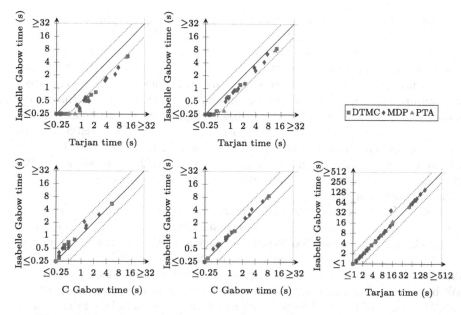

Fig. 4. SCCs only   **Fig. 5.** SCCs + glue code   **Fig. 6.** Topological LP time

mobench yields a CSV file with all measurements, and log files for each individual
benchmark run. We then use the MODEST TOOLSET's moplot utility to generate
the scatter plots shown in the remainder of this paper. Each benchmark instance
results in one point (x, y) indicating that the x-axis task took x seconds to
complete while the y-axis task took y seconds for this instance. We note that
the "consensus" instance with parameter values K = 2, N = 8 ran out of memory,
and the "zeroconf" model caused the LP solver to time out on both its instances.
We thus omit these 3 failed instances in our plots.

7.3 Benchmarking Results

Figure 4 compares the runtime of all three implementations of the core SCC-
finding algorithms, excluding any time used by the glue code described in Sect. 6.
Replacing the C# Tarjan implementation by the verified one of Gabow's algorithm appears to boost the performance, with benchmarks that are more than
twice as fast. We suspect the two most important reasons for the difference in
performance to be that the Tarjan implementation additionally sorts the MDP's
states on-the-fly, and that we compare two different algorithms. However, we
have no reliable data to determine the influence on the performance for the latter, if it exists. On the other hand, the manual C implementation of Gabow's
algorithm appears to perform similarly to the verified implementation, with the
manual implementation having a slight edge in general. This is expected as we
have more control over micro-optimizations in the manual implementation.

Figure 5 shows the same comparison but including the time spent in the "glue code" that sorts the MDP's states by SCC for the topological LP solver. Recall that, for Tarjan's algorithm in mcsta, this is done on-the-fly, so we cannot measure it separately. The "fair" difference in performance for these two implementations thus lies between what is shown in Figs. 4 and 5. As expected, the runtime shifts in favour of the Tarjan implementation here, yet the performance boost remains considerable, with speedups of up to two times. This is because the glue code generally takes much less time than the actual SCC algorithm. When comparing the manual C implementation to the verified Isabelle LLVM implementation in this setting, the manual implementation still wins. Both implementations use the same glue code, so effectively we see a fixed offset added to both runtimes.

Finally, Fig. 6 compares the entire model checking procedure, including state space exploration and LP solving (using mcsta's default LP solver, which is currently GLOP, part of the Google OR Tools). We see that, in the grand scheme of things, we maintain the performance of mcsta by replacing the existing unverified Tarjan implementation by a verified implementation of Gabow's algorithm. We improved the performance of the SCC calculation, but since this is only a small fragment of the model checking procedure it does not show in the figure. It does however mean that we have replaced an important part of our model checker without affecting the performance.

We see one outlier in Fig. 6, which is the instance of the "ij" model with parameters num_tokens_var = 20. This is caused by a combination of two effects: First, mcsta converts the probabilities in the model to floating-point numbers at some point, which incurs a rounding error and may lead to the accumulation of imprecisions on further processing. This instance works with very small numbers, causing the imprecisions to accumulate along the topology, eventually resulting in a linear program that the LP solver considers infeasible. This causes mcsta to abort with a corresponding error message to the user[2]. Second, topological orderings are not unique, and different implementations of different SCC-finding algorithms can produce different orderings. For this benchmark instance, our implementations of Tarjan's and Gabow's algorithms in fact produce different orderings; and the one obtained by Tarjan's finds an infeasible SCC much later than the one of Gabow's. As a result, the topological LP procedure—solving the SCCs in reverse topological order—aborts much earlier on the Tarjan ordering.

Another notable benchmark instance was of the "zeroconf" model, where the LP solver did not terminate for unknown reasons no matter which SCC-finding algorithm we used (and which was therefore excluded from Figs. 4, 5 and 6). This highlights the need to verify code—especially for the core components such as SCC finding or LP solving of safety-critical software like a model checker.

---

[2] Despite the error, we did not exclude this instance from the figures because the error is after the SCC computation, so mobench did not flag it as a problem—and ultimately, this provides an interesting insight.

8 Conclusion

We have replaced the SCC-finding algorithm of the state-of-the-art probabilistic model checker mcsta, part of the MODEST TOOLSET, by a verified version, without negatively affecting mcsta's overall performance. We see this work as a first step in gradually replacing the unverified components of a probabilistic model checker by verified ones. While this approach does not immediately produce a fully verified model checker, we can benchmark and optimize each verified component to avoid performance regressions, while decreasing the trusted code base of the model checker with each replacement step. To avoid expensive copying of data representations at the interface between verified and unverified components, the verified algorithms have to work on the same data structures as the original model checker. To this end, we used a stepwise refinement approach to obtain verified LLVM code which can readily be linked with mcsta.

Our verification is based on an existing verification of a rather inefficient purely functional SCC algorithm, which we significantly extended: we generalized the abstract algorithm to support duplicate successor nodes, and clarified the proof by introducing a ghost variable. Moreover, we added additional data structure invariants that are required for in-bounds checks when refining to 64-bit integers. Finally, we replaced the whole implementation by an efficient imperative one. In particular, we accurately modelled mcsta's graph data structure.

We embedded the resulting verified LLVM code into mcsta, and extensively benchmarked it. Our verified algorithm in isolation is faster than the original unverified one used by mcsta, so its use has no negative effect on mcsta's overall performance. To explore the optimisation potential for future work, we also benchmarked a hand-optimized C implementation.

Future Work. The biggest bottleneck in the current implementation is the glue code. We aim to remove this by means of a different encoding, by removing from mcsta the need for states to be sorted by SCC, or by extending the verified implementation by an on-the-fly sorting. Beyond that, our experiments suggest that further optimizing our verified SCC implementation will only have a minute effect on the overall performance. Thus, it is also worth looking at other components of the model checker: Maximal end component finding algorithms [1] are required for sound (i.e. guaranteed ϵ-correct) MDP solution algorithms like interval iteration [15]. As they require an SCC algorithm as a subroutine, they are an obvious next candidate for verification. Interval iteration itself is a further promising verification target, in particular its floating-point-correct variants [16]. To this end, we are already working on extending the IRF to reason about floating-point numbers.

Data Availibility Statement. Our supplementary material, proofs, and the tools used to obtain the results presented in this paper are archived and available at DOI 10.4121/aff9f553-0e9e-4ec2-90e0-20c5b6152862 [21].

References

1. de Alfaro, L.: Formal verification of probabilistic systems. Ph.D. thesis, Stanford University, USA (1997). https://searchworks.stanford.edu/view/3910936
2. Baier, C., de Alfaro, L., Forejt, V., Kwiatkowska, M.: Model checking probabilistic systems. In: Clarke, E.M., Henzinger, T.A., Veith, H., Bloem, R. (eds.) Handbook of Model Checking, pp. 963–999. Springer, Cham (2018). https://doi.org/10.1007/978-3-319-10575-8_28
3. Ballarin, C.: Locales and locale expressions in Isabelle/Isar. In: Berardi, S., Coppo, M., Damiani, F. (eds.) TYPES 2003. LNCS, vol. 3085, pp. 34–50. Springer, Heidelberg (2004). https://doi.org/10.1007/978-3-540-24849-1_3
4. Balyo, T., Heule, M.J.H., Iser, M., Järvisalo, M., Suda, M. (eds.): Proceedings of SAT Competition 2022: Solver and Benchmark Descriptions, Department of Computer Science Series of Publications B, vol. B-2022-1. Department of Computer Science, University of Helsinki (2022). http://hdl.handle.net/10138/318450
5. Bengtsson, J., Yi, W.: Timed automata: semantics, algorithms and tools. In: Desel, J., Reisig, W., Rozenberg, G. (eds.) ACPN 2003. LNCS, vol. 3098, pp. 87–124. Springer, Heidelberg (2004). https://doi.org/10.1007/978-3-540-27755-2_3
6. Brunner, J., Lammich, P.: Formal verification of an executable LTL model checker with partial order reduction. J. Autom. Reason. **60**(1), 3–21 (2017). https://doi.org/10.1007/s10817-017-9418-4
7. Chen, R., Lévy, J.-J.: A semi-automatic proof of strong connectivity. In: Paskevich, A., Wies, T. (eds.) VSTTE 2017. LNCS, vol. 10712, pp. 49–65. Springer, Cham (2017). https://doi.org/10.1007/978-3-319-72308-2_4
8. Dai, P., Goldsmith, J.: Topological value iteration algorithm for Markov decision processes. In: Veloso, M.M. (ed.) 20th International Joint Conference on Artificial Intelligence (IJCAI), pp. 1860–1865 (2007). http://ijcai.org/Proceedings/07/Papers/300.pdf
9. D'Argenio, P.R., Jeannet, B., Jensen, H.E., Larsen, K.G.: Reduction and refinement strategies for probabilistic analysis. In: Hermanns, H., Segala, R. (eds.) PAPM-PROBMIV 2002. LNCS, vol. 2399, pp. 57–76. Springer, Heidelberg (2002). https://doi.org/10.1007/3-540-45605-8_5
10. Esparza, J., Lammich, P., Neumann, R., Nipkow, T., Schimpf, A., Smaus, J.-G.: A fully verified executable LTL model checker. In: Sharygina, N., Veith, H. (eds.) CAV 2013. LNCS, vol. 8044, pp. 463–478. Springer, Heidelberg (2013). https://doi.org/10.1007/978-3-642-39799-8_31
11. Fleury, M.: Optimizing a verified SAT solver. In: Badger, J.M., Rozier, K.Y. (eds.) NFM 2019. LNCS, vol. 11460, pp. 148–165. Springer, Cham (2019). https://doi.org/10.1007/978-3-030-20652-9_10
12. Forejt, V., Kwiatkowska, M., Norman, G., Parker, D.: Automated verification techniques for probabilistic systems. In: Bernardo, M., Issarny, V. (eds.) SFM 2011. LNCS, vol. 6659, pp. 53–113. Springer, Heidelberg (2011). https://doi.org/10.1007/978-3-642-21455-4_3
13. Gabow, H.N.: Path-based depth-first search for strong and biconnected components. Inf. Process. Lett. **74**(3), 107–114 (2000). https://doi.org/10.1016/S0020-0190(00)00051-X
14. Haddad, S., Monmege, B.: Reachability in MDPs: refining convergence of value iteration. In: Ouaknine, J., Potapov, I., Worrell, J. (eds.) RP 2014. LNCS, vol. 8762, pp. 125–137. Springer, Cham (2014). https://doi.org/10.1007/978-3-319-11439-2_10

15. Haddad, S., Monmege, B.: Interval iteration algorithm for MDPs and IMDPs. Theor. Comput. Sci. **735**, 111–131 (2018). https://doi.org/10.1016/j.tcs.2016.12. 003

16. Hartmanns, A.: Correct probabilistic model checking with floating-point arithmetic. In: Fisman, D., Rosu, G. (eds.) TACAS 2022. LNCS, vol. 13244, pp. 41–59. Springer, Cham (2022). https://doi.org/10.1007/978-3-030-99527-0_3

17. Hartmanns, A., Hermanns, H.: The Modest Toolset: an integrated environment for quantitative modelling and verification. In: Ábrahám, E., Havelund, K. (eds.) TACAS 2014. LNCS, vol. 8413, pp. 593–598. Springer, Heidelberg (2014). https://doi.org/10.1007/978-3-642-54862-8_51

18. Hartmanns, A., Junges, S., Quatmann, T., Weininger, M.: A practitioner's guide to MDP model checking algorithms. In: Sankaranarayanan, S., Sharygina, N. (eds.) TACAS 2023. LNCS, vol. 13993, pp. 469–488. Springer, Cham (2023). https://doi.org/10.1007/978-3-031-30823-9_24

19. Hartmanns, A., Kaminski, B.L.: Optimistic value iteration. In: Lahiri, S.K., Wang, C. (eds.) CAV 2020. LNCS, vol. 12225, pp. 488–511. Springer, Cham (2020). https://doi.org/10.1007/978-3-030-53291-8_26

20. Hartmanns, A., Klauck, M., Parker, D., Quatmann, T., Ruijters, E.: The quantitative verification benchmark set. In: Vojnar, T., Zhang, L. (eds.) TACAS 2019. LNCS, vol. 11427, pp. 344–350. Springer, Cham (2019). https://doi.org/10.1007/978-3-030-17462-0_20

21. Hartmanns, A., Kohlen, B., Lammich, P.: Artifact for the paper "Fast verified SCCs for probabilistic model checking". 4TU.Centre for Research Data (2023). https://doi.org/10.4121/aff9f553-0e9e-4ec2-90e0-20c5b6152862

22. Hensel, C., Junges, S., Katoen, J.P., Quatmann, T., Volk, M.: The probabilistic model checker Storm. Int. J. Softw. Tools Technol. Transf. **24**(4), 589–610 (2022). https://doi.org/10.1007/s10009-021-00633-z

23. Heule, M., Hunt, W., Kaufmann, M., Wetzler, N.: Efficient, verified checking of propositional proofs. In: Ayala-Rincón, M., Muñoz, C.A. (eds.) ITP 2017. LNCS, vol. 10499, pp. 269–284. Springer, Cham (2017). https://doi.org/10.1007/978-3-319-66107-0_18

24. Hölzl, J.: Markov chains and Markov decision processes in Isabelle/HOL. J. Autom. Reason. **59**(3), 345–387 (2016). https://doi.org/10.1007/s10817-016-9401-5

25. Holzmann, G.J.: The model checker SPIN. IEEE Trans. Softw. Eng. **23**(5), 279–295 (1997). https://doi.org/10.1109/32.588521

26. Kwiatkowska, M., Norman, G., Parker, D.: PRISM 4.0: verification of probabilistic real-time systems. In: Gopalakrishnan, G., Qadeer, S. (eds.) CAV 2011. LNCS, vol. 6806, pp. 585–591. Springer, Heidelberg (2011). https://doi.org/10.1007/978-3-642-22110-1_47

27. Kwiatkowska, M.Z., Norman, G., Parker, D., Sproston, J.: Performance analysis of probabilistic timed automata using digital clocks. Formal Methods Syst. Des. **29**(1), 33–78 (2006). https://doi.org/10.1007/s10703-006-0005-2

28. Kwiatkowska, M.Z., Norman, G., Segala, R., Sproston, J.: Automatic verification of real-time systems with discrete probability distributions. Theor. Comput. Sci. **282**(1), 101–150 (2002). https://doi.org/10.1016/S0304-3975(01)00046-9

29. Lammich, P.: Automatic data refinement. In: Blazy, S., Paulin-Mohring, C., Pichardie, D. (eds.) ITP 2013. LNCS, vol. 7998, pp. 84–99. Springer, Heidelberg (2013). https://doi.org/10.1007/978-3-642-39634-2_9

30. Lammich, P.: Verified efficient implementation of Gabow's strongly connected component algorithm. In: Klein, G., Gamboa, R. (eds.) ITP 2014. LNCS, vol. 8558, pp. 325–340. Springer, Cham (2014). https://doi.org/10.1007/978-3-319-08970-6_21

31. Lammich, P.: Refinement to Imperative/HOL. In: Urban, C., Zhang, X. (eds.) ITP 2015. LNCS, vol. 9236, pp. 253–269. Springer, Cham (2015). https://doi.org/10.1007/978-3-319-22102-1_17

32. Lammich, P.: Generating verified LLVM from Isabelle/HOL. In: Harrison, J., O'Leary, J., Tolmach, A. (eds.) 10th International Conference on Interactive Theorem Proving (ITP). LIPIcs, vol. 141, pp. 22:1–22:19. Schloss Dagstuhl - Leibniz-Zentrum für Informatik (2019). https://doi.org/10.4230/LIPIcs.ITP.2019.22

33. Lammich, P.: Efficient verified (UN)SAT certificate checking. J. Autom. Reason. **64**(3), 513–532 (2019). https://doi.org/10.1007/s10817-019-09525-z

34. Lammich, P.: Refinement of parallel algorithms down to LLVM. In: Andronick, J., de Moura, L. (eds.) 13th International Conference on Interactive Theorem Proving (ITP). LIPIcs, vol. 237, pp. 24:1–24:18. Schloss Dagstuhl - Leibniz-Zentrum für Informatik (2022). https://doi.org/10.4230/LIPIcs.ITP.2022.24

35. Lammich, P., Tuerk, T.: Applying data refinement for monadic programs to Hopcroft's algorithm. In: Beringer, L., Felty, A. (eds.) ITP 2012. LNCS, vol. 7406, pp. 166–182. Springer, Heidelberg (2012). https://doi.org/10.1007/978-3-642-32347-8_12

36. Mansour, M.A., Schäffeler, M.: Formally verified solution methods for Markov decision processes. In: 37th AAAI Conference on Artificial Intelligence, pp. 15073–15081 (2022). https://doi.org/10.1609/aaai.v37i12.26759

37. Neumann, R.: Using Promela in a fully verified executable LTL model checker. In: Giannakopoulou, D., Kroening, D. (eds.) VSTTE 2014. LNCS, vol. 8471, pp. 105–114. Springer, Cham (2014). https://doi.org/10.1007/978-3-319-12154-3_7

38. Nipkow, T., Wenzel, M., Paulson, L.C. (eds.): Isabelle/HOL – A Proof Assistant for Higher-Order Logic. LNCS, vol. 2283. Springer, Heidelberg (2002). https://doi.org/10.1007/3-540-45949-9

39. Pottier, F.: Depth-first search and strong connectivity in Coq. In: Vingt-sixièmes journées francophones des langages applicatifs (JFLA) (2015)

40. Puterman, M.L.: Markov decision processes. Handb. Oper. Res. Manag. Sci. **2**, 331–434 (1990)

41. Quatmann, T., Katoen, J.-P.: Sound value iteration. In: Chockler, H., Weissenbacher, G. (eds.) CAV 2018. LNCS, vol. 10981, pp. 643–661. Springer, Cham (2018). https://doi.org/10.1007/978-3-319-96145-3_37

42. Vajjha, K., Shinnar, A., Trager, B.M., Pestun, V., Fulton, N.: CertRL: formalizing convergence proofs for value and policy iteration in Coq. In: Hritcu, C., Popescu, A. (eds.) 10th ACM SIGPLAN International Conference on Certified Programs and Proofs (CPP), pp. 18–31. ACM (2021). https://doi.org/10.1145/3437992.3439927

43. Wimmer, S., Herbreteau, F., van de Pol, J.: Certifying emptiness of timed Büchi automata. In: Bertrand, N., Jansen, N. (eds.) FORMATS 2020. LNCS, vol. 12288, pp. 58–75. Springer, Cham (2020). https://doi.org/10.1007/978-3-030-57628-8_4

44. Wimmer, S., Lammich, P.: Verified model checking of timed automata. In: Beyer, D., Huisman, M. (eds.) TACAS 2018. LNCS, vol. 10805, pp. 61–78. Springer, Cham (2018). https://doi.org/10.1007/978-3-319-89960-2_4

45. Wimmer, S., Mutius, J.: Verified certification of reachability checking for timed automata. In: Biere, A., Parker, D. (eds.) TACAS 2020. LNCS, vol. 12078, pp. 425–443. Springer, Cham (2020). https://doi.org/10.1007/978-3-030-45190-5_24

Bi-objective Lexicographic Optimization in Markov Decision Processes with Related Objectives

Damien Busatto-Gaston[1], Debraj Chakraborty[2]([✉]),
Anirban Majumdar[3], Sayan Mukherjee[3], Guillermo A. Pérez[4],
and Jean-François Raskin[3]

[1] Université Paris Est Créteil, LACL, 94010 Créteil, France
`damien.busatto-gaston@u-pec.fr`
[2] Masaryk University, Brno, Czech Republic
`chakraborty@fi.muni.cz`
[3] Université Libre de Bruxelles, Brussels, Belgium
`{anirban.majumdar,sayan.mukherjee,jean-francois.raskin}@ulb.be`
[4] University of Antwerp – Flanders Make, Antwerp, Belgium
`guillermo.perez@uantwerpen.be`

Abstract. We consider lexicographic bi-objective problems on Markov Decision Processes (MDPs), where we optimize one objective while guaranteeing optimality of another. We propose a two-stage technique for solving such problems when the objectives are related (in a way that we formalize). We instantiate our technique for two natural pairs of objectives: minimizing the (conditional) expected number of steps to a target while guaranteeing the optimal probability of reaching it; and maximizing the (conditional) expected average reward while guaranteeing an optimal probability of staying safe (w.r.t. some safe set of states). For the first combination of objectives, which covers the classical frozen lake environment from reinforcement learning, we also report on experiments performed using a prototype implementation of our algorithm and compare it with what can be obtained from state-of-the-art probabilistic model checkers solving optimal reachability.

Keywords: Markov decision processes · Multi-objective · Synthesis

1 Introduction

Probabilistic model-checkers, such as STORM [17] or PRISM [19], have been developed to solve the model-checking problem for logics like PCTL and models like

G. A. Pérez—Supported by the iBOF "DESCARTES" and FWO "SAILor" projects. Debraj Chakraborty, Anirban Majumdar, Sayan Mukherjee and Jean-François Raskin were supported by the EOS project *Verifying Learning Artificial Intelligent Systems* (F.R.S.-FNRS and FWO). Debraj Chakraborty was also supported by MASH (MUNI/I/1757/2021) of Masaryk University.

É. André and J. Sun (Eds.): ATVA 2023, LNCS 14215, pp. 203–223, 2023.
https://doi.org/10.1007/978-3-031-45329-8_10

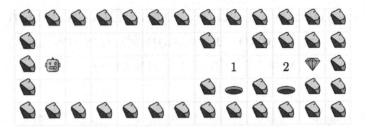

Fig. 1. In the game of Frozen Lake, a robot moves in a slippery grid. It has to reach the target (the gem) while avoiding holes in the grid. The robot can no longer move once in a hole. Part of the grid contains walls and the robot cannot move into them. The frozen surface of the lake being slippery, when the robot tries to move by picking a cardinal direction, the next state is determined stochastically over adjacent directions. For example, trying to move right would result on the robot going to the cell on the right with probability 0.8 but going up or down with probability 0.1 for each.

Markov decision processes. These tools can be used to compute strategies (or schedulers) that maximize the probability of, for instance, reaching a set of states. As a concrete example, they can be used to solve the Frozen Lake problem shown in Fig. 1, where a robot must navigate from an initial point to a target while avoiding holes in the ice. The ground is frozen and so the movements of the robot are subject to stochastic dynamics. While model-checkers provide optimal strategies for the probability of reaching the target, those strategies may not be efficient in terms of the expected number of steps required to reach it. For instance, the strategy returned by STORM for the grid given in Fig. 1 requires on average 345 steps to reach the target, while there are other strategies that are optimal for reachability that can reach the target in just 34 steps on average. Indeed, a strategy can be optimal in terms of the probability to reach the target while (seemingly) behaving like a random walk on the grid (on portions without holes in particular). In the worst case, one could expect to reach the target after large number of steps (even on grids where there is a short and direct path to target), which can be considered useless for practical purposes.[1] Therefore, in this context, we aim to not only *maximize the probability* of reaching the target, but also *minimize the expected number of steps* required to reach it, which is thus a multi-objective problem. Unfortunately, multi-objective optimization is not yet standard for probabilistic model checkers and most of them support it only for specific combinations of some objectives. For instance, STORM can solve the optimal reachability problem and compute the minimal expected cost to target, but only for target sets that can be reached with probability one. The

---

[1] In particular, the strategy could be used as a component of some larger approach dealing with a more challenging problem too difficult for exact methods. In these cases, such as [8], one frequently relies on machine-learning techniques (*e.g.* Monte-Carlo methods or reinforcement learning) that run simulations for a fixed number of steps. Thus, a strategy that takes needlessly too many steps to reach a target will not help with learning practical and relevant strategies.

latter is not usually the case in the Frozen Lake problem: the robot may need to walk next to a hole, and risk falling into it, in order to reach the target. In this paper, we demonstrate how to address the problems we have identified with the Frozen Lake example by leveraging the algorithms implemented in STORM.

We identify a family of bi-objective optimization problems that can be solved in two steps using readily available model-checking tools. This family of problems is formalized as follows. Let $\mathcal{M}$ be an MDP and $\Sigma(\mathcal{M})$ the set of all strategies for it. We study reward functions that map strategies $\sigma \in \Sigma(\mathcal{M})$ to real numbers via the induced MC $\mathcal{M}_\sigma$. Concretely, let $f, g : \Sigma(\mathcal{M}) \to \mathbb{R}$. We say a strategy $\sigma \in \Sigma(\mathcal{M})$ is f-optimal if $f(\sigma) = \sup_{\tau \in \Sigma(\mathcal{M})} f(\tau)$ and write Σ_f for the set of all f-optimal strategies.

There are multiple ways in which one can approach the problem of finding optimal strategies with respect to both f and g (see, e.g., [11] and references therein). In this work, we fix a lexicographic order on the functions. Formally, we want to compute a strategy σ such that the following holds:

$$\sigma \in \Sigma_f \text{ and } g(\sigma) = \sup_{\tau \in \Sigma_f} g(\tau) \tag{1}$$

Our Contribution. In this paper, we discuss the problem described above for two concrete cases of f and g. First, we tackle the motivating example from Frozen Lake and detail how to find strategies that maximize f, the probability of reaching a set of target states, while minimizing the conditional expected number of steps to reach them, encoded as g. It is not clear how to obtain an exact finite representation of the set Σ_f of all optimal strategies for f. To solve this problem, we first compute an over-approximation Σ_f^{over} of Σ_f. We then prune the original MDP in such a way that the set of all strategies in the pruned MDP is exactly Σ_f^{over}. In this context, Σ_f^{over} will be the set of strategies that only play actions used by at least one optimal strategy for reachability. We then optimize a modified objective g' in the pruned MDP, that, in turn, optimizes both f and g in the lexicographic order in the original MDP. The pruned MDP may contain actions from states that are part of some strategy maximizing the probability of reaching a target but which (taken together) do not make any progress towards the target (for example, a self-loop). These actions, however, are not part of the strategies that optimize g' in the pruned MDP and hence they are also not part of the strategies that are returned by our algorithm. Secondly, we also consider the problem of maximizing the probability of remaining in a safe set of states, encoded as f, while maximizing the expected mean-payoff along safe paths, encoded as g. Unlike the case for reachability, in this problem, we can in fact construct an exact finite representation of Σ_f in the form of an MDP (Theorem 2), which we again construct by pruning the original one. Similar to the reachability case, we then optimize a modified objective g' in the pruned MDP. In both of these cases, we prove (in Theorems 1 and 3) that the strategies optimizing g' in the pruned MDP, are solutions to Eq. 1.

Note that, the solution to the second problem is related to the *shielding* [2] framework and similar works [12,18], where one computes an exact representation of the set of all optimal strategies for the first objective and then solves for the second objective within that space. However, as remarked earlier, it is unclear how to get an exact representation of Σ_f in the first problem.

In both cases, our solution to these (lexicographic) bi-objective problems can be implemented by using two calls to off-the-shelf tools like STORM or PRISM, thus resulting in a polynomial-time solution. We report on experimental results for the Frozen Lake example that validate the need and practicality of our approach. Finally, we discuss other instances of multi-objective problems where our approach naturally generalizes.

Related Works. The strategy synthesis problem in MDPs (or stochastic games, their 2.5-players extension) can be defined for a wide variety of temporal objectives and quantitative rewards. Multi-objective problems are particularly challenging, as they need to optimize for multiple, potentially conflicting, goals. [10] detailed a strategy synthesis algorithm for lexicographic combinations of ω-regular objectives. This problem has also been studied with model-free, reinforcement learning approaches [16]. However, these approaches do not consider objectives that maximize quantitative rewards, and cannot optimize for properties such as the time to reach a target. In [6], one can mix LTL objectives with mean-payoff rewards and in [21] a lexicographic combination of discounted-sum rewards is considered. Moreover, a discounted semantics of LTL[2] is studied in [1], and can be used as a way to optimize for the time until a target is reached. Combinations of LTL and total-reward objectives have been considered in works such as [15] and [13], under assumptions that exclude our problem. Indeed, while minimizing the time to reach a target can be encoded as optimizing the total-reward of a slightly modified structure (where costs are 1 at every move before the target is reached then 0 forever), these works are not directly applicable to our problem: applying [15] requires the assumption that the optimal probability to reach a target is 1 in order to minimize the expected time to target, and [13] searches for a strategy on the Pareto frontier instead of optimizing for a lexicographic combination of objectives.

Note that minimizing the time to reach a target (a variant of the *stochastic shortest path problem* [5]) is only well-defined under the condition that the target is reached, so that our example requires studying *conditional* probabilities. This notion has been studied in single-objective settings, so that for example probabilistic model-checkers can optimize for the (conditional) probability of satisfying an ω-regular event under the condition that another ω-regular event holds [3]. In particular, [4] details how to maximize the expected total-reward until a target is reached, under the assumption that the target is indeed reached with positive probability. This does not solve our motivating example however, as it may yield a strategy that is suboptimal for the probability of reaching the target. Finally, we note that tools such as [9] can handle settings similar to our second example (optimizing for safety and mean-payoff), but they do not consider conditional mean-payoff.

---

[2] This allows one to express constraints on the number of steps needed to satisfy an Until operator.

Overall, our general two-stage technique covers combinations of objectives that are subcases of problems previously studied (e.g. in [10]) but it is also applicable to combinations not previously considered. Interestingly, and to the best of our knowledge, optimizing for a reachability objective while minimizing the conditional time to satisfy is not formally covered by previous work on multi-objective strategy synthesis, and is not an available feature of probabilistic model-checkers. It may be possible that this problem can be reduced to finding *bias-optimal strategies* [14] in a slightly modified MDP. However, this does not generalize to other objectives.

The missing proofs can be found in the longer version of the paper [7].

2 Preliminaries

A *probability distribution* on a countable set S is a function $d : S \to [0,1]$ such that $\sum_{s \in S} d(s) = 1$. We denote the set of all probability distributions on set S by $\mathcal{D}(S)$. The support of a distribution $d \in \mathcal{D}(S)$ is $\mathsf{Supp}(d) = \{s \in S \mid d(s) > 0\}$.

2.1 Markov Chain

Definition 1 (Markov chain). *A (discrete-time) Markov chain or an MC is a tuple $M = (S, P)$, where S is a countable set of states and P is a mapping from S to $\mathcal{D}(S)$.*

For states $s, s' \in S$, $P(s)(s')$ denotes the probability of moving from state s to state s' in a single transition and we denote this probability $P(s)(s')$ as $P(s, s')$.

For a Markov chain M, a *finite path* $\rho = s_0 s_1 \dots s_i$ of length $i > 0$ is a sequence of $i + 1$ consecutive states such that for all $t \in [0, i-1]$, $s_{t+1} \in \mathsf{Supp}(P(s_t))$. We also consider states to be paths of length 0. Similarly, An *infinite path* is an infinite sequence $\rho = s_0 s_1 s_2 \dots$ of states such that for all $t \in \mathbb{N}$, $s_{t+1} \in \mathsf{Supp}(P(s_t))$. For a finite or infinite path $\rho = s_0 s_1 \dots$, we denote its $(i+1)^{th}$ state by $\rho[i] = s_i$. We denote the last state of a finite path $\rho = s_0 s_1 \dots s_n$ by $\mathsf{last}(\rho) = s_n$. Let $\rho = s_0 s_1 \dots s_i$ and $\rho' = s_0' s_1' \dots s_j'$ be two paths such that $s_i = s_0'$. Then, $\rho \cdot \rho'$ denotes the path $s_0 s_1 \dots s_i s_1' \dots s_j'$. For a finite or infinite path $\rho = s_0 s_1 \dots$, we denote its *i-length prefix* as $\rho_{|_i} = s_0 s_1 \dots s_i$.

For a finite path $\rho \in \mathsf{Paths}_M$, we use $\mathsf{Paths}_M^\omega(\rho)$ to denote the set of all paths $\rho' \in \mathsf{Paths}_M^\omega$ such that there exists $\rho'' \in \mathsf{Paths}_M^\omega$ with $\rho' = \rho \cdot \rho''$. $\mathsf{Paths}_M^\omega(\rho)$ is called the *cylinder set* of ρ.

The σ-algebra associated with the MC M is the smallest σ-algebra that contains the cylinder sets $\mathsf{Paths}_M^\omega(\rho)$ for all $\rho \in \mathsf{Paths}_M$. For a state s in S, a measure is defined for the cylinder sets as –

$$\mathbb{P}_{M,s}(\mathsf{Paths}_M^\omega(s_0 s_1 \dots s_i)) = \begin{cases} \prod_{t=0}^{i-1} P(s_t)(s_{t+1}) & \text{if } s_0 = s \\ 0 & \text{otherwise.} \end{cases}$$

We also have $\mathbb{P}_{M,s}(\mathsf{Paths}_M^\omega(s)) = 1$ and $\mathbb{P}_{M,s}(\mathsf{Paths}_M^\omega(s')) = 0$ for $s' \neq s$. This can be extended to a unique probability measure $\mathbb{P}_{M,s}$ on the aforementioned

σ-algebra. In particular, if $\mathcal{C} \subseteq \mathsf{Paths}_M$ is a set of finite paths forming pairwise disjoint cylinder sets, then $\mathbb{P}_{M,s}(\cup_{\rho \in \mathcal{C}} \mathsf{Paths}_M^\omega(\rho)) = \sum_{\rho \in \mathcal{C}} \mathbb{P}_{M,s}(\mathsf{Paths}_M^\omega(\rho))$. Moreover, if $\Pi \in \mathsf{Paths}_M^\omega$ is the complement of a measurable set Π', then $\mathbb{P}_{M,s}(\Pi) = 1 - \mathbb{P}_{M,s}(\Pi')$.

2.2 Markov Decision Process

Definition 2 (Markov decision process). *A Markov decision process or an MDP is a tuple $\mathcal{M} = (S, A, P)$, where S is a finite set of states, A is a finite set of actions, and P is a (partial) mapping from $S \times A$ to $\mathcal{D}(S)$.*

$P(s,a)(s')$ denotes the probability that action a in state s leads to state s' and we denote this probability $P(s,a)(s')$ as $P(s,a,s')$. Note that not all actions may be *legal* from a state. Therefore, if an action a is legal from a state s, we will have $\sum_{s' \in S} P(s,a,s') = 1$. Otherwise, we will have $P(s,a,s')$ is undefined (denoted by $\perp$) for all $s' \in S$.

The definitions and notations used for paths in Markov chain can be extended in the case of MDPs. In an MDP, a *path* is a sequence of states and actions.

For an MDP $\mathcal{M}$, a (probabilistic) *strategy* is a function $\sigma : \mathsf{Paths}_\mathcal{M} \to \mathcal{D}(A)$ that maps a finite path ρ to a probability distribution in $\mathcal{D}(A)$. For a path $\rho \in \mathsf{Paths}_\mathcal{M}$ and a strategy σ, we will write $\sigma(\rho, a)$ in place of $\sigma(\rho)(a)$. A strategy σ is *deterministic* if the support of the probability distributions $\sigma(\rho)$ has size 1. A strategy σ is *memoryless* if $\sigma(\rho)$ depends only on $\mathsf{last}(\rho)$, i.e. if σ satisfies that for all $\rho, \rho' \in \mathsf{Paths}_\mathcal{M}$, $\mathsf{last}(\rho) = \mathsf{last}(\rho') \Rightarrow \sigma(\rho) = \sigma(\rho')$. We denote the set of all finite paths in $\mathcal{M}$ starting from s following σ by $\mathsf{Paths}_\mathcal{M}(s, \sigma)$.

An MDP $\mathcal{M}$ induced by a strategy σ defines an MC $\mathcal{M}_\sigma$. Intuitively, this is obtained by unfolding $\mathcal{M}$ using the strategy σ and using the probabilities in $\mathcal{M}$ to define the transition probabilities. Formally, $\mathcal{M}_\sigma = (\mathsf{Paths}_\mathcal{M}, P_\sigma)$ where for all paths $\rho \in \mathsf{Paths}_\mathcal{M}$, $P_\sigma(\rho)(\rho \cdot as) = \sigma(\rho)(a) \cdot P(\mathsf{last}(\rho), a)(s)$. Thus, a state ρ in $\mathsf{Paths}_\mathcal{M}$ uniquely *matches* a finite path ρ' in $\mathcal{M}_\sigma$ where $\mathsf{last}(\rho') = \rho$. This way when a strategy σ and a state s is fixed, the probability measure $\mathbb{P}_{\mathcal{M}_\sigma, s}$ defined in $\mathcal{M}_\sigma$ is also extended for paths in $\mathsf{Paths}_\mathcal{M}$. We write the expected value of a random variable X with respect to the probability distribution $\mathbb{P}_{\mathcal{M}_\sigma, s}$ as $\mathbb{E}_{\mathcal{M}_\sigma, s}(X)$. For the ease of notation, we write $\mathbb{P}_{\mathcal{M}_\sigma, s}$ and $\mathbb{E}_{\mathcal{M}_\sigma, s}$ as $\mathbb{P}_{\sigma, s}$ and $\mathbb{E}_{\sigma, s}$ respectively, if the MDP $\mathcal{M}$ is clear from the context. Also, we write $\mathsf{Paths}_{\mathcal{M}_\sigma}^\omega(\rho)$ as $\mathsf{Cyl}_\sigma(\rho)$, if the MDP $\mathcal{M}$ is clear from the context.

In the sequel, we make use of (technical) lemmas that follow from the extensive literature on Markov chains and MDPs. However, for completeness, and to give the reader intuition regarding the presented objectives, we also give proofs for some of them.

3 Length-Optimal Strategy for Reachability

We begin by considering the multi-objective problem motivated by the game of frozen lake – the robot tries to reach a target with as few steps as possible while not compromising on the probability of reaching a target. More formally, in this section, we find a strategy in an MDP that minimizes the expected number of steps to reach some goal states among those strategies that maximize the probability of reaching the goal states.

We consider a set of target states $T \subseteq S$ in $\mathcal{M}$, and assume that every state in T is a sink state, that is, it has only one outgoing action to itself with probability 1. Given a path ρ in an MC $M = (S, P)$, we use $\text{len}_T(\rho)$ to denote the length of the shortest prefix of ρ that reaches one of the states of T, that is, $\text{len}_T(\rho) = i$ if $\rho[i] \in T$ and for all $j < i$, $\rho[j] \notin T$.

For an MDP $\mathcal{M} = (S, A, P)$, let $\mathbb{P}_{\sigma,s}(\Diamond T)$ be the probability of reaching a state in T, starting from $s \in S$, following the strategy σ in $\mathcal{M}$. Then, let $\text{Val}_{\mathcal{M}}(s) = \max_{\sigma} \mathbb{P}_{\sigma,s}(\Diamond T)$ be the maximum probability to reach T from s, and $\Sigma_{\mathcal{M},s}(\Diamond T) = \arg\max_{\sigma} \mathbb{P}_{\sigma,s}(\Diamond T)$ be the set of all optimal strategies.

Problem statement.

Given an MDP $\mathcal{M}$, an initial state s_0 and a set of goal states T, our objective is to find a strategy that minimizes $\mathbb{E}_{\sigma,s_0}(\text{len}_T \mid \Diamond T)$ among the strategies in $\Sigma_{\mathcal{M},s_0}(\Diamond T)$, that is, the strategies which maximize $\mathbb{P}_{\sigma,s_0}(\Diamond T)$.

For the rest of this section, we fix the MDP $\mathcal{M} = (S, A, P)$ and a set of target states $T \subseteq S$. Note that, in this case, the functions $\sigma \mapsto \mathbb{P}_{\sigma,s_0}(\Diamond T)$ and $\sigma \mapsto -\mathbb{E}_{\sigma,s_0}(\text{len}_T \mid \Diamond T)$ correspond to the two functions f and g, respectively, and the set $\Sigma_{\mathcal{M},s_0}(\Diamond T)$ corresponds to Σ_f, described in the introduction (Eq. 1).

3.1 Maximizing Probability to Reach a Target

We denote the set $\{(s, a) \in S \times A \mid \text{Val}_{\mathcal{M}}(s) = \sum_{s'} P(s, a, s') \cdot \text{Val}_{\mathcal{M}}(s')\}$ by $\text{Opt}_{\mathcal{M}}$. For $s \in S$, let $\text{Opt}_{\mathcal{M}}(s)$ be the set $\{a \mid (s, a) \in \text{Opt}_{\mathcal{M}}\}$. Finally, we use $\Sigma_{\mathcal{M}}^{\text{Opt}}$ to represent the set of strategies that takes actions according to $\text{Opt}_{\mathcal{M}}$, that is, $\Sigma_{\mathcal{M}}^{\text{Opt}} = \{\sigma \mid \forall \rho, \forall a \in \text{Supp}(\sigma(\rho)); (\text{last}(\rho), a) \in \text{Opt}_{\mathcal{M}}\}$.

Lemma 1. *For every state $s \in S$ and for every $a \in A$,*

$$\text{Val}_{\mathcal{M}}(s) \geq \sum_{s'} P(s, a, s') \cdot \text{Val}_{\mathcal{M}}(s').$$

Proof. Suppose, there is a state $s \in S$ and an action $a \in A$ such that $\text{Val}_{\mathcal{M}}(s) < \sum_{s'} P(s, a, s') \cdot \text{Val}_{\mathcal{M}}(s')$. Now, consider the strategy σ' that takes action a from s and then from paths $s \cdot as'$ follows a strategy $\sigma_{s'} \in \Sigma_{\mathcal{M},s'}(\Diamond T)$ that maximizes the probability to reach states in T from s'. Formally,

$$\sigma'(\rho) = \begin{cases} a & \text{if } \rho = s \\ \sigma_{s'}(\rho') & \text{if } \rho = s \cdot as' \cdot \rho' \end{cases}$$

Then, $\mathbb{P}_{\sigma',s}(\Diamond T) = \sum_{s'} P(s, a, s') \cdot \mathbb{P}_{\sigma_{s'},s'}(\Diamond T) = \sum_{s'} P(s, a, s') \cdot \text{Val}_{\mathcal{M}}(s') > \text{Val}_{\mathcal{M}}(s)$, which is a contradiction as $\text{Val}_{\mathcal{M}}(s) \geq \mathbb{P}_{\sigma,s}(\Diamond T)$ for any σ. $\qquad\square$

Lemma 2. *For every state $s \in S$, $\Sigma_{\mathcal{M},s}(\Diamond T) \subseteq \Sigma_{\mathcal{M}}^{\mathsf{Opt}}$.*

Proof. Towards a contradiction, suppose that, there is a strategy $\sigma^* \in \Sigma_{\mathcal{M},s}(\Diamond T)$ such that $\sigma^* \notin \Sigma_{\mathcal{M}}^{\mathsf{Opt}}$. Then there exists a path ρ and an action $a \in \mathsf{Supp}(\sigma^*(\rho))$ such that $(\mathsf{last}(\rho), a) \notin \mathsf{Opt}_{\mathcal{M}}$. Let $\mathsf{last}(\rho) = t$. Then, from Lemma 1 and the fact that $(t, a) \notin \mathsf{Opt}_{\mathcal{M}}$, we get:

$$\mathsf{Val}_{\mathcal{M}}(t) > \sum_{s'} P(t, a, s') \cdot \mathsf{Val}_{\mathcal{M}}(s'), \tag{2}$$

and for every other action $a' \neq a$,

$$\mathsf{Val}_{\mathcal{M}}(t) \geq \sum_{s'} P(t, a', s') \cdot \mathsf{Val}_{\mathcal{M}}(s'). \tag{3}$$

Consider the strategy $\overline{\sigma}^*$ that differs from σ^* only on paths with ρ as prefix: on every path having ρ as a prefix, $\overline{\sigma}^*$ takes the next action according to a strategy $\sigma_t \in \Sigma_{\mathcal{M},t}(\Diamond T)$ that maximizes the probability to reach a state in T from t, whereas, it takes action according to σ^* on every other path. Formally,

$$\overline{\sigma}^*(\rho') = \begin{cases} \sigma_t(\rho'') & \text{if } \rho' = \rho \cdot \rho'' \\ \sigma^*(\rho') & \text{otherwise.} \end{cases}$$

Note that, for every strategy σ, and for all $a' \in A$, $\mathbb{P}_{\mathcal{M}_{\sigma^*},\rho \cdot a' s'}(\Diamond T) \leq \mathsf{Val}_{\mathcal{M}}(s')$.

Therefore, $\mathbb{P}_{\sigma^*,\rho}(\Diamond T) = \sum_{a'} \left(\sigma^*(\rho, a') \cdot \sum_{s'} \left(P(t, a', s') \cdot \mathbb{P}_{\sigma^*, \rho \cdot a' s'}(\Diamond T) \right) \right)$

$$\leq \sum_{a'} \left(\sigma^*(\rho, a') \cdot \sum_{s'} \left(P(t, a', s') \cdot \mathsf{Val}_{\mathcal{M}}(s') \right) \right)$$

$$< \sum_{a'} \sigma^*(\rho, a') \cdot \mathsf{Val}_{\mathcal{M}}(t) \quad \text{[from Eq. 2 and 3]}$$

$$= \mathsf{Val}_{\mathcal{M}}(t)$$

So, $\mathbb{P}_{\overline{\sigma}^*,\rho}(\Diamond T) = \mathbb{P}_{\sigma_t,t}(\Diamond T) = \mathsf{Val}_{\mathcal{M}}(t) > \mathbb{P}_{\sigma^*,\rho}(\Diamond T)$. For a finite path ρ and an infinite path ρ', we write $\rho \sqsubseteq \rho'$ if there exists an infinite path ρ'' such that $\rho' = \rho \cdot \rho''$. Now note that, for every strategy σ,

$$\mathbb{P}_{\sigma,s}(\Diamond T) = \mathbb{P}_{\sigma,s}(\rho' \models \Diamond T \wedge \rho \sqsubseteq \rho') + \mathbb{P}_{\sigma,s}(\rho' \models \Diamond T \wedge \rho \not\sqsubseteq \rho')$$
$$= \mathbb{P}_{\sigma,s}(\mathsf{Cyl}_{\sigma}(\rho)) \cdot \mathbb{P}_{\sigma,\rho}(\Diamond T) + \mathbb{P}_{\sigma,s}(\rho' \models \Diamond T \wedge \rho \not\sqsubseteq \rho') \tag{4}$$

Since for any ρ' such that $\rho \not\sqsubseteq \rho'$, $\sigma^*(\rho') = \overline{\sigma}^*(\rho')$, we have $\mathbb{P}_{\sigma^*,s}(\mathsf{Cyl}_{\sigma}(\rho))$ is equal to $\mathbb{P}_{\overline{\sigma}^*,s}(\mathsf{Cyl}_{\overline{\sigma}^*}(\rho))$, and furthermore, $\mathbb{P}_{\sigma^*,s}(\rho' \models \Diamond T \wedge \rho \not\sqsubseteq \rho')$ is equal to $\mathbb{P}_{\overline{\sigma}^*,s}(\rho' \models \Diamond T \wedge \rho \not\sqsubseteq \rho')$. Plugging this into Eq. 4 for σ^* and $\overline{\sigma}^*$, and the fact that $\mathbb{P}_{\sigma^*,\rho}(\Diamond T) < \mathbb{P}_{\overline{\sigma}^*,\rho}(\Diamond T)$, we conclude $\mathbb{P}_{\sigma^*,s}(\Diamond T) < \mathbb{P}_{\overline{\sigma}^*,s}(\Diamond T)$, which contradicts the fact that σ^* is an optimal strategy. $\qquad\square$

3.2   Minimizing Expected Conditional Length to Target

In the following, we propose a simple two-step pruning algorithm to solve the multi-objective problem defined earlier in this section. Towards that direction, we first modify the given MDP $\mathcal{M}$ in the following manner.

Definition 3. *We define the* pruned MDP $\mathcal{M}' = (S', A, P')$ *with* $S' = \{s \in S \mid \mathsf{Val}_{\mathcal{M}}(s) > 0\}$ *and* P' *constructed from* P *in the following way:*

$$P'(s, a, s') = \begin{cases} P(s, a, s') \cdot \frac{\mathsf{Val}_{\mathcal{M}}(s')}{\mathsf{Val}_{\mathcal{M}}(s)} & \text{if } (s, a) \in \mathsf{Opt}_{\mathcal{M}} \text{ and } s, s' \in S' \\ \bot & \text{otherwise.} \end{cases}$$

Note that $\mathcal{M}' = (S', A, P')$ is well-defined, since P' is a probability distribution. Indeed, $\sum_{s'} P'(s, a, s') = \sum_{s'} P(s, a, s') \cdot \frac{\mathsf{Val}_{\mathcal{M}}(s')}{\mathsf{Val}_{\mathcal{M}}(s)} = \frac{\mathsf{Val}_{\mathcal{M}}(s)}{\mathsf{Val}_{\mathcal{M}}(s)} = 1$.

From the construction of $\mathcal{M}'$, we get that the set $\Sigma(\mathcal{M}')$ of all strategies in $\mathcal{M}'$ is, in fact, $\Sigma_{\mathcal{M}}^{\mathsf{Opt}}$. Following similar notation as introduced earlier, for a strategy $\sigma \in \Sigma(\mathcal{M}')$, we write $\mathbb{P}_{\mathcal{M}'_{\sigma}, s}$ and $\mathbb{E}_{\mathcal{M}'_{\sigma}, s}$ as $\mathbb{P}'_{\sigma, s}$ and $\mathbb{E}'_{\sigma, s}$, respectively. Also, we write $\mathsf{Paths}_{\mathcal{M}'_{\sigma}}^{\omega}(\rho)$ as $\mathsf{Cyl}'_{\sigma}(\rho)$.

We now have all the ingredients to present the algorithm:

Algorithm 1

Input: $\mathcal{M} = (S, A, P)$, $s_0 \in S$ and $T \subseteq S$.

1: Create MDP $\mathcal{M}' = (S', A, P')$ according to Definition 3.
2: Find a strategy σ^* that minimizes the expected length in $\mathcal{M}'$:

$$\sigma^* \in \arg\min_{\sigma} \mathbb{E}'_{\sigma, s_0}(\mathsf{len}_T).$$

3: **return** σ^*.

Note that, the strategies present in the pruned MDP $\mathcal{M}'$ contain every strategy of $\mathcal{M}$ that optimizes the probability of reaching a target (Lemma 2). To show that Algorithm 1 indeed returns a length-optimal strategy maximizing the probability of reachability in $\mathcal{M}$, we need to show the following:

- the strategy given by Algorithm 1 is indeed a strategy that optimizes the probability to reach a target, and
- for every strategy $\sigma \in \Sigma_{\mathcal{M}, s_0}(\Diamond T)$, the conditional expected length to a target state $\mathbb{E}_{\sigma, s_0}(\mathsf{len}_T \mid \Diamond T)$ in $\mathcal{M}$ is the same as $\mathbb{E}'_{\sigma, s_0}(\mathsf{len}_T)$ in $\mathcal{M}'$. Therefore, it is enough to minimize the expected length in $\mathcal{M}'$.

We first show a relation between the measures of cylinder sets in $\mathcal{M}$ and $\mathcal{M}'$.

Lemma 3. *For every strategy* $\sigma \in \Sigma_{\mathcal{M}}^{\mathsf{Opt}}$ *and for every path* $\rho = s_0 a_0 s_1 \ldots s_n \in ((S' \setminus T) \cdot A)^* T \cap \mathsf{Paths}_{\mathcal{M}'}(s_0, \sigma)$, $\mathbb{P}'_{\sigma, s_0}(\mathsf{Cyl}'_{\sigma}(\rho)) = \frac{\mathbb{P}_{\sigma, s_0}(\mathsf{Cyl}_{\sigma}(\rho))}{\mathsf{Val}_{\mathcal{M}}(s_0)}$.

Proof. As $s_n \in T$, $\mathsf{Val}_\mathcal{M}(s_n) = 1$. So,

$$\mathbb{P}'_{\sigma,s_0}(\mathsf{Cyl}'_\sigma(\rho)) = \prod_{i=0}^{n-1} \sigma(\rho_{|i}, a_i) \cdot P'(s_i, a_i, s_{i+1})$$

$$= \prod_{i=0}^{n-1} \sigma(\rho_{|i}, a_i) \cdot P(s_i, a_i, s_{i+1}) \cdot \frac{\mathsf{Val}_\mathcal{M}(s_{i+1})}{\mathsf{Val}_\mathcal{M}(s_i)}$$

$$= \mathbb{P}_{\sigma,s_0}(\mathsf{Cyl}_\sigma(\rho)) \cdot \frac{\mathsf{Val}_\mathcal{M}(s_n)}{\mathsf{Val}_\mathcal{M}(s_0)} = \frac{\mathbb{P}_{\sigma,s_0}(\mathsf{Cyl}_\sigma(\rho))}{\mathsf{Val}_\mathcal{M}(s_0)} .$$

$\square$

Using Lemma 3 we will prove that (cf. Corollary 1) every strategy that maximizes the probability of reaching a target state in $\mathcal{M}$, reaches a target state in $\mathcal{M}'$ with probability 1, and vice versa.

Lemma 4. *For every strategy* $\sigma \in \Sigma_\mathcal{M}^{\mathsf{Opt}}$, $\mathbb{P}'_{\sigma,s_0}(\Diamond T) = \frac{\mathbb{P}_{\sigma,s_0}(\Diamond T)}{\mathsf{Val}_\mathcal{M}(s_0)}$.

Proof. Note that, $\mathsf{Paths}_{\mathcal{M}'}(s_0) \cap ((S' \setminus T) \cdot A)^* T = \mathsf{Paths}_\mathcal{M}(s_0) \cap ((S \setminus T) \cdot A)^* T$, since in the construction of $\mathcal{M}'$ we only remove states of $\mathcal{M}$ from which no state in T is reachable. Therefore, using Lemma 3, we get:

$$\mathbb{P}'_{\sigma,s_0}(\Diamond T) = \sum_{\rho \in \mathsf{Paths}_{\mathcal{M}'}(s_0) \cap ((S' \setminus T)A)^* T} \mathbb{P}'_{\sigma,s_0}(\mathsf{Cyl}'_\sigma(\rho))$$

$$= \sum_{\rho \in \mathsf{Paths}_\mathcal{M}(s_0) \cap ((S \setminus T)A)^* T} \frac{\mathbb{P}_{\sigma,s_0}(\mathsf{Cyl}_\sigma(\rho))}{\mathsf{Val}_\mathcal{M}(s_0)}$$

$$= \frac{\mathbb{P}_{\sigma,s_0}(\Diamond T)}{\mathsf{Val}_\mathcal{M}(s_0)} .$$

$\square$

Corollary 1. *For every* $\sigma \in \Sigma(\mathcal{M})$, $\sigma \in \Sigma_{\mathcal{M},s_0}(\Diamond T)$ *iff* $\mathbb{P}'_{\sigma,s_0}(\Diamond T) = 1$.

Since for every $\sigma \in \Sigma_{\mathcal{M},s_0}(\Diamond T)$, $\mathbb{P}_{\sigma,s_0}(\Diamond T \mid \Diamond T) = 1$, we can write:

$$\mathbb{E}_{\sigma,s_0}(\mathsf{len}_T \mid \Diamond T) = \sum_{r=0}^{\infty} r \cdot \frac{\mathbb{P}_{\sigma,s_0}(\{\rho \mid \rho \models \Diamond T \wedge \mathsf{len}_T(\rho) = r\})}{\mathbb{P}_{\sigma,s_0}(\Diamond T)}$$

$$= \sum_{r=0}^{\infty} r \cdot \sum_{\rho \in \mathsf{Paths}_\mathcal{M}(s_0) \cap ((S \setminus T)A)^* T : \mathsf{len}_T(\rho) = r} \frac{\mathbb{P}_{\sigma,s_0}(\mathsf{Cyl}_\sigma(\rho))}{\mathsf{Val}_\mathcal{M}(s_0)} .$$

We now relate the expected length of reaching a target state in $\mathcal{M}'$ with the expected conditional length of reaching a target state in $\mathcal{M}$.

Lemma 5. *For any strategy* $\sigma \in \Sigma_{\mathcal{M},s_0}(\Diamond T)$, $\mathbb{E}'_{\sigma,s_0}(\mathsf{len}_T) = \mathbb{E}_{\sigma,s_0}(\mathsf{len}_T \mid \Diamond T)$.

Proof. Using $\mathsf{Paths}_{\mathcal{M}'}(s_0) \cap ((S' \setminus T) \cdot A)^*T = \mathsf{Paths}_{\mathcal{M}}(s_0) \cap ((S \setminus T) \cdot A)^*T$, Lemma 3 and Corollary 1, we get:

$$\mathbb{E}'_{\sigma,s_0}(\mathrm{len}_T) = \sum_{r=0}^{\infty} r \cdot \mathbb{P}'_{\sigma,s_0}(\{\rho \mid \rho \models \Diamond T \wedge \mathrm{len}_T(\rho) = r\})$$

$$= \sum_{r=0}^{\infty} r \cdot \sum_{\rho \in \mathsf{Paths}_{\mathcal{M}'}(s_0) \cap ((S'\setminus T)A)^*T : \mathrm{len}_T(\rho) = r} \mathbb{P}'_{\sigma,s_0}(\mathsf{Cyl}'_{\sigma}(\rho))$$

$$= \sum_{r=0}^{\infty} r \cdot \sum_{\rho \in \mathsf{Paths}_{\mathcal{M}}(s_0) \cap ((S\setminus T)A)^*T : \mathrm{len}_T(\rho) = r} \frac{\mathbb{P}_{\sigma,s_0}(\mathsf{Cyl}_{\sigma}(\rho))}{\mathsf{Val}_{\mathcal{M}}(s_0)}$$

$$= \mathbb{E}_{\sigma,s_0}(\mathrm{len}_T \mid \Diamond T).$$

$\square$

Finally, we prove the correctness of Algorithm 1:

Theorem 1. *Given an MDP $\mathcal{M} = (S, A, P)$, a state $s_0 \in S$ and $T \subseteq S$, let σ^* be the strategy returned by Algorithm 1. Then,*

1. $\mathbb{P}_{\sigma^*,s_0}(\Diamond T) = \mathsf{Val}_{\mathcal{M}}(s_0)$.
2. $\mathbb{E}_{\sigma^*,s_0}(\mathrm{len}_T \mid \Diamond T) = \min\limits_{\sigma \in \Sigma_{\mathcal{M},s_0}(\Diamond T)} \mathbb{E}_{\sigma,s_0}(\mathrm{len}_T \mid \Diamond T)$

Proof. From Corollary 1, we get that $\mathbb{E}'_{\sigma,s_0}(\mathrm{len}_T) \neq \infty$ iff $\sigma \in \Sigma_{\mathcal{M},s_0}(\Diamond T)$. So if $\sigma^* \notin \Sigma_{\mathcal{M},s_0}(\Diamond T)$, then $\mathbb{E}'_{\sigma^*,s_0}(\mathrm{len}_T) = \infty$. But since for any strategy σ in $\Sigma_{\mathcal{M},s_0}(\Diamond T)$, $\mathbb{E}'_{\sigma,s_0}(\mathrm{len}_T) < \infty$, it contradicts the fact that σ^* minimizes $\mathbb{E}'_{\sigma,s_0}(\mathrm{len}_T)$. Therefore, $\sigma^* \in \Sigma_{\mathcal{M},s_0}(\Diamond T)$, and hence $\mathbb{P}_{\sigma^*,s_0}(\Diamond T) = \mathsf{Val}_{\mathcal{M}}(s_0)$.

From Lemma 5, we get for any $\sigma \in \Sigma_{\mathcal{M},s_0}(\Diamond T)$,

$$\mathbb{E}_{\sigma,s_0}(\mathrm{len}_T \mid \Diamond T) = \mathbb{E}'_{\sigma,s_0}(\mathrm{len}_T)$$

$$\implies \arg\min_{\sigma \in \Sigma_{\mathcal{M},s_0}(\Diamond T)} \mathbb{E}_{\sigma,s_0}(\mathrm{len}_T \mid \Diamond T) = \arg\min_{\sigma \in \Sigma_{\mathcal{M},s_0}(\Diamond T)} \mathbb{E}'_{\sigma,s_0}(\mathrm{len}_T)$$

Hence, $\sigma^* \in \arg\min_{\sigma \in \Sigma_{\mathcal{M},s_0}(\Diamond T)} \mathbb{E}_{\sigma,s_0}(\mathrm{len}_T \mid \Diamond T)$ and therefore, we conclude, $\mathbb{E}_{\sigma^*,s_0}(\mathrm{len}_T \mid \Diamond T) = \min\limits_{\sigma \in \Sigma_{\mathcal{M},s_0}(\Diamond T)} \mathbb{E}_{\sigma,s_0}(\mathrm{len}_T \mid \Diamond T)$. $\square$

Note that, constructing the MDP $\mathcal{M}'$ (Line 1 of Algorithm 1) takes polynomial time. Finding a strategy that optimizes $\mathbb{E}'_{\sigma,s_0}(\mathrm{len}_T)$ also takes polynomial time [5]. Therefore, the overall algorithm terminates in polynomial time.

4   Experimental Results

We have made a prototype implementation of the pruning-based algorithm (Algorithm 1) described in Sect. 3. In this section, we compare the performance (expected number of steps to reach the goal states) of our algorithm with the strategies generated by STORM that (only) maximize the probability of reaching the goal states.

Table 1. Comparison of the expected conditional length to reach the target for the strategies given by Algorithm 1 ($v_{DistOpt}$) and STORM (v_{Storm}) on some of the randomly generated layouts, sorted by their ratio. 'Shortest distance' refer to the length of the shortest path to the target (without considering the stochastic dynamics of Frozen Lake) and 'Val$_{\mathcal{M}}(s_0, \Diamond T)$' represents the maximum probability of reaching the target from the initial position of the robot (s_0).

layouts ($\mathcal{M}$)	Val$_{\mathcal{M}}(s_0, \Diamond T)$	Shortest distance	$v_{DistOpt}$	v_{Storm}
1	0.66	9	76.48	76.48
2	0.52	18	299.75	629.16
3	1.00	2	2.40	12.12
4	1.00	3	3.44	34.47
5	1.00	6	7.71	137.56
6	0.68	10	264.04	9598.81
7	1.00	5	112.69	9367.02
8	0.91	10	11.49	5879.63
9	1.00	3	3.66	5711.76
10	0.91	5	12.89	149357.57

In our MDP, when the robot tries to move by picking a direction, the next state is determined randomly over the neighbouring positions of the robot, according to the following distribution weights: the intended direction gets a weight of 10, and other directions that are not a wall and not the reverse direction of the intended one get a weight of 1, the distribution is then normalized so that the weights sum up to 1.

We generated 100 layouts of size 10×10 where we placed walls in (i) each cell in the border of the grid and (ii) with probability 0.1, at each of other cells. We then placed holes in the remaining empty cells with the same probability. Finally, we chose the position of the target and the starting position from the remaining empty cells uniformly at random.

From these layouts, we constructed MDPs described in the PRISM language, a format supported by STORM. For each MDP, we extracted two strategies: (i) a strategy $\sigma_{Storm} \in \Sigma_{\mathcal{M},s}(\Diamond T)$ that is produced by STORM that optimizes the probability to reach the target, and (ii) $\sigma_{DistOpt}$, a strategy that is derived from Algorithm 1. Note that, both of these strategies are optimal for the probability to reach the target. However, the first strategy does not focus on optimizing the length to reach the target. For both of these strategies, we calculate the expected conditional distance to the target in their induced Markov chains. Table 1 reports on our experimental results for a representative subset of the 100 layouts we generated, one of each decile (one layout from the 10 best percents, one from the $10 - 20\%$ range, etc.).

Observe that the strategy given by Algorithm 1 does not necessarily suggest following the shortest path, as this may not optimize the first objective (reaching the target with maximum probability). For example, in the layout in Fig. 1, the 'shortest' path to the target has length 10. But if we need to maximize the probability to reach the target, from the cell in the grid marked with 1, instead of going right, a better strategy would be to keep going to the cell above and then coming back. This way, the agent will avoid the hole below with certainty, and will eventually go to the right. This is the strategy that Algorithm 1 provides, which has expected conditional length to the target 33.85. On the other hand, the expected conditional length to the target while following the optimal strategy produced by STORM is much larger (345.34). This is because it asks the robot to loop in the 6×3 area in the left. Because of the stochastic dynamics it eventually leaves this area and reaches the target, but it may take a long time, increasing the expected conditional length.

While performing the experiments on the 100 randomly generated layouts, we observed that in 9 layouts out of 10, the expected conditional length (v_{Storm}) for the strategy σ_{Storm} is at least twice the expected conditional length (v_{DistOpt}) for the strategy σ_{DistOpt}. In 69% of the layouts, v_{Storm} values are 10 times worse than the v_{DistOpt} values. In the worst cases (23% of the layouts), v_{Storm} values are at least a 1000 times worse than the v_{DistOpt} values.

5   Safety and Expected Mean Payoff

In this section, we consider another multi-objective problem – as a first objective, we maximize the probability of avoiding a set of states in an MDP, and as a second objective, we maximize the expected conditional Mean Payoff. We propose a pruning-based algorithm, similar to Algorithm 1, to solve this problem.

For this section, we augment the definition of an MDP $\mathcal{M}$ with a *reward function* $R : S \times A \rightarrow \mathbb{R}$, where S, A and P are the same as in the previous sections. Furthermore, we consider a set of states $\text{Bad} \subset S$ in $\mathcal{M}$ and assume that every state in Bad is a sink state.

For an MDP $\mathcal{M} = (S, A, P, R)$, let $\mathbb{P}_{\mathcal{M}_\sigma,s}(\Box \neg \text{Bad})$ be the probability of avoiding all states in Bad, starting from $s \in S$, following the strategy σ in $\mathcal{M}$. Then, let $\text{Val}_{\mathcal{M}}(s) = \max_\sigma \mathbb{P}_{\mathcal{M}_\sigma,s}(\Box \neg \text{Bad})$ be the maximum probability to avoid Bad from s, and $\Sigma_{\mathcal{M},s}(\Box \neg \text{Bad}) = \arg\max_\sigma \mathbb{P}_{\mathcal{M}_\sigma,s}(\Box \neg \text{Bad})$ be the set of all optimal strategies for safety.

To formally define the second objective, we first define the *total reward* of horizon n for a path $\rho = s_0 a_0 \ldots$ as $\text{Rew}_n(\rho) = \sum_{i=0}^{n-1} R(s_i, a_i)$. Then, for a strategy σ and a state s, the *expected mean-payoff* is defined as

$$\mathbb{E}_{\sigma,s}(\text{MP}) = \liminf_{n \to \infty} \frac{1}{n} \mathbb{E}_{\sigma,s}(\text{Rew}_n).$$

The optimal *expected average reward* starting from a state s in an MDP $\mathcal{M}$ is defined over all strategies σ in $\mathcal{M}$ as $\sup_\sigma \mathbb{E}_{\sigma,s}(\text{MP})$. One can restrict the supremum to the deterministic memoryless strategies [20, section 9.1.4].

We use $\mathbb{E}_{\sigma,s}(\text{Rew}_n \mid \Box \neg \text{Bad})$ to denote the *expected conditional finite horizon reward*. Then the *expected conditional mean-payoff* is defined as

$$\mathbb{E}_{\sigma,s}(\text{MP} \mid \Box \neg \text{Bad}) = \liminf_{n \to \infty} \frac{1}{n} \mathbb{E}_{\sigma,s}(\text{Rew}_n \mid \Box \neg \text{Bad}).$$

Intuitively, it represents the expected mean-payoff one would obtain by following the strategy σ and staying safe.

Problem statement.

Given an MDP $\mathcal{M}$, an initial state s_0 and a set of states Bad where $\mathsf{Val}_{\mathcal{M}}(s_0) > 0$, our objective is to find a strategy that maximizes $\mathbb{E}_{\mathcal{M}_\sigma, s_0}(\mathsf{MP} \mid \Box\neg\mathsf{Bad})$ among the strategies in $\Sigma_{\mathcal{M}, s_0}(\Box\neg\mathsf{Bad})$, i.e., the strategies maximizing $\mathbb{P}_{\mathcal{M}_\sigma, s_0}(\Box\neg\mathsf{Bad})$.

For the rest of this section, we fix the MDP $\mathcal{M} = (S, A, P, R)$ and a set of bad states $\mathsf{Bad} \subset S$. Note that, in this case, the functions $\sigma \mapsto \mathbb{P}_{\sigma, s_0}(\Box\neg\mathsf{Bad})$ and $\sigma \mapsto \mathbb{E}_{\sigma, s_0}(\mathsf{MP} \mid \Box\neg\mathsf{Bad})$ correspond to the two functions f and g, respectively, and $\Sigma_{\mathcal{M}, s_0}(\Box\neg\mathsf{Bad})$ corresponds to Σ_f, described in the introduction (Eq. 1).

5.1   Maximizing Probability of Staying Safe

We denote the set $\{(s, a) \in S \times A \mid \mathsf{Val}_{\mathcal{M}}(s) = \sum_{s'} P(s, a, s') \cdot \mathsf{Val}_{\mathcal{M}}(s')\}$ using $\mathsf{Opt}_{\mathcal{M}}$. For $s \in S$, let $\mathsf{Opt}_{\mathcal{M}}(s)$ be the set $\{a \mid (s, a) \in \mathsf{Opt}_{\mathcal{M}}\}$. Finally, we use $\Sigma_{\mathcal{M}}^{\mathsf{Opt}}$ to represent the set of strategies that takes actions according to $\mathsf{Opt}_{\mathcal{M}}$, that is, $\Sigma_{\mathcal{M}}^{\mathsf{Opt}} = \{\sigma \mid \forall \rho, \forall a \in \mathsf{Supp}(\sigma(\rho)); (\mathsf{last}(\rho), a) \in \mathsf{Opt}_{\mathcal{M}}\}$.

We first state the following results, analogous to Lemma 1 and 2 respectively, which can be proved similarly as in the case of reachability.

Lemma 6. *For every state $s \in S \setminus \mathsf{Bad}$ and for every action a,*

$$\mathsf{Val}_{\mathcal{M}}(s) \geq \sum_{s'} P(s, a, s') \cdot \mathsf{Val}_{\mathcal{M}}(s').$$

Lemma 7. *For every state $s \in S$, $\Sigma_{\mathcal{M}, s}(\Box\neg\mathsf{Bad}) \subseteq \Sigma_{\mathcal{M}}^{\mathsf{Opt}}$.*

Furthermore, we will show that, unlike reachability, in this case, the other direction of the containment also holds:

Lemma 8. *For every state $s \in S$, $\Sigma_{\mathcal{M}, s}(\Box\neg\mathsf{Bad}) \supseteq \Sigma_{\mathcal{M}}^{\mathsf{Opt}}$.*

In order to prove Lemma 8, we first develop a few intermediate results. We start with defining the following notations:

$$\mathsf{UPre}^0(\mathsf{Bad}) = \mathsf{Bad}, \quad \mathsf{UPre}^{i+1}(\mathsf{Bad}) = \{s \mid \forall a, \exists s' \in \mathsf{UPre}^i(\mathsf{Bad}), P(s, a, s') > 0\},$$

$$\mathsf{UPre}^*(\mathsf{Bad}) = \bigcup_{i=0}^{\infty} \mathsf{UPre}^i(\mathsf{Bad}).$$

Furthermore, we define $\mathsf{Good} = S \setminus \mathsf{UPre}^*(\mathsf{Bad})$, $V = S \setminus (\mathsf{Good} \cup \mathsf{Bad})$.

Lemma 9. *For every state $s \in S$, $\mathsf{Val}_{\mathcal{M}}(s) = 1$ iff $s \in \mathsf{Good}$.*

Proof. For $s \in \mathsf{Good}$, $\exists a$ such that $\mathsf{Supp}(P(s, a)) \subseteq \mathsf{Good}$. This gives a strategy to surely avoid Bad, and hence $\mathsf{Val}_{\mathcal{M}}(s) = 1$.

If $s \notin \mathsf{Good}$, then either (i) $s \in \mathsf{Bad}$, in which case $\mathsf{Val}_{\mathcal{M}}(s) = 0$, or (ii) $s \in \mathsf{UPre}^*(\mathsf{Bad})$, and hence $s \in \mathsf{UPre}^i(\mathsf{Bad}) \setminus \mathsf{UPre}^{i-1}(\mathsf{Bad})$ for some i. Then, for every action a, $\mathsf{Supp}(P(s, a)) \cap \mathsf{UPre}^{i-1}(\mathsf{Bad}) \neq \emptyset$. This implies, for any strategy σ, there is a path from s of length at most i reaching Bad following σ. Since this path has a non-zero probability, we therefore get that $\mathsf{Val}_{\mathcal{M}}(s) < 1$. $\qquad\Box$

For a strategy σ and a finite path ρ, we define the strategy σ_ρ as follows: for any finite path ρ' starting from $\mathsf{last}(\rho)$, $\sigma_\rho(\rho') = \sigma(\rho \cdot \rho')$.

Lemma 10. *For every strategy $\sigma \in \Sigma_\mathcal{M}^{\mathsf{Opt}}$, and every finite path ρ in $\mathcal{M}$ following σ, $\mathbb{P}_{\sigma_\rho,\mathsf{last}(\rho)}(\Box\neg\mathsf{Bad}) = 1$ iff $\mathsf{last}(\rho) \in \mathsf{Good}$.*

Proof. We denote $\mathsf{last}(\rho)$ by s. First, let $s \in \mathsf{Good}$. Then we can show that $\forall a \in \mathsf{Opt}_\mathcal{M}(s), \mathsf{Supp}(P(s,a)) \subseteq \mathsf{Good}$. Indeed, if there exists an action $a \in \mathsf{Opt}_\mathcal{M}(s)$ and a state $s' \in \mathsf{Supp}(P(s,a))$ such that $s' \notin \mathsf{Good}$, then from Lemma 9, $\mathsf{Val}(s') < 1$, which would further imply that

$$\mathsf{Val}_\mathcal{M}(s) = \sum_{s'} P(s,a,s') \cdot \mathsf{Val}_\mathcal{M}(s') < \sum_{s'} P(s,a,s') = 1\,,$$

which contradicts the fact that $s \in \mathsf{Good}$ (using Lemma 9). So for every strategy σ in $\Sigma_\mathcal{M}^{\mathsf{Opt}}$, every path from s following σ_ρ only visits states from Good. Therefore, $\mathbb{P}_{\sigma_\rho,s}(\Box\neg\mathsf{Bad}) = 1$.

To conclude, observe that if $s \in S \setminus \mathsf{Good}$, $\mathbb{P}_{\sigma_\rho,s}(\Box\neg\mathsf{Bad}) \le \mathsf{Val}_\mathcal{M}(s) < 1$. □

In the following, for the ease of notation, for any state $s \in S$ and a strategy σ, we denote $\mathbb{P}_{\sigma,s}(\mathsf{Cyl}_\sigma(\rho))$ by $\mathbf{P}_{\sigma,s}(\rho)$. Recall that, for any action $a \in \mathsf{Opt}_\mathcal{M}(s)$, $\mathsf{Val}_\mathcal{M}(s) = \sum_{s'} P(s,a,s') \cdot \mathsf{Val}_\mathcal{M}(s')$. We can then expand $\mathsf{Val}_\mathcal{M}(s)$ as:

$$\mathsf{Val}_\mathcal{M}(s) = \sum_{a} \sigma(s,a)\mathsf{Val}_\mathcal{M}(s) = \sum_{a} \sigma(s,a) \sum_{s'} P(s,a,s') \cdot \mathsf{Val}_\mathcal{M}(s')\,.$$

We can generalize the above statement by unfolding $\mathsf{Val}_\mathcal{M}(\cdot)$ for n steps:

Lemma 11. *For every state $s \in S$ and for every strategy $\sigma \in \Sigma_\mathcal{M}^{\mathsf{Opt}}$,*

$$\mathsf{Val}_\mathcal{M}(s) = \sum_{\rho \in (VA)^n V} \mathbf{P}_{\sigma,s}(\rho) \cdot \mathsf{Val}_\mathcal{M}(\mathsf{last}(\rho)) + \sum_{\rho \in (VA)^{<n}\mathsf{Good}} \mathbf{P}_{\sigma,s}(\rho)$$

The summation in the first term of the above expression is taken over all paths that reach neither Good nor Bad within n steps, whereas the summation in the second term is over all paths that reach some state in Good within n steps. The result in Lemma 11 follows from the following result:

Lemma 12. *For every finite path $\rho = s_0 a_0 s_1 \dots s_n$ of length n and for every strategy σ in $\Sigma_\mathcal{M}^{\mathsf{Opt}}$, for all $k < n$:*

$$\mathsf{Val}_\mathcal{M}(s_k) = \sum_{\rho' \in (VA)^{n-k} V} \mathbf{P}_{\sigma_{\rho|_k},s_k}(\rho') \cdot \mathsf{Val}_\mathcal{M}(\mathsf{last}(\rho')) + \sum_{\rho' \in (VA)^{<n-k}\mathsf{Good}} \mathbf{P}_{\sigma_{\rho|_k},s_k}(\rho')\,.$$

Using Lemma 12, we can now prove Lemma 11:

Proof of Lemma 11. Putting $k = 0$ in Lemma 12, we get:

$$\mathsf{Val}_\mathcal{M}(s_0) = \sum_{\rho' \in (VA)^n V} \mathbf{P}_{\sigma,s_0}(\rho') \cdot \mathsf{Val}_\mathcal{M}(\mathsf{last}(\rho')) + \sum_{\rho' \in (VA)^{<n}\mathsf{Good}} \mathbf{P}_{\sigma,s_0}(\rho')\,.$$

□

We now characterize $\mathbb{P}(\cdot)$ in the same way as we did for $\mathsf{Val}(\cdot)$. Note that, for any state s and any strategy σ, we can expand $\mathbb{P}_{\sigma,s}(\square\neg\mathsf{Bad})$ as

$$\mathbb{P}_{\sigma,s}(\square\neg\mathsf{Bad}) = \sum_a \sigma(s,a) \sum_{s'} P(s,a,s') \cdot \mathbb{P}_{\sigma_{sas'},s'}(\square\neg\mathsf{Bad}).$$

Analogous to Lemma 11, we can generalize this statement by unfolding $\mathbb{P}(\cdot)$ for n steps:

Lemma 13. *For every state $s \in S$ and for every strategy $\sigma \in \Sigma_{\mathcal{M}}^{\mathsf{Opt}}$,*

$$\mathbb{P}_{\sigma,s}(\square\neg\mathsf{Bad}) = \sum_{\rho \in (VA)^n V} \mathbf{P}_{\sigma,s}(\rho) \cdot \mathbb{P}_{\sigma_\rho,\mathsf{last}(\rho)}(\square\neg\mathsf{Bad}) + \sum_{\rho \in (VA)^{<n}\,\mathsf{Good}} \mathbf{P}_{\sigma,s}(\rho).$$

Lemma 14. *For every $s \in S$, and every $\sigma \in \Sigma_{\mathcal{M}}^{\mathsf{Opt}}$, $\mathsf{Val}_{\mathcal{M}}(s) = \mathbb{P}_{\sigma,s}(\square\neg\mathsf{Bad})$.*

Proof. If $s \in \mathsf{Good}$, $\mathsf{Val}_{\mathcal{M}}(s) = \mathbb{P}_{\sigma,s}(\square\neg\mathsf{Bad}) = 1$. If $s \in \mathsf{Bad}$, $\mathsf{Val}_{\mathcal{M}}(s) = \mathbb{P}_{\sigma,s}(\square\neg\mathsf{Bad}) = 0$. Finally, if $s \in V$, from Lemma 11 and Lemma 13,

$$\mathsf{Val}_{\mathcal{M}}(s) - \mathbb{P}_{\sigma,s}(\square\neg\mathsf{Bad}) = \sum_{\rho \in (VA)^n V} \mathbf{P}_{\sigma,s}(\rho) \cdot (\mathsf{Val}_{\mathcal{M}}(\mathsf{last}(\rho)) - \mathbb{P}_{\sigma_\rho,\mathsf{last}(\rho)}(\square\neg\mathsf{Bad}))$$

$$< \sum_{\rho \in (VA)^n V} \mathbf{P}_{\sigma,s}(\rho) \quad [\text{Using Lemma 10}]$$

For $s \in \mathsf{UPre}^*(\mathsf{Bad})$, there is a path of length at most $|V|$ reaching Bad in $\mathcal{M}_\sigma$. So $\lim_{n\to\infty} \sum_{\rho \in (VA)^n V} \mathbf{P}_{\sigma,s}(\rho) = 0$. □

Lemma 8 follows directly from Lemma 14. Then, using Lemma 7 and 8, we conclude the following theorem:

Theorem 2. *For every state $s \in S$, $\Sigma_{\mathcal{M},s}(\square\neg\mathsf{Bad}) = \Sigma_{\mathcal{M}}^{\mathsf{Opt}}$.*

5.2 Maximizing Expected Conditional Mean Payoff

We propose a simple two-step pruning algorithm, similar to Algorithm 1, to solve the multi-objective problem defined by safety and mean-payoff. We first modify the given MDP $\mathcal{M}$ in the following manner.

Definition 4. *Let $S' = \{s \in S \mid \mathsf{Val}_{\mathcal{M}}(s) > 0\}$. We define $\mathcal{M}' = (S', A, P', R)$ where P' is defined as follows:*

$$P'(s,a,s') = \begin{cases} P(s,a,s') \cdot \frac{\mathsf{Val}_{\mathcal{M}}(s')}{\mathsf{Val}_{\mathcal{M}}(s)} & \text{if } (s,a) \in \mathsf{Opt}_{\mathcal{M}} \text{ and } s \in S' \\ \bot & \text{otherwise.} \end{cases}$$

Note that $\mathcal{M}'$ is again well-defined. We now present the two-step algorithm:

For a state s_0, a strategy σ, and a finite path $\rho = s_0 a_0 s_1 \ldots s_n \in (S'A)^*S' \cap \mathsf{Paths}_{\mathcal{M}'}(s_0,\sigma)$, we define, $\mathsf{GoodCyl}_\sigma(\rho) = \mathsf{Cyl}_\sigma(\rho) \cap \{\rho' \mid \rho' \models \square\neg\mathsf{Bad}\}$. Then, using Lemma 14, we get that if $\sigma \in \Sigma_{\mathcal{M}}^{\mathsf{Opt}}$, then

$$\mathbb{P}_{\sigma,s_0}(\mathsf{GoodCyl}_\sigma(\rho)) = \mathbb{P}_{\sigma,s_0}(\mathsf{Cyl}_\sigma(\rho)) \cdot \mathbb{P}_{\sigma_\rho,s_n}(\square\neg\mathsf{Bad}) = \mathbb{P}_{\sigma,s_0}(\mathsf{Cyl}_\sigma(\rho)) \cdot \mathsf{Val}_{\mathcal{M}}(s_n). \quad (5)$$

Algorithm 2

Input: $\mathcal{M} = (S, A, P, R)$, $s_0 \in S$, Bad $\subseteq S$

1: Create the MDP $\mathcal{M}' = (S', A, P', R')$ according to Definition 4.
2: Find a strategy σ^* that maximizes the expected mean payoff in $\mathcal{M}'$:

$$\sigma^* \in \arg\max_\sigma \mathbb{E}'_{\sigma,s_0}(\mathsf{MP}).$$

3: **return** σ^*.

Lemma 15. *For every strategy* $\sigma \in \Sigma_{\mathcal{M}}^{\mathsf{Opt}}$, $s_0 \in S'$ *and every finite path* $\rho = s_0 a_0 s_1 \ldots s_n \in (S'A)^* S' \cap \mathsf{Paths}_{\mathcal{M}'}(s_0, \sigma)$, $\mathbb{P}'_{\sigma,s_0}(\mathsf{Cyl}'_\sigma(\rho)) = \frac{\mathbb{P}_{\sigma,s_0}(\mathsf{GoodCyl}_\sigma(\rho))}{\mathsf{Val}_{\mathcal{M}}(s_0)}$.

Proof.

$$\mathbb{P}'_{\sigma,s_0}(\mathsf{Cyl}'_\sigma(\rho)) = \prod_{i=0}^{n-1} \sigma(\rho_{|i}, a_i) \cdot P'(s_i, a_i, s_{i+1})$$

$$= \prod_{i=0}^{n-1} \sigma(\rho_{|i}, a_i) \cdot P(s_i, a_i, s_{i+1}) \cdot \frac{\mathsf{Val}_{\mathcal{M}}(s_{i+1})}{\mathsf{Val}_{\mathcal{M}}(s_i)}$$

$$= \mathbb{P}_{\sigma,s_0}(\mathsf{Cyl}_\sigma(\rho)) \cdot \frac{\mathsf{Val}_{\mathcal{M}}(s_n)}{\mathsf{Val}_{\mathcal{M}}(s_0)} = \frac{\mathbb{P}_{\sigma,s_0}(\mathsf{GoodCyl}_\sigma(\rho))}{\mathsf{Val}_{\mathcal{M}}(s_0)} \quad \text{[from Eq. 5]}$$

$\square$

We now show the following correlation between the expected mean-payoff in $\mathcal{M}'$ and the expected conditional mean-payoff in $\mathcal{M}$:

Lemma 16. *For every strategy* σ, $\mathbb{E}'_\sigma(\mathsf{MP}) = \mathbb{E}_\sigma(\mathsf{MP} \mid \Box \neg \mathsf{Bad})$

Proof. For $r \in \mathbb{R}$, we define $\xi_r = \{\rho \in \mathsf{Paths}_{\mathcal{M}}(s_0) \cap (SA)^n S \mid \mathsf{Rew}_n(\rho) = r\}$ and $\xi'_r = \{\rho \in \mathsf{Paths}_{\mathcal{M}'}(s_0) \cap (S'A)^n S' \mid \mathsf{Rew}_n(\rho) = r\}$. Note that for a fixed n, there are finitely many such non-empty ξ_r. From the definition of the conditional expected reward in $\mathcal{M}$, we get:

$$\mathbb{E}_{\sigma,s_0}(\mathsf{Rew}_n \mid \Box \neg \mathsf{Bad}) = \sum_r r \cdot \frac{\mathbb{P}_{\sigma,s_0}(\{\rho \mid \mathsf{Rew}_n(\rho) = r\} \cap \Box \neg \mathsf{Bad})}{\mathbb{P}_{\sigma,s_0}(\Box \neg \mathsf{Bad})}$$

$$= \sum_r r \cdot \sum_{\rho \in \xi_r} \frac{\mathbb{P}_{\sigma,s_0}(\mathsf{Cyl}_\sigma(\rho) \cap \Box \neg \mathsf{Bad})}{\mathsf{Val}_{\mathcal{M}}(s_0)}$$

$$= \sum_r r \cdot \sum_{\rho \in \xi_r} \frac{\mathbb{P}_{\sigma,s_0}(\mathsf{GoodCyl}_\sigma(\rho))}{\mathsf{Val}_{\mathcal{M}}(s_0)}.$$

Then, $\mathbb{E}'_{\sigma,s_0}(\mathrm{Rew}_n) = \sum_r r \cdot \mathbb{P}'_{\sigma,s_0}(\{\rho \mid \mathrm{Rew}_n(\rho) = r\}) = \sum_r r \cdot \sum_{\rho \in \xi'_r} \mathbb{P}'_{\sigma,s_0}(\mathsf{Cyl}'_\sigma(\rho))$

$$= \sum_r r \cdot \sum_{\rho \in \xi'_r} \frac{\mathbb{P}_{\sigma,s_0}(\mathsf{GoodCyl}_\sigma(\rho))}{\mathsf{Val}_{\mathcal{M}}(s_0)}$$

$$= \sum_r r \cdot \sum_{\rho \in \xi_r} \frac{\mathbb{P}_{\sigma,s_0}(\mathsf{GoodCyl}_\sigma(\rho))}{\mathsf{Val}_{\mathcal{M}}(s_0)} \qquad (6)$$

$$= \mathbb{E}_{\sigma,s_0}(\mathrm{Rew}_n \mid \Box\neg\mathsf{Bad}) \qquad (7)$$

The equality in Eq. 6 is due to the fact that for any finite path $\rho = s_0 \ldots s_n \in (SA)^n S \setminus (S'A)^n S'$, $\exists i$ s.t. $\mathsf{Val}_{\mathcal{M}}(s_i) = 0$, which implies, $\mathbb{P}_{\sigma,s_0}(\mathsf{GoodCyl}_\sigma(\rho)) \le \mathbb{P}_{\sigma,s_0}(\mathsf{GoodCyl}_\sigma(s_0 \ldots s_i)) = \mathbb{P}_{\sigma,s_0\ldots s_i}(\Box\neg\mathsf{Bad}) \le \mathsf{Val}_{\mathcal{M}}(s_i) = 0$.

Finally, dividing by n and taking limit on the both sides of Eq. 7, we get $\mathbb{E}'_{\sigma,s_0}(\mathsf{MP}) = \mathbb{E}_{\sigma,s_0}(\mathsf{MP} \mid \Box\neg\mathsf{Bad})$. $\qquad\Box$

Now we prove the correctness of Algorithm 2:

Theorem 3. *Given an MDP $\mathcal{M} = (S, A, P, R)$, a state $s_0 \in S$ and $\mathsf{Bad} \subset S$, let σ^* be the strategy returned by Algorithm 2. Then,*

1. $\mathbb{P}_{\sigma^*,s_0}(\Box\neg\mathsf{Bad}) = \mathsf{Val}_{\mathcal{M}}(s_0)$.
2. $\mathbb{E}_{\sigma^*,s_0}(\mathsf{MP} \mid \Box\neg\mathsf{Bad}) = \max\limits_{\sigma \in \Sigma_{\mathcal{M},s_0}(\Box\neg\mathsf{Bad})} \mathbb{E}_{\sigma,s_0}(\mathsf{MP} \mid \Box\neg\mathsf{Bad})$

Proof. From Theorem 2, for any σ in $\Sigma_{\mathcal{M}}^{\mathsf{Opt}}$, $\mathbb{P}_{\sigma,s_0}(\Box\neg\mathsf{Bad}) = \mathsf{Val}_{\mathcal{M}}(s_0)$. Note that a strategy in $\mathcal{M}'$ would be in $\Sigma_{\mathcal{M}}^{\mathsf{Opt}}$. Therefore, $\mathbb{P}_{\sigma^*,s_0}(\Box\neg\mathsf{Bad}) = \mathsf{Val}_{\mathcal{M}}(s_0)$.

From Lemma 16, we get for any σ,

$$\mathbb{E}_{\sigma,s_0}(\mathsf{MP} \mid \Box\neg\mathsf{Bad}) = \mathbb{E}'_{\sigma,s_0}(\mathsf{MP})$$

$$\Rightarrow \quad \arg\max_{\sigma \in \Sigma_{\mathcal{M},s_0}(\Box\neg\mathsf{Bad})} \mathbb{E}_{\sigma,s_0}(\mathsf{MP} \mid \Box\neg\mathsf{Bad}) = \arg\max_{\sigma \in \Sigma_{\mathcal{M},s_0}(\Box\neg\mathsf{Bad})} \mathbb{E}'_{\sigma,s_0}(\mathsf{MP})$$

Hence, $\sigma^* \in \arg\max_{\sigma \in \Sigma_{\mathcal{M},s_0}(\Box\neg\mathsf{Bad})} \mathbb{E}_{\sigma,s_0}(\mathsf{MP} \mid \Box\neg\mathsf{Bad})$ and therefore, we conclude, $\mathbb{E}_{\sigma^*,s_0}(\mathsf{MP} \mid \Box\neg\mathsf{Bad}) = \max\limits_{\sigma \in \Sigma_{\mathcal{M},s_0}(\Box\neg\mathsf{Bad})} \mathbb{E}_{\sigma,s_0}(\mathsf{MP} \mid \Box\neg\mathsf{Bad})$. $\qquad\Box$

Note that, constructing the MDP $\mathcal{M}'$ (Line 1 of Algorithm 2) takes polynomial time. Finding a strategy that optimizes $\mathbb{E}'_{\sigma,s_0}(\mathsf{MP})$ also takes polynomial time [20, Chapter 9]. Therefore, the overall algorithm takes polynomial time.

6 Discussion

The work presented in this article proposes a pruning-based approach (Algorithms 1, 2) that can be used to solve certain multi-objective problems in MDPs. The algorithms work by first pruning the given MDP based on the first objective, and then solving the (possibly simplified) second objective on the pruned MDP. Note that, optimizing the second objective, in turn, optimizes both of the objectives in the lexicographic order.

The case where the first objective is to maximize the probability of reaching a set of (target) states in an MDP and the second objective is to minimize the conditional expected time to reach the same set of states, has been discussed in Sect. 3. Note that one can consider more general (positive) cost functions and try to minimize the conditional expected cost to reach the target states as a secondary objective, keeping the first objective unchanged.

Based on a suggestion by Jakob Piribauer, we conjecture that the second objective considered in this paper can, in fact, be replaced by any measurable function. More precisely, when the first objective is to remain safe, our technique can be applied to solve the bi-objective problem where the second objective is to optimize the expected value of a measurable function g, conditioned on the event that safety is satisfied. To this end, we can prove the following result: every strategy in the original MDP $\mathcal{M}$ that maximizes $\mathbb{E}(g \mid \Box\neg\mathsf{Bad})$ while maximizing the probability of staying safe, also maximizes the expected value of g in the pruned MDP $\mathcal{M}'$, that is,

$$\sup_{\sigma \in \Sigma_{\mathsf{Safe}}^{\mathcal{M}}} \mathbb{E}_\sigma(g \mid \Box\neg\mathsf{Bad}) = \sup_{\sigma \in \Sigma(\mathcal{M}')} \mathbb{E}'_\sigma(g)$$

where $\Sigma_{\mathsf{Safe}}^{\mathcal{M}}$ denotes the set of all strategies that maximize the probability of staying safe in $\mathcal{M}$. We believe this result can be proved by generalizing the proof of Lemma 16.

Similarly, when the primary objective is to reach a set of target states with as high probability as possible, we believe our technique will be able to compute the optimal strategy when the secondary objective is given by any measurable function g. We conjecture that the following result will hold: any strategy in $\mathcal{M}$ that first maximizes the probability to reach a target and further maximizes the expected value of a measurable function g conditioned on reaching a target state, will also maximize the (unconditional) expected value of g in the pruned MDP $\mathcal{M}'$, among the strategies that reach a target almost surely, that is, with probability 1. More formally, we can obtain the following result:

$$\sup_{\sigma \in \Sigma_{\mathsf{Reach}}^{\mathcal{M}}} \mathbb{E}_\sigma(g \mid \Diamond T) = \sup_{\sigma \in \Sigma_{\mathsf{a.s.Reach}}^{\mathcal{M}'}} \mathbb{E}'_\sigma(g)$$

where $\Sigma_{\mathsf{a.s.Reach}}^{\mathcal{M}'}$ is the set of all strategies in $\mathcal{M}'$ that, when followed, forces $\mathcal{M}'$ to reach a target state with probability 1. Further, if it is the case that every strategy in $\mathcal{M}'$ maximizing the (unconditional) expected value of g reaches a target with probability 1 (which was the case in the pair of objectives considered in Sect. 3), then the problem reduces to finding a strategy in $\mathcal{M}'$ that maximizes the (unconditional) expected value of g among all strategies, that is,

$$\sup_{\sigma \in \Sigma_{\mathsf{Reach}}^{\mathcal{M}}} \mathbb{E}_\sigma(g \mid \Diamond T) = \sup_{\sigma \in \Sigma(\mathcal{M}')} \mathbb{E}'_\sigma(g).$$

While we studied only two-dimensional lexicographic objectives for the sake of clarity and simplicity, we note that our work can be straight-forwardly extended to more than two reward structures. For example, one may want to optimize for safety first, reachability second, and minimal expected time to reach a target as a third objective. In this case, we would proceed in three steps: a first pruning of the MDP that solves the safety problem, a second pruning that over-approximate the winning strategies for reachability, and finally we would minimize the expected distance.

References

1. Almagor, S., Boker, U., Kupferman, O.: Discounting in LTL. In: Ábrahám, E., Havelund, K. (eds.) TACAS 2014. LNCS, vol. 8413, pp. 424–439. Springer, Heidelberg (2014). https://doi.org/10.1007/978-3-642-54862-8_37
2. Alshiekh, M., Bloem, R., Ehlers, R., Könighofer, B., Niekum, S., Topcu, U.: Safe reinforcement learning via shielding. In: Proceedings of the 32nd AAAI Conference on Artificial Intelligence, (AAAI 2018), pp. 2669–2678. AAAI Press (2018)
3. Baier, C., Klein, J., Klüppelholz, S., Märcker, S.: Computing conditional probabilities in Markovian models efficiently. In: Ábrahám, E., Havelund, K. (eds.) TACAS 2014. LNCS, vol. 8413, pp. 515–530. Springer, Heidelberg (2014). https://doi.org/10.1007/978-3-642-54862-8_43
4. Baier, C., Klein, J., Klüppelholz, S., Wunderlich, S.: Maximizing the conditional expected reward for reaching the goal. In: Legay, A., Margaria, T. (eds.) TACAS 2017. LNCS, vol. 10206, pp. 269–285. Springer, Heidelberg (2017). https://doi.org/10.1007/978-3-662-54580-5_16
5. Bertsekas, D.P., Tsitsiklis, J.N.: An analysis of stochastic shortest path problems. Math. Oper. Res. **16**(3), 580–595 (1991). https://doi.org/10.1287/moor.16.3.580
6. Bohy, A., Bruyère, V., Filiot, E., Raskin, J.-F.: Synthesis from LTL specifications with mean-payoff objectives. In: Piterman, N., Smolka, S.A. (eds.) TACAS 2013. LNCS, vol. 7795, pp. 169–184. Springer, Heidelberg (2013). https://doi.org/10.1007/978-3-642-36742-7_12
7. Busatto-Gaston, D., Chakraborty, D., Majumdar, A., Mukherjee, S., Pérez, G.A., Raskin, J.F.: Bi-objective lexicographic optimization in Markov decision processes with related objectives (2023). https://arxiv.org/abs/2305.09634
8. Chakraborty, D., Busatto-Gaston, D., Raskin, J., Pérez, G.A.: Formally-sharp dagger for MCTS: lower-latency monte Carlo tree search using data aggregation with formal methods. In: Agmon, N., An, B., Ricci, A., Yeoh, W. (eds.) Proceedings of the 2023 International Conference on Autonomous Agents and Multiagent Systems, AAMAS 2023, London, United Kingdom, 29 May 2023–2 June 2023, pp. 1354–1362. ACM (2023). https://dl.acm.org/doi/10.5555/3545946.3598783
9. Chatterjee, K., Henzinger, T.A., Jobstmann, B., Singh, R.: QUASY: quantitative synthesis tool. In: Abdulla, P.A., Leino, K.R.M. (eds.) TACAS 2011. LNCS, vol. 6605, pp. 267–271. Springer, Heidelberg (2011). https://doi.org/10.1007/978-3-642-19835-9_24
10. Chatterjee, K., Katoen, J.P., Mohr, S., Weininger, M., Winkler, T.: Stochastic games with lexicographic objectives. Form. Methods Syst. Des. (2023). https://doi.org/10.1007/s10703-023-00411-4
11. Chatterjee, K., Majumdar, R., Henzinger, T.A.: Markov decision processes with multiple objectives. In: Durand, B., Thomas, W. (eds.) STACS 2006. LNCS, vol. 3884, pp. 325–336. Springer, Heidelberg (2006). https://doi.org/10.1007/11672142_26

12. Chatterjee, K., Novotný, P., Pérez, G.A., Raskin, J., Zikelic, D.: Optimizing expectation with guarantees in POMDPs. In: Singh, S., Markovitch, S. (eds.) Proceedings of the Thirty-First AAAI Conference on Artificial Intelligence, 4–9 February 2017, San Francisco, California, USA, pp. 3725–3732. AAAI Press (2017). http://aaai.org/ocs/index.php/AAAI/AAAI17/paper/view/14354

13. Chen, T., Kwiatkowska, M., Simaitis, A., Wiltsche, C.: Synthesis for multi-objective stochastic games: an application to autonomous urban driving. In: Joshi, K., Siegle, M., Stoelinga, M., D'Argenio, P.R. (eds.) QEST 2013. LNCS, vol. 8054, pp. 322–337. Springer, Heidelberg (2013). https://doi.org/10.1007/978-3-642-40196-1_28

14. Denardo, E.V.: Computing a bias-optimal policy in a discrete-time Markov decision problem. Oper. Res. 18(2), 279–289 (1970). http://www.jstor.org/stable/168684

15. Forejt, V., Kwiatkowska, M., Norman, G., Parker, D., Qu, H.: Quantitative multi-objective verification for probabilistic systems. In: Abdulla, P.A., Leino, K.R.M. (eds.) TACAS 2011. LNCS, vol. 6605, pp. 112–127. Springer, Heidelberg (2011). https://doi.org/10.1007/978-3-642-19835-9_11

16. Hahn, E.M., Perez, M., Schewe, S., Somenzi, F., Trivedi, A., Wojtczak, D.: Model-free reinforcement learning for lexicographic omega-regular objectives. In: Huisman, M., Păsăreanu, C., Zhan, N. (eds.) FM 2021. LNCS, vol. 13047, pp. 142–159. Springer, Cham (2021). https://doi.org/10.1007/978-3-030-90870-6_8

17. Hensel, C., Junges, S., Katoen, J., Quatmann, T., Volk, M.: The probabilistic model checker Storm. Int. J. Softw. Tools Technol. Transf. 24(4), 589–610 (2022). https://doi.org/10.1007/s10009-021-00633-z

18. Junges, S., Jansen, N., Dehnert, C., Topcu, U., Katoen, J.-P.: Safety-constrained reinforcement learning for MDPs. In: Chechik, M., Raskin, J.-F. (eds.) TACAS 2016. LNCS, vol. 9636, pp. 130–146. Springer, Heidelberg (2016). https://doi.org/10.1007/978-3-662-49674-9_8

19. Kwiatkowska, M., Norman, G., Parker, D.: PRISM 4.0: verification of probabilistic real-time systems. In: Gopalakrishnan, G., Qadeer, S. (eds.) CAV 2011. LNCS, vol. 6806, pp. 585–591. Springer, Heidelberg (2011). https://doi.org/10.1007/978-3-642-22110-1_47

20. Puterman, M.L.: Markov Decision Processes: Discrete Stochastic Dynamic Programming. Wiley Series in Probability and Statistics, Wiley (1994). https://doi.org/10.1002/9780470316887

21. Skalse, J., Hammond, L., Griffin, C., Abate, A.: Lexicographic multi-objective reinforcement learning. In: Raedt, L.D. (ed.) Proceedings of the Thirty-First International Joint Conference on Artificial Intelligence, IJCAI-22, pp. 3430–3436. International Joint Conferences on Artificial Intelligence Organization (2022). https://doi.org/10.24963/ijcai.2022/476. Main Track

Synthesis

Model Checking Strategies
from Synthesis over Finite Traces

Suguman Bansal[1]($\boxtimes$) (iD), Yong Li[2]($\boxtimes$) (iD), Lucas M. Tabajara[3]($\boxtimes$) (iD),
Moshe Y. Vardi[4]($\boxtimes$) (iD), and Andrew Wells[4]($\boxtimes$) (iD)

[1] Georgia Institute of Technology, Atlanta, GA, USA
suguman@gatech.edu
[2] University of Liverpool, Liverpool, UK
liyong@liverpool.ac.uk
[3] Runtime Verification, Champaign, Illinois, USA
l.martinelli.tabajara@gmail.com
[4] Rice University, Houston, TX, USA
vardi@cs.rice.edu, andrew.wells@rice.edu

Abstract. The innovations in reactive synthesis from *Linear Temporal Logics over finite traces* (LTLf) will be amplified by the ability to verify the correctness of the strategies generated by LTLf synthesis tools. This motivates our work on LTLf *model checking*. LTLf model checking, however, is not straightforward. The strategies generated by LTLf synthesis may be represented using *terminating* transducers or *non-terminating* transducers where executions are of finite-but-unbounded length or infinite length, respectively. For synthesis, there is no evidence that one type of transducer is better than the other since they both demonstrate the same complexity and similar algorithms.

In this work, we show that for model checking, the two types of transducers are fundamentally different. Our central result is that LTLf model checking of non-terminating transducers is *exponentially harder* than that of terminating transducers. We show that the problems are EXPSPACE-complete and PSPACE-complete, respectively. Hence, considering the feasibility of verification, LTLf synthesis tools should synthesize terminating transducers. This is, to the best of our knowledge, the *first* evidence to use one transducer over the other in LTLf synthesis.

1 Introduction

Linear Temporal Logic over finite traces [14] (LTLf) is the finite-horizon counterpart of the well-known Linear Temporal Logic (LTL) over infinite traces [24]. LTLf is rapidly gaining popularity among real-world applications where behaviors are better expressed over a finite but unbounded horizon [7,11,12,19,35].

Reactive synthesis from LTLf specifications, or LTLf synthesis [2,8,10,13, 15,18,29,37] has amassed so much interest that the 2023 Reactive Synthesis

---

[1] http://www.syntcomp.org/news/.

A. Wells—Work was performed while the author was at Rice University.

Competition (SYNTCOMP) will inaugurate an LTLf track[1]. Consequently, LTLf synthesis tools have been growing in complexity [2,9,18,29,37]. Their correctness, however, is rarely verified. To continue the innovations in synthesis and to successfully conduct large-scale competitions like SYNTCOMP there is, therefore, a need to verify the correctness of the synthesized strategies/transducers. Verifying the results as opposed to verifying the tools has been advocated in various contexts, including translation validation [27], program checking [6], and equivalence checking [22]. For LTL synthesis, result checking is simply LTL *model checking*. For LTLf synthesis, we need LTLf *model checking*. But this is a topic that has *not* been studied so far, hence this work.

We observe that LTLf model checking for LTLf synthesis tools is *not* as straightforward as one might have thought to be. The standard approach in the literature on LTLf synthesis generates *non-terminating transducers*. This includes the seminal work on synthesis [13] and the SYNTCOMP guidelines [20]. The executions of non-terminating transducers are of infinite length. Since LTLf formulas are defined on finite traces only, an execution of a non-terminating transducer is said to satisfy an LTLf formula if there *exists* a finite-length prefix that satisfies the formula [13]. Few works on synthesis do mention the possibility of *terminating transducers* as the output [2,37]. Since their executions are of finite length, LTLf satisfaction is defined naturally on terminating transducers. When it comes to synthesis, there is no clear evidence that one type of transducer is better than the other, since the complexity and algorithms of synthesis are the same for both types. We believe this is why existing works on LTLf synthesis do *not* make a clear distinction between the two. For implementations, however, most works use non-terminating transducers as they directly correspond to standard Mealy/Moore machines (See state-of-the-art tools, e.g., Syft [37], Lisa [2], and Lydia [9]). This work shows, however, that from the *model-checking* perspective, the two types of transducers are *fundamentally different* and bear a significant impact on synthesis.

Our central result is that LTLf model checking of non-terminating transducers is *exponentially harder* than LTLf model checking of terminating transducers. We demonstrate that under LTLf specifications, model checking non-terminating transducers is EXPSPACE-complete, whereas model checking terminating transducers is PSPACE-complete. An immediate implication of this result is that for non-terminating transducers, LTLf model checking is exponentially harder than LTL model checking, which is known to be PSPACE-complete [33]. This result is unexpected because a factor behind the increasing popularity of LTLf is the perception that problems using LTLf are at most as hard as those using LTL, if not simpler (See Table 1). This is because LTLf formulas can be expressed by automata over finite words [14], which allow for practically scalable algorithms for automata constructions [30]. Conversely, LTL formulas require automata over infinite words [36], for which the automata manipulation is harder in theory [17,26,31,32] and in practice [16,21]. It is no wonder that an exponential increase in the model-checking complexity seems surprising at first.

The exponential blow-up in LTLf model-checking of non-terminating transducers arises from subtlety in the problem definition. A transducer satisfies a

Table 1. LTL vs. LTLf: Complexity w.r.t. specification. NT and T abbreviate non-terminating and terminating models, respectively.

	LTL	LTLf
Non-deterministic Automata	(NBA) Exponential	(NFA) Exponential
Satisfiability	PSPACE-complete [28]	PSPACE-complete [14]
Synthesis	2EXPTIME-complete [25]	2EXPTIME-complete [13]
Model Checking (NT)	PSPACE-complete [33]	EXPSPACE-complete (New!)
Model Checking (T)	Undefined	PSPACE-complete (New!)

formula if there are no counterexamples. In non-terminating transducers, an infinite execution is a counterexample if *every* finite prefix does not satisfy the LTLf formula. Formally, for an LTLf formula ϕ, let $\mathsf{pref}(\phi)$ represent the language consisting of all infinite executions for which every prefix satisfies ϕ. Then, a non-terminating transducer $\mathcal{M}$ satisfies an LTLf formula ϕ iff $\mathcal{L}(\mathcal{M}) \cap \mathsf{pref}(\neg\phi) = \emptyset$, where $\mathcal{L}(\mathcal{M})$ is the set of all executions of $\mathcal{M}$. This is where LTLf model checking fundamentally differs from LTL model checking, as counterexamples in LTL are obtained simply from an automaton for the negation of the formula [33]. W.l.o.g., we show that while $\mathsf{pref}(\phi)$ is ω-regular for all LTLf formulas ϕ, the size of their non-deterministic Büchi automata (NBA) is doubly exponential in the size of the formula, i.e., $2^{2^{O(|\phi|)}}$ and $2^{2^{\Omega(\sqrt{|\phi|})}}$. Once again, this differs from LTL model checking, where the size of the NBAs for counterexamples is singly exponential in the size of the formula. As a result, we show LTLf model checking of non-terminating transducers is in EXPSPACE using on-the-fly emptiness checking of $\mathcal{L}(\mathcal{M}) \cap \mathsf{pref}(\neg\phi)$. We establish EXPSPACE-hardness from first principles.

In contrast, we show that LTLf model checking of terminating transducers is PSPACE-complete. Due to their finite-length executions, counterexamples in terminating transducers are completely characterized by the negation of the formula, lending the same complexity as LTL model checking.

Thus, our results offer a clear recommendation between the two types of transducers in LTLf synthesis. We argue that synthesis tools should account for the feasibility of the verification of the synthesized transducers. Consequently, we recommend that synthesis tools should generate terminating transducers rather than non-terminating transducers. We believe this is the *first* work to offer *theoretical* evidence to use one transducer over the other in synthesis. Furthermore, these results could be applied immediately to run the LTLf track in SYNTCOMP.

Outline. Sect. 2 outlines preliminaries on LTLf and LTLf synthesis. Section 3 motivates and defines LTLf model checking. Section 4 is dedicated to $\mathsf{pref}(\phi)$. Section 5 develops the complexity of model checking. Lastly, Sect. 6 concludes.

2   Preliminaries and Notations

We use the standard notions of deterministic and non-deterministic finite automata (DFAs and NFAs, respectively) as well as deterministic and non-deterministic Büchi automata (DBAs and NBAs, respectively). For an automaton, we use the notation $\mathcal{A} = (\Sigma, S, \iota, \delta, F)$ where Σ is a finite set of symbols (called an alphabet), S is a finite set of states, $\iota \in S$ is the initial state, $F \subseteq S$ is the set of accepting states, and $\delta \subseteq S \times \Sigma \times S$ is the transition relation. We use standard semantics for all automata, hence refer details to the appendix of [3].

2.1 Linear Temporal Logic over Finite Traces (LTLf)

LTLf [1,14] extends propositional logic with finite-horizon temporal operators. In effect, LTLf is a variant of LTL [24] that is interpreted over finite rather than infinite traces. The syntax of an LTLf formula over a finite set of propositions Prop is identical to LTL, and defined as

$$\varphi := \text{true} \mid \text{false} \mid a \in \text{Prop} \mid \neg\varphi \mid \varphi_1 \wedge \varphi_2 \mid X\varphi \mid \varphi_1 U \varphi_2$$

where X (Next) and U (Until), are temporal operators. We also include their dual operators, N (Weak Next) and R (Release), defined as $N\varphi \equiv \neg X \neg \varphi$ and $\varphi_1 R \varphi_2 \equiv \neg(\neg\varphi_1 U \neg\varphi_2)$. We also use typical abbreviations such as $F\varphi \equiv \text{true}U\varphi$, $G\varphi \equiv \text{false}R\varphi$, $\varphi_1 \vee \varphi_2 = \neg(\neg\varphi_1 \wedge \neg\varphi_2)$, $\varphi_1 \rightarrow \varphi_2 \equiv \neg\varphi_1 \vee \varphi_2$. We denote by $|\phi|$ the length/size of a formula ϕ, i.e., the number of operators in ϕ.

The semantics of LTLf is similar to LTL but is interpreted over finite traces. A finite sequence ρ over 2^{Prop} is said to satisfy an LTLf formula ϕ over Prop, denoted by $\rho \models \phi$, if $\rho, 0 \models \phi$ where for all positions $0 \leq i < |\rho|$, $\rho, i \models \phi$ is defined inductively on ϕ as follows:

- $\rho, i \models \text{true}$; $\rho, i \not\models \text{false}$; $\rho, i \models a$ iff $a \in \rho_i$;
- $\rho, i \models \neg\varphi$ iff $\rho, i \not\models \varphi$;
- $\rho, i \models \phi_1 \wedge \phi_2$ iff $\rho, i \models \phi_1$ and $\rho, i \models \phi_2$;
- $\rho, i \models X\phi$ iff $i + 1 < |\rho|$ and $\rho, i + 1 \models \phi$;
- $\rho, i \models \phi_1 U \phi_2$ iff there exists j s.t. $i \leq j < |\rho|$ and $\rho, j \models \phi_2$, and for all k, $i \leq k < j$, we have $\rho, k \models \phi_1$.

Observe that X requires that there *exists* a next position; In the context of *finite* traces, its negation also contains the situation that no next position exists, formulated as $\neg(X\text{true})$ or equivalently $N\text{false}$. This differs from LTL where the Next operator is applied to all positions. Also, note that LTLf formulas are evaluated on traces of non-zero length.

The language of an LTLf formula ϕ over Prop is the set of all finite sequences ρ over 2^{Prop} such that $\rho \models \phi$. The language of an LTLf formula is regular. The NFA and DFA representing LTLf are of size singly exponential and doubly exponential, respectively, in the size of the formula [14]. We note that a letter $\sigma \in \Sigma$ of the NFA/DFA corresponds to a valuation over the set Prop of propositions.

2.2 LTLf Synthesis and Transducers

Let LTLf formula ϕ be defined over propositional variables partitioned into $\mathcal{I}$ and $\mathcal{O}$ representing the input and output variables, respectively. Given such an

LTLf formula ϕ, the problem of LTLf *realizability* is to determine whether there exists a strategy $f : (2^{\mathcal{I}})^* \to 2^{\mathcal{O}}$ such that for all $\lambda_{\mathcal{I}} = I_0, I_1, \cdots \in (2^{\mathcal{I}})^\omega$, there is an integer $k \geq 0$ such that the finite trace $\rho = (I_0 \cup f(\varepsilon)), (I_1 \cup f(I_0)), \cdots, (I_k \cup f(I_0, I_1, \cdots, I_{k-1}))$ satisfies ϕ. The LTLf *synthesis problem* is to generate such a function, if the given formula is realizable [13]. Intuitively, LTLf synthesis can be viewed as a game between two agents, an environment and a system, who continually take turns to assign values to the input and output variables, respectively, to generate a sequence of input and output variables. W.l.o.g., we assume the system plays first, followed by the environment, and so on. The goal of synthesis is to generate a strategy for the system agent so that all resulting plays with the environment satisfy the given specification. We note that our model-checking results also hold when the environment plays first, as we will model strategies as transition systems in model checking for generality (cf. Section 3).

Non-terminating Transducers. The standard in LTLf synthesis is to represent the strategy f using (non-terminating) transducers [13,20]. W.l.o.g., a transducer is a *Moore machine* $\mathcal{M} = (Q, q_0, \mathcal{I}, \mathcal{O}, \delta, G)$ where Q is a finite set of states, $q_0 \in Q$ is the initial state, and $\mathcal{I}$ and $\mathcal{O}$ are finite sets of input and output variables, respectively. Functions $\delta : Q \times 2^{\mathcal{I}} \to Q$ and $G : Q \to 2^{\mathcal{O}}$ are the *transition function* and the *output function*, respectively. Given an input sequence $\lambda_{\mathcal{I}} = I_0, I_1, \cdots \in (2^{\mathcal{I}})^\omega$, the output sequence is $\lambda_{\mathcal{O}} = G(q_0), G(q_1), \cdots \in (2^{\mathcal{O}})^\omega$ where q_0 is the initial state and $q_{i+1} = \delta(q_i, I_i)$ for all $i \geq 0$.

Then, given an LTLf formula with variables partitioned into $\mathcal{I}$ and $\mathcal{O}$ the realizability and synthesis problem is to generate a Moore machine $\mathcal{M}$ such that for all input sequences $\lambda = I_0, I_1, \cdots \in (2^{\mathcal{I}})^\omega$, there exists an integer $k \geq 0$ such that $\rho = (I_0, G(q_0)), (I_1, G(q_1)) \ldots (I_k, G(q_k))$ satisfies ϕ. Intuitively, the system and environment play indefinitely, where the system plays as per the transducer. The play (an execution in the transducer) satisfies an LTLf formula if there exists a finite-length prefix that satisfies the formula.

Terminating Transducers. The strategy f can also be represented using terminating transducers [2,37]. W.l.o.g., a terminating transducer is a *Terminating Moore machine* $\mathcal{M} = (Q, q_0, \mathcal{I}, \mathcal{O}, \delta, G, F)$ where Q, q_0, $\mathcal{I}$, $\mathcal{O}$, δ, and G are as defined for Moore machines and $\emptyset \neq F \subseteq Q$ are the *terminal states*. An input sequence $\lambda_{\mathcal{I}} = I_0, I_1, \cdots I_k \in (2^{\mathcal{I}})^*$ generates an output sequence $\lambda_{\mathcal{O}} = G(q_0), G(q_1), \ldots G(q_k) \in (2^{\mathcal{O}})^*$ where q_0 is the initial state and $q_{i+1} = \delta(q_i, I_i)$ for all $0 \leq i < k$.

Then, given an LTLf formula with variables partitioned into $\mathcal{I}$ and $\mathcal{O}$, the realizability and synthesis problem is to generate a terminating Moore machine $\mathcal{M}$ such that for all input sequence $\lambda = I_0, I_1, \cdots \in (2^{\mathcal{I}})^\omega$, there exists an integer $k \geq 0$ such that $\rho = (I_0, G(q_0)), (I_1, G(q_1)) \ldots (I_k, G(q_k))$ with $q_{k+1} = \delta(q_k, I_k) \in F$ and ρ satisfies ϕ. Intuitively, the synthesized terminating transducer is such that as soon as a play lands in a terminal state of the transducer, the system agent controlling the output variables wins the game and this play is over as it is guaranteed that the play seen so far satisfies the given formula. On the contrary, in non-terminating transducers, the system agent does not have the ability to terminate a game as it is never informed of whether it has seen a satisfying prefix.

3 LTLf Model Checking

In addition to being of independent interest, our motivation behind LTLf model checking is to support the ongoing development of LTLf synthesis tools. As synthesis tools continue to become more complex, it is imperative that we design automatic approaches to check their correctness. One way is to evaluate whether the result generated from these tools is correct. In the case of LTLf synthesis, result checking corresponds to LTLf model checking. Finally, an immediate application of LTLf model checking could be in running the inaugural LTLf track in the Reactive Synthesis Competition (SYNTCOMP) [20].

We begin by defining the model-checking problem. As described in Sect. 2.2, the result of LTLf synthesis could be a terminating or a non-terminating transducer. Since LTLf satisfaction on executions in the two types of transducers differ, we define model-checking on them separately. For the sake of generality, we define model-checking with respect to *transition systems* (TS) as opposed to transducers. Translations from transducers to transition systems are standard and polynomial [23]. Hence, the translation details have been omitted.

Non-Terminating Transition Systems are those that run indefinitely, i.e., their executions are of infinite length (e.g. network servers). Formally, a non-terminating TS is a structure $\mathcal{M} = (\Sigma, S, T, \iota, L)$, where Σ is a finite propositional alphabet, S is a finite set of states, relation $T \subseteq S \times S$ is the transition relation with no sink states, ι is the initial state, and $L : S \to 2^{\Sigma}$ is the *labeling function*. An *execution* $\rho = s_0 s_1 \cdots$ in $\mathcal{M}$ is an infinite sequence of consecutive states beginning with the initial state, i.e., $s_0 = \iota$ and $(s_i, s_{i+1}) \in T$ for all $i \geq 0$. The *label sequence* of ρ is the sequence $L(\rho) = L(s_0)L(s_1)\cdots$. The n-length finite prefix of ρ and its label sequence are given by $\rho[0, n] = s_0 \cdots s_{n-1}$ and $L(\rho[0, n]) = L(s_0) \cdots L(s_{n-1})$, respectively, for $n > 0$.

Since executions are of infinite-length and LTLf formulas are interpreted over finite-length sequences only, we say an *execution ρ in $\mathcal{M}$ satisfies an* LTLf *formula* ϕ, denoted by $\rho \models \mathcal{M}$, as follows

$$\rho \models \phi \text{ iff } \exists n > 0 \text{ s.t. } L(\rho[0, n]) \models \phi,$$

i.e., there exists a finite-length prefix of the execution that satisfies the formula.

Terminating Transition Systems are those that terminate after a finite but unbounded amount of steps (e.g. a terminating program). Formally, a terminating TS is given by a structure $\mathcal{M} = (\Sigma, S, T, \iota, L, F)$, where $\Sigma, S, T \subseteq S \times S$, ι, and $L : S \to 2^{\Sigma}$ are defined as for nonterminating transition systems and $\emptyset \neq F \subseteq S$ are the *terminal states*, which are the only states that are allowed to be sink states. An *execution* $\rho = s_0 \cdots s_n$ in $\mathcal{M}$ is a finite sequence of consecutive states beginning with the initial state and ending in a terminal state, i.e., $s_0 = \iota$ and $(s_i, s_{i+1}) \in T$ for all $0 \leq i < n$, and $s_n \in F$. Its *label sequence* is the sequence $L(\rho) = L(s_0) \cdots L(s_n)$.

An *execution* ρ *in* $\mathcal{M}$ *satisfies an* LTLf *formula* ϕ, denoted by $\rho \models \phi$,

$$\rho \models \phi \text{ iff } L(\rho) \models \phi.$$

Model Checking. We first define *satisfaction* and then *model checking*.

Definition 1 ($\mathcal{M} \models \phi$). *Given a non-terminating (resp., terminating) transition system* $\mathcal{M}$ *and an* LTLf *formula* ϕ, *we say TS* $\mathcal{M}$ *satisfies* ϕ, *denoted by* $\mathcal{M} \models \phi$, *if for all (resp., finite) executions* ρ *of* $\mathcal{M}$, *we have that* $\rho \models \phi$.

Definition 2 (Model Checking). *Given a non-terminating (resp. terminating) transition system* $\mathcal{M}$ *and an* LTLf *formula* φ, *the problem of* LTLf *model checking of non-terminating (resp. terminating) models is to determine whether* $\mathcal{M}$ *satisfies* φ.

Note on abuse of notation. The notation $\models$ has been overloaded to express satisfaction at several occasions, namely, in LTLf semantics, in defining when executions of non-terminating and terminating systems satisfy a formula, and when a system satisfies a formula. We overload notation to avoid new symbols for each case, as the context is clear from the L.H.S.

4 Prefix Language of LTLf Formulas

This section builds the basic blocks for LTLf model checking of non-terminating systems. Recall from Sect. 3, an (infinite-length) execution in a non-terminating system $\mathcal{M}$ violates an LTLf formula ϕ if *all* of its finite prefixes violate ϕ. So, the counterexamples are captured by the language that accepts an infinite word iff all of its finite prefixes violate ϕ (or satisfy $\neg\phi$). We call this the *prefix language* of an LTLf formula $\neg\phi$. Then, clearly, $\mathcal{M} \models \phi$ iff the intersection of $\mathcal{M}$ with the prefix language of $\neg\phi$ is empty, making the prefix language a basic block to model-check non-terminating systems.

We first observe that the prefix languages for LTLf formulas are ω-regular. We then show that one can construct a DBA accepting the prefix language of an LTLf formula, which incurs a doubly exponential blow-up (Sect. 4.1). One may expect that the complexity of the construction can be improved if we target at NBAs. We show, however, that the doubly exponential blow-up is *not* due to a lack of better construction, but a fundamental trait of the problem itself (Theorem 2). This is in contrast to the construction of NBA/NFA for LTL/ LTLf, where only deterministic automata constructions incur doubly exponential blow-ups and nondeterministic automata constructions incur singly exponential blow-ups, hinting at the hardness of model checking. Finally, we identify a fragment of LTLf formulas for which a singly exponential construction of NBAs for their prefix languages can be obtained via a translation from LTLf to LTL (Sect. 4.2).

4.1 Prefix Automata for LTLf

This section formally defines the prefix language/automata for LTLf formulas and proves that their automata constructions involve an unavoidable double-exponential blow-up. The upper and lower bounds are shown in Theorem 1 and Theorem 2, respectively.

Definition 3 (Prefix Language). *Given an* LTLf *formula ϕ, the prefix language of ϕ, denoted by* pref(ϕ), *is such that an (infinite-length) word $w \in$ pref(ϕ) iff every finite prefix of w satisfies ϕ, i.e., $\forall n > 0.w[0,n] \models \phi$.*

Recall that the semantics of LTLf requires traces of non-zero length only (see Sect. 2). So we only need $n > 0$, instead of $n \geq 0$, ignoring the empty word. By abuse of notation, we let pref(ϕ) denote both the prefix language and its corresponding automaton, called the *prefix automaton*.

We start by showing pref(ϕ) is ω-regular for LTLf formula ϕ:

Theorem 1 (Prefix automata: Upper bound). *For an* LTLf *formula ϕ, the language* pref(ϕ) *is ω-regular. The Büchi automaton recognizing* pref(ϕ) *has $2^{2^{O(|\phi|)}}$ states.*

Proof. Given LTLf formula ϕ, we construct a DBA for pref(ϕ) as follows:

1. Construct a DFA $D = (\Sigma, Q, \iota, \delta, F)$ for $\neg\phi$, i.e., $\mathcal{L}(D) = \mathcal{L}(\neg\phi)$.
   We require D to be *complete* in the sense that for every state s and every alphabet $a \in \Sigma$, there exists a successor $t = \delta(s, a)$.
2. Obtain a DBA $C = (\Sigma, Q, \iota, \delta', F)$ by converting all accepting states F of D to accepting sink states in C. For this, replace all outgoing transitions from all accepting states in D with self loops on all letters.
   Formally, replace every $\delta(f, a) = t$ in DFA D with $f = \delta'(f, a)$ in DBA C, for all $f \in F$ and $a \in \Sigma$. For all other states, let δ' behaves identically to δ.
3. Obtain the desired Büchi automaton $B = (\Sigma, Q, \iota, \delta', \mathcal{F} = Q \setminus F)$ by swapping accepting and non-accepting states of C.

Since C is a DBA with accepting sink states, C is the complement of B. Hence, it suffices to show that C accepts $w \in \Sigma^\omega$ iff there exists a finite prefix of w that satisfies $\neg\phi$. Clearly, $w \in \mathcal{L}(C)$ then w must have a finite-prefix satisfying $\neg\phi$ since the accepting states of C and D are identical. Conversely, we need to show that despite δ and δ' being different, C will accept all words that contain a finite prefix satisfying $\neg\phi$. For this, we show that for every such word, C retains the transitions to accept the shortest prefix satisfying $\neg\phi$. Details can be found in the appendix of [3]. Finally, the number of states of C are bounded by those of D which is doubly exponential in $|\phi|$ [14].   □

Observe that the Büchi automaton B constructed above is *deterministic*. One of our key discoveries is that the doubly exponential blow-up appears even in the construction of NBAs for pref(ϕ), demonstrating that the blow-up is fundamentally unavoidable. Theorem 2 presents such an LTLf formula to demonstrate the blow-up. The rest of the section builds up to that construction.

We observe that the blow-up is caused by the combination of two aspects: First is the universal quantification on prefixes of words in $\mathsf{pref}(\phi)$; Second is the ability of an LTLf formula to identify the k-th last positions of finite words using the X (Next) modality. At first, we identify an ω-regular language, parameterized with $n \geq 1$, such that all NBAs accepting the language have at least 2^{2^n} states. Let $n \in \mathbb{N}$ and $\Sigma = \{0, 1, \#, \&\}$. Consider the language $L_n \subseteq \Sigma^\omega$ where

$$u \cdot \& \cdot v \in L_n \text{ s.t. if } \#w\# \text{ appears in } v \text{ then } \#w\# \text{ also appears in } u,$$

where $w \in \{0,1\}^n$, $u \in \{0,1,\#\}^*$ and $v \in \{0,1,\#\}^\omega$. Intuitively, L_n consists of infinite words that are (a) split into two parts by a special character "$\&$" and (b) all words of the form $\#w\#$ appearing after "$\&$" must have appeared before "$\&$", for all n-length words $w \in \{0,1\}^n$. Essentially, L_n is a bit-level adaption of the language K_d where $x \cdot \& \cdot y \in K_d$ if digits appearing in y are a subset of digits appearing in x, where $x \in D^*$ and $y \in D^\omega$ for $D = \{0, 1, \cdots, d-1\}$. Obviously, the words $14\&1$ and $134\&4$ are good prefixes of a word $x \cdot \& \cdot y \in K_d$ when $d > 5$. There are also less obvious good prefixes, such as a permutation of D followed by the letter $\&$. We need to recognize all good prefixes in order to accept the language K_d. So, it is necessary to keep track of the digits (i.e., subsets of D) that the automaton has seen so far in an input word. Hence, the NBA of K_d needs $2^{\Omega(d)}$ states. The same proof can be adapted to show that the NBA of L_n consists of $2^{2^{\Omega(n)}}$ states. We refer to [3] for more detailed proofs.

Next, we need to identify a regular language F_n such that, by abuse of notation, $\mathsf{pref}(F_n)$ corresponds to L_n and F_n can be represented by an LTLf formula of polynomial length in the parameter $n > 0$. A natural choice would be to let F_n to be the finite-word version of L_n. In other words, $u \cdot \& \cdot v \in F_n$ s.t. if $\#w\#$ appears in v then $\#w\#$ must have appeared in u for all $w \in \{0,1\}^n$ and $u, v \in \{0,1,\#\}^*$. The issue is that F_n cannot be represented by a short LTLf formula for the same reason why L_n cannot be expressed by a short LTL formula.

We need F_n to be a *simpler* language. The roadmap would be to leverage the universal quantification over all prefixes to generate L_n. This is also where we leverage the ability of LTLf to refer to the last k-th positions of a finite trace. Keeping these goalposts, we define regular language $F_n \subseteq \Sigma^*$ as

$$u \cdot \& \cdot v \in F_n \text{ s.t. if the last } n + 2 \text{ characters of } v \text{ are of the form } \#w\#$$
$$\text{then } \#w\# \text{ also appears in } u,$$

where $w \in \{0,1\}^n$ and $u, v \in \{0,1,\#\}^*$. Intuitively, by applying universal quantification on all finite-length prefixes, focusing on the last $n + 2$ characters of words in F_n is sufficient to ensure that every occurrence of the form $\#w\#$ after the symbol "$\&$" appears in the portion before the "$\&$".

There is one last caveat. There are infinitely many prefixes of words in L_n that may not contain the symbol $\&$. This issue can be easily remedied by including words without symbol $\&$ to both languages. We overload the notation of $\mathsf{pref}(L)$ to refer to the prefix language of a language over finite words L. Then,

Lemma 1. *Let L_n and F_n be as defined above. Then*

$$L_n \uplus \{0,1,\#\}^\omega = \mathsf{pref}(F_n \uplus \{0,1,\#\}^*).$$

Proof (Proof Sketch). To see why $L_n \uplus \{0,1,\#\}^\omega \subseteq \mathsf{pref}(F_n \uplus \{0,1,\#\}^*)$, observe that the prefixes of a word $w \in L_n \uplus \{0,1,\#\}^\omega$ either contain the symbol & or they don't. If the prefix falls under the latter, then the prefix is contained in $\{0,1,\#\}^*$. Otherwise, if the last $n+2$ characters are not in the form $\#w\#$ for $w \in \{0,1\}^n$ then the prefix is contained in F_n by definition of F_n. If the last $n+2$ characters are in form $\#w\#$ for $w \in \{0,1\}^n$, then, by properties of words in L_n, $\#w\#$ must have appeared before &. Once again, the prefix is contained in F_n. Thus, all prefixes of w are contained in $F_n \uplus \{0,1,\#\}^*$.

The converse, i.e., $\mathsf{pref}(F_n \uplus \{0,1,\#\}^*) \subseteq L_n \uplus \{0,1,\#\}^\omega$, can be proven by a similar case-by-case analysis. Details can be found in the appendix of [3]. □

The last piece is to show that the language $F_n \uplus \{0,1,\#\}^*$ can be expressed using an LTLf formula ϕ_n of length polynomial in n, as shown below:

Theorem 2 (Prefix automata: Lower bound). *There exists an LTLf formula ψ such that the number of states in all NBAs for $\mathsf{pref}(\psi)$ is $2^{2^{\Omega(\sqrt{|\psi|})}}$.*

Proof. Let $n \in \mathbb{N} \setminus \{0\}$ and $\Sigma = \{0,1,\#,\&\}$. Let L_n and F_n be as defined above.

Since all NBAs of L_n are of size $2^{2^{\Omega(n)}}$ and L_n is disjoint from $\{0,1,\#\}^\omega$ by containing the "&" symbol, it is easy to show that all NBAs of $L_n \uplus \{0,1,\#\}^\omega$ require $2^{2^{\Omega(n)}}$ states as well.

From Lemma 1, it is sufficient to show that $F_n \uplus \{0,1,\#\}^*$ can be represented by an LTLf formula of length $\mathcal{O}(n^2)$. So, let us construct the desired LTLf formula ϕ_n. By abuse of notation, let the propositions be given by $\mathsf{Prop} = \{0,1,\#,\&\}$ with the interpretation that the symbol holds when its proposition is true. Recall that a letter σ in the finite alphabet Σ corresponds to a valuation over the atomic propositions Prop. For instance, $\& \in \Sigma$ is interpreted as the valuation $\neg 0 \wedge \neg 1 \wedge \neg \# \wedge \&$ over Prop. Then, the LTLf formula ϕ_n is a conjunction of the following three:

(R1). At all times, only one proposition can be true.
(R2). If "&" holds at some place, it occurs exactly once.
(R3). If "&" holds at some place, then if the end of the word has the form $\#w\#$, for $w \in \{0,1\}^n$, $\#w\#$ must have appeared before "&".

The LTLf formulation of (R1), denoted by $\mathsf{OnlyOneProp}$, is quite straightforward and has been deferred to the supplementary material of [3]. The formulation of (R2) is $\mathsf{F}\& \to \mathsf{ExactOne}\&$, where $\mathsf{ExactOne}\&$ expresses that "&" occurs exactly once:

$$\mathsf{ExactOne}\& := (\neg\&\mathsf{U}(\& \wedge (\neg(\mathsf{Xtrue}) \vee \mathsf{X}(\mathsf{G}\neg\&)))).$$

Intuitively, the "&" symbol is not seen *until* it is seen somewhere, after which either the trace *terminates* (i.e., $\neg(\mathsf{Xtrue})$ holds) or the trace does not see "&" *globally* (i.e., $\mathsf{X}(\mathsf{G}\neg\&)$ holds). In fact, we also have $\neg(\mathsf{Xtrue}) \vee \mathsf{X}(\mathsf{G}\neg\&) \equiv \mathsf{N}(\mathsf{G}\neg\&)$.

To express (R3), we first introduce two formulas. The first is EndWith#w#
to express that the end of the word has the form #w#. The second is
End#w#AppearsBefore& to express that the word #w# must appear before
"&". So, (R3) is expressed by

$$F\& \rightarrow (\mathsf{EndWith}\#w\# \rightarrow \mathsf{End}\#w\#\mathsf{AppearsBefore}\&)$$

For EndWith#w#, we introduce shorthands, namely $\mathsf{Ends} := X^{n+1}(\neg(X\mathsf{true}))$,
and $\mathsf{Appear}\#w\# := \# \wedge X^{n+1}\# \wedge \bigwedge_{i=1}^{n} X^i(0 \vee 1)$. Note that Ends is true only at
the $(n+2)$-th last position of a trace and Appear#w# enforces that the current
and next $n+1$ positions have the form #w# for $w \in \{0,1\}^n$. Then,

$$\mathsf{EndWith}\#w\# := G(\mathsf{Ends} \rightarrow \mathsf{Appear}\#w\#)$$

Also, End#w#AppearsBefore& :=

$$F\left(\mathsf{Appear}\#w\# \wedge F\& \wedge \bigwedge_{i=1}^{n}[(X^i0 \wedge G(\mathsf{Ends} \rightarrow X^i0)) \vee (X^i1 \wedge G(\mathsf{Ends} \rightarrow X^i1))]\right)$$

Intuitively, when defining End#w#AppearsBefore&, we assume that we are
standing at the first position of a word of the form #w# that appears before
"&". So, we require that Appear#w# holds and later F& holds. Next, we require
the same word w to appear at the end. So we require that if in the i-th position,
0 (resp. 1) holds, at the i-th position from where Ends holds, 0 (resp. 1) must
also hold. This is formulated as $(X^i0 \wedge G(\mathsf{Ends} \rightarrow X^i0)) \vee (X^i1 \wedge G(\mathsf{Ends} \rightarrow X^i1))$.
    Finally, the whole formula ϕ_n is given as follows:

$\phi_n = \mathsf{OnlyOneProp}$
$\quad \wedge (F\& \rightarrow (\mathsf{ExactOne\&} \wedge ((\mathsf{EndWith}\#w\# \rightarrow \mathsf{End}\#w\#\mathsf{AppearsBefore}\&))))$

Clearly, when F& does not hold, all words satisfying ϕ_n would be in
$\{0,1,\#\}^\omega$. If F& holds, then all words should meet (R2) and (R3). One can
easily verify that ϕ_n specifies the language $F_n \uplus \{0,1,\#\}^*$. Thus, $\mathsf{pref}(\phi_n) = L_n \uplus \{0,1,\#\}^\omega$.
    Last but not the least, the length of ϕ_n is in $\mathcal{O}(n^2)$ since End#w#
AppearsBefore& has length of $\mathcal{O}(n^2)$.   □

    Note that the LTLf formulation makes heavy use of Ends, which in turn uses
the X modality. Essentially, Ends serves as a unique identifier of a specific position
at the end of all traces. This enables us to anchor at that location without any
artificial constructs and to express the desiderata accordingly. This is a crucial
difference between LTLf and LTL.

4.2   Prefix Automata for LTLf Fragment

In this section, we show that a singly exponential construction of NBAs is possible for a fragment of LTLf formulas. Through an exposition of the prefix language

for fragments of LTLf, we highlight some of the peculiarities of the prefix language. Consider the fragment of LTLf, denoted as $\mathsf{LTLf}_{\backslash\{R,\vee\}}$, which permits all but the R (Release) modality and allows $\neg$ and $\vee$ on literals only, as defined below:

$$\psi := \ell \mid \neg\ell \mid \psi \wedge \psi \mid \mathrm{X}\psi \mid \mathrm{N}\psi \mid \mathrm{F}\psi \mid \mathrm{G}\psi \mid \psi\mathrm{U}\psi$$

where $\ell := a \in \mathsf{Prop} \mid \neg a \mid \ell \wedge \ell \mid \ell \vee \ell$. We show that the prefix language of this fragment is equivalently represented by an LTL formula of the same size, hence its NBA is singly exponential in the size of the formula. The said LTL formula can be obtained using the translation $t : \mathsf{LTLf}_{\backslash\{R,\vee\}} \to$ LTL described below (Since LTL and LTLf share the same syntax, to avoid confusion, we add the subscript ∞ to temporal operators in LTL, indicating that we have $|\rho| = \infty$. For instance, Globally in LTL becomes G_∞):

- $t(\ell) = \ell,\ t(\neg\ell) = \neg\ell$
- $t(\mathrm{X}\psi) = \mathsf{false},\ t(\mathrm{N}\psi) = \mathrm{X}_\infty t(\psi)$
- $t(\psi_1 \wedge \psi_2) = t(\psi_1) \wedge t(\psi_2)$
- $t(\mathrm{F}\psi) = t(\psi)$
- $t(\psi_1\mathrm{U}\psi_2) = t(\psi_2)$
- $t(\mathrm{G}\psi) = \mathrm{G}_\infty(t(\psi))$

The insight behind this translation is to identify that the criteria for a formula to hold on all finite-length prefixes simplifies to the formula holding on a prefix of length one. The proof is presented below:

Lemma 2. *Let $\phi \in \mathsf{LTLf}_{\backslash\{R,\vee\}}$ and let LTL $t(\phi)$ be as defined above. Then, $\mathcal{L}(t(\phi)) = \mathsf{pref}(\phi)$ and $\mathcal{O}(|\phi|) = \mathcal{O}(|t(\phi)|)$.*

Proof. Trivially, $\mathcal{O}(|\phi|) = \mathcal{O}(|t(\phi)|)$ holds. We prove that $\mathcal{L}(t(\phi)) = \mathsf{pref}(\phi)$ by structural induction on ϕ. In the interest of space, we skip the base cases (ℓ and $\neg\ell$). We also skip the $\wedge$ and G modalities, as they are intuitive. We present the argument for X, N, F, and U. The full proof can be found in the appendix of [3].

We set up notations: for $w = w_0 w_1 \cdots \in \Sigma^\omega$, let $w[i,j] = w_i \cdots w_{j-1}$ denote subsequences of w for $0 \le i < j$. So, $w[0,n]$ is the n-length prefix of w for $n > 0$. By inductive hypothesis (I.H.), we assume $\mathcal{L}(t(\gamma)) = \mathsf{pref}(\gamma)$ for $\gamma \in \{\psi, \psi_1, \psi_2\}$.

Case Fψ: The critical observation is that for Fψ to hold on all finite prefixes, Fψ must hold on the prefix of length 1, which in turn is possible only if the first position of the word satisfies ψ. Formally, first we show that $\mathsf{pref}(\mathrm{F}\psi) \subseteq \mathcal{L}(t(\mathrm{F}\psi))$. Let $w \in \mathsf{pref}(\mathrm{F}\psi)$. Then, in particular $w[0,1] \models \mathrm{F}\psi$. This is possible only if $w[0,1] \models \psi$. Thus, for all $n > 0$, we get $w[0,n] \models \psi$. So, $w \in \mathsf{pref}(\psi)$. By I.H., $w \in \mathcal{L}(t(\psi))$. By translation, this means $w \in \mathcal{L}(t(\mathrm{F}\psi))$. Next, we show $\mathcal{L}(t(\mathrm{F}\psi)) \subseteq \mathsf{pref}(\mathrm{F}\psi)$. Let $w \in \mathcal{L}(t(\mathrm{F}\psi))$. By translation, $w \in \mathcal{L}(t(\psi))$. By I.H., $w \in \mathsf{pref}(\psi)$. Now, if ψ holds, then Fψ also holds for all non-zero lengths. Hence, $w \in \mathsf{pref}(\mathrm{F}\psi)$.

Case $\psi_1\mathrm{U}\psi_2$: As earlier, the critical observation is for $\psi_1\mathrm{U}\psi_2$ to hold on a prefix of length one. For this, ψ_2 must hold. The proof is similar to the earlier case.

Case Xψ: The issue is that Xψ can never be true on a word of length one, since there does not exist a next position on length one words. Hence, $\mathsf{pref}(\mathrm{X}\psi) = \emptyset = \mathcal{L}(\mathsf{False}) = \mathcal{L}(t(\mathrm{X}\psi))$.

Case $N\psi$: N (Weak Next) doesn't have the issue faced by X. If a word is of length one, $N\psi$ trivially holds. For words of all other lengths, it requires $X\psi$ to hold. Formally, first we show that $\mathsf{pref}(N\psi) \subseteq \mathcal{L}(t(N\psi))$. Let $w \in \mathsf{pref}(N\psi)$. Then, by semantics of LTLf, it follows that the second position on w must satisfy ψ, i.e., $w[1, 2] \models \psi$. In particular, for all $i > 1$, $w[1, i] \models \psi$. So, $w[1, \infty] \in \mathsf{pref}(\psi)$. By I.H., $w[1, \infty] \in \mathcal{L}(t(\psi))$. Hence, $w \in \mathcal{L}(X_\infty t(\psi)) = \mathcal{L}(t(N\psi))$. Conversely, let $w \in \mathcal{L}(t(N\psi))$. By translation, $w \in \mathcal{L}(X_\infty t(\psi))$. Hence, by I.H., we get for all $i > 1$, $w[0, i] \models X\psi$ and $w[0, 1] \models N\psi$ since $w[1, \infty] \in \mathcal{L}(t(\psi)) = \mathsf{pref}(\psi)$. In other words, $w \in \mathsf{pref}(N\psi)$.   □

An immediate consequence of Lemma 2 is that the prefix automata for $\mathsf{LTLf}_{\backslash\{R,\vee\}}$ are singly exponential in the size of the formula [34]:

Corollary 1. *Let* $\phi \in \mathsf{LTLf}_{\backslash\{R,\vee\}}$. *The NBA for* $\mathsf{pref}(\phi)$ *contains* $2^{\mathcal{O}(|\phi|)}$ *states.*

Note that, in all the cases above, every conjunct holds on *all* finite prefixes. This may not be true if $\vee$ (or) is permitted in the formula. For example, consider $\phi = Ga \vee Fb$. Now, the word $w = \{a\}\{b\}\{\}^\omega \in \mathsf{pref}(\phi)$ since the prefix of length one satisfies Ga and all other prefixes satisfy Fb. Hence, with disjunction, different prefixes can satisfy *different* disjuncts. In fact, the LTL formula for $\mathsf{pref}(\phi)$ is $aU_\infty b \vee G_\infty a$. However, such translations may increase the formula length because of duplicating the formula under G_∞ modality. An open problem here is to identify the largest fragment for which the prefix automata have only singly exponential blow-up. This goes hand-in-hand with uncovering the core behind the doubly exponential blow-up for prefix automata.

5 Complexity of LTLf Model Checking

We present the complexity of LTLf model checking. Section 5.1 develops the lower bound for model checking non-terminating systems and Sect. 5.2 presents the completeness argument for both terminating and non-terminating systems.

5.1 EXPSPACE Lower Bound for Non-terminating Systems

We prove EXPSPACE-hardness of LTLf model checking of non-terminating systems by a polynomial-time reduction from the problem of whether an exponential-space Turing machine $T = (Q, \Gamma, \delta, q_0, F)$ accepts an input word $x = x_1 \ldots x_n$. The components of the Turing machine are defined as follows:

- Q is the set of states and $q_0 \in Q$ is the initial state.
- Γ is the tape alphabet, which is assumed to include the blank symbol $\emptyset$.
- $\delta : Q \times \Gamma \to Q \times \Gamma \times \{\leftarrow, \to\}$ is the transition function. $\delta(q, \gamma) = (q', \gamma', d)$ means that if the machine is in state q and the head reads symbol γ, it moves to state q', writes symbol γ', and moves the head in direction d.
- $F \subseteq Q$ is the set of accepting states. The machine accepts if it reaches a state in F.

Since T is an exponential-space Turing machine, we can assume that its tape has 2^{cn} cells, where n is the size of the input and c is a constant.

High-Level Idea. Given a Turing machine T and an input x, our reduction will construct a non-terminating system M and an LTLf formula φ s.t. T accepts x iff every execution of M has a finite prefix that satisfies φ, i.e., $M \models \varphi$.

In this reduction, we will encode runs of the Turing machine as label sequences of the system. A *cell* in the tape is encoded as a sequence of $cn + 1$ propositional assignments. The first assignment encodes the content of the cell, which can be either a symbol $\gamma \in \Gamma$ or a symbol γ along with a state $q \in Q$, the latter indicating that the head is on that cell and is in state q. The remaining cn assignments encode the position of the cell in the tape as a cn-bit number (since the tape has 2^{cn} cells). The concatenation of 2^{cn} cells encodes a *configuration* of the Turing machine. Therefore, each configuration is encoded by $2^{cn}(cn + 1)$ assignments in total. The concatenation of configurations encodes a *run* of the Turing machine. Note, however, that for such a run to be consistent with the run of T on x, certain consistency conditions must hold:

1. For every configuration, the encoding of the position of the first cell must be 0, and the encoding must increase by 1 for each successive cell.
2. The first configuration must start with x on the tape and the head on the first cell and in the initial state q_0.
3. Successive configurations must be consistent with the transition function δ.

One way is to enforce all consistency conditions through the system M. However, since each configuration consists of 2^{cn} cells, this would require the system to have an exponential number of states. Therefore, to allow for a polynomial reduction, we enforce the consistency conditions through the formula φ.

For this, we construct an LTLf formula $\varphi := \varphi_{cons} \rightarrow \varphi_{acc}$ where φ_{cons} expresses the the consistency conditions and φ_{acc} expresses the property of reaching an accepting configuration. Therefore, every execution with a finite prefix that satisfies φ is either inconsistent or an accepting run of T on x. Since T is deterministic, there is exactly one execution of M that is consistent with T. Every other execution will necessarily satisfy $\neg\varphi_{cons}$, and this execution will satisfy φ_{acc} if and only if T accepts x. Therefore, if every execution of M has a finite prefix that satisfies φ, then the run of T on input x is accepting, and vice-versa.

We now provide the details of the system M and the formula φ.

Atomic Propositions. The propositions used by system M are the following:

- $part_0$ indicates that the current assignment represents the first part of the cell encoding, encoding the cell's content.
- $part_i$, for $1 \leq i \leq cn$, indicates that the current assignment represents the i-th bit of the encoding of the cell's position. Only one of $part_0, \ldots, part_{cn}$ is true at any given time.

– $cell_\lambda$, for $\lambda \in \Gamma \cup (Q \times \Gamma)$, indicates that the content of the cell is λ (a tape symbol with or without the head). This proposition can only be true if $part_0$ is true.
– bit gives the current bit of the cell's position. This proposition can only be true if $part_0$ is false.

The Model. We define the transition system $M = (\Sigma, S, T, \iota, L)$ as follows:

– $\Sigma = \{part_0, \ldots, part_{cn}\} \cup \{cell_\lambda \mid \lambda \in \Gamma \cup (Q \times \Gamma)\} \cup \{bit\}$
– $S = \{(0, \lambda) \mid \lambda \in \Gamma \cup (Q \times \Gamma)\} \cup \{(i, b) \mid 1 \le i \le cn, b \in \{0, 1\}\}$
– $\iota = (0, (q_0, \emptyset))$
– $(s, s') \in T$ if and only if one of the following is true (for some λ, b, b'):
  • $s = (0, \lambda)$ and $s' = (1, b)$.
  • $s = (i, b)$ for $1 \le i < cn$, and $s' = (i + 1, b')$.
  • $s = (cn, b)$ and $s' = (0, \lambda)$.
– $L((0, \lambda)) = \{part_0, cell_\lambda\}$
– $L((i, b)) = \{part_i\} \cup \{bit \mid b = 1\}$

The propositional alphabet Σ consists of the set of propositions described above. The states of the M are either of the form $(0, \lambda)$, where λ is the content of a cell, or (i, b) for $1 \le i \le cn$, where b is the current bit in the encoding of the cell's position. The initial state is $(0, (q_0, \emptyset))$, indicating that a) this is the first part of the cell's encoding, b) the head is on this cell, c) the machine is in the initial state q_0, and d) the cell is blank (this should be the cell immediately to the left of the input word x).

The transition relation ensures only that the system progresses consistently from part 0 of the encoding to part 1, part 2, part 3, and so on until part cn, after which it resets back to part 0 (of the next cell). Note that the values of λ and b are unconstrained, as these will be handled by the formula φ. Observe the three consistency conditions required for runs of T are not wired into the model.

Finally, the labeling function L simply converts the state into an appropriate propositional representation.

The Formula. We now construct the LTLf formula φ over the propositional alphabet Σ. As mentioned before, we want φ to be such that, if an execution of the system M has a prefix that satisfies φ, then either that execution violates a consistency condition or it is an accepting run. To achieve this, we construct $\varphi = \neg\varphi_{cons} \vee \varphi_{acc}$. φ_{acc} is defined as follows:

$$\varphi_{acc} = \bigvee_{q \in F} \bigvee_{\gamma \in \Gamma} \mathrm{F}\, cell_{(q, \gamma)}.$$

It is easy to see that an execution of M has a prefix that satisfies φ_{acc} iff that execution reaches a state $(0, (q, \gamma))$ where q is an accepting state of T.

Meanwhile, we define φ_{cons} as a conjunction of formulas, such that if an execution has a prefix that violates one of these formulas then the execution is inconsistent, and every inconsistent execution has a prefix that violates one of these formulas. We classify these formulas into three groups, one for each of the three consistency conditions described above:

(C1). Consistency within a configuration (the binary encoding of each cell's position is correct)
(C2). Consistency with the input word (the first configuration is correct)
(C3). Consistency with the transition function (every configuration follows from the previous one)

The first two conditions (C1) and (C2) are relatively straightforward to encode as formulas of polynomial size. For details, we refer to the appendix of [3].

The third condition (C3) is where the biggest challenge lies. This condition requires reasoning about changes from one configuration to the next. The difficulty lies in accessing the segment that represents the same cell in the next configuration using a polynomial-sized formula. Recall that a cell is represented by $cn + 1$ assignments in the trace and each configuration is composed of 2^{cn} cells. Since the size of each configuration is exponential, formulas may require exponential size. For instance, if the segment representing a cell begins at assignment i in the trace, then the same cell in the next configuration will start at assignment $i + 2^{cn}(cn + 1)$. Referring to this assignment directly in the formula would require $2^{cn}(cn + 1)$ nested X operators. Alternatively, the cell in the next configuration can be identified by being the first cell where the binary encoding of its position on the tape is the same as the current cell. However, this may require enumeration on all possible assignments of the $cn + 1$ bits.

To circumvent this problem and compare corresponding cells in two different configurations using a formula of polynomial size, we take advantage of the fact that we are dealing with finite prefixes of the trace. The insight is that we can use the last position in the trace as an anchor, so that instead of having to find the cell in the next configuration with the same position encoding, we can instead look at the last cell in the trace and test if a) it is in the next configuration, and b) it has the same position encoding. Since the formula is checked for every prefix, eventually we will find a prefix where this holds. We can then check if the contents of the cells are consistent with the transition function.

We now go into details of the formula for (C3). Consistency condition (C3) says that every configuration follows from the previous one according to T's transition function δ. As mentioned before, to ensure that we get a formula of polynomial size, the formula that we construct actually expresses the following condition: for all cells c in the prefix, if the last cell c_{Last} of the prefix is in the same position as c but in the next configuration, then c_{Last} follows from c based on the transition function. Since the formula must hold for all prefixes, its satisfaction implies the original consistency condition.

We start by defining the useful shorthand $L^{-i}\phi \equiv F(\phi \wedge X^{i-1}\neg X\,\text{true})$, which denotes that ϕ holds i positions before the end of the prefix (e.g. $L^{-1}\phi$ means that ϕ holds at the last position of the prefix). This is expressed by saying that at some point in the future ϕ holds, and $i-1$ positions after that is the last position of the prefix (by the semantics of LTLf, $\neg X$ true only holds at the last position). We then define the formula MatchLastCell, which checks if the cell c in the current position corresponds to the last cell c_{Last} of the prefix, as follows:

$$\text{MatchLastCell} \equiv part_0 \wedge L^{-cn}part_0 \wedge \bigwedge_{i=1}^{cn}(X^i bit \leftrightarrow L^{-cn}X^i bit)$$

$$\wedge\, X\Big(\neg\text{NewConfig U}\,(\text{NewConfig} \wedge X\,G\,\neg\text{NewConfig})\Big)$$

where $\text{NewConfig} \equiv (part_0 \wedge \bigwedge_{i=1}^{cn}(X^i \neg bit))$ denotes the start of a new configuration (a cell whose position in the tape is encoded as 0). MatchLastCell expresses that (a) we are at the start of a cell c ($part_0$); (b) the last cn positions of the prefix encode another cell c_{Last} ($L^{-cn}part_0$); (c) c and c_{Last} are in the same tape position ($\bigwedge_{i=1}^{cn}(X^i bit \leftrightarrow L^{-cn}X^i bit)$); and (d) we start a new configuration exactly once between c and c_{Last} ($X(\neg\text{NewConfig U}\,(\text{NewConfig} \wedge X\,G\,\neg\text{NewConfig}))$). In other words, c and c_{Last} are the same cell in successive configurations. We can then encode the consistency condition by the formula

$$G(\text{MatchLastCell} \to \varphi_\delta) \wedge G(\text{MatchLastCell} \to \varphi_\delta^{\leftarrow})$$

$$\wedge\, G(X^{cn+1}\,\text{MatchLastCell} \to \varphi_\delta^{\rightarrow}) \wedge G(X^{cn+1}\,\text{MatchLastCell} \to \varphi_\delta^0)$$

where each of φ_δ, $\varphi_\delta^{\leftarrow}$, $\varphi_\delta^{\rightarrow}$, and φ_δ^0 expresses one way in which the contents of the cell c can change (or not change) in the next configuration:

- φ_δ expresses that if the head is on c ($cell_{(q,\gamma)}$), then in c_{Last} the head must have moved to a different cell and written the appropriate symbol γ' given by the transition relation ($L^{-cn}\,cell_{\gamma'}$)
- $\varphi_\delta^{\leftarrow}$ expresses that if the head is on the cell to the *right* of c ($X^{cn+1}\,cell_{(q,\gamma_2)}$), and the transition relation requires it to move left, then in the next configuration the head must have moved to c_{Last} ($L^{-cn}\,cell_{(q',\gamma_1)}$))
- $\varphi_\delta^{\rightarrow}$ expresses that if the head is on the cell to the *left* of c ($cell_{(q,\gamma_1)}$), and the transition relation requires it to move right, then in the next configuration the head must have moved to c_{Last} ($L^{-cn}\,cell_{(q',\gamma_2)}$))
- Finally, φ_δ^0 expresses that if the head is neither on c nor on the cells adjacent to it ($cell_{\gamma_1} \wedge X^{cn+1}\,cell_{\gamma_2} \wedge X^{2(cn+1)}\,cell_{\gamma_3}$), then the contents of the cell don't change ($L^{-cn}\,cell_{\gamma_2}$)

Note that in the latter two formulas c is the cell to the right of the current cell ($X^{cn+1}\,\text{MatchLastCell}$) this is necessary so that $\varphi_\delta^{\rightarrow}$ and φ_δ^0 can refer to the cell to the left of c. Formula for φ_δ, $\varphi_\delta^{\leftarrow}$, $\varphi_\delta^{\rightarrow}$, and φ_δ^0 have been presented in the appendix of [3]. The size of each formula is polynomial in the size of the transition relation of the Turing Machine.

Theorem 3 (LTLf Model Checking. Lower bound). LTLf *model checking of non-terminating systems is EXPSPACE-hard.*

Proof. Let the non-terminating system M and LTLf formula $\varphi = \neg\varphi_{cons} \vee \varphi_{acc}$ be as described above. We show that an exponential-space Turing machine T accepts an input word x iff every execution of M has a finite prefix that satisfies φ, i.e., $M \models \varphi$. Note that since T is deterministic, its execution on the input word x is unique. Therefore, there is exactly one trace π of M that simulates the execution of T on x. By construction, a trace has a finite prefix that satisfies $\neg\varphi_{cons}$ iff that trace violates one of the consistency conditions. This holds for every trace of M except π. So, because no finite prefix of π satisfies $\neg\varphi_{cons}$, M model checks if and only if π has a prefix that satisfies φ_{acc}, which means that π eventually reaches an accepting state. Since π simulates T on x, this happens if and only if T accepts x. $\qquad\square$

5.2 Final Complexity Results

Finally, we present the complexity of model-checking non-terminating systems:

Theorem 4 (MC. Non-terminating. Complexity). LTLf *model checking of non-terminating systems is EXPSPACE-complete.*

Proof. Recall, a non-terminating system $\mathcal{M}$ satisfies an LTLf formula ϕ iff $\mathcal{L}(\mathcal{M}) \cap \mathsf{pref}(\neg\phi) = \emptyset$. A naive algorithm would explicitly construct $\mathsf{pref}(\neg\phi)$ and require doubly exponential space in the size of ϕ. Instead, the approach is to construct $\mathsf{pref}(\phi)$ on-the-fly in exponential space and simultaneously evaluate the emptiness of $\mathcal{M} \cap \mathsf{pref}(\neg\phi)$. Given all three steps in the construction of $\mathsf{pref}(\phi)$ are amenable to on-the-fly constructions, this procedure follows standard on-the-fly procedures [33]. Thus, LTLf model checking of non-terminating models is in EXPSPACE. Theorem 3 establishes the matching lower bound. $\quad\square$

This result is unexpected as it implies that LTLf model checking is exponentially harder than LTL model checking for non-terminating systems, contrary to the prior perception that problems in LTLf tend to be as hard if not easier than their counterparts in LTL (See Table 1).

Next, we present the complexity of model-checking terminating systems:

Theorem 5 (MC. Terminating. Complexity). LTLf *model checking of terminating systems is PSPACE-complete.*

Proof. Recall that a terminating system M satisfies an LTLf formula ϕ if every execution of M satisfies ϕ. So, $M \models \phi$ iff $\mathcal{L}(M \cap A_{\neg\phi}) = \emptyset$ where $A_{\neg\phi}$ is the NFA for $\neg\phi$. Since the NFA is exponential in the size of the LTLf formula [14], an on-the-fly algorithm for non-emptiness checking of $M \cap A_{\neg\phi}$ can be performed in PSPACE. PSPACE-hardness can be proven by a trivial reduction from LTLf *satisfiability*, which is PSPACE-complete [14]. $\quad\square$

For LTLf synthesis, these results imply that it is much harder to verify a non-terminating transducer than a terminating transducer. Hence, to test the correctness of an LTLf synthesis tool by verifying its output strategy, it would be better for LTLf synthesis tools to generate terminating transducers. This, to the best of our knowledge, is the *first* theoretically sound evidence to use one transducer over the other in LTLf synthesis.

6   Concluding Remarks

Motivated by the recent surge in LTLf synthesis tools that are rarely verified for result correctness, this work is the *first* to investigate the problem of LTLf model checking. Noting that LTLf synthesis can generate both terminating and non-terminating transducers, we examine LTLf model checking for both possibilities. Our central result is that LTLf model checking of non-terminating models is exponentially harder than terminating models. Their complexities are EXPSPACE-complete and PSPACE-complete, respectively. This is surprising at first as it implies that LTLf model checking is harder than LTL model checking for non-terminating models, contrary to the expectation from prior comparisons between LTLf and LTL (See Table 1). In addition to being of independent interest, our results immediately lend several broad impacts:

1. They present the first theoretical evidence for the use of terminating transducers to represent the synthesized strategies in LTLf synthesis, as it would be easier to verify the correctness of the synthesized transducer.
2. Implementations of our LTLf model checking algorithms could be deployed in large-scale competitions such as the LTLf track in SYNTCOMP 2023.
3. They invite further exploration into LTLf vs LTL, as it breaks the prior perception that problems in LTLf are *as hard if not simpler* than their LTL counterparts.

One may envision our results to be used to automatically verify the correctness of synthesized models in the LTLf track in synthesis competitions. It would be interesting to see how the practical implementations for LTLf model checking compare under terminating and non-terminating semantics, even though terminating models are preferred in theory. The development of practical tools presents several new challenges, including efficient and scalable construction of $pref(\phi)$ and its tractable fragments. Our results also inspire future work in the development of LTLf model checking in more complex domains such as probabilistic models or under asynchrony [4,5].

Acknowledgements. We thank the anonymous reviewers for their valuable feedback. This work has been supported by the Engineering and Physical Sciences Research Council [grant number EP/X021513/1], NASA 80NSSC17K0162, NSF grants IIS-1527668, CCF-1704883, IIS-1830549, CNS-2016656, DoD MURI grant N00014-20-1-2787, and an award from the Maryland Procurement Office.

References

1. Baier, J.A., McIlraith, S.: Planning with temporally extended goals using heuristic search. In: ICAPS, pp. 342–345. AAAI Press (2006)
2. Bansal, S., Li, Y., Tabajara, L., Vardi, M.: Hybrid compositional reasoning for reactive synthesis from finite-horizon specifications. In: AAAI, vol. 34, pp. 9766–9774 (2020)

3. Bansal, S., Li, Y., Tabajara, L.M., Vardi, M.Y., Wells, A.M.: Model checking strategies from synthesis over finite traces. CoRR abs/2305.08319 (2023). https://doi.org/10.48550/arXiv.2305.08319

4. Bansal, S., Namjoshi, K.S., Sa'ar, Y.: Synthesis of coordination programs from linear temporal specifications. Proc. ACM Program. Lang. (POPL) 4, 1–27 (2019)

5. Bansal, S., Namjoshi, K.S., Sa'ar, Y.: Synthesis of asynchronous reactive programs from temporal specifications. In: Chockler, H., Weissenbacher, G. (eds.) CAV 2018. LNCS, vol. 10981, pp. 367–385. Springer, Cham (2018). https://doi.org/10.1007/978-3-319-96145-3_20

6. Blum, M., Kannan, S.: Designing programs that check their work. J. ACM 42(1), 269–291 (1995)

7. Brafman, R.I., De Giacomo, G.: Planning for LTLf/LDLf goals in non-Markovian fully observable nondeterministic domains. In: IJCAI, pp. 1602–1608 (2019)

8. Camacho, A., Icarte, R.T., Klassen, T.Q., Valenzano, R.A., McIlraith, S.A.: LTL and beyond: formal languages for reward function specification in reinforcement learning. In: IJCAI, vol. 19, pp. 6065–6073 (2019)

9. De Giacomo, G., Favorito, M.: Compositional approach to translate LTLf/LDLf into deterministic finite automata. In: Proceedings of the International Conference on Automated Planning and Scheduling, vol. 31, pp. 122–130 (2021)

10. De Giacomo, G., Favorito, M., Li, J., Vardi, M.Y., Xiao, S., Zhu, S.: LTLf synthesis as AND-OR graph search: knowledge compilation at work. In: Proceedings of IJCAI (2022)

11. De Giacomo, G., Iocchi, L., Favorito, M., Patrizi, F.: Foundations for restraining bolts: reinforcement learning with LTLf/LDLf restraining specifications. In: ICAPS, vol. 29, pp. 128–136 (2019)

12. De Giacomo, G., Rubin, S.: Automata-theoretic foundations of fond planning for LTLf and LDLf goals. In: IJCAI, pp. 4729–4735 (2018)

13. De Giacomo, G., Vardi, M.: Synthesis for LTL and LDL on finite traces. In: IJCAI, pp. 1558–1564. AAAI Press (2015)

14. De Giacomo, G., Vardi, M.Y.: Linear temporal logic and linear dynamic logic on finite traces. In: IJCAI, pp. 854–860. AAAI Press (2013)

15. De Giacomo, G., Vardi, M.Y.: LTLf and LDLf synthesis under partial observability. In: IJCAI, vol. 2016, pp. 1044–1050 (2016)

16. Duret-Lutz, A., et al.: From spot 2.0 to spot 2.10: What's new? In: Shoham, S., Vizel, Y. (eds.) CAV 2022, Part II. Lecture Notes in Computer Science, vol. 13372, pp. 174–187. Springer, Cham (2022). https://doi.org/10.1007/978-3-031-13188-2_9

17. Esparza, J., Křetínský, J., Sickert, S.: A unified translation of linear temporal logic to ω-automata. J. ACM (JACM) 67(6), 1–61 (2020)

18. Favorito, M.: Forward LTLf synthesis: DPLL at work. arXiv preprint arXiv:2302.13825 (2023)

19. He, K., Lahijanian, M., Kavraki, L.E., Vardi, M.Y.: Reactive synthesis for finite tasks under resource constraints. In: IROS, pp. 5326–5332. IEEE (2017)

20. Jacobs, S., Perez, G.A., Schlehuber-Caissier, P.: The temporal logic synthesis format TLSF v1.2 (2023)

21. Křetínský, J., Meggendorfer, T., Sickert, S.: Owl: a library for ω-words, automata, and LTL. In: Lahiri, S.K., Wang, C. (eds.) ATVA 2018. LNCS, vol. 11138, pp. 543–550. Springer, Cham (2018). https://doi.org/10.1007/978-3-030-01090-4_34

22. Kuehlmann, A., van Eijk, C.A.: Combinational and sequential equivalence checking. In: Hassoun, S., Sasao, T. (eds.) Logic Synthesis and Verification. The Springer International Series in Engineering and Computer Science, vol. 654, pp. 343–372. Springer, Boston (2002). https://doi.org/10.1007/978-1-4615-0817-5_13

23. De Nicola, R., Vaandrager, F.: Action versus state based logics for transition systems. In: Guessarian, I. (ed.) LITP 1990. LNCS, vol. 469, pp. 407–419. Springer, Heidelberg (1990). https://doi.org/10.1007/3-540-53479-2_17
24. Pnueli, A.: The temporal logic of programs. In: FOCS, pp. 46–57. IEEE (1977)
25. Pnueli, A., Rosner, R.: On the synthesis of a reactive module. In: POPL, pp. 179–190 (1989)
26. Safra, S.: On the complexity of omega -automata. In: FOCS, pp. 319–327 (1988)
27. Siegel, M., Pnueli, A., Singerman, E.: Translation validation. In: Proceedings of TACAS, pp. 151–166 (1998)
28. Sistla, A.P., Clarke, E.M.: The complexity of propositional linear temporal logics. J. ACM (JACM) **32**(3), 733–749 (1985)
29. Tabajara, L.M., Vardi, M.Y.: Partitioning techniques in LTLf synthesis. In: IJCAI, pp. 5599–5606. AAAI Press (2019)
30. Tabakov, D., Rozier, K., Vardi, M.Y.: Optimized temporal monitors for SystemC. Formal Meth. Syst. Des. **41**(3), 236–268 (2012)
31. Thomas, W., et al.: Automata, Logics, and Infinite Games: A Guide to Current Research, vol. 2500. Springer, Berlin (2002)
32. Vardi, M.Y.: The büchi complementation saga. In: Thomas, W., Weil, P. (eds.) STACS 2007. LNCS, vol. 4393, pp. 12–22. Springer, Heidelberg (2007). https://doi.org/10.1007/978-3-540-70918-3_2
33. Vardi, M.Y., Wolper, P.: An automata-theoretic approach to automatic program verification. In: LICS. IEEE Computer Society (1986)
34. Vardi, M.Y., Wolper, P.: Reasoning about infinite computations. Inf. Comput. **115**(1), 1–37 (1994)
35. Wells, A.M., Lahijanian, M., Kavraki, L.E., Vardi, M.Y.: LTLf synthesis on probabilistic systems. arXiv preprint arXiv:2009.10883 (2020)
36. Wolper, P., Vardi, M.Y., Sistla, A.P.: Reasoning about infinite computation paths. In: FOCS, pp. 185–194. IEEE (1983)
37. Zhu, S., Tabajara, L.M., Li, J., Pu, G., Vardi, M.Y.: Symbolic LTLf synthesis. In: IJCAI, pp. 1362–1369. AAAI Press (2017)

Reactive Synthesis of Smart Contract Control Flows

Bernd Finkbeiner[1], Jana Hofmann[2](✉), Florian Kohn[1],
and Noemi Passing[1]

[1] CISPA Helmholtz Center for Information Security, Saarbrücken, Germany
{finkbeiner,florian.kohn,noemi.passing}@cispa.de
[2] Azure Research, Microsoft, Cambridge, UK
t-jhofmann@microsoft.com

Abstract. Smart contracts are small but highly error-prone programs that implement agreements between multiple parties. We present a reactive synthesis approach for the automatic construction of smart contract state machines. Towards this end, we extend temporal stream logic (TSL) with universally quantified parameters over infinite domains. Parameterized TSL is a convenient logic to specify the temporal control flow, i.e., the correct order of transactions, as well as the data flow of the contract's fields. We develop a two-step approach that 1) synthesizes a finite representation of the – in general – infinite-state system and 2) splits the system into a compact hierarchical architecture that enables the implementation of the state machine in Solidity. We implement the approach in our prototype tool SCSYNT, which – within seconds – automatically constructs Solidity code that realizes the specified control flow.

Keywords: Reactive Synthesis · Temporal Stream Logic · Parameterized Synthesis · Smart Contracts

1 Introduction

Smart contracts are small programs that implement digital contracts between multiple parties. They are deployed on the blockchain and thereby remove the need for a trusted third party that enforces a correct execution of the contract. Recent history, however, has witnessed numerous bugs in smart contracts, some of which led to substantial monetary losses. One critical aspect is the implicit state machine of a contract: to justify the removal of a trusted third party – a major selling point for smart contracts – all parties must trust that the contract indeed enforces the agreed order of transactions.

Formal methods play a significant role in the efforts to improve the trustworthiness of smart contracts. Indeed, the *code is law* paradigm is shifting towards a *specification is law* paradigm [1]. Formal verification has been successfully applied to prove the correctness of the implicit state machine of smart contracts, for example, by verifying the contract against temporal logic specifications [31,33,34] or a given state machine [36]. Other approaches model the control flow with state machines and construct Solidity code from it [4,24,27,37].

© The Author(s), under exclusive license to Springer Nature Switzerland AG 2023
É. André and J. Sun (Eds.): ATVA 2023, LNCS 14215, pp. 248–269, 2023.
https://doi.org/10.1007/978-3-031-45329-8_12

Synthesis, i.e., the automatic construction of Solidity code *directly* from a temporal specification, has hardly been studied so far (except for a first step [35], see related work).

In this paper, we study the synthesis of smart contracts state machines from temporal stream logic (TSL), which we equip with universally quantified parameters. TSL extends linear-time temporal logic (LTL) with data cells and uninterpreted functions and predicates. These features enable us to reason about the order of transactions as well as the data flow of the contract's fields. To distinguish method calls from different callers, we extend the logic with universally quantified parameters. For example, the following parameterized TSL formula expresses that every voter can only vote once and that a field numVotes is increased with every vote.

$$\forall m. \; \square(\texttt{vote(m)} \; \rightarrow \; [\![\texttt{numVotes} \leftarrow \texttt{numVotes} + 1]\!] \; \wedge \bigcirc\square\neg\texttt{vote(m)}))$$

The above formula demonstrates the challenges associated with parameterized TSL synthesis. First of all, a part of the formula restricts the allowed method calls, which are inputs in the synthesis problem. To make specifications realizable, we restrict ourselves to safety properties, which we express in the past-time fragment of parameterized TSL. Second, as the contract might interact with arbitrarily many voters, the above formula ranges over an infinite domain. However, we need to find a finite representation of the system that can be translated into feasible Solidity code.

We tackle this challenge in two steps. First, we translate the parameterized pastTSL formula to pastTSL to synthesize a finite representation of the system. Unfortunately, we show that the realizability problem of pastTSL is undecidable, even without parameters. As a remedy, we employ a sound approximation in LTL [11] to make synthesis possible.

In a second step, we split the resulting state machine into a hierarchical structure of smaller, distributed state machines. This architecture can be interpreted as an infinite-state system realizing the original formula. It also minimizes the number of transactions needed to keep the system up to date at runtime.

We implement the approach in our prototype SCSYNT, which, due to the past-time fragment, leverages efficient symbolic algorithms. We specify ten different smart contract specifications and obtain an average synthesis time of two seconds. Our largest specification is based on Avolab's NFT auction [2] and produces a state machine with 12 states in 12 s. To summarize, we

- show how to specify smart contract control flows in parameterized pastTSL,
- prove undecidability of the general realizability problem of pastTSL,
- and present a sound (but necessarily incomplete) synthesis approach for parameterized pastTSL formulas that generates a hierarchy of state machines to enable a compact representation of the system in Solidity.

Related Work. Formal approaches for smart contracts range from the automatic construction of contracts from state machines [27,28], over the verification against temporal logics [31,33,34] and state machines [21,36], to deductive verification approaches [6,16]. Closest to our work is a synthesis approach based on LTL specifications [35]. The approach does not reason about the contract's data: neither about the current value of the fields, nor about parameters like the method's caller. To quote the authors of [35]: the main challenge in the synthesis of smart contracts is "how to strike a balance between simplicity and expressivity [...] to allow effective synthesis of practical smart contracts". In this paper, we opt for a more expressive temporal logic and simultaneously aim to keep the specifications readable.

TSL has been successfully applied to synthesize FPGA controllers [12] and functional reactive programs [10]. To include domain-specific reasoning, TSL has been extended with theories [8] and SMT solvers [25]. A recent approach combines TSL reactive synthesis with SyGus to synthesize implementations for TSL's uninterpreted functions [3]. Parameterized synthesis has so far focused on distributed architectures parameterized in the number of components [15,17,18, 26]. Orthogonal to this work, these approaches rely on a reduction to bounded isomorphic synthesis [15,17,18] or apply a learning-based approach [26].

Overview. We first provide some brief preliminaries on state machines, reactive synthesis, and TSL. In Sect. 3, we introduce parameterized TSL and demonstrate how it can be used for specifying smart contract control flows. Subsequently, we discuss the high-level idea and associated challenges of our synthesis approach in Sect. 4 and discuss synthesis from plain pastTSL in Sect. 5. demonstrate how to specify smart contracts using pure pastTSL and prove the undecidability of its realizability problem. We proceed with the main part of the approach, a splitting algorithm for state machines, in Sect. 6. Finally, we discuss the implementation of SCSYNT and its evaluation in Sect. 7.

2   Preliminaries

We assume familiarity with linear-time temporal logic (LTL). A definition with past-time temporal operators can be found in [5,13]. We only assume basic knowledge about smart contracts; for an introduction we refer to [7].

2.1   State Machines, Safety Properties and Reactive Synthesis

We give a brief introduction to Mealy machines, safety properties, and reactive synthesis. In this work, we represent smart contract control flows as *Mealy state machines* [30], which separate the alphabet into inputs I and outputs O. A Mealy machine $\mathcal{M}$ is a tuple (S, s_0, δ) of states S, initial state s_0, and transition relation $\delta \subseteq S \times I \cup O \times S$. For a compact representation, we attach the outputs also to transitions, not to the states. We call $\mathcal{M}$ *finite-state* if both $\Sigma = I \cup O$ and S are finite, and *infinite-state* otherwise. An infinite sequence $t \in \Sigma^\omega$ is a *trace* of $\mathcal{M}$ if there is an infinite sequence of states $r \in S^{\omega}$ such that $r[0] = s_0$ and $(r[i], t[i], r[i+1]) \in \delta$ for all points in time $i \in \mathbb{N}$. A finite sequence of states $r \in S^{+}$ results in a finite trace $t \in \Sigma^{+}$.

In this paper, we work with specifications that are *safety properties*(see, e.g., [20,22]). A safety property can be equivalently expressed as a Mealy machine $\mathcal{M}$ that describes the set of traces that satisfy the property ($\mathcal{M}$ is called the *safety region* of the property). For a safety specification, the *reactive synthesis* problem is to determine the *winning region*, i.e., the maximal subset of its safety region such that for every combination of state and input, there is a transition into said subset. A *strategy* is a subset of the winning region such that in each state, there is exactly one outgoing transition for every input.

2.2 Past-Time Temporal Stream Logic

PastTSL is the past-time variant of TSL [11], a logic that extends LTL with cells that can hold data from a possibly infinite domain. To abstract from concrete data, TSL includes uninterpreted functions and predicates. *Function terms* $\tau_f \in \mathcal{T}_F$ are recursively defined by

$$\tau_f ::= \mathsf{s} \mid f\ \tau_f^1 \dots \tau_f^n$$

where s is either a cell $\mathsf{c} \in \mathbb{C}$ or an input $i \in \mathbb{I}$, and $f \in \Sigma_F$ is a function symbol. *Constants* $\Sigma_F^0 \subseteq \Sigma_F$ are 0-ary function symbols. *Predicate terms* $\tau_p \in \mathcal{T}_P$ are obtained by applying a predicate symbol $p \in \Sigma_P$ with $\Sigma_P \subseteq \Sigma_F$ to a tuple of function terms. PastTSL formulas are built according to the following grammar:

$$\varphi, \psi ::= \neg\varphi \mid \varphi \wedge \psi \mid \ominus\varphi \mid \varphi\, \mathcal{S}\, \psi \mid \tau_p \mid [\![\mathsf{c} \hookleftarrow \tau_f]\!]$$

An *update term* $[\![\mathsf{c} \hookleftarrow \tau_f]\!] \in \mathcal{T}_U$ denotes that cell c is overwritten with τ_f. The temporal operators are called "Yesterday" $\ominus$ and "Since" $\mathcal{S}$. Inputs, function symbols, and predicate symbols a purely syntactic objects. To assign meaning to them, let $\mathcal{V}$ be the set of values with $\mathbb{B} \subseteq \mathcal{V}$. We denote by $\mathcal{I} : \mathbb{I} \to \mathcal{V}$ the evaluation of inputs. An *assignment function* $\langle \cdot \rangle : \Sigma_F \to \mathcal{F}$ assigns function symbols to functions $\mathcal{F} = \bigcup_{n \in \mathbb{N}} \mathcal{V}^n \to \mathcal{V}$.

The type $\mathcal{C} = \mathbb{C} \to \mathcal{T}_F$ describes an update of all cells. For every cell $\mathsf{c} \in \mathbb{C}$, let $init_{\mathsf{c}}$ be its initial value. The evaluation function $\eta_{\langle \cdot \rangle} : \mathcal{C}^{\omega} \times \mathcal{I}^{\omega} \times \mathbb{N} \times \mathcal{T}_F \to \mathcal{V}$ evaluates a function term at point in time i with respect to an *input stream* $\iota \in \mathcal{I}^{\omega}$ and a *computation* $\varsigma \in \mathcal{C}^{\omega}$:

$$\eta_{\langle \cdot \rangle}(\varsigma, \iota, i, \mathsf{s}) := \begin{cases} \iota\ i\ \mathsf{s} & \text{if } \mathsf{s} \in \mathbb{I} \\ init_{\mathsf{s}} & \text{if } \mathsf{s} \in \mathbb{C} \wedge i = 0 \\ \eta_{\langle \cdot \rangle}(\varsigma, \iota, i-1, \varsigma\ (i-1)\ \mathsf{s}) & \text{if } \mathsf{s} \in \mathbb{C} \wedge i > 0 \end{cases}$$

$$\eta_{\langle \cdot \rangle}(\varsigma, \iota, i, f\ \tau_0 \dots \tau_{m-1}) := \langle f \rangle\ \eta_{\langle \cdot \rangle}(\varsigma, \iota, i, \tau_0)\ \dots\ \eta_{\langle \cdot \rangle}(\varsigma, \iota, i, \tau_{m-1})$$

Note that $\iota\ i\ \mathsf{s}$ denotes the value of s at position i according to ι. Likewise, $\varsigma\ i\ \mathsf{s}$ is the function term that ς assigns to s at position i. With the exception of update and predicate terms, the semantics of pastTSL is similar to that of LTL.

$$\varsigma, \iota, t \models_{\langle \cdot \rangle} \neg \varphi \qquad \text{iff} \qquad \varsigma, \iota, t \not\models_{\langle \cdot \rangle} \varphi$$

$$\varsigma, \iota, t \models_{\langle \cdot \rangle} \varphi \wedge \psi \qquad \text{iff} \qquad \varsigma, \iota, t \models_{\langle \cdot \rangle} \varphi \text{ and } \varsigma, \iota, t \models_{\langle \cdot \rangle} \psi$$

$$\varsigma, \iota, t \models_{\langle \cdot \rangle} \ominus \varphi \qquad \text{iff} \qquad t > 0 \wedge \varsigma, \iota, t - 1 \models_{\langle \cdot \rangle} \varphi$$

$$\varsigma, \iota, t \models_{\langle \cdot \rangle} \varphi \mathcal{S} \psi \qquad \text{iff} \qquad \exists\, 0 \le t' \le t.\ \varsigma, \iota, t' \models_{\langle \cdot \rangle} \psi \text{ and}$$
$$\forall t' < k \le t.\ \varsigma, \iota, k \models_{\langle \cdot \rangle} \varphi$$

$$\varsigma, \iota, t \models_{\langle \cdot \rangle} [\![\mathbf{v} \leftharpoonup \tau]\!] \qquad \text{iff} \qquad \varsigma\, t\, \mathbf{v} \equiv \tau$$

$$\varsigma, \iota, t \models_{\langle \cdot \rangle} p\ \tau_0 \dots \tau_m \qquad \text{iff} \qquad \eta_{\langle \cdot \rangle}(\varsigma, \iota, t, p\ \tau_0 \dots \tau_m\ )$$

We use $\equiv$ to syntactically compare two terms. We derive three additional operators: $\ominus\varphi := \neg \ominus \neg\varphi$, $\diamondsuit\varphi := true\ \mathcal{S}\ \varphi$, and $\boxminus\varphi := \neg \diamondsuit \neg\varphi$. The difference between $\ominus$ and "Weak Yesterday" $\ominus$ is that $\ominus$ evaluates to *false* in the first step and $\ominus$ to *true*. We use pastTSL formulas to describe safety properties. Therefore, we define that computation ς and an input stream ι satisfy a pastTSL formula φ, written $\varsigma, \iota \models_{\langle \cdot \rangle} \varphi$, if $\forall i \in \mathbb{N}.\, \varsigma, \iota, i \models_{\langle \cdot \rangle} \psi$.

The realizability problem of a pastTSL formula ψ asks whether there exists a strategy that reacts to predicate evaluations with cell updates according to ψ. Formally, a strategy is a function $\sigma : (2^{\mathcal{T}_P})^+ \to \mathcal{C}$. For $\iota \in \mathcal{I}^\omega$, we write $\sigma(\iota)$ for the computation obtained from σ:

$$\sigma(\iota)(i) = \sigma(\{\tau_p \in \mathcal{T}_P \mid \eta_{\langle \cdot \rangle}(\sigma(\iota), \iota, 0, \tau_p)\} \dots \{\tau_p \in \mathcal{T}_P \mid \eta_{\langle \cdot \rangle}(\sigma(\iota), \iota, i, \tau_p)\})$$

Note that in order to define $\sigma(\iota)(i)$, the definition uses $\sigma(\iota)$. This is well-defined since the evaluation function $\eta_{\langle \cdot \rangle}(\varsigma, \iota, i, \tau)$ only uses $\varsigma\, 0 \dots \varsigma\,(i-1)$.

Definition 1 ([11]). *A pastTSL formula ψ is* realizable *if, and only if, there exists a strategy $\sigma : (2^{\mathcal{T}_P})^+ \to \mathcal{C}$ such that for every input stream $\iota \in \mathcal{I}^\omega$ and every assignment function $\langle \cdot \rangle : \Sigma_F \to \mathcal{F}$ it holds that $\sigma(\iota), \iota \models_{\langle \cdot \rangle} \psi$.*

3 Parameterized TSL for Smart Contract Specifications

In this section, we introduce parameterized pastTSL and show how the past-time fragment of the logic can be used for specifying smart contract state machines.

3.1 Parameterized TSL

Parameterized TSL extends TSL with universally quantified parameters. Let P be a set of parameters and $\mathbb{C}_P$ a set of parameterized cells, where each cell is of the form $c(p_1, \dots, p_m)$ with $p_1, \dots, p_m \in P$. A parameterized TSL formula is a formula $\forall p_1, \dots, \forall p_n.\ \psi$, where ψ is a TSL formula with cells from $\mathbb{C}_P$ and which may use parameters as base terms in function and predicate terms. We require that the formula is closed, i.e., every parameter occurring in ψ is bound in the quantifier prefix.

Parameterized TSL formulas are evaluated with respect to a domain $\mathbb{P}$ for the parameters. We use a function $\mu : P \to \mathbb{P}$ to instantiate parameters. Given a parameterized TSL formula $\forall p_1, \ldots, \forall p_n. \psi$, $\psi[\mu]$ is the formula obtained by replacing all parameters according to μ. To simplify our constructions, we want $\psi[\mu]$ to be a TSL formula. Therefore, we assume that $\mathbb{P}$ is a subset of the set of constants and that $c(\mu(p_1), \ldots, \mu(p_m)) \in \mathbb{C}$, i.e., the instantiation of a parameterized cell refers to a normal, non-parameterized cell. Given a computation ς and an input stream ι, we define $\varsigma, \iota \models \forall p_1, \ldots, \forall p_n. \psi$ iff $\forall \mu : P \to \mathbb{P}. \varsigma, \iota \models \psi[\mu]$.

3.2   Example: ERC20 Contract

We illustrate how parameterized pastTSL can be used to specify the state machine logic of smart contract with an ERC20 token system. An ERC20 token system provides a platform to transfer tokens between different accounts. We follow the Open Zeppelin documentation [32]. The special feature of the contract is the possibility to transfer not only tokens from one's own account but, after approval, also from a different account. The core contract consists of methods `transfer`, `transferFrom`, and `approve`. We do not model getters like `totalSupply` or `balanceOf` as they are not relevant for the temporal behavior of the contract. The Open Zeppelin ERC20 contract describes various extensions to the core contract, one of which is the ability to pause transfers. We distinguish between pausing transfers globally (**pause**) and from one's own account (**pause(m)**).

Our specifications describe the temporal control flow of the contract's method calls and the data flow of its fields. We distinguish between *requirements, obligations,* and *assumptions*. Requirements enforce the right order of method calls with correct arguments. Obligations describe the data flow in the fields of the contract. Assumptions restrict the space of possible predicate evaluations. For this example, we do not need any assumptions. A typical assumption in other specifications would be that x > y and y > x cannot hold at the same time.

To emphasize that all past-time formulas are required to hold globally, we add a $\square$ operator to formulas. We use two parameters m and n, where m always refers to the address from which tokens are subtracted and parameter n, whenever different from m, to the address that initiates the transfer. We start with the requirements. First, any transfer from m must be backed by sufficient funds.

$$\square(\texttt{transfer(m)} \lor \texttt{transferFrom(m,n)} \; \to \; \texttt{suffFunds(m, arg@amount)})$$

Second, no method call can happen after **pause** until **unpause** is called:

$$\square(\texttt{transferFrom(m,n)} \lor \texttt{transfer(m)} \lor \texttt{approve(m,n)} \lor \texttt{localPause(m)} \lor$$
$$\texttt{localUnpause(m)} \; \to \; (\neg\texttt{pause}\; S\; \texttt{unpause}) \lor \boxminus \neg\texttt{pause})$$

In contrast, `localPause(m)` only stops method calls from m's account:

$$\square(\texttt{transferFrom(m,n)} \lor \texttt{transfer(m)} \lor \texttt{approve(m,n)}$$
$$\to \; ((\neg\texttt{localPause(m)})\; S\; \texttt{localUnpause(m)}) \lor \boxminus \neg\texttt{localPause(m)})$$

Finally, **pause** and **unpause** can only be called by the owner of the contract. Additionally, they cannot be called twice without the respective other in between and **unpause** cannot be called if **pause** has not been called at least once.

$\Box(\text{unpause} \rightarrow \text{msg.sender} = \text{owner}() \land \ominus(\neg \text{unpause } \mathcal{S} \text{ pause}))$

$\Box(\text{pause} \rightarrow \text{msg.sender} = \text{owner}() \land \ominus(\neg \text{pause } \mathcal{S} \text{ unpause}) \lor \ominus \boxminus \neg \text{pause})$

mgs.sender is an input, whereas owner() is a constant. For the obligations, we need to make sure that the approved field is updated correctly. We use TSL's cell mechanism to model fields and use parameterized cells for mappings.

$\Box(\text{approve}(\text{m,n}) \rightarrow [\![\text{approved}(\text{m,n}) \leftarrowtail \text{arg@amount}]\!])$

$\Box(\text{transferFrom}(\text{m,n}) \rightarrow [\![\text{approved}(\text{m,n}) \leftarrowtail \text{approved}(\text{m,n}) - \text{arg@amount}]\!])$

$\Box(\neg(\text{transferFrom}(\text{m}) \lor \text{approve}(\text{m,n})) \rightarrow [\![\text{approved}(\text{m,n}) \leftarrowtail \text{approved}(\text{m,n})]\!])$

Transitions that do not change the content of a cell are indicated by self-updates like $[\![\text{approved}(\text{m,n}) \leftarrowtail \text{approved}(\text{m,n})]\!]$.

4   Synthesis Approach

The synthesis goal of this paper is to construct a state machine that satisfies parameterized pastTSL specifications like the one given in the last section.

4.1   Problem Statement

Our specifications are split into assumptions φ_A, requirements φ_R, and obligations φ_O, all of which are parameterized pastTSL formulas. Each of them can be given as invariant φ^{inv} or as initial formula φ^{init}. For synthesis, we compose them to the following formula, which, according to the definition of (parameterized) pastTSL, is required to hold globally.

$$\varphi := \forall \mathtt{p}_1, \dots, \mathtt{p}_m.$$
$$(\ominus false \rightarrow \varphi_A^{init} \land \varphi_R^{init}) \land (\boxminus(\varphi_A^{inv} \land \varphi_R^{inv})) \rightarrow (\ominus false \rightarrow \varphi_O^{init}) \land \varphi_O^{inv}$$

Here, $\mathtt{p}_1, \dots, \mathtt{p}_m$ are the parameters occurring in the inner formulas φ_A^{init}, φ_R^{init}, φ_O^{init}, φ_A^{inv}, φ_R^{inv}, and φ_O^{inv}. We use $\ominus false$ to refer to the first position of a trace.

It might seem counter-intuitive that we include requirements on the left side of the implication. The reason is that requirements describe a monitor on the method calls, which, from a synthesis perspective, constitute system inputs. Thus, if we conjuncted requirements with obligations, the specification would be unrealizable. Instead, we leverage the fact that all specifications describe safety properties. Thus, state machines satisfying φ have a shape as depicted in Fig. 1.

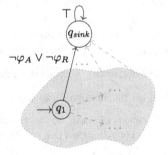

Fig. 1. Sketch of the system synthesized from φ. The dotted blue area implements the contract.

Whenever an assumption or a requirement is violated, the machine enters an accepting sink state. To obtain the desired result, we reject any method call

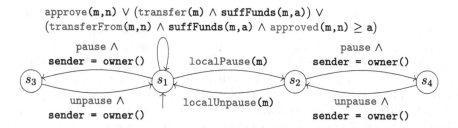

Fig. 2. System $\mathcal{W}$ for the ERC20 contract. Irrelevant predicates and all cell updates are omitted for readability. We also write a instead of **arg@amount**.

for which the system moves to the sink state. Like this, the remaining system enforces the requirements on method calls and also satisfies the obligations. For the rest of the paper, we depict state machines synthesized from φ without the sink state.

On Safety Properties. We restrict ourselves to safety properties for three reasons. First of all, as we consider the synthesis problem, our requirements can only describe a monitor on the method calls. Liveness properties are known not to be monitorable. For future work, one could consider model-checking the synthesized state machine with regard to liveness properties like "eventually, method X is *callable*". Second, the restriction to safety automata enables the splitting algorithm described in Sect. 6, which is essential for our approach in order to efficiently implement the state machine in Solidity. Lastly, synthesis from safety properties is less complex than full LTL synthesis (c.f. Section 7), which enables us to synthesize non-trivial state machines within seconds.

4.2 High-Level Description of the Approach

Challenges. We need to address two major challenges. First, as parameters range over an infinite domain $\mathbb{P}$, parameterized pastTSL formulas describe (in general) *infinite-state systems.* Second, even if we managed to synthesize some representation of the infinite-state system, we still need to translate it to Solidity code. In Solidity, every computation costs gas. Therefore, we need to find a compact representation of the system that minimizes the number of computation steps needed to update the system after a method call.

Approach in a Nutshell. We address these challenges in two steps. First, we interpret the specification as being unquantified, i.e., we remove all quantifiers and tread the parameters as normal constants (e.g., in case of **suffFunds(m, arg@amount)**) or as part of the cells' name (e.g., in case of **approved(m,n)**). Like that, we obtain a plain pastTSL formula that describes the finite-state system representing the correct control flow for every parameter instantiation. We synthesize the winning region from that formula, which we call $\mathcal{W}$. For the running ERC20 example, $\mathcal{W}$ can be found in Fig. 2.

Of course, the contract can be in different states of $\mathcal{W}$ depending on the parameter instantiation. In theory, we would therefore like to keep the necessary number of copies of $\mathcal{W}$. For example, if `approve(m=1,n=2)` is called, we would execute the corresponding transition in system $\mathcal{W}_{(m=1,n=2)}$. The problem with this naive approach is that calling a method parameterized with only a subset of the parameters would lead to updates of several systems. For example, if `localPause(m=1)` is called, this would have to be recorded in all $\mathcal{W}_{(m=1,n=v)}$ for any value v of `n` observed so far. Updating all these state machines after each method call would lead to a quick explosion of the gas consumption in Solidity. Instead, addressing the second challenge, we split $\mathcal{W}$ into a hierarchical structure of state machines, one for each subset of parameters. As a result, we only have to update a single state machine per method call and still maintain the correct state of each instance (we describe this approach in more detail in Sect. 6.1). To summarize, we proceed as follows.

1. Interpret the parameterized pastTSL formula φ as a pastTSL formula ψ and synthesize the winning region $\mathcal{W}$ from it.
2. Split $\mathcal{W}$ into a hierarchical structure $\mathcal{W}_1, \ldots, \mathcal{W}_n$ and show how these systems can be interpreted as an infinite-state machine $\mathcal{M}$ satisfying φ.
3. Generate Solidity code that implements transitions according to $\mathcal{W}_1, \ldots, \mathcal{W}_n$.

In the following sections, we discuss each of these steps in detail.

5   PastTSL Synthesis

Let φ be a parameterized pastTSL formula as described in Sect. 4.1. We first translate φ to pastTSL. This is easy: just remove all quantifiers and interpret parameters as constants (i.e., $P \subseteq \Sigma_F^0$) and parameterized cells as normal cells (i.e., $\mathbb{C}_P \subseteq \mathbb{C}$).

Unfortunately, even though past-time fragments usually simplify logical problems, we establish that the realizability problem of pastTSL is undecidable. We obtain this result by a reduction from the universal halting problem of lossy counter machines [29].

An *n-counter machine (nCM)* consists of a finite set of instructions $l_1, \ldots, l_m$, which modify n counters $c_1, \ldots, c_n$. Each instruction l_i is of one of the following forms, where $1 \le x \le n$ and $1 \le j, k \le m$.

- l_i: $c_x := c_x + 1$; goto l_j
- l_i: if $c_x = 0$ then goto l_j else $c_x := c_x - 1$; goto l_k
- l_i: halt

A configuration of a nCM is a tuple $(l_i, v_1, \ldots, v_n)$, where l_i is the next instruction to be executed, and $v_1, \ldots, v_n$ denote the values of the counters. Compared to non-lossy nCMs, the counters of a lossy nCM may spontaneously decrease. We employ a version of lossiness where a counter can become zero if it is tested for zero (see [29] for details). A lossy nCM halts from an initial configuration if it eventually reaches a state with the halting instruction.

Theorem 1. *The pastTSL realizability problem is undecidable.*

Proof. We reduce from the universal halting problem of lossy nCMs, which is undecidable [29]. We spell out the main ideas. Our formulas consist of one constant $z()$, one function f, and one predicate p. There are no inputs. Applying an idea from [23], we use two cells for every counter c_x: c_x^{inc} to count increments and c_x^{dec} to count decrements. Applying f to c_x^{inc} increments the counter, applying f to c_x^{dec} decrements it. If the number of increments and decrements is equal, the counter is zero. In TSL, we use the formula $\psi_x^0 := p(c_x^{inc}) \leftrightarrow p(c_x^{dec})$ to test if a counter is zero. Note that if the counter really is zero, then the test for zero *must* evaluate to *true* by the TSL semantics. For all other cases, it *may* evaluate to *true*. If the equivalence evaluates to *true* even though the counter is non-zero, we interpret it as a spontaneous reset. Initially, the value of the counters need to be arbitrary. We reflect this by making no assumptions on the first step, thereby allowing the strategy to set the counter cells to any valid function term $f^*(z())$. We use n cells $l_1, \ldots, l_n$ for encoding the instructions. Globally, all instruction cells but the one indicating the next instruction, indicated by $[\![l_i \hookleftarrow f(l_i)]\!]$, need to self-update. We spell out the encoding of an instruction of the second type.

$$\Box(\ominus[\![l_i \hookleftarrow f(l_i)]\!] \to (\psi_x^0 \to [\![l_j \hookleftarrow f(l_j)]\!] \wedge [\![c_x^{inc} \hookleftarrow z()]\!] \wedge [\![c_x^{dec} \hookleftarrow z()]\!])$$
$$\wedge (\neg\psi_x^0 \to [\![l_k \hookleftarrow f(l_k)]\!] \wedge [\![c_x^{inc} \hookleftarrow c_x^{inc}]\!] \wedge [\![c_x^{dec} \hookleftarrow f(c_x^{dec})]\!]))$$

The formula tests if the instruction to be executed is l_i. If so, we test the counter c_x for zero and set the corresponding cell to $z()$ if that is the case. Furthermore, the correct next instruction is updated by applying f. Finally, we encode that we never reach a halting state: $\Box \neg[\![l_{halt} \hookleftarrow f(l_{halt})]\!]$. The resulting pastTSL formula is realizable if, and only if, there is an initial state such that the machine never halts. Thus, undecidability of the pastTSL realizability problem follows. $\qed$

5.1 PastTSL Synthesis via PastLTL Approximation

As pastTSL realizability is undecidable, we have to approximate the synthesis problem. To do so, we employ a reduction proposed in [11], which approximates TSL synthesis in LTL, for which realizability is decidable. The reduction replaces all predicate terms and update terms of a TSL formula ψ with unique atomic propositions, e.g., a_{p_x} for $p(\mathbf{x})$ and $a_{x\_to\_f\_x}$ for $[\![\mathbf{x} \hookleftarrow f(\mathbf{x})]\!]$. Additionally, the reduction adds a formula that ensures that every cell is updated with exactly one function term in each step. Given a pastTSL formula ψ, the reduction produces an LTL approximation ψ_{LTL} that also falls into the past-time fragment. The reduction is sound but not complete [11], i.e., ψ might be realizable even if ψ_{LTL} is not. For the smart contract specifications we produced for our evaluation, however, we never encountered spurious unrealizability.

Let AP be the set of atomic propositions of ψ_{LTL}. From every trace t over AP, we can directly generate a computation $comp(t) \in \mathcal{C}^\omega$ as follows:

$$comp(t)(i)(\mathbf{c}) = \tau_f \quad \text{if } a_{\mathbf{c}\_to\_\tau_f} \in t(i)$$

For the other direction, given a computation ς, an input stream ι, and an assignment function $\langle \cdot \rangle$, we write $LTL(\iota, \varsigma, \langle \cdot \rangle)$ for the corresponding trace over AP.

$$LTL(\iota, \varsigma, \langle \cdot \rangle)(i) = \{\{a_{\tau_p} \mid \eta_{\langle \cdot \rangle}(\varsigma, \iota, i, \tau_p)\}\} \cup \{a_{c\_to\_\tau_f} \mid \varsigma(i)(c) = \tau_f\}$$

The following proposition follows from the soundness of the approximation.

Proposition 1. *For every assignment function $\langle \cdot \rangle$, input stream ι, and computation ς, $LTL(\iota, \varsigma, \langle \cdot \rangle) \models \psi_{LTL}$ iff $\varsigma, \iota \models_{\langle \cdot \rangle} \psi$.*

Parameterized Atomic Propositions. In our case, the pastTSL formula ψ is obtained from a parameterized pastTSL formula φ. Thus, the atomic propositions of ψ_{LTL} contain parameters, e.g., $a_{transferFrom\_m\_n}$. To enable correctness reasoning in the next section, we lift the instantiation of parameters to the level of atomic propositions and LTL formulas.

For $a \in AP$, we write $a(p_1, \ldots, p_m)$ if a contains parameters $p_1, \ldots, p_m$. We usually denote the sequence $p_1, \ldots, p_m$ with some P_i, for which we also use set notation. We assume that every proposition occurs with only one sequence of parameters, i.e., there are no $a(P_i), a(P_j) \in AP$ with $P_i \neq P_j$.

Given $\mu : P \to \mathbb{P}$, $P_i[\mu]$ denotes $(\mu(p_1), \ldots, \mu(p_m))$ and $a[\mu]$ denotes $a(P_i[\mu])$. For example, for $a_{transferFrom\_m\_n}[m \mapsto 1, n \mapsto 2]$, we obtain $a_{transferFrom\_1\_2}$. We also write $\psi_{LTL}[\mu]$ for an LTL formula where every atomic proposition is instantiated according to μ. We define $AP_\mathbb{P} = \{a[\mu] \mid a \in AP, \mu : P \to \mathbb{P}\}$. As there are no two $a(P_i), a(P_j) \in AP$ with $P_i \neq P_j$, for any $\alpha \in AP_\mathbb{P}$, there is exactly one a such that $a[\mu] = \alpha$ for some μ.

6   Splitting Algorithm

In the last section, we discussed that we need to approximate the parameterized pastTSL formula φ to an LTL formula ψ_{LTL} to synthesize $\mathcal{W}$. Note that $\mathcal{W}$ alone does not implement a strategy for φ as each parameter instance might be in a different state of $\mathcal{W}$ (c.f. Section 4.2). In this section, we discuss how to split up $\mathcal{W}$ to enable an efficient implementation in Solidity while at the same time making sure that the generated traces realize the original formula φ.

6.1   Idea of the Algorithm

The idea of the algorithm is to split $\mathcal{W}$ into multiple subsystems $\mathcal{W}_1, \ldots, \mathcal{W}_n$ such that each $\mathcal{W}_i$ contains the transitions for method calls with parameters P_i. For the ERC20 example, we produce the three systems $\mathcal{W}_\emptyset$, $\mathcal{W}_{\{m\}}$, and $\mathcal{W}_{\{m,n\}}$ depicted in Fig. 3. For each of these systems, at runtime, we create a copy for every instantiation of their parameters.

If a method with parameters P_i is called and $\mathcal{W}_i$ is in state q, then the transition from q labeled with that method call is the candidate transition to be executed. This means that compared to the naive solution (c.f. Section 4.2) a

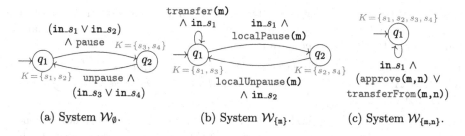

Fig. 3. State machines for all non-empty parameter sets. For readability, we omit cell updates and all predicates apart from method calls.

call to localPause(m=1) only has to be recorded in a single transition system (namely $\mathcal{W}_{\{m=1\}}$).

Crucially, however, we now need to ensure that we only produce traces of $\mathcal{W}$. For example, if localPause(m=1) is called, we move from state q_1 to q_2 in system $\mathcal{W}_{\{m=1\}}$. This corresponds to a transition from s_1 to s_2 in $\mathcal{W}$. Now, for instances with m=1, calls to all methods except localUnpause(m=1) and pause need to be rejected (according to $\mathcal{W}$), even though these would technically be possible in systems $\mathcal{W}_{\{m=1,n=v\}}$ (for any v). To do so, we synchronize the systems with the help of transition guards in_s_i and additional state labels K.

A guard in_s_i indicates that the transition can only be taken in state s_i of $\mathcal{W}$. To check if this requirement is satisfied, the systems share their knowledge about the state $\mathcal{W}$ would currently be in. A knowledge label $K = \{s_1, s_2\}$ in state q of $\mathcal{W}_i$ means that $\mathcal{W}$ could be in state s_1 or state s_2 if $\mathcal{W}_i$ is in state q. Each system is a projection to some transitions of $\mathcal{W}$ and therefore has different knowledge labels.

The systems share their knowledge in order to determine which state $\mathcal{W}$ would be in for a trace of one parameter instantiation. For each method call, the systems must come to a conclusion if that call would be allowed in the current state of $\mathcal{W}$. However, $\mathcal{W}_i$ may only use the knowledge of systems $\mathcal{W}_j$ with $P_j \subseteq P_i$ as these are the parameters for which there is currently a value available. To guarantee that an unambiguous conclusion is always possible to achieve, we formulate two simple requirements and an independence check.

6.2   Construction

Let ψ_{LTL} be given. The formula is the approximation of a pastTSL formula and therefore ranges over $AP = I \cup O$, where I are the atomic propositions obtained from predicate terms and O are the ones obtained from update terms. For $A \subseteq AP$, we write $A_{|O}$ instead of $A \cap O$. We denote the set of atomic propositions that correspond to some method call $\mathtt{f}(P_i)$ by $I_{call} \subseteq I$ and the set of output propositions that denote self-updates by $O_{self} \subseteq O$.

Let $\mathcal{W} = (S_{\mathcal{W}}, s_{\mathcal{W}}^0, \delta_{\mathcal{W}})$ be the finite-state machine over AP that constitutes the winning region of ψ_{LTL}. $\delta_{\mathcal{W}}$ its transition relation. We state two requirements on $\mathcal{W}$, which are needed to enable a sound splitting of $\mathcal{W}$ and can be checked easily by inspecting all its transitions. First, we require that calls to a method parameterized with parameter sequence P_i only result in cell updates parameterized with the same parameter sequence.

Requirement 1 (Local Updates). *For every transition $(s, A, s') \in \delta_W$, if $o(P_i) \in A_{|O}$ and $o(P_i) \notin O_{self}$, then there is a method call proposition $f(P_i) \in A$.*

Second, whether a method can be called at a given state must not depend on predicates with parameters that are not included in the current method call.

Requirement 2 (Independence of Irrelevant Predicates). *For every $(s, A, s') \in \delta_W$, if $f(P_i) \in A$, then for every $a(P_j) \in I$ with $P_j \not\subseteq P_i$ and $a(P_j) \notin I_{call}$, there is a transition (s, A', s') with $a(P_j) \in A$ iff $a(P_j) \notin A'$ and $A_{|O} = A'_{|O}$.*

The above requirement is needed to unify software and state machine reasoning. In state machines, the value of all propositions needs to be known to determine the right transition. In software, however, if `localPause(m)` is called, the value of n is undefined and we cannot evaluate predicates depending on n.

If W satisfies the above requirements, we construct $W_1, \ldots, W_n$ for each parameter subset P_i. Each W_i projects W to the method calls with parameters P_i. The algorithm to construct the projections combines several standard automata-theoretic concepts:

1. Introduce a new guard proposition in_s for every state $s \in S_W$ of W. For every transition $(s, A, s') \in \delta_W$, replace A with $A \cup \{in\_s\}$.
2. Label all transitions $(s, A, s') \in \delta_W$ for which there is no $f(P_i) \in A$ with ϵ. The result is a nondeterministic safety automaton with ϵ-edges.
3. W_i is obtained by determinizing the safety automaton using the standard subset construction. This removes all ϵ transitions. During the construction, we label each state with the subset of S_W it represents, these are the knowledge labels K.

We use S_i for the states of W_i, δ_i for its transition relation, and $K_i : S_i \to 2^{S_W}$ for the knowledge labels. Note that every transition in W is labeled with exactly one method call proposition and is therefore present in exactly one W_i. The following two propositions follow from the correctness of the subset construction for the determinization of finite automata. The first proposition states that the outgoing transitions of a state $s_i \in W_i$ are exactly the outgoing transitions of all states $s \in K_i(s_i)$.

Proposition 2. *For every state $s_i \in S_i$, if $s \in K_i(s_i)$, then for all $s' \in S$ and $A \subseteq AP$, $(s, A, s') \in \delta_W$ iff $(s_i, A \cup \{in\_s\}, s'_i) \in \delta_i$ for some $s'_i \in S_i$.*

The second one states that the knowledge labels in W_i are consistent with the transitions of W.

Proposition 3. *Let $(s, A, s') \in \delta_W$ with $f(P_i) \in A$. Then, for every state $s_i \in S_i$ with $s \in K_i(s_i)$, and every transition $(s_i, A \cup \{in\_s\}, s'_i) \in \delta_i$, it holds that $s' \in K_i(s'_i)$. Furthermore, for every s_j of W_j with $i \neq j$, if $s \in K_j(s_j)$, then $s' \in K_j(s_j)$.*

6.3   Check for Independence

We now define the check if transitions in $\mathcal{W}_i$ can be taken independently of the current state of all $\mathcal{W}_j$ with $P_j \not\subseteq P_i$. If the check is positive, we can implement the system efficiently in Solidity: when a method $f(P_i)$ is called, we only need to update the single system $\mathcal{W}_i$ and whether the transition can be taken only depends on the available parameters.

Let s_i and s_i' be states in $\mathcal{W}_i$ and $A \subseteq AP$. Let $G_{(s_i,A,s_i')} = \{s \mid (s_i, A \cup \{\text{in\_s}\}, s_i') \in \delta_i\}$ be the set of all guard propositions that occur on transitions from s_i to s_i' with A. Let $P_{j_1}, \ldots P_{j_l}$ be the maximum set of parameter subsets such that $P_{j_k} \subseteq P_i$ for $1 \leq k \leq l$. A transition (s_i, A, s_i') is *independent* if for all states $s_{j_1}, \ldots, s_{j_l}$ with $s_{j_k} \in S_{j_k}$ either

(i) $K_i(s_i) \cap \bigcap_{1 \leq k \leq l} K_{j_k}(s_{j_k}) \subseteq G_{(s_i,A,s_i')}$ or
(ii) $(K_i(s_i) \cap \bigcap_{1 \leq k \leq l} K_{j_k}(s_{j_k})) \cap G_{(s_i,A,s_i')} = \emptyset$.

The check combines the knowledge of $\mathcal{W}_i$ in state s_i with the knowledge of each combination of states from $\mathcal{W}_{j_1}, \ldots, \mathcal{W}_{j_l}$. For each potential combination, it must be possible to determine whether transition (s_i, A, s_i') can be taken. If the first condition is satisfied, then the combined knowledge leads to the definite conclusion that $\mathcal{W}$ is currently in a state where an A-transition can be taken. If the second condition is satisfied, it definitely cannot be taken. If none of the two is satisfied, then the combined knowledge of P_i and all P_{j_k} is insufficient to reach a definite answer.

Note that some state combinations $s_i, s_{j_1}, \ldots, s_{j_l}$ might be impossible to reach. But then, we have that $K_i(s_i) \cap \bigcap_{1 \leq k \leq l} K_{j_k}(s_{j_k}) = \emptyset$ and the second condition is satisfied. The check is successful if all transitions (s_i, A, s_i') in all δ_i are independent.

6.4   Interpretation as Infinite-State Machine

The goal of this section is to construct a state machine $\mathcal{M}$ from $\mathcal{W}_1, \ldots \mathcal{W}_n$ such that the original parameterized pastTSL formula φ is satisfied. To simplify the presentation, we define $\mathcal{M}$ as a state machine over $AP_{\mathbb{P}}$. Due to the direct correspondence of atomic propositions in $AP_{\mathbb{P}}$ to predicate and update terms $T_P \cup T_U$, a state machine for φ can easily be obtained from that. In the following, we assume that $\mathcal{W}$ satisfies Requirements 1 and 2 and that $\mathcal{W}_1, \ldots, \mathcal{W}_n$ pass the check for independence. We construct $\mathcal{M}$ as follows.

A state in $\mathcal{M}$ is a collection of $n = |2^P|$ functions $f_1, \ldots, f_n$, where $f_i : \mathbb{P}^m \to S_i$ if $P_i = (p_{i_1}, \ldots, p_{i_m})$. Each f_i indicates in which state of $\mathcal{W}_i$ instance μ currently is. The initial state is the collection of functions that all map to the initial states of their respective $\mathcal{W}_i$. For every state $s = (f_1, \ldots, f_n)$ of $\mathcal{M}$, every $P_i \subseteq P$, and every instance μ, we add a transition where $P_i[\mu]$ takes a step and all other instances stay idle. Let $f_i(P_i[\mu]) = s_i$, $s_i' \in S_i$, $A \subseteq AP$, and $G_{(s_i,A,s_i')} = \{s \mid (s_i, A \cup \{\text{in\_s}\}, s_i') \in \delta_i\}$. Let $P_{j_1}, \ldots P_{j_l}$ be all subsets of P_i. If

$K_i(s_i) \cap \bigcap_{1 \leq k \leq l} K_{j_k}(f_{j_k}(P_{j_k}[\mu])) \subseteq G_{(s_i, A, s'_i)}$, we add the transition (s, A', s') to $\mathcal{M}$, where A' and s' are defined as follows.

$$A' = \{a[\mu] \mid a \in A\} \cup \{o[\mu'] \mid o \in O_{self}, o[\mu'] \neq o[\mu]\}$$
$$s' = (f_1, \ldots, f_i[P_i[\mu] \mapsto s'_i], \ldots, f_n)$$

The label A' sets all propositions of instance μ as in A and sets all other input propositions to *false*. Of all other outputs propositions, it only sets those denoting self-updates to *true*.

6.5   Correctness

Finally, we argue that $\mathcal{M}$ as defined above satisfies the original specification φ for all instantiations of its parameters.

Trace Projection. To obtain a compact state machine, our specifications require that in each step, exactly one method is called. Like that, the resulting specification describes the control flow projected on each instance. To argue that $\mathcal{M}$ satisfies φ, we therefore need to project its traces to the steps relevant for an instance μ. These are the steps that either include a method call to μ or a non-self-update of one of μ's cells.

For $A \subseteq AP_{\mathbb{P}}$, we define A_μ as $\{\alpha \in A \mid \exists a \in AP. \alpha = a[\mu]\}$. Let $traces(\mathcal{M})$ be the set of infinite traces produced by $\mathcal{M}$. Given $t \in traces(\mathcal{M})$, let $t' = (t[0])_\mu (t[1])_\mu \ldots$. Now, we define t_μ to be the trace obtained from t' by deleting all positions i such that $(t[i]_\mu)_{|O} \subseteq O_{self}$ and $\neg \exists f(P_i) \in I_{call}. f(P_i)[\mu] \in t'[i]$. Note that t_μ might be a finite trace even if t is infinite. Since t_μ only deletes steps from t that do not change the value of the cells, t_μ still constitutes a sound computation regarding the TSL semantics. We define $traces_\mu(\mathcal{M}) = \{t_\mu \mid t \in traces(\mathcal{M})\}$.

Correctness Proof. Most of the work is done in the following lemma. We define $\mathcal{W}_\mu$ as the state machine that replaces the transition labels of $\mathcal{W}$ with their instantiations according to μ, i.e., if $(s, A, s') \in \mathcal{W}$, then $(s, A[\mu], s') \in \mathcal{W}_\mu$. Not every infinite run of $\mathcal{M}$ corresponds to an infinite run in $\mathcal{W}_\mu$ for every μ. However, we show that if the run has infinitely many μ-transitions, then it can be mapped to an infinite trace in $\mathcal{W}_\mu$. The proof of the lemma can be found in the full version of this paper [9].

Lemma 1. *For every instance μ, $traces_\mu(\mathcal{M}) = traces(\mathcal{W}_\mu)$.*

From the above lemma we directly obtain the desired correctness result.

Theorem 2. *Let $\varphi = \forall p_1, \ldots p_m. \psi$ be a parameterized pastTSL formula and ψ_{LTL} its LTL approximation. If $\mathcal{W}$ is the winning region of ψ_{LTL}, $\mathcal{W}$ satisfies Requirements 1 and 2, and can be split into $\mathcal{W}_1, \ldots, \mathcal{W}_n$ such that the check for independence is successful, then for every μ, $\mathcal{M}$ defines a strategy for $\varphi[\mu]$.*

Proof. Let $\mu : P \to \mathbb{P}$ be an instantiation of the parameters $p_1, \ldots p_m$, $\iota \in \mathcal{I}^\omega$ be an input stream, and $\langle \cdot \rangle$ be an assignment function. First, for any trace $t \in traces_\mu(\mathcal{M})$ with $LTL(\iota, comp(t), \langle \cdot \rangle) = t$ (see Sect. 5.1 for the definition), we have that $t \in traces(\mathcal{W}_\mu)$ because of Lemma 1. As all traces of $\mathcal{W}$ satisfy ψ_{LTL}, $t \models \psi_{\mathrm{LTL}}[\mu]$ (since μ is only a renaming of atomic propositions on the LTL-level). By Proposition 1, we obtain $\iota, comp(t) \models \psi[\mu]$. Second, as $\mathcal{W}$ implements the set of all strategies satisfying ψ_{LTL}, with the same reasoning, there is at least one t in $\mathcal{M}$ with $LTL(\iota, comp(t), \langle \cdot \rangle) = t$.

6.6 Extension to Existential Quantifiers

Currently, our approach cannot handle existential quantifiers. In the example of the ERC20 contract, this forbids us to use a field funds(m) to store the balance of all users of the contract. If we were to try, we could use an additional parameter r for the recipient of the tokens and state the following.

$$\forall m, n, r. \,\Box(\texttt{transferFrom(m,n,r)} \lor \texttt{transfer(m,r)}$$
$$\to [\![\texttt{funds(m)} \leftarrowtail \texttt{funds(m)} - \texttt{arg@amount}]\!]$$
$$\land [\![\texttt{funds(r)} \leftarrowtail \texttt{funds(r)} + \texttt{arg@amount}]\!])$$

However, for completeness, we would have to specify that the funds field does not spuriously increase, which would require existential quantifiers.

$$\forall r. \,\Box([\![\texttt{funds(r)} \leftarrowtail \texttt{funds(r)} + \texttt{arg@amount}]\!]$$
$$\to \exists m. \,\exists n. \,\texttt{transferFrom(m,n,r)} \lor \texttt{transfer(m,r)})$$

A similar limitation stems from Requirement 1, which requires that a field parameterized with set P_i can only be updated by a method that is also parameterized with P_i. As for existential quantifiers, we would otherwise not be able to distinguish spurious updates from intended updates of cells. While it might be challenging to extend the approach with arbitrary existential quantification, it should be possible for future work to include existential quantification that prevents spurious updates. One could, for example, define some sort of "lazy synthesis", which only does a non-self-update when necessary.

7 Implementation and Evaluation

7.1 Implementation

We implemented our approach in a toolchain consisting of several steps. First, we translate the pastTSL specification into a pastLTL formula using TSLtools [19], which we adapted to handle past-time operators. We then synthesize a state machine using BDD-based symbolic synthesis. To make our lives easier, we implemented a simple analysis to detect free choices and deadlocks, which both indicate potential specification errors. If the specification contains parameters, we split the resulting state machine as described in Sect. 6. Lastly, the state machines are translated to Solidity code. The toolchain is implemented in our tool SCSYNT consisting of approximately 3000 lines of Python code (excluding TSLtools). From a user perspective, we obtain the workflow depicted in Fig. 4.

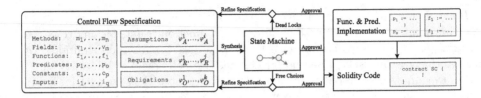

Fig. 4. Workflow of our smart contract control flow synthesis.

Synthesis from PastLTL. The first part of our toolchain implements a symbolic synthesis algorithm for pastLTL. As such, it can also be employed outside the context of smart contract synthesis. We are not aware of any other tool that implements pastLTL synthesis. We first build the safety automaton of the specification using a representation as BDDs. For pastLTL, a symbolic approach is especially efficient due to the long-known fact that for evaluating a pastLTL formula at time point i, it is sufficient to know the value of all subformulas at point $i - 1$ [13]. Afterwards, we symbolically extract the winning region from the safety region with a classic fixpoint attractor construction. Finally, we minimize the resulting state machine using an explicit implementation of Hopcroft's minimization algorithm [14].

State Machine Analysis. We analyze the winning region for free choices and potential deadlocks, which both usually indicate specification errors. A free choice is a state which, for the same input, has multiple outgoing transitions into the winning region. If there are free choices and the developer has no preference which one is chosen, SCSYNT nondeterministically commits to one option. For the deadlock detection, we require the user to label *determined predicate terms*. We call a predicate determined if either 1) it becomes a constant at some time or 2) only method calls can change its value. An example of class 1 are predicates over the time, e.g., `time > cTime()`: if it is *true* at some point, it will never be *false* again. A class 2 example would be a predicate that counts whether the number stored in a field has passed a fixed threshold. A predicate like `msg.sender = owner()`, on the other hand, is not determined as the evaluation changes with the input `msg.sender`. SCSYNT automatically detects if, at some point, there is an evaluation of the determined predicate terms that is allowed by the assumptions but for which there is no valid transition. It then warns of a potential deadlock.

Translation to Solidity. For the translation, the developer needs to provide the implementation of all predicates and functions, as they are uninterpreted (which makes the synthesis feasible after all). Some of the most common functions and predicates (e.g., equality and addition) are automatically replaced by SCSYNT. The `owner` and `msg.sender` keywords are translated automatically; the owner is set in the constructor. Conceptually, the translation to Solidity is straightforward. For each method of the contract, we create a function that contains the state machine logic for that particular method. For parameterized specifications,

Table 1. Sizes of the specifications and state machines as well as the average running time of SCSYNT. #Forms. is the number of individual past-time formulas, #Nodes is the number of nodes of the AST. The state machine size is the sum of the states/transitions of the split state machines. The synthesis and translation times are the respective average on 10 runs of the same benchmark.

Contract	Specification		State Machine		Avg. Time (s)	
	#Forms.	#Nodes	#States	#Trans.	Synth.	Transl.
Asset Transfer	36	216	8	14	5.9996	0.0053
Blinded Auction	19	218	5	8	1.5446	0.0026
Coin Toss	27	154	5	7	1.6180	0.0029
Crowd Funding	17	100	4	8	0.2178	0.0026
ERC20	15	140	9	5	0.4812	0.0033
ERC20 Extended	19	244	10	7	1.9608	0.0040
NFT Auction	30	325	12	15	12.1853	0.0080
Simple Auction	15	83	4	7	0.1362	0.0026
Ticket System	13	97	4	6	0.1812	0.0028
Voting	17	98	6	5	0.1478	0.0023

the contract is augmented with a mapping recording the knowledge labels (c.f. Section 6). The parameters other than the sender are included as arguments. Following [27], we also add automatic protection against reentrancy attacks by setting a Boolean flag if a method is currently executing.

7.2 Evaluation

The goal of our evaluation is to show that 1) parameterized pastTSL is indeed a suitable logic for specifying smart contract state machines and 2) that our implemented toolchain is efficient. To do so, we specified and synthesized ten different smart contracts with a non-trivial temporal control flow using pastTSL specifications with and without parameters. A detailed description of all benchmarks is provided in the full version of this paper [9]. The most challenging benchmark to specify was the NFT auction, a parameterized specification for a contract actively maintained by Avolabs. Its reference implementation has over 1400 lines of code. We manually extracted 30 past-time formulas from the README of the contract provided on the GitHub of Avolabs [2].

All experiments were run on a 2020 Macbook with an Apple M1 chip, 16GB RAM, running MacOS. The results are shown in Table 1. We report the size of the specification and of the resulting state machine as well as the running time of the synthesis procedure itself and the translation to Solidity code. Most importantly, the evaluation shows that specifying and automatically generating the non-trivial state machine logic of a smart contract is possible. We successfully synthesized Solidity code for state machines of up to 12 states. The evaluation also shows that our toolchain is efficient: synthesis itself took up to 12 s; in most cases, SCSYNT synthesizes a state machine in less than two seconds. The translation of the state machine into Solidity code is nearly instantaneous.

8   Conclusion

We have described the synthesis of Solidity code from specifications given in pastTSL equipped with universally quantified parameters. Our approach is the first that facilitates a comprehensive specification of the implicit state machine of a smart contract, including the data flow of the contract's fields and guards on the methods' arguments. The algorithm proceeds in two steps: first, we translate the specification to pastTSL. While we have shown that pastTSL realizability without parameters is undecidable in general, solutions can be obtained via a sound reduction to LTL. In a second step, we split the resulting system into a hierarchical structure of multiple systems, which constitutes a finite representation of a system implementing the original formula and also enables a feasible handling when translated to Solidity. Our prototype tool SCSYNT implements the synthesis toolchain, including an analysis of the state machine regarding potential specification errors.

For future work, we aim to extend our approach to specifications given in pastTSL with alternating parameter quantifiers. There are also several exciting possibilities to combine our work with other synthesis and verification techniques. One avenue is to automatically prove necessary assumptions in deductive verification tools [6], especially for assumptions that state invariants maintained by method calls. Another possibility is to synthesize function and predicate implementations in the spirit of [3]. Finally, now that we have developed the algorithmic foundations and implemented a first prototype, we aim to conduct a thorough evaluation of our approach in comparison to hand-written (non-formal) approaches.

Acknowledgements. This work was supported by the European Research Council (ERC) Grant HYPER (No. 101055412) and by DFG grant 389792660 as part of TRR 248.

References

1. Antonino, P., Ferreira, J., Sampaio, A., Roscoe, A.W.: Specification is law: safe creation and upgrade of ethereum smart contracts. CoRR abs/2205.07529 (2022). https://doi.org/10.48550/arXiv.2205.07529
2. Avolabs: NFT auction reference contract. https://github.com/avolabs-io/nft-auction (2022). Accessed 05 July 2022

3. Choi, W., Finkbeiner, B., Piskac, R., Santolucito, M.: Can reactive synthesis and syntax-guided synthesis be friends? In: 43rd ACM SIGPLAN Conference on Programming Language Design and Implementation (PLDI) (2022). https://publications.cispa.saarland/3674/
4. Ciccio, C.D., et al.: Blockchain support for collaborative business processes. Inform. Spektrum **42**(3), 182–190 (2019). https://doi.org/10.1007/s00287-019-01178-x
5. Cimatti, A., Roveri, M., Sheridan, D.: Bounded verification of past LTL. In: Hu, A.J., Martin, A.K. (eds.) FMCAD 2004. LNCS, vol. 3312, pp. 245–259. Springer, Heidelberg (2004). https://doi.org/10.1007/978-3-540-30494-4_18
6. Dharanikota, S., Mukherjee, S., Bhardwaj, C., Rastogi, A., Lal, A.: Celestial: a smart contracts verification framework. In: Proceedings of the 21st Conference on Formal Methods in Computer-Aided Design (FMCAD 2021), pp. 133–142 (2021)
7. Ethereum: Introduction to ethereum (2021). https://ethereum.org/en/developers/docs/intro-to-ethereum/ . Accessed 05 July 2022
8. Finkbeiner, B., Heim, P., Passing, N.: Temporal stream logic modulo theories. In: FoSSaCS 2022. LNCS, vol. 13242, pp. 325–346. Springer, Cham (2022). https://doi.org/10.1007/978-3-030-99253-8_17
9. Finkbeiner, B., Hofmann, J., Kohn, F., Passing, N.: Reactive synthesis of smart contract control flows (2023)
10. Finkbeiner, B., Klein, F., Piskac, R., Santolucito, M.: Synthesizing functional reactive programs. In: Eisenberg, R.A. (ed.) Proceedings of the 12th ACM SIGPLAN International Symposium on Haskell, Haskell@ICFP 2019, Berlin, Germany, 18–23 August 2019, pp. 162–175. ACM (2019). https://doi.org/10.1145/3331545.3342601
11. Finkbeiner, B., Klein, F., Piskac, R., Santolucito, M.: Temporal stream logic: synthesis beyond the bools. In: Dillig, I., Tasiran, S. (eds.) CAV 2019. LNCS, vol. 11561, pp. 609–629. Springer, Cham (2019). https://doi.org/10.1007/978-3-030-25540-4_35
12. Geier, G., Heim, P., Klein, F., Finkbeiner, B.: Syntroids: synthesizing a game for FPGAS using temporal logic specifications. CoRR abs/2101.07232 (2021). https://arxiv.org/abs/2101.07232
13. Havelund, K., Roşu, G.: Synthesizing monitors for safety properties. In: Katoen, J.-P., Stevens, P. (eds.) TACAS 2002. LNCS, vol. 2280, pp. 342–356. Springer, Heidelberg (2002). https://doi.org/10.1007/3-540-46002-0_24
14. Hopcroft, J.: An n log n algorithm for minimizing states in a finite automaton. In: Theory of Machines and Computations, pp. 189–196. Elsevier (1971)
15. Jacobs, S., Bloem, R.: Parameterized synthesis. Log. Methods Comput. Sci. **10**(1) (2014). https://doi.org/10.2168/LMCS-10(1:12)2014
16. Kalra, S., Goel, S., Dhawan, M., Sharma, S.: ZEUS: analyzing safety of smart contracts. In: 25th Annual Network and Distributed System Security Symposium, NDSS 2018, San Diego, California, USA, 18-21 February 2018. The Internet Society (2018). https://doi.org/10.14722/ndss.2018.23082
17. Khalimov, A., Jacobs, S., Bloem, R.: PARTY parameterized synthesis of token rings. In: Sharygina, N., Veith, H. (eds.) CAV 2013. LNCS, vol. 8044, pp. 928–933. Springer, Heidelberg (2013). https://doi.org/10.1007/978-3-642-39799-8_66
18. Khalimov, A., Jacobs, S., Bloem, R.: Towards efficient parameterized synthesis. In: Giacobazzi, R., Berdine, J., Mastroeni, I. (eds.) VMCAI 2013. LNCS, vol. 7737, pp. 108–127. Springer, Heidelberg (2013). https://doi.org/10.1007/978-3-642-35873-9_9
19. Klein, F., Santolucito, M.: TSL tools (2019). https://github.com/kleinreact/tsltools

20. Kupferman, O., Vardi, M.Y.: Model checking of safety properties. In: Halbwachs, N., Peled, D. (eds.) CAV 1999. LNCS, vol. 1633, pp. 172–183. Springer, Heidelberg (1999). https://doi.org/10.1007/3-540-48683-6_17

21. Lahiri, S.K., Chen, S., Wang, Y., Dillig, I.: Formal specification and verification of smart contracts for azure blockchain. CoRR abs/1812.08829 (2018). https://arxiv.org/abs/1812.08829

22. Lamport, L.: Proving the correctness of multiprocess programs. IEEE Trans. Softw. Eng. **3**(2), 125–143 (1977). https://doi.org/10.1109/TSE.1977.229904

23. Lisitsa, A., Potapov, I.: Temporal logic with predicate lambda-abstraction. In: 12th International Symposium on Temporal Representation and Reasoning (TIME 2005), 23–25 June 2005, Burlington, Vermont, USA, pp. 147–155. IEEE Computer Society (2005). https://doi.org/10.1109/TIME.2005.34

24. López-Pintado, O., García-Bañuelos, L., Dumas, M., Weber, I., Ponomarev, A.: Caterpillar: a business process execution engine on the ethereum blockchain. Softw. Pract. Exp. **49**(7), 1162–1193 (2019). https://doi.org/10.1002/spe.2702

25. Maderbacher, B., Bloem, R.: Reactive synthesis modulo theories using abstraction refinement. CoRR abs/2108.00090 (2021). https://arxiv.org/abs/2108.00090

26. Markgraf, O., Hong, C.-D., Lin, A.W., Najib, M., Neider, D.: Parameterized synthesis with safety properties. In: Oliveira, B.C.S. (ed.) APLAS 2020. LNCS, vol. 12470, pp. 273–292. Springer, Cham (2020). https://doi.org/10.1007/978-3-030-64437-6_14

27. Mavridou, A., Laszka, A.: Designing secure ethereum smart contracts: a finite state machine based approach. In: Meiklejohn, S., Sako, K. (eds.) FC 2018. LNCS, vol. 10957, pp. 523–540. Springer, Heidelberg (2018). https://doi.org/10.1007/978-3-662-58387-6_28

28. Mavridou, A., Laszka, A., Stachtiari, E., Dubey, A.: VeriSolid: correct-by-design smart contracts for ethereum. In: Goldberg, I., Moore, T. (eds.) FC 2019. LNCS, vol. 11598, pp. 446–465. Springer, Cham (2019). https://doi.org/10.1007/978-3-030-32101-7_27

29. Mayr, R.: Undecidable problems in unreliable computations. Theor. Comput. Sci. **297**(1–3), 337–354 (2003). https://doi.org/10.1016/S0304-3975(02)00646-1

30. Mealy, G.H.: A method for synthesizing sequential circuits. Bell Syst. Tech. J. **34**(5), 1045–1079 (1955). https://doi.org/10.1002/j.1538-7305.1955.tb03788.x

31. Nehai, Z., Piriou, P.Y., Daumas, F.: Model-checking of smart contracts. In: 2018 IEEE International Conference on Internet of Things (iThings) and IEEE Green Computing and Communications (GreenCom) and IEEE Cyber, Physical and Social Computing (CPSCom) and IEEE Smart Data (SmartData), pp. 980–987. IEEE (2018)

32. Open Zeppelin: Erc20 token system documentation from open zeppelin (2022). https://docs.openzeppelin.com/contracts/2.x/api/token/erc20. Accessed 05 July 2022

33. Permenev, A., Dimitrov, D.K., Tsankov, P., Drachsler-Cohen, D., Vechev, M.T.: VerX: safety verification of smart contracts. In: 2020 IEEE Symposium on Security and Privacy, SP 2020, San Francisco, CA, USA, 18–21 May 2020, pp. 1661–1677. IEEE (2020). https://doi.org/10.1109/SP40000.2020.00024

34. Stephens, J., Ferles, K., Mariano, B., Lahiri, S.K., Dillig, I.: SmartPulse: automated checking of temporal properties in smart contracts. In: 42nd IEEE Symposium on Security and Privacy, SP 2021, San Francisco, CA, USA, 24–27 May 2021, pp. 555–571. IEEE (2021). https://doi.org/10.1109/SP40001.2021.00085

35. Suvorov, D., Ulyantsev, V.: Smart contract design meets state machine synthesis: Case studies. CoRR abs/1906.02906 (2019). https://arxiv.org/abs/1906.02906

36. Wang, Y., et al.: Formal verification of workflow policies for smart contracts in azure blockchain. In: Chakraborty, S., Navas, J.A. (eds.) VSTTE 2019. LNCS, vol. 12031, pp. 87–106. Springer, Cham (2020). https://doi.org/10.1007/978-3-030-41600-3_7

37. Zupan, N., Kasinathan, P., Cuellar, J., Sauer, M.: Secure smart contract generation based on petri nets. In: Rosa Righi, R., Alberti, A.M., Singh, M. (eds.) Blockchain Technology for Industry 4.0. BT, pp. 73–98. Springer, Singapore (2020). https://doi.org/10.1007/978-981-15-1137-0_4

Synthesis of Distributed Protocols by Enumeration Modulo Isomorphisms

Derek Egolf[✉] and Stavros Tripakis

Northeastern University, Boston, MA, USA
{egolf.d,stavros}@northeastern.edu

Abstract. Synthesis of distributed protocols is a hard, often undecidable, problem. *Completion* techniques provide partial remedy by turning the problem into a search problem. However, the space of candidate completions is still massive. In this paper, we propose optimization techniques to reduce the size of the search space by a factorial factor by exploiting symmetries (*isomorphisms*) in functionally equivalent solutions. We present both a theoretical analysis of this optimization as well as empirical results that demonstrate its effectiveness in synthesizing both the Alternating Bit Protocol and Two Phase Commit. Our experiments show that the optimized tool achieves a speedup of approximately 2 to 10 times compared to its unoptimized counterpart.

1 Introduction

Distributed protocols are at the heart of the internet, data centers, cloud services, and other types of infrastructure considered indispensable in a modern society. Yet distributed protocols are also notoriously difficult to get right, and have therefore been one of the primary application domains of formal verification [15,19,20,22,31]. An even more attractive proposition is distributed protocol *synthesis*: given a formal correctness specification ψ, automatically generate a distributed protocol that satisfies ψ, i.e., that is *correct-by-construction*.

Synthesis is a hard problem in general, suffering, like formal verification, from scalability and similar issues. Moreover, for distributed systems, synthesis is generally undecidable [12,23,29,30]. Techniques such as program *sketching* [26, 27] remedy scalability and undecidability concerns essentially by turning the synthesis problem into a *completion* problem [2,3]: given an *incomplete* system M_0 and a specification ψ, automatically synthesize a completion M of M_0, such that M satisfies ψ.

For example, the synthesis of the well-known *alternating-bit protocol* (ABP) is considered in [4] as a completion problem: given an ABP system containing the incomplete $Sender_0$ and $Receiver_0$ processes shown in Fig. 1, complete these two processes (by adding but not removing any transitions, and not adding nor removing any states), so that the system satisfies a given set of requirements.

É. André and J. Sun (Eds.): ATVA 2023, LNCS 14215, pp. 270–291, 2023.
https://doi.org/10.1007/978-3-031-45329-8_13

In cases where the space of all possible completions is finite, completion turns synthesis into a decidable problem.[1] However, even then, the number of possible completions can be prohibitively large, even for relatively simple protocols. For instance, as explained in [4], the number of all possible completions in the ABP example is $512^4 \cdot 36$, i.e., approximately 2.5 trillion candidate completions.

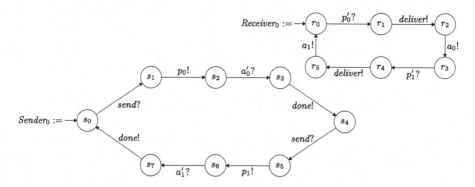

Fig. 1. The incomplete ABP Sender and Receiver processes of [4]

Not only is the number of candidate completions typically huge, but it is often also interesting to generate not just one correct completion, but many. For instance, suppose both M_1 and M_2 are (functionally) correct solutions. We may want to evaluate M_1 and M_2 also for *efficiency* (perhaps using a separate method) [10]. In general, we may want to synthesize (and then evaluate w.r.t. performance or other metrics) not just one, but in principle *all* correct completions. We call this problem the completion *enumeration* problem, which is the main focus of this paper.

Enumeration is harder than *1-completion* (synthesis of just one correct solution), since the number of correct solutions might be very large. For instance, in the case of the ABP example described above, the number of correct completions is 16384 and it takes 88 min to generate all of them [4].

The key idea in this paper is to exploit the notion of *isomorphisms* in order to reduce the number of correct completions, as well as the search space of candidate completions in general. To illustrate the idea, consider a different incomplete $Sender_0$ process, shown in Fig. 2. Two possible completions of this $Sender_0$ are shown in Fig. 3. Although these two completions are in principle different, they are identical except that states s_3 and s_7 are swapped. Our goal is to develop a technique which considers these two completions *equivalent up to isomorphism*, and only explores (and returns) one of them.

---

[1] We emphasize that no generality is lost in the sense that one can augment the search for correct completions with an outer loop that keeps adding extra *empty* states (with no incoming or outgoing transitions), which the inner completion procedure then tries to complete. Thus, we can keep searching for progressively larger systems (in terms of number of states) until a solution is found, if one exists.

272   D. Egolf and S. Tripakis

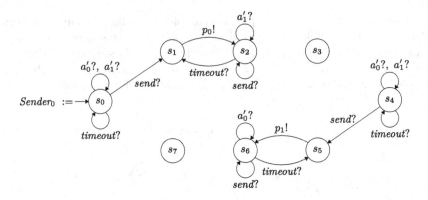

Fig. 2. An incomplete ABP Sender with permutable states s_3, s_7

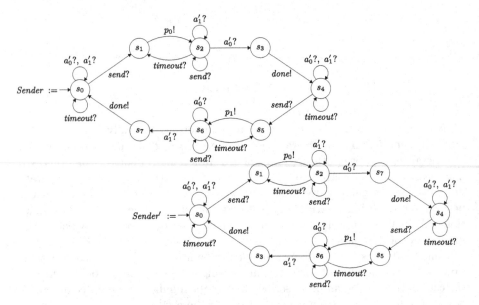

Fig. 3. Two synthesized completions of the incomplete process of Fig. 2. Observe that the two completions are identical except that states s_3 and s_7 are flipped.

To achieve this goal, we adopt the *guess-check-generalize* paradigm (GCG) [1, 2,13,26,27]. In a nutshell, GCG works as follows: (1) pick a candidate completion M; (2) check whether M satisfies ψ: if it does, M is one possible solution to the synthesis problem; (3) if M violates ψ, *prune* the search space of possible completions by excluding a *generalization* of M, and repeat from step (1). In the most trivial case, the generalization of M contains only M itself. Ideally, however, and in order to achieve a more significant pruning of the search space, the generalization of M should contain many more "bad" completions which are somehow "similar" (for instance, isomorphic) to M.

A naive way to generalize based on isomorphism is to keep a list of completions encountered thus far and perform an isomorphism check against every element of this list whenever a new candidate is picked. Our approach is smarter: in fact, it does not involve any isomorphism checks whatsoever. Instead, our approach guarantees that no isomorphic completions are ever picked to begin with by pruning them from the search space. This is ultimately done using syntactic transformations of completion representations. The details are left for Sect. 4.

Furthermore, our notion of "encountering" a completion is quite wide. Rather than just pruning completions that are isomorphic to *candidates*, we also prune completions that are isomorphic to any completion in the *generalizations of* the candidates (with respect to some prior, unextended notion of generalization). Between the trivial approach involving isomorphism checks and our own approach are several other approaches which are good, but not excellent. Indeed, a categorization of the subtle differences between such approaches is a key contribution of this paper (see Sect. 4.3). These subtleties are easy to miss.

In summary, the main contributions of this paper are the following: (1) we define the 1-completion and completion-enumeration problems *modulo isomorphisms*; (2) we examine new methods to solve these problems based on the GCG paradigm; (3) we identify properties that an efficient GCG modulo isomorphisms algorithm should have; (4) we propose two instances of such an algorithm, using a naive and a sophisticated notion of generalization; (5) we evaluate our methods on the synthesis of two simple distributed protocols: the ABP and Two Phase Commit (2PC) and demonstrate speedups with respect to the unoptimized method of approximately 2 to 10 times.

2   Preliminaries

Labeled Transition Systems. A (finite) *labeled transition system* (LTS) M is a tuple $\langle \Sigma, Q, Q_0, \Delta \rangle$, where

- Σ is a finite set of transition *labels*
- Q is a finite set of *states*
- $Q_0 \subseteq Q$ is the set of *initial states*
- $\Delta \subseteq Q \times \Sigma \times Q$ is the *transition relation*.

We write the transition $(p, a, q) \in \Delta$ as $p \xrightarrow{a} q$.

A *run* of M is an infinite sequence $q_0 \xrightarrow{a_0} q_1 \xrightarrow{a_1} q_2 \xrightarrow{a_2} ...$, where $q_0 \in Q_0$ and for each i we have $(q_i, a_i, q_{i+1}) \in \Delta$. The *trace* produced by this run is $a_0 a_1 a_2 \cdots$. Semantically, an LTS M represents a set of infinite traces, denoted $[\![M]\!] \subseteq \Sigma^\omega$. Specifically, a trace $a_0 a_1 a_2 \cdots$ is in $[\![M]\!]$ exactly when there exists a run $q_0 \xrightarrow{a_0} q_1 \xrightarrow{a_1} q_2 \xrightarrow{a_2} ...$ of M.

Correctness Specification. We will assume that we have some formal notion of *specification* and some formal notion of *satisfaction* between an LTS M and a specification ψ. We write $M \vDash \psi$ to denote that M satisfies ψ. Our work is agnostic to what exactly ψ might be (e.g., a temporal logic formula, etc.).

Completions and Syntactic Constraints. Suppose that M and M_0 are two LTSs with the same set of labels Σ, the same set of states Q, the same set of initial states Q_0, and with transition relations Δ and Δ_0, respectively. We say that M *is a completion of* M_0 exactly when $\Delta_0 \subseteq \Delta$. That is, M completes M_0 by adding more transitions to it (and not removing any). For example, each of the two LTSs of Fig. 3 is a completion of the LTS shown in Fig. 2.

Often, we wish to impose some constraints on the kind of synthesized processes that we want to obtain during automated synthesis, other than the global constraints imposed on the system by the correctness specification. For example, in the formal distributed protocol model proposed in [4], synthesized processes such as the ABP *Sender* and *Receiver* are constrained to satisfy a number of requirements, including absence of deadlocks, determinism of the transition relation, the constraint that each state is either an *input state* (i.e., it only receives inputs) or an *output state* (i.e., it emits a unique output), the constraint that input states are *input-enabled* (i.e., they do not block any inputs), and so on. Such properties are often syntactic or structural and can be inferred statically by observing the transition relation. The fact that an LTS is a completion of another LTS can also be captured by such constraints.

Constraints like the above are application-specific, and our approach is agnostic to their precise form and meaning. We will therefore abstract them away, and assume that there is a propositional logic formula Φ which captures the set of all syntactically well-formed candidate completions. The variable space of Φ and its precise meaning is application-specific. We will give a detailed construction of Φ for LTS in Sect. 3. We write $M \vDash \Phi$ when LTS M satisfies the *syntactic constraints* Φ. Let $[\![\Phi]\!] = \{M \mid M \vDash \Phi\}$.

We say that an LTS is *correct* if it satisfies both the syntactic constraints imposed by Φ and the semantic constraints imposed by ψ.

Computational Problems

Problem 1 (Model-Checking). Given LTS M, specification ψ, and constraints Φ, check whether $M \vDash \psi$ and $M \vDash \Phi$.

A solution to the model-checking problem is an algorithm, MC, such that for all M, Φ, ψ, if $M \vDash \Phi$ and $M \vDash \psi$ then $\text{MC}(M, \Phi, \psi) = 1$; otherwise, $\text{MC}(M, \Phi, \psi) = 0$.

Problem 2 (Synthesis). Given specification ψ and constraints Φ, find, if one exists, LTS M such that $M \vDash \psi$ and $M \vDash \Phi$.

Problem 3 (Completion). Given LTS M_0, specification ψ, and constraints Φ, find, if one exists, a completion M of M_0 such that $M \vDash \psi$ and $M \vDash \Phi$.

Problem 4 (Completion enumeration). Given LTS M_0, specification ψ, and constraints Φ, find all completions M of M_0 such that $M \vDash \psi$ and $M \vDash \Phi$.

3 The Guess-Check-Generalize Paradigm

In this section we first propose a generic GCG algorithm and reason about its correctness (Sect. 3.1). We then show how to instantiate this algorithm to solve Problems 3 and 4 (Sect. 3.2).

3.1 A Generic GCG Algorithm and Its Correctness

Algorithm 1 is a formal description of a generic GCG algorithm. The algorithm takes as input: (1) a set of syntactic constraints in the form of a propositional formula Φ, as described in Sect. 2; (2) a specification ψ as described in Sect. 2; and (3) a *generalizer* function γ, described below.

Algorithm 1: GCG$[\Phi, \psi, \gamma]$

---

1 **while** Φ *is satisfiable* **do**
2 $\quad \sigma := \text{SAT}(\Phi);$
3 $\quad$ **if** $\text{MC}(M_\sigma, \Phi, \psi) = 1$ **then**
4 $\quad\quad$ **return** σ;
5 $\quad\quad \Phi := \Phi \wedge \neg\sigma;$
6 $\quad$ **else**
7 $\quad\quad \Phi := \Phi \wedge \neg\gamma(\sigma);$

Φ is a propositional logic formula (over a certain set of boolean variables that depends on the application domain at hand) encoding all possible syntactically valid completions. Every satisfying assignment σ of Φ corresponds to one completion, which we denote as M_σ. Observe that GCG does not explicitly take an initial (incomplete) model M_0 as input: this omission is not a problem because M_0 can be encoded in Φ, as mentioned in Sect. 2. We explain specifically how to do that in the case of LTS in Sect. 3.2.

The algorithm works as follows: while Φ is satisfiable: Line 2: pick a candidate completion σ allowed by Φ by calling a SAT solver. Line 3: model-check the corresponding model M_σ against ψ (by definition, M_σ satisfies Φ because σ satisfies Φ). Line 4: if M_σ satisfies ψ then we have found a correct model: we can return it and terminate if we are solving Problem 3, or return it and continue our search for additional correct models if we are solving Problem 4. In the latter case, in line 5 we exclude σ from Φ (slightly abusing notation, we treat σ as a formula satisfied exactly and only by σ, so that $\neg\sigma$ is the formula satisfied by all assignments except σ). Line 7: if M_σ violates ψ, then we exclude from Φ the *generalization* $\gamma(\sigma)$ of σ, and continue our search.

Generalizers. A *generalizer* is a function γ which takes an assignment σ and returns a propositional logic formula $\gamma(\sigma)$ that encodes all "bad" assignments that we wish to exclude from Φ. Ideally, however, $\gamma(\sigma)$ will encode many more assignments (and therefore candidate completions), so as to prune as large a part of the search space as possible. A concrete implementation of γ may require additional information other than just σ. For example, γ may consult the specification ψ, counter-examples returned by the model-checker (which are themselves a function of ψ and σ), and so on. We avoid including all this information in the inputs of γ to ease presentation. We note that ψ does not change during a run of Algorithm 1 and therefore ψ can be "hardwired" into γ without loss of generality.

A valid generalizer should include the assignment being generalized and it should only include bad assignments (i.e., it should exclude correct completions). Formally, a generalizer γ is said to be *proper* if for all σ such that $\sigma \vDash \Phi$ and $M_\sigma \nvDash \psi$, the following conditions hold: (1) *Self-inclusion:* $\sigma \vDash \gamma(\sigma)$, and (2) *Correct-exclusion:* for any ϱ, if $\varrho \vDash \Phi$ and $M_\varrho \vDash \psi$ then $\varrho \nvDash \gamma(\sigma)$.

The Correctness of GCG

Lemma 1. *If γ is proper then* GCG$[\Phi, \psi, \gamma]$ *terminates.*

Proof. If γ is proper then $\gamma(\sigma)$ is guaranteed to include at least σ. Φ is a propositional logic formula, therefore it only has a finite set of satisfying assignments. Every iteration of the loop removes at least one satisfying assignment from Φ, therefore the algorithm terminates. □

During a run, Algorithm 1 returns a (possibly empty) set of assignments Sol $= \{\sigma_1, \sigma_2, ..., \sigma_n\}$, representing the solution to Problems 3 or 4. Also during a run, the algorithm guesses candidate assignments by calling the subroutine SAT (line 2). Let Cand be the set of all these candidates. Note that Sol $\subseteq$ Cand, since every solution returned (line 4) has been first guessed in line 2.

Whenever the algorithm reassigns $\Phi := \Phi \wedge \neg\varphi$, we say that it *prunes* φ, i.e., the satisfying assignments of φ are now excluded from the search. We will need to reason about the set of assignments that have been pruned after a certain *partial run* of the program. In such cases we can imagine running the algorithm for some amount of time and pausing it. Then the set Pruned denotes the set of assignments that have been pruned up until that point. It is true that after the program terminates Pruned $= [\![\Phi]\!]\backslash$Cand, but this equality does not necessarily hold for all partial runs.

Theorem 1. *(1)* GCG$[\Phi, \psi, \gamma]$ *is sound, i.e., for all $\sigma \in$ Sol, we have $\sigma \vDash \Phi$ and $M_\sigma \vDash \psi$. (2) If γ is proper then* GCG$[\Phi, \psi, \gamma]$ *is complete, i.e., for all $\sigma \vDash \Phi$, if $M_\sigma \vDash \psi$ then $\sigma \in$ Sol.*

Proof. Every $\sigma \in$ Sol satisfies Φ (line 2) and the corresponding M_σ satisfies ψ (line 3), therefore GCG$[\Phi, \psi, \gamma]$ is sound. Now, suppose that γ is proper, and take ϱ such that $\varrho \vDash \Phi$ and $M_\varrho \vDash \psi$. To show completeness, it suffices to show that $\varrho \in$ Cand. Then, we also have $\varrho \in$ Sol because M_ϱ passes the model-checking test in line 3. Suppose, for a contradiction, that $\varrho \notin$ Cand, i.e., that ϱ is pruned. Then there must exist some σ such that $\varrho \vDash \gamma(\sigma)$ (line 7). But $\sigma \vDash \Phi$ (line 2), which means that ϱ violates the *correct-exclusion* property of γ. Contradiction. □

3.2   A Concrete Instance of GCG for LTS

Algorithm 1 is *generic* in the sense that depending on how exactly we instantiate Φ, ψ, and γ, we can encode different completion enumeration (and more generally model enumeration) problems, as well as solutions. We now show how to instantiate Algorithm 1 to solve Problems 3 and 4 concretely for LTS.

Encoding LTSs and Completions in Propositional Logic. Let $M_0 = \langle \Sigma, Q, Q_0, \Delta_0 \rangle$ be an incomplete LTS. Then we can define a set of boolean variables

$$V := \{p \looparrowright^a q \mid p, q \in Q \wedge a \in \Sigma\}$$

so that boolean variable $p \looparrowright^a q$ encodes whether transition $p \xrightarrow{a} q$ is present or not (if $p \xrightarrow{a} q$ is present, then $p \looparrowright^a q$ is true, otherwise it is false). More formally, let ASGN_V be the set of all assignments over V. An assignment $\sigma \in \mathrm{ASGN}_V$ represents LTS M_σ with transition relation $\Delta_\sigma = \{(p, a, q) \mid \sigma(p \looparrowright^a q) = 1\}$. To enforce M_σ to be a completion of M_0, we need to enforce that $\Delta_0 \subseteq \Delta_\sigma$. We do so by initializing our syntactic constraints Φ as $\Phi := \Phi_{\Delta_0}$, where

$$\Phi_{\Delta_0} := \bigwedge_{p \xrightarrow{a} q \in \Delta_0} p \looparrowright^a q.$$

We can then add extra constraints to Φ such as determinism or absence of deadlocks, as appropriate.

A Concrete Generalizer for LTS. Based on the principles of [4], we can construct a *concrete generalizer* $\gamma_{LTS}(\sigma)$ for LTS as $\gamma_{LTS}(\sigma) := \gamma_{safe}(\sigma) \vee \gamma_{live}(\sigma)$, which we separate into a disjunction of a safety violation generalizer and a liveness violation generalizer. The safety component γ_{safe} works on the principle that if LTS M_σ violates a safety property, then adding extra transitions will not solve this violation. Thus:

$$\gamma_{safe}(\sigma) := \bigwedge_{\{x \in V \mid \sigma(x) = 1\}} x.$$

The liveness component γ_{live} can be defined based on a notion of reachable, "bad" cycles that enable something to happen infinitely often. Thus, $\neg \gamma_{live}$ captures all LTSs that disable these bad cycles by breaking them or making them unreachable.

It can be shown that the concrete generalizer γ_{LTS} is proper. Therefore, the concrete instance $\mathrm{GCG}[\Phi, \psi, \gamma_{LTS}]$ is sound, terminating, and complete, i.e., it solves Problems 3 and 4.

Even though the concrete generalizer is correct, it is not very effective. In particular, it does not immediately prune isomorphisms. There may be $O(n!)$ trivially equivalent completions up to state reordering, where n is the number of states in the LTS. In the next section we present two optimizations exploiting isomorphisms.

4   Synthesis Modulo Isomorphisms

4.1   LTS Isomorphisms

Intuitively, two LTS are isomorphic if we can rearrange the states of one to obtain the other. For synthesis purposes, we often wish to provide as a constraint a set of *permutable states* A, so as to exclude rearrangements that move states outside of A. If we can still rearrange the states of an LTS M_1 to obtain another LTS M_2 subject to this constraint, then we say that M_1 *and* M_2 *are isomorphic up to* A. For example, the two LTSs of Fig. 3 are isomorphic up to the set of permutable states $A = \{s_3, s_7\}$. Strictly speaking, they are permutable up to any set of their states, but we choose A to reflect the fact that those two states have no incoming or outgoing transitions in Fig. 2. Permuting any other states would yield an LTS that is not a completion of Fig. 2.

We now define isomorphisms formally. Let M_0, M_1, and M_2 be LTSs with the same Σ, Q, Q_0, and with transition relations Δ_0, Δ_1, and Δ_2, respectively. Suppose that M_1 and M_2 are both completions of M_0. Let $A \subseteq Q \backslash Q_0$. Then we say M_1 and M_2 are isomorphic up to A, denoted $M_1 \overset{A}{\simeq} M_2$, if and only if there exists a bijection $f : A \to A$ (i.e., a *permutation*) such that

$$p \overset{a}{\to} q \in \Delta_1 \text{ if and only if } f(p) \overset{a}{\to} f(q) \in \Delta_2.$$

By default, we will assume that A is the set of non-initial states that have no incoming or outgoing transitions in M_0. In that case we will omit A and write $M_1 \simeq M_2$.

Lemma 2. *LTS isomorphism is an equivalence relation, i.e., it is reflexive, symmetric, and transitive.*

We use $[M]$ to denote the *equivalence class* of M, i.e., $[M] = \{M' \mid M' \simeq M\}$.

Lemma 3. *If* $M_1 \overset{A}{\simeq} M_2$ *then* $[\![M_1]\!] = [\![M_2]\!]$.

Lemma 3 states that LTS isomorphism preserves traces. More generally, we will assume that our notion of specification is preserved by LTS isomorphism, namely, that if $M_1 \overset{A}{\simeq} M_2$ then for any specification ψ, $M_1 \vDash \psi$ iff $M_2 \vDash \psi$.

Isomorphic Assignments. Two assignments σ and ϱ are isomorphic if the LTSs that they represent are isomorphic. Hence we write $\sigma \simeq \varrho$ if and only if $M_\sigma \simeq M_\varrho$. We write $[\varrho]$ to denote the equivalence class of ϱ, i.e., the set of all assignments that are isomorphic to ϱ. These equivalence classes partition Φ since $\simeq$ is an equivalence relation.

4.2   Completion Enumeration Modulo Isomorphisms

Isomorphisms allow us to focus our attention to Problem 5 instead of Problem 4:

Problem 5 (Completion enumeration modulo isomorphisms). Given LTS M_0, specification ψ, and constraints Φ, find the set

$$\{[M] \mid M \text{ is a completion of } M_0 \text{ such that } M \vDash \psi \text{ and } M \vDash \Phi\}.$$

Problem 5 asks that only significantly different (i.e., non-isomorphic) completions are returned to the user. Problem 5 can be solved by a simple modification to Algorithm 1, namely, to exclude the entire equivalence class $[\sigma]$ of any discovered solution σ, as shown in Algorithm 2, line 5.

Algorithm 2: $\text{GCG}_{\simeq}[\Phi, \psi, \gamma]$ solving Problem 5

---
1 **while** Φ *is satisfiable* **do**
2      $\sigma := \text{SAT}(\Phi)$;
3   **if** $\text{MC}(M_\sigma, \Phi, \psi) = 1$ **then**
4   **return** σ;
5         $\Phi := \Phi \wedge \neg[\sigma]$;
6   **else**
7         $\Phi := \Phi \wedge \neg\gamma(\sigma)$;

4.3 Properties of an Efficient GCG Algorithm

We begin by presenting a list of properties that an efficient instance of GCG ought to satisfy. Except for Property 1, satisfaction of these properties generally depends on the generalizer used.

Property 1. For all σ that satisfy Φ, $[\sigma] \cap \text{Sol}$ has 0 or 1 element(s). In other words, we return at most one solution per equivalence class.

Property 1 asks that only significantly different (i.e., non-isomorphic) completions are returned to the user, thereby solving Problem 5, which is our main goal. In addition, this property implies that the number of completions is kept small, which is important when these are fed as inputs to some other routine (e.g., one that selects a "highly fit" completion among all valid completions).

$\text{GCG}_{\simeq}$ satisfies Property 1, regardless of the parameters. However, we can go further, by ensuring that not only we do not return isomorphic completions, but we do not even consider isomorphic candidate completions in the first place:

Property 2. For all σ that satisfy Φ, $[\sigma] \cap \text{Cand}$ has 0 or 1 element(s). In other words, we consider at most one candidate per equivalence class.

Maintaining Property 2 now guarantees that we only call the most expensive subroutines at most once for each equivalence class. Note that, since $\text{Sol} \subseteq \text{Cand}$, Property 2 implies Property 1.

Property 2 is still not entirely satisfactory. For instance, suppose the algorithm generates σ as a candidate and then prunes $\gamma(\sigma)$. Now suppose that $\varrho \simeq \sigma$. Property 2 implies that we *cannot* call/prune $\gamma(\varrho)$. Property 3 rectifies this:

280   D. Egolf and S. Tripakis

Property 3 (invariant). Suppose that GCG$_\simeq$ invokes $\Phi := \Phi \wedge \neg\gamma(\sigma)$. Then for any $\varrho \simeq \sigma$, we should have $[\![\gamma(\varrho)]\!] \subseteq$ Pruned. In other words, if we prune $\gamma(\sigma)$, we should also prune $\gamma(\varrho)$ for every ϱ isomorphic to σ.

We note that, contrary to Properties 1 and 2 which need only hold after termination, Property 3 is an *invariant*: we want it to hold for all *partial executions* of the algorithm.

Theorem 2. *Suppose γ is proper. If* GCG$_\simeq[\Phi, \psi, \gamma]$ *maintains Property 3 as an invariant, then* GCG$_\simeq[\Phi, \psi, \gamma]$ *also maintains Property 2.*

Maintaining Property 3 increases the rate at which the search space is pruned, but is still not enough. Suppose that $\tau \vDash \gamma(\sigma)$ and that $\tau' \simeq \tau$. If we prune the members of $\gamma(\sigma)$, then we will prune τ, but not necessarily τ'. This possibility is unsatisfactory, since τ and τ' should both be treated whenever one of them is.

Property 4 (invariant). Suppose $\tau \in$ Pruned and $\tau' \simeq \tau$. Then $\tau' \in$ Pruned or $\tau' \in$ Sol. In other words, if we prune τ we should also prune any isomorphic τ', unless τ' happens to be a solution. (Note that Property 1 guarantees that this exception applies to at most one τ').

Maintaining Property 4 as an invariant further accelerates pruning. Under certain conditions, Property 3 implies Property 4. In particular, Property 3 implies Property 4 if γ is *invertible*, a concept that we define next.

Invertible Generalizers. Let γ be a generalizer and let τ be an assignment. We define the *inverse* $\gamma^{-1}(\tau)$, to be the propositional logic formula satisfied by all σ such that $\tau \vDash \gamma(\sigma)$. That is, $\sigma \vDash \gamma^{-1}(\tau)$ iff $\tau \vDash \gamma(\sigma)$.

Let φ and φ' be propositional logic formulas. Suppose that for every $\sigma \vDash \varphi$, there exists a $\sigma' \vDash \varphi'$ such that $\sigma' \simeq \sigma$. Then we say that φ *subsumes φ' up to isomorphism*. If φ and φ' both subsume each other, then we say that they are *equivalent up to isomorphism*.

A generalizer γ is *invertible* if for all assignments τ, τ' that satisfy Φ, if $\tau \simeq \tau'$ then $\gamma^{-1}(\tau)$ and $\gamma^{-1}(\tau')$ are equivalent up to isomorphism. Now if $\tau \vDash \gamma(\sigma)$ and $\tau' \simeq \tau$, invertibility guarantees that we can point to a $\sigma' \simeq \sigma$ such that $\tau' \vDash \gamma(\sigma')$.

Theorem 3. *Suppose γ is proper and invertible. If* GCG$_\simeq[\Phi, \psi, \gamma]$ *maintains Property 3 as an invariant, then* GCG$_\simeq[\Phi, \psi, \gamma]$ *also maintains Property 4 as an invariant.*

Proof. Let γ be a proper, invertible generalizer. We will proceed by contradiction. Assume that we have run the algorithm for some amount of time and paused its execution, freezing the state of Pruned. Suppose that GCG$_\simeq[\Phi, \psi, \gamma]$ satisfies Property 3 at this point, but that it does not satisfy Property 4. From the negation of Property 4, we have at this point in the execution two assignments τ and τ' such that (1) $\tau \simeq \tau'$, (2) $\tau \in$ Pruned, (3) $\tau' \notin$ Pruned, and (4) $\tau' \notin$ Sol.

There are two cases that fall out of (2). Either τ was pruned using a call to γ, or exactly $[\tau]$ was pruned. In the second case, we quickly reach a contradiction since it implies that $\tau' \in$ Pruned, violating assumption (3).

So instead, we assume $\tau \vDash \gamma(\sigma)$ for some σ and that this call to γ was invoked at some point in the past. So $\sigma \vDash \gamma^{-1}(\tau)$. But then by invertibility and (1) there exists $\sigma' \simeq \sigma$ such that $\sigma' \vDash \gamma^{-1}(\tau')$ and hence $\tau' \vDash \gamma(\sigma')$. Property 3 tells us then that $\tau' \in$ Pruned, but this conclusion also violates assumption (3). $\qquad\square$

It can be shown that the generalizer γ_{LTS} is invertible. Essentially, this is because γ_{LTS} does not depend on state names (for example, the structure of cycles and paths is independent of state names). Still, $\text{GCG}_\simeq[\Phi, \psi, \gamma_{LTS}]$ satisfies only Property 1 above. Therefore, we will next describe an optimized generalization method that exploits isomorphism to satisfy all properties.

4.4 Optimized Generalization

Equivalence Closure. If γ is a generalizer and $\simeq$ is an equivalence relation, then let

$$\tilde{\tilde{\gamma}}(\varrho) := \bigvee_{\sigma \in [\varrho]} \gamma(\sigma)$$

be the *equivalence closure* of γ. If $\gamma(\sigma) \equiv \tilde{\tilde{\gamma}}(\sigma)$ for all σ, we say that γ is *closed under equivalence*.

Note that $\tilde{\tilde{\gamma}}$ is itself a generalizer. An instance of $\text{GCG}_\simeq$ that uses $\tilde{\tilde{\gamma}}$ is correct and satisfies all the efficiency properties identified above:

Theorem 4. *If γ is a proper generalizer, then $\text{GCG}_\simeq[\Phi, \psi, \tilde{\tilde{\gamma}}]$ is sound, terminating, and complete up to isomorphisms.*

Theorem 5. *If γ is proper, then $\text{GCG}_\simeq[\Phi, \psi, \tilde{\tilde{\gamma}}]$ maintains Properties 1 and 2. Furthermore, the algorithm maintains Property 3 as an invariant.*

Theorem 6. *If γ is both proper and invertible, then: (1) $\tilde{\tilde{\gamma}}$ is invertible; (2) $\text{GCG}_\simeq[\Phi, \psi, \tilde{\tilde{\gamma}}]$ maintains Property 4 as an invariant.*

Computation Options for $\tilde{\tilde{\gamma}}$. The naive way to compute $\tilde{\tilde{\gamma}}$ is to iterate over all $\sigma_1, \sigma_2, \cdots, \sigma_k \in [\varrho]$, compute each $\gamma(\sigma_i)$, and then return the disjunction of all $\gamma(\sigma_i)$. We call this the *naive generalization* approach. The problem with this approach is that we have to call γ as many as $n!$ times, where n is the number of permutable states. The experimental results in Sect. 5 indicate empirically that this naive method does not scale well.

We thus propose a better approach, which is *incremental*, in the sense that we only have to compute γ once, for $\gamma(\sigma_1)$; we can then perform simple *syntactic transformations* on $\gamma(\sigma_1)$ to obtain $\gamma(\sigma_2)$, $\gamma(\sigma_3)$, and so on. As we will show, these transformations are much more efficient than computing each $\gamma(\sigma_i)$ from scratch. So-called *permuters* formalize this idea:

Permuters. A *permuter* is a function π that takes as input an assignment ϱ and the generalization $\gamma(\sigma)$ for some $\sigma \simeq \varrho$, and returns a propositional logic formula $\pi(\sigma, \gamma(\varrho))$ such that $\forall \varrho \vDash \Phi, \forall \sigma \simeq \varrho :: M_\varrho \nvDash \psi \rightarrow \pi(\varrho, \gamma(\sigma)) \equiv \gamma(\varrho)$. That is, assuming ϱ is "bad" ($M_\varrho \nvDash \psi$), $\pi(\varrho, \gamma(\sigma))$ is equivalent to $\gamma(\varrho)$. However, contrary to γ, π can use the extra information $\gamma(\sigma)$ to compute the generalization of ϱ. Then, instead of $\tilde{\tilde{\gamma}}(\varrho)$, we can compute the logically equivalent formula

$$\gamma_\pi(\varrho) := \bigvee_{\sigma \in [\varrho]} \pi(\sigma, \gamma(\varrho)).$$

Theorem 7. *Theorems 4, 5, and 6 also hold for* $\mathrm{GCG}_\simeq[\Phi, \psi, \gamma_\pi]$.

Proof. Follows from the fact that for any ϱ, $\gamma_\pi(\varrho) \equiv \tilde{\tilde{\gamma}}(\varrho)$.   □

A Concrete Permuter for LTS. We now explain how to compute π concretely in our application domain, namely LTS. Let M_0 be an incomplete LTS. Let σ_1, σ_2 be two assignments encoding completions M_{σ_1} and M_{σ_2} of M_0. Suppose $M_{\sigma_1} \overset{A}{\simeq} M_{\sigma_2}$. Recall that A is the set of permutable states (the non-initial states with no incoming/outgoing transitions by default). Then there is a permutation $f : A \rightarrow A$, such that applying f to the states of M_{σ_1} yields M_{σ_2}. f allows us to transform one LTS to another, but it also allows us to transform the generalization formula for σ_1, namely $\gamma(\sigma_1)$, to the one for σ_2, namely $\gamma(\sigma_2)$.

For example, let M_0 be the leftmost LTS in Fig. 4, with alphabet $\Sigma = \{a\}$, states $Q = \{p_0, p_1, p_2, p_3\}$, initial state p_0, and the empty transition relation. Let M_{σ_1} and M_{σ_2} be the remaining LTSs shown in Fig. 4. Let $A = \{p_1, p_2, p_3\}$ and let f be the permutation mapping p_1 to p_3, p_3 to p_2, and p_2 to p_1. Then $M_{\sigma_1} \overset{A}{\simeq} M_{\sigma_2}$ and f is the witness to this isomorphism.

Let $\gamma(\sigma_1) = (p_0 \leftrightsquigarrow^a p_1) \wedge (p_1 \leftrightsquigarrow^a p_2) \wedge (p_2 \leftrightsquigarrow^a p_3)$. $\gamma(\sigma_1)$ captures the four LTSs in Fig. 5. The key idea is that we can compute $\gamma(\sigma_2)$ by transforming $\gamma(\sigma_1)$ *purely syntactically*. In particular, we apply the permutation f to all p_i appearing in the variables of the formula. Doing so, we obtain $\gamma(\sigma_2) = (p_0 \leftrightsquigarrow^a p_3) \wedge (p_3 \leftrightsquigarrow^a p_1) \wedge (p_1 \leftrightsquigarrow^a p_2)$. This formula in turn captures the four LTSs in Fig. 6, which are exactly the permutations of those in Fig. 5 after applying f.

We now describe this transformation formally. Observe that M_{σ_1} and M_{σ_2} have the same set of states, say Q. We extend the permutation to $f : Q \rightarrow Q$ by defining $f(q) = q$ for all states $q \notin A$. Now, we extend this permutation of states to permutations of the set V (the set of boolean variables encoding transitions). Specifically we extend f to permute V by defining: $f(p \leftrightsquigarrow^a q) := f(p) \leftrightsquigarrow^a f(q)$ and we extend it to propositional formulas by applying it to all variables in the formula. Then we define $\pi_{LTS}(\sigma_2, \gamma(\sigma_1)) := f(\gamma(\sigma_1))$.

In essence, the permuter π_{LTS} identifies the permutation f witnessing the fact that $\sigma_1 \simeq \sigma_2$. It then applies f to the variables of $\gamma(\sigma_1)$. Applying f to $\gamma(\sigma_1)$ is equivalent to applying f to all assignments that satisfy $\gamma(\sigma_1)$.

It can be shown that π_{LTS} is a permuter for LTS. It follows then that the concrete instance $\mathrm{GCG}_\simeq[\Phi, \psi, \gamma_\pi]$ (where $\gamma := \gamma_{LTS}$ and $\pi := \pi_{LTS}$) satisfies

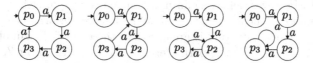

Fig. 4. An incomplete LTS M_0 and two possible completions, M_{σ_1} and M_{σ_2}

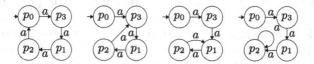

Fig. 5. LTSs represented by $(p_0 \looparrowright^a p_1) \wedge (p_1 \looparrowright^a p_2) \wedge (p_2 \looparrowright^a p_3)$

Theorem 7, i.e., it is sound, terminating, complete up to isomorphisms, and satisfies all Properties 1–4.

Fig. 6. LTSs represented by $(p_0 \looparrowright^a p_3) \wedge (p_3 \looparrowright^a p_1) \wedge (p_1 \looparrowright^a p_2)$

5   Implementation and Evaluation

Implementation and Experimental Setup. We evaluate the three algorithms discussed so far: the *unoptimized* algorithm $\mathrm{GCG}[\Phi, \psi, \gamma_{LTS}]$ of [2,4] (Sect. 3.2); and the *naive optimization* $\mathrm{GCG}_\sim[\Phi, \psi, \tilde{\tilde{\gamma}}]$ and *permuter optimization* $\mathrm{GCG}_\sim[\Phi, \psi, \gamma_\pi]$ algorithms of Sect. 4.4. These are respectively labeled 'unopt.', 'naive opt.', and 'perm. opt.' in the tables that follow.

In addition, we evaluate the unoptimized algorithm outfitted with an additional optimization, which we call the dead transition optimization. We say that a transition of an LTS is *dead* if this transition is never taken in any run. If M with states Q is correct and has k dead transitions, then there are $|Q|^k$ solutions that are equivalent modulo dead transitions, since we can point a dead transition anywhere while maintaining correctness. The dead transition optimization prunes all solutions which are equivalent modulo dead transitions. It is equivalent to the unoptimized algorithm in cases where there are no solutions or where we are looking for only one solution. Therefore, we evaluate the dead transition optimization side-by-side with the unoptimized solution only when we are enumerating all correct completions. The naive and permuter optimizations both include the dead transition optimization.

We use [28], the Python implementation of $\textsc{gcg}[\Phi, \psi, \gamma_{LTS}]$ made publicly available by the authors of [2,4], and we implement our optimizations on top of [28] in order to keep the comparison fair. The tool can handle completion of distributed systems, rather than of single LTSs. Distributed systems are represented as networks of communicating LTSs similar to those in [4]. Specifications are represented using safety and liveness (Büchi) monitors, again similar to those in [4]. However, let us again mention that our approach is not specific to any particular specification logic; it should allow for performance gains whenever the cost of model-checking is greater than the cost of the simple syntactic transformations applied by the permuter. We use the SAT solver Z3 [7] to pick candidates from the search space. Our experimental results can be reproduced using a publicly available artifact [9].

For our experiments we use the ABP case study as presented in [4] as well as our own two phase commit (2PC) case study. We consider three use cases: (1) *completion enumeration*: enumerate all correct completions; (2) *realizable 1-completion*: return the first correct completion and stop, where we ensure that a correct completion exists; and (3) *unrealizable 1-completion*: return the first correct completion, except that we ensure that none exists (and therefore the tool has to explore the entire candidate space in vain).

We consider a *many-process synthesis* scenario, where the goal is to synthesize two or more processes, and a *1-process synthesis* scenario, where the goal is to synthesize a single process. In both of these scenarios across both the ABP and 2PC case studies, the synthesized processes are composed with additional environment processes and safety and liveness monitors. The results of the many-process synthesis scenario are presented shortly. Due to lack of space, the results of the 1-process synthesis scenario are presented in Appendix A.2 of [11]. The latter results do not add much additional insight, except that 1-process synthesis tends to take less time.

Each experiment was run on a dedicated 2.40 GHz CPU core located on the Northeastern Discovery Cluster. All times are in seconds, rounded up to the second.

Many-Process Synthesis Experiments. In all these experiments, there are multiple LTSs that must both be completed. In the case of ABP: (1) the incomplete ABP *Receiver$_0$* of Fig. 1 without further modification; (2) an incomplete sender process, which is obtained by removing some set of transitions from process *Sender* of Fig. 3. The set of transitions removed from *Sender* are all incoming and all outgoing transitions from all states designated as permutable for that experiment (column A in the tables that follow). For instance, in experiment $\{s_1, s_2\}$ of Table 1 we remove all incoming and outgoing transitions from states s_1 and s_2 of *Sender*, and similarly for the other experiments. And in the case of 2PC: (1) two incomplete 2PC database managers (see Fig. 8 in Appendix A.1 of [11]) (2) an incomplete transaction manager, which is obtained by removing some set of transitions from a complete transaction manager (see Fig. 7 in Appendix A.1 of [11]).

Table 1. Many-Process Synthesis, Completion Enumeration

Case Study; A	unopt.			dead opt.			naive opt.			perm. opt.		
	sol.	iter.	time	sol.	iter.	time	sol.	iter.	time	sol.	iter.	time
2PC; $\{p_1, p_2\}$	4	536	47	4	536	46	2	274	34	2	274	28
2PC; $\{p_2, p_3\}$	48	1417	130	4	1352	124	2	735	93	2	735	77
2PC; $\{p_3, p_4\}$	336	2852	266	6	2600	231	3	1328	161	3	1328	134
2PC; $\{p_4, p_8\}$	576	1813	168	4	1237	112	2	575	75	2	648	66
ABP; $\{s_1, s_2\}$	64	628	27	8	574	21	4	289	18	4	304	12
ABP; $\{s_2, s_3\}$	64	1859	75	8	1832	70	4	946	55	4	943	37
ABP; $\{s_3, s_4\}$	32	374	18	4	353	13	2	188	12	2	192	8
ABP; $\{s_4, s_5\}$	32	3728	177	4	3638	170	2	1913	160	2	1833	93
ABP; $\{s_5, s_6\}$	64	449	27	8	412	21	4	199	18	4	201	11
ABP; $\{s_6, s_7\}$	64	1518	94	8	1481	87	4	769	80	4	752	47
2PC; $\{p_2, p_3, p_4\}$	2016	17478	1896	36	15646	1677	6	2693	719	6	2693	466
2PC; $\{p_3, p_4, p_8\}$	$^{7939}\!/$	101278	TO	36	23044	2498	6	4079	1064	6	3997	682
ABP; $\{s_1, s_2, s_3\}$	192	5641	226	24	5499	207	4	968	155	4	937	49
ABP; $\{s_2, s_3, s_4\}$	3072	23025	1470	48	19114	934	8	3639	722	8	3331	225
ABP; $\{s_3, s_4, s_5\}$	96	14651	748	12	15108	760	2	2599	567	2	2520	172
ABP; $\{s_4, s_5, s_6\}$	1536	14405	876	24	13269	686	4	2458	554	4	2215	151
ABP; $\{s_5, s_6, s_7\}$	192	4686	287	24	4559	268	4	809	241	4	748	57
2PC; $\{p_1, p_2, p_3, p_4\}$	$^{8064}\!/$	70250	TO	144	62280	11915	6	2770	2844	6	2719	1564
ABP; $\{s_1, s_2, s_3, s_4\}$	12288	90031	8143	192	76591	5458	8	3704	2931	8	3271	628
ABP; $\{s_3, s_4, s_5, s_6\}$	6144	59838	4777	96	52935	3543	4	2896	2655	4	2351	431
ABP; $\{s_4, s_5, s_6, s_7\}$	$^{100}\!/$	108929	TO	$^{38}\!/_{96}$	111834	TO	$^{3}\!/_{4}$	10443	TO	4	8639	7480

Completion Enumeration. Table 1 presents the results for the completion enumeration use case and many-process synthesis scenario. Columns labeled *sol.* and *iter.* record the number of solutions (i.e., |Sol|) and loop iterations of Algorithm 2 (i.e., the number of candidates |Cand|, i.e., the number of times the SAT routine is called), respectively. Pilot experiments showed negligible variance across random seeds, so reported times are for one seed. TO denotes a timeout of 4 h, in which case p/q means the tool produced p out of the total q solutions. For the dead opt. column, we know that $q = 24 \cdot n$, where n is the number of solutions/equivalence classes found by the permuter optimization and $24 = 4!$ is the number of isomorphisms for 4 states. Since the naive optimization produces equivalence classes, $q = n$ for the naive opt. column.

The results in Table 1 are consistent with our theoretical analyses. When there are 2 permutable states, the naive and permuter optimizations explore about half the number of candidates as the dead transitions method. For 3 permutable states, the optimized methods explore about $3! = 6$ times fewer candidates. For 4 permutable states, the optimized methods explore about $4! = 24$ times fewer candidates than the dead transitions method in the only experiment where the unoptimized method does not timeout. Notably, the permuter optimization does not timeout on any of these experiments.

Realizable 1-Completion. Table 2 presents the results for the realizable 1-completion use case (return the first solution found and stop) and many-process synthesis scenario. Our experiments and those of [4] suggest that there is more time variability for this task depending on the random seed provided to Z3. Thus, for Table 2 we run the tools for 10 different random seeds and report average times and number of iterations, rounded up. In one case (last row of Table 2), for a single seed out of the 10 seeds, the program timed out before finding a solution. As the true average is unknown in this case, we report it as TO.

Table 2. Many-Process Synthesis, Realizable 1-Completion

Case Study; A	unopt.		naive opt.		perm. opt.	
	iter.	time	iter.	time	iter.	time
2PC; $\{p_1, p_2\}$	199	19	157	20	157	17
2PC; $\{p_2, p_3\}$	483	47	429	55	426	46
2PC; $\{p_3, p_4\}$	798	72	696	84	666	69
2PC; $\{p_4, p_8\}$	380	37	319	44	311	34
ABP; $\{s_1, s_2\}$	111	4	110	7	100	4
ABP; $\{s_2, s_3\}$	220	9	205	13	200	9
ABP; $\{s_3, s_4\}$	106	5	102	7	105	5
ABP; $\{s_4, s_5\}$	1669	75	909	73	1202	60
ABP; $\{s_5, s_6\}$	102	5	95	8	102	5
ABP; $\{s_6, s_7\}$	507	28	294	28	294	17
2PC; $\{p_2, p_3, p_4\}$	440	48	590	147	561	89
2PC; $\{p_3, p_4, p_8\}$	954	94	861	205	796	121
ABP; $\{s_1, s_2, s_3\}$	332	12	225	36	240	13
ABP; $\{s_2, s_3, s_4\}$	2462	108	904	170	1028	64
ABP; $\{s_3, s_4, s_5\}$	2267	102	1040	219	819	52
ABP; $\{s_4, s_5, s_6\}$	2735	130	1513	333	1327	92
ABP; $\{s_5, s_6, s_7\}$	361	21	264	69	308	22
2PC; $\{p_1, p_2, p_3, p_4\}$	806	81	495	387	572	220
ABP; $\{s_1, s_2, s_3, s_4\}$	1957	85	1068	760	890	122
ABP; $\{s_3, s_4, s_5, s_6\}$	5425	261	1003	860	1601	234
ABP; $\{s_4, s_5, s_6, s_7\}$	16098	1088	TO	TO	4159	1158

Unrealizable 1-Completion. Table 3 presents the results for the unrealizable 1-completion use case and many-process synthesis scenario. For these experiments, we artificially modify the ABP *Sender* by completely removing state s_7, which results in no correct completion existing. A similar change is applied to *tx. man.*

in the case of 2PC. Thus, the tools explore the entire search space and terminate without finding a solution. As can be seen, the permuter optimization significantly prunes the search space and achieves considerable speedups.

Table 3. Many-Process Synthesis, Unrealizable 1-Completion

Case Study; A	unopt.		naive opt.		perm. opt.	
	iter.	time	iter.	time	iter.	time
2PC; $\{p_1, p_2\}$	3207	292	1658	206	1655	175
2PC; $\{p_2, p_3\}$	9792	978	4996	646	4982	552
2PC; $\{p_3, p_4\}$	14911	1527	7645	1053	7589	878
2PC; $\{p_4, p_8\}$	5123	494	2537	339	2555	282
ABP; $\{s_1, s_2\}$	1650	58	879	52	853	33
ABP; $\{s_2, s_3\}$	4300	173	2384	171	2374	106
ABP; $\{s_3, s_4\}$	327	13	173	11	164	7
ABP; $\{s_4, s_5\}$	3108	143	1592	130	1710	89
ABP; $\{s_5, s_6\}$	333	16	172	15	168	9
2PC; $\{p_2, p_3, p_4\}$	66088	TO	19717	10867	19850	9610
2PC; $\{p_3, p_4, p_8\}$	70586	TO	26343	TO	26516	14340
ABP; $\{s_1, s_2, s_3\}$	20858	1022	3705	798	3668	253
ABP; $\{s_2, s_3, s_4\}$	58974	4021	10516	2673	10496	1052
ABP; $\{s_3, s_4, s_5\}$	12323	596	2231	504	2167	146
ABP; $\{s_4, s_5, s_6\}$	11210	557	2104	491	1985	136
2PC; $\{p_1, p_2, p_3, p_4\}$	67659	TO	10365	TO	12308	TO
ABP; $\{s_1, s_2, s_3, s_4\}$	129264	TO	12096	TO	14739	TO
ABP; $\{s_3, s_4, s_5, s_6\}$	45056	2869	2466	2392	2004	339

6   Related Work

Synthesis of Distributed Protocols: Distributed system synthesis has been studied both in the reactive synthesis setting [23] and in the setting of discrete-event systems [29, 30]. More recently, synthesis of distributed protocols has been studied using completion techniques in [2–4, 17]. [2, 4] study completion of finite-state protocols such as ABP but they do not focus on enumeration. [3] considers infinite-state protocols and focus on synthesis of symbolic expressions (guards and assignments). None of [2–4] propose any reduction techniques. We propose reduction modulo isomorphisms.

[17] studies synthesis for a class of parameterized distributed agreement-based protocols for which verification is efficiently decidable. Another version of the

paper [16] considers permutations of process indices. These are different from our permutations over process states.

Synthesis of parameterized distributed systems is also studied in [21] using the notion of *cutoffs*, which guarantee that if a property holds for all systems up to a certain size (the cutoff size) then it also holds for systems of any size. Cutoffs are different from our isomorphism reductions.

Bounded Synthesis: The bounded synthesis approach [12] limits the search space of synthesis by setting an upper bound on certain system parameters, and encodes the resulting problem into a satisfiability problem. Bounded synthesis is applicable to many application domains, including distributed system synthesis, and has been successfully used to synthesize systems such as distributed arbiters and dining philosophers [12]. Symmetries have also been exploited in bounded synthesis. Typically, such symmetries encode similarity of processes (e.g., all processes having the same state-transition structure, as in the case of dining philosophers). As such, these symmetries are similar to those exploited in parameterized systems, and different from our LTS isomorphisms.

Symmetry Reductions in Model-Checking: Symmetries have been exploited in model-checking [5]. The basic idea is to take a model M and construct a new model M_G which has a much smaller state space. This construction exploits the fact that many states in M might be functionally equivalent, in the sense of incoming and outgoing transitions. The key distinction between this work and ours is that our symmetries are over the space of models rather than the space of states of a fixed model. This distinction allows us to exploit symmetries for completion enumeration rather than model-checking.

Symmetry-Breaking Predicates: Symmetry-breaking predicates have been used to solve SAT [6], SMT [8], and even graph search problems [14], more efficiently. Our work is related in the sense that we are also trying to prune a search space. But our approach differs both in the notion of symmetry used (LTS isomorphism) as well as the application domain (distributed protocols). Moreover, rather than trying to eliminate all but one member of each equivalence class at the outset, say, by somehow adding a global (and often prohibitively large) symmetry-breaking formula Ξ to Φ, we do so *on-the-fly* for each candidate solution.

Canonical Forms: In program synthesis work [25], a candidate program is only checked for correctness if it is in some normal form. [25] is not about synthesis of distributed protocols, and as such the normal forms considered there are very different from our LTS isomorphisms. In particular, as with symmetry-breaking, the normal forms used in [25] are global, defined *a-priori* for the entire program domain, whereas our generalizations are computed on-the-fly. Moreover, the approach of [25] may still generate two equivalent programs as candidates (prior to verification), i.e., it does not satisfy our Property 2.

Sketching, CEGIS, OGIS, Sciduction: Completion algorithms such as GCG belong to the same family of techniques as sketching [27], counter-example guided inductive synthesis (CEGIS) [1,13,26,27], oracle-guided inductive synthesis (OGIS) [18], and sciduction [24].

7 Conclusions

We proposed a novel distributed protocol synthesis approach based on completion enumeration modulo isomorphisms. Our approach follows the *guess-check-generalize* synthesis paradigm, and relies on non-trivial optimizations of the generalization step that exploit state permutations. These optimizations allow to significantly prune the search space of candidate completions, achieving speedups of factors approximately 2 to 10 and in some cases completing experiments in minutes instead of hours. To our knowledge, ours is the only work on distributed protocol enumeration using reductions such as isomorphism.

As future work, we plan to employ this optimized enumeration approach for the synthesis of distributed protocols that achieve not only correctness, but also performance objectives. We also plan to address the question *where do the incomplete processes come from?* If not provided by the user, such incomplete processes might be automatically generated from example scenarios as in [2,4], or might simply be "empty skeletons" of states, without any transitions. We also plan to extend our approach to infinite-state protocols, as well as application domains beyond protocols, as Algorithm 2 is generic and thus applicable to a wide class of synthesis domains.

Acknowledgements. Derek Egolf's research has been initially supported by a Northeastern University PhD fellowship. This material is based upon work supported by the National Science Foundation Graduate Research Fellowship under Grant No. (1938052). Any opinion, findings, and conclusions or recommendations expressed in this material are those of the authors(s) and do not necessarily reflect the views of the National Science Foundation. We thank Christos Stergiou for his work on the distributed protocol completion tool that we built upon. We also thank the anonymous reviewers for their helpful comments and feedback.

References

1. Alur, R., et al.: Syntax-guided synthesis. In: Formal Methods in Computer-Aided Design, FMCAD, pp. 1–17 (2013)
2. Alur, R., Martin, M., Raghothaman, M., Stergiou, C., Tripakis, S., Udupa, A.: Synthesizing finite-state protocols from scenarios and requirements. In: Yahav, E. (ed.) HVC 2014. LNCS, vol. 8855, pp. 75–91. Springer, Cham (2014). https://doi.org/10.1007/978-3-319-13338-6_7
3. Alur, R., Raghothaman, M., Stergiou, C., Tripakis, S., Udupa, A.: Automatic completion of distributed protocols with symmetry. In: Kroening, D., Păsăreanu, C.S. (eds.) CAV 2015. LNCS, vol. 9207, pp. 395–412. Springer, Cham (2015). https://doi.org/10.1007/978-3-319-21668-3_23

4. Alur, R., Tripakis, S.: Automatic synthesis of distributed protocols. SIGACT News **48**(1), 55–90 (2017)

5. Clarke, E.M., Emerson, E.A., Jha, S., Sistla, A.P.: Symmetry reductions in model checking. In: Hu, A.J., Vardi, M.Y. (eds.) CAV 1998. LNCS, vol. 1427, pp. 147–158. Springer, Heidelberg (1998). https://doi.org/10.1007/BFb0028741

6. Crawford, J.M., Ginsberg, M.L., Luks, E.M., Roy, A.: Symmetry-breaking predicates for search problems. In: Aiello, L.C., Doyle, J., Shapiro, S.C. (eds.) Proceedings of the Fifth International Conference on Principles of Knowledge Representation and Reasoning (KR 1996), Cambridge, Massachusetts, USA, 5–8 November 1996, pp. 148–159. Morgan Kaufmann (1996)

7. de Moura, L., Bjørner, N.: Z3: an efficient SMT solver. In: Ramakrishnan, C.R., Rehof, J. (eds.) TACAS 2008. LNCS, vol. 4963, pp. 337–340. Springer, Heidelberg (2008). https://doi.org/10.1007/978-3-540-78800-3_24

8. Dingliwal, S., Agarwal, R., Mittal, H., Singla, P.: CVC4-SymBreak: derived SMT solver at SMT competition 2019. CoRR, abs/1908.00860 (2019)

9. Egolf, D.: ATVA2023 artifact. https://github.com/egolf-cs/synge_reproducible

10. Egolf, D., Tripakis, S.: Decoupled fitness criteria for reactive systems. arXiv eprint arXiv:2212.12455 (2022)

11. Egolf, D., Tripakis, S.: Synthesis of distributed protocols by enumeration modulo isomorphisms. arXiv eprint arXiv:2306.02967 (2023)

12. Finkbeiner, B., Schewe, S.: Bounded synthesis. Int. J. Softw. Tools Technol. Transf. **15**(5–6), 519–539 (2013). https://doi.org/10.1007/s10009-012-0228-z

13. Gulwani, S., Polozov, O., Singh, R.: Program synthesis. Found. Trends Program. Lang. **4**(1–2), 1–119 (2017)

14. Heule, M.J.H.: The quest for perfect and compact symmetry breaking for graph problems. In: Davenport, J.H., et al. (eds.) 18th International Symposium on Symbolic and Numeric Algorithms for Scientific Computing, SYNASC 2016, Timisoara, Romania, 24–27 September 2016, pp. 149–156. IEEE (2016)

15. Holzmann, G.: Design and Validation of Computer Protocols. Prentice Hall (1991)

16. Jaber, N., Jacobs, S., Kulkarni, M., Samanta, R.: Parameterized synthesis for distributed applications with consensus. https://www.cs.purdue.edu/homes/roopsha/papers/discoveri.pdf

17. Jaber, N., Wagner, C., Jacobs, S., Kulkarni, M., Samanta, R.: Synthesis of distributed agreement-based systems with efficiently-decidable parameterized verification. CoRR, abs/2208.12400 (2022)

18. Jha, S., Seshia, S.A.: A theory of formal synthesis via inductive learning. Acta Informatica **54**(7), 693–726 (2017). https://doi.org/10.1007/s00236-017-0294-5

19. Lamport, L.: Specifying Systems, The TLA+ Language and Tools for Hardware and Software Engineers. Addison-Wesley, Boston (2002)

20. Lynch, N.A.: Distributed Algorithms. Morgan Kaufmann Publishers Inc., San Francisco (1996)

21. Mirzaie, N., Faghih, F., Jacobs, S., Bonakdarpour, B.: Parameterized synthesis of self-stabilizing protocols in symmetric networks. Acta Informatica **57**(1–2), 271–304 (2020). https://doi.org/10.1007/s00236-019-00361-7

22. Newcombe, C., Rath, T., Zhang, F., Munteanu, B., Brooker, M., Deardeuff, M.: How amazon web services uses formal methods. Commun. ACM **58**(4), 66–73 (2015)

23. Pnueli, A., Rosner, R.: Distributed reactive systems are hard to synthesize. In: Proceedings of the 31th IEEE Symposium on Foundations of Computer Science, pp. 746–757 (1990)

24. Seshia, S.A.: Sciduction: combining induction, deduction, and structure for verification and synthesis. In: Groeneveld, P., Sciuto, D., Hassoun, S. (eds.) The 49th Annual Design Automation Conference 2012, DAC 2012, San Francisco, CA, USA, 3–7 June 2012, pp. 356–365. ACM (2012)
25. Smith, C., Albarghouthi, A.: Program synthesis with equivalence reduction. In: Enea, C., Piskac, R. (eds.) VMCAI 2019. LNCS, vol. 11388, pp. 24–47. Springer, Cham (2019). https://doi.org/10.1007/978-3-030-11245-5_2
26. Solar-Lezama, A., Tancau, L., Bodik, R., Seshia, S., Saraswat, V.: Combinatorial sketching for finite programs. SIGOPS Oper. Syst. Rev. 40(5), 404–415 (2006)
27. Solar-Lezama, A.: Program sketching. Int. J. Softw. Tools Technol. Transf. 15(5–6), 475–495 (2013). https://doi.org/10.1007/s10009-012-0249-7
28. Stergiou, C.: Distributed protocol completion tool. https://github.com/stavros7167/distributed_protocol_completion
29. Thistle, J.G.: Undecidability in decentralized supervision. Syst. Control Lett. 54(5), 503–509 (2005)
30. Tripakis, S.: Undecidable problems of decentralized observation and control on regular languages. Inf. Process. Lett. 90(1), 21–28 (2004)
31. Zave, P.: Reasoning about identifier spaces: how to make chord correct. IEEE Trans. Softw. Eng. 43(12), 1144–1156 (2017)

Controller Synthesis for Reactive Systems with Communication Delay by Formula Translation

J. S. Sajiv Kumar⬤ and Raghavan Komondoor[✉]⬤

Indian Institute of Science, Bengaluru, India
{sajiv,raghavan}@iisc.ac.in

Abstract. The problem of automated reactive synthesis has been well studied by researchers. We consider a setting that is common in practice, wherein there is a communication delay between the (synthesized) controller and the (controlled) plant, such that symbols emitted by either component reach the other component after a delay. We address the problem of synthesizing a controller that can assure the given temporal property at the remote plant despite delay. We consider two variants of this setting, one where the delay is a constant over the entire trace, and the other where the delay could increase over time (upto an upper bound), and propose approaches for both these settings. We state and prove soundness and completeness results for both our approaches. We have implemented our approaches, and evaluated them on the standard SYNTCOMP 2022 suite of temporal properties. The results provide evidence for the robustness and practicality of our approaches.

1 Introduction

Reactive synthesis is the problem of automatically inferring a correct-by- construction *controller*, that can control an *environment* or *plant* to ensure that all runs of the plant satisfy a given temporal property. This is a classical problem, that has been extensively studied over several decades. We cite a selection of papers [5,6,10,13], and refer the interested reader to a recent book chapter [1] for a comprehensive view.

The classical controller synthesis setting assumes instant (delay-free) communication of input and output symbols between the controller and the controlled plant. However, delay in the flow of information between controller and plant is common in real life settings, due to issues like distance between the plant and controller, or network congestion. For instance, this is recognized in the *Controller Area Network (CAN)* protocol for vehicular control [4,19], and in protocols for the remote control of satellites [2,11]. Researchers often devise carefully handcrafted solutions to account for delay in individual protocols [15,18], but this can be complicated and error prone.

The formal methods research community has been aware of this issue, and has proposed a few techniques that can synthesize controllers while accounting

É. André and J. Sun (Eds.): ATVA 2023, LNCS 14215, pp. 292–311, 2023.
https://doi.org/10.1007/978-3-031-45329-8_14

for communication delay [3,5,16]. Our work has the same broad objective, and we address the scenario where we are given a *Linear Temporal Logic* (LTL) property as specification. We make the following contributions in this paper:

- Previous researchers have focused on the setting where the delay between the two sides is *fixed* and constant throughout the infinite trace (e.g., 2 time units of delay). For the first time in the literature to the best of our knowledge, we identify the issue of *variable delay* that can arise in real systems, formulate this problem mathematically, and propose an approach to solve it.
- We propose a novel approach that reduces controller synthesis from LTL specifications in the presence of delay to the problem of LTL synthesis without delay. We devise techniques (for fixed delay and variable delay) that emit a delay-adjusted, translated LTL formula. This formula can be fed to any classical (no-delay) LTL synthesis tool. This makes our approach efficient, flexible, and capable of leveraging future advances in classical synthesis. Previous approaches [3,5], in contrast, involved extensions to specific synthesis approaches. (Additionally, they did not address variable delay.)
- We implement our approach, and evaluate it on a standard set of 1075 benchmarks. Our results show that our approach is more efficient than a baseline approach [3] that targets fixed delay, and gives acceptable performance in the more-complex variable delay setting.

The rest of this paper is organized as follows. Section 2 provides background that is required in the rest of the paper. Section 3 presents our fixed-delay approach, while Sect. 4 presents our variable-delay approach. Section 5 presents an add-on feature to our approach – an unrealizability filter. Section 6 presents our implementation and evaluation, Sect. 7 discusses related work, while Sect. 8 concludes the paper and suggests future work directions.

2   Background

In this section we provide brief background on classical notions of plant, controller, and controller synthesis, in the absence of delay.

We are concerned with *synchronous, reactive* systems. Such a system consists of two *players*, the first player being the *controller*, while the second player being the *plant* (or *environment*). A *trace* of the system is an infinite sequence of *steps*. The plant observes a subset of *signals* from a given *output set* O in each step, and emits a subset of signals from a given *input set* I in each step. Each subset of I is called an *input symbol* while each subset of O is called an *output* symbol.

Definition 1 (Controller).   *A controller is a transducer* $C = (Q, 2^I, 2^O, \delta, \omega, q_0)$ *where Q is the finite set of controller states, q_0 is the initial controller state, 2^I is the input alphabet of the transducer, 2^O is the output alphabet of the transducer, $\delta : Q \times 2^I \to Q$ is the state transition function, and $\omega : Q \times 2^I \to 2^O$ is the output function.*

Definition 2 (Trace generated by a controller). *A trace generated by a controller* $(Q, 2^I, 2^O, \delta, \omega, q_0)$ *is a function* $t : \mathbb{N} \to 2^{I \cup O}$, *such that:*

$t[0] \cap O = \omega(q_0, t[0] \cap I)$,

$\forall i > 0. \; t[i] \cap O = \omega(\delta^i(q_0, t), t[i] \cap I)$,

where $\delta^i(q_0, t) = q_0$, *if* $i = 0$, *and* $\delta^i(q_0, t) = \delta(\delta^{i-1}(q_0, t), t[i - 1])$, *if* $i > 0$

Note, we use $t[i]$ to denote the symbols mapped to $i \in \mathbb{N}$ by the trace t, which is intuitively the content of the trace t at step i. Intuitively, the controller, while in a state $q \in Q$ in step i of the current trace t, receives the input symbol $t[i] \cap I$ emitted by the plant in step i, and responds by emitting the output symbol $t[i] \cap O \equiv \omega(q, t[i] \cap I)$ and by transitioning to the state $\delta(q, t[i] \cap I)$ in the same step.

A *linear temporal logic* [12] (LTL) formula on symbol set $I \cup O$ is syntactically defined using the following grammar:

$$\Psi = x \mid \neg\Psi \mid \Psi \wedge \Psi \mid \Psi \vee \Psi \mid X\Psi \mid F\Psi \mid G\Psi \mid \Psi U \Psi, \text{ where } x \in I \cup O.$$

Definition 3 (Trace satisfying LTL specification).

If t *is a trace, then for any* $i \geq 0$, *the suffix of* t *starting at step* i, *denoted as* $t(i)$, *is said to satisfy an LTL formula as defined below.*

$$t(i) \models \begin{cases} x & \text{if } x \in t[i], x \in (I \cup O) \\ \neg\Psi & \text{if } t(i) \not\models \Psi \\ \psi \wedge \varphi & \text{if } t(i) \models \psi \text{ and } t(i) \models \varphi \\ \psi \vee \varphi & \text{if } t(i) \models \psi \text{ or } t(i) \models \varphi \\ X\Psi & \text{if } t(i + 1) \models \Psi \\ F\Psi & \text{if } \exists k \geq i. \, t(k) \models \Psi \\ G\Psi & \text{if } \forall k \geq i. \, t(k) \models \Psi \\ \psi U \varphi & \text{if } \exists k \geq i. \, t(k) \models \varphi \text{ and } \forall n \in [i \ldots k). \, t(n) \models \psi \end{cases}$$

The trace t *is said to satisfy a LTL formula* Ψ *if* $t(0) \models \Psi$.

Definition 4 (Controller meeting a temporal specification). *A controller is said to meet a given temporal specification* Ψ *(*Ψ *being an LTL formula) if and only if every trace generated by the controller satisfies* Ψ.

Definition 5 (Realizable specification). *A specification* Ψ *is said to be realizable (under no delay) if and only if there exist a controller that meets the specification.*

Figure 1(a) depicts a controller that meets the specification given in the caption of the figure. The part before the '/' on each transition denotes an input symbol, the part after the '/' denotes the corresponding output symbol according to the ω function, while the target state of the transition denotes the result of the δ function. A "-" indicates that any symbol is ok. In this example, the set $I = \{r\}$ while the set $O = \{g\}$. In fact, in illustrations throughout this paper,

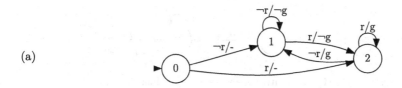

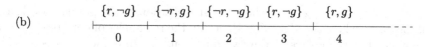

Fig. 1. (a) Controller C_1, meeting specification $G((r \Rightarrow X(g \vee X(g))) \wedge (\neg r \Rightarrow \neg X(g \wedge (X(g)))))$, (b) A trace generated by the controller

we will assume this same input set I and output set O. We use the notation '$\neg x$' in a set to indicate that the signal x is not an element of the set.

Note that if a given plant provides certain guarantees on its behavior, e.g., that it will not emit signal r in two consecutive steps, such guarantees can be encoded in LTL and treated as an *assumption*. The given *specification* can be amended to the form *assumption $\Rightarrow$ specification*, and a controller that meets this amended specification can be constructed.

Automatically synthesizing a controller that meets a given LTL-formula specification is a theoretically and practically important problem. It is important because it enables correctness by construction. It is a well-studied problem, and many interesting approaches have been proposed in the literature [1]. Numerous practical tools have been developed for this problem [7], and in fact our approach, which we present in the subsequent sections, is designed to be able to use any of these approaches as a blackbox.

3   Fixed Delay

The setting we address is that of delay between the plant and controller. That is, the output symbol emitted by either player at a step will potentially reach the other player at a later step. This effectively means the reactive system evolves as a *pair* of traces t_c, t_p, where t_c is the trace observed by the controller and t_p is the trace observed by the plant, rather than as a single trace t that is commonly visible to both players. This notion of a trace pair has not been proposed in closely related previous works. In this section and the next, we consider the setting where delay is *fixed* in both directions; i.e., there exist a pair of constants (d_{cp}, d_{pc}), both being non-negative integers, such that each output symbol (resp. input symbol) from the controller (resp. plant) reaches the plant (resp. controller) after d_{cp} (resp. d_{pc}) steps. This delay setting has been considered by previous researchers [3,5] as well. It can be easily seen that in this setting, it is enough to consider delay in one direction (any one direction). That is, a controller that meets an LTL-formula specification in the presence of

Fig. 2. Controller feasible under delay = 2

delays (d_{cp}, d_{pc}) will also meet the same specification in the presence of delays $(d, 0)$ or $(0, d)$, where $d = d_{pc} + d_{cp}$. Hence, in the remainder of our presentation, we assume that the delays in the two directions are $(0, d)$, where d is a given constant.

3.1 Definitions

Definition 6 (Trace pair under delay). *A trace pair (t_c, t_p) under delay d is a pair of traces t_c and t_p such that: (1) The first d steps of t_c have the special ϵ_i in place of an input symbol, indicating that no input symbol has arrived so far from the plant. Every other step in both traces has an input symbol and an output symbol, similar to the no-delay setting, (2) For any step i, $t_c[i] \cap O = t_p[i] \cap O$, meaning the symbol emitted by the controller reaches the plant without any delay, and (3) For any step i, $t_c[i+d] \cap I = t_p[i] \cap I$, meaning input symbols reach the controller after d steps of delay.*

Definition 7 (Trace pair satisfying a specification). *A trace pair (t_c, t_p) under delay d is said to satisfy a specification if t_p satisfies the specification.*

Definition 8 (Controller feasible under delay). *A controller (see Definition 1) is said to be feasible under delay d if there is a path of d consecutive transitions going out from the initial state q_0 such that all transitions in this path are labeled "-" for the input symbol. (Such edges can be traversed upon receiving any input symbol or even upon ϵ_i.)*

Definition 9 (Trace pair generated by a controller). *A trace pair (t_c, t_p) under delay d is said to be generated by a controller C if t_c is generated by C (see Definition 2).*

Definition 10 (Controller meeting a specification under delay). *A controller is said to meet a given specification Ψ under delay d if and only if each trace pair (t_c, t_p) under delay d that is generated by the controller is such that t_p satisfies Ψ.*

Definition 11 (Realizable specification under delay). *A specification Ψ is said to be realizable under delay d if and only if there exists a controller that meets the specification under delay d.*

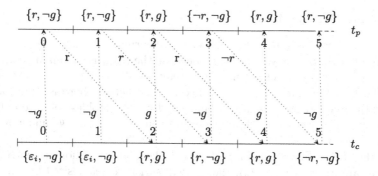

Fig. 3. A sample trace pair (t_c, t_p) under delay $= 2$. (t_c, t_p) satisfies the specification $G((r \Rightarrow X(g \lor X(g))) \land (\neg r \Rightarrow \neg X(g \land (X(g)))))$.

Figure 2 depicts a controller that is feasible under delay $d = 2$. This controller can be seen to meet the specification given in the caption of Fig. 1 under delay $d = 2$. The trace pair depicted in Fig. 3 is under delay $= 2$, and can be seen to be generated by the controller in Fig. 2. This trace pair satisfies the specification. The dashed arrows in Fig. 3 indicate of the flow of symbols in both directions.

3.2 Results on Control Under Delay

An specification that is realizable without delay may not be realizable in the presence of delay. For instance, consider the specification $G(r \Leftrightarrow g)$, where r is an input signal and g is an output signal. A controller that emits g (resp. $\emptyset \in O$) in the same step when it sees r (resp. $\emptyset \in I$) meets the specification when there is no delay. However, this specification is not realizable in the presence of any delay $d > 0$, as whatever the controller emits in the first step (without knowledge of the input), the plant could potentially emit a symbol in the first step to violate the specification. Similarly, a specification that is realizable under a certain delay may not remain realizable under higher values of delay.

Say a specification is realizable under delay d_1 and under delay d_2, $d_1 < d_2$. A controller that meets the specification under delay d_1 may not necessarily meet the same specification under delay d_2. For instance, the controller in Fig. 1 can meet the specification in the caption of that figure under no delay, but not under delay $= 2$ because in the first two steps t_c will neither satisfy r nor $\neg r$. As mentioned earlier, the controller in Fig. 2 meets this specification under delay $= 2$.

A controller that meets a specification under delay d_2 can be easily shown to meet the same specification under any d_1 such that $d_1 < d_2$ (and hence no delay also). The input symbols emitted by the plant can be held in a buffer and delayed by an extra $d_2 - d_1$ steps, and then any trace pair generated by the controller will satisfy the specification. In other words, the set of realizable specifications under (fixed) delay is a strict subset of realizable specifications under no delay.

3.3 Controller Synthesis

It is natural for a user to specify a temporal formula Ψ that they require all plant-side traces to satisfy. This is the because the plant is the main component of interest to the user, and normally one requires all plant-side traces to satisfy a specification that one requires irrespective of whether there is delay or not, or what the amount of delay is. We hence address the problem of automatically synthesizing a controller C that meets a given specification Ψ under a given amount of delay d.

By the definitions given in Sect. 3.1, if the above-mentioned controller C generates any trace pair (t_c, t_p), then t_p will satisfy Ψ (as desired by the user). However, t_c may not satisfy Ψ. Our approach is to construct a *transformed* LTL formula $tr_f(\Psi)$, such that any such t_c satisfies $tr_f(\Psi)$. $tr_f(\Psi)$ is obtained by replacing every leaf x in the formula Ψ, where x is an element of the input set I, with $X^d(x)$, where X^d means d (nested) occurrences of the LTL "next" operator X, and d is the given total delay. We then supply $tr_f(\Psi)$ to any existing (no-delay) controller synthesis approach, treating the approach as a blackbox, and return the controller synthesized by the approach as the desired controller C that meets Ψ under delay d.

To illustrate our approach, consider our running example specification $\Psi = G((\ r\ \Rightarrow X(g \lor X(g))) \land (\neg\ r\ \Rightarrow \neg X(g \land (X(g)))))$. The transformed LTL formula $tr_f(\Psi)$, with $d = 2$, is $G((\ X(X(r))\ \Rightarrow X(g \lor X(g))) \land (\neg\ X(X(r))\ \Rightarrow \neg X(g \land (X(g)))))$. The to-be transformed leaves and the transformed portions have been highlighted for clarity. The controller shown in Fig. 2 was obtained using the synthesis tool *Strix* [10] by providing $tr_f(\Psi)$ as input. We already discussed in Sect. 3.1 that this controller meets the specification Ψ under delay $= 2$.

As another example, consider the specification $\Psi = G(r \Leftrightarrow g)$. The transformed specification in this case with $d = 2$ is $G(X(X(r)) \Leftrightarrow g)$. This formula is unrealizable in reality (and as per *Strix*), and indeed this specification Ψ is unrealizable under delay $= 2$ as we had discussed in Sect. 3.2.

3.4 Soundness and Completeness

Lemma 1. *For any trace pair (t_c, t_p) under delay d, for any LTL formula Ψ, t_p satisfies Ψ iff t_c satisfies $tr_f(\Psi)$.*

Intuitively, the above property holds because t_c is identical to t_p except that the input symbol in each step of t_p has been shifted to the right by d steps in t_c, and that is the exact difference between Ψ and $tr_f(\Psi)$ as well. We give a proof for the above lemma in an appendix (the proof is by structural induction on Ψ). The appendix is available in a long-term repository https://doi.org/10.6084/m9.figshare.c.6608452 associated with this paper.

Theorem 1 (Soundness). *Any controller C synthesized by our approach meets the given specification Ψ under the given delay d.*

Proof: *By construction of C, all traces generated by C satisfy $tr_f(\Psi)$. This means, for any trace pair (t_c, t_p) generated by C, t_c satisfies $tr_f(\Psi)$. Therefore, by Lemma 1, for any trace pair (t_c, t_p) generated by C, t_p satisfies Ψ.* □

Theorem 2 (Completeness). *Our approach returns a controller whenever the given specification Ψ is realizable under the given delay d.*

Proof: *If Ψ is realizable under delay d, it means there exists a controller C' that is feasible under delay d and that meets the given property Ψ under delay d. That is, every trace pair (t_c, t_p) under delay d that is generated by C' is such that t_p satisfies Ψ. It is easy to see that for any trace t'_c that C' can generate, there exists a (unique) trace t'_p such that (t'_c, t'_p) is a trace pair under delay d. Therefore, by Lemma 1, it follows that all traces generated by C' satisfy $tr_f(\Psi)$. This means that the controller synthesis approach that we invoke as a black box with input specification $tr_f(\Psi)$ will necessarily this declare this specification to be realizable, and will necessarily return a controller C (which may or may not be equal to C').* □

4 Variable Delay

In this section we consider the more challenging setting of *variable delay*. Here, as the trace (pair) evolves over time, the delay from each side to the other can increase. At each step, the delay can be equal to or greater than the delay in the previous step, subject to given minimum and maximum delays, d_l and d_u, applicable in each direction over the entire trace. Variable delay occurs in practice due to variations in environmental conditions (such as network congestion, or interference) that cause delays. To our knowledge ours is the first paper to propose, formulate, and solve the problem of controller synthesis in the presence of variable delay.

4.1 Definitions

Definition 12 (Trace pair under variable delay). *A trace pair under variable delay (d_l, d_u), where d_l and d_u are non-negative integers such that $d_u \geq d_l$, (we drop the word variable in the rest of this section for brevity), is a pair of traces t_c and t_p such that:*

1. *There exist two infinite sequences d_{cp} and d_{pc} corresponding to this trace pair, each one being a monotonically non-decreasing sequence of integers from the interval $[d_l, d_u]$.*
2. *The output symbol emitted by t_c at its step 0 will reach t_p at its step 0. That is, intuitively, the plant trace starts when it receives the first output symbol from the controller. Subsequently, for each $i > 0$, the output symbol emitted at the controller's step i will reach the plant at its step $i + d_{cp}[i] - d_{cp}[0]$. In other words, $t_c[i] \cap O = t_p[i + d_{cp}[i] - d_{cp}[0]] \cap O$, for all $i \geq 0$.*

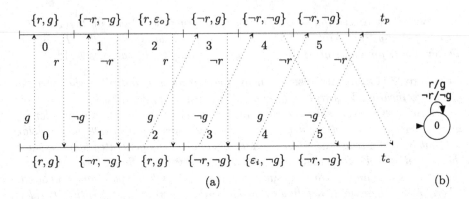

Fig. 4. (a) A sample trace pair (t_c, t_p) under variable delay $(0, 1)$. (t_c, t_p) satisfies the specification $G((r \Rightarrow (g \vee X(g \vee Xg))) \wedge (\neg r \Rightarrow \neg(g \wedge (X(g \wedge Xg)))))$. (b) A controller that meets this specification under variable delay.

3. For any index k such that there exists no i such that $i + d_{cp}[i] - d_{cp}[0]$ is equal k, $t_p[k] \cap O$ will be empty, and $t_p[k]$ will contain the special symbol ϵ_o to indicate that no output symbol was received in this step (due to increase in delay in the controller to plant direction). We assume that the communication channel between the plant and controller is enhanced in a way that it assures this behavior.

4. The input symbol emitted by t_p at its ith step, for any $i \geq 0$, reaches the plant in its step $corr(i)$, where $corr(i)$ is equal to $i + d_{cp}[0] + d_{pc}[i]$. In other words, $t_p[i] \cap I = t_c[corr(i)] \cap I$, for all $i \geq 0$. ($d_{cp}[0]$ gets added to account for the delayed start of t_p relative to t_c, as discussed in the previous point.)

5. Analogous to ϵ_o, the controller receives a special symbol ϵ_i in any step in which it receives no input symbol from the plant due to increase in delay in the plant to controller direction.

Intuitively, $d_{cp}[i]$ indicates the delay (in number of steps) from controller to plant for the symbol emitted by the controller in its ith step. d_{pc} has an analogous meaning, but from the plant to the controller. Note, the transition from a lower delay to a higher delay can happen anywhere in the (infinite) trace, or need not happen at all, and a bounded number of delay transitions can occur in each direction (at most $d_u - d_l$, to be particular).

Figure 4(a) depicts a sample trace pair under delay $(0, 1)$. Here, $d_{cp}[0]$ and $d_{cp}[1]$ are zero, while the remaining entries in the d_{cp} sequence are one. $d_{pc}[0]$ to $d_{pc}[3]$ are zero, while $d_{pc}[4]$ onward are one. Notice the presence of ϵ_o and ϵ_i at the delay transition points. The dashed arrows indicate the flow of symbols visually.

We update the definition of a trace satisfying an LTL formula (see Definition 3), to say that if trace t_c (resp. t_p) has ϵ_i (resp. ϵ_o) in index $t_c[i]$ (resp. $t_p[i]$), then it is interpreted as $t_c[i]$ (resp. $t_p[i]$) not satisfying x (and satisfying $\neg x$) for any $x \in I$ (resp. $x \in O$).

The analogues of Definition 7 and Definitions 9–11 apply in the variable delay setting as well, simply by substituting each occurrence of the wording "under delay d" with "under delay (d_l, d_u)". Since ϵ_i's can arrive at any point in the controller-side trace t_c (and not necessarily in the beginning), and since ϵ_i is interpreted as all input signals being off, any controller (see Definition 1) is also a feasible controller under variable delay.

Figure 4(b) depicts a controller that meets the specification shown in the caption of the figure. Part (a) in the figure depicts one of the trace pairs generated by this controller. Note that in $t_c[4]$, the controller interprets ϵ_i as $\neg g$ and hence emits $\neg g$.

4.2 Results on Control Under Variable Delay

A temporal property Ψ that is realizable under fixed delay $d = d_u + d_u$ is not necessarily realizable under variable delay (d_l, d_u). In other words, the set of realizable specifications under variable delay is a strict subset of realizable specifications under fixed delay. As an example, consider the specification $G(g)$, where g is an output element. This specification is met by the controller that emits g continuously, both under no delay and any amount of fixed delay. However, this specification is not realizable under variable delay for any delay bound, because t_p can receive up to d_u ϵ_o's, and the steps where it receives ϵ_o's do not satisfy g.

Any controller C that meets any specification Ψ under variable delay (d_l, d_u) also necessarily meets the same specification under fixed delay $d_u + d_u$. This is because any fixed-delay trace pair under delay $d_u + d_u$ is also a trace pair under variable delay, with all elements of d_{pc} and d_{cp} being equal to d_u.

4.3 Controller Synthesis

As in the fixed delay setting, we propose a LTL formula translation scheme tr_v. The approach then is to use any (no-delay) synthesis approach as a blackbox to synthesize a controller that realizes the property $tr_v(\Psi)$, where Ψ is the given LTL formula.

A Naive Proposal. A naive proposal would be to model the translation similar to our fixed delay approach, and basically replace every leaf $x \in I$ in Ψ with the disjunction $X^{2d_l}x \vee X^{2d_l+1}x \vee \ldots \vee X^{2d_u}x$ (in place of $X^d x$ in the fixed delay setting). The intuitive reason for this proposal is that if (t_c, t_p) are a trace pair under delay (d_l, d_u), and if x and y are the input and output symbols at a plant step $t_p[i]$, and if y was earlier emitted by the controller at step $t_c[k]$, then x would be received by the controller in the range of steps $t_c[k + 2d_l]$ to $t_c[k + 2d_u]$ due to the properties of trace pairs under delay. Therefore, since we would like t_p to satisfy Ψ and t_c to satisfy $tr_v(\Psi)$, input symbol leaves in Ψ would need to be moved forward by $2d_l$ to $2d_u$ steps, and this is implemented using the transformation proposed above.

However, the proposal above is not sound. Consider the LTL specification $G(g)$. Its translation would be $G(g)$ itself (as it does not refer to the input symbol r). Now, $G(g)$ is realizable under no-delay, but the controller that results from synthesis, which emits g continuously, does not meet the specification in the presence of variable delay as the steps of t_p that receive ϵ_o do not satisfy g. This motivates the need for a more sophisticated transformation scheme.

Our Proposed Scheme. In order to solve the issue above, we introduce a set of *reflected* elements $R = \{o' \mid o \in O\} \cup \{\epsilon'_o\}$. We also demand a (further) enhancement to the communication medium such that if the plant emits $x \in 2^I$ to the controller at any step $t_p[i]$, then the communication medium actually sends out $x \cup \{y' \mid y$ is in O or y is $\epsilon_o, y \in t_p[i]\}$ to the controller at this step. For instance, in Fig. 4, $\{r, g'\}$ would be sent out at $t_p[0]$ and would reach the controller at $t_c[0]$, with g' being *reflected* back because g was received in $t_p[0]$. Similarly, ϵ'_o would be reflected back from $t_p[2]$, and therefore $\{r, \epsilon'_o\}$ would reach the controller at $t_c[2]$. Only ϵ_i would reach $t_c[4]$, with no input or reflected elements reaching. And $t_p[4]$ would not reflect g' as g was not received in this step. Intuitively, reflected elements give information to the controller on when its (previously emitted) output symbols reached the plant.

$$tr_v^g(\Psi) = \begin{cases} x, & \text{if } \Psi = x \text{ and } x \in I \\ y', & \text{if } \Psi = y \text{ and } y \in O \\ \neg tr_v^g(\Psi_1), & \text{if } \Psi = \neg\Psi_1 \\ tr_v^g(\Psi_1) \wedge tr_v^g(\Psi_2), & \text{if } \Psi = \Psi_1 \wedge \Psi_2 \\ tr_v^g(\Psi_1) \vee tr_v^g(\Psi_2), & \text{if } \Psi = \Psi_1 \vee \Psi_2 \\ X\big(\epsilon_i \, U \, (\neg\epsilon_i \wedge tr_v^g(\Psi_1))\big), & \text{if } \Psi = X\Psi_1 \\ F\big(\neg\epsilon_i \wedge tr_v^g(\Psi_1)\big), & \text{if } \Psi = F\Psi_1 \\ G\big(\epsilon_i \, U \, (\neg\epsilon_i \wedge tr_v^g(\Psi_1))\big), & \text{if } \Psi = G\Psi_1 \\ (\epsilon_i \, U \, (\neg\epsilon_i \wedge tr_v^g(\Psi_1))) \, U \, (\epsilon_i \, U \, (\neg\epsilon_i \wedge tr_v^g(\Psi_2))), & \text{if } \Psi = \Psi_1 \, U \, \Psi_2 \end{cases}$$

The translation function tr_v^g defined above forms the core of our translation scheme. We now illustrate it with a couple of examples. For now, treat $tr_v(\Psi)$ as being equal to $\epsilon_i \, U \, (\neg\epsilon_i \wedge tr_v^g(\Psi))$. $tr_v(G(g))$ yields $\epsilon_i \, U \, (\neg\epsilon_i \wedge (G(\epsilon_i \, U \, (\neg\epsilon_i \wedge g'))))$. The intuition behind the translation is that if g is to occur in all steps of t_p, then the reflected g' must occur infinitely often in t_c (once corresponding to each step in t_p), and any steps of t_c that do not have g' must have received nothing (i.e., ϵ_i) from the plant. The other cases in the definition above follow the same intuition. Note, during controller synthesis from the translated formula, the reflected elements as well as ϵ'_o (in addition to the elements in I) must be treated as input elements, as they come from the plant to the controller.

A formula such as $F(g)$ is realizable under variable delay. A controller that continually emits g meets this specification under variable delay (for any (d_l, d_u)). However, $tr_v(F(g)) = \epsilon_i \, U \, (\neg\epsilon_i \wedge (F(\neg\epsilon_i \wedge g')))$ is not realizable and will not yield a controller when fed to a blackbox synthesis tool, as g' is technically an input symbol and hence appears to be entirely in the hands of the (adversial) plant. What is missing in the translation tr_v^g is an assertion that the controller can at any time force a g' to appear later in its input by emitting a g at this time. We therefore **define** $tr_v(\Psi)$ **to be equal to** $\Psi_{as} \Rightarrow \epsilon_i U (\neg\epsilon_i \wedge (tr_v^g(\Psi)))$, where:

$$\Psi_{as} = \bigwedge_{y \in O} G\left(y \Rightarrow \bigvee_{i \in [2d_l, 2d_u]} X^i y'\right) \wedge \bigwedge_{x \in I \cup R} G(x \Rightarrow \neg\epsilon_i) \wedge$$

$$\bigwedge_{y \in O} (GF(y') \Rightarrow GF(y)) \wedge \bigwedge_{y \in O} (GF(\neg y') \Rightarrow GF(\neg y)) \wedge FG(\neg\epsilon_i)$$

We call Ψ_{as} a *trace pair characterization*, which is a formula that specifies properties of any trace t_c such that there exists a t_p such that (t_c, t_p) is a trace pair. The first conjunct in the definition above captures the assertion that we had mentioned above, while the remaining four conjuncts capture other properties of trace pairs under delay when reflection is employed. Coming back to the example, it is easy to see that $\Psi_{as} \Rightarrow \epsilon_i U (\neg\epsilon_i \wedge (F(\neg\epsilon_i \wedge g')))$ is realizable, and is met by the controller that continually emits g. Intuitively, the last conjunct in the definition of Ψ_{as} assures that at some point ϵ_i's will stop appearing (reason: there can be atmost d_u occurrences of ϵ_i's in a trace), while the first conjunct assures that after ϵ_i's stop appearing each g emitted by the controller will cause g' to appear in a subsequent step.

4.4 Properties of Our Approach

Lemma 2. *For any trace pair (t_c, t_p) under variable delay (d_l, d_u), for any LTL formula Ψ, and for any index i, $t_p(i)$ satisfies Ψ iff $t_c(corr(i))$ satisfies $tr_v^g(\Psi)$, where $corr(i)$ equals the expression $i + d_{cp}[0] + d_{pc}[i]$. (Proof provided in appendix.)*

Theorem 3 (Soundness). *Any controller C synthesized by our approach meets the given specification Ψ under the given delay (d_l, d_u).*

Proof: *Consider any trace pair (t_c, t_p) under delay (d_l, d_u) generated by C. C was constructed to realize the formula $\Psi_{as} \Rightarrow \epsilon_i U (\neg\epsilon_i \wedge (tr_v^g(\Psi)))$. It can be seen that by definition of Ψ_{as}, since (t_c, t_p) is a trace pair under delay (d_l, d_u), t_c must satisfy Ψ_{as}. Since t_c was generated by C, it then follows that t_c also satisfies $\epsilon_i U (\neg\epsilon_i \wedge (tr_v^g(\Psi)))$. From this, and by the properties possessed by trace pairs under delay, it follows that $t_c(corr(0))$ satisfies $tr_v^g(\Psi)$. Therefore, by Lemma 2, $t_p(0)$ (i.e., t_p) satisfies Ψ.* □

Unlike, in the fixed delay setting, our approach as presented above does *not* offer a completeness guarantee. That is, a specification that is realizable under delay may be declared as unrealizable. For example, consider the property $\Psi = G(\neg g)$. This specification is in reality met by the controller that continually emits $\neg g$. However, the translated formula $tr_v(\Psi) = \Psi_{as} \Rightarrow$

$\epsilon_i\, U\,(\neg\epsilon_i \wedge (G(\epsilon_i\, U\,(\neg\epsilon_i \wedge (\neg g')))))$ will be declared as unrealizable when it is fed to any no-delay controller synthesis tool. Intuitively, the reason is that Ψ_{as} should ideally also assert that for any $i, i+1$, the steps of t_c between $t_c[corr(i)]$ and $t_c[corr(i+1)]$ contain only ϵ_i's, but it does not.

To summarize, the Ψ_{as} we have defined is a *sound* trace pair characterization, but not a *complete* one. A trace pair characterization is sound if for any trace pair (t_c, t_p) under delay (d_l, d_u), t_c is guaranteed to satisfy the characterization. This soundness was invoked in the proof of Theorem 3 above. A trace pair characterization can be called complete, if, for any trace t_c that satisfies the characterization, there exists a trace t_p such that (t_c, t_p) is trace pair under delay (d_l, d_u). Our approach is basically parametric on the trace pair characterization used, and our approach will be sound (resp. complete) if the characterization is sound (resp. complete). It may be possible to devise a complete trace pair characterization, but it is likely to lead to high synthesis complexity.

5   Unrealizability Filter

A lot practical properties tend to be unrealizable under delay, and the black-box synthesis approach may expend a lot of time to detect unrealizability of the transformed formula in such cases. We therefore propose a novel, efficient, syntax-based heuristic that detects if a given formula is unrealizable under delay. The heuristic is sound, in that it never mis-classifies a realizable property as unrealizable. The heuristic is not guaranteed to detect all unrealizable properties, so whenever it does not give a classification, the synthesis blackbox will need to be invoked.

We first introduce a pre-requisite function IOIS that is used by the filters. For the given property Ψ, IOIS(Ψ) returns a logical formula in conjunctive normal form. Any atomic fact in the formula is of the form (x, l), where x is an *input literal* or an *output literal*. Input literals are input elements or their negations (e.g., r, $\neg r$), while output literals are output elements or their negations (e.g., g, $\neg g$). l is in general a finite set of closed intervals in the non-negative integers domain. Due to space limitations, we provide the full definition of IOIS in the appendix. For illustration, if $\Psi \equiv G((r \Rightarrow Xg) \wedge (\neg r \Rightarrow X\neg g))$, then IOIS($\Psi$) happens to yield the following formula, which is a conjunction of two conjuncts: $((\neg r, [0,0]) \vee (g, [1,1])) \wedge ((r, [0,0]) \vee (\neg g, [1,1]))$. The intuition is that any plant side trace t_p can satisfy Ψ *only if* it satisfies IOIS(Ψ). An atomic fact (x, l) is satisfied by a trace t_p iff for some index $i \in l$, $t_p[i]$ satisfies x.

Two literals are said to be *contradictory* if one is a negation of the other. For e.g., $\neg r$ and r. For a given non-negative integer d, a conjunct C_i is said to be *d-bounded* if it contains exactly one atomic fact with an output literal, contains at least one atomic fact with an input literal, and $\max(W) - \min(V) < d$, where W is the interval-set associated with the output literal in the conjunct, and V is the union of the interval sets associated with all input intervals in the conjunct. A conjunct is said to be a *tautology* if it contains two contradictory input literals, and the interval-sets associated with these two input literals are overlapping.

We now define the **fixed-delay filter** for a given total delay d as follows: It classifies the given Ψ as unrealizable if $IOIS(\Psi)$ contains two conjuncts C_i and C_j such that (a) both conjuncts contain exactly one output literal each, (b) these two output literals are contradictory, (c) the interval sets associated with both these output literals are the same, and each of these interval sets is a unit-interval (i.e., of total width 1), (d) C_i or C_j (or both) are d-bounded, and (e) neither conjunct is a tautology.

The intuition is that a d-bounded conjunct contains input literals and an output literal close enough that the controller cannot use the input symbols in t_c to decide whether to emit the output literal or its negation in order to satisfy the conjunct. Therefore, if two conjuncts have opposite output literals required at the same step in the trace, whichever conjunct the controller tries to satisfy, the other conjunct can be falsified by the adversarial plant.

The example provided earlier in this section indeed gets classified as unrealizable by our filter when $d = 2$. Intuitively, the property is unrealizable because the controller has to send a g or a $\neg g$ *before* it comes to know whether the step in t_p that precedes the step where this g or $\neg g$ will be received emitted r or $\neg r$.

We now define two **variable-delay filters**. The first filter for the variable-delay setting simply invokes the fixed-delay filter defined above with $d = d_u + d_u$ (see Sect. 4.2 for the justification). The second filter classifies the given Ψ as unrealizable if $IOIS(\Psi)$ contains a conjunct C such that (a) all output literals in the conjunct are *positive* (i.e., not of the form '$\neg g$'), (b) the total number of positions in the union of the interval sets corresponding to the output literals in the conjunct (i.e., not counting more than once the positions that occur in multiple interval-sets) is less than or equal to $d_u - d_l$, and (c) the conjunct is not a tautology. The intuition is that such a conjunct becomes falsified if $d_u - d_l$ ϵ_i's happen to occur in all positions in the above-mentioned union.

6   Empirical Evaluation

We have implemented both our fixed delay and variable delay approaches. Our approaches accept LTL specifications in the standard *TLSF* format. We use *Syfco* [9] as a front-end to parse TLSF, and implement our formula translation using Haskell (as that is Syfco's supported language). Our filter implementations are also Syfco and Haskell based. We selected *Strix* [10] as the blackbox tool to perform synthesis using our translated formulas. Strix was in Number 1 position among all competing synthesis tools in SYNTCOMP 2022 synthesis competition [7,8]. SYNTCOMP is a pre-eminent annual contest for (no-delay) synthesis tools. For our evaluations, we selected all 1075 TLSF benchmarks (i.e., LTL specifications) used in the SYNTCOMP 2022 contest.

We are not aware of any other tool that performs delay synthesis from given LTL specifications. Therefore, to serve as a baseline, we obtained a recently released tool by Chen et al. [3], from the web site mentioned in their paper. This tool addresses strategy inference from safety games under fixed-delay. Since they do not accept LTL as input directly, and only accept a game graph with a

Table 1. Summary of results

Run	# Realizable	# Unrealizable	# timeouts	# Strix errors	Time (s)
No delay	500	388	187		145404
FD $d = 4$	248	463 + 124 = 587	238	2	192952
FD $d = 10$	206	463 + 40 = 503	364	2	278480
VD (1,2)	39	542 + 25 = 567	82	387	107850
VD (1,5)	37	697 + 3 = 700	66	272	77190
Chen $d = 4$	90	170	618	197	460890

safety winning condition, we need to first translate LTL specifications to safety game graphs. We do this using the "k-bounded safety approximation" feature provided in *Owl* [14], which is a widely used library for analysis of automata and LTL specifications. The bound specifies the maximum number of visits to final states tolerated during safety game translation (as any finite number of visits is winning). For any LTL property, there exists a (potentially exponentially high) value of k at which the translation is guaranteed sound. To keep the translation time tractable, we have specified an upper limit of $k = 10$. Therefore, Owl will stop at this value of 10, or at a value less than 10 if it finds a sound safety game for this lower value. In cases where Owl stops at value 10, the safety game graph Owl returns may not be sound. However, we enforce the limit of $k = 10$ so that Owl will finish within practical time limits. Empirically we observe a loss of soundness in some cases (details of which we will provide later). The running times comparison is hence the more interesting takeaway from this baseline study.

6.1   Our Results

Table 1 summarizes the results from our runs. Each row represents a run of a tool or approach on all 1075 benchmarks. To keep the total time of the runs tractable, and also to facilitate uniform comparisons, we use a timeout of 720 s per benchmark in each run. The columns indicate the name of the run, number of benchmarks found realizable, number of benchmarks found unrealizable, number of benchmarks on which analysis was stopped due to the timeout being hit, number of benchmarks on which the corresponding tool encountered errors/exceptions during processing, and finally the total wall clock time of the run (on all 1075 benchmarks). All our runs were done on a server with an Intel Xeon W-2295 processor and 256 GB of RAM. Our tool, and certain artifacts from our runs, are available in our repository https://doi.org/10.6084/m9.figshare.c.6608452.

The 'No delay' run is a baseline, and represents a run of Strix directly on the given benchmarks, without any delay translation. 187 benchmarks hit the timeout, while the rest were declared realizable (500 of them) or unrealizable (388 of them). The average time to process a single benchmark is 136 s.

Fixed Delay. We now discuss the next two rows, which depict information about runs of our fixed-delay approach, with delay $d = 4$ and $d = 10$, respectively. For each benchmark, out of the 720 s allotted, we use the first 20 s to run two separate filters sequentially. The first filter is our filter, described in Sect. 5. The second is a run of Strix on the untranslated formula, to see if declares unrealizability. Recall that as per the discussion in Sect. 3.2, if a specification is unrealizable with no-delay, it must be unrealizable with delay. Our run script kills each filter after 10 s, and proceeds to run Strix on the translated formula of the benchmark (with a budget of 700 s) if neither filter declares unrealizability.

The '# Realizable' column indicates that 248 benchmarks (out of a maximum possible 500) were found realizable with delay $d = 4$, while 206 were found realizable when the delay is increased to $d = 10$. This is consistent with our theoretical claims of higher-delay realizability implying lower-delay realizability and delay realizability implying no-delay realizable. Note that what used to be a realizable or unrealizable benchmark under no-delay could have migrated to the timeouts category in the fixed-delay runs.

The '# Unrealizable' column shows the break up of the number of benchmarks found unrealizable by the filters (the number before the "+") and the number of benchmarks not removed by the filters but subsequently found to be unrealizable by Strix when applied on the translated formula. It is notable that the filters are very effective, and identify 463 benchmarks are unrealizable (under both delay values). This is a major reason why the fixed-delay total wall-clocks times are not very high. It only 33% higher than the no-delay wall-clock time at $d = 4$, and 91% higher at the very high delay value of $d = 10$. It is notable that since our fixed-delay approach is *sound* and *complete*, any benchmark that is declared as realizable (resp. unrealizable) will necessarily belong to the declared category. It is also notable that with $d = 4$, the number of timeout runs we encounter is only a little more than with the no-delay run despite the complexity of having to account for delay. We are very encouraged by this result about the efficiency of our approach.

Variable Delay. In the variable-delay runs, we employ a total of four filters sequentially, with a time budget of 10 s for each filter (per benchmark). The first two filters were presented at the end of Sect. 5. The next two filters are (a) a run of Strix on the original untranslated formula Ψ, and (b) a run of Strix on Ψ after it is translated as per the fixed-delay translation, with $d = d_u + d_u$. The reasoning behind these two applications of Strix as filters is provided in Sect. 4.2. If none of the four filters detects a benchmark as unrealizable, then we proceed to run Strix on the (variable-delay) translated formula, with a budget of 680 s.

The next two rows in Table 1 depict information about runs of our variable-delay approach, with delay $(1, 2)$ and $(1, 5)$ respectively. Recall that if a specification is realizable under variable delay $(1, 2)$ (resp. $(1, 5)$), it must be realizable under fixed-delay with $d = 4$ (resp. $d = 10$). The data indicates that a substantially smaller number of benchmarks were found to be realizable. Part of the reason for this is that realizability indeed is less likely to hold with variable delay than with fixed delay, based on manual analysis of real specifications. But the other reason is the substantial numbers of benchmarks on which Strix threw exceptions when applied to the translated properties (even though they were syntactically valid). Many of these exceptions contained a message such as "Too many elements to create power set: 65 > 30". We suspect that many of these translated formulas may be too large for Strix. We have some future work ideas to try to mitigate this effect, which we discuss at the end of the paper.

In the variable delay runs, the benchmarks found unrealizable by the filters are guaranteed to be unrealizable. However, due to the incompleteness of our trace pair characterization Ψ_{as}, some of the benchmarks that were declared unrealizable by Strix (25 in the $(1, 2)$ run and 3 in the $(1, 5)$ run) could potentially be realizable. Despite the prevalence of Strix errors, we are encouraged that on 56% to 69% of benchmarks, i.e., $567 + 39$ with delay $(1, 2)$ and $700 + 37$ with delay $(1, 5)$, our approach gives definitive results. In all cases, our formula translation is very fast (less than 1 s per benchmark).

Sample Properties. To give a taste for what kind of properties become unrealizable under different settings, we manually extract core unrealizable portions from real properties and present them here. Properties $(FG(\neg r_0)) \Leftrightarrow (GF(g))$ and $G(r_0 \Leftrightarrow (Xr_1))$ are unrealizable even without delay. The property $G(r \Leftrightarrow (Xg))$ is realizable without delay but not realizable under fixed delay $d = 2$. The specification $(G((r_0) \rightarrow (((r_1) \leftrightarrow (X(g_1))) U (g_0))))$ is realizable under fixed-delay $d = 2$ but unrealizable under variable delay $(1, 2)$. The design of our unrealizability filter gives a more principled feel for causes of unrealizability (applicable in many, not all, benchmarks).

6.2 Comparison with Chen et al.'s Tool

The last row in Table 1 depicts information about our run of Chen et al.'s synthesis tool. This row is to be compared with the "FD $d = 4$" row which is about our corresponding approach. From the last row, it is seen that 618 benchmarks faced a timeout. Among these, 524 faced the 720 s timeout during the LTL to safety game translation within Owl itself, while the remaining 94 faced a timeout within the synthesis tool. To ensure the uniform total 720 s budget, the time budget we gave to the synthesis tool was 720 s minus the time taken during the LTL to safety game translation. The 197 error cases were all encountered within their synthesis tool.

Of the 90 benchmarks declared realizable, 17 were found unrealizable by our tool. Additionally, 40 of the declared unrealizable specifications were declared realizable by our tool. Since our fixed-delay tool is provably sound and complete, and because their synthesis tool is also presumably correct, we suspect these misclassifications occur due to potential unsoundness in the initial LTL to safety game translation, as discussed at the beginning of this section.

We cannot conclude about the efficiency of Chen et al.'s tool per-se from this comparison. However, LTL to safety game conversion is inherently an expensive operation. Whereas, LTL synthesis tools like Strix are heavily optimized using heuristics. The takeaway is that when one's input is an LTL specification, it is useful to have a way to synthesize directly than to have to go via a determinized safety game construction.

7 Related Work

There is a rich literature in the *classical* LTL synthesis space, where the problem is to synthesize a controller from an LTL specification, with the controller and plant communicating via input/output symbols, in the absence of delay. Pnueli et al. [13] propose a seminal solution for this problem, based on determinization of Büchi automata. This approach has been extended with numerous practical optimizations, and is in fact used in the tool Strix that we have used in our evaluations. The time complexity of classical synthesis is in general double exponential in the size of the LTL specification.

An early work that investigated controller synthesis in the presence of delay was by Tripakis et al. [16]. They address the problem of *supervisory control*, and not input/output symbol based control, which is our setting. In supervisory control, the controller can block the plant from taking a transition by observing the event associated with the proposed transition. They address a restricted class of specifications of the form that every event a must eventually be followed by an event b. They allow multiple controllers to simultaneously control the plant; each controller can observe a subset of events without any delay, and observes the events corresponding to the other controllers' subsets with delay. There is no empirical evaluation reported in this paper.

Finkbeiner et al. [5] studied various extended versions of the controller synthesis for symbol-based control. Their approach is to construct an alternating parity automaton from the given LTL specification, which accepts (infinite) *run trees* that represent winning strategies for the controller. The authors describe how the automaton can be transformed to handle distributed systems, where there are multiple controllers, and environments where there is (fixed) delay. There is no empirical evaluation in this paper. The practical tool *Bosy* [6] that was introduced subsequently is based on this approach, and uses a SAT-solver formulation to try to find a controller within a given size bound k whose unfoldings are accepted run trees. This tool does not appear to support delay.

Winter et al. [17] recently investigated a problem that they call *delay games*. Their notion of delay is not similar to ours, and does not model communication delay between plant and controller. Rather, the controller is allowed to skip playing in its turns, while the plant keeps playing and emitting input symbols. Effectively the controller gains a lookahead into the plant's behavior before it chooses to play, and hence this *broadens* the class of realizable specifications beyond what is realizable under no-delay.

The closest related work to ours is by Chen et al. [3]. We have partially described their work already in Sect. 6. They address fixed delay only, that too on a given 2-player game graph with a safety winning condition. They first present a naive proposal that reduces the strategy inference problem to delay-free games by exploding the game graph by pairing each game graph state with a queue configuration. As this is expensive, they subsequently present an optimized strategy that increases the queue lengths iteratively, pruning uncontrollable states along the way, until the queue lengths reach the given delay d. They do not explicitly address LTL specifications. LTL specifications would first need to be determinized to obtain a game graph, and this incurs exponential cost.

8 Conclusions and Future Work

In conclusion, to the best of our knowledge, our work is the first one to identify and address the problem of variable delay. We also investigate how variable delay relates theoretically to fixed delay. Ours is also the first approach to solve delay synthesis using LTL formula translation. The advantages of this approach are its relative simplicity, flexibility in terms of being able to automatically leverage efficiency improvements to classical (no-delay) synthesis approaches that may emerge in the future, and substantial empirically observed performance gain compared to a closely related and recent baseline approach [3].

In future work we plan to investigate if our variable delay translation can be made more efficient, and can possibly be made complete. Both of these would need (differing) changes to the trace pair characterization Ψ_{as}. We would like to try blackbox synthesis tools other than Strix within our implementation. Conceptually, we would like to extend our approach to distributed control, where there are multiple controllers, with differing delays to the plant.

References

1. Bloem, R., Chatterjee, K., Jobstmann, B.: Graph games and reactive synthesis. In: Clarke, E., Henzinger, T., Veith, H., Bloem, R. (eds.) Handbook of Model Checking, pp. 921–962. Springer, Cham (2018). https://doi.org/10.1007/978-3-319-10575-8_27
2. Book, G.: Space data link protocols-summary of concept and rationale (2012)
3. Chen, M., Fränzle, M., Li, Y., Mosaad, P.N., Zhan, N.: Indecision and delays are the parents of failure—taming them algorithmically by synthesizing delay-resilient control. Acta Informatica **58**(5), 497–528 (2020). https://doi.org/10.1007/s00236-020-00374-7
4. Di Natale, M,, Zeng, H., Giusto, P., Ghosal, A.: Understanding and Using the Controller Area Network Communication Protocol: Theory and Practice. Springer, Heidelberg (2012). https://doi.org/10.1007/978-1-4614-0314-2
5. Finkbeiner, B., Schewe, S.: Uniform distributed synthesis. In: 20th Annual IEEE Symposium on Logic in Computer Science (LICS 2005), pp. 321–330 (2005). https://doi.org/10.1109/LICS.2005.53
6. Finkbeiner, B., Schewe, S.: Bounded synthesis. Int. J. Softw. Tools Technol. Transfer **15**(5–6), 519–539 (2013). https://doi.org/10.1007/s10009-012-0228-z
7. Jacobs, S.: The reactive synthesis competition (SYNTCOMP) (2022). http://www.syntcomp.org/
8. Jacobs, S., et al.: The reactive synthesis competition (syntcomp): 2018–2021. arXiv preprint arXiv:2206.00251 (2022)

9. Klein, F.: Syfco: Synthesis format conversion tool (2023). https://github.com/ reactive-systems/syfco
10. Meyer, P.J., Sickert, S., Luttenberger, M.: Strix: explicit reactive synthesis strikes back! In: Chockler, H., Weissenbacher, G. (eds.) CAV 2018. LNCS, vol. 10981, pp. 578–586. Springer, Cham (2018). https://doi.org/10.1007/978-3-319-96145-3_31
11. Nguyen, T.M.: Future satellite system architectures and practical design issues: an overview. Satellite Systems-Design, Modeling, Simulation and Analysis (2020)
12. Pnueli, A.: The temporal logic of programs. In: 18th Annual Symposium on Foundations of Computer Science, pp. 46–57. IEEE (1977). https://doi.org/10.1109/SFCS.1977.32
13. Pnueli, A., Rosner, R.: On the synthesis of a reactive module. In: Proceedings of the 16th ACM SIGPLAN-SIGACT Symposium on Principles of Programming Languages, pp. 179–190 (1989). https://doi.org/10.1145/75277.75293
14. Sickert, S.: OWL: a command-line tool and a library for omega-words, omega-automata and linear temporal logic (LTL) (2023). https://owl.model.in.tum.de/
15. Tindell, K., Burns, A., Wellings, A.J.: Calculating controller area network (CAN) message response times. Control Eng. Pract. **3**(8), 1163–1169 (1995)
16. Tripakis, S.: Decentralized control of discrete-event systems with bounded or unbounded delay communication. IEEE Trans. Autom. Control **49**(9), 1489–1501 (2004). https://doi.org/10.1109/TAC.2004.834116
17. Winter, S., Zimmermann, M.: Finite-state strategies in delay games. Inf. Comput. **272**, 104500 (2020). https://doi.org/10.1016/j.ic.2019.104500
18. Zhang, H., Shi, Y., Wang, J., Chen, H.: A new delay-compensation scheme for networked control systems in controller area networks. IEEE Trans. Ind. Electron. **65**(9), 7239–7247 (2018). https://doi.org/10.1109/TIE.2018.2795574
19. Zhang, Y., Chen, M., Guizani, N., Wu, D., Leung, V.C.: SOVCAN: safety-oriented vehicular controller area network. IEEE Commun. Mag. **55**(8), 94–99 (2017). https://doi.org/10.1109/MCOM.2017.1601185

Statistical Approach to Efficient and Deterministic Schedule Synthesis for Cyber-Physical Systems

Shengjie Xu$^{(\boxtimes)}$ ⓘ, Bineet Ghosh ⓘ, Clara Hobbs ⓘ, Enrico Fraccaroli ⓘ, Parasara Sridhar Duggirala ⓘ, and Samarjit Chakraborty ⓘ

University of North Carolina at Chapel Hill, Chapel Hill, NC 27599, USA
{sxunique,bineet,cghobbs,enrifrac,psd,samarjit}@cs.unc.edu

Abstract. Correctness of controller implementations rely on real-time guarantees that all control tasks finish execution by their prescribed deadlines. However, with increased complexity and heterogeneity in hardware, the worst-case execution time estimates are becoming very conservative. Thus, for efficient usage of hardware resources, some control tasks might have to miss their deadlines. Recent work has shown that a system can still abide by its safety requirements even after missing some of its deadlines. This paper investigates an approach to synthesize a scheduler for control tasks that miss some deadlines without compromising its safety requirements. But given that the number of possible schedules increase combinatorially with the number of tasks involved, our scheduler synthesis uses an efficient automata representation to search for the appropriate schedule. We incorporate statistical verification techniques to construct this automaton and accelerate the search process. Statistical verification is advantageous compared to deterministic verification in the synthesis process in two ways: first, it enables us to synthesize schedules that would not be possible otherwise, and second, it drastically reduces the time taken to synthesize such a schedule. We demonstrate both these advantages through a case study with five controllers having different safety specifications, but sharing the same computational resource.

1 Introduction

Modern-day cars (and other autonomous systems) have several millions of lines of code deployed on various *electronic control units* (ECUs). Each ECU implements multiple feedback control software tasks managing important functions such as engine control, brake control, suspension and vibration control. The typical workflow for implementing these control tasks in software is a two-step process. In the first step, a control designer would design the feedback function using principles of control design. In the second step, the embedded systems engineer would schedule the control tasks such that each task would meet its prescribed deadline. This separation of concerns allows for communication between control

---

This work was supported by the NSF grant #2038960.

É. André and J. Sun (Eds.): ATVA 2023, LNCS 14215, pp. 312–333, 2023.
https://doi.org/10.1007/978-3-031-45329-8_15

designers and software engineers through task deadlines and allows for parallel development of software architecture and feedback control mechanisms.

However, the rapid increase in the volume of software being deployed in autonomous systems to enable additional *autonomous features* poses a challenge to this design flow. First, due to increased complexity in hardware, safe estimates of Worst-Case Execution Time (WCET) are overly conservative, and thus, applying traditional design flow with the estimated WCET would result in considerable waste of computational resources. Second, scheduling multiple tasks on a shared computational resource with optimistic estimates of WCET would risk missing task deadlines arbitrarily and the system not satisfying its performance requirements. As a result, it is challenging to (a) ensure that none of the control tasks miss their deadlines, and (b) synthesize a scheduler that tolerates these deadline misses while satisfying performance requirements. Further, automotive in-vehicle architectures are moving away from one function per ECU or "federated", to multiple functions sharing resources, or "integrated" architectures. The clear trend is that future architectures will be less static than before, as indicated by developments like AUTOSTAR Adaptive and service-oriented paradigms [3,9]. Thus, it is necessary to rethink the design flows for autonomous systems with new software and hardware architectures.

Schedule Synthesis Problem: Consider the setting where a shared computational resource is used to implement multiple controller tasks, but it is not powerful enough to ensure that all tasks meet their deadlines all the time. *i.e.,* the utilization of the tasks on this resource is greater than 1. Instead of having to reduce the number of controller tasks or use more powerful and therefore expensive hardware, this paper proposes a new *correct-by-construction* approach for synthesizing control implementations. *Our primary observation is that the safety and performance specification can be satisfied even when some of the control jobs miss their deadlines.* This is because the feedback control mechanisms are often robust to delays in sensing and actuation. In particular, with some delays, the dynamics of the closed-loop system deviates only slightly from the dynamics when no tasks miss their deadlines. The question is: which deadline misses cause acceptable deviation in the system dynamics, and can we synthesize task schedules that exploit such deadline miss patterns? We leverage this observation for synthesizing the task scheduler that (a) incorporates deadline miss patterns of control tasks—specified as weakly hard constraints [15,16,32], and (b) the control performance, specified as deviation in system dynamics from the dynamics under ideal timing behavior, when control tasks are scheduled with these weakly hard constraints. The proposed approach thus has two steps. The first step involves checking whether a set of weakly hard timing constraints satisfy a control performance specification, *viz.,* a maximum deviation in dynamics from the system dynamics with no task deadline misses. The second step collects such weakly hard constraints for all the control tasks to be implemented and synthesizes a scheduler that is compatible with the weakly hard constraints of all the tasks. This workflow is illustrated in Fig. 1, where for each control task,

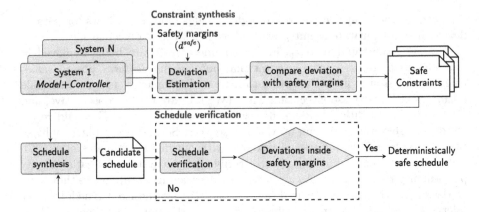

Fig. 1. Overview of the proposed method.

we first synthesize a collection of weakly hard constraints, and then a scheduler for the task set is synthesized from these constraints.

Contributions: One of the important contributions of this paper is the use of statistical model checking. In the literature, various deterministic techniques have been proposed for ensuring that a controller implementation is compatible with the scheduling of the underlying control tasks [8,17,19,36,42]. These techniques either employ bounded model checking techniques, abstract interpretation, or software model checking techniques. However, due to the non-deterministic nature of the weakly hard constraints, deterministic techniques are often overly conservative and suffer from scalability issues [18,39]. As a result, the landscape of compatibility between feedback control design and scheduling with weakly hard real-time constraints is poorly explored. To overcome this challenge, we use statistical model checking approaches for exploring the compatibility between a given weakly hard constraint and the safety specification of the controller. That is, instead of ensuring that a weakly hard constraint *always* satisfies the performance specification, we check whether the constraint satisfies the specification *with high probability*. This begs the question: how can we provide *deterministic* performance guarantees when the compatibility is checked using statistical guarantees? We provide deterministic guarantees by checking if the final schedule (that is deterministic) satisfies all the performance requirements of the individual controllers—a sanity check. If the final schedule does not satisfy all the performance requirements, the schedule synthesizer would search the space of other compatible weakly hard constraints and continue the search process.

Using a statistical approach for listing all the compatible weakly hard constraints for a given controller and synthesizing the scheduler using a sanity check has several advantages. First, statistical model checking approaches are highly scalable as they only require *opaque-box* access to the plant and its corresponding feedback controller. Second, statistical model checking techniques are less conservative as the guarantees are based on the behaviors of the controller that are sampled during the verification process. Finally, the scheduler synthesized using statistical model checking is provably at least as good as the schedule synthesized using traditional model checking approaches. We demonstrate the advantages of our method to synthesize a schedule for various control tasks sharing the same computational platform. To the best of the authors' knowledge, this is the first approach that leverages a statistical model checking approach for synthesizing a deterministic scheduler.

1.1   Related Work

A number of papers have studied the characterization of deadline misses in real-time settings. Notably, the work in [1] proposes a systematic method for characterizing deadline hit/miss patterns. These so-called weakly hard constraints have been studied in a number of settings, including schedulability analysis, formal verification, and runtime monitoring, with [4,19,30] being some recent examples. A significant body of recent research exists on checking control safety properties, such as stability, under deadline misses [23,30,31]. These studies are related to the general problem of ensuring control performance when software tasks implementing feedback controllers experience timing uncertainties. Techniques for isolating different tasks have been investigated in [25]. Joint scheduler and control strategy design – to satisfy stability and other performance constraints – have been proposed [6,7,14]. On the other hand, timing analysis of control software has also been studied [20,21] to provide tighter timing estimates by exploiting the structure of the programs [5]. There has also been considerable work on testing [37] and verification [22,24] of control software to ensure that mathematical models of controllers are preserved in a software implementation that is subjected to artifacts like delays, bounded precision arithmetic, and side effects introduced by a compiler.

In particular, this work has been inspired by a number of recent works [12,17] that relate *quantitative* safety properties—such as the maximum deviation of a system's trajectory from an ideal trajectory—with the maximum number of consecutive deadline misses. These works use deterministic reachable set-based methods, or rely on Statistical Hypothesis Testing (SHT), to provide a deviation upper bound with a statistical guarantee. However, there has been considerably less focus on the synthesis of task schedules that satisfy control safety properties, particularly those beyond stability, which is the central topic of this paper. The study in [41] explored scheduling to satisfy safety constraints, but its deterministic deviation estimation suffers from a tradeoff between exponentially growing execution time and large overestimation of the deviation, similar to [17]. At a philosophical level, the current work is also similar to program synthesis using stochastic search [34] and neuro-symbolic synthesis [29]. In these program synthesis approaches, the search for the *correct program* is conducted using a stochastic process such as random search or generative neural network and the final program returned is verified to satisfy the specification.

2   Background

This section introduces the system formulation, its behavior under deadline misses, and the characterization of deadline miss patterns that affect system behavior. These concepts will be used throughout the rest of the paper.

2.1   System Formulation

Control systems are dynamic in nature and are often described using differential equations. These are called *state equations*, and each one describes the relationship between the time derivative of a single state variable with respect to other state variables and the system's inputs. For instance, an autonomous vehicle system might be described with equations regarding its velocity, acceleration, and steering angle. A state equation for it is of the form:

$$\dot{x}(t) = f(x, u, t), \tag{1}$$

where $x(t) \in \mathbb{R}^n$ represents the states of the system and $u(t) \in \mathbb{R}^p$ the inputs to the system. Certain characteristics of a control system can influence the representational forms of its dynamics. If the differential equations describing the system are time-invariant and linear, then the system dynamics can be expressed by the state-space model

$$\dot{x}(t) = Ax(t) + Bu(t), \tag{2}$$

where $A \in \mathbb{R}^{n \times n}$, and $B \in \mathbb{R}^{n \times p}$ represent the constant *continuous-time* transition matrix and the input matrix, respectively. Equation (2) shows that the rate of change of the system state $\dot{x}(t)$ depends both on the current state $x(t)$ and the control input $u(t)$. When the controller is implemented as a software task, the state-space model needs to be discretized and assumes the form of

$$x[t+1] = A_d x[t] + B_d u[t]. \tag{3}$$

where A_d and B_d represent the *discrete* counterparts of A and B respectively, and are computed as:

$$A_d = e^{AP}, \qquad B_d = \int_0^P e^{A\tau} B \, d\tau \tag{4}$$

Here, P is the sampling period for sensing the environment and actuation. We focus on closed-loop systems, where the state measurement is used to determine the control input of the next actuation. In practice, this is done by a periodic real-time task running on a processor and is assumed to be of the form

$$u[t] = Kx[t-1], \tag{5}$$

where $K \in \mathbb{R}^{p \times n}$ is the *feedback gain*. We follow the logical execution time (LET) paradigm, where the deadline equals the sampling period. A new control input is always applied at the deadline of the control job, *i.e.*, the system state is sampled at time $t-1$ and used to compute the control input for time t, where the state and control input is computed according to Eqs. (3) and (5). This is also in line with popular time-triggered implementations of control tasks [13].

2.2   System Behavior Under Deadline Misses

The correct behavior of the control system described in Sect. 2.1 relies on the timely computation of the control input u by the end of each period. If the periodic real-time task computing the control input misses its deadline, then Eq. (5) no longer holds, and the system may deviate from its ideal behavior and become unsafe. However, the safety of the system depends on the amount of deviation from its ideal behavior, and most systems can tolerate a certain degree of deviation before it becomes unsafe. In this section, we quantify the deviation from a system's ideal behavior and define the set of safe trajectories.

We consider the behavior of the system only over a finite time horizon H. Thus, the states of the system will be recorded at time points $0, 1, \ldots, H$. For ease of exposition, we also assume that the initial state of the system is $z[0] \in \mathbb{R}^n$. Setting the initial state as $z[0]$, we define the *nominal trajectory*, denoted as τ_{nom}, of the system as the trajectory resulting from no deadline misses as follows.

Definition 1 (Nominal Trajectory). *A nominal trajectory (τ_{nom}) of a system is the sequence of states of length $H + 1$ of the form $x[0], x[1] \ldots, x[H]$, where $x[0] = z[0]$ is the initial state, $x[t + 1]$ is computed with Eq. (3) and $u[t]$ is computed with Eq. (5).*

Let $\mathcal{T}$ be the set of sequences of length $H + 1$ over $\mathbb{R}^n$ where the control task has missed some deadlines. For each $\tau \in \mathcal{T}$, $\tau = \tau[0], \tau[1] \ldots, \tau[H]$ where $\tau[i] \in \mathbb{R}^n$ and $\tau[0] = z[0]$. Intuitively, $\mathcal{T}$ denotes the set of *all* possible trajectories of length $H + 1$ in the state space starting from the initial state $z[0]$. We wish to find a subset of $\mathcal{T}$ that does not deviate from the nominal trajectory τ_{nom} by more than a safety bound d^{safe}. This requires a way to quantify deviations from the nominal trajectory. With a metric $\mathrm{dis}(\cdot)$ defined between two points in $\mathbb{R}^n$, we define the distance between a pair of trajectories (τ, τ'), also denoted as $\mathrm{dis}(\cdot)$, as follows:

$$\mathrm{dis}(\tau, \tau') \doteq \max_{0 \leq t \leq H} \mathrm{dis}(\tau[t], \tau'[t]). \tag{6}$$

We now fix a safety margin $d^{safe} > 0$. This leads to the set of safe trajectories $\mathcal{T}_{safe} \subset \mathcal{T}$, defined as

$$\mathcal{T}_{safe} = \{\tau \mid \mathrm{dis}(\tau, \tau_{nom}) \leq d^{safe}\}. \tag{7}$$

This is the set of trajectories that do not exceed the safety margin around the nominal trajectory, *i.e.*, trajectories that do not deviate more than d^{safe} from the nominal trajectory. Clearly, the nominal trajectory is also a member of $\mathcal{T}_{safe}$.

2.3   Characterizing Deadline Miss Patterns

We now characterize the pattern of deadline misses and its connection to deviation in system behavior. The *weakly hard constraints*, proposed in [1], provide an alternative to the traditional hard/soft classification of real-time systems and have been studied in a number of settings including schedulability analysis and formal verification [4,19,30]. The $\binom{m}{k}$ constraint is one of the four types of constraints proposed in [1] and states that out of any k consecutive deadlines of the task, *at least* m of them must be met. A notable result from [1] is that weakly hard constraints are regular languages over $\{0,1\}$, provided that a deadline hit is represented by 1 and miss by 0. We denote the regular language representing $\binom{m}{k}$ as $\mathcal{L}_{(m,k)}$.

Finally, suppose $\gamma \in \{0,1\}^H$ is a sequence of length H representing a pattern of deadline hits and misses. A unique trajectory τ_γ is defined for γ where $\tau_\gamma[0] = z[0]$, $\tau_\gamma[t+1]$ is computed with Eq. (3), and

$$u[t] = \begin{cases} K\tau_\gamma[t-1], & \gamma[t] = 1 \\ u[t-1], & \gamma[t] = 0. \end{cases} \tag{8}$$

This leads to

$$\mathcal{T}_{(m,k)} = \{\tau_\gamma \mid \gamma \in \mathcal{L}_{(m,k)}\}. \tag{9}$$

In other words, $\mathcal{T}_{(m,k)}$ is the set of all trajectories resulting from deadline hit/miss patterns in the regular language $\mathcal{L}_{(m,k)}$. We call the system *safe* under $\binom{m}{k}$ if and only if $\mathcal{T}_{(m,k)} \subseteq \mathcal{T}_{safe}$, which is equivalent to checking the following inequality

$$\max_{\tau \in \mathcal{T}_{(m,k)}} \mathrm{dis}(\tau, \tau_{nom}) \leq d^{safe}. \tag{10}$$

Intuitively, it means the system is safe under $\binom{m}{k}$ if and only if the maximum deviation of all trajectories $\tau \in \mathcal{T}_{(m,k)}$ is less than or equal to the safety margin of the system.

3   Statistical Hypothesis Testing

Computing the exact maximum deviation pertaining to a given constraint (*e.g.*, weakly hard constraints), in the worst case, might require computing deviation of 2^H trajectories, where H is the time horizon. This is clearly infeasible for practical values of H. To address this issue, [17] proposed a deterministic technique that employs reachable sets to compute an upper bound on the maximum deviation for a given constraint, rather than the exact maximum deviation. This approach enables safe deviation bounds (*i.e.*, an upper bound) to be computed for large time bounds. However, this technique has two main issues. Firstly, because it relies on reachable-set-based methods, the resulting upper bound is often overly conservative, rendering it ineffective for the safety verification in some instances. Secondly, because computing reachable sets can be computationally intensive, it was unable to compute a bound in a reasonable amount of time (1 h) for some applications, limiting its applicability.

In contrast to deterministic methods, a novel method presented in [12] uses statistical hypothesis testing (SHT) to compute a bound on the maximum deviation with a high level of confidence that is determined by the user. This technique demonstrates better performance than the deterministic method proposed

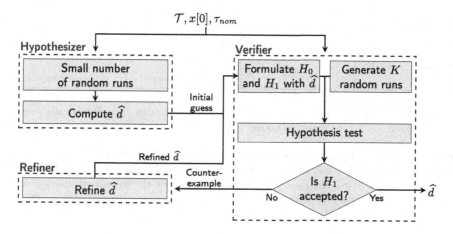

Fig. 2. Statistical hypothesis testing approach proposed in [12]. The Hypothesizer module makes an initial guess for the upper bound on the maximum deviation and sends it to the Verifier module for verification. If the verification fails, the counterexample is generated and sent to the Refiner module, which refines the guessed deviation based on the counterexample and sends it back to the Verifier module. This iteration continues until a successful verification is achieved, at which point the computed bound $\widehat{d}$ on the maximum deviation is returned.

in [17], both in terms of the tightness of the computed bound and computation time. In the rest of this section, we briefly review the technique proposed in [12] and present an illustrative example of the technique.

The proposed method in [12] employs a statistical hypothesis testing framework—specifically, Jeffreys's Bayes factor-based method—alongside a counterexample-based refinement strategy to compute a deviation upper bound with probabilistic guarantees. It comprises three main modules, namely the Hypothesizer module, the Verifier module, and the Refiner module. First, the inputs—the system model, the initial state, and the *nominal trajectory* of the system—are provided to the Hypothesizer module, which then makes an initial *guess* of the upper bound on the maximum deviation. Subsequently, the guessed upper bound is forwarded to the Verifier module, which uses SHT to verify its correctness. If the guessed deviation bound is incorrect, the Verifier module generates a counterexample and passes it on to the Refiner module. The Refiner module refines the guessed deviation based on the counterexample and sends it back to the Verifier module for re-verification. This iterative process continues until a successful verification occurs, with the desired level of confidence specified by the user. At this point, the computed bound on the maximum deviation is returned. The method is illustrated in Fig. 2.

We now give a more detailed review of the statistical hypothesis testing procedure employed within the Verifier module. The purpose of the Verifier module is to verify, using SHT, whether a given bound on the maximum deviation $\widehat{d}$ is indeed correct with the specified confidence level. For a given value of confidence c, the null and alternate hypotheses can be formulated as follows:

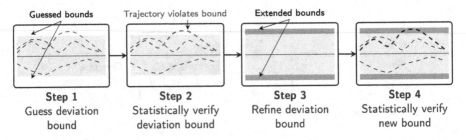

Guessed bounds	Trajectory violates bound	**Extended bounds**	

Step 1	Step 2	Step 3	Step 4
Guess deviation bound	Statistically verify deviation bound	Refine deviation bound	Statistically verify new bound

Fig. 3. Steps to compute deviation using the SHT method [12]. The nominal trajectory is the solid line in the center, while randomly generated trajectories are shown as dashed lines. The light blue envelope represents the calculated upper bound on deviation. (Color figure online)

$$H_0 : \mathcal{P}rob\left[\mathcal{T}, x[0], \tau_{nom}, \widehat{d}\right] < c \qquad (11)$$

$$H_1 : \mathcal{P}rob\left[\mathcal{T}, x[0], \tau_{nom}, \widehat{d}\right] \geq c \qquad (12)$$

where $\mathcal{P}rob\left[\mathcal{T}, x[0], \tau_{nom}, \widehat{d}\right]$ is the probability that a randomly selected trajectory τ has a deviation that remains within the deviation upper bound $\widehat{d}$. Intuitively, the null hypothesis H_0 represents the rejection of $\widehat{d}$ as the correct deviation upper bound, while the alternative hypothesis H_1 represents the acceptance of $\widehat{d}$. The Verifier tests the two hypotheses by first generating a set of K samples from the assumed distribution of executions, denoted by $X = \{\tau_1, \tau_2, \ldots, \tau_K\}$. The sample size K is derived from the Bayes factor B and confidence level c selected by the user. It then examines whether *all* members of X satisfy the upper bound constraint of $\widehat{d}$ (*i.e.*, the deviation of all the trajectories in X, from the nominal trajectory τ_{nom}, is less than $\widehat{d}$). If all members of X satisfy this condition, we accept the alternative hypothesis H_1 and report $\widehat{d}$ as the estimated bound. However, if at least one counterexample exists, then the Verifier rejects *devub* and send the counterexample to the Refiner module.

3.1   Example of Statistical Hypothesis Testing

In this section, we demonstrate how the SHT framework from [12] is used to compute the upper bound on the deviation $\widehat{d}$ for a specific weakly hard constraint. Figure 3 illustrates the overall process. We use the linearized motion of an F1Tenth [28] model car as an example, discretized with the period $P = 20$ ms:

$$x[t+1] = \begin{bmatrix} 1.000 & 0.1300 \\ 0 & 1.0000 \end{bmatrix} x[t] + \begin{bmatrix} 0.0256 \\ 0.3937 \end{bmatrix} u[t]$$

In this example, we compute the deviation upper bound for the weakly hard constraint $\left(\frac{1}{3}\right)$ from a nominal trajectory with no deadline misses, starting with the initial state $x[0] = [1\ 1]^T$. We assume a time horizon of $H = 5$ periods.

When a deadline is missed, the overrun job is killed and the control input from the previous period is held, consistent with the *Hold&Kill* policy [23]. The SHT framework compute the deviation upper bound $\widehat{d}$ with the following steps:

1. The `Hypothesizer` *guesses* an upper bound by considering a small sample of random sequences of deadline hit/miss that satisfy the weakly hard constraint $\left(\frac{1}{3}\right)$: 10110, 11001 (0 indicates miss, 1 indicates hit). The maximum deviation from the two random samples, 0.0482, is used as the initial guess $\widehat{d_0}$.
2. The guessed upper bound $\widehat{d_0} = 0.0482$ is verified by the `Verifier`, which returns *False*. *i.e.*, a counterexample is found whose deviation from nominal trajectory $d = 0.3157$ exceeds the initial guess $\widehat{d_0} = 0.0482$.
3. Since the guessed bound $\widehat{d_0}$ was not verified, the `Refiner` takes the counterexample produced by the `Verifier` and updates the previous deviation upper bound, $\widehat{d_0} = 0.0482$, to the deviation obtained from the counterexample, $\widehat{d_1} = 0.3157$.
4. The refined upper bound $\widehat{d_1} = 0.3157$ is again sent to the `Verifier` module for re-checking. This time, the `Verifier` module accepts the $\widehat{d_1} = 0.3157$ as a valid upper bound up to the desired probabilistic guarantees, and terminates the procedure

We note that the $\widehat{d} = 0.3157$ computed from the SHT is the same as the deviation produced by the reachability analysis method used in [41] for this example. This is because the small number of total deadline hit/miss sequences (as a result of the small time horizon $H = 5$) enables both methods to find the exact trajectory corresponding to the deviation upper bound. However, this is no longer the case as H increases due to the exponentially growing number of total deadline hit/miss sequences.

4   Proposed Schedule Synthesis

The schedule synthesis problem we wish to solve is as follows:

Problem 1 (Schedule Synthesis). Given a set of N controller tasks with the same period, their respective safety margins d^{safe}, and an implementation platform where at most $J < N$ controllers can be scheduled in each period, determine if a schedule over the time horizon H exists where all the controller tasks can be scheduled without deviating more than their safety margin. Furthermore, synthesize a schedule if one exists.

We propose an efficient solution to Problem 1, using the deviation upper bound estimation methods proposed in [12]. Our approach involves three stages:

1. *Compute* the collection of all weakly hard constraints that are statistically safe.
2. *Synthesize* a candidate schedule using the list of safe constraints from each task.
3. *Verify* the safety of the candidate schedule. If it is unsafe, go back to step 2; if it is safe, exit with the safe schedule.

Our approach is similar to the two-stage schedule synthesis scheme proposed by [41]. However, our method is different from theirs in two important aspects: First, the method in [41] deploys a deterministic technique to determine a list of safe constraints. This causes issues where lengthy execution time and substantial overestimation of deviation upper bounds significantly restrict the pool of weakly hard constraints available for schedule synthesis considerably. In contrast, our scheduler synthesis method capitalizes on the speed and tightness advantages of the SHT-based method proposed in [12]. Second, given that the deviation guarantee provided by the SHT-based method is probabilistic, our method incorporates an additional schedule verification phase. This step verifies the safety of the schedule produced by the schedule synthesis step. It is important to note that, because the exact deviations for the trajectories corresponding to the final schedule can be exactly determined, the schedules generated by our method are *deterministically* safe despite its reliance on a statistical method for constraint checking. This is different from the [12], where the gain in performance and tightness is at the price of only obtaining a probabilistic guarantee (*e.g.*, with confidence $c = 0.99$).

Constraint Checking. Given a control task T_i and its safety margin d_i^{safe}, constraint checking determines the set of weakly hard constraints under which the system is safe. This amounts to checking if $\mathbf{d}(m, k) \leq d_i^{safe}$, where $\mathbf{d}(m, k)$ is the maximum deviation of the trajectories in $\mathcal{T}_{(m,k)}$ from the nominal trajectory of T_i. More precisely,

$$\mathbf{d}(m, k) = \max\{\text{dis}(\tau, \tau_{nom}) \mid \tau \in \mathcal{T}_{(m,k)}\}. \tag{13}$$

However, checking this directly is expensive, due to the exponential number of hit/miss patterns of length H. To get around this, we compute an upper bound $\widehat{d}(m, k)$ on $\mathbf{d}(m, k)$ with confidence c using the SHT-based method in [12]. It then suffices to check that $\widehat{d}(m, k) \leq d^{safe}$ to derive a probabilistic guarantee of the safety of the system under $\binom{m}{k}$. We then iterate through all weakly hard constraints (up to a maximum window size $k_{max} \ll H$) and compute $\widehat{d}(m, k)$ using the SHT-based method for each constraint $\binom{m}{k}$. If $\widehat{d}(m, k) \leq d_i^{safe}$, we conclude that the system is safe under $\binom{m}{k}$ with confidence c and add $\binom{m}{k}$ to the set of safe constraints.

Schedule Synthesis. As introduced in Sect. 2.3, a weakly hard constraint $\binom{m}{k}$ is a regular language $\mathcal{L}(m, k)$ over $\{0, 1\}$, where a string represents a hit/miss pattern satisfying $\binom{m}{k}$. We denote such an automaton for the control task T_i by $\mathbb{A}_i = \langle L^i, \Sigma, \delta^i, F^i, \ell_0^i \rangle$, where L^i is a set of states, $\Sigma = \{0,1\}$ is the input alphabet (miss/hit), $\delta^i = L^i \times \Sigma \to L^i$ is the transition function, F^i is the set of accepting states, and ℓ_0^i is the initial state. With this construction, an accepting run of $\mathbb{A}_i$ is a hit/miss pattern that satisfies at least one safe weakly hard constraint for the corresponding controller task T_i. We use these individual finite automata for each task i to construct a *scheduler automaton* as follows:

Definition 2 (Scheduler Automaton). *A **scheduler automaton** $\mathbb{A}^S$ for a set of N controllers whose constraints are represented by the automata of the form $\mathbb{A}_i = \langle L^i, \Sigma, \delta^i, F^i, \ell_0^i \rangle$, where at most J controllers can be scheduled in each time slot, is defined as an automaton $\langle L^S, \Sigma^S, \delta^S, F^S, \ell_0^S \rangle$:*

L^S *set of states,* $L^S = \prod_i L^i$*;*
Σ^S *input alphabet,* $\Sigma^S \subset \{0,1\}^N$*. A sequence* $\sigma \in \{0,1\}^N$ *is in* Σ^S *if and only if* $\sum_i \sigma^i \leq J$*;*
δ^S *transition function,* $\delta^S(\ell, \sigma) = \prod_i \delta^i(\ell^i, \sigma^i)$*;*
F^S *accepting states of the automaton,* $F^S = \prod_i F^i$*;*
ℓ_0^S *initial state of the automaton,* $\ell_0^S = \prod_i \ell_0^i$*.*

The set of states L^S is a Cartesian product of the controller automaton states: $L^S = L^1 \times L^2 \times \cdots \times L^N$, where each state $\ell \in L^S$ is a tuple of individual states from each controller: $\ell = \langle \ell^1, \ell^2, \ldots, \ell^N \rangle$. The set of actions $\Sigma^S \subset \{0,1\}^N$ now captures hits and misses for all controllers, and an action $\sigma = \langle \sigma^1, \sigma^2, \ldots, \sigma^N \rangle$ is valid if and only if $\sum_i \sigma^i \leq J$. For example, $N = 3, J = 1$ results in $\Sigma^S = \{000, 001, 010, 100\}$, where $\sigma = 010$ indicates that only the second controller is scheduled. The transition function δ^S is the Cartesian product of individual transition functions $\prod_i \delta^i$. Concretely, assuming $\sigma \in \Sigma^S$ is a valid action for the scheduler automaton $\mathbb{A}^S$, the transition function δ^S becomes:

$$\delta^S(\ell, \sigma) = \langle \delta^1(\ell^1, \sigma^1), \delta^2(\ell^2, \sigma^2), \ldots, \delta^N(\ell^N, \sigma^N) \rangle.$$

The set of accepting states F is the Cartesian product of the individual accepting states. A state $\ell = \langle \ell^1, \ell^2, \ldots, \ell^N \rangle$ is an accepting state if and only if $\ell^i \in F^i$ for all $i \in [1, N]$. Intuitively, this means that the schedule is valid only if all the controllers operate within their safety margin; if any of the controller automaton $\mathbb{A}_i$ transition to a non-accepting (unsafe) state, the scheduler automaton will also transition to a non-accepting state.

Under this formulation, an accepting run of length $H + 1$ of the scheduler automaton is a schedule that satisfies at least one weakly hard constraint in the set of safe constraints for each control task. The existence of safe schedules can be checked by running emptiness checking on the scheduler automaton, and schedules can be generated using breadth-first search (BFS).

Schedule Verification. Given a synthesized schedule, we verify if the actual deviation of each system is within its safety margin. Toward this, we first calculate the exact trajectory of each system τ^i using the synthesized schedule for that system γ^i from the previous stage. The actual deviation of that system can be then calculated using the with $d^i = \text{dis}(\tau^i, \tau^i_{nom})$. If $d^i < d^{safe}_i$ for all systems, the schedule is verified to be safe. Note that since the exact deviation for each system is determined by the schedule, the schedule is *deterministically* safe despite the probabilistic guarantee given by the SHT-based method in Constraint Synthesis. Otherwise, the verification fails and a different schedule must be synthesized. If no schedule has passed the verification step and no more candidate schedules are available from schedule synthesis, the process terminates and returns `No Schedule`.

Since the safety guarantee obtained for each system by SHT has a confidence of at least c, the probability that a schedule produced by schedule synthesis is safe for N controllers is at least c^N. For $N = 20$ and $c = 0.99$, this translates to a probability of at least $0.99^{20} \approx 0.81$ and an expected $\frac{1}{0.81} = 1.23$ repetitions until a safe schedule is verified. We think this is reasonable and won't become a bottleneck for the scalability of the proposed approach.

4.1   Comparison with Deterministic Method Proposed in [41]

We now demonstrate that our scheduler synthesis technique that uses stochastic hypothesis testing for generating all the weakly hard constraints is at least as good as scheduler synthesis that uses deterministic verification process.

Lemma 1. *Consider the controller T_i that is scheduled satisfying the weakly hard constraint $\binom{m}{k}$ leading to at most $d(m, k)$ deviation from the nominal trajectory. For such controller, if the SHT estimates the deviation $\hat{d}(m, k)$ and a deterministic verification method provides an upper bound of $\tilde{d}(m, k)$, then, $\hat{d}(m, k) \le d(m, k) \le \tilde{d}(m, k)$.*

Since the deterministic verification techniques would compute a conservative overapproximation of all behaviors, $d(m, k) \le \tilde{d}(m, k)$. Since the estimation of the deviation during SHT is generated from one of the counterexamples, there exists at least one behavior with deviation $\hat{d}(m, k) \le d(m, k)$.

Theorem 1. *If the scheduler synthesis procedure using the deterministic verification technique for collecting the set of all the safe weakly hard constraints successfully generates a schedule, then the SHT-based constraint generation would also eventually generate it.*

Proof. Suppose that the deterministic verification method returned a safe schedule where the weakly hard constraint for each task T_i is $\binom{m}{k}_i$. From Lemma 1, we know that the same weakly hard constraint $\binom{m}{k}_i$ would also be considered safe using the SHT method. Therefore, the scheduler automaton generated using constraints using SHT would either terminate early with a safe schedule or eventually construct the scheduler automaton with weakly hard constraints $\binom{m}{k}_i$ for the task i. Therefore, the scheduler automaton, in the worst case, returns the same schedule obtained using deterministic verification.

5   Evaluation

To evaluate the effectiveness of our approach in scheduler synthesis, we implemented the proposed method in *Julia* [2] and conducted experiments on a system where five different controllers share the same computational platform. Our goal is to answer the following research questions:

1. Is our approach capable of synthesizing safe schedules where existing methods cannot?
2. How does the execution time of our approach compare to existing methods?

5.1   Benchmarks

We use five dynamical system models from the automotive domain. All systems are discretized with a period $P = 20$ ms, and controllers for each system are computed with LQR using a one-period delay.

RC Network (RC). Our first model is a resistor-capacitor network [10] with the following model:

$$\dot{x}(t) = \begin{bmatrix} -6.0 & 1.0 \\ 0.2 & -0.7 \end{bmatrix} x(t) + \begin{bmatrix} 5.0 \\ 0.5 \end{bmatrix} u(t).$$

F1Tenth Car (F1). Our second model is the linearized motion of an F1Tenth model car [28]:

$$\dot{x}(t) = \begin{bmatrix} 0 & 6.5 \\ 0 & 0 \end{bmatrix} x(t) + \begin{bmatrix} 0 \\ 19.685 \end{bmatrix} u(t).$$

Our next three plant models are selected from [33] and also represent subsystems from the automotive domain.

DC Motor (DC). Our third model is the speed controller for a DC motor adapted from [38]:

$$\dot{x}(t) = \begin{bmatrix} -10 & 1 \\ -0.02 & -2 \end{bmatrix} x(t) + \begin{bmatrix} 0 \\ 2 \end{bmatrix} u(t).$$

Car Suspension (CS). Our fourth model is a suspension system adapted from [35]:

$$\dot{x}(t) = \begin{bmatrix} 0 & 1 & 0 & 0 \\ -8 & -4 & 8 & 4 \\ 0 & 0 & 0 & 1 \\ 80 & 40 & -160 & -60 \end{bmatrix} x(t) + \begin{bmatrix} 0 \\ 80 \\ 20 \\ -1120 \end{bmatrix} u(t).$$

Table 1. Initial states and safety margins of the five models used in experiments.

	Initial State	Safety Margin
RC Network	$[1\ 1]^T$	0.07
F1 Tenth Car	$[1\ 1]^T$	0.56
DC Motor	$[100\ 100]^T$	0.1
Car Suspension	$[100\ 100\ 100\ 100]^T$	0.8
Cruise Control	$[1\ 1\ 1]^T$	0.06

Cruise Control (CC). Our final model is a cruise control system adapted from [27]:

$$\dot{x}(t) = \begin{bmatrix} 0 & 1 & 0 \\ 0 & 0 & 1 \\ -6.0476 & -5.2856 & -0.238 \end{bmatrix} x(t) + \begin{bmatrix} 0 \\ 0 \\ 2.4767 \end{bmatrix} u(t).$$

5.2   Experiments

We compared the effectiveness and performance of the proposed SHT-based method with the existing deterministic method [41]. For each method, the five models in Sect. 5.1 are used with a starting state x_0 that is offset from the origin in the state-space. The goal of all controllers is to bring the state x to the origin. The starting states and safety margins for the five systems are shown in Table 1. We assume that the controller tasks of the five systems are implemented on the same processor. During each period of $P = 20$ ms, we also assume that only two out of the five tasks can be run (*i.e.*, $J = 2$). The limitation that at most two tasks can be executed in each slot is very similar to the scheduling in AUTOSTAR Adaptive, where several tasks with the same period are combined together for scheduling purposes.

We used Julia 1.8 for all experiments. The parameters used in the experiments are as follows: The maximum window size for weakly hard constraint k_{max} is 6; the Bayes factor B is $4.15 * 10^5$; the time horizon H is 100; the confidence level c for statistical hypothesis testing is 0.99. We used Euclidean distance for all deviation estimations.

We recognize that some of the parameters (*e.g.*, $k_{max} = 6$ and $N = 5$) are relatively small. These values are selected primarily for the ease of comparison against the existing deterministic method. Additionally, as the majority of computation effort is spent on the constraint synthesis phase, whose execution time grows linearly with the number of controllers N, increasing N has a mostly linear effect on the overall execution time. On the other hand, as a max window size of $k_{max} = 6$ already covers cases as extreme as only 1 deadline hit in every 6 consecutive invocations of the task, we believe that the potential benefit of experimenting with even higher values of k_{max} is outweighed by the increased computation.

Table 2. Deviation upper bounds $\widehat{d}$ for each system and weakly hard constraint, computed by the SHT-based method.

	Window Size (k)	Minimum Hits (m)					
		1	2	3	4	5	6
RC Network $d^{safe} = 0.07$	1	0.0	–	–	–	–	–
	2	0.036	0.0	–	–	–	–
	3	0.0656	0.036	0.0	–	–	–
	4	0.0899	0.0656	0.036	0.0	–	–
	5	0.11	0.0899	0.0656	0.036	0.0	–
	6	0.126	0.11	0.0899	0.0656	0.036	0.0
F1 Tenth Car $d^{safe} = 0.56$	1	0.0	–	–	–	–	–
	2	0.179	0.0	–	–	–	–
	3	0.364	0.179	0.0	–	–	–
	4	0.557	0.364	0.179	0.0	–	–
	5	0.75	0.557	0.364	0.179	0.0	–
	6	0.949	0.75	0.557	0.364	0.179	0.0
DC Motor $d^{safe} = 0.1$	1	0.0	–	–	–	–	–
	2	0.0546	0.0	–	–	–	–
	3	0.107	0.0546	0.0	–	–	–
	4	0.156	0.107	0.0546	0.0	–	–
	5	0.204	0.157	0.107	0.0546	0.0	–
	6	0.248	0.204	0.157	0.107	0.0546	0.0
Car Suspension $d^{safe} = 0.8$	1	0.0	–	–	–	–	–
	2	0.16	0.0	–	–	–	–
	3	0.34	0.16	0.0	–	–	–
	4	0.53	0.34	0.159	0.0	–	–
	5	0.729	0.529	0.339	0.159	0.0	–
	6	0.908	0.717	0.526	0.338	0.158	0.0
Cruise Control $d^{safe} = 0.06$	1	0.0	–	–	–	–	–
	2	0.0138	0.0	–	–	–	–
	3	0.0298	0.0115	0.0	–	–	–
	4	0.0368	0.0212	0.0117	0.0	–	–
	5	0.0455	0.0323	0.0194	0.0115	0.0	–
	6	0.0584	0.0423	0.0262	0.0201	0.0116	0.0

5.3 RQ1: Effectiveness of the Proposed Approach to Synthesize Safe Schedules

To answer RQ1, we applied our SHT-based constraint and schedule synthesis method to the systems in Sect. 5.1. We also ran the deterministic method in [41]

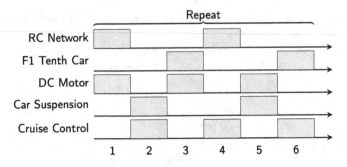

Fig. 4. Schedule synthesized by the SHT-based method.

with iteration parameter $n = 15$. **Result**: the proposed SHT-based method was able to synthesize a safe schedule, shown in Fig. 4, while the deterministic method failed to find a safe schedule.

Detailed results of constraint and schedule synthesis are outlined in Table 2 and Table 3, respectively. In Table 2, the value at row k and column m in Table 2 represents the deviation upper bound $\widehat{d}(m, k)$ associated with weakly hard constraint $\binom{m}{k}$, computed by the SHT-based method. If $\widehat{d}(m, k) < d^{safe}$, then $\binom{m}{k}$ is added to the safe list of constraints for that system. The safe values are highlighted in Table 2, where values highlighted with ▉ are safe according to both the SHT-based method and the deterministic method ($\widehat{d}, \tilde{d} < d^{safe}$), and values highlighted with light green ▢ are safe according to the SHT-based only and unsafe according to the deterministic method ($\widehat{d} \leq d^{safe} \leq \tilde{d}$). As shown in Lemma 1, any constraint deemed safe by the deterministic method is always deemed safe by the SHT-based method too. We observe from Table 2 that while the deterministic method and the SHT-based method performed similarly for the RC Network and DC Motor systems, the SHT-based method is able to produce tighter estimates for the F1 Tenth Car, Car Suspension and Cruise Control systems. The Car Suspension and Cruise Control systems especially see a large increase in safe constraints.

Table 3 shows the exact deviation for each system under the schedule in Fig. 4, per the schedule verification procedure described in Sect. 4. We observe that the schedule for each individual system closely matches one of the safe constraints for that system. For example, the schedule for RC Network matches the weakly hard constraint $\binom{1}{3}$. We compared the actual deviation with the estimated $\widehat{d}(m, k)$ for that constraint. For two out of five systems, the deterministic method estimates deviation upper bounds $\tilde{d}$ higher than the safety margin d^{safe}; the SHT-based method estimates values closer to the actual deviation that are all within the safety margin. This matches the result in Table 2, where the deterministic method greatly overestimates the deviation upper bound for the Car Suspension and Cruise Control systems. Finally, we note that the scheduler passed the schedule verifier on the first try. This is expected, given the high confidence level $c = 0.99$ used during the constraint synthesis step.

Table 3. Exact deviation values for each system when scheduled according to Fig. 4. All systems have deviation values within their respective safety margin, *i.e.*, the schedule is deterministically safe.

	Safety Margin	Closest Constraint	Estimated $\widehat{d}(m,k)$	Estimated $\tilde{d}(m,k)$	Actual Deviation
RC Network	0.07	$\left(\frac{1}{3}\right)$	0.0656	0.0656	0.0092
F1 Tenth Car	0.56	$\left(\frac{1}{3}\right)$	0.364	0.364	0.303
DC Motor	0.1	$\left(\frac{1}{2}\right)$	0.0546	0.0546	0.157
Car Suspension	0.8	$\left(\frac{1}{3}\right)$	0.34	1.04	0.13
Cruise Control	0.06	$\left(\frac{1}{2}\right)$	0.0138	0.0712	0.00578

These results suggest that our SHT-based approach effectively produces *deterministically* safe schedules, even when the existing method fails to do so.

5.4 RQ2: Reduction of Execution Time Using the Proposed Approach

In addition to the two configurations used in Sect. 5.3, we also ran an additional configuration of the deterministic approach in [41] with parameter $n = 18$. We ran this additional configuration because a higher n value correlates to a tighter deviation estimation, and we incremented the n value progressively until the deterministic method returns a valid schedule with $n = 18$. The execution times for the constraint synthesis and schedule synthesis using the two methods are outlined in Table 4.

We observe that the SHT-based method delivers a 30× to 600× speed up for constraint synthesis of individual systems compared to the deterministic method. In total, the SHT-based method is 55× and 394× faster than the deterministic method with $n = 15$ and $n = 18$, respectively. Second, the procedure of schedule synthesis and verification accounts for a relatively small fraction of the overall execution time. Third, our method takes roughly the same amount of time for each system, whereas the deterministic method takes much more time to compute the Car Suspension system than other systems. Finally, we note that although the deterministic method is able to synthesize a safe schedule for the benchmarks with parameter $n = 18$, it does so using exponentially more time as n increases [17]. The SHT-based method eliminates the need for finding the suitable n value, which in itself is a time-consuming process.

In summary, the deterministic method takes orders of magnitudes more time than the SHT-based method to execute and requires a suitable n value to synthesize a safe schedule. The SHT-based is able to synthesize a schedule much faster while eliminating the need to find the n value through trial and error, further reducing execution time.

Table 4. Execution times for the SHT-based and deterministic methods.

	SHT ($c = 0.99$)	DET ($n = 15$)	DET ($n = 18$)
RC Network	2.17 s	115.35 s	818.92 s
F1 Tenth Car	2.09 s	115.96 s	817.70 s
DC Motor	2.78 s	112.95 s	820.18 s
Car Suspension	3.10 s	292.35 s	2071.46 s
Cruise Control	3.33 s	111.65 s	799.89 s
Schedule Synthesis	0.017 s	0.106 s	0.012 s
Schedule Verification	0.008 s	–	–
Total	13.50 s	748.37 s	5328.16 s
Schedulable?	Yes	No	Yes

6   Concluding Remarks

Ensuring traditional real-time guarantees that no task misses its deadline has become increasingly challenging because of (a) the increased volume of software being deployed in modern autonomous systems, and (b) the increased complexity of the hardware in such systems. Consequently, some feedback control tasks may miss their deadlines and their behavior would deviate from the nominal behavior. This causes a divergence between the design and implementation of autonomous systems, posing a major hurdle in their certification. Our approach to overcome this hurdle is to synthesize a *correct-by-construction* control system implementation for all control tasks sharing computational resources. By allowing tasks to miss their deadlines *by design*, the pessimism associated with software timing analysis is partly mitigated. We demonstrated that incorporating probabilistic model checking to collect a collection of weakly hard constraints in the scheduler synthesis (1) enables us to schedule tasks that could not be scheduled using deterministic verification techniques, and (2) reduces the computational effort required for synthesizing such schedules. We demonstrated these two advantages by scheduling a task set on a system, where five controllers share the same computational resource.

Currently, our work requires that all the controllers have the same period and are scheduled on a uni-processor. While these restrictions are compatible with the AUTOSTAR Dynamic framework of scheduling groups of processes that share a control period, we plan to extend this work to controllers that have different sampling periods as a part of future work.

There are a number of optimization and extensions of the work that we are interested in exploring. For example, in addition to the $\binom{m}{k}$ constraints used in this work, several other types of weakly hard constraints exist and may be applicable to the problem, such as the $\langle m \rangle$ constraint that specifies no more than m consecutive misses can occur [39]. Finally, while this paper is on synthesizing schedules by focusing on "*system-level properties*," like control safety, instead of "secondary" properties like timing behavior, this idea is applicable more generally. For example, when messages are not *fully* encrypted or authenticated for security [26,40], it might be shown that a safety property of the form studied in this paper cannot be violated even if the system is under attack. Similar results may also be established in the case of ensuring system reliability [11].

References

1. Bernat, G., Burns, A., Liamosi, A.: Weakly hard real-time systems. IEEE Trans. Comput. **50**(4), 308–321 (2001)
2. Bezanson, J., Edelman, A., Karpinski, S., Shah, V.B.: Julia: a fresh approach to numerical computing. SIAM Rev. **59**(1), 65–98 (2017)
3. Bordoloi, U.D., Chakraborty, S., Jochim, M., Joshi, P., Raghuraman, A., Ramesh, S.: Autonomy-driven emerging directions in software-defined vehicles. In: Design, Automation & Test in Europe Conference & Exhibition (DATE) (2023)
4. von der Brüggen, G., et al.: Efficiently approximating the probability of deadline misses in real-time systems. In: Euromicro Conference on Real-Time Systems. ECRTS (2018)
5. Chakraborty, S., Erlebach, T., Thiele, L.: On the complexity of scheduling conditional real-time code. In: Dehne, F., Sack, J.-R., Tamassia, R. (eds.) WADS 2001. LNCS, vol. 2125, pp. 38–49. Springer, Heidelberg (2001). https://doi.org/10.1007/3-540-44634-6_5
6. Chakraborty, S., et al.: Automotive cyber-physical systems: a tutorial introduction. IEEE Des. Test **33**(4), 92–108 (2016)
7. Chang, W., Chakraborty, S.: Resource-aware automotive control systems design: a cyber-physical systems approach. Found. Trends Electron. Des. Autom. **10**(4), 249–369 (2016)
8. Duggirala, P.S., Viswanathan, M.: Analyzing real time linear control systems using software verification. In: IEEE Real-Time Systems Symposium (RTSS) (2015)
9. Fraccaroli, E., Joshi, P., Xu, S., Shazzad, K., Jochim, M., Chakraborty, S.: Timing predictability for SOME/IP-based service-oriented automotive in-vehicle networks. In: Design, Automation & Test in Europe Conference & Exhibition (DATE) (2023)
10. Gabel, R.A., Roberts, R.A.: Signals and Linear Systems. Wiley, Hoboken (1987)
11. Georgakos, G., et al.: Reliability challenges for electric vehicles: from devices to architecture and systems software. In: 50th Annual Design Automation Conference (DAC) (2013)
12. Ghosh, B., et al.: Statistical hypothesis testing of controller implementations under timing uncertainties. In: 28th IEEE International Conference on Embedded and Real-Time Computing Systems and Applications (RTCSA) (2022)
13. Goswami, D., Lukasiewycz, M., Schneider, R., Chakraborty, S.: Time-triggered implementations of mixed-criticality automotive software. In: Design, Automation & Test in Europe Conference & Exhibition (DATE) (2012)
14. Goswami, D., Schneider, R., Chakraborty, S.: Re-engineering cyber-physical control applications for hybrid communication protocols. In: Design, Automation and Test in Europe (DATE) (2011)
15. Hamdaoui, M., Ramanathan, P.: A dynamic priority assignment technique for streams with (m, k)-firm deadlines. IEEE Trans. Comput. **44**(12), 1443–1451 (1995)

16. Hammadeh, Z., Ernst, R., Quinton, S., Henia, R., Rioux, L.: Bounding deadline misses in weakly-hard real-time systems with task dependencies. In: Design, Automation & Test in Europe Conference & Exhibition (DATE) (2017)
17. Hobbs, C., Ghosh, B., Xu, S., Duggirala, P.S., Chakraborty, S.: Safety analysis of embedded controllers under implementation platform timing uncertainties. IEEE Trans. Comput.-Aided Des. Integr. Circ. Syst. 41(11), 4016–4027 (2022)
18. Huang, C., Chang, K.-C., Lin, C.-W., Zhu, Q.: SAW: a tool for safety analysis of weakly-hard systems. In: Lahiri, S.K., Wang, C. (eds.) CAV 2020. LNCS, vol. 12224, pp. 543–555. Springer, Cham (2020). https://doi.org/10.1007/978-3-030-53288-8_26
19. Huang, C., Li, W., Zhu, Q.: Formal verification of weakly-hard systems. In: 22nd ACM International Conference on Hybrid Systems: Computation and Control (HSCC) (2019)
20. Ju, L., Huynh, B.K., Roychoudhury, A., Chakraborty, S.: Timing analysis of Esterel programs on general-purpose multiprocessors. In: 47th Design Automation Conference (DAC) (2010)
21. Ju, L., et al.: Context-sensitive timing analysis of Esterel programs. In: 46th Design Automation Conference (DAC) (2009)
22. Kumar, P., Goswami, D., Chakraborty, S., Annaswamy, A., Lampka, K., Thiele, L.: A hybrid approach to cyber-physical systems verification. In: The 49th Annual Design Automation Conference (DAC) (2012)
23. Maggio, M., Hamann, A., Mayer-John, E., Ziegenbein, D.: Control-system stability under consecutive deadline misses constraints. In: 32nd Euromicro Conference on Real-Time Systems (ECRTS) (2020)
24. Majumdar, R., Saha, I., Zamani, M.: Synthesis of minimal-error control software. In: 12th International Conference on Embedded Software (EMSOFT) (2012)
25. Masrur, A., et al.: VM-based real-time services for automotive control applications. In: 16th IEEE International Conference on Embedded and Real-Time Computing Systems and Applications (RTCSA) (2010)
26. Mundhenk, P., et al.: Security analysis of automotive architectures using probabilistic model checking. In: 52nd Annual Design Automation Conference (DAC) (2015)
27. Osman, K., Rahmat, M.F., Ahmad, M.A.: Modelling and controller design for a cruise control system. In: 5th International Colloquium on Signal Processing & Its Applications (2009)
28. O'Kelly, M., Zheng, H., Karthik, D., Mangharam, R.: F1TENTH: an open-source evaluation environment for continuous control and reinforcement learning. In: Proceedings of the NeurIPS 2019 Competition and Demonstration Track. PMLR (2020). https://proceedings.mlr.press/v123/o-kelly20a.html
29. Parisotto, E., Mohamed, A.R., Singh, R., Li, L., Zhou, D., Kohli, P.: Neuro-symbolic program synthesis. arXiv preprint arXiv:1611.01855 (2016)
30. Pazzaglia, P., et al.: Adaptive design of real-time control systems subject to sporadic overruns. In: Design Automation and Test in Europe (DATE) (2021)
31. Pazzaglia, P., Mandrioli, C., Maggio, M., Cervin, A.: DMAC: deadline-miss-aware control. In: Euromicro Conference on Real-Time Systems (ECRTS) (2019)
32. Pazzaglia, P., Sun, Y., Natale, M.D.: Generalized weakly hard schedulability analysis for real-time periodic tasks. ACM Trans. Embed. Comput. Syst. 20(1), 1–26 (2020). https://doi.org/10.1145/3404888
33. Roy, D., Zhang, L., Chang, W., Goswami, D., Chakraborty, S.: Multi-objective co-optimization of FlexRay-based distributed control systems. In: IEEE Real-Time and Embedded Technology and Applications Symposium (RTAS) (2016)

34. Schkufza, E., Sharma, R., Aiken, A.: Stochastic superoptimization. ACM SIGARCH Comput. Archit. News **41**(1), 305–316 (2013)
35. Schneider, R., Goswami, D., Zafar, S., Chakraborty, S., Lukasiewycz, M.: Constraint-driven synthesis and tool-support for FlexRay-based automotive control systems. In: 2011 Proceedings of the Ninth IEEE/ACM/IFIP International Conference on Hardware/Software Codesign and System Synthesis (CODES+ISSS) (2011)
36. Schneider, R., et al.: Multi-layered scheduling of mixed-criticality cyber-physical systems. J. Syst. Archit. **59**(10-D), 1215–1230 (2013)
37. Tibba, G., Malz, C., Stoermer, C., Nagarajan, N., Zhang, L., Chakraborty, S.: Testing automotive embedded systems under X-in-the-loop setups. In: 35th International Conference on Computer-Aided Design (ICCAD) (2016)
38. Tilbury, D., Messner, B.: Control Tutorials for MATLAB and Simulink. https://ctms.engin.umich.edu/CTMS/index.php?aux=Home
39. Vreman, N., Pates, R., Maggio, M.: WeaklyHard.jl: scalable analysis of weakly-hard constraints. In: 28th IEEE Real-Time and Embedded Technology and Applications Symposium (RTAS) (2022)
40. Waszecki, P., et al.: Automotive electrical and electronic architecture security via distributed in-vehicle traffic monitoring. IEEE Trans. Comput. Aided Des. Integr. Circ. Syst. **36**(11), 1790–1803 (2017)
41. Xu, S., Ghosh, B., Hobbs, C., Thiagarajan, P.S., Chakraborty, S.: Safety-aware flexible schedule synthesis for cyber-physical systems using weakly-hard constraints. In: 28th Asia and South Pacific Design Automation Conference (ASP-DAC) (2023)
42. Zhang, L., Goswami, D., Schneider, R., Chakraborty, S.: Task-and network-level schedule co-synthesis of ethernet-based time-triggered systems. In: 19th Asia and South Pacific Design Automation Conference (ASP-DAC) (2014)

Compositional High-Quality Synthesis

Rafael Dewes$^{(\boxtimes)}$ and Rayna Dimitrova

CISPA Helmholtz Center for Information Security, Saarbrücken, Germany
`rafael.dewes@cispa.de`

Abstract. Over the last years, there has been growing interest in synthesizing reactive systems from quantitative specifications, with the goal of constructing correct and high-quality systems. Considering quantitative requirements in systems consisting of multiple components is challenging not only because of scalability limitations but also due to the intricate interplay between the different possibilities of satisfying a specification and the required cooperation between components. Compositional synthesis holds the promise of addressing these challenges.

We study the compositional synthesis of reactive systems consisting of multiple components, from requirements specified in a fragment of the logic LTL[F], which extends LTL with quality operators. We consider specifications that are combinations of local and shared quantitative requirements. We present a sound decomposition rule that allows for synthesizing one component at a time. The decomposition requires assume-guarantee contracts between the components, and we provide a method for iteratively refining the assumptions and guarantees. We evaluate our approach with a prototype implementation, demonstrating its advantages over monolithic synthesis and ability to generate decompositions.

1 Introduction

Reactive synthesis can be used to automatically construct correct-by-design reactive systems from high-level specifications. The correctness requirements are typically specified using temporal logics such as Linear Temporal Logic (LTL). However, logics like LTL have limited ability to capture preferences on the quality of the synthesized system, such as resource requirements, efficiency, or prioritization of tasks. Over the last decades, the study of quantitative specification formalisms and the development of synthesis techniques for constructing high-quality implementations has attracted significant attention. Specification formalisms include weighted automata [8] and temporal logics equipped with propositional quality operators and discounting operators [1,2].

In the development of synthesis algorithms for quantitative specifications, the focus has been predominantly on single-component synthesis. Extensions have considered quantitative specifications in assume-guarantee form, for instance expressed in the GR(1)[$\mathcal{F}$] fragment [4], as well as relaxations of the synthesis problem, such as good-enough synthesis [3], where the system is required to produce an output satisfying the specification with a certain value only if the environment provides an input sequence for which such an output exists.

© The Author(s), under exclusive license to Springer Nature Switzerland AG 2023
É. André and J. Sun (Eds.): ATVA 2023, LNCS 14215, pp. 334–354, 2023.
https://doi.org/10.1007/978-3-031-45329-8_16

While such extensions focus on the explicit or implicit assumptions made about the environment, they do not study the interaction between cooperating components within the synthesized system in the presence of quantitative specifications. It has been widely recognized that compositional approaches are necessary in order to make reactive synthesis applicable to complex systems of multiple components.

In this paper we propose a *compositional method* for good-enough synthesis [3] for specifications expressed in a fragment of the logic LTL[$\mathcal{F}$] [2]. LTL[$\mathcal{F}$] extends LTL with quality operators, and instead of true or false, the satisfaction values of formulas are real values in $[0, 1]$. A higher value of satisfaction of a formula by an execution trace corresponds to a higher quality. Good-enough synthesis, introduced in [3], is a relaxation of the classical synthesis problem. For specifications in LTL[$\mathcal{F}$] this means that for each input sequence the synthesized system is required to ensure the highest value possible for this input sequence.

We study the problem of decomposing the good-enough synthesis task over multiple components. To this end, we consider LTL[$\mathcal{F}$] specifications that are a *combination of local specifications* for the individual components *and a shared specification*. The local specification φ^c_{local} for a component c captures requirements that are local to c, while the shared specification Ψ_{shared} captures requirements pertaining to multiple components. We furthermore make some natural assumptions about the specifications, which we make use of in order to provide a sound decomposition of the synthesis problem. We assume for each local specification that it does not refer to the output variables of other components, and that the shared specification is a safety property. These assumptions are meaningful in a setting where components have their own individual objectives, but must in addition jointly guarantee that some safety requirement is fulfilled.

The task we study is to synthesize in a compositional manner a system of *cooperating* components that ensures for each input sequence the *highest possible value for the combined specification*. Our goal is to decompose this task into synthesis tasks for the individual components, which for each component c consider only φ^c_{local} and Ψ_{shared}, and in addition, assumptions on the other components and additional guarantees that c provides to the other components when necessary. We illustrate the problem on an example.

Example. Suppose that our goal is to synthesize a system consisting of two components, where i is a Boolean variable input from the external environment, o_1 is a Boolean output of component 1, and o_2 is a Boolean output of component 2. We assume that each component has full information, that is, observes all environment inputs and outputs of other components. We consider implementations in the form of Moore machines, i.e., the output of each component at a given step can only depend on past inputs and outputs of other components.

The system must satisfy the specification $\Phi = \varphi^1_{local} \wedge \varphi^2_{local} \wedge \Psi_{shared}$, where $\varphi^1_{local} = (\Box\Diamond o_1) \oplus_{\frac{1}{2}} (\Box\Diamond(i \wedge \bigcirc\neg o_1))$ is the specification of component 1, and $\varphi^2_{local} = \Box\Diamond o_2$ is the local specification of component 2, and $\Psi_{shared} = \Box(o_1 \rightarrow \bigcirc\neg o_2)$ is the shared specification.

Here, the local specification φ^2_{local}, which requires that o_2 is true infinitely often, and the shared specification Ψ_{shared}, which requires that every time when

o_1 is true then o_2 must be false in the next step, are both qualitative LTL specifications. Hence, each has two possible values, 0 and 1.

The local specification φ^1_{local} of component 1 uses the weighted sum operator $\oplus_{\frac{1}{2}}$ with weight $\frac{1}{2}$ for each of the subformulas. Hence, an execution of the system where o_1 is true infinitely often will result in value of at least $\frac{1}{2}$ for φ^1_{local}. If additionally $i \wedge \bigcirc \neg o_1$ is true infinitely often on that execution then the value of φ^1_{local} will be 1. If both are false, the value of φ_1 is 0. Since Φ is the conjunction of the three specifications, its value is the minimum of their values.

The task is then to synthesize a system $\mathcal{S}$ that satisfies the following: for any value v and infinite sequence σ_I of values of i provided by the environment, if there is a sequence of outputs σ_O, such that the value of Φ on $\sigma_I \parallel \sigma_O$ is v, then, for the output $\mathcal{S}(\sigma_I)$ of $\mathcal{S}$ on σ_I, the value of Φ on $\sigma_I \parallel \mathcal{S}(\sigma_I)$ must be at least v.

Consider the monolithic system that has three (global) states s_1, s_2, s_3, and such that in s_1 the output is $(o_1 := \text{true}, o_2 := \text{true})$, and in the other two states it is $(o_1 := \text{false}, o_2 := \text{false})$. From s_1 the system always transitions to s_2 and from s_3 it always transitions to s_1. From s_2 it goes to s_1 if i is false and to s_3 if i is true. Thus, if i is infinitely often true, then this system implementation ensures value 1, since it also guarantees that each of o_1 and o_2 is true infinitely often and Ψ_{shared} holds. If i is *not* true infinitely often, then the maximal value of Φ that is possible is $\frac{1}{2}$, which is also what the implementation ensures.

Such a system can be synthesized by applying to Φ the algorithm presented in [3] for good-enough synthesis for LTL$[\mathcal{F}]$ specifications.

Our goal is to decompose the synthesis problem, such that we *consider the local specifications of the two components in isolation*. That is, to synthesize an implementation for component 1 considering φ^1_{local} and Ψ_{shared}, and similarly for component 2. Each component cannot on its own enforce the maximal possible values for both the shared and its local specification. Thus, it needs to make assumptions on the behavior of the other component. Here, component 1 needs to make an assumption, A_1, on the behavior of component 2, which in this case is Ψ_{shared} itself. Component 2 also needs to make an assumption, A_2, that requires that o_1 is false infinitely often, to be able to satisfy both φ^2_{local} and Ψ_{shared}. Component 1 can guarantee the assumption A_2, while ensuring the maximal possible value for φ^1_{local} and Ψ_{shared} (under assumption A_1). The components obtained by projection from the system above satisfy these requirements.

An *assume-guarantee contract* between the components, like the one above, allows for the decomposition of the synthesis task for Φ into local synthesis tasks for the individual components. We study the problem of establishing such a decomposition and automatically deriving assume guarantee contracts.

Contributions. We provide a decomposition rule that identifies conditions on the LTL$[\mathcal{F}]$ specifications of the above form, which guarantee that an assume-guarantee decomposition is sound. In particular, we define the notion of *good-enough* tuples of assumptions, and describe a method for automatically deriving assume-guarantee contracts for quantitative specifications. We have implemented the proposed approach in a prototype and demonstrate on a set of examples that the compositional synthesis technique outperforms the monolithic one.

Related Work. Compositional approaches for synthesis from qualitative specifications have been studied extensively. In assume-guarantee synthesis [9,11,18, 21] the synthesis problem is decomposed using an assume-guarantee contract to capture the interface and dependencies between components. Other techniques are based on a decomposition of the given specification into independent specifications by analysis of the dependencies between components [17], or by semantic analysis of the language descried by the specification [16]. None of these approaches consider good-enough synthesis for quantitative specifications.

The notion of good-enough synthesis [3], where the system must only ensure the satisfaction value made possible by the environment, is closely related to the notions of dominant strategies [13], that is, strategies that perform as good as the best alternative, as well as admissible strategies [10], which are strategies that are not dominated by another strategy. Dominant strategies have been used for compositional synthesis [13,17], by making use of the fact that implementations must be dominant strategies and reducing the synthesis problem to a sequence of synthesis tasks treating the processes in the system one at a time. These compositional techniques are only studied in the qualitative setting and when the components have a common objective, while in our case we consider quantitative specifications and components have both shared and local specifications. In rational synthesis [20], the environment of the system being synthesized consists of rational agents with their own objectives. In contrast, we consider cooperating components as part of the system and aim to synthesize them compositionally.

The automatic generation of assumptions for qualitative specifications has been studied extensively. [12] presents a game-based method for deriving environment assumptions that turn an unrealizable specification into a realizable one. [5,6] propose techniques for correcting unrealizable specifications in the form of implications between assumptions and guarantees. In [21] the authors present an iterative procedure, called negotiation, for deriving assumption-guarantee pairs. Their assumption-generation method, similarly to ours, is based on [12]. Our iterative strengthening of assumptions follows the idea of their negotiation process. Neither of these works considers quantitative specifications.

A number of techniques have been developed for compositional synthesis for conjunctions of multiple specifications. In [15] this is done for solving games compositionally in the context of bounded synthesis, and [7] presents a technique for compositional synthesis for conjunctions of Safety LTL specifications. The method we use to treat the conjunctions of multiple combinations of values in our good-enough synthesis procedure is similar to these techniques, but in the context of the construction of the safety games in bounded synthesis.

2 Preliminaries

2.1 Languages and Automata over Infinite Words

Let Σ be a finite alphabet. The set of finite (infinite) words over Σ is denoted by Σ^* (respectively Σ^ω). For a word $\sigma = \sigma_0, \sigma_1, \ldots \in \Sigma^\omega$, we denote with $\sigma[i] = \sigma_i$ the letter at position i, and with $\sigma[i, \infty) = \sigma_i, \sigma_{i+1}, \ldots$ the suffix of σ starting at position i. For a finite word $\sigma' \in \Sigma^*$ and a word $\sigma'' \in \Sigma^* \cup \Sigma^\omega$, we denote with $\sigma' \cdot \sigma''$ the concatenation of the prefix σ' and the suffix σ''. A language $L \subseteq \Sigma^\omega$ is a safety language if and only if for every $\sigma \in \Sigma^\omega \setminus L$ there exists a finite prefix σ' of σ such that for every $\sigma'' \in \Sigma^\omega$ it holds that $\sigma' \cdot \sigma'' \notin L$.

For a set X, we denote with 2^X the powerset of X. For a word σ over alphabet 2^X and a subset $Y \subseteq X$ we denote with $\mathsf{proj}(\sigma, Y)$ the projection of σ onto the alphabet 2^Y. Given disjoint sets $X_1, \ldots, X_m$ and for each $i \in \{1, \ldots, m\}$ a word σ_i over the alphabet 2^{X_i}, we define the parallel composition $\|_{i=1}^m \sigma_i$ of the words $\sigma_1, \ldots, \sigma_m$ such that $(\|_{i=1}^m \sigma_i)[j] = \bigcup_{i=1}^m \sigma_i[j]$ for all j.

We will use several types of automata over infinite words, whose definitions we recall in this subsection, together with some operations and properties.

A *generalized nondeterministic Büchi automaton* (GNBA) over an alphabet Σ is a tuple $\mathcal{A} = (\Sigma, Q, \delta, Q_0, \alpha)$, where Q is a finite set of states, $Q_0 \subseteq Q$ is a set of initial states, $\delta : Q \times \Sigma \to 2^Q$ is the transition function, and $\alpha \subseteq 2^Q$ a set of sets of accepting states. A run of $\mathcal{A} = (\Sigma, Q, \delta, Q_0, \alpha)$ on an infinite word $\sigma \in \Sigma^\omega$ is an infinite sequence $\rho \in Q^\omega$ of states such that $q_0 \in Q_0$, and for every $i \in \mathbb{N}$ it holds that $\rho[i+1] \in \delta(\rho[i], \sigma[i+1])$. A run ρ of a GNBA is accepting if and only if for every $F \in \alpha$ it holds that for every $i \in \mathbb{N}$ there exists $j \geq i$ such that $\rho[j] \in F$, i.e., ρ visits each set in α infinitely often. An infinite word σ is accepted by a GNBA $\mathcal{A}$ if there exists an accepting run of $\mathcal{A}$ on σ.

A *nondeterministic Büchi automaton* (NBA) is a GNBA $\mathcal{A} = (\Sigma, Q, \delta, Q_0, \alpha)$ with $|\alpha| = 1$. When $\mathcal{A}$ is an NBA we will also write $\mathcal{A} = (\Sigma, Q, \delta, Q_0, F)$ where $F \subseteq Q$ is the single set of accepting states. A *safety automaton* is a Büchi automaton in which all states are accepting. Hence, for safety automata every infinite run is accepting, and words that are not accepted have no infinite run. An automaton is *deterministic* if $|Q_0| = 1$ and $|\delta(q, a)| \leq 1$ for all $q \in Q$, $a \in \Sigma$.

A *universal co-Büchi automaton* (UCB) is a tuple $\mathcal{A} = (\Sigma, Q, \delta, Q_0, F)$, where Σ, Q, δ and Q_0 are as in NBA, but now $F \subseteq Q$ is a set of *rejecting states*. A run ρ of a UCB is accepting if and only if there exists $i \in \mathbb{N}$ such that for every $j \geq i$ it holds that $\rho[j] \notin F$, i.e., ρ visits the set F only finitely many times. A UCB $\mathcal{A}$ accepts an infinite word σ if *all* infinite runs of $\mathcal{A}$ on σ are accepting.

For $\mathcal{A}$ over alphabet Σ, we define $\mathcal{L}(\mathcal{A}) := \{\sigma \in \Sigma^\omega \mid \sigma \text{ is accepted by } \mathcal{A}\}$.

For NBA $\mathcal{A} = (\Sigma, Q, \delta, Q_0, F)$ it holds for the UCB $\mathcal{U} := (\Sigma, Q, \delta, Q_0, F)$ that $\mathcal{L}(\mathcal{U}) = \Sigma^\omega \setminus \mathcal{L}(\mathcal{A})$. Thus, a UCB for a language $L \subseteq \Sigma^\omega$ can be obtained from an NBA for the complement language. For GNBA $\mathcal{A}_i = (\Sigma, Q^i, \delta^i, Q_0^i, \alpha^i)$ for $i \in \{1, 2\}$, the product automaton is defined as $\mathcal{A}_1 \times \mathcal{A}_2 := (\Sigma, Q^1 \times Q^2, \delta_\times, Q_0^1 \times Q_0^2, \alpha^1 \cup \alpha^2)$ where $(q_1', q_2') \in \delta_\times((q_1, q_2), a)$ if and only if $q_i' \in \delta^i(q_i, a)$ for all $i \in \{1, 2\}$. It holds that $\mathcal{L}(\mathcal{A}_1 \times \mathcal{A}_2) = \mathcal{L}(\mathcal{A}_1) \cap \mathcal{L}(\mathcal{A}_1)$. The union is defined as $\mathcal{A}_1 \cup \mathcal{A}_2 := (\Sigma, Q^1 \cup Q^2, \delta_\cup, Q_0^1 \cup Q_0^2, \{F_1 \cup Q^2 \mid F_1 \in \alpha^1\} \cup \{F_2 \cup Q^1 \mid F_2 \in \alpha^2\})$, where $q' \in \delta_\cup(q, a)$ if and only if $q' \in \delta^i(q, a)$ for some $i \in \{1, 2\}$. It holds that $\mathcal{L}(\mathcal{A}_1 \cup \mathcal{A}_2) = \mathcal{L}(\mathcal{A}_1) \cup \mathcal{L}(\mathcal{A}_2)$.

For a GNBA $\mathcal{A} = (2^{AP}, Q, \delta, Q_0, \alpha)$ and $AP' \subseteq AP$, we define the existential projection of $\mathcal{A}$ with respect to AP' to be the GNBA $\mathsf{proj}_\exists(\mathcal{A}, AP') \overset{\text{def}}{=} (2^{AP}, Q, \delta', Q_0, \alpha)$ with $\delta'(q, a) = \bigcup_{b \in 2^{AP'}} \delta(q, \mathsf{proj}(a, 2^{AP \setminus AP'}) \cup b)$. By definition, the projection automaton has the language $\mathcal{L}(\mathsf{proj}_\exists(\mathcal{A}, AP')) = \{\sigma \in (2^{AP})^\omega \mid \exists \sigma' \in (2^{AP'})^\omega. \ \mathsf{proj}(\sigma, 2^{AP \setminus AP'}) \parallel \sigma' \in \mathcal{L}(\mathcal{A})\}$.

2.2   The Temporal Logic LTL[$\mathcal{F}$]

In this section, we recall the temporal logic $LTL[\mathcal{F}]$ introduced in [2]. Let AP be a set of Boolean atomic propositions, and $\mathcal{F} \subseteq \{f : [0,1]^k \to [0,1] \mid k \in \mathbb{N}\}$ a set of functions. The LTL[$\mathcal{F}$] formulas are generated by the grammar $\varphi ::= p \mid$ true $\mid$ false $\mid f(\varphi_1, \ldots, \varphi_k) \mid \bigcirc\varphi \mid \varphi_1 \mathcal{U} \varphi_2$, where $p \in AP$, and $f \in \mathcal{F}$.

We consider sets $\mathcal{F}$ that include functions that allow us to express the usual Boolean operators, i.e., $\{f_\neg, f_\wedge, f_\vee\} \subseteq \mathcal{F}$, where $f_\neg(x) \stackrel{\text{def}}{=} 1 - x$, $f_\wedge(x,y) \stackrel{\text{def}}{=}$ $\min\{x,y\}$ and $f_\vee(x,y) \stackrel{\text{def}}{=} \max\{x,y\}$. For ease of notation, we use the operators $\neg, \wedge, \vee$ instead of the corresponding functions. As noted in [2], LTL coincides with LTL[$\mathcal{F}$] when $\mathcal{F} = \{\neg, \wedge, \vee\}$. One useful function is weighted average $x \oplus_\lambda y \stackrel{\text{def}}{=}$ $\lambda \cdot x + (1 - \lambda) \cdot y$, where $\lambda \in \{0,1\}$. We define the temporal operators *finally* $\Diamond\varphi \stackrel{\text{def}}{=}$ true$\mathcal{U}\varphi$ and *globally* $\Box\varphi \stackrel{\text{def}}{=} \neg(\Diamond\neg\varphi)$.

For an LTL[$\mathcal{F}$] formula φ, we denote with $Vars(\varphi)$ the set of atomic propositions occurring in φ, and with $|\varphi|$ the description size of φ.

The semantics of LTL[$\mathcal{F}$] is defined with respect to words in $(2^{AP})^\omega$, and maps an LTL[$\mathcal{F}$] formula φ and a word $\sigma \in (2^{AP})^\omega$, to a value $[\![\varphi, \sigma]\!] \in [0,1]$. For $f \in \mathcal{F}$, we define $[\![f(\varphi_1, \ldots, \varphi_k), \sigma]\!] := f([\![\varphi_1, \sigma]\!], \ldots, [\![\varphi_k, \sigma]\!])$. The semantics of *until* is $[\![\varphi_1 \mathcal{U} \varphi_2, \sigma]\!] := \max_{i \geq 0}\{\min\{[\![\varphi_2, \sigma[i, \infty)]\!], \min_{0 \leq j < i}[\![\varphi_1, \sigma[j, \infty)]\!]\}\}$. We refer the reader to [2] for the full formal definition of the semantics of LTL[$\mathcal{F}$]. We denote with $Vals(\varphi) \stackrel{\text{def}}{=} \{[\![\varphi, \sigma]\!] \mid \sigma \in (2^{AP})^\omega\}$ the set of possible values of an LTL[$\mathcal{F}$] formula φ. In [2] it was established that for every LTL[$\mathcal{F}$] formula φ it holds that $|Vals(\varphi)| \leq 2^{|\varphi|}$. That is, each formula's set of possible values is finite, and its cardinality is at most exponential in the size of φ.

Theorem 1 ([2]). *Let φ be an LTL[$\mathcal{F}$] formula over AP and $V \subseteq [0,1]$ be a set of values. There exists an GNBA $\mathcal{A}_{\varphi,V}$ such that for every $\sigma \in (2^{AP})^\omega$ it holds that $[\![\varphi, \sigma]\!] \in V$ if and only if $\sigma \in \mathcal{L}(\mathcal{A}_{\varphi,V})$. Furthermore, $\mathcal{A}_{\varphi,V}$ has at most $2^{(|\varphi|^2)}$ states and at most $|\varphi|$ sets of accepting states.*

One relevant property of the construction in the proof of Theorem 1 for our automata-based compositional synthesis procedure is that the set of values V only plays a role in the construction of the set of initial states. In particular, one can construct the automaton $\mathcal{A}_{\varphi, Vals(\varphi)} = (2^{AP}, Q, \delta, Q, \alpha)$ where every state is initial. From $\mathcal{A}_{\varphi, Vals(\varphi)}$ we can obtain the respective automaton $\mathcal{A}_{\varphi,V}$ for every V by instantiating the corresponding set of initial states based on V. Intuitively, these are the states in Q where the formula φ has some value $v \in V$.

3   Good-Enough Assume-Guarantee Decomposition

We begin this section by formally introducing the problem we study in the paper, namely, the synthesis of multi-component reactive systems from LTL[$\mathcal{F}$] specifications. We first describe the system model we consider.

3.1   Multi-component Reactive Systems

We consider reactive systems with a finite set I of *input atomic propositions* and a finite set O of *output atomic propositions* that are disjoint, i.e., $I \cap O = \emptyset$. We call the words in $(2^{AP})^\omega$ *(execution) traces*.

A *reactive component* is a Moore machine $M = (I_M, O_M, S, s^{init}, \rho, Out)$, where I_M and O_M are M's sets of input and output propositions respectively, S is a finite set of states, $s^{init} \in S$ is the initial state, $\rho : S \times 2^{I_M} \to S$ is the transition function, and $Out : S \to 2^{O_M}$ is the output labeling function. Given an input trace $\sigma_{I_M} \in (2^{I_M})^\omega$, M produces the output trace $M(\sigma_{I_M}) \in (2^{O_M})^\omega$ such that $M(\sigma_{I_M})[i] = Out(s_i)$, where the infinite sequence $s_0, s_1, \ldots$ of states is such that $s_0 = s^{init}$, and $s_{i+1} = \rho(s_i, \sigma_{I_M}[i])$ for every $i \in \mathbb{N}$.

A *multi-component reactive system* is a tuple $\mathcal{S} = (I, O, \mathcal{M})$, where I and O are the sets of input and output propositions respectively, $\mathcal{M} = \langle M_1, \ldots M_n \rangle$ is a tuple of reactive components $M_c = (I_c, O_c, S_c, s_c^{init}, \rho_c, Out_c)$ such that (1) for every $c, c' \in \{1, \ldots, n\}$ with $c \neq c'$ it holds that $O_c \cap O_{c'} = \emptyset$, (2) $\biguplus_{c=1}^n O_c = O$, and (3) $I_c = I \cup (O \setminus O_c)$. Conditions (1) and (2) stipulate that the sets of output propositions of the individual components partition O. Condition (3) stipulates that each component can read all input propositions I and all output propositions of the other components. We denote with $O_{\bar{c}} = \bigcup_{c' \in \{1, \ldots, n\} \setminus \{c\}} O_{c'}$ the set of outputs of components different from c. Given an input trace $\sigma_I \in (2^I)^\omega$, a multi-component reactive system generates an output trace $\sigma_O \in (2^O)^\omega$, which we denote by $(\|_{c=1}^n M_c)(\sigma_I)$, such that $\mathsf{proj}(\sigma_O, O_c) = M_c(\sigma_I \| \mathsf{proj}(\sigma_O, O_{\bar{c}}))$ for all c. That is, $(\|_{c=1}^n M_c)(\sigma_I)$ is the composition of all the output traces of the components in $\mathcal{S}$.

3.2   Good-Enough Realizability and Synthesis from LTL[$\mathcal{F}$]

We study the problem of synthesizing multi-component reactive systems from LTL[$\mathcal{F}$] specifications, precisely formulated below.

Problem 1. Given an LTL[$\mathcal{F}$] formula Φ over atomic propositions $AP = I \uplus O$, and a partitioning $O_1, \ldots, O_n$ of the set of output propositions, decide whether there exists a multi-component reactive system $\mathcal{S}$ such that $\mathcal{S} = (I, O, \mathcal{M})$ where O_c is the set of output propositions of component $c \in \{1, \ldots, n\}$, such that for every $\sigma_I \in (2^I)^\omega$ and every $v \in Vals(\Phi)$ the following condition (1) holds.

$$\text{If there exists } \sigma_O \in (2^O)^\omega \text{ with } \llbracket \Phi, \sigma_I \| \sigma_O \rrbracket = v, \\ \text{then } \llbracket \Phi, \sigma_I \| (\|_{c=1}^n M_c)(\sigma_I) \rrbracket \geq v. \tag{1}$$

Since our definition of multi-component reactive systems allows for components to observe all inputs and outputs of other components, the above problem can be solved by considering the monolithic synthesis problem for the composed system. This problem is known to be 2EXPTIME-complete [3]. When a monolithic system is synthesized, it can be easily decomposed using projection. However, this creates a dependency between the implementations of the individual components. Furthermore, for specifications that combine both local requirements on the components and shared system properties, a synthesis approach that treats such specifications compositionally is desirable.

For the remaining sections, we consider the problem of synthesizing n components, which we label with indices $c \in \{1, \ldots, n\}$, and fix a corresponding partitioning $O_1, \ldots, O_n$ of the set of output propositions.

3.3 Good-Enough Decomposition

As stated in Sect. 1, we consider specifications Φ expressed as a combination of local specifications for the individual components, as well as a shared requirement. Formally, we assume that $\Phi = comb(\varphi_{local}^1, \ldots, \varphi_{local}^n, \Psi_{shared})$, where the function $comb : [0,1]^{n+1} \rightarrow [0,1]$ is non-decreasing in each subset of its arguments, that is, for every $v_1, \ldots, v_{n+1}$ and $v_1', \ldots, v_{n+1}'$, if we have $comb(v_1', \ldots, v_{n+1}') < comb(v_1, \ldots, v_{n+1})$, then, $v_i' < v_i$ for some i.

We refer to Ψ_{shared} as the *shared specification* and to each φ_{local}^c as the *local specification of component c*. Below is an example of such a specification.

Example 1. Let $I = \{i\}$, $O_1 = \{o_1\}$, $O_2 = \{o_2\}$ and consider the specification $\Phi = (\varphi_{local}^1 \oplus_{\frac{1}{3}} (\varphi_{local}^2 \oplus_{\frac{1}{2}} \Psi_{shared}))$, where the function $comb$ is a weighted sum in which each part is weighted $\frac{1}{3}$ and the individual specifications are

$$\varphi_{local}^1 = \Box o_1 \oplus_{\frac{1}{2}} \Box \Diamond o_1, \quad \varphi_{local}^2 = \Box o_2 \oplus_{\frac{1}{2}} \Box \Diamond o_2,$$

$$\Psi_{shared} = \Box(i \rightarrow (\bigcirc \neg o_1 \oplus_{\frac{1}{2}} \bigcirc \neg o_2)).$$

If for some $\sigma \in (2^{AP})^\omega$ we have $[\![\varphi_{local}^1, \sigma]\!] = 1$, $[\![\varphi_{local}^2, \sigma]\!] = \frac{1}{2}$ and $[\![\Psi_{shared}, \sigma]\!] = 0$, then we have the value $[\![\Phi, \sigma]\!] = \frac{1}{2}$ for the overall specification.

As mentioned in Sect. 1, we furthermore assume that the specification Φ satisfies two additional conditions, under which we establish the soundness of our compositional synthesis approach. The first condition restricts the shared specifications, while the second condition restricts the local specifications.

Condition 1. The shared specifications Ψ_{shared} is a *safety* LTL[$\mathcal{F}$] specification.

Definition 1 (Safety LTL[$\mathcal{F}$] specifications). *We say that an LTL[$\mathcal{F}$] formula is a safety specification if and only if for every word $\sigma \in (2^{AP})^\omega$ and every value $v \in Vals(\varphi)$, if $[\![\varphi, \sigma]\!] < v$, then there exists a prefix σ' of σ, such that for every possible infinite continuation $\sigma'' \in (2^{AP})^\omega$ of σ' we have $[\![\varphi, \sigma' \cdot \sigma'']\!] < v$.*

If we consider the LTL fragment of LTL[$\mathcal{F}$], then the above notion coincides with the notion of LTL-definable safety languages. To see this, note that for an LTL formula φ we have $Vals(\varphi) = \{0,1\}$. Thus, $[\![\varphi, \sigma]\!] < 1$ corresponds to φ being violated by σ, and the condition corresponds to the existence of a bad prefix. In Example 1 above, the shared specification is a safety specification.

Condition 2. For each component c, the local specification φ_{local}^c refers only to output propositions in O_c and input propositions in I, i.e., $Vars(\varphi_{local}^c) \cap O \subseteq O_c$.
Note that Ψ_{shared} can refer to all the input and output signals.

Under the above assumptions, we consider the synthesis problem for LTL[$\mathcal{F}$] specifications of the above form in a compositional manner. We call a specification that satisfies all of the conditions *compositional*.

Our compositional synthesis approach is based on assume-guarantee contracts, which formalize the interface properties between the components.

Definition 2 (Assume-guarantee contract). *An* assume-guarantee contract *is a tuple* $\langle (A_c, G_c) \rangle_{c=1}^{n}$ *where* $A_c \subseteq (2^{AP})^\omega$ *is called the* assumption *of component* c, *and* $G_c \subseteq (2^{AP})^\omega$ *is called the* guarantee *of component* c, *where each* A_c *and* G_c *are safety languages*, $\bigcap_{c' \in \{1,\dots,n\} \setminus \{c\}} G_{c'} \subseteq A_c$, *and*

- *Let* $\sigma \in (2^{AP})^*$ *be a finite word such that there exists an infinite word* $\sigma' \in (2^{AP})^\omega$ *such that* $\sigma \cdot \sigma' \in A_c$. *Then, for every* $o_c \in 2^{O_c}$, *there exists* $\sigma'' \in (2^{AP})^\omega$ *such that* $\sigma \cdot \sigma'' \in A_c$ *and* $\mathsf{proj}(\sigma''[0], O_c) = o_c$.
- *Let* $\sigma \in (2^{AP})^*$ *be a finite word such that there exists an infinite word* $\sigma' \in (2^{AP})^\omega$ *such that* $\sigma \cdot \sigma' \in G_c$. *Then, for every* $o_{\bar{c}} \in 2^{O_{\bar{c}}}$, *there exists* $\sigma'' \in (2^{AP})^\omega$ *such that* $\sigma \cdot \sigma'' \in G_c$ *and* $\mathsf{proj}(\sigma''[0], O_{\bar{c}}) = o_{\bar{c}}$.

The first condition ensures that component c cannot on its own violate its assumption A_c by selecting a bad output o_c. The second condition states that the remaining components cannot violate the guarantee which c must provide, by selecting some bad output $o_{\bar{c}}$. We will employ assume-guarantee contracts to decompose the synthesis problem for Φ into local synthesis problems for the individual components. To guarantee soundness, we impose a condition on the assumptions, which we call *good-enough assumptions*. Intuitively, good-enough assumptions do not "eliminate" possible values of Ψ_{shared}.

We are now ready to state our compositional synthesis problem.

Definition 3 (Good-enough assumptions). *Let* $\langle A_1, \dots A_n \rangle$ *be assumptions for the components in* $\{1, \dots, n\}$. *We say that* $\langle A_1, \dots A_n \rangle$ *is a good-enough tuple of assumptions if and only if for all* $\sigma_I \in (2^I)^\omega$, *for all* $v \in Vals(\Psi_{shared})$:

$$
\begin{aligned}
&\text{if there exists } \sigma_O \in (2^O)^\omega \text{ with } [\![\Psi_{shared}, \sigma_I \parallel \sigma_O]\!] = v, \\
&\text{then there exists } \sigma'_O \in (2^O)^\omega \text{ with } [\![\Psi_{shared}, \sigma_I \parallel \sigma'_O]\!] \geq v \\
&\qquad\qquad\qquad\quad \text{and } (\sigma_I \parallel \sigma'_O) \in \bigcap_{c \in \{1,\dots,n\}} A_c.
\end{aligned}
\tag{2}
$$

Problem 2. Given a compositional LTL[$\mathcal{F}$] specification Φ over atomic propositions $AP = I \uplus O$ with partitioning $O_1, \dots, O_n$ of the set of output propositions, decide whether there exists a multi-component reactive system $\mathcal{S} = (I, O, \mathcal{M})$ where O_c is the set of output propositions of component $c \in \{1, \dots, n\}$, such that for each component $c \in \{1, \dots, n\}$ the conditions below are satisfied

$$
\begin{aligned}
&\forall \sigma_I \in (2^I)^\omega, \forall \sigma_{O_{\bar{c}}} \in (2^{O_{\bar{c}}})^\omega, \forall u \in Vals(\varphi^c_{local}), \forall w \in Vals(\Psi_{shared}): \\
&\text{if there exists } \sigma_{O_c} \in (2^{O_c})^\omega, \text{ with } [\![\varphi^c_{local}, \sigma_I \parallel \sigma_{O_c} \parallel \sigma_{O_{\bar{c}}}]\!] = u, \\
&\qquad\qquad\qquad \text{and } [\![\Psi_{shared}, \sigma_I \parallel \sigma_{O_c} \parallel \sigma_{O_{\bar{c}}}]\!] = w \\
&\text{and if } (\sigma_I \parallel M_c(\sigma_I \parallel \sigma_{O_{\bar{c}}}) \parallel \sigma_{O_{\bar{c}}}) \in A_c, \\
&\text{then } [\![\varphi^c_{local}, \sigma_I \parallel M_c(\sigma_I \parallel \sigma_{O_{\bar{c}}}) \parallel \sigma_{O_{\bar{c}}}]\!] \geq u \text{ and} \\
&\qquad [\![\Psi_{shared}, \sigma_I \parallel M_c(\sigma_I \parallel \sigma_{O_{\bar{c}}}) \parallel \sigma_{O_{\bar{c}}}]\!] \geq w
\end{aligned}
\tag{3}
$$

$$\forall \sigma_I \in (2^I)^\omega, \forall \sigma_{O_{\bar{c}}} \in (2^{O_{\bar{c}}})^\omega : (\sigma_I \parallel M_c(\sigma_I \parallel \sigma_{O_{\bar{c}}}) \parallel \sigma_{O_{\bar{c}}}) \in \overline{A}_c \cup G_c, \quad (4)$$

where $\langle (A_1, G_1), \ldots, (A_n, G_n) \rangle$ is an assume-guarantee contract for components $\{1, \ldots, n\}$ such that $\langle A_1, \ldots A_n \rangle$ is a good-enough tuple of assumptions.

Intuitively, in *Problem* 2 we consider only φ^c_{local} and Ψ_{shared} for each component c, without the remaining context of Φ, that is, the function *comb* and the local specifications of the other components. To ensure soundness of the decomposition, we consider *all possible* pairs (u, w) of values of φ^c_{local} an Ψ_{shared} and require that *for each pair for values that is possible*, the component's strategy ensures at least these values. In that way, an implementation for a component c that satisfies condition (3) does not restrict the possible values of Ψ_{shared} unnecessarily. We will see below that this results in the decomposition rule being sound but incomplete. But first, we show a simple example that demonstrates why we imposed the two conditions on the individual specifications in Φ.

Example 2. Let $I = \{i\}, O_1 = \{o_1\}, O_2 = \{o_2\}$ and $\Phi = \mathsf{true} \wedge \mathsf{true} \wedge \Psi_{shared}$, where $\Psi_{shared} = ((\Box i) \leftrightarrow (\Diamond o_1)) \wedge ((\Box i) \leftrightarrow (\Diamond o_2))$. Here the shared specification Ψ_{shared} is not a safety property. While for any $\sigma_I \in (2^I)^\omega$ there exist sequences of outputs that satisfy Φ, there is no system that satisfies Φ for every σ_I, as it would have to make a correct guess about the future inputs.

Consider an implementation of component $c \in \{1, 2\}$ that waits until the other component outputs true, and then does so itself, and otherwise outputs false. Such a pair of implementations satisfies condition (3), as it only requires that Φ is satisfied if the environment *and the other component* made it possible. However, the composition of these two implementations never sets any of o_1 and o_2 to true, and thus does not satisfy the conditions in *Problem* 1.

If we allow local specifications to refer to outputs of other components we can transform the above example into one with local specifications.

The next example shows a specification where the local synthesis problems in *Problem* 2 are realizable without any extra assumptions.

Example 3. Let $I = \{i\}, O_1 = \{o_1\}, O_2 = \{o_2\}$ and $\Phi = \varphi^1_{local} \wedge \varphi^2_{local} \wedge \Psi_{shared}$, where $\varphi^c_{local} = \Box o_c \oplus_{\frac{1}{2}} \Box \Diamond o_c$ for each c and $\Psi_{shared} = \Box(\neg i \rightarrow \bigcirc(\neg o_1 \wedge \neg o_2))$.

A system in which each component c sets o_c to true whenever i was true in the step before satisfies condition (1) for each input sequence and value v of Φ.

Taking $A_1 = G_1 = A_2 = G_2 = (2^{AP})^\omega$ we have that the same system satisfies conditions (3) and (4) for each component. This is because condition (3) only requires component c to ensure value 1 for Ψ_{shared} shared when i is false and $o_{\bar{c}}$ is false, and hence no explicit assumption is needed. This is in general not the case, and in many cases, cooperation and assumptions are necessary.

The next theorem establishes the soundness of the decomposition.

Theorem 2 (Soundness of GE A/G decomposition). *Let Φ be a compositional LTL[$\mathcal{F}$] specification with a partitioning $\{O_1, \ldots, O_n\}$ of the output propositions. Let $\langle (A_1, G_1), \ldots, (A_n, G_n) \rangle$ be an assume-guarantee contract for* *components* $\{1, \ldots, n\}$ *such that* $\langle A_1, \ldots A_n \rangle$ *is a good-enough tuple of assumptions. Then, every multi-component reactive system* $\mathcal{S} = (I, O, \mathcal{M})$ *that is a solution to* Problem 2 *is also a solution to* Problem 1.

The converse to the statement of Theorem 2 is not true, as the following example demonstrates. That is, the decomposition rule is sound, but not complete.

Example 4 (Incompleteness of the Decomposition).
Let $I = \{i\}$, $O_1 = \{o_1\}$, $O_2 = \{o_2\}$ and $\Phi = \varphi^1_{local} \wedge \varphi^2_{local} \wedge \Psi_{shared}$, where
$$\varphi^1_{local} = \Box((i \to \bigcirc o_1) \oplus_{\frac{1}{2}} \Diamond o_1), \quad \varphi^2_{local} = \Box((i \to \bigcirc o_2) \oplus_{\frac{2}{3}} \Diamond o_2)$$
$$\Psi_{shared} = \Box(i \oplus_{\frac{1}{2}} \bigcirc \neg(o_1 \wedge o_2))$$
For the input trace $\sigma_I = \{i\}^\omega$ there exists σ_O such that $[\![\Phi, \sigma_I \| \sigma_O]\!] = \frac{1}{2}$, and this is the best value achievable by the system for this input sequence. The system that outputs $o_1 = o_2 = $ true if i held in the previous step, and alternates between o_1 and o_2 otherwise, achieves this value and satisfies the conditions of *Problem 1*. However, there exists no implementation that satisfies the conditions of the decomposition in *Problem 2*. To see this, note that for each c we have that for $\sigma_I = \{i\}^\omega$ and $\sigma_{O_{\bar{c}}} = \{o_{\bar{c}}\}^\omega$ there exists σ_{O_c} such that $[\![\varphi^c_{local}, \sigma_I \| \sigma_{O_c} \| \sigma_{O_{\bar{c}}}]\!] = 1$ and there exists σ_{O_c} such that $[\![\Psi_{shared}, \sigma_I \| \sigma_{O_c} \| \sigma_{O_{\bar{c}}}]\!] = 1$, but there is no implementation for c that ensures both values, and hence there is no implementation that satisfies (3).

4   Compositional Good-Enough Synthesis

We propose an approach to solving *Problem 2* using bounded synthesis, which we describe in this section. In a first step, our synthesis procedure constructs several automata from the given specifications and assume-guarantee contract (if given). In order to facilitate the generation of assumptions, we present a compositional synthesis method based on bounded synthesis [19], where for a given bound on the size of the implementations, a safety game is constructed from the automata constructed in the first step. If the current set of assumptions is insufficient, that is, the local synthesis problems for some component c has no solution, we present a method for strengthening the assumption A_c of component c.

4.1   Automata Constructions

We begin by detailing the different automata constructed by our procedure.

Automata for the Specifications. Consider φ^c_{local} and Ψ_{shared}. Using the construction from Theorem 1, we construct the automata

- $\mathcal{B}_c = \mathcal{A}_{\varphi^c_{local}, Vals(\varphi^c_{local})} = (2^{AP}, Q^c, \delta^c, Q^c, \alpha^c)$, the GNBA for φ^c_{local} and
- $\mathcal{B}_s = \mathcal{A}_{\Psi_{shared}, Vals(\Psi_{shared})} = (2^{AP}, Q^s, \delta^s, Q^s, \alpha^s)$, the GNBA for Ψ_{shared}.

Both $\mathcal{B}_c$ and $\mathcal{B}_s$ are constructed for the respective full set of formula values. We then construct the GNBA $\mathcal{B}'_{cs} = \mathsf{proj}_\exists(\mathcal{B}_c \times \mathcal{B}_s, O_c)$ and $\mathcal{B}''_{cs} = \mathcal{B}_c \cup \mathcal{B}_s$, which accept the existential projection of the product on O_c and the union.

Assumptions as Automata. We consider assume-guarantee contracts represented as automata. The assumptions A_c and the complement languages $2^{AP} \backslash G_c$ of the guarantees of all components are represented respectively as the NBA

- $\mathcal{A}_c = (2^{AP}, Q^{c,a}, \delta^{c,a}, Q_0^{c,a}, \alpha^{c,a})$ is the assumption of component c.
- $\overline{\mathcal{G}}_c = (2^{AP}, Q^{c,g}, \delta^{c,g}, Q_0^{c,g}, \alpha^{c,g})$ is the complement of the guarantee of c.

Combining Specifications and Contract. From the automata $\mathcal{B}_c, \mathcal{B}_s, \mathcal{A}_c$ and $\overline{\mathcal{G}}_c$, we construct the GNBA $\mathcal{B} = (2^{AP}, \widehat{Q}, \widehat{\delta}, \widehat{Q}_0, \widehat{\alpha}) := (\mathcal{B}'_{cs} \times \mathcal{A}_c \times \mathcal{B}''_{cs}) \cup (\mathcal{A}_c \times \overline{\mathcal{G}}_c)$.

We will use the GNBA $\mathcal{B}$ to characterize the language of the traces that violate at least one of conditions (3) and (4).

In the construction, we ensure that the states of $\mathcal{B}$ are of one of the forms (1) $(q_\exists^c, q_\exists^s, q^{ca}, q^{cs})$, where $q_\exists^c \in Q^c$, $q_\exists^s \in Q^s$, $q^{ca} \in Q^{c,a}$, $q^{cs} \in (Q^c \cup Q^s)$, or (2) $q^{cg} \in Q^{c,a} \times Q^{c,g}$. The set of initial states in $\mathcal{B}$ is $\widehat{Q}_0 = Q^c \times Q^s \times Q_0^{c,a} \times (Q^c \cup Q^s) \cup (Q_0^{c,a} \times Q_0^{c,g})$. With that, the states of the first form assign values to the formulas φ_{local}^c and Ψ_{shared} in the respective sub-states.

Let $u \in Vals(\varphi_{local}^c)$ and $w \in Vals(\Psi_{shared})$. The above property of $\mathcal{B}$ allows us to devise from $\mathcal{B}$ an automaton $\mathcal{B}_{(u,w)}$ as follows. First, for $\sim \in \{<, \geq, =\}$, let

$$Q_{\sim u}^c := \{q \in Q^c \mid q(\varphi_{local}^c) \sim u\} \text{ and } Q_{\sim w}^s := \{q \in Q^s \mid q(\Psi_{shared}) \sim w\}.$$

We define the set of initial states in $\mathcal{B}$ for the pair of values (u, w) as the set

$$\widehat{Q}_0^{(u,w)} := (Q_{\geq u}^c \times Q_{\geq w}^s \times Q_0^{c,a} \times (Q_{<u}^c \cup Q_{<w}^s)) \cup (Q_0^{c,a} \times Q_0^{c,g}).$$

With that, we define the automaton $\mathcal{B}_{(u,w)} := (2^{AP}, \widehat{Q}, \widehat{\delta}, \widehat{Q}_0^{(u,w)}, \widehat{\alpha})$.

Intuitively, the language of the automaton $\mathcal{B}_{(u,w)}$ consists of the traces that violate at least one of conditions (3) and (4) for the value pair (u, w).

Proposition 1. *For the GNBA $\mathcal{B}_{(u,w)}$ constructed above it holds that for $\sigma \in (2^{AP})^\omega$ we have $\sigma \in \mathcal{L}(\mathcal{B}_{(u,w)})$ iff $\sigma \notin (\overline{A}_c \cup G_c)$ or all of the following hold:*

- *there exists $\sigma_{O_c} \in (2^O)^\omega$ such that $[\![\varphi_{local}^c, \text{proj}(\sigma, I \cup O_{\overline{c}}) \parallel \sigma_{O_c}]\!] \geq u$ and $[\![\Psi_{shared}, \text{proj}(\sigma, I \cup O_{\overline{c}}) \parallel \sigma_{O_c}]\!] \geq w$, and $\sigma \in A_c$,*
- *$[\![\varphi_{local}^c, \sigma]\!] < u$ or $[\![\Psi_{shared}, \sigma]\!] < w$.*

Transformation to UCB. From the GNBA $\mathcal{B}$ constructed above, we obtain an NBA, which we then interpret as a UCB for the complement language.

For φ_{local}^c, Ψ_{shared}, A_c and $\overline{\mathcal{G}}_c$, we denote with $\text{UCB}_c(\mathcal{B}_c, \mathcal{B}_s, A_c, \overline{\mathcal{G}}_c)$ the universal co-Büci automaton obtained in this way from the GNBA $\mathcal{B}_c$ and $\mathcal{B}_s$.

Given $\mathcal{U} := \text{UCB}_c(\mathcal{B}_c, \mathcal{B}_s, A_c, \overline{\mathcal{G}}_c)$, $u \in Vals(\varphi_{local}^c)$ and $w \in Vals(\Psi_{shared})$, we denote with $\text{Instantiate}_c(\mathcal{U}, u, w)$ the UCB obtained from the GNBA $\mathcal{B}_{(u,w)}$.

Proposition 1 provides us with a basis for a solution to *Problem* 2 when we are given an assume-guarantee contract. For a given component c, using the product of the automata $\text{Instantiate}_c(\mathcal{U}_c, u, w)$, for all $u \in Vals(\varphi_{local}^c)$ and $w \in Vals(\Psi_{shared})$, we can apply any suitable reactive synthesis method.

However, in order to facilitate the generation of assumptions, we propose a procedure based on bounded synthesis. In the next two subsections we first describe our compositional synthesis procedure with given assumptions, and then present the iterative generation of contracts.

function CompSynt $(\langle\varphi_{local}^c\rangle_{c=1}^n, \Psi_{shared}, \mathcal{B}_s, \langle\mathcal{B}_c\rangle_{c=1}^n, \langle\mathcal{A}_c, \overline{\mathcal{G}}_c\rangle_{c=1}^n, b_{init}, b_{max})$

1   **if** ¬GoodEnough($\langle\mathcal{A}_c\rangle_{c=1}^n, \mathcal{B}_s$) **then return** ⊥

2    $b := b_{init}$

3   **while true do**

4        $done :=$ true

5   **for** $c = 1, \ldots, n$ **do**

6            $\mathcal{U}_c := \mathsf{UCB}_c(\mathcal{B}_c, \mathcal{B}_s, \mathcal{A}_c, \overline{\mathcal{G}}_c)$

7            $M_c := \mathsf{LocalSynt}(\mathcal{U}_c, I, O_c, O_{\overline{c}}, Vals(\varphi_{local}^c), Vals(\Psi_{shared}), b)$

8   **if** $M_c = \bot$ **then** $done :=$ false; **break**

9   **if** $done$ **then return** $\langle M_c\rangle_{c=1}^n$

10   **if** $b < b_{max}$ **then** $b :=$ increment(b) **else return** unknown

Algorithm 1: Compositional bounded synthesis for a combined specification $\Phi = comb(\varphi_{local}^1, \ldots, \varphi_{local}^n, \Psi_{shared})$, with a given assume-guarantee contract consisting of assumptions $\langle\mathcal{A}_c\rangle_{c=1}^n$ and negated guarantees $\langle\overline{\mathcal{G}}_c\rangle_{c=1}^n$. The automata $\mathcal{B}_s = \mathcal{A}_{\Psi_{shared}, Vals(\Psi_{shared})}$ and $\mathcal{B}_c := \mathcal{A}_{\varphi_{local}^c, Vals(\varphi_{local}^c)}$ are given as input.

function LocalSynt $(\mathcal{U}_c, I, O_c, O_{\overline{c}}, U, W, b)$

1   **let** $\mathcal{D}$ be a deterministic safety automaton for the language $(2^{AP})^\omega$

2   **for** $(u, w) \in U \times W$ **do**

3        $\mathcal{U}_{(u,w)} := \mathsf{Instantiate}_c(\mathcal{U}_c, u, w)$; $\mathcal{D} := \mathsf{Safety}(\mathcal{U}_{(u,w)}, b, \mathcal{D})$

4        $(Win, strategy) := \mathsf{SolveSafetyGame}(\mathcal{D}, I \uplus O_{\overline{c}}, O_c)$

5   **if** $Win := \bot$ **then return** ⊥

6        $\mathcal{D} := \mathsf{PruneLosing}(\mathcal{D}, Win, I \uplus O_{\overline{c}}, O_c)$

7   **return** $\mathsf{ToMoore}(strategy, I, O_c, O_{\overline{c}})$

Algorithm 2: Bounded synthesis for a single component c, with specification given by the UCB $\mathcal{U}_c$ and sets of values U and W defining the initial states. I is the set of inputs, O_c is the set of outputs c, $O_{\overline{c}}$ are the outputs of the remaining components. b is the bound for the bounded synthesis algorithm.

4.2   Synthesis with a Given Assume-Guarantee Contract

For a given component c, our method, based on bounded synthesis, processes the automata for the different value pairs incrementally in the construction of the safety game for a given bound. The compositional synthesis procedure CompSynt described below is detailed in Algorithm 1, and the incremental bounded synthesis method LocalSynt for a single component in Algorithm 2.

The procedure CompSynt first verifies that the assumptions meet the good-enough condition by calling the function GoodEnough (described later). If this is the case, CompSynt iterates over the components, constructing the UCB $\mathcal{U}_c := \mathsf{UCB}_c(\mathcal{B}_c, \mathcal{B}_s, \mathcal{A}_c, \overline{\mathcal{G}}_c)$ and invoking LocalSynt (described later), which performs incremental bounded synthesis for a component c. If an implementation is found by LocalSynt for all c, then CompSynt returns a multi-component reactive system. Otherwise, the bound is increased if the maximum (given as parameter) is not reached. If the latter is the case, CompSynt returns unknown.

Checking for Good-Enough Assumptions. The function GoodEnough verifies that a tuple of assumptions represented as automata $\langle \mathcal{A}_c \rangle_{c=1}^{n}$ is good-enough. It uses the GNBA $\mathcal{B}_s$ representing the shared specification Ψ_{shared}. For every $v \in Vals(\Psi_{shared})$ the procedure constructs the GNBA

- $\mathcal{D}_s^{=v}$ obtained from $\mathsf{proj}_{\exists}(\mathcal{B}_s, O)$ by setting the set of initial states to $Q_{=v}^{s}$,
- $\mathcal{D}_s^{\geq v}$ obtained from $\mathsf{proj}_{\exists}(\mathcal{B}_s \cap \bigcap_{c \in \{1,\ldots,n\}} \mathcal{A}_c, O)$ with init. states $Q_{\geq v}^{s} \times Q_0^{c,a}$.

Then, we verify that $\langle \mathcal{A}_c \rangle_{c=1}^{n}$ is good-enough by checking if the language inclusion $\mathcal{L}(\mathcal{D}_s^{=v}) \subseteq \mathcal{L}(\mathcal{D}_s^{\geq v})$, which directly corresponds to condition (2), holds.

Incremental Bounded Synthesis. The procedure LOCALSYNT iterates over the pairs of values in the set $U \times W$, where $U := Vals(\varphi_{local}^{c})$, $W := Vals(\Psi_{shared})$. For each (u, w), it constructs the UCB $\mathsf{Instantiate}_c(\mathcal{U}_c, u, w)$ instantiated from $\mathcal{U}_c$ for this value pair. It then constructs and solves incrementally a safety game.

Function Safety constructs a deterministic safety automaton from the UCB $\mathcal{U}_{(u,w)}$ for bound $b \in \mathbb{N}$. Different from the single automaton case, in LOCAL-SYNT we are constructing a deterministic safety automaton for the product of all $\mathsf{Instantiate}_c(\mathcal{U}_c, u, w)$ for $(u, w) \in U \times W$. We perform the construction incrementally. LOCALSYNT maintains a deterministic safety automaton $\mathcal{D}$ which is the product constructed thus far. $\mathcal{D}$ is passed as an argument to Safety and used in an on-the-fly construction to prune losing choices from the deterministic safety automaton constructed from the current $\mathcal{U}_{(u,w)}$.

Function SolveSafetyGame applied to $\mathcal{D}$ performs the standard construction of transforming a deterministic automaton into a two-player game by splitting the input propositions $I \uplus O_{\bar{c}}$ (note that here the output of other components is treated as input) and the output propositions O_c. The safety game is solved and SolveSafetyGame returns a pair $(Win, strategy)$, where Win is either $\bot$, in the case when the initial state of $\mathcal{D}$ is not winning for the output player, or otherwise Win is the set of states winning for the output player, and $strategy$ is the most permissive winning strategy for the output player. Function PruneLosing takes as input the automaton $\mathcal{D}$ and the winning region $Win \neq \bot$ computed by SolveSafetyGame and prunes from $\mathcal{D}$ the choices of the output player that do not lead to states in Win. Since the implementation must satisfy (3) for all (u, w), all the calls to SolveSafetyGame must be successful to return an implementation.

4.3 Synthesis with Iterative Assumption Generation

Assume-guarantee contracts can be difficult to design, especially for the synthesis of good-enough implementations of quantitative specifications. We present a method for iterative generation of good-enough assumptions, inspired by the notion of negotiation introduced in [21]. The idea is to consider the components in turn, and, if the local synthesis problem is not realizable for a component, to generate assumptions on the behavior on the other components. The generated assumption is added to the guarantees of the other components, which can generate assumptions on their own. This process continues until finding an assume-guarantee contract that makes all local synthesis problems realizable.

function CompSyntAGen $(\langle\varphi_{local}^c\rangle_{c=1}^n, \Psi_{shared}, \mathcal{B}_s, \langle\mathcal{B}_c\rangle_{c=1}^n, b_{init}, b_{max})$

1   **let** $\mathcal{A}_c^0$ be a safety automaton for $(2^{AP})^\omega$ for every $c \in \{1, \ldots, n\}$

2    $b := b_{init}$

3   **while** $b \leq b_{max}$ **do**

4      $done := \mathsf{true}$

5   **for** $c = 1, \ldots, n$ **do**

6        $\overline{\mathcal{G}}_c := \mathsf{Augment}(\bigcup_{\overline{c}\in\{1,\ldots,n\}\setminus\{c\}} \overline{\mathcal{A}}_c^0, O_{\overline{c}})$; $\mathcal{U}_c := \mathsf{UCB}_c(\mathcal{B}_c, \mathcal{B}_s, \mathcal{A}_c, \overline{\mathcal{G}}_c)$

7        $M_c := \mathsf{LocalSynt}(\mathcal{U}_c, I, O_c, O_{\overline{c}}, \mathit{Vals}(\varphi_{local}^c), \mathit{Vals}(\Psi_{shared}), b)$

8   **if** $M_c = \bot$ **then**

9          $done := \mathsf{false}$

10          $(\mathcal{A}_c^0, \mathcal{A}_c) := \mathsf{GenAssumption}(\mathcal{U}_c, b, I, O_c, O_{\overline{c}}, \langle\mathcal{A}_c^0\rangle_{c=1}^n, \langle\mathcal{A}_c\rangle_{c=1}^n)$

11   **if** $(\mathcal{A}_c^0, \mathcal{A}_c) = (\bot, \bot)$ **then** $restart := \mathsf{true}$; **break**

12   **if** $done$ **then return** $\langle M_c\rangle_{c=1}^n$

13   **if** $restart$ **then** $b := \mathsf{increment}(b)$

14   **return** unknown

Algorithm 3: Compositional synthesis for a combined specification $\Phi = comb(\varphi_{local}^1, \ldots, \varphi_{local}^n, \Psi_{shared})$ with iterative assumption generation. The automata $\mathcal{B}_s = \mathcal{A}_{\Psi_{shared}, \mathit{Vals}(\Psi_{shared})}$ and $\mathcal{B}_c := \mathcal{A}_{\varphi_{local}^c, \mathit{Vals}(\varphi_{local}^c)}$ are given as input.

Our compositional synthesis method with assumption generation is shown in Algorithm 3. Similarly to Algorithm 1, the method is based on incremental bounded synthesis. Here the guarantees are obtained from the assumptions, which initially permit any trace in $(2^{AP})^\omega$. When the current assumption is not sufficient for the local synthesis problem for some component c to be realizable, the procedure GenAssumption, shown in Algorithm 4 is invoked. We maintain two automata for the assumption for each component: $\mathcal{A}_c$ is the actual assumption, and the automaton $\mathcal{A}_c^0$ is used to represent the combination of the languages constructed from the assumption generation procedure before the transformation to $\mathcal{A}_c$. We explain this when we present the assumption generation.

Assumption Generation. To find an assumption for a locally unrealizable (with the given bound) specification $\mathcal{U}_c$ for component c, GenAssumption considers the synthesis problem where all the components collaborate on realizing $\mathcal{U}_c$. In the resulting safety game all the output propositions $O_c \uplus O_{\overline{c}}$ are under the control of the output player. If the initial state is winning for the output player, then the winning region Win represents the most general cooperative strategy. Function ExtractAssumption uses Win to generate a new assumption $\mathcal{A}_{new}$, represented as a safety automaton. $\mathcal{A}_{new}$ must satisfy the following conditions:

(i) The local specification for component c constructed with the updated tuple of assumptions must be realizable by component c alone.

(ii) The combined assumption of component c and the newly generated guarantees of the other components must satisfy the conditions of Definition 2.

(iii) The updated tuple of assumptions $\langle\mathcal{A}_1, \ldots, \mathcal{A}_c \cap \mathcal{A}_{new}, \ldots, \mathcal{A}_n\rangle$ must be good-enough with respect to the shared specification Ψ_{shared}.

function GENASSUMPTION($\mathcal{U}_c, b, I, O_c, O_{\overline{c}}, \langle \mathcal{A}_c^0 \rangle_{c=1}^n, \langle \mathcal{A}_c \rangle_{c=1}^n$)

1   **let** $\mathcal{D}$ be a deterministic safety automaton for the language $(2^{AP})^\omega$

2   **for** $(u, w) \in U \times W$ **do**

3       $\mathcal{U}_{(u,w)} := \mathsf{Instantiate}_c(\mathcal{U}_c, u, w)$; $\mathcal{D} := \mathsf{Safety}(\mathcal{U}_{(u,w)}, b, \mathcal{D})$

4       $(Win, strategy) := \mathsf{SolveSafetyGame}(\mathcal{D}, I, O_c \uplus O_{\overline{c}})$

5   **if** $Win := \bot$ **then return** $\bot$

6       $\mathcal{D} := \mathsf{PruneLosing}(\mathcal{D}, Win, I, O_c \uplus O_{\overline{c}})$

7     $Invalid := \emptyset$

8   **while true do**

9       $\mathcal{A}_{new}^0 := \mathsf{ExtractAssumption}(\mathcal{D}, Win, I, O_c, O_{\overline{c}}, Invalid)$

10   **if** $\mathsf{GoodEnough}(\langle \mathcal{A}_1, \ldots, \mathsf{Augment}(\mathcal{A}_c^0 \cap \mathcal{A}_{new}^0, O_c), \ldots, \mathcal{A}_n \rangle, \mathcal{B}_s)$ **then**

11   **return** $(\mathcal{A}_c^0 \cap \mathcal{A}_{new}^0, \mathsf{Augment}(\mathcal{A}_c^0 \cap \mathcal{A}_{new}^0, O_c))$

12      $Invalid := Invalid \cup \{\mathcal{A}_{new}^0\}$

Algorithm 4: Generation of a good enough assumption for component c from the winning region in the cooperative synthesis game for the specification $\mathcal{U}_c$.

Additionally, we give preference to assumptions that do not unnecessarily restrict the other components, although we do not give guarantees on minimality.

The function $\mathsf{ExtractAssumption}$ constructs an intermediate safety automaton $\mathcal{A}_{new}^0$ which is obtained from $\mathcal{D}$ and Win. It receives as additional input the set $Invalid$, which consists of the previously extracted assumptions that violate condition (iii) above. The extraction process checks against $Invalid$ to avoid repeating the failed assumptions. We now give the construction of $\mathcal{A}_{new}^0$.

Let $\mathcal{D} = (2^{AP}, Q, \delta, Q_0, Q)$ be the deterministic safety automaton. Note that since the output player wins the safety game defined by $\mathcal{D}$, we have $Q_0 \subseteq Win$.

First we define a function $f_c : (Q \cap Win) \times 2^I \to 2^{O_c}$ such that for each $q \in Q \cap Win$, $i \in 2^I$ and all $\tilde{o} \in 2^{O_c}$ it holds that: $\{o_{\overline{c}} \in 2^{O_{\overline{c}}} \mid \exists q' \in Win.\ q' \in \delta(q, i \cup f_c(q, i)) \cup o_{\overline{c}})\}| \geq |\{o_{\overline{c}} \in 2^{O_{\overline{c}}} \mid \exists q' \in Win.\ q' \in \delta(q, i \cup \tilde{o} \cup o_{\overline{c}})\}|$.

That is, f_c maps each $q \in Q \cap Win$ and $i \in 2^I$ to the output of component c that allows for the maximal number of possible choices for the remaining components from $q \in Q \cap Win$ and $i \in 2^I$ landing in Win. This choice ensures local minimality of the restrictions on the other components.

Then, we define the function $f_{\overline{c}} : (Q \cap Win) \times 2^I \to 2^{2^{O_{\overline{c}}}}$ such that $f_{\overline{c}}(q, i) := \{o_{\overline{c}} \in 2^{O_{\overline{c}}} \mid \exists q' \in Win.\ q' \in \delta(q, i \cup f_c(q, i)) \cup o_{\overline{c}})\}$. Intuitively, $f_{\overline{c}}$ maps $q \in Q \cap Win$ and $i \in 2^I$ to the outputs of the components other than c that together with $f_c(q, i)$ lead to a state $q' \in Win$. Thus, the outputs of the other components are chosen such that they allow component c to realize $\mathcal{U}_c$ following f_c.

The automaton $\mathcal{A}_{new}^0$ is then constructed based on the function $f_{\overline{c}}$. We let $\mathcal{A}_{new}^0 := (2^{AP}, Q \cap Win, \delta^0, Q_0, Q \cap Win)$, where for every $q \in Q \cap Win$, $i \in 2^I$, $o_c \in 2^{O_c}$, $o_{\overline{c}} \in 2^{O_{\overline{c}}}$ and $q' \in Q \cap Win$ we have $q' \in \delta^0(q, i \cup o_c \cup o_{\overline{c}})$ if and only if $o_{\overline{c}} \in f_{\overline{c}}(q, i)$. Thus, the transition function δ^0 includes all transitions to states in $Q \cap Win$, where the output agrees with the function $f_{\overline{c}}$.

The automaton $\mathcal{A}_{new}^0$ satisfies condition (i). It does not necessarily satisfy (ii), since the outputs on the labels on the transitions in δ^0 are defined based on the

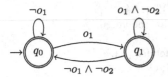

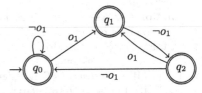

(a) Automaton $\mathcal{A}_1$ representing the assumption made by component 1 (guarantee provided by component 2).

(b) Automaton $\mathcal{A}_2$ representing the assumption made by component 2 (guarantee provided by component 1)

Fig. 1. Assume-guarantee contract computed for Example 5

function $f_{\overline{c}}$ that depends on f_c. Thus, it is possible that outputs of component c disagreeing with f_c could result in words rejected by $\mathcal{A}_{new}^0$, that is they will be violating the new assumption. To this end, we augment $\mathcal{A}_{new}^0$ by adding the missing transitions, to ensure that such words are included in the language of the assumption automaton. We denote with $\mathsf{Augment}(\mathcal{A}_c^0 \cap \mathcal{A}_{new}^0, O_c)$ the augmented version of the new assumption, and with $\mathsf{Augment}(\bigcup_{\overline{c} \in \{1,\ldots,n\} \setminus \{c\}} \overline{\mathcal{A}}_c^0, O_{\overline{c}})$ the augmented updated guarantee.

With that, the updated assumption automaton for component c is obtained by constructing $\mathsf{Augment}(\mathcal{A}_c^0 \cap \mathcal{A}_{new}^0, O_c)$. What remains is to ensure condition (iii). The procedure GENASSUMPTION keeps generating candidate assumptions until an updated assumption for c satisfies all the three conditions, or no more new assumptions can be generated from the given winning region Win. In such case it returns $(\bot, \bot)$, upon which COMPSYNTAGEN restarts with larger bound.

Theorem 3 (Soundness). *Let Φ be a compositional LTL[$\mathcal{F}$] specification. If* COMPSYNTAGEN *returns a multi-component reactive system $\mathcal{S} = (I, O, \mathcal{M})$, then $\mathcal{S}$ is a solution to* Problem 1.

We illustrate the process of iterative assumption generation on an example.

Example 5. Let $I = \{i\}$, $O_1 = \{o_1\}$, $O_2 = \{o_2\}$ and consider the specification $\Phi = \varphi_{local}^1 \wedge \varphi_{local}^2 \wedge \Psi_{shared}$, where the individual specifications are

$$\varphi_{local}^1 = (\square \lozenge o_1) \oplus_{\frac{1}{2}} \square \lozenge (i \wedge \bigcirc \neg o_1), \quad \varphi_{local}^2 = \square \lozenge o_2,$$

$$\Psi_{shared} = \square(o_1 \rightarrow \bigcirc \neg o_2).$$

The first call to procedure LOCALSYNT for component 1 in COMPSYNTAGEN determines that there exists no implementation for component 1 that is a solution to the local synthesis problem with bound 2. The local synthesis problem with specifications φ_{local}^1 and Ψ_{shared} is not good-enough realizable by component 1 on its own, because the satisfaction of Ψ_{shared} depends on the future values of variable o_2, which is not under the control of component 1. In particular, since φ_{local}^1 requires setting o_1 to true infinitely often in order to achieve a good enough satisfaction value, component 1 is unable to avoid the requirement that Ψ_{shared} puts on o_2. Thus, procedure GENASSUMPTION is invoked to generate an assumption on the behavior of component 2. GENASSUMPTION solves a safety game in which o_2 is controllable output. In this game, the system player has a winning strategy, from which the assumption $\mathcal{A}_1$ made by component 1, depicted in Fig. 1a, is extracted. This assumption is added to the guarantee $\mathcal{G}_2$ of component 2, after which procedure LOCALSYNT is applied to component 2.

Again, there exists no implementation for component 2 that is a solution to the local good-enough synthesis problem with bound 2. The reason is that the local specification φ_{local}^2 cannot be satisfied in conjunction with the guarantee $\mathcal{G}_2$ in case o_1 is always set to true. Following that, GENASSUMPTION is invoked to generate an assumption on the behavior of component 1. GENASSUMPTION solves the cooperative safety game constructed for bound 2, and generates the assumption that component 1 does not set o_1 to true twice in a row (as the bound is 2). The generated safety automaton $\mathcal{A}_2$ is given in Fig. 1b. With the assume-guarantee contract in Fig. 1, the subsequent calls to LOCALSYNT for both components succeed, producing a multi-component reactive system.

5   Experimental Evaluation

We implemented our compositional synthesis procedure in a prototype. The tool takes the compositional $LTL[\mathcal{F}]$ specification as input. If realizable, it produces a set of implementations, one for each component, that satisfy the conditions of *Problem 2*. Should the specification require cooperation between the components, the tool iteratively generates additional assumptions in the form of automata. Our tool uses *Spot* [14] (v2.10.6) for the automata operations and for solving the safety games in bounded synthesis.

We compare the compositional approach and the monolithic approach using our prototype, demonstrating the benefits of compositional synthesis for the same underlying implementation. We extract the UCB before starting the construction of the safety game to apply sdf[1] for reference, which takes this UCB as input and performs bounded synthesis. To our knowledge, there are currently no other tools available that would apply to our setting or could easily be extended.

We performed experiments on several examples on a laptop with an Intel Core i7 processor at 2.8 GHz and 16 GB of memory. Table 1 shows the results.

The first three examples are realizable without explicit assumptions. The others need additional assumptions, which can be given or derived. Example intro_ex is the one described in Sect. 1.

The results show that the compositional synthesis scales better than the monolithic approach on the considered benchmarks. In particular, most specifications can only be handled when treated in the decomposition. This is expected, as the decomposed specifications are smaller, and in the monolithic case the automata become prohibitively large. It should be noted that even in the cases when assumptions are necessary and require multiple iterations to be generated,

---

[1]   https://github.com/5nizza/sdf-hoa.

Table 1. Experimental results, time in seconds, timeout of 30 min. Size is the size of initial automata for $(\varphi_l^1, \varphi_l^2, \ldots, \Psi_s)$, and largest final UCB. We differentiate between compositional with iterative assumptions (iter.), predefined assumptions (pred.), or no assumptions (none). In some cases (n/a.), there were no automata to execute sdf on.

Example	n	Autom. size		Monolithic	Compositional			Using sdf	
		init	UCB		none	iter.	pred.	mono.	comp.
max_use	2	13,7,7	108	335	25.73	–	–	TO	51.26
use_if_req2	2	17,17,17	671	TO	79.10	–	–	TO	TO
use_if_req3	3	17,17,17,29	2612	TO	1074.81	–	–	TO	TO
intro_ex	2	9,5,7	1115	290.37	–	57.73	17.6	TO	11.4
color_change	2	6,6,13	689	196.45	–	108.19	23.15	TO	34.8
two_foll_one	2	33,8,7	672	TO	–	442.74	215.12	TO	TO
perm_to_r3	3	7,7,8,13	3363	TO	–	286.42	194.84	n/a	TO
perm_to_r4	4	7,7,7,11,25	5558	TO	–	TO	TO	n/a	TO

the compositional approach is still faster than the monolithic one. For example color_change, it takes half the time to complete and the size of the UCB in the monolithic case is around the combined size for both components separately.

When increasing the number of components, the monolithic specification necessarily increases in size, whereas, depending on the specification, it can remain small for the individual components. Still, constructing the safety game from the UCB is the most time-consuming step, and is performed for each component once per iteration. As the local synthesis problems become more complex, the timeout may be reached before iterating through all components, such as in perm_to_r4.

Also apparent from these results is that our prototype implementation does not scale well yet. Growing use_if_req2 to three components in use_if_req3 increases the runtime significantly. For perm_to_r3 and perm_to_r4, it runs into the timeout going from three to four. It should be noted that for these benchmarks sdf reaches the timeout as well, when executed with the resulting UCB.

As expected, with assumptions given a priori, the performance of the compositional approach improves as each component is considered only once. The challenge here lies in manually finding suitable assumptions.

Lastly, when using sdf, we can only compare to the execution of our prototype without assumption generation. Applicable cases are when assumptions are not needed or are given, and the monolithic case. For larger automata, sdf was in most cases unable to finish within the timeout. This is expected as the extracted UCB encodes the behavior for all pairs of values.

6   Conclusion

We investigated the compositional synthesis problem for good-enough synthesis from specifications in a fragment of LTL[$\mathcal{F}$], considering fully-informed components with shared and local specifications. We identified sufficient conditions on the specifications that guarantee the soundness of the proposed decomposition rule. One of the directions for future work is the development of a more sophisticated analysis of the combination of local and shared specifications, to allow taking weights and other factors into account in the local synthesis problem. Another direction is the consideration of partial information. In order for the technique to be viable, we plan to improve the scalability of our prototype.

References

1. Almagor, S., Boker, U., Kupferman, O.: Discounting in LTL. In: Ábrahám, E., Havelund, K. (eds.) TACAS 2014. LNCS, vol. 8413, pp. 424–439. Springer, Heidelberg (2014). https://doi.org/10.1007/978-3-642-54862-8_37
2. Almagor, S., Boker, U., Kupferman, O.: Formally reasoning about quality. J. ACM **63**(3), 24:1–24:56 (2016)
3. Almagor, S., Kupferman, O.: Good-enough synthesis. In: Lahiri, S.K., Wang, C. (eds.) CAV 2020, Part II. LNCS, vol. 12225, pp. 541–563. Springer, Cham (2020). https://doi.org/10.1007/978-3-030-53291-8_28
4. Almagor, S., Kupferman, O., Ringert, J.O., Velner, Y.: Quantitative assume guarantee synthesis. In: Majumdar, R., Kunčak, V. (eds.) CAV 2017, Part II. LNCS, vol. 10427, pp. 353–374. Springer, Cham (2017). https://doi.org/10.1007/978-3-319-63390-9_19
5. Alur, R., Moarref, S., Topcu, U.: Counter-strategy guided refinement of GR(1) temporal logic specifications. In: Formal Methods in Computer-Aided Design, FMCAD 2013, Portland, OR, USA, 20–23 October 2013, pp. 26–33. IEEE (2013)
6. Alur, R., Moarref, S., Topcu, U.: Pattern-based refinement of assume-guarantee specifications in reactive synthesis. In: Baier, C., Tinelli, C. (eds.) TACAS 2015. LNCS, vol. 9035, pp. 501–516. Springer, Heidelberg (2015). https://doi.org/10.1007/978-3-662-46681-0_49
7. Bansal, S., De Giacomo, G., Di Stasio, A., Li, Y., Vardi, M.Y., Zhu, S.: Compositional Safety LTL Synthesis. In: Lal, A., Tonetta, S. (eds.) VSTTE 2022. LNCS, vol. 13800, pp. 1–19. Springer, Cham (2023). https://doi.org/10.1007/978-3-031-25803-9_1
8. Bloem, R., Chatterjee, K., Henzinger, T.A., Jobstmann, B.: Better quality in synthesis through quantitative objectives. In: Bouajjani, A., Maler, O. (eds.) CAV 2009. LNCS, vol. 5643, pp. 140–156. Springer, Heidelberg (2009). https://doi.org/10.1007/978-3-642-02658-4_14
9. Bloem, R., Chatterjee, K., Jacobs, S., Könighofer, R.: Assume-guarantee synthesis for concurrent reactive programs with partial information. In: Baier, C., Tinelli, C. (eds.) TACAS 2015. LNCS, vol. 9035, pp. 517–532. Springer, Heidelberg (2015). https://doi.org/10.1007/978-3-662-46681-0_50
10. Brenguier, R., Raskin, J.-F., Sankur, O.: Assume-admissible synthesis. Acta Inform. **54**(1), 41–83 (2017)
11. Chatterjee, K., Henzinger, T.A.: Assume-guarantee synthesis. In: Grumberg, O., Huth, M. (eds.) TACAS 2007. LNCS, vol. 4424, pp. 261–275. Springer, Heidelberg (2007). https://doi.org/10.1007/978-3-540-71209-1_21
12. Chatterjee, K., Henzinger, T.A., Jobstmann, B.: Environment assumptions for synthesis. In: van Breugel, F., Chechik, M. (eds.) CONCUR 2008. LNCS, vol. 5201, pp. 147–161. Springer, Heidelberg (2008). https://doi.org/10.1007/978-3-540-85361-9_14

13. Damm, W., Finkbeiner, B.: Automatic compositional synthesis of distributed systems. In: Jones, C., Pihlajasaari, P., Sun, J. (eds.) FM 2014. LNCS, vol. 8442, pp. 179–193. Springer, Cham (2014). https://doi.org/10.1007/978-3-319-06410-9_13

14. Duret-Lutz, A., et al.: From spot 2.0 to spot 2.10: what's new? In: Shoham, S., Vizel, Y. (eds.) CAV 2022. LNCS, vol. 13372, pp. 174–187. Springer, Cham (2022). https://doi.org/10.1007/978-3-031-13188-2_9

15. Filiot, E., Jin, N., Raskin, J.-F.: Antichains and compositional algorithms for LTL synthesis. Formal Methods Syst. Des. **39**(3), 261–296 (2011)

16. Finkbeiner, B., Geier, G., Passing, N.: Specification decomposition for reactive synthesis. In: Dutle, A., Moscato, M.M., Titolo, L., Muñoz, C.A., Perez, I. (eds.) NFM 2021. LNCS, vol. 12673, pp. 113–130. Springer, Cham (2021). https://doi.org/10.1007/978-3-030-76384-8_8

17. Finkbeiner, B., Passing, N.: Dependency-based compositional synthesis. In: Hung, D.V., Sokolsky, O. (eds.) ATVA 2020. LNCS, vol. 12302, pp. 447–463. Springer, Cham (2020). https://doi.org/10.1007/978-3-030-59152-6_25

18. Finkbeiner, B., Passing, N.: Compositional synthesis of modular systems. Innov. Syst. Softw. Eng. **18**(3), 455–469 (2022)

19. Finkbeiner, B., Schewe, S.: Bounded synthesis. Int. J. Softw. Tools Technol. Transf. **15**(5–6), 519–539 (2013)

20. Kupferman, O., Perelli, G., Vardi, M.Y.: Synthesis with rational environments. Ann. Math. Artif. Intell. **78**(1), 3–20 (2016). https://doi.org/10.1007/s10472-016-9508-8

21. Majumdar, R., Mallik, K., Schmuck, A.-K., Zufferey, D.: Assume-guarantee distributed synthesis. IEEE Trans. Comput. Aided Des. Integr. Circuits Syst. **39**(11), 3215–3226 (2020)

Neural Networks

Learning Provably Stabilizing Neural Controllers for Discrete-Time Stochastic Systems

Matin Ansaripour[1], Krishnendu Chatterjee[2], Thomas A. Henzinger[2],
Mathias Lechner[3], and Đorđe Žikelić[2(✉)]

[1] Sharif University of Technology, Tehran, Iran
[2] Institute of Science and Technology Austria (ISTA), Klosterneuburg, Austria
{krishnendu.chatterjee,tah,djordje.zikelic}@ist.ac.at
[3] Massachusetts Institute of Technology, Cambridge, MA, USA
mlechner@mit.edu

Abstract. We consider the problem of learning control policies in discrete-time stochastic systems which guarantee that the system stabilizes within some specified stabilization region with probability 1. Our approach is based on the novel notion of stabilizing ranking supermartingales (sRSMs) that we introduce in this work. Our sRSMs overcome the limitation of methods proposed in previous works whose applicability is restricted to systems in which the stabilizing region cannot be left once entered under any control policy. We present a learning procedure that learns a control policy together with an sRSM that formally certifies probability 1 stability, both learned as neural networks. We show that this procedure can also be adapted to formally verifying that, under a given Lipschitz continuous control policy, the stochastic system stabilizes within some stabilizing region with probability 1. Our experimental evaluation shows that our learning procedure can successfully learn provably stabilizing policies in practice.

Keywords: Learning-based control · Stochastic systems · Martingales · Formal verification · Stabilization

1 Introduction

Machine learning based methods and in particular reinforcement learning (RL) present a promising approach to solving highly non-linear control problems. This has sparked interest in the deployment of learning-based control methods in safety-critical autonomous systems such as self-driving cars or healthcare devices. However, the key challenge for their deployment in real-world scenarios is that they do not consider hard safety constraints. For instance, the main objective of RL is to maximize expected reward [46], but doing so provides no guarantees of the system's safety. A more recent paradigm in safe RL considers constrained Markov decision processes (cMDPs) [3,4,21,26,50], which are equiped with both

© The Author(s), under exclusive license to Springer Nature Switzerland AG 2023
É. André and J. Sun (Eds.): ATVA 2023, LNCS 14215, pp. 357–379, 2023.
https://doi.org/10.1007/978-3-031-45329-8_17

a reward function and an auxiliary cost function. The goal of these works is then to maximize expected reward while keeping expected cost below some tolerable threshold. While these methods do enhance safety, they only ensure empirically that the expected cost function is below the threshold and do not provide any formal guarantees on constraint satisfaction.

This is particularly concerning for safety-critical applications, in which unsafe behavior of the system might have fatal consequences. Thus, a fundamental challenge for deploying learning-based methods in safety-critical autonomous systems applications is *formally certifying* safety of learned control policies [5,25].

Stability is a fundamental safety constraint in control theory, which requires the system to converge to and eventually stay within some specified stabilizing region with probability 1, a.k.a. almost-sure (a.s.) asymptotic stability [31,33]. Most existing research on learning policies for a control system with formal guarantees on stability considers *deterministic* systems and employs Lyapunov functions [31] for certifying the system's stability. In particular, a Lyapunov function is learned jointly with the control policy [1,8,15,42]. Informally, a Lyapunov function is a function that maps system states to nonnegative real numbers whose value decreases after every one-step evolution of the system until the stabilizing region is reached. Recently, [37] proposed a learning procedure for learning *ranking supermartingales (RSMs)* [11] for certifying a.s. asymptotic stability in discrete-time stochastic systems. RSMs generalize Lyapunov functions to supermartingale processes in probability theory [54] and decrease in value in *expectation* upon every one-step evolution of the system.

While these works present significant advances in learning control policies with formal stability guarantees as well as formal stability verification, they are either only applicable to deterministic systems or assume that the stabilizing set is *closed under system dynamics*, i.e., the agent cannot leave it once entered. In particular, the work of [37] reduces stability in stochastic systems to an *a.s. reachability* condition by assuming that the agent cannot leave the stabilization set. However, this assumption may not hold in real-world settings because the agent may be able to leave the stabilizing set with some positive probability due to the existence of stochastic disturbances, see Fig. 1. We illustrate the importance of relaxing this assumption on the classical example of balancing a pendulum in the upright position, which we also study in our experimental evaluation. The closedness under system dynamics assumption implies that, once the pendulum is in an upright position, it is ensured to stay upright and not move away. However, this is not a very realistic assumption due to possible existence of minor disturbances which the controller needs to balance out. The closedness under system dynamics assumption essentially assumes the existence of a balancing control policy which takes care of this problem. In contrast, our method does not assume such a balancing policy and learns a control policy which ensures that both (1) the pendulum reaches the upright position and (2) that the pendulum eventually stays upright with probability 1.

While the removal of the assumption that a stabilizing region cannot be left may appear to be a small improvement, in formal methods this is well-understood to be a significant and difficult step. With the assumption, the desired controller has an a.s. reachability objective. Without the assumption, the desired controller has an a.s. persistence (or co-Büchi) objective, namely, to reach and stay in the stabilizing region with probability 1. Verification or synthesis for reachability conditions allow in general much simpler techniques than verification or synthesis for persistence conditions. For example, in non-stochastic systems, reachability can be expressed in alternation-free μ-calculus (i.e., fixpoint computation), whereas persistence requires alternation (i.e., nested fixpoint computation). Technically, reachability conditions are found on the first level of the Borel hierarchy, while persistence conditions are found on the second level [13]. It is, therefore, not surprising that also over continuous and stochastic state spaces, reachability techniques are insufficient for solving persistence problems.

In this work, we present the following three contributions.

1. **Theoretical Contributions.** In this work, we introduce *stabilizing ranking supermartingales (sRSMs)* and prove that they certify a.s. asymptotic stability in discrete-time stochastic systems even when the stabilizing set is not assumed to be closed under system dynamics. The key novelty of our sRSMs compared to RSMs is that they also impose an expected decrease condition within a part of the stabilizing region. The additional condition ensures that, once entered, the agent leaves the stabilizing region with probability at most $p < 1$. Thus, we show that the probability of the agent entering and leaving the stabilizing region N times is at most p^N, which by letting $N \to \infty$ implies that the agent eventually stabilizes within the region with probability 1. The key conceptual novelty is that we combine the convergence results of RSMs which were also exploited in [37] with a *concentration bound* on the supremum value of a supermartingale process. This combined reasoning allows us to formally guarantee a.s. asymptotic stability even for systems in which the stabilizing region is not closed under system dynamics. We remark that our proof that sRSMs certify a.s. asymptotic stability is not an immediate application of results from martingale theory, but that it introduces a novel method to reason about eventual stabilization within a set. We present this novel method in the proof of Theorem 1. Finally, we show that sRSMs not only present qualitative results to certify a.s. asymptotic stability but also present quantitative upper bounds on the number of time steps that the system may spend outside of the stabilization set prior to stabilization.

2. **Algorithmic Contributions.** Following our theoretical results on sRSMs, we present an algorithm for learning a control policy jointly with an sRSM that certifies a.s. asymptotic stability. The method parametrizes both the policy and the sRSM as neural networks and draws insight from established procedures for learning neural network Lyapunov functions [15] and RSMs [37]. It loops between a learner module that jointly trains a policy and an sRSM candidate and a verifier module that certifies the learned sRSM candidate by formally checking whether all sRSM conditions are satisfied. If the sRSM candidate violates some sRSM conditions, the verifier module produces counterexamples that are added to the learner module's training set to guide the

learner in the next loop iteration. Otherwise, if the verification is successful and the algorithm outputs a policy, then the policy guarantees a.s. asymptotic stability. By fixing the control policy and only learning and verifying the sRSM, our algorithm can also be used to verify that a given control policy guarantees a.s. asymptotic stability. This verification procedure only requires that the control policy is a Lipschitz continuous function.

3. **Experimental Contributions.** We experimentally evaluate our learning procedure on 2 stochastic RL tasks in which the stabilizing region is not closed under system dynamics and show that our learning procedure successfully learns control policies with a.s. asymptotic stability guarantees for both tasks.

Organization. The rest of this work is organized as follows. Section 2 contains preliminaries. In Sect. 3, we introduce our novel notion of stabilizing ranking supermartingales and prove that they provide a sound certificate for a.s. asymptotic stability, which is the main theoretical contribution of our work. In Sect. 4, we present the learner-verifier procedure for jointly learning a control policy together with an sRSM that formally certifies a.s. asymptotic stability. In Sect. 5, we experimentally evaluate our approach. We survey related work in Sect. 6. Finally, we conclude in Sect. 7.

2 Preliminaries

We consider a discrete-time stochastic dynamical system of the form

$$\mathbf{x}_{t+1} = f(\mathbf{x}_t, \pi(\mathbf{x}_t), \omega_t),$$

where $f : \mathcal{X} \times \mathcal{U} \times \mathcal{N} \to \mathcal{X}$ is a dynamics function, $\pi : \mathcal{X} \to \mathcal{U}$ is a control policy and $\omega_t \in \mathcal{N}$ is a stochastic disturbance vector. Here, we use $\mathcal{X} \subseteq \mathbb{R}^n$ to denote the state space, $\mathcal{U} \subseteq \mathbb{R}^m$ the action space and $\mathcal{N} \subseteq \mathbb{R}^p$ the stochastic disturbance space of the system. In each time step, ω_t is sampled according to a probability distribution d over $\mathcal{N}$, independently from the previous samples.

A sequence $(\mathbf{x}_t, \mathbf{u}_t, \omega_t)_{t \in \mathbb{N}_0}$ of state-action-disturbance triples is a trajectory of the system, if $\mathbf{u}_t = \pi(\mathbf{x}_t)$, $\omega_t \in \mathsf{support}(d)$ and $\mathbf{x}_{t+1} = f(\mathbf{x}_t, \mathbf{u}_t, \omega_t)$ hold for each $t \in \mathbb{N}_0$. For each state $\mathbf{x}_0 \in \mathcal{X}$, the system induces a Markov process and defines a probability space over the set of all trajectories that start in $\mathbf{x}_0$ [41], with the probability measure and the expectation operators $\mathbb{P}_{\mathbf{x}_0}$ and $\mathbb{E}_{\mathbf{x}_0}$.

Assumptions. The state space $\mathcal{X} \subseteq \mathbb{R}^n$, the action space $\mathcal{U} \subseteq \mathbb{R}^m$ and the stochastic disturbance space $\mathcal{N} \subseteq \mathbb{R}^p$ are all assumed to be Borel-measurable. Furthermore, we assume that the system has a *bounded maximal step size* under any policy π, i.e. that there exists $\Delta > 0$ such that for every $\mathbf{x} \in \mathcal{X}$, $\omega \in \mathcal{N}$ and policy π we have $||\mathbf{x} - f(\mathbf{x}, \pi(\mathbf{x}), \omega)||_1 \leq \Delta$. Note that this is a realistic assumption that is satisfied in many real-world scenarios, e.g. a self-driving car can only traverse a certain maximal distance within each time step whose bounds depend on the maximal speed that the car can develop.

For our learning procedure in Sect. 4, we assume that $\mathcal{X} \subseteq \mathbb{R}^n$ is compact and that f is Lipschitz continuous, which are common assumptions in control theory. Given two metric spaces (X, d_X) and (Y, d_Y), a function $g : X \to Y$ is said to be *Lipschitz continuous* if there exists a constant $L > 0$ such that for every $x_1, x_2 \in X$ we have $d_Y(g(x_1), g(x_2)) \leq L \cdot d_X(x_1, x_2)$. We say that L is a Lipschitz constant of g. For the verification procedure when the control policy π is given, we also assume that π is Lipschitz continuous. This is also a common assumption in control theory and RL that allows for a rich class of policies including neural network policies, as all standard activation functions such as ReLU, sigmoid or tanh are Lipschitz continuous [47]. Finally, in Sect. 4 we assume that the stochastic disturbance space $\mathcal{N}$ is bounded or that d is a product of independent univariate distributions, which is needed for efficient sampling and expected value computation.

Almost-Sure Asymptotic Stability. There are several notions of stability in stochastic systems. In this work, we consider the notion of almost-sure asymptotic stability [33], which requires the system to eventually *converge and stay within* the stabilizing set. In order to define this formally, for each $x \in \mathcal{X}$ let $d(\mathbf{x}, \mathcal{X}_s) = \inf_{\mathbf{x}_s \in \mathcal{X}_s} ||\mathbf{x} - \mathbf{x}_s||_1$, where $|| \cdot ||_1$ is the l_1-norm on $\mathbb{R}^m$.

Definition 1. *A Borel-measurable set $\mathcal{X}_s \subseteq \mathcal{X}$ is* almost-surely (a.s.) asymptotically stable, *if for each initial state $\mathbf{x}_0 \in \mathcal{X}$ we have*

$$\mathbb{P}_{\mathbf{x}_0}\left[\lim_{t \to \infty} d(\mathbf{x}_t, \mathcal{X}_s) = 0\right] = 1.$$

The above definition slightly differs from that of [33] which considers the special case of a singleton $\mathcal{X}_s = \{\mathbf{0}\}$. The reason for this difference is that, analogously to [37] and to the existing works on learning stabilizing policies in deterministic systems [8,15,42], we need to consider stability with respect to an open neighborhood of the origin for learning to be numerically stable.

3   Theoretical Results

We now introduce our novel notion of stabilizing ranking supermartingales (sRSMs). We then show that sRSMs can be used to formally certify a.s. asymptotic stability with respect to a fixed policy π *without* requiring that the stabilizing set is closed under system dynamics. To that end, in this section we assume that the policy π is fixed. In the next section, we will then present our learning procedure.

Prior Work – Ranking Supermartingales (RSMs). In order to motivate our sRSMs and to explain their novelty, we first recall ranking supermartingales (RSMs) [11] that were used in [37] for certifying a.s. asymptotic stability under a given policy π, when the stabilizing set is assumed to be closed under system dynamics. If the stabilizing set is assumed to be closed under system dynamics, then a.s. asymptotic stability of $\mathcal{X}_s$ is equivalent to *a.s. reachability* since the agent cannot leave $\mathcal{X}_s$ once entered.

Intuitively, an RSM is a non-negative continuous function $V : \mathcal{X} \to \mathbb{R}$ whose value at each state in $\mathcal{X} \backslash \mathcal{X}_s$ strictly decreases in expected value by some $\epsilon > 0$ upon every one-step evolution of the system under the policy π.

Definition 2 (Ranking supermartingales [11,37]). *A continuous function* $V : \mathcal{X} \to \mathbb{R}$ *is a* ranking supermartingale (RSM) *for* $\mathcal{X}_s$ *if* $V(\mathbf{x}) \geq 0$ *for each* $\mathbf{x} \in \mathcal{X}$ *and if there exists* $\epsilon > 0$ *such that for each* $\mathbf{x} \in \mathcal{X} \backslash \mathcal{X}_s$ *we have*

$$\mathbb{E}_{\omega \sim d}\Big[V(f(\mathbf{x}, \pi(\mathbf{x}), \omega))\Big] \leq V(\mathbf{x}) - \epsilon.$$

It was shown that, if a system under policy π admits an RSM *and* the stabilizing set $\mathcal{X}_s$ is assumed to be closed under system dynamics, then $\mathcal{X}_s$ is a.s. asymptotically stable. The intuition behind this result is that V needs to strictly decrease in expected value until $\mathcal{X}_s$ is reached while remaining bounded from below by 0. Results from martingale theory can then be used to prove that the agent must eventually converge and reach $\mathcal{X}_s$ with probability 1, due to a strict decrease in expected value by $\epsilon > 0$ outside of $\mathcal{X}_s$ which prevents convergence to any other state. However, apart from nonnegativity, the defining conditions on RSMs do not impose any conditions on the RSM once the agent reaches $\mathcal{X}_s$. In particular, if the stabilizing set $\mathcal{X}_s$ is *not* closed under system dynamics, then the defining conditions of RSMs do not prevent the agent from leaving and reentering $\mathcal{X}_s$ infinitely many times and thus never stabilizing. In order to formally ensure stability, the defining conditions of RSMs need to be strengthened and in the rest of this section we solve this problem.

Our New Certificate – Stabilizing Ranking Supermartingales (sRSMs). We now define our sRSMs, which certify a.s. asymptotic stability even when the stabilizing set is not assumed to be closed under system dynamics and thus overcome the limitation of RSMs of [37] that was discussed above. Recall, we use Δ to denote the maximal step size of the system.

Definition 3 (Stabilizing ranking supermartingales). *Let* $\epsilon, M, \delta > 0$. *A Lipschitz continuous function* $V : \mathcal{X} \to \mathbb{R}$ *is said to be an* (ϵ, M, δ)-stabilizing ranking supermartingale $((\epsilon, M, \delta)$-sRSM$)$ *for* $\mathcal{X}_s$ *if the following conditions hold:*

1. Nonnegativity. $V(\mathbf{x}) \geq 0$ *holds for each* $\mathbf{x} \in \mathcal{X}$.
2. Strict expected decrease if $V \geq M$. *For each* $\mathbf{x} \in \mathcal{X}$, *if* $V(\mathbf{x}) \geq M$ *then*

$$\mathbb{E}_{\omega \sim d}\Big[V\Big(f(\mathbf{x}, \pi(\mathbf{x}), \omega)\Big)\Big] \leq V(\mathbf{x}) - \epsilon.$$

3. Lower bound outside $\mathcal{X}_s$. $V(\mathbf{x}) \geq M + L_V \cdot \Delta + \delta$ *holds for each* $\mathbf{x} \in \mathcal{X} \backslash \mathcal{X}_s$, *where* L_V *is a Lipschitz constant of* V.

An example of an sRSM for a 1-dimensional stochastic dynamical system is shown in Fig. 1. The intuition behind our new conditions is as follows. Condition 2 in Definition 3 requires that, at each state in which $V \geq M$, the value of V decreases in expectation by $\epsilon > 0$ upon one-step evolution of the system.

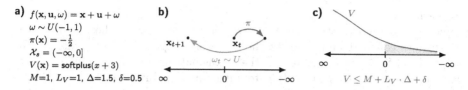

a) $f(\mathbf{x}, \mathbf{u}, \omega) = \mathbf{x} + \mathbf{u} + \omega$
$\omega \sim U(-1, 1)$
$\pi(\mathbf{x}) = -\frac{1}{2}$
$\mathcal{X}_s = (-\infty, 0]$
$V(\mathbf{x}) = \text{softplus}(x + 3)$
$M{=}1,\ L_V{=}1,\ \Delta{=}1.5,\ \delta{=}0.5$

b)

c)

Fig. 1. Example of a 1-dimensional stochastic dynamical system for which the stabilizing set $\mathcal{X}_s$ is not closed under system dynamics since from every system state any other state is reachable with positive probability. **a)** System definition and an sRSM that it admits. **b)** Illustration of a single time step evolution of the system. **c)** Visualization of the sRSM and the corresponding level set used to bound the probability of leaving the stabilizing region.

As we show below, this ensures probability 1 convergence to the set of states $S = \{\mathbf{x} \in \mathcal{X} \mid V(\mathbf{x}) \le M\}$ from any other state of the system. On the other hand, condition 3 in Definition 3 requires that $V \ge M + L_V \cdot \Delta + \delta$ outside of the stabilizing set $\mathcal{X}_s$, thus $S \subseteq \mathcal{X}_s$. Moreover, if the agent is in a state where $V \le M$, the value of V in the next state has to be $\le M + L_V \cdot \Delta$ due to Lipschitz continuity of V and Δ being the maximal step size of the system. Therefore, even if the agent leaves S, for the agent to actually leave $\mathcal{X}_s$ the value of V has to *increase* from a value $\le M + L_V \cdot \Delta$ to a value $\ge M + L_V \cdot \Delta + \delta$ while satisfying the strict expected *decrease* condition imposed by condition 2 in Definition 3 at every intermediate state that is not contained in S. The following theorem is the main result of this section.

Theorem 1. *If there exist $\epsilon, M, \delta > 0$ and an (ϵ, M, δ)-sRSM for $\mathcal{X}_s$, then $\mathcal{X}_s$ is a.s. asymptotically stable.*

Proof sketch, full proof in the extended version [6]. In order to prove Theorem 1, we need to show that $\mathbb{P}_{\mathbf{x}_0}[\lim_{t \to \infty} d(\mathbf{x}_t, \mathcal{X}_s) = 0] = 1$ for every $\mathbf{x}_0 \in \mathcal{X}$. We show this by proving the following two claims. First, we show that, from each initial state $\mathbf{x}_0 \in \mathcal{X}$, the agent converges to and reaches $S = \{\mathbf{x} \in \mathcal{X} \mid V(\mathbf{x}) \le M\}$ with probability 1. The set S is a subset of $\mathcal{X}_s$ by condition 3 in Definition 3 of sRSMs. Second, we show that once the agent is in S it may leave $\mathcal{X}_s$ with probability at most $p = \frac{M + L_V \cdot \Delta}{M + L_V \cdot \Delta + \delta} < 1$. We then prove that the two claims imply Theorem 1.

Claim 1. For each initial state $\mathbf{x}_0 \in \mathcal{X}$, the agent converges to and reaches $S = \{\mathbf{x} \in \mathcal{X} \mid V(\mathbf{x}) \le M\}$ with probability 1.

To prove Claim 1, let $\mathbf{x}_0 \in \mathcal{X}$. If $\mathbf{x}_0 \in S$, then the claim trivially holds. So suppose w.l.o.g. that $\mathbf{x}_0 \notin S$. We consider the probability space $(\Omega_{\mathbf{x}_0}, \mathcal{F}_{\mathbf{x}_0}, \mathbb{P}_{\mathbf{x}_0})$ of all system trajectories that start in $\mathbf{x}_0$, and define a *stopping time* $T_S : \Omega_{\mathbf{x}_0} \to \mathbb{N}_0 \cup \{\infty\}$ which to each trajectory assigns the first hitting time of the set S and is equal to ∞ if the trajectory does not reach S. Furthermore, for each $i \in \mathbb{N}_0$, we define a random variable X_i in this probability space via

$$X_i(\rho) = \begin{cases} V(\mathbf{x}_i), & \text{if } i < T_S(\rho) \\ V(\mathbf{x}_{T_S(\rho)}), & \text{otherwise} \end{cases} \tag{1}$$

for each trajectory $\rho = (\mathbf{x}_t, \mathbf{u}_t, \omega_t)_{t \in \mathbb{N}_0} \in \Omega_{\mathbf{x}_0}$. In words, X_i is equal to the value of V at the i-th state along the trajectory until S is reached, upon which it becomes constant and equal to the value of V upon first entry into S. We prove that $(X_i)_{i=0}^{\infty}$ is an instance of the mathematical notion of ϵ-*ranking super-martingales* (ϵ-*RSMs*) [11] for the stopping time T_S. Intuitively, an ϵ-RSM for T_S is a stochastic process which is non-negative, decreases in expected value upon every one-step evolution of the system and furthermore the decrease is strict and by $\epsilon > 0$ until the stopping time T_S is exceeded. If ϵ is allowed to be 0 as well, then the process is simply said to be a *supermartingale* [54]. It is a known result in martingale theory that, if an ϵ-RSM exists for T_S, then $\mathbb{P}_{\mathbf{x}_0}[T_S < \infty] = \mathbb{P}_{\mathbf{x}_0}[\text{Reach}(S)] = 1$. Thus, by proving that $(X_i)_{i=0}^{\infty}$ defined above is an ϵ-RSM for T_S, we also prove Claim 1. We provide an overview of martingale theory results used in this proof in the extended version of the paper [6].

Claim 2. $\mathbb{P}_{\mathbf{x}_0}[\exists t \in \mathbb{N}_0 \text{ s.t. } \mathbf{x}_t \notin \mathcal{X}_s] = p < 1$ where $p = \frac{M + L_V \cdot \Delta}{M + L_V \cdot \Delta + \delta}$, for each $\mathbf{x}_0 \in S$.

To prove Claim 2, recall that $S = \{\mathbf{x} \in \mathcal{X} \mid V(\mathbf{x}) \leq M\}$. Thus, as V is Lipschitz continuous with Lipschitz constant L_V and Δ is the maximal step size of the system, it follows that the value of V immediately upon the agent leaving the set S is $\leq M + L_V \cdot \Delta$. Hence, for the agent to leave $\mathcal{X}_s$ from $\mathbf{x}_0 \in S$, it first has to reach a state $\mathbf{x}_1$ with $M < V(\mathbf{x}_1) \leq M + L_V \cdot \Delta$ and then to also reach a state $\mathbf{x}_2 \notin \mathcal{X}_s$ from $\mathbf{x}_1$ without reentering S. By condition 3 in Definition 3 of sRSMs, we have $V(\mathbf{x}_2) \geq M + L_V \cdot \Delta + \delta$. We claim that this happens with probability at most $p = \frac{M + L_V \cdot \Delta}{M + L_V \cdot \Delta + \delta}$. To prove this, we use another result from martingale theory which says that, if $(Z_i)_{i=0}^{\infty}$ is a nonnegative supermartingale and $\lambda > 0$, then $\mathbb{P}[\sup_{i \geq 0} Z_i \geq \lambda] \leq \frac{\mathbb{E}[Z_0]}{\lambda}$ (see the extended version for full proof [6]). We apply this theorem to the process $(X_i')_{i=0}^{\infty}$ defined analogously as in Eq. 1, but in the probability space of trajectories that start in $\mathbf{x}_1$. Then, since in this probability space we have that X_0 is equal to $V(\mathbf{x}_1) \leq M + L_V \cdot \Delta$, by plugging in $\lambda = M + L_V \cdot \Delta + \delta$ we conclude that the probability of the process ever leaving $\mathcal{X}_s$ and thus reaching a state in which $V \geq M + L_V \cdot \Delta + \delta$ is

$$\mathbb{P}_{\mathbf{x}_0}[\exists t \in \mathbb{N}_0 \text{ s.t. } \mathbf{x}_t \notin \mathcal{X}_s]$$
$$\leq \mathbb{P}_{\mathbf{x}_0}[\sup_{i \geq 0} X_i \geq M + L_V \cdot \Delta + \delta]$$
$$\leq \mathbb{P}_{\mathbf{x}_1}[\sup_{i \geq 0} X_i' \geq M + L_V \cdot \Delta + \delta]$$
$$\leq \frac{M + L_V \cdot \Delta}{M + L_V \cdot \Delta + \delta} = p < 1,$$

so Claim 2 follows. The above inequality is formally proved in the extended version [6].

Claim 1 and Claim 2 Imply Theorem 1. Finally, we show that these two claims imply the theorem statement. By Claim 1, the agent with probability 1 converges to and reaches $S \subseteq \mathcal{X}_s$ from any initial state. On the other hand, by Claim 2, upon reaching a state in S the probability of leaving $\mathcal{X}_s$ is at most $p < 1$. Furthermore, even if $\mathcal{X}_s$ is left, by Claim 1 the agent is guaranteed to again converge to and reach S. Hence, due to the system dynamics under a fixed policy satisfying Markov property, the probability of the agent leaving and reentering S more than N times is bounded from above by p^N. By letting $N \to \infty$, we conclude that the probability of the agent leaving $\mathcal{X}_s$ and reentering infinitely many times is 0, so the agent with probability 1 eventually enters and S and does not leave $\mathcal{X}_s$ after that. This implies that $\mathcal{X}_s$ is a.s. asymptotically stable. □

Bounds on Stabilization Time. We conclude this section by showing that our sRSMs not only certify a.s. asymptotic stability of $\mathcal{X}_s$, but also provide bounds on the number of time steps that the agent may spend outside of $\mathcal{X}_s$. This is particularly relevant for safety-critical applications in which the goal is not only to ensure stabilization but also to ensure that the agent spends as little time outside the stabilization set as possible. For each trajectory $\rho = (\mathbf{x}_t, \mathbf{u}_t, \omega_t)_{t \in \mathbb{N}_0}$, let $\mathsf{Out}_{\mathcal{X}_s}(\rho) = |\{t \in \mathbb{N}_0 \mid \mathbf{x}_t \notin \mathcal{X}_s\}| \in \mathbb{N}_0 \cup \{\infty\}$.

Theorem 2 (Proof in the extended version [6]). *Let $\epsilon, M, \delta > 0$ and suppose that $V : \mathcal{X} \to \mathbb{R}$ is an (ϵ, M, δ)-sRSM for $\mathcal{X}_s$. Let $\Gamma = \sup_{\mathbf{x} \in \mathcal{X}_s} V(\mathbf{x})$ be the supremum of all possible values that V can attain over the stabilizing set $\mathcal{X}_s$. Then, for each initial state $\mathbf{x}_0 \in \mathcal{X}$, we have that*

1. $\mathbb{E}_{\mathbf{x}_0}[\mathsf{Out}_{\mathcal{X}_s}] \leq \frac{V(\mathbf{x}_0)}{\epsilon} + \frac{(M + L_V \cdot \Delta) \cdot (\Gamma + L_V \cdot \Delta)}{\delta \cdot \epsilon}$.
2. $\mathbb{P}_{\mathbf{x}_0}[\mathsf{Out}_{\mathcal{X}_s} \geq t] \leq \frac{V(\mathbf{x}_0)}{t \cdot \epsilon} + \frac{(M + L_V \cdot \Delta) \cdot (\Gamma + L_V \cdot \Delta)}{\delta \cdot \epsilon \cdot t}$, *for any time $t \in \mathbb{N}$.*

4 Learning Stabilizing Policies and sRSMs on Compact State Spaces

In this section, we present our method for learning a stabilizing policy together with an sRSM that formally certifies a.s. asymptotic stability. As stated in Sect. 2, our method assumes that the state space $\mathcal{X} \subseteq \mathbb{R}^n$ is compact and that f is Lipschitz continuous with Lipschitz constant L_f. We prove that, if the method outputs a policy, then it guarantees a.s. asymptotic stability. After presenting the method for learning control policies, we show that it can also be adapted to a formal verification procedure that learns an sRSM for a given Lipschitz continuous control policy π.

Outline of the Method. We parameterize the policy and the sRSM via two neural networks $\pi_\theta : \mathcal{X} \to \mathcal{U}$ and $V_\nu : \mathcal{X} \to \mathbb{R}$, where θ and ν are vectors of neural network parameters. To enforce condition 1 in Definition 3, which requires the sRSM to be a nonnegative function, our method applies the softplus activation function $x \mapsto \log(\exp(x) + 1)$ to the output of V_ν. The remaining layers of π_θ and V_ν apply ReLU activation functions, therefore π_θ and V_ν are also Lipschitz continuous [47]. Our method draws insight from the algorithms of [15,55] for learning policies together with Lyapunov functions or RSMs and it comprises

---

Algorithm 1. Learner-verifier procedure

1: **Input** Dynamics function f, stochastic disturbance distribution d, stabilizing region $\mathcal{X}_s \subseteq \mathcal{X}$, Lipschitz constant L_f

2: **Parameters** $\tau > 0$, $N_{\text{cond } 2} \in \mathbb{N}$, $N_{\text{cond } 3} \in \mathbb{N}$, ϵ_{train}, δ_{train}

3: $\widetilde{\mathcal{X}} \leftarrow$ centers of cells of a discretization rectangular grid in $\mathcal{X}$ with mesh τ

4: $B \leftarrow$ centers of grid cells of a subgrid of $\widetilde{\mathcal{X}}$

5: $\pi_\theta \leftarrow$ policy trained by using PPO [44]

6: $M \leftarrow 1$

7: **while** timeout not reached **do**

8:     $\pi_\theta, V_\nu \leftarrow$ jointly trained by minimizing the loss in (2) on dataset B

9:     $\widetilde{\mathcal{X}}_{\geq M} \leftarrow$ centers of cells over which $V_\nu(\mathbf{x}) \geq M$

10:     $L_\pi, L_V \leftarrow$ Lipschitz constants of π_θ, V_ν

11:     $K \leftarrow L_V \cdot (L_f \cdot (L_\pi + 1) + 1)$

12:     $\widetilde{\mathcal{X}}_{ce} \leftarrow$ counterexamples to condition 2 on $\widetilde{\mathcal{X}}_{\geq M}$

13:     **if** $\widetilde{\mathcal{X}}_{ce} = \{\}$ **then**

14:         Cells$_{\mathcal{X} \setminus \mathcal{X}_s} \leftarrow$ grid cells that intersect $\mathcal{X} \setminus \mathcal{X}_s$

15:         $\Delta_\theta \leftarrow$ max. step size of the system with policy π

16:         **if** $\underline{V}_\nu(\text{cell}) > M + L_V \cdot \Delta_\theta$ for all cell $\in$ Cells$_{\mathcal{X} \setminus \mathcal{X}_s}$ **then**

17:             **return** π_θ, V_ν, "$\mathcal{X}_s$ is a.s. asymptotically stable under π_θ"

18:         **end if**

19:     **else**

20:         $B \leftarrow (B \setminus \{\mathbf{x} \in B | V_\nu(\mathbf{x}) < M\}) \cup \widetilde{\mathcal{X}}_{ce}$

21:     **end if**

22: **end while**

23: **Return** Unknown

---

of a *learner* and a *verifier* module that are composed into a loop. In each loop iteration, the learner module first trains both π_θ and V_ν on a training objective in the form of a differentiable approximation of the sRSM conditions 2 and 3 in Definition 3. Once the training has converged, the verifier module formally checks whether the learned sRSM candidate satisfies conditions 2 and 3 in Definition 3. If both conditions are fulfilled, our method terminates and returns a policy together with an sRSM that formally certifies a.s. asymptotic stability. If at least one sRSM condition is violated, the verifier module enlarges the training set of the learner by counterexample states that violate the condition in order to guide the learner towards fixing the policy and the sRSM in the next learner iteration. This loop is repeated until either the verifier successfully verifies the learned sRSM and outputs the control policy and the sRSM, or until some specified timeout is reached in which case no control policy is returned by the method. The pseudocode of the algorithm is shown in Algorithm 1. In what follows, we provide details on algorithm initialization (lines 3–6, Algorithm 1) and on the learner and the verifier modules (lines 7–22, Algorithm 1).

4.1   Initialization

State Space Discretization. The key challenge in verifying an sRSM candidate is to check the expected decrease condition imposed by condition 2 in Definition 3. To check this condition, following the idea of [8] and [37] our method first computes a discretization of the state space $\mathcal{X}$. A *discretization* $\widetilde{\mathcal{X}}$ of $\mathcal{X}$ with *mesh* $\tau > 0$ is a finite subset $\widetilde{\mathcal{X}} \subseteq \mathcal{X}$ such that for every $\mathbf{x} \in \mathcal{X}$ there exists $\widetilde{\mathbf{x}} \in \widetilde{\mathcal{X}}$ with $\|\widetilde{\mathbf{x}} - \mathbf{x}\|_1 < \tau$. Our method computes the discretization by considering *centers of cells of a rectangular grid* of sufficiently small cell size (line 3, Algorithm 1). The discretization will later be used by the verifier in order to reduce verification of condition 2 to checking a slightly stricter condition at discretization vertices, due to all involved functions being Lipschitz continuous (more details Sect. 4.3).

The algorithm also collects the set B of grid cell centers of a subgrid of $\widetilde{\mathcal{X}}$ of larger mesh (line 4, Algorithm 1). This set will be used as the initial training set for the learner, and will then be gradually expanded by counterexamples computed by the verifier.

Policy Initialization. We initialize parameters of the neural network policy π_θ by running several iterations of the proximal policy optimization (PPO) [44] RL algorithm (line 5, Algorithm 1). In particular, we induce a Markov decision process (MDP) from the given system by using the reward function $r : \mathcal{X} \to \mathbb{R}$ defined via

$$r(\mathbf{x}) = \begin{cases} 1, & \text{if } \mathbf{x} \in \mathcal{X}_s \\ 0, & \text{otherwise} \end{cases}$$

in order to learn an initial policy that drives the system toward the stabilizing set. The practical importance of initialization for learning stabilizing policies in deterministic systems was observed in [15].

Fix the Value $M = 1$. As the last initialization step, we observe that one may always rescale the value of an sRSM by a strictly positive constant factor while preserving all conditions in Definition 3. Therefore, without loss of generality, we fix the value $M = 1$ in Definition 3 for our sRSM (line 6, Algorithm 1).

4.2   Learner

The policy and the sRSM candidate are learned by minimizing the loss

$$\mathcal{L}(\theta, \nu) = \mathcal{L}_{\text{cond } 2}(\theta, \nu) + \mathcal{L}_{\text{cond } 3}(\theta, \nu) \tag{2}$$

(line 8, Algorithm 1). The two loss terms guide the learner towards an sRSM candidate that satisfies conditions 2 and 3 in Definition 3.

We define the loss term for condition 2 via

$$\mathcal{L}_{\text{cond } 2}(\theta, \nu) = \frac{1}{|B|} \sum_{\mathbf{x} \in B} \Big(\max \Big\{$$
$$\sum_{\omega_1, \dots, \omega_{N_{\text{cond } 2}} \sim d} \frac{V_\nu \big(f(\mathbf{x}, \pi_\theta(\mathbf{x}), \omega_i) \big)}{N_{\text{cond } 2}} - V_\nu(\mathbf{x}) + \epsilon_{\text{train}}, 0 \Big\} \Big).$$

Intuitively, for each element $\mathbf{x} \in B$ of the training set, the corresponding term in the sum incurs a loss whenever condition 2 is violated at $\mathbf{x}$. Since the expected value of V_ν at a successor state of $\mathbf{x}$ does not admit a closed form expression due to V_ν being a neural network, we approximate it as the mean of values of V_ν at $N_{\text{cond 2}}$ independently sampled successor states of $\mathbf{x}$, with $N_{\text{cond 2}}$ being an algorithm parameter.

For condition 3, the loss term samples $N_{\text{cond 3}}$ system states from $\mathcal{X}\backslash\mathcal{X}_s$ with $N_{\text{cond 3}}$ an algorithm parameter and incurs a loss whenever condition 3 is not satisfied at some sampled state:

$$\mathcal{L}_{\text{cond3}}(\theta, \nu) = \max\left\{M + L_{V_\nu} + \Delta_\theta + \delta_{\text{train}} - \min_{x_1,...x_{N_{\text{cond 3}}}\sim\mathcal{X}\backslash\mathcal{X}_s} V_\nu(x_i), 0\right\}.$$

Regularization Terms in the Implementation. In our implementation, we also add two regularization terms to the loss function used by the learner. The first term favors learning an sRSM candidate whose global minimum is within the stabilizing set. The second term penalizes large Lipschitz bounds of the networks π_θ and V_ν by adding a regularization term. While these two loss terms do not directly enforce any particular condition in Definition 3, we observe that they help the learning and the verification process and decrease the number of needed learner-verifier iterations. See the extended version [6] for details on regularization terms.

4.3 Verifier

The verifier formally checks whether the learned sRSM candidate satisfies conditions 2 and 3 in Definition 3. Recall, condition 1 is satisfied due to the softplus activation function applied to the output of V_ν.

Formal Verification of Condition 2. The key challenge in checking the expected decrease condition in condition 2 is that the expected value of a neural network function does not admit a closed-form expression, so we cannot evaluate it directly. Instead, we check condition 2 by first showing that it suffices to check a slightly stricter condition at vertices of the discretization $\tilde{\mathcal{X}}$, due to all involved functions being Lipschitz continuous. We then show how this stricter condition is checked at each discretization vertex.

To verify condition 2, the verifier first collects the set $\tilde{\mathcal{X}}_{\geq M}$ of centers of all grid cells that contain a state $\mathbf{x}$ with $V_\nu(\mathbf{x}) \geq M$ (line 9, Algorithm 1). This set is computed via interval arithmetic abstract interpretation (IA-AI) [22,27], which for each grid cell propagates interval bounds across neural network layers in order to bound from below the minimal value that V_ν attains over that cell. The center of the grid cell is added to $\tilde{\mathcal{X}}_{\geq M}$ whenever this lower bound is smaller than M. We use the method of [27] to perform IA-AI with respect to a neural network function V_ν so we refer the reader to [27] for details on this step.

Once $\tilde{\mathcal{X}}_{\geq M}$ is computed, the verifier uses the method of [47, Section 4.3] to compute the Lipschitz constants L_π and L_V of neural networks π_θ and V_ν, respectively (line 10, Algorithm 1). It then sets $K = L_V \cdot (L_f \cdot (L_\pi + 1) + 1)$ (line 11, Algorithm 1). Finally, for each $\widetilde{\mathbf{x}} \in \widetilde{\mathcal{X}}_{\geq M}$ the verifier checks the following stricter inequality

$$\mathbb{E}_{\omega \sim d}\left[V_\nu\left(f(\widetilde{\mathbf{x}}, \pi_\theta(\widetilde{\mathbf{x}}), \omega)\right)\right] < V_\nu(\widetilde{\mathbf{x}}) - \tau \cdot K, \tag{3}$$

and collects the set $\widetilde{\mathcal{X}}_{ce} \subseteq \widetilde{\mathcal{X}}_{\geq M}$ of counterexamples at which this inequality is violated (line 12, Algorithm 1). The reason behind checking this stronger constraint is that, due to Lipschitz continuity of all involved functions and due to τ being the mesh of the discretization, we can show (formally done in the proof of Theorem 3) that this condition being satisfied for each $\widetilde{\mathbf{x}} \in \widetilde{\mathcal{X}}_{\geq M}$ implies that the expected decrease condition $\mathbb{E}_{\omega \sim d}[V_\nu(f(\mathbf{x}, \pi_\theta(\widetilde{\mathbf{x}}), \omega))] < V_\nu(\mathbf{x})$ is satisfied for all $\mathbf{x} \in \mathcal{X}$ with $V(\mathbf{x}) \geq M$. Then, due to both sides of the inequality being continuous functions and $\{\mathbf{x} \in \mathcal{X} \mid V_\nu(\mathbf{x}) \geq M\}$ being a compact set, their difference admits a strictly positive global minimum $\epsilon > 0$ so that $\mathbb{E}_{\omega \sim d}[V_\nu(f(\mathbf{x}, \pi_\theta(\widetilde{\mathbf{x}}), \omega))] \leq V_\nu(\mathbf{x}) - \epsilon$ is satisfied for all $\mathbf{x} \in \mathcal{X}$ with $V(\mathbf{x}) \geq M$. We show in the paragraph below how our method formally checks whether the inequality in (3) is satisfied at some $\widetilde{\mathbf{x}} \in \widetilde{\mathcal{X}}_{\geq M}$.

If (3) is satisfied for each $\widetilde{\mathbf{x}} \in \widetilde{\mathcal{X}}_{\geq M}$ and so $\widetilde{\mathcal{X}}_{ce} = \emptyset$, the verifier concludes that V_ν satisfies condition 2 in Definition 3 and proceeds to checking condition 3 in Definition 3 (lines 14–18, Algorithm 1). Otherwise, any computed counterexample to this constraint is added to B to help the learner fine-tune an sRSM candidate (line 20, Algorithm 1) and the algorithm proceeds to the start of the next learner-verifier iteration (line 7, Algorithm 1).

Checking Inequality (3) *and Expected Value Computation.* To check (3) at some $\widetilde{\mathbf{x}} \in \widetilde{\mathcal{X}}_{\geq M}$, we need to compute the expected value $\mathbb{E}_{\omega \sim d}[V_\nu(f(\widetilde{\mathbf{x}}, \pi_\theta(\widetilde{\mathbf{x}}), \omega))]$. Note that this expected value does not admit a closed form expression due to V_ν being a neural network function, so we cannot evaluate it directly. Instead, we use the method of [37] in order to compute an upper bound on this expected value and use this upper bound to formally check whether (3) is satisfied at $\widetilde{\mathbf{x}}$. For completeness of our presentation, we briefly describe this expected value bound computation below. Recall, in our assumptions in Sect. 2, we said that our algorithm assumes that the stochastic disturbance space $\mathcal{N}$ is bounded or that d is a product of independent univariate distributions.

First, consider the case when $\mathcal{N}$ is bounded. We partition the stochastic disturbance space $\mathcal{N} \subseteq \mathbb{R}^p$ into finitely many cells $\text{cell}(\mathcal{N}) = \{\mathcal{N}_1, \ldots, \mathcal{N}_k\}$. We denote by $\text{maxvol} = \max_{\mathcal{N}_i \in \text{cell}(\mathcal{N})} \text{vol}(\mathcal{N}_i)$ the maximal volume of any cell in the partition with respect to the Lebesgue measure over $\mathbb{R}^p$. The expected value can then be bounded from above via

$$\mathbb{E}_{\omega \sim d}\left[V_\nu\left(f(\widetilde{\mathbf{x}}, \pi_\theta(\widetilde{\mathbf{x}}), \omega)\right)\right] \leq \sum_{\mathcal{N}_i \in \text{cell}(\mathcal{N})} \text{maxvol} \cdot \sup_{\omega \in \mathcal{N}_i} F(\omega)$$

where $F(\omega) = V_\nu(f(\widetilde{\mathbf{x}}, \pi_\theta(\widetilde{\mathbf{x}}), \omega)$. Each supremum on the right-hand-side is then bounded from above by using the IA-AI-based method of [27].

Second, consider the case when $\mathcal{N}$ is unbounded but d is a product of independent univariate distributions. Note that in this case we cannot directly follow the above approach since maxvol $= \max_{\mathcal{N}_i \in \text{cell}(\mathcal{N})} \text{vol}(\mathcal{N}_i)$ would be infinite. However, since d is a product of independent univariate distributions, we may first apply the Probability Integral Transform [39] to each univariate distribution in d to transform it into a finite support distribution and then proceed as above.

Formal Verification of Condition 3. To formally verify condition 3 in Definition 3, the verifier collects the set Cells$_{\mathcal{X}\setminus\mathcal{X}_s}$ of all grid cells that intersect $\mathcal{X}\setminus\mathcal{X}_s$ (line 14, Algorithm 1). Then, for each cell $\in$ Cells$_{\mathcal{X}\setminus\mathcal{X}_s}$, it uses IA-AI to check

$$\underline{V}_\nu(\text{cell}) > M + L_V \cdot \Delta_\theta, \tag{4}$$

with $\underline{V}_\nu(\text{cell})$ denoting the lower bound on V_ν over the cell computed by IA-AI (lines 15–16, Algorithm 1). If this holds, then the verifier concludes that V_ν satisfies condition 3 in Definition 3 with $\delta = \min_{\text{cell}\in\text{Cells}_{\mathcal{X}\setminus\mathcal{X}_s}}\{\underline{V}_\nu(\text{cell}) - M - L_V \cdot \Delta_\theta\}$. Hence, as conditions 2 and 3 have both been formally verified to be satisfied, the method returns the policy π_θ and the sRSM V_ν which formally proves that $\mathcal{X}_s$ is a.s. asymptotically stable under π_θ (line 17, Algorithm 1). Otherwise, the method proceeds to the next learner-verifier loop iteration (line 7, Algorithm 1).

Algorithm Correctness. The following theorem establishes the correctness of Algorithm 1. In particular, it shows that if the verifier confirms that conditions 2 and 3 in Definition 3 are satisfied and therefore Algorithm 1 returns a control policy π_θ and an sRSM V_ν, then it holds that V_ν is indeed an sRSM and that $\mathcal{X}_s$ is a.s. asymptotically stable under π_θ.

Theorem 3 (Algorithm correctness, proof in the extended version [6]). *Suppose that the verifier shows that V_ν satisfies (3) for each $\tilde{\mathbf{x}} \in \tilde{\mathcal{X}}_{\geq M}$ and (4) for each cell $\in$ Cells$_{\mathcal{X}\setminus\mathcal{X}_s}$, so Algorithm 1 returns π_θ and V_ν. Then V_ν is an sRSM and $\mathcal{X}_s$ is a.s. asymptotically stable under π_θ.*

4.4   Adaptation into a Formal Verification Procedure

To conclude this section, we show that Algorithm 1 can be easily adapted into a formal verification procedure for showing that $\mathcal{X}_s$ is a.s. asymptotically stable under some given control policy π. This adaptation only assumes that π is Lipschitz continuous with a given Lipschitz constant L_π, or alternatively that it is a neural network policy with Lipschitz continuous activation functions in which case we use the method of [47] to compute its Lipschitz constant L_π.

Instead of jointly learning the control policy and the sRSM, the formal verification procedure now only learns a neural network sRSM V_ν. This is done by executing the analogous learner-verifier loop described in Algorithm 1. The only difference happens in the learner module, where now only the parameters ν of the sRSM neural network are learned. Hence, the loss function in (2) that is used

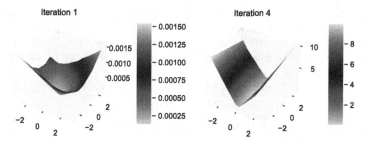

Fig. 2. Visualization of the sRSM candidate after 1 and 4 iterations of our algorithm for the inverted pendulum task. The candidate after 1 iteration does not satisfy all sRSM conditions, while the candidate after 4 iterations is an sRSM.

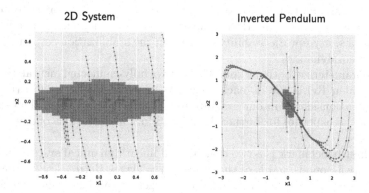

Fig. 3. Visualization of the learned stabilizing sets in green, in which the system will remain with probability 1. (Color figure online)

in (line 8, Algorithm 1) has the same form as in Sect. 4.2, but now it only takes parameters ν as input:

$$\mathcal{L}(\nu) = \mathcal{L}_{\text{cond } 2}(\nu) + \mathcal{L}_{\text{cond } 3}(\nu).$$

Additionally, the control policy initialization in (line 5, Algorithm 1) becomes redundant because the control policy π is given. Apart from these two changes, the formal verification procedure remains identical to Algorithm 1 and its correctness follows from Theorem 3.

5   Experimental Results

In this section, we experimentally evaluate the effectiveness of our method[1]. We consider the same experimental setting and the two benchmarks studied in [37]. However, in contrast to [37], we do not assume that the stabilization sets are

---

[1] Our implementation is available at https://github.com/mlech26l/neural_martingales/tree/ATVA2023.

Table 1. Results of our experimental evaluation. The first column shows benchmark names. The second column shows the numer of learner-verifier loop iterations needed to successfully learn and verify a control policy and an sRSM. The third column shows the mesh of the used discretization grid. The fourth column shows runtime in seconds.

Benchmark	Iters.	Mesh (τ)	Runtime
2D system	5	0.0007	3660 s
Pendulum	4	0.003	2619 s

closed under system dynamics and that the system stabilizes immediately upon reaching the stabilization set. In our evaluation, we modify both environments so that this assumption is violated. The goal of our evaluation is to confirm that our method based on sRSMs can in practice learn policies that formally guarantee a.s. asymptotic stability even when the stabilization set is not closed under system dynamics.

We parameterize both π_θ and V_ν by two fully-connected neural networks with 2 hidden ReLU layers, each with 128 neurons. Below we describe both benchmarks considered in our evaluation, and refer the reader to the extended version of the paper [6] for further details and formal definitions of environment dynamics.

The first benchmark is a two-dimensional linear dynamical system with non-linear control bounds and is of the form $x_{t+1} = Ax_t + Bg(u_t) + \omega$, where ω is a stochastic disturbance vector sampled from a zero-mean triangular distribution. The function g clips the action to stay within the interval $[1, -1]$. The state space is $\mathcal{X} = \{x \mid |x_1| \leq 0.7, |x_2| \leq 0.7\}$ and we want to learn a policy for the stabilizing set

$$\mathcal{X}_s = \mathcal{X} \setminus \Big(\{x \mid -0.7 \leq x_1 \leq -0.6, -0.7 \leq x_2 \leq -0.4\}$$
$$\bigcup \{x \mid 0.6 \leq x_1 \leq 0.7, 0.4 \leq x_2 \leq 0.7\} \Big).$$

The second benchmark is a modified version of the inverted pendulum problem adapted from the OpenAI gym [9]. Note that this benchmark has non-polynomial dynamics, as its dynamics function involves a sine function (see the extended version [6]). The system is expressed by two state variables that represent the angle and the angular velocity of the pendulum. Contrary to the original task, the problem considered here introduces triangular-shaped random noise to the state after each update step. The state space is define as $\mathcal{X} = \{x \mid |x_1| \leq 3, |x_2| \leq 3\}$, and objective of the agent is to stabilize the pendulum within the stabilizing set

$$\mathcal{X}_s = \mathcal{X} \setminus \Big(\{x \mid -3 \leq x_1 \leq -2.9, -3 \leq x_2 \leq 0\}$$
$$\bigcup \{x \mid 2.9 \leq x_1 \leq 3, 0 \leq x_2 \leq 3\} \Big).$$

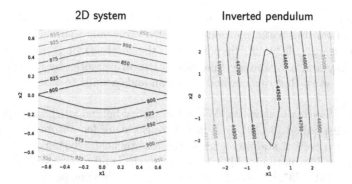

Fig. 4. Contour lines of the expected stabilization time implied by Theorem 2 for the 2D system task on the left and the inverted pendulum task on the right.

For both tasks, our algorithm could find valid sRSMs and prove stability. The runtime characteristics, such as the number of iterations and total runtime, is shown in Table 1. In Fig. 2 we plot the sRSM found by our algorithm for the inverted pendulum task. We also visualize for both tasks in Fig. 3 in green the subset of $\mathcal{X}_s$ implied by the learned sRSM in which the system stabilizes. Finally, in Fig. 4 we show the contour lines of the expected stabilization time bounds that are obtained by applying Theorem 2 to the learned sRSMs.

Limitations. We conclude by discussing limitations of our approach. Verification of neural networks is inherently a computationally difficult problem [8,30,43]. Our method is subject to this barrier as well. In particular, the complexity of the grid decomposition routine for checking the expected decrease condition is exponential in the dimension of the system state space. Consideration of different grid decomposition strategies and in particular non-uniform grids that incorporate properties of the state space is an interesting direction of future work towards improving the scalability of our method. However, a key advantage of our approach is that the complexity is only linear in the size of the neural network policy. Consequently, our approach allows learning and verifying networks that are of the size of typical networks used in reinforcement learning [44]. Moreover, our grid decomposition procedure runs entirely on accelerator devices, including CPUs, GPUs, and TPUs, thus leveraging future advances in these computing devices. A technical limitation of our learning procedure is that it is restricted to compact state spaces. Our theoretical results are applicable to arbitrary (potentially unbounded) state spaces, as shown in Fig. 1.

6 Related Work

Stability for Deterministic Systems. Most early works on control with stability constraints rely either on hand-designed certificates or their computation via sum-of-squares (SOS) programming [28,40]. Automation via SOS programming is restricted to problems with polynomial dynamics and does not scale well with dimension. Learning-based methods present a promising approach to overcome these limitations [14,29,42]. In particular, the methods of [1,15] also learn a control policy and a Lyapunov function as neural networks by using a learner-verifier framework that our method builds on and extends to stochastic systems.

Stability for Stochastic Systems. While the theory behind stochastic system stability is well studied [33,34], only a few works consider automated controller synthesis with formal stability guarantees for stochastic systems with continuous dynamics. The methods of [23,51] are numerical and certify weaker notions of stability. Recently, [37,55] used RSMs and learn a stabilizing policy together with an RSM that certifies a.s. asymptotic stability. However, this method assumes closedness under system dynamics and essentially considers the stability problem as a reachability problem. In contrast, our proof in Sect. 3 introduces a new type of reasoning about supermartingales which allows us to handle stabilization without prior knowledge of a set that is closed under the system dynamics.

Reachability and Safety for Stochastic Systems. Comparatively more works have studied controller synthesis in stochastic systems with formal reachability and safety guarantees. A number of methods abstract the system as a finite-state Markov decision process (MDP) and synthesize a controller for the MDP to provide formal reachability or safety guarantees over finite time horizon [10,35,45,53]. An abstraction based method for obtaining infinite time horizon PAC-style guarantees on the probability of reach-avoidance in linear stochastic systems was proposed in [7]. A method for formal controller synthesis in infinite time horizon non-linear stochastic systems with guarantees on the probability of co-safety properties was proposed in [52]. A learning-based approach for learning a control policy that provides formal reachability and avoidance infinite time horizon guarantees was proposed in [56].

Safe Exploration RL. Safe exploration RL restricts exploration of RL algorithms in a way that a given safety constraint is satisfied. This is typically ensured by learning the system dynamics' uncertainty and limiting exploratory actions within a high probability safe region via Gaussian Processes [32,49], linearized models [24], deep robust regression [38] and Bayesian neural networks [36].

Probabilistic Program Analysis. Ranking supermartingales were originally proposed for proving a.s. termination in probabilistic programs (PPs) [11]. Since then, martingale-based methods have been used for termination [2,16,17,19] safety [18,20,48] and recurrence and persistence [12] analysis in PPs, with the latter being equivalent to stability. However, the persistence certificate of [12] is substantially different from ours. In particular, the certificate of [12] requires strict expected decrease outside the stabilizing set and non-strict expected decrease within the stabilizing set. In contrast, our sRSMs require strict expected decrease outside and only within a small part of the stabilizing set (see Definition 3). We also note that the certificate of [12] cannot be combined with our learner-verifier procedure. Indeed, since our verifier module discretizes the state space and verifies a stricter condition at discretization vertices, if we tried to verify an instance of the certificate of [12] then we would be verifying the strict expected decrease condition over the whole state space. But this condition is not satisfiable over compact state spaces, as any continuous function must admit a global minimum.

7   Conclusion

In this work, we developed a method for learning control policies for stochastic systems with formal guarantees about the systems' a.s. asymptotic stability. Compared to the existing literature, which assumes that the stabilizing set is closed under system dynamics and cannot be left once entered, our approach does not impose this assumption. Our method is based on the novel notion of stabilizing ranking supermartingales (sRSMs) that serve as a formal certificate of a.s. asymptotic stability. We experimentally showed that our learning procedure is able to learn stabilizing policies and stability certificates in practice.

Acknowledgement. This work was supported in part by the ERC-2020-AdG 101020093, ERC CoG 863818 (FoRM-SMArt) and the European Union's Horizon 2020 research and innovation programme under the Marie Skłodowska-Curie Grant Agreement No. 665385.

References

1. Abate, A., Ahmed, D., Giacobbe, M., Peruffo, A.: Formal synthesis of Lyapunov neural networks. IEEE Control. Syst. Lett. **5**(3), 773–778 (2021). https://doi.org/10.1109/LCSYS.2020.3005328
2. Abate, A., Giacobbe, M., Roy, D.: Learning probabilistic termination proofs. In: Silva, A., Leino, K.R.M. (eds.) CAV 2021. LNCS, vol. 12760, pp. 3–26. Springer, Cham (2021). https://doi.org/10.1007/978-3-030-81688-9_1
3. Achiam, J., Held, D., Tamar, A., Abbeel, P.: Constrained policy optimization. In: International Conference on Machine Learning, pp. 22–31. PMLR (2017)
4. Altman, E.: Constrained Markov Decision Processes, vol. 7. CRC Press (1999)
5. Amodei, D., Olah, C., Steinhardt, J., Christiano, P.F., Schulman, J., Mané, D.: Concrete problems in AI safety. CoRR abs/1606.06565 (2016). https://arxiv.org/abs/1606.06565
6. Ansaripour, M., Chatterjee, K., Henzinger, T.A., Lechner, M., Zikelic, D.: Learning provably stabilizing neural controllers for discrete-time stochastic systems. CoRR abs/2210.05304 (2022). https://doi.org/10.48550/arXiv.2210.05304
7. Badings, T.S., et al.: Robust control for dynamical systems with non-gaussian noise via formal abstractions. J. Artif. Intell. Res. **76**, 341–391 (2023). https://doi.org/10.1613/jair.1.14253
8. Berkenkamp, F., Turchetta, M., Schoellig, A.P., Krause, A.: Safe model-based reinforcement learning with stability guarantees. In: Guyon, I., et al. (eds.) Advances in Neural Information Processing Systems 30: Annual Conference on Neural Information Processing Systems 2017, Long Beach, CA, USA, 4–9 December 2017, pp. 908–918 (2017). https://proceedings.neurips.cc/paper/2017/hash/766ebcd59621e305170616ba3d3dac32-Abstract.html

9. Brockman, G., et al.: OpenAI gym. arXiv preprint arXiv:1606.01540 (2016)
10. Cauchi, N., Abate, A.: Stochy-automated verification and synthesis of stochastic processes. In: Proceedings of the 22nd ACM International Conference on Hybrid Systems: Computation and Control, pp. 258–259 (2019)
11. Chakarov, A., Sankaranarayanan, S.: Probabilistic program analysis with martingales. In: Sharygina, N., Veith, H. (eds.) CAV 2013. LNCS, vol. 8044, pp. 511–526. Springer, Heidelberg (2013). https://doi.org/10.1007/978-3-642-39799-8_34
12. Chakarov, A., Voronin, Y.-L., Sankaranarayanan, S.: Deductive proofs of almost sure persistence and recurrence properties. In: Chechik, M., Raskin, J.-F. (eds.) TACAS 2016. LNCS, vol. 9636, pp. 260–279. Springer, Heidelberg (2016). https://doi.org/10.1007/978-3-662-49674-9_15
13. Chang, E., Manna, Z., Pnueli, A.: Characterization of temporal property classes. In: Kuich, W. (ed.) ICALP 1992. LNCS, vol. 623, pp. 474–486. Springer, Heidelberg (1992). https://doi.org/10.1007/3-540-55719-9_97
14. Chang, Y., Gao, S.: Stabilizing neural control using self-learned almost Lyapunov critics. In: IEEE International Conference on Robotics and Automation, ICRA 2021, Xi'an, China, 30 May–5 June 2021, pp. 1803–1809. IEEE (2021). https://doi.org/10.1109/ICRA48506.2021.9560886
15. Chang, Y., Roohi, N., Gao, S.: Neural Lyapunov control. In: Wallach, H.M., Larochelle, H., Beygelzimer, A., d'Alché-Buc, F., Fox, E.B., Garnett, R. (eds.) Advances in Neural Information Processing Systems 32: Annual Conference on Neural Information Processing Systems 2019, NeurIPS 2019, Vancouver, BC, Canada, 8–14 December 2019, pp. 3240–3249 (2019). https://proceedings.neurips.cc/paper/2019/hash/2647c1dba23bc0e0f9cdf75339e120d2-Abstract.html
16. Chatterjee, K., Fu, H., Goharshady, A.K.: Termination analysis of probabilistic programs through Positivstellensatz's. In: Chaudhuri, S., Farzan, A. (eds.) CAV 2016. LNCS, vol. 9779, pp. 3–22. Springer, Cham (2016). https://doi.org/10.1007/978-3-319-41528-4_1
17. Chatterjee, K., Fu, H., Novotný, P., Hasheminezhad, R.: Algorithmic analysis of qualitative and quantitative termination problems for affine probabilistic programs. In: Bodík, R., Majumdar, R. (eds.) Proceedings of the 43rd Annual ACM SIGPLAN-SIGACT Symposium on Principles of Programming Languages, POPL 2016, St. Petersburg, FL, USA, 20–22 January 2016, pp. 327–342. ACM (2016). https://doi.org/10.1145/2837614.2837639
18. Chatterjee, K., Goharshady, A.K., Meggendorfer, T., Zikelic, D.: Sound and complete certificates for quantitative termination analysis of probabilistic programs. In: Shoham, S., Vizel, Y. (eds.) CAV 2022. LNCS, vol. 13371, pp. 55–78. Springer, Cham (2022). https://doi.org/10.1007/978-3-031-13185-1_4
19. Chatterjee, K., Goharshady, E.K., Novotný, P., Zárevúcky, J., Žikelić, Đ: On lexicographic proof rules for probabilistic termination. In: Huisman, M., Păsăreanu, C., Zhan, N. (eds.) FM 2021. LNCS, vol. 13047, pp. 619–639. Springer, Cham (2021). https://doi.org/10.1007/978-3-030-90870-6_33
20. Chatterjee, K., Novotný, P., Zikelic, D.: Stochastic invariants for probabilistic termination. In: Castagna, G., Gordon, A.D. (eds.) Proceedings of the 44th ACM SIGPLAN Symposium on Principles of Programming Languages, POPL 2017, Paris, France, 18–20 January 2017, pp. 145–160. ACM (2017). https://doi.org/10.1145/3009837.3009873
21. Chow, Y., Nachum, O., Duénez-Guzmán, E.A., Ghavamzadeh, M.: A Lyapunov-based approach to safe reinforcement learning. In: Bengio, S., Wallach, H.M., Larochelle, H., Grauman, K., Cesa-Bianchi, N., Garnett, R. (eds.) Advances in

Neural Information Processing Systems 31: Annual Conference on Neural Information Processing Systems 2018, NeurIPS 2018, Montréal, Canada, 3–8 December 2018, pp. 8103–8112 (2018). https://proceedings.neurips.cc/paper/2018/hash/4fe5149039b52765bde64beb9f674940-Abstract.html

22. Cousot, P., Cousot, R.: Abstract interpretation: a unified lattice model for static analysis of programs by construction or approximation of fixpoints. In: Graham, R.M., Harrison, M.A., Sethi, R. (eds.) Conference Record of the Fourth ACM Symposium on Principles of Programming Languages, Los Angeles, California, USA, January 1977, pp. 238–252. ACM (1977). https://doi.org/10.1145/512950.512973

23. Crespo, L.G., Sun, J.: Stochastic optimal control via Bellman's principle. Automatica 39(12), 2109–2114 (2003). https://doi.org/10.1016/S0005-1098(03)00238-3

24. Dalal, G., Dvijotham, K., Vecerík, M., Hester, T., Paduraru, C., Tassa, Y.: Safe exploration in continuous action spaces. arXiv abs/1801.08757 (2018)

25. García, J., Fernández, F.: A comprehensive survey on safe reinforcement learning. J. Mach. Learn. Res. 16, 1437–1480 (2015). https://dl.acm.org/citation.cfm?id=2886795

26. Geibel, P.: Reinforcement learning for MDPs with constraints. In: Fürnkranz, J., Scheffer, T., Spiliopoulou, M. (eds.) ECML 2006. LNCS (LNAI), vol. 4212, pp. 646–653. Springer, Heidelberg (2006). https://doi.org/10.1007/11871842_63

27. Gowal, S., et al.: On the effectiveness of interval bound propagation for training verifiably robust models. CoRR abs/1810.12715 (2018). https://arxiv.org/abs/1810.12715

28. Henrion, D., Garulli, A.: Positive Polynomials in Control, vol. 312. Springer, Heidelberg (2005)

29. Jin, W., Wang, Z., Yang, Z., Mou, S.: Neural certificates for safe control policies. CoRR abs/2006.08465 (2020). https://arxiv.org/abs/2006.08465

30. Katz, G., Barrett, C., Dill, D.L., Julian, K., Kochenderfer, M.J.: Reluplex: an efficient SMT solver for verifying deep neural networks. In: Majumdar, R., Kunčak, V. (eds.) CAV 2017. LNCS, vol. 10426, pp. 97–117. Springer, Cham (2017). https://doi.org/10.1007/978-3-319-63387-9_5

31. Khalil, H.: Nonlinear Systems. Pearson Education, Prentice Hall (2002)

32. Koller, T., Berkenkamp, F., Turchetta, M., Krause, A.: Learning-based model predictive control for safe exploration. In: 2018 IEEE Conference on Decision and Control (CDC), pp. 6059–6066 (2018)

33. Kushner, H.J.: On the stability of stochastic dynamical systems. Proc. Natl. Acad. Sci. U.S.A. 53(1), 8 (1965)

34. Kushner, H.J.: A partial history of the early development of continuous-time nonlinear stochastic systems theory. Automatica 50(2), 303–334 (2014). https://doi.org/10.1016/j.automatica.2013.10.013

35. Lavaei, A., Khaled, M., Soudjani, S., Zamani, M.: AMYTISS: parallelized automated controller synthesis for large-scale stochastic systems. In: Lahiri, S.K., Wang, C. (eds.) CAV 2020. LNCS, vol. 12225, pp. 461–474. Springer, Cham (2020). https://doi.org/10.1007/978-3-030-53291-8_24

36. Lechner, M., Zikelic, D., Chatterjee, K., Henzinger, T.A.: Infinite time horizon safety of Bayesian neural networks. In: Ranzato, M., Beygelzimer, A., Dauphin, Y.N., Liang, P., Vaughan, J.W. (eds.) Advances in Neural Information Processing Systems 34: Annual Conference on Neural Information Processing Systems 2021, NeurIPS 2021, 6–14 December 2021, Virtual, pp. 10171–10185 (2021). https://proceedings.neurips.cc/paper/2021/hash/544defa9fddff50c53b71c43e0da72be-Abstract.html

37. Lechner, M., Zikelic, D., Chatterjee, K., Henzinger, T.A.: Stability verification in stochastic control systems via neural network supermartingales. In: Thirty-Sixth AAAI Conference on Artificial Intelligence, AAAI 2022, Thirty-Fourth Conference on Innovative Applications of Artificial Intelligence, IAAI 2022, The Twelveth Symposium on Educational Advances in Artificial Intelligence, EAAI 2022 Virtual Event, 22 February–1 March 2022, pp. 7326–7336. AAAI Press (2022). https://ojs.aaai.org/index.php/AAAI/article/view/20695

38. Liu, A., Shi, G., Chung, S.J., Anandkumar, A., Yue, Y.: Robust regression for safe exploration in control. In: L4DC (2020)

39. Murphy, K.P.: Machine Learning - A Probabilistic Perspective. Adaptive Computation and Machine Learning Series. MIT Press (2012)

40. Parrilo, P.A.: Structured semidefinite programs and semialgebraic geometry methods in robustness and optimization. California Institute of Technology (2000)

41. Puterman, M.L.: Markov Decision Processes: Discrete Stochastic Dynamic Programming. Wiley Series in Probability and Statistics. Wiley (1994). https://doi.org/10.1002/9780470316887

42. Richards, S.M., Berkenkamp, F., Krause, A.: The Lyapunov neural network: adaptive stability certification for safe learning of dynamical systems. In: 2nd Annual Conference on Robot Learning, CoRL 2018, Zürich, Switzerland, 29–31 October 2018, Proceedings. Proceedings of Machine Learning Research, vol. 87, pp. 466–476. PMLR (2018). https://proceedings.mlr.press/v87/richards18a.html

43. Sälzer, M., Lange, M.: Reachability is NP-complete even for the simplest neural networks. In: Bell, P.C., Totzke, P., Potapov, I. (eds.) RP 2021. LNCS, vol. 13035, pp. 149–164. Springer, Cham (2021). https://doi.org/10.1007/978-3-030-89716-1_10

44. Schulman, J., Wolski, F., Dhariwal, P., Radford, A., Klimov, O.: Proximal policy optimization algorithms. arXiv preprint arXiv:1707.06347 (2017)

45. Soudjani, S.E.Z., Gevaerts, C., Abate, A.: FAUST^2: formal abstractions of uncountable-state stochastic processes. In: Baier, C., Tinelli, C. (eds.) TACAS 2015. LNCS, vol. 9035, pp. 272–286. Springer, Heidelberg (2015). https://doi.org/10.1007/978-3-662-46681-0_23

46. Sutton, R.S., Barto, A.G.: Reinforcement Learning: An Introduction. MIT Press, Cambridge (2018)

47. Szegedy, C., et al.: Intriguing properties of neural networks. In: Bengio, Y., LeCun, Y. (eds.) 2nd International Conference on Learning Representations, ICLR 2014, Banff, AB, Canada, 14–16 April 2014, Conference Track Proceedings (2014). https://arxiv.org/abs/1312.6199

48. Takisaka, T., Oyabu, Y., Urabe, N., Hasuo, I.: Ranking and repulsing supermartingales for reachability in randomized programs. ACM Trans. Program. Lang. Syst. **43**(2), 5:1–5:46 (2021). https://doi.org/10.1145/3450967

49. Turchetta, M., Berkenkamp, F., Krause, A.: Safe exploration for interactive machine learning. In: NeurIPS (2019)

50. Uchibe, E., Doya, K.: Constrained reinforcement learning from intrinsic and extrinsic rewards. In: 2007 IEEE 6th International Conference on Development and Learning, pp. 163–168. IEEE (2007)

51. Vaidya, U.: Stochastic stability analysis of discrete-time system using Lyapunov measure. In: American Control Conference, ACC 2015, Chicago, IL, USA, 1–3 July 2015, pp. 4646–4651. IEEE (2015). https://doi.org/10.1109/ACC.2015.7172061

52. Van Huijgevoort, B., Schön, O., Soudjani, S., Haesaert, S.: SySCoRe: synthesis via stochastic coupling relations. In: Proceedings of the 26th ACM International Conference on Hybrid Systems: Computation and Control, HSCC 2023. Association for Computing Machinery (2023). https://doi.org/10.1145/3575870.3587123

53. Vinod, A.P., Gleason, J.D., Oishi, M.M.K.: SReachTools: a MATLAB stochastic reachability toolbox. In: Ozay, N., Prabhakar, P. (eds.) Proceedings of the 22nd ACM International Conference on Hybrid Systems: Computation and Control, HSCC 2019, Montreal, QC, Canada, 16–18 April 2019, pp. 33–38. ACM (2019). https://doi.org/10.1145/3302504.3311809

54. Williams, D.: Probability with Martingales. Cambridge Mathematical Textbooks. Cambridge University Press (1991)

55. Zikelic, D., Lechner, M., Chatterjee, K., Henzinger, T.A.: Learning stabilizing policies in stochastic control systems. CoRR abs/2205.11991 (2022). https://doi.org/10.48550/arXiv.2205.11991

56. Zikelic, D., Lechner, M., Henzinger, T.A., Chatterjee, K.: Learning control policies for stochastic systems with reach-avoid guarantees. In: Proceedings of the AAAI Conference on Artificial Intelligence, vol. 37, no. 10, pp. 11926–11935 (2023). https://doi.org/10.1609/aaai.v37i10.26407

An Automata-Theoretic Approach to Synthesizing Binarized Neural Networks

Ye Tao[1], Wanwei Liu[1]($\boxtimes$), Fu Song[2,3,4], Zhen Liang[5], Ji Wang[5], and Hongxu Zhu[1]

[1] College of Computer Science and Technology,
National University of Defense Technology, Changsha, China
{taoye0117,wwliu,zhuhongxu}@nudt.edu.cn

[2] School of Information Science and Technology, ShanghaiTech University,
Shanghai, China
songfu@shanghaitech.edu.cn

[3] Institute of Software, Chinese Academy of Sciences and University of Chinese
Academy of Sciences, Beijing, China

[4] Automotive Software Innovation Center, Shanghai, China

[5] Institute for Quantum Information and State Key Laboratory for High Performance
Computing, National University of Defense Technology, Changsha, China
{liangzhen,wj}@nudt.edu.cn

Abstract. Deep neural networks, (DNNs, a.k.a. NNs), have been widely used in various tasks and have been proven to be successful. However, the accompanied expensive computing and storage costs make the deployments in resource-constrained devices a significant concern. To solve this issue, quantization has emerged as an effective way to reduce the costs of DNNs with little accuracy degradation by quantizing floating-point numbers to low-width fixed-point representations. Quantized neural networks (QNNs) have been developed, with binarized neural networks (BNNs) restricted to binary values as a special case. Another concern about neural networks is their vulnerability and lack of interpretability. Despite the active research on trustworthy of DNNs, few approaches have been proposed to QNNs. To this end, this paper presents an automata-theoretic approach to synthesizing BNNs that meet designated properties. More specifically, we define a temporal logic, called BLTL, as the specification language. We show that each BLTL formula can be transformed into an automaton on finite words. To deal with the state-explosion problem, we provide a tableau-based approach in real implementation. For the synthesis procedure, we utilize SMT solvers to detect the existence of a model (i.e., a BNN) in the construction process. Notably, synthesis provides a way to determine the hyper-parameters of the network before training. Moreover, we experimentally evaluate our approach and demonstrate its effectiveness in improving the individual fairness and local robustness of BNNs while maintaining accuracy to a great extent.

É. André and J. Sun (Eds.): ATVA 2023, LNCS 14215, pp. 380–400, 2023.
https://doi.org/10.1007/978-3-031-45329-8_18

1 Introduction

Deep Neural Networks (DNNs) are increasingly used in a variety of applications, from image recognition to autonomous driving, due to their high accuracy in classification and prediction tasks [27, 30]. However, two critical challenges emerge, high-cost and a lack of trustworthiness, that impede their further development.

On the one hand, a modern DNN typically contains a large number of parameters which are typically stored as 32-bit floating-point numbers (e.g., GPT-4 contains about 100 trillion parameters [14]), thus an inference often demands more than a billion floating-point operations. As a result, deploying a modern DNN requires huge computing and storage resources, thus it is challenging for resource-constrained embedding devices. To tackle this issue, quantization has been introduced, which compresses a network by converting floating-point numbers to low-width fixed-point representations, so that it can significantly reduce both memory and computing costs using fixed-point arithmetic with a relatively small side-effect on the network's accuracy [23].

On the other hand, neural networks are known to be vulnerable to input perturbations, namely, slight input disturbance may dramatically change their output [3–7, 12, 28, 36]. In addition, NNs are often treated as black box [17], and we are truly dearth of understanding of the decision-making process inside the "box". As a result, a natural concern is whether NNs can be trustworthy, especially in some safety-critical scenarios, where erroneous behaviors might lead to serious consequences. One promising way to tackle this problem is formal verification, which defines properties that we expect the network to satisfy and rigorously checks whether the network meets our expectations. Numerous verification approaches have been proposed recently aiming at this purpose [17]. Nevertheless, these approaches in general ignore rounding errors in quantized computations, making them unable to apply for quantized neural networks (QNNs). It has been demonstrated that specifications that hold for a floating-point numbered DNN may not necessarily hold after quantizing the inputs and/or parameters of the DNN [3, 13]. For instance, a DNN that is robust to given input perturbations might become non-robust after quantization. Compared to DNN verification [15, 17–21, 37], verifying QNN is truly a more challenging and less explored problem. Evidences show that the verification problem for QNNs is harder than DNNs [16], and only few works are specialized for verifying QNNs [1, 8, 13, 16, 24, 26, 32–35].

In this paper, we concentrate on BNNs (i.e., binarized neural networks), a special type of QNN. Although formal verification has been the primary explored approach to verifying (quantized) neural networks, we pursue another promising line, synthesizing the expected binarized neural networks directly. In other words, we aim to construct a neural network that satisfies the expected properties we specify, rather than verifying an existing network's compliance with those properties. To achieve this, we first propose, BLTL, an extension of LTL_f (namely, LTL defined on finite words), as the specification language. This logic can conveniently describe data-related properties of BNNs. We then provide an approach to converting a BLTL formula to an equivalent automaton. The synthesis task is then boiled down to find a path from an initial state to an accepting state in the automaton.

Unfortunately, such a method suffers from the state-exploration problem. To mitigate this issue, we observe that it is not necessary to synthesize the entire BNN since the desired properties are only related to some specific hyper-parameters of the network. To this end, we propose a tableau-based approach: To judge whether a path is successfully detected, we check the satisfiability of the associated BLTL formulas, and convert the problem into an IDL-solving problem, which can be efficiently solved. Besides, we prove the existence of a tracing-back threshold, which allows us to do backtracking earlier to avoid doing trace searching that is unlikely to lead to a solution. The solution given by the solver provides the hyper-parameters of the BNN, including the length of the network and crucial input-output relations of blocks. Afterwards, one can perform a block-wise training to obtain a desired BNN.

We implement a prototype synthesizing tool and evaluate our approach on local robustness and individual fairness. The experiments demonstrate that our approach can effectively improve the network's reliability compared to the baseline, especially for individual fairness.

The main contributions of this work are summarized as follows:

- We present a new temporal logic, called BLTL, for describing properties of BNNs, and provide an approach to transforming BLTL formulas into equivalent finite-state automata.
- We propose an automata-theoretic synthesis approach that determines the hyper-parameters of a BNN model before training.
- We implement a prototype synthesis tool and evaluate the effectiveness on two concerning properties, demonstrating the feasibility of our method.

Related Work. For BNNs, several verification approaches have been proposed. Earlier work reduces the BNN verification problem to hardware verification (i.e., verifying combinatorial circuits), for which SAT solvers are harnessed [8]. Following this line, [24] proposes a direct encoding from the BNN verification problem into the SAT problem. [25] studies the effect of BNN architectures on the performance of SAT solvers and uses this information to train SAT-friendly BNNs. [1] provides a framework for approximately quantitative verification of BNNs with PAC-style guarantees via approximate SAT model counting. Another line of BNN verification encodes a BNN and its input region into a binary decision diagram (BDD), and then one can verify some properties of the network by analyzing BDD. [26] proposes an Angluin-style learning algorithm to compile a BNN on a given input region into a BDD, and utilize a SAT solver as an equivalence oracle to query. [33] has developed a more efficient BDD-based quantitative verification framework by exploiting the internal structure of BNNs. Few work has been dedicated to QNN verification so far. [13] shows that the properties guaranteed by the DNN are not preserved after quantization. To resolve this issue, they introduce an approach to verifying QNNs by using SMT solvers in bit-vector theory. Later, [16] proves that verifying QNN with bit-vector specifications is **PSPACE**-Hard. More recently, [32,35] reduce the verification problem into integer linear constraint solving which are significantly more efficient than the SMT-based one.

Outline. The rest of the paper is organized as follows: In Sect. 2, we introduce preliminaries. We present the specification language BLTL in Sect. 3. In Sect. 4, we show how to translate a BLTL formula into an equivalent automaton, which is the basic of tableau-based approach for synthesis, and technical details are given in Sect. 5. The proposed approach is implemented and evaluated in Sect. 6. We conclude the paper in Sect. 7.

2   Preliminaries

We denote by $\mathbb{R}$, $\mathbb{N}$, and $\mathbb{B}$ the set of real numbers, natural numbers, and Boolean domain $\{0, 1\}$, respectively. We use $\mathbb{R}^n$ and $\mathbb{B}^n$ to denote the set of real number vectors and binary vectors with n elements, respectively. For $n \in \mathbb{N}$, let $[n]$ be the set $\{0, 1, 2, \ldots, n-1\}$. We will interchangeably use the terminologies 0–1 vector and binary vector in this paper. For a binary vector $\boldsymbol{b}$, we use $\mathsf{dec}(\boldsymbol{b})$ to denote its corresponding decimal number, and conversely let $\mathsf{bin}(d)$ be the corresponding binary vector which encodes the number d. For example, let $\boldsymbol{b} = (0, 1, 1)^\mathrm{T}$, then we have $\mathsf{dec}(\boldsymbol{b}) = 3$. Note that $\mathsf{bin}(\mathsf{dec}(\boldsymbol{b})) = \boldsymbol{b}$ and $\mathsf{dec}(\mathsf{bin}(d)) = d$. For two binary vectors $\boldsymbol{a} = (a_0, \ldots, a_{n-1})^\mathrm{T}$ and $\boldsymbol{b} = (b_0, \ldots, b_{n-1})^\mathrm{T}$ with the same length, we denote by $\boldsymbol{a} \sim \boldsymbol{b}$ if $a_i \sim b_i$ for all $i \in [n]$, otherwise $\boldsymbol{a} \not\sim \boldsymbol{b}$, where $\sim \in \{>, \geq, <, \leq, =\}$. Note that $\boldsymbol{a} \neq \boldsymbol{b}$ if $a_i \neq b_i$ for some $i \in [n]$.

A (vectorized) Boolean function takes a 0–1 vector as input and returns another 0–1 vector. Hence, it is essentially a mapping from integers to integers when each 0–1 vector $\boldsymbol{b}$ is viewed as an integer $\mathsf{dec}(\boldsymbol{b})$. We denote by $\boldsymbol{I}_n$ the identity function such that $\boldsymbol{I}_n(\boldsymbol{b}) = \boldsymbol{b}$, for any $\boldsymbol{b} \in \mathbb{B}^n$, where the subscript n may be dropped when it is clear from the context. We use *composition* operation $\circ$ to represent the function composition among Boolean functions.

A *binarized neural network* (BNN) is a feed-forward neural network, composed of several internal blocks and one output block [26,33]. Each internal block is comprised of 3 layers and can be viewed as a mapping $f : \{-1, 1\}^n \to \{-1, 1\}^m$. Slightly different from internal blocks, the output block outputs the classification label to which the highest activation corresponds, thus, can be seen as a mapping $\mathsf{out} : \{-1, 1\}^n \to \mathbb{R}^p$, where p is the number of classification labels of the network.

Since the binary values -1 and $+1$ can be represented as their Boolean counterparts 0 and 1 respectively, each internal block can be viewed as a Boolean function $f : \mathbb{B}^n \to \mathbb{B}^m$ [33]. Therefore, ignoring the slight difference in the output block, an n-block BNN $\mathcal{N}$ can be encoded via a series of Boolean functions $f_i : \mathbb{B}^{\ell_i} \to \mathbb{B}^{\ell_{i+1}}$ ($i = 0, 1, \ldots, n-1$), and $\mathcal{N}$ works as the combination of these Boolean functions, namely, it corresponds to the function,

$$f_{\mathcal{N}} = f_{n-1} \circ f_{n-2} \circ \cdots \circ f_1 \circ f_0.$$

Integer difference logic (IDL) is a fragment of linear integer arithmetic, in which atomic formulas must be of the form $x - y \sim c$ where x and y are integer variables, and c is an integer constant, $\sim\in\{\le,\ge,<,>,=,\ne\}$. All these atomic formulas can be transformed into constraints of the form $x - y \le c$ [2]. For example, $x - y = c$ can be transformed into $x - y \le c \wedge x - y \ge c$.

The task of an IDL-problem is to check the satisfiability of an IDL formula in conjunctive normal form (CNF)

$$(x_1 - y_1 \le c_1) \wedge \cdots \wedge (x_n - y_n \le c_n),$$

which can be in general converted into the cycle detection problem in a weighted, directed graph with $O(n)$ nodes and $O(n)$ edges, and solved by e.g., Bellman-Ford or Dijkstra's algorithm, in $O(n^2)$ time [22]. IDL can be generalized to Boolean combinations of atomic formulas of the form $x - y \sim c$.

3   The Temporal Logic BLTL

3.1   Syntax and Semantics of BLTL

Let us fix a signature Σ, consisting of a set of desired Boolean functions and 0-1 vectors. Particularly, let Σ_V be the subset of Σ containing only 0-1 vectors.

Terms of BLTL are described via BNF as follows:

$$t ::= \boldsymbol{b} \mid f(t) \mid \triangleright^k t$$

where $\boldsymbol{b} \in \Sigma_V$ is a 0-1 vector, called *vector constant*, $f \in \Sigma \setminus \Sigma_V$ is a Boolean function, and $k \in \mathbb{N}$ is a constant, and $\triangleright^k$ in $\triangleright^k t$ denotes k placeholders for k consecutive blocks of a BNN (i.e., k Boolean functions) to be applied onto the term t. We remark that $\triangleright^0 t = t$.

BLTL formulas are given via the following grammar:

$$\psi ::= \top \mid t \sim t \mid \neg\psi \mid \psi \vee \psi \mid \mathsf{X}\psi \mid \psi\mathsf{U}\psi$$

where $\sim\in\{\le,\ge,<,>,=\}$, X is the *Next* operator and U is the *Until* operator.

We define the following derived Boolean operators, quantifiers with finite domain, and temporal operators:

$$\psi_1 \wedge \psi_2 \overset{\text{def}}{=} \neg(\neg\psi_1 \vee \neg\psi_2) \qquad\qquad \mathsf{F}\psi \overset{\text{def}}{=} \top\mathsf{U}\psi \qquad\qquad \mathsf{G}\psi \overset{\text{def}}{=} \neg\mathsf{F}\neg\psi$$

$$\psi_1 \to \psi_2 \overset{\text{def}}{=} (\neg\psi_1) \vee \psi_2 \qquad\qquad \psi_1\mathsf{R}\psi_2 \overset{\text{def}}{=} \neg(\neg\psi_1\mathsf{U}\neg\psi_2) \qquad \overline{\mathsf{X}}\psi \overset{\text{def}}{=} \neg\mathsf{X}\neg\psi$$

$$\forall \boldsymbol{x} \in \mathbb{B}^k.\psi \overset{\text{def}}{=} \bigwedge_{\boldsymbol{b}\in\mathbb{B}^k\cap\Sigma_V} \psi[\boldsymbol{x}/\boldsymbol{b}] \qquad\qquad \exists \boldsymbol{x} \in \mathbb{B}^k.\psi \overset{\text{def}}{=} \neg\forall\boldsymbol{x} \in \mathbb{B}^k.\neg\psi$$

where $\psi[\boldsymbol{x}/\boldsymbol{b}]$ denotes the BLTL formula obtained from ψ by replacing each occurrence of $\boldsymbol{x}$ with $\boldsymbol{b}$.

The semantics of BLTL formulas is defined w.r.t. a BNN $\mathcal{N}$ given by the composition of Boolean functions $f_\mathcal{N} = f_{n-1} \circ f_{n-2} \circ \cdots \circ f_1 \circ f_0$, and a position $i \in \mathbb{N}$. We first define the semantics of terms, which is given by the function $[\![\bullet]\!]_{\mathcal{N},i}$, inductively:

- $[\![\boldsymbol{b}]\!]_{\mathcal{N},i} = \boldsymbol{b}$ for each vector constant $\boldsymbol{b}$;

- $[\![f(t)]\!]_{\mathcal{N},i} = f([\![t]\!]_{\mathcal{N},i});$
- $[\![\triangleright^k t]\!]_{\mathcal{N},i} = \begin{cases} (f_{i+\mathsf{slen}(t)+k-1} \circ \cdots \circ f_{i+\mathsf{slen}(t)})([\![t]\!]_{\mathcal{N},i}), & \text{if } k \geq 1; \\ [\![t]\!]_{\mathcal{N},i}, & \text{if } k = 0; \end{cases}$

where f_i is the identity Boolean function $\boldsymbol{I}$ if $i \geq n$, $\mathsf{slen}(\boldsymbol{b}) = 0$, $\mathsf{slen}(f(t)) = \mathsf{slen}(t) + 1$ and $\mathsf{slen}(\triangleright^k t) = \mathsf{slen}(t) + k$.

Note that we assume the widths of Boolean functions and their argument vectors are compatible.

Proposition 1. *We have:* $[\![\triangleright^k \triangleright^{k'} t]\!]_{\mathcal{N},i} = [\![\triangleright^{k+k'} t]\!]_{\mathcal{N},i}.$

Subsequently, the semantics of BLTL formulas is characterized via the *satisfaction* relation $\models$, inductively:

- $\mathcal{N}, i \models \top$ always holds;
- $\mathcal{N}, i \models t_1 \sim t_2$ iff $[\![t_1]\!]_{\mathcal{N},i} \sim [\![t_2]\!]_{\mathcal{N},i}$;
- $\mathcal{N}, i \models \neg\varphi$ iff $\mathcal{N}, i \not\models \varphi$;
- $\mathcal{N}, i \models \varphi_1 \vee \varphi_2$ iff $\mathcal{N}, i \models \varphi_1$ or $\mathcal{N}, i \models \varphi_1$;
- $\mathcal{N}, i \models \mathsf{X}\psi$ iff $i < n - 1$ and $\mathcal{N}, i+1 \models \psi$;
- $\mathcal{N}, i \models \psi_1\mathsf{U}\psi_2$ iff there is j such that $i \leq j < n$, $\mathcal{N}, j \models \psi_2$ and $\mathcal{N}, k \models \psi_1$ for each $i \leq k < j$;

We may write $\mathcal{N} \models \psi$ in the case of $i = 0$. In the sequel, we denote by $\mathscr{L}(\psi)$ the set of BNNs $\{\mathcal{N} \mid \mathcal{N} \models \varphi\}$ for each formula φ, and denote by $\psi_1 \equiv \psi_2$ if $\mathcal{N}, i \models \psi_1 \Leftrightarrow \mathcal{N}, i \models \psi_2$ for every BNN $\mathcal{N}$ and i.

Proposition 2. *The following statements hold:*

1. $\mathsf{G}\psi \equiv \bot\mathsf{R}\psi;$
2. $\mathsf{F}\psi \equiv \psi \vee \mathsf{XF}\psi;$
3. $\mathsf{G}\psi \equiv \psi \wedge \overline{\mathsf{X}}\mathsf{G}\psi;$
4. $\psi_1\mathsf{U}\psi_2 \equiv \psi_2 \vee (\psi_1 \wedge \mathsf{X}(\psi_1\mathsf{U}\psi_2));$
5. $\psi_1\mathsf{R}\psi_2 \equiv \psi_2 \wedge (\psi_1 \vee \overline{\mathsf{X}}(\psi_1\mathsf{R}\psi_2)).$

For a BLTL formula φ and a BNN $\mathcal{N}$, the *model checking* problem w.r.t. φ and $\mathcal{N}$ is to decide whether $\mathcal{N} \models \varphi$ holds.

With the above derived operators, together with the patterns $\neg\neg\psi \equiv \psi$ and $\neg(t_1 \sim t_2) \equiv t_1 \not\sim t_2$, BLTL formulas can be transformed into *negation normal form* (NNF) by pushing the negations ($\neg$) inward, till no the negations are involved. Given two sets of formulas Γ and Γ' in NNF, we say that Γ' is a *proper closure* of Γ, if the following conditions hold:

- $\Gamma \subseteq \Gamma'$.
- $\psi_1 \wedge \psi_2 \in \Gamma'$ implies that both $\psi_1 \in \Gamma'$ and $\psi_2 \in \Gamma'$.
- $\psi_1 \vee \psi_2 \in \Gamma'$ implies that either $\psi_1 \in \Gamma'$ or $\psi_2 \in \Gamma'$.
- $\psi_1\mathsf{U}\psi_2 \in \Gamma'$ implies $\psi_2 \vee (\psi_1 \wedge \mathsf{X}(\psi_1\mathsf{U}\psi_2)) \in \Gamma'$.
- $\psi_1\mathsf{R}\psi_2 \in \Gamma'$ implies $\psi_2 \wedge (\psi_1 \vee \overline{\mathsf{X}}(\psi_1\mathsf{R}\psi_2)) \in \Gamma'$.

We denote by $\mathsf{Cl}(\Gamma)$ the set consisting of all proper closures of Γ (note that $\mathsf{Cl}(\Gamma)$ is a family of formula sets.) We also denote by $\mathsf{Sub}(\psi)$ the set of the subformulas of ψ except that

- if $\psi_1\mathsf{U}\psi_2 \in \mathsf{Sub}(\psi)$, then $\psi_2 \vee (\psi_1 \wedge \mathsf{X}(\psi_1\mathsf{U}\psi_2)) \in \mathsf{Sub}(\psi)$;
- if $\psi_1\mathsf{R}\psi_2 \in \mathsf{Sub}(\psi)$, then $\psi_2 \wedge (\psi_1 \vee \overline{\mathsf{X}}(\psi_1\mathsf{R}\psi_2)) \in \mathsf{Sub}(\psi)$.

3.2   Illustrating Properties Expressed by BLTL

In this section, we demonstrate the expressiveness of BLTL. Since BLTL has the ability to express Boolean logic and arithmetic operations, we can see that many concerning properties can be specified using BLTL.

We can partition a vector into segments of varying widths, and then define a Boolean function, denoted by e_i, to extract the i-th segment with width of n, namely, $e_i : \mathbb{B}^m \to \mathbb{B}^n$, where m is the width of vector $\boldsymbol{b}$. We use $\boldsymbol{b}[i]$ to refer to $e_i(\boldsymbol{b})$ in the case that $e_i(\boldsymbol{b}) \in \mathbb{B}$.

Local Robustness. Given a BNN $\mathcal{N}$ and a n-width input $\boldsymbol{u}$, $\mathcal{N}$ is robust w.r.t. $\boldsymbol{u}$, if all inputs in the region $B(\boldsymbol{u}, \epsilon)$, are classified into the same class as $\boldsymbol{u}$ [1]. Here, we consider $B(\boldsymbol{u}, \epsilon)$ as the set of vectors that differ from $\boldsymbol{u}$ in at most ϵ positions, where ϵ is the maximum number of positions at which the values differ from those of $\boldsymbol{u}$. The local robustness can be described as follows:

$$\forall \boldsymbol{x} \in \mathbb{B}^n. \sum_{i=1}^{|\boldsymbol{u}|} (\boldsymbol{x}[i] \oplus \boldsymbol{u}[i]) \leq \epsilon \to \mathcal{N}(\boldsymbol{x}) = \mathcal{N}(\boldsymbol{u})$$

Individual Fairness. In the context of a BNN $\mathcal{N}$ with an input of t attributes and n-width, where the s-th attribute is considered sensitive, $\mathcal{N}$ is fair w.r.t the s-th attribute, when no two input vectors in its domain differ only in the value of the s-th attribute and yield different outputs [31,38]. The individual fairness can be formulated as:

$$\forall \boldsymbol{a}, \boldsymbol{b} \in \mathbb{B}^n. (\neg (e_s(\boldsymbol{a}) = e_s(\boldsymbol{b})) \wedge \forall i \in [t] - \{s\}.e_i(\boldsymbol{a}) = e_i(\boldsymbol{b})) \to \mathcal{N}(\boldsymbol{a}) = \mathcal{N}(\boldsymbol{b})$$

where e_i denotes the extraction of the i-th attribute, $\mathbb{B}^n$ is the domain of $\mathcal{N}$, and $\boldsymbol{a}$, $\boldsymbol{b}$ are input vectors.

In practice, it is possible to select inputs in the $\mathbb{B}^n$, and modify the sensitive attribute to obtain the proper pairs, which only differ in the sensitive attribute. For any such pair $(\boldsymbol{b}, \boldsymbol{b}')$, we formulate the specification as $\mathcal{N}(\boldsymbol{b}) = \mathcal{N}(\boldsymbol{b}')$.

Specification for Internal Blocks. BLTL can specify block-level properties. For instance, the formula

$$\forall \boldsymbol{x} \in \mathbb{B}^4. \mathsf{F}(\boldsymbol{x} \geq \boldsymbol{a} \to \rhd \boldsymbol{x} = \boldsymbol{a})$$

states that there exists a block in the network that behaves as follows: for any 4-bit input whose value is greater than or equal to $\boldsymbol{a}$, the corresponding output is equal to $\boldsymbol{a}$.

4   From BLTL to Automata

In this section, we present both an explicit and an implicit construction that translate a BLTL formula into an equivalent finite-state automaton. We first show how to eliminate the placeholders $\rhd^k$ in terms $\rhd^k t$ and atomic formulas $t_1 \sim t_2$.

4.1   Eliminating Placeholders

To eliminate the placeholders $\rhd^k$ in terms $\rhd^k t$, we define the *apply operator* $[\,] : T \times \Sigma \setminus \Sigma_V \to T$, where T denotes the set of terms. $[t, f]$, written as $t[f]$, is called the *application* of the term t w.r.t. the Boolean function $f \in \Sigma$, which instantiates the innermost placeholder of the term t by the Boolean function f. Below, we give a formal description of the application.

Let us fix a term t. According to Proposition 1, t can be equivalently transformed into the following canonical form

$$\rhd^{\ell_k} g_{k-1} \left(\rhd^{\ell_{k-1}} g_{k-2} \left(\cdots g_0 \left(\rhd^{\ell_0} b \right) \cdots \right) \right)$$

where b is a vector constant, $\ell_0 \geq 0$ and $\ell_i > 0$ for each $i > 0$. Hereafter, we assume that t is in the canonical form, and let $\mathsf{len}(t) = \sum_{i=0}^{k} \ell_i$.

When t is $\rhd$-free, i.e., $\mathsf{len}(t) = 0$, we let $t[f] = t$. When $\mathsf{len}(t) > 0$, we say that the Boolean function $f \in \Sigma$ is *applicable* w.r.t. the term t, if:

1. $b \in \mathsf{dom}\, f$;
2. if $\ell_0 = 1$, then $\mathsf{ran}\, f = \mathsf{dom}\, g_0$.

Intuitively, the above two conditions ensure that $f(b)$ and $g_0 \circ f$ are well-defined.

If $f \in \Sigma$ is applicable w.r.t. the term t, we let $t[f]$ be the term:

$$t[f] = \begin{cases} \rhd^{\ell_k} g_{k-1} \left(\rhd^{\ell_{k-1}} g_{k-2} \left(\cdots g_0 \left(\rhd^{\ell_0 - 1} b' \right) \cdots \right) \right), & \text{if } \ell_0 > 1 \\ \rhd^{\ell_k} g_{k-1} \left(\rhd^{\ell_{k-1}} g_{k-2} \left(\cdots g_1 \left(\rhd^{\ell_1} b'' \right) \cdots \right) \right), & \text{if } \ell_0 = 1 \end{cases}$$

where $b' = f(b)$ and $b'' = (g_0 \circ f)(b)$.

It can be seen that $\mathsf{len}(t[f]) = \mathsf{len}(t) - 1$. By iteratively applying this operator, the placeholders $\rhd^k$ in the term t can be eliminated. For convenience, we write $t[f_0, f_1, \ldots, f_i]$ for the shorthand of

$$t[f_0][f_1] \cdots [f_i],$$

provided that each Boolean function f_i is applicable w.r.t. $t[f_0][f_1] \cdots [f_i]$. Likewise, we call $t[f_0, f_1, \ldots, f_i]$ the *application* of t w.r.t. the Boolean functions $f_0, f_1, \cdots, f_i$.

In particular, the *collapsion* of term t, denoted by $t \downarrow$, is the term $t[\underbrace{I, \ldots, I}_{\mathsf{len}(t)}]$, namely, $t \downarrow$ is obtained from t w.r.t. $\mathsf{len}(t)$ identity functions.

We hereafter denote by $\mathsf{Cons}(\Sigma)$ the set of constraints $t_1 \sim t_2$ over the signature Σ and lift the apply operator $[\,]$ from terms to atomic formulas $t_1 \sim t_2$. For a constraint $\gamma = t_1 \sim t_2 \in \mathsf{Cons}(\Sigma)$, we denote by $\gamma[f]$ the constraint $t_1[f] \sim t_2[f]$; and by $\gamma \downarrow$ the constraint $t_1 \downarrow \sim t_2 \downarrow$. Note that the former implicitly assumes that the Boolean function f is applicable w.r.t. both terms t_1 and t_2 (in this case, we call that f is applicable w.r.t. γ), whereas the latter requires that the terms $t_1 \downarrow$ and $t_2 \downarrow$ have the same width (we call that t_1 and t_2 are *compatible* w.r.t. collapsion). In addition, we let $\mathsf{len}(\gamma) = \max(\mathsf{len}(t_1), \mathsf{len}(t_2))$, and in the case that $\mathsf{len}(\gamma) = 0$, we let $\gamma[f] = \top$ (resp. $\gamma[f] = \bot$) for any Boolean function f if γ is evaluated to true (resp. false).

We subsequently extend the above notations to constraint sets. Suppose that $\Gamma \subseteq \mathsf{Cons}(\Sigma)$, we let $\Gamma[f] \overset{\text{def}}{=} \{\gamma[f] \mid \gamma \in \Gamma\}$, and let $\Gamma \downarrow \overset{\text{def}}{=} \{\gamma \downarrow \mid \gamma \in \Gamma\}$. Remind that the notation $\Gamma[f]$ makes sense only if the Boolean function f is *applicable* w.r.t. Γ, namely f is applicable w.r.t. each constraint $\gamma \in \Gamma$. Likewise, the notation $\Gamma \downarrow$ indicates that t_1 and t_2 is compatible w.r.t. collapse for each constraint $t_1 \sim t_2 \in \Gamma$.

Theorem 1. *For a BNN $\mathcal{N}$ given by $f_{\mathcal{N}} = f_{n-1} \circ f_{n-2} \circ \cdots \circ f_1 \circ f_0$, and a constraint $\gamma \in \mathsf{Cons}(\Sigma)$, we have:*

1. *$\mathcal{N}, i \models \gamma$ iff $\mathcal{N}, i+1 \models \gamma[f_i]$ for each $i < n$.*
2. *$\mathcal{N}, i \models \gamma$ iff $\mathcal{N}, i \models \gamma \downarrow$ for each $i \geq n$.*

Indeed, since $\gamma \downarrow$ must have the form $b_1 \sim b_2$, where both b_1 and b_2 are Boolean constants, then the truth value of $\gamma \downarrow$ can always be directly evaluated.

4.2   Automata Construction

Given a BLTL formula φ in NNF, we can construct a finite-state automaton $\mathcal{A}_\varphi = (Q_\varphi, \Sigma, \delta_\varphi, I_\varphi, F_\varphi)$, where:

- $Q_\varphi = \bigcup_{\Gamma \subseteq \mathsf{Sub}(\varphi)} \mathsf{Cl}(\Gamma)$. Recall that $\mathsf{Cl}(\Gamma) \subseteq 2^{\mathsf{Sub}(\varphi)}$ if $\Gamma \subseteq \mathsf{Sub}(\varphi)$, thus each state must be a subset of $\mathsf{Sub}(\varphi)$.
- For each $q \in Q_\varphi$, let $\mathsf{Cons}(q) \overset{\text{def}}{=} q \cap \mathsf{Cons}(\Sigma)$, let $q' = \{\psi \mid \mathsf{X}\psi \in q\}$ and let $q'' = \{\psi \mid \overline{\mathsf{X}}\psi \in q\}$. Then, for each Boolean function $f \in \Sigma$, we have

$$\delta_\varphi(q, f) = \begin{cases} \emptyset, & \bot \in q \\ \mathsf{Cl}(q' \cup q'' \cup \mathsf{Cons}(q)[f]), & \bot \notin q \end{cases}.$$

- $I_\varphi = \{q \in Q_\varphi \mid \varphi \in q\}$ is the set of initial states.
- F_φ is the set of accepting states such that for every state $q \in Q_\varphi$, $q \in F_\varphi$ only if $\{\psi \mid \mathsf{X}\psi \in q\} = \emptyset$, $\bot \notin q$ and $\mathsf{Cons}(q) \downarrow$ is evaluated true.

For a BNN $\mathcal{N}$ given by $f_{\mathcal{N}} = f_{n-1} \circ f_{n-2} \circ \cdots \circ f_1 \circ f_0$, we denote by $\mathcal{N} \in \mathscr{L}(\mathcal{A}_\varphi)$ if the sequence of the Boolean functions $f_0, f_1, \cdots, f_{n-1}$, regarded as a finite word, is accepted by the automaton $\mathcal{A}_\varphi$.

Intuitively, $\mathcal{N}$ accepts an input word iff it has an accepting run $q_0, q_1 \cdots, q_n$, where q_i is constituted with a set of formulas that make the specification φ valid at the position i. In this situation, I_φ refers to the states involving φ and $q_0 \in I_\varphi$. For the transition $q_i \xrightarrow{f_i} q_{i+1}$, q_i' and q_i'' indicate the sets of formulas which should be satisfied in the next position $i+1$ according to the semantics of *next* (X) and *weak next* ($\overline{\mathsf{X}}$). Additionally, $\mathsf{Cons}(q_{i+1})$ is obtained by applying the Boolean function f_i to the constraints in q_i.

The following theorem reveals the relationship between φ and $\mathcal{A}_\varphi$.

Theorem 2. *Let $\mathcal{N}$ be a BNN given by a sequence of Boolean functions for a BLTL formula φ, we have:*

$$\mathcal{N} \models \varphi \text{ if and only if } \mathcal{N} \in \mathscr{L}(\mathcal{A}_\varphi).$$

The proof and an example of the construction refer to [29].

4.3 Tableau-Based Construction

We have successfully provided a process for converting an BLTL formula into an automaton on finite words. At first glance, it seems that the model checking problem w.r.t. BNN can be immediately boiled down to a word-problem of finite automata. Nevertheless, a careful analysis shows that this would result in a prohibitively high cost. Actually, for a BLTL formula φ, the state set of $\mathcal{A}_\varphi$ is $\bigcup_{\Gamma \subseteq \mathsf{Sub}(\varphi)} \mathsf{Cl}(\Gamma) \subseteq 2^{\mathsf{Sub}(\varphi)}$, thus the number of states is exponential in the size of the length of φ. To avoid explicit construction, we provide an "on-the-fly" approach when performing synthesis.

Suppose the BLTL φ is given in NNF and the BNN $\mathcal{N}$ is given as a sequence of Boolean functions $f_0, f_1, \ldots, f_{n-1}$, using the following approach, we may construct a tree $\mathcal{T}_{\varphi,\mathcal{N}}$ which fulfills the followings:

- $\mathcal{T}_{\varphi,\mathcal{N}}$ is rooted at $\langle 0, \{\varphi\}\rangle$;
- For an internal node $\langle i, \Gamma\rangle$ with $i < n - 1$, it has a child $\langle j, \Gamma'\rangle$ only if there is a tableau rule

$$\begin{array}{c|c} i & \Gamma \\ \hline j & \Gamma' \end{array}$$

  where j is either i or $i + 1$.
- A leaf $\langle i, \Gamma\rangle$ of $\mathcal{T}_{\varphi,\mathcal{N}}$ is a (MODAL)-node with $i = n - 1$, where nodes to which only the rule (MODAL) can be applied are called (MODAL)-nodes.

$$\text{(AND)} \quad \begin{array}{c|c} i & \Gamma, \varphi_1 \wedge \varphi_2 \\ \hline i & \Gamma, \varphi_1, \varphi_2 \end{array} \qquad \text{(OR-j)} \quad \begin{array}{c|c} i & \Gamma, \varphi_1 \vee \varphi_2 \\ \hline i & \Gamma, \varphi_j \end{array} \quad (j = 1, 2)$$

$$\text{(TRUE)} \quad \begin{array}{c|c} i & \Gamma, \boldsymbol{t}_1 \sim \boldsymbol{t}_2 \\ \hline i & \Gamma, \top \end{array} \qquad \text{(FALSE)} \quad \begin{array}{c|c} i & \Gamma, \boldsymbol{t}_1 \sim \boldsymbol{t}_2 \\ \hline i & \Gamma, \bot \end{array}$$

$$\text{(UNTIL)} \quad \begin{array}{c|c} i & \Gamma, \varphi_1 \mathsf{U}\varphi_2 \\ \hline i & \Gamma, \varphi_2 \vee (\varphi_1 \wedge \mathsf{X}(\varphi_1 \mathsf{U}\varphi_2)) \end{array}$$

$$\text{(RELEASE)} \quad \begin{array}{c|c} i & \Gamma, \varphi_1 \mathsf{R}\varphi_2 \\ \hline i & \Gamma, \varphi_2 \wedge (\varphi_1 \vee \mathsf{X}(\varphi_1 \mathsf{R}\varphi_2)) \end{array}$$

$$\text{(MODAL)} \quad \begin{array}{c|c} i & \Gamma, \mathsf{X}\psi_1, \ldots, \mathsf{X}\psi_m, \overline{\mathsf{X}}\varphi_1, \ldots, \overline{\mathsf{X}}\varphi_k \\ \hline i+1 & \{\gamma[f_i] \mid \gamma \in \Gamma, \mathsf{len}(\gamma) > 0\}, \psi_1, \ldots, \psi_m, \varphi_1, \ldots, \varphi_k \end{array}$$

Fig. 1. Tableau rules for Automata Construction

Tableau rules are listed in Fig. 1. For the rule (MODAL), we require that Γ consists of atomic formulas being of the form $t_1 \sim t_2$. In the rules (TRUE) and (FALSE), we require that $\mathsf{len}(t_1 \sim t_2) = 0$ and it is evaluated to true and false, respectively.

Suppose $\langle n, \Gamma \cup \{\mathsf{X}\psi_1, \ldots, \mathsf{X}\psi_m\} \cup \{\overline{\mathsf{X}}\varphi_1, \ldots, \overline{\mathsf{X}}\varphi_k\}\rangle$ is a leaf of $\mathcal{T}_{\varphi,\mathcal{N}}$. We say it is *successful* if $m = 0$ and $\Gamma \downarrow$ is evaluated to true. In addition, we say a path of $\mathcal{T}_{\varphi,\mathcal{N}}$ is *successful* if it ends with a successful leaf, and no node along this path contains $\bot$.

In the process of the on-the-fly construction, we start by creating the root node, then apply the tableau rules to rewrite the formulas in the subsequent nodes. In addition, before the rule (MODAL) or (OR-j) is applied, we preserve the set of formulas, which allows us to trace back and construct other parts of the automaton afterward. We exemplify how to achieve the synthesis task via the construction in Sect. 5.

Theorem 3. $\mathcal{N} \models \varphi$ *if and only if* $\mathcal{T}_{\varphi,\mathcal{N}}$ *has a successful path.*

Proof. Let $\mathcal{A}_\varphi$ be the automaton corresponding to φ. According to Theorem 2, it suffices to show that $\mathcal{N} \in \mathscr{L}(\mathcal{A}_\varphi)$ iff $\mathcal{T}_{\varphi,\mathcal{N}}$ has a successful path.

Suppose, $\mathcal{N}$ is accepted by $\mathcal{A}_\varphi$ with the run $q_0, q_1, \ldots, q_n$, we also create the root node $\langle 0, \Gamma_0 = \{\varphi\}\rangle$. Inductively, we have the followings statements for each node $\langle i, \Gamma_j \rangle$ which is already constructed:

1) $\Gamma_j \subseteq q_i$;
2) $\mathcal{N}, i \models \psi$ for each $\psi \in q_i$ (see the proof of Theorem 2)

Then, if $\langle i, \Gamma_j\rangle$ is not a leaf, we create a new node $\langle i', \Gamma_j'\rangle$ in the following way:

- $i' = i$ if $\langle i, \Gamma_j\rangle$ is not a (MODAL)-node, otherwise $i' = i + 1$;
- if rule (OR-k) ($k = 1, 2$) is applied to $\langle i, \Gamma_j\rangle$ to some $\varphi_1 \vee \varphi_2 \in \Gamma_j$, we require that $\varphi_k \in \Gamma_j'$; for other cases, Γ_j' is uniquely determined by Γ_j and the tableau rule which is applied.

It can be checked that both Items 1) and 2) still hold at $\langle i', \Gamma_j'\rangle$. Then, we can see that the path we constructed is successful since q_n is an accepting state of $\mathcal{A}_\varphi$.

For the other way round, suppose that $\mathcal{T}_{\varphi,\mathcal{N}}$ involves a successful path

$$\langle 0, \Gamma_{0,0}\rangle, \langle 0, \Gamma_{0,1}\rangle, \ldots, \langle 0, \Gamma_{0,\ell_0}\rangle, \langle 1, \Gamma_{1,0}\rangle, \langle 1, \Gamma_{1,1}\rangle, \ldots, \langle 1, \Gamma_{1,\ell_1}\rangle, \ldots,$$
$$\langle i, \Gamma_{i,0}\rangle, \langle i, \Gamma_{i,1}\rangle, \ldots, \langle i, \Gamma_{i,\ell_i}\rangle, \ldots, \langle n, \Gamma_{n,0}\rangle, \langle n, \Gamma_{n,1}\rangle, \ldots, \langle n, \Gamma_{n,\ell_n}\rangle$$

then, the state sequence $q_0, q_1, \ldots, \ldots, q_n$ yields an accepting run of $\mathcal{A}_\varphi$ on $\mathcal{N}$, where $q_i = \bigcup_{j=0}^{\ell_i} \Gamma_{i,j}$. $\qquad\square$

5   BNN Synthesis

Let us now consider a more challenging task: Given a BLTL specification φ, to find some BNN $\mathcal{N}$ such that $\mathcal{N} \models \varphi$. In the synthesis task, the parameters of the desired BNN are not given, even, we are not aware of the length (i.e., the number of blocks) of the network. To address this challenge, we leverage the tableau-based method (cf. Sect. 4.3) to construct the automaton for the given specification φ and check the existence of the desired BNN at the same time. But when performing the tableau-based rewriting, we need to view each block (i.e., a Boolean function) f_i as an unknown variable (called *block variable* in what follows).

The construction of the tableau-tree starts from the root node $\langle 0, \varphi \rangle$ in a depth-first search manner. During the construction, for each internal node $\langle i, \Gamma \rangle$, the following steps are taken: Firstly, rules other than (OR-1) and (MODAL) are applied to Γ until no further changes occur. Then rule (OR-j) is applied to the disjunctions in the formula set, and we always first try rule (OR-1) when the rewriting is performed. Lastly, rule (MODAL) is applied to generate node $\langle i+1, \Gamma' \rangle$, which becomes the next node in the path, and the Boolean function f_i used in the rewriting is just a block variable. Particularly, we retain a stack of nodes on which either rule (OR-j) or (MODAL) is applied for backtracing. A node is called a (OR-j) node if rule (OR-j) is applied onto it. Once an X-free (MODAL)-node is reached, we verify the success of the path. However, since now the blocks are no longer concrete in this setting, an atomic formula of the form $\gamma[f_i, \ldots, f_{i+k}]$ cannot be immediately evaluated even if it is $\triangleright$-free. As a result, whether a path is *successful* cannot be evaluated directly.

To address this issue, we invoke an integer different logic (IDL) solver to examine the satisfiability of the atomic formulas in the (MODAL)-nodes along the path, and we declare success if all of them are satisfiable and in addition, it ends up with an X-free (MODAL)-node. Meanwhile, the model given by the solver would reveal hyper-parameters of the BNN, which then we adopt to obtain the expected BNN. For a node $\langle i, \Gamma \rangle$, we call i to be the *depth counter*. Once the infeasibility is reported by the IDL solver, or some specific depth counter (call it the *threshold*) is reached, a trace-back to the nearest (OR-1) node is required: all the nodes under the nearest (OR-1) node (including itself) are popped from the stack and then apply rule (OR-2) to that node (it becomes a (OR-2) node), but this time we do not push anything into the stack, because both choices for the disjunctive formula have been tried so far. If no (OR-1) nodes remains in the stack when doing trace-back, we declare the failure of the synthesis.

Now, there are two issues to deal with during that process. The first is, how to determine if the aforementioned 'threshold' is reached; second, how can we convert the satisfiability testing into IDL-solving.

5.1   The Threshold

There exists a naïve bound for the first problem, which is just the state number of $\mathcal{A}_\varphi$. However, this bound is in general not compact (i.e., doubly exponential in the size of the formula φ), and thus we provide a tighter bound.

We first introduce the following notion. Two modal nodes $\langle i, \Gamma \rangle$ and $\langle j, \Gamma' \rangle$ are *isomorphic*, denoted by $\langle i, \Gamma \rangle \cong \langle j, \Gamma' \rangle$, if Γ can be transformed into Γ'

under a (block) variable bijection. The following lemma about isomorphic model nodes is straightforward.

Lemma 1. *If $\langle i, \Gamma \rangle \cong \langle j, \Gamma' \rangle$ and the node $\langle i, \Gamma \rangle$ could lead to a successful leaf (i.e., satisfiable leaf), then so does the node $\langle j, \Gamma' \rangle$.*

Thus, given φ, the threshold can be the number of equivalence classes w.r.t. $\cong$. To make the analysis clearer, we here introduce some auxiliary notions.

- We call an atomic constraint γ occurring in φ to be an *original constraint* (or, *non-padded constraint*); and call a formula being of the form $\gamma[f_i, \ldots, f_j]$ *padded constraint*, where $f_i, \ldots, f_j$ are block variables.
- A (padded or non-padded) constraint with length 0 (i.e., $\triangleright$-free) is called *saturated*. In general, such a constraint is obtained from a non-padded constraint γ via applying k layer variables, where $k = \mathsf{len}(\gamma)$.

Theorem 4. *Let φ be a closed BLTL formula, and let*

- $c = \#(Cons(\Sigma) \cap Sub(\varphi))$, *i.e., the number of (non-padded) constraints occurring in φ;*
- $k = \max\{\mathsf{len}(\gamma) \mid \gamma \in Cons(\Sigma) \cap Sub(\varphi)\}$, *i.e., the maximum length of non-padded constraints occurring in φ;*
- p *be the number of temporal operators in φ*

then, $2^{(k+1)c+p} + 1$ is a threshold for synthesis.

The proof refers to [29].

5.2   Encoding with IDL Problem

Another problem is how to convert the satisfiability testing into IDL-solving. To tackle this problem, we present a method that transforms BLTL atomic formulas to IDL constraints.

We may temporarily view a Boolean function $g : \mathbb{B}^m \to \mathbb{B}^n$ as a (partial) integer function with domain $[2^m]$, namely, we equivalently view g maps $\mathsf{dec}(\boldsymbol{b})$ to $\mathsf{dec}(g(\boldsymbol{b}))$.

For a $\triangleright$-free term $\boldsymbol{t} = (f_k \circ f_{k-1} \circ \cdots \circ f_0)(\boldsymbol{b})$, we say that $(f_i \circ f_{i-1} \circ \cdots \circ f_0)(\boldsymbol{b})$ is an *intermediate term* of $\boldsymbol{t}$ where $i \leq k$. In what follows, we denote by $\boldsymbol{T}$ the set of all intermediate terms that may occur in the process of IDL-solving, which is a part of synthesis that check the satisfiability of atomic formulas in successful leaves.

Remind that in a term or an intermediate term, a symbol g may either be a fixed function or a variable that needs to be determined by the IDL-solver (i.e., *block variables*). To make it clearer, we in general use $g_0, g_1, \ldots$ to designate the former functions, whereas use f_0, f_1, etc. for the latter cases.

The theory of IDL is limited to handling the Boolean combinations of the form $x - y \sim c$, where x, y are integer variables and c is an integer constant. However, since functions occur in the terms, they cannot be expressed using IDL.

To this end, we note that we merely care about partial input-output relations of the functions, which consist of mappings among T, and then the finite mappings can be expressed by integer constraints. Thus, for each intermediate term $t \in T$, we introduce an integer variable v_t.

Then, all constraints describing the synthesis task are listed as follows.

(1) For each BLTL constraint $t_1 \sim t_2$, we have a conjunct $v_{t_1} \sim v_{t_2}$.
(2) For each block variable $f : \mathbb{B}^n \to \mathbb{B}^m$ and each $f(t) \in T$, we add the bound constraints $0 \leq v_{f(t)}$ and $v_{f(t)} \leq 2^m$.
(3) For each block variable f and every pair of terms $t_1, t_2 \in T$, we have the constraint: $v_{t_1} = v_{t_2} \to v_{f(v_1)} = v_{f(v_2)}$, which guarantees f to be a mapping.
(4) For every fixed function g, we impose the constraint $v_{g(t)} = \mathsf{dec}(g(\mathsf{bin}(v_t)))$ for every $t \in T$.

Once the satisfiability is reported by the IDL-solver, we extract partial mapping information of f_i's from the solver's model, by analyzing equations of the form $v_t = c$, where c is an integer called the value of t. We iterate over the model and record the value of terms, when we encounter an equation in the form of $v_{f_i(t)} = c$, we query the value of t, and obtain one input-output relation of f_i. Eventually, we get partial essential mapping information of such f_i's.

5.3 Utilize the Synthesis

A BNN that satisfies the specification can be obtained via block-wise training, namely, training each block independently to fulfill its generated input-output mapping relation, which is extracted by the IDL-solver during the synthesis process. Indeed, such training is not only in general lightweight but also able to reuse the pre-trained blocks.

Let us now consider a more general requirement that we have both high-level temporal specification (such as fairness, robustness) and data constraints (i.e., labels on a dataset), and is asked to obtain a BNN to meet all these obligations.

A straightforward idea is to express all data constraints with BLTL, and then perform a monolithic synthesis. However, such a solution seems to be infeasible, because the large amount of data constraints usually produces a rather complicated formula, and it makes the synthesis extremely difficult.

An alternative approach is to first perform the synthesis w.r.t. the high-level specification, then do a retraining upon the dataset. However, the second phase may distort the result of the first phase. In general, one need to conduct an iterative cycle composed of synthesis-training-verification, yet the convergence of such process cannot be guaranteed. Thus, we need make a trade-off between these two types of specifications.

More practically, synthesis can be used as an "enhancement" procedure. Suppose, we already have some BNN trained with the given dataset, then we are aware the hyper-parameters of that. This time, we have more information when doing synthesis, e.g., the threshold is replaced by the length of the network, and the shape (i.e., the width of input and output) of each block are also given. With this, we may perform a more effective IDL-solving process, and then retrain each block individually. Definitely, this might affect the accuracy of network, and some compromise also should be done.

6   Experimental Evaluation

We implement a prototype tool in Python, which uses Z3 [9] as the off-the-shelf IDL solver and PyTorch to train blocks and BNNs. To the best of our knowledge, few existing work on synthesizing BNN has been done so far. Hence, we mainly investigate the feasibility of our approach by exploring how much the trustworthiness of BNN can be enhanced, and the corresponding trade-off on accuracy degradation. The first two experiments focus on evaluating the effectiveness of synthesis in enhancing the properties of BNNs. We set BNNs with diverse architectures as baselines, and synthesize models via the "enhancement" procedure, wherein the threshold matches the length of the baselines, and the shape of blocks are constrained to maintain the same architecture as the baselines. Eventually, the blocks are retrained to fulfill the partial mapping, and the synthesized model is obtained through retraining on the dataset. We compare the synthesized models and their baselines on two properties: *local robustness* and *individual fairness*. Moreover, we also study the potential of our approach to assist in determining the network architecture.

Datasets. We train models and evaluate our approach over two classical datasets, MNIST [10] and UCI Adult [11]. MNIST is a dataset of handwritten digits, which contains 70,000 gray-scale images with 10 classes, and each image has 28×28 pixels. In the experiments, we downscale the images to 10×10, and binarize the normalized images, and then transform them into 100-width vectors. UCI Adult contains 48,842 entries with 14 attributes, such as age, gender, workclass and occupation. The classification task on the dataset UCI Adult is to predict whether an individual's annual salary is greater than 50K. We first remove unusable data, retain 45,221 entries, and then transform the real-value data into 66-dimension binarized vectors as input.

Experimental Setup. In the block-wise training, different loss functions are employed for internal and output blocks: the MSE loss function for internal blocks and the cross-entropy loss function for output blocks. The training process entails a fixed number of epochs, with 150 epochs for internal blocks and 30 epochs for output blocks. The experiments are conducted on a 3.6G HZ CPU

Table 1. BNN baselines.

Name	Arch	Acc	Name	Arch	Acc
R1	100-32-10	82.62%	F1	66-32-2	80.12%
R2	100-50-10	84.28%	F2	66-20-2	79.88%
R3	100-50-32-10	83.50%	F3	66-32-20-2	78.13%

with 12 cores and 32 GB RAM, and the blocks and BNNs are trained using a single GeForce RTX 3070 Ti GPU.

Baseline. We use six neural networks with different architectures as baselines, where three models **R1–R3** are trained on the MNIST for 10 epochs with a learning rate of 10^{-4} to study local robustness. For individual fairness, we train 3 models (**F1–F3**) on the UCI Adult for 10 epochs, with a learning rate of 10^{-3}, and split the dataset into a training set and a test set in a 4:1 ratio. The detailed information is listed in Table 1, Column (Name) indicates the name of BNNs, and Column (Arch) presents their architectures. The architecture of each network is described as by a sequence $\{n_i\}_{i=0}^{s}$, where s is the number of the blocks in the network, and n_i and n_{i+1} indicate the input and output dimensions of the i-th block. For instance, 100-32-10 indicates that the BNN has two blocks, input dimensions of these blocks are 100 and 32 respectively, and the number of classification labels is 10. Column (Acc) shows the accuracy of the models on the test set.

6.1 Local Robustness

In this section, we evaluate the effectiveness of our approach for enhancing the robustness of models in different cases. We use the metric, called Adversarial Attack Success Rate (ASR), to measure a model's resistance to adversarial attacks. ASR is calculated as the proportion of perturbed inputs that leads to a different prediction result compared to the original input.

We choose 30 image vectors from the training set, and set the maximum perturbation to four levels, $\epsilon \in \{1, 2, 3, 4\}$. The value of ϵ indicates the maximum number of positions that can be modified in one image vector. One selected input vector, one maximum perturbation ϵ and one baseline model constitute a case, resulting in a total of 360 cases.

For each of the 360 cases, we make a synthesized model individually and compare its ASR with the corresponding baseline. For the local robustness property (cf. Sect. 3.2), since the input space is too large to enumerate, we need to sample inputs within $B(\boldsymbol{u}, \epsilon)$ when describing the specification, which is formulated as $\bigwedge_{i=1}^{k} (\mathcal{N}(\boldsymbol{u}) = \mathcal{N}(\boldsymbol{b}_i))$, where each $\boldsymbol{b}_i$ is a sample and k is the number of samples. We here sample 100 points within the maximum perturbation limit ϵ. The specification is written as $\bigwedge_{i=1}^{k} (\triangleright^n \boldsymbol{u} = \triangleright^n \boldsymbol{b}_i)$, where n is the number of the block of the baseline. Subsequently, we use the block constraint (cf. Sect. 5.2), $0 \leq v_{f_i(t)} \leq 2^m$, to specify the range of output of each block. To make the bound tighter, we retain the maximal and minimal activations of each block using calibration data run on the baseline, and then take the recorded values as bounds. Eventually, the generated mappings are used in the block-wise training, and then the enhanced BNN is obtained through retraining on the MNIST dataset.

We also take 100 samples for each case and compare the ASR for baselines and their synthesized counterparts. The results are shown in Fig. 2, where blue bars represent the baselines, while green bars represent synthesized models. We use the sign + to denote the synthesized models. Figure 2(a) (resp. Fig. 2(b) and

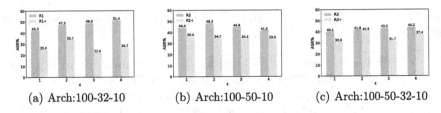

(a) Arch:100-32-10   (b) Arch:100-50-10   (c) Arch:100-50-32-10

Fig. 2. Results of local robustness.

Fig. 2(c)) depicts the percentage of average ASR of **R1** (resp. **R2** and **R3**) and the counterpart **R1+** (resp. **R2+** and **R3+**) (the vertical axis), with different ϵ (1, 2, 3, 4) (the horizontal axis). The results demonstrate a decrease in ASR by an average of 43.45%, 22.12%, and 16.95% for **R1**, **R2** and **R3**, respectively.

Whilst the models' robustness are enhanced, their accuracy are slightly decreased. Table 2 shows the results of the accuracy of the models, where Acc+ represents the average accuracy for synthesized models with the same architectures.

Table 2. The average accuracy of **R1**–**R3** and their synthesized models.

	R1	R2	R3
Acc	82.62%	84.28%	83.50%
Acc+	81.33%	81.72%	78.75%

6.2 Individual Fairness

In this section, we investigate the individual fairness w.r.t two sensitive features, namely, sex (Male and Female) and race (White and Black) on the UCI Adult dataset.

We consider **F1**–**F3** as baselines, and randomly select 1000 entries for both **F1** and **F2**, and 200 entries for **F3** from the training dataset, and then generate proper pairs by modifying the value of the sensitive attribute while keeping all other attributes the same. For example, we modify the value of Male to Female. After forming specifications using the approach mentioned in Sect. 3.2 with the pairs, we proceed with the "enhancement" procedure and retraining to obtain the synthesized models. We then evaluate the models on the test dataset by measuring the fairness score. We count the number of the fair pairs (i.e., the pairs only differ in the sensitive attribute, and yield the same predication result): *fair num*, and compute the fairness score, $\frac{fair\ num}{test\ size}$, where *test size* is the size of the test set.

The results are listed in Table 3, where the baselines and the sensitive attributes are shown in Columns 1,2. Columns 3,4 (Acc/Acc+) demonstrate the

Table 3. Results of individual fairness.

Model	Feature	Acc	Acc+	Fair	Fair+	Synthesis Time(s)
F1	sex	80.12%	74.53%	92.91%	99.94%	241.67
F1	race	80.12%	74.54%	92.92%	100%	216.46
F2	sex	79.88%	75.71%	95.68%	97.83%	215.61
F2	race	79.88%	75.18%	94.64%	98.47%	212.46
F3	sex	78.13%	74.48%	89.67%	99.83%	90.39
F3	race	79.88%	74.09%	89.16%	98.27%	95.75

Table 4. The synthesized models whose architectures are given by our tool.

Attr	Arch	Len	#Mapping	Acc	Fair
sex	66-10-10-2	3	1117	74.38%	99.51%
sex	66-8-2	2	559	74.69%	99.72%
race	66-9-8-2	3	952	74.38%	94.59%
race	66-8-2	2	567	74.13%	99.71%

accuracy of baselines and synthesized models, and Columns 5,6 (Fair/Fair+) show their fairness scores. The results show that all the models' individual fairness is significantly improved, some of which even reach 100% (e.g., Row 2, the fairness score increase from 92.92% to 100%). However, the enhancement is accompanied by the accuracy loss, Columns 3,4 show that all models suffer from a certain degree of accuracy decrease. Our tool efficiently synthesized the hyper-parameters within a few minutes, as shown in Column 7.

Furthermore, we examine the ability of our approach on helping determine the architecture of the BNNs. For both sex and race, we sample 200 entries in the training dataset to generate proper pairs, and formulate the specification without using the bound constraints or fixing the number of block, as follows,

$$\mathsf{F}(\bigwedge_i^k (\boldsymbol{x}_i = \boldsymbol{y}_i)) \wedge (\bigwedge_i^k (\boldsymbol{x}_i = \triangleright^2 \boldsymbol{a}_i \wedge \boldsymbol{y}_i = \triangleright^2 \boldsymbol{b}_i) \vee (\bigwedge_i^k (\boldsymbol{x}_i = \triangleright^3 \boldsymbol{a}_i \wedge \boldsymbol{y}_i = \triangleright^3 \boldsymbol{b}_i)))$$

where $(\boldsymbol{a}_i, \boldsymbol{b}_i)$ is the proper pair, and k is the number of samples. The formula indicates the presence of consecutive blocks in the model, with a length of either 2 or 3. For each proper pair $(\boldsymbol{a}_i, \boldsymbol{b}_i)$, their respective outputs $(\boldsymbol{x}_i, \boldsymbol{y}_i)$ must be equal.

After synthesizing the partial input-output relation of block functions f_i's, we determine the length of the network by selecting the maximum i among the block functions f_i's. The dimensions of the blocks are set to the maximum input and output dimensions in the partial relation obtained for the corresponding f_i.

We make a slight adjustment to the synthesis framework, when finding a group of hyper-parameters, we continue searching for one more feasible group, resulting in two groups of hyper-parameters for sex and race. We showcase the synthesized models in Table 4. Column 1 indicates the sensitive attribute of interest, and Columns 2,3 give the architecture and the length of the BNNs respectively. Column 4 shows the number of partial mappings we obtained in the synthesis task. Our tool successfully generates models with varying architectures and high individual fairness, which are presented in Columns 5,6 respectively.

7   Conclusion

In this paper, we have presented an automata-based approach to synthesizing binarized neural networks. Specifying BNNs' properties with the designed logic BLTL, the synthesis framework uses the tableau-based construction approach and the IDL-solver to determine hyper-parameters of BNNs and relations among some parameters. Subsequently, we may perform a block-wise training. We implemented a prototype tool and the experiments demonstrate the effectiveness of our approach in enhancing the local robustness and individual fairness of BNNs. Although our approach shows the feasibility of synthesizing trustworthy BNNs, there is still a need to further explore this line of work. In the future, beyond the input-output relation of BNNs, we plan to focus on specifying properties between the intermediate blocks. Additionally, we aim to extend the approach to handle the synthesis task of multi-bits QNNs.

Acknowledgement. This work is partially supported by the National Key R & D Program of China (2022YFA1005101), the National Natural Science Foundation of China (61872371, 62072309, 62032024), CAS Project for Young Scientists in Basic Research (YSBR-040), and ISCAS New Cultivation Project (ISCAS-PYFX-202201).

References

1. Baluta, T., Shen, S., Shinde, S., Meel, K.S., Saxena, P.: Quantitative verification of neural networks and its security applications. In: Proceedings of the 2019 ACM SIGSAC Conference on Computer and Communications Security, pp. 1249–1264 (2019)
2. Barrett, C., Stump, A., Tinelli, C., et al.: The SMT-lib standard: version 2.0. In: Proceedings of the 8th International Workshop on Satisfiability Modulo Theories (Edinburgh, UK), vol. 13, p. 14 (2010)
3. Bu, L., Zhao, Z., Duan, Y., Song, F.: Taking care of the discretization problem: a comprehensive study of the discretization problem and a black-box adversarial attack in discrete integer domain. IEEE Trans. Dependable Secur. Comput. **19**(5), 3200–3217 (2022)
4. Chen, G., et al.: Who is real bob? Adversarial attacks on speaker recognition systems. In: Proceedings of the 42nd IEEE Symposium on Security and Privacy (SP), pp. 694–711 (2021)
5. Chen, G., Zhang, Y., Zhao, Z., Song, F.: QFA2SR: query-free adversarial transfer attacks to speaker recognition systems. In: Proceedings of the 32nd USENIX Security Symposium (2023)

6. Chen, Get al.: Towards understanding and mitigating audio adversarial examples for speaker recognition. IEEE Trans. Dependable Secur. Comput. **20**(5), 3970–3987 (2022)
7. Chen, G., Zhao, Z., Song, F., Chen, S., Fan, L., Liu, Y.: AS2T: arbitrary source-to-target adversarial attack on speaker recognition systems. IEEE Trans. Dependable Secur. Comput. 1–17 (2022)
8. Cheng, C.-H., Nührenberg, G., Huang, C.-H., Ruess, H.: Verification of binarized neural networks via inter-neuron factoring. In: Piskac, R., Rümmer, P. (eds.) VSTTE 2018. LNCS, vol. 11294, pp. 279–290. Springer, Cham (2018). https://doi.org/10.1007/978-3-030-03592-1_16
9. de Moura, L., Bjørner, N.: Z3: an efficient SMT solver. In: Ramakrishnan, C.R., Rehof, J. (eds.) TACAS 2008. LNCS, vol. 4963, pp. 337–340. Springer, Heidelberg (2008). https://doi.org/10.1007/978-3-540-78800-3_24
10. Deng, L.: The MNIST database of handwritten digit images for machine learning research. IEEE Signal Process. Mag. **29**(6), 141–142 (2012)
11. Dua, D., Graff, C.: UCI machine learning repository (2017). https://archive.ics.uci.edu/ml
12. Eykholt, Ket al.: Robust physical-world attacks on deep learning visual classification. In: Proceedings of the IEEE Conference on Computer Vision and Pattern Recognition, pp. 1625–1634 (2018)
13. Giacobbe, M., Henzinger, T.A., Lechner, M.: How many bits does it take to quantize your neural network? In: TACAS 2020, Part II. LNCS, vol. 12079, pp. 79–97. Springer, Cham (2020). https://doi.org/10.1007/978-3-030-45237-7_5
14. GPT-4. https://openai.com/product/gpt-4
15. Guo, X., Wan, W., Zhang, Z., Zhang, M., Song, F., Wen, X.: Eager falsification for accelerating robustness verification of deep neural networks. In: Proceedings of the 32nd IEEE International Symposium on Software Reliability Engineering, pp. 345–356 (2021)
16. Henzinger, T.A., Lechner, M., Zikelic, D.: Scalable verification of quantized neural networks. In: Proceedings of the AAAI Conference on Artificial Intelligence, vol. 35, pp. 3787–3795 (2021)
17. Huang, X., et al.: A survey of safety and trustworthiness of deep neural networks: verification, testing, adversarial attack and defence, and interpretability. Comput. Sci. Rev. **37**, 100270 (2020)
18. Li, J., Liu, J., Yang, P., Chen, L., Huang, X., Zhang, L.: Analyzing deep neural networks with symbolic propagation: towards higher precision and faster verification. In: Chang, B.-Y.E. (ed.) SAS 2019. LNCS, vol. 11822, pp. 296–319. Springer, Cham (2019). https://doi.org/10.1007/978-3-030-32304-2_15
19. Liang, Z., Ren, D., Liu, W., Wang, J., Yang, W., Xue, B.: Safety verification for neural networks based on set-boundary analysis. In: David, C., Sun, M. (eds.) TASE 2023. LNCS, vol. 13931, pp. 248–267. Springer, Cham (2023). https://doi.org/10.1007/978-3-031-35257-7_15
20. Liu, C., et al.: Algorithms for verifying deep neural networks. Found. Trends® Optim. **4**(3–4), 244–404 (2021)
21. Liu, W.W., Song, F., Zhang, T.H.R., Wang, J.: Verifying ReLU neural networks from a model checking perspective. J. Comput. Sci. Technol. **35**, 1365–1381 (2020)
22. Lösbrock, C.D.: Implementing an incremental solver for difference logic. Master's thesis, RWTH Aachen University (2018)
23. Nagel, M., Fournarakis, M., Amjad, R.A., Bondarenko, Y., Van Baalen, M., Blankevoort, T.: A white paper on neural network quantization. arXiv preprint arXiv:2106.08295 (2021)

24. Narodytska, N., Kasiviswanathan, S., Ryzhyk, L., Sagiv, M., Walsh, T.: Verifying properties of binarized deep neural networks. In: Proceedings of the AAAI Conference on Artificial Intelligence, vol. 32 (2018)
25. Narodytska, N., Zhang, H., Gupta, A., Walsh, T.: In search for a SAT-friendly binarized neural network architecture. In: International Conference on Learning Representations (2020)
26. Shih, A., Darwiche, A., Choi, A.: Verifying binarized neural networks by Angluin-style learning. In: Janota, M., Lynce, I. (eds.) SAT 2019. LNCS, vol. 11628, pp. 354–370. Springer, Cham (2019). https://doi.org/10.1007/978-3-030-24258-9_25
27. Simonyan, K., Zisserman, A.: Very deep convolutional networks for large-scale image recognition. arXiv preprint arXiv:1409.1556 (2014)
28. Song, F., Lei, Y., Chen, S., Fan, L., Liu, Y.: Advanced evasion attacks and mitigations on practical ml-based phishing website classifiers. Int. J. Intell. Syst. **36**(9), 5210–5240 (2021)
29. Tao, Y., Liu, W., Song, F., Liang, Z., Wang, J., Zhu, H.: An automata-theoretic approach to synthesizing binarized neural networks (2023). https://songfu1983.github.io/publications/ATVA23full.pdf
30. FSD chip-tesla. https://en.wikichip.org/wiki/tesla_(car_company)/fsd_chip
31. Zhang, P., et al.: White-box fairness testing through adversarial sampling. In: Proceedings of the ACM/IEEE 42nd International Conference on Software Engineering, pp. 949–960 (2020)
32. Zhang, Y., Song, F., Sun, J.: QEBVerif: quantization error bound verification of neural networks. In: Proceedings of the 35th International Conference on Computer Aided Verification, pp. 413–437 (2023)
33. Zhang, Y., Zhao, Z., Chen, G., Song, F., Chen, T.: **BDD4BNN**: a BDD-based quantitative analysis framework for binarized neural networks. In: Silva, A., Leino, K.R.M. (eds.) CAV 2021, Part I. LNCS, vol. 12759, pp. 175–200. Springer, Cham (2021). https://doi.org/10.1007/978-3-030-81685-8_8
34. Zhang, Y., Zhao, Z., Chen, G., Song, F., Chen, T.: Precise quantitative analysis of binarized neural networks: a BDD-based approach. ACM Trans. Softw. Eng. Methodol. **32**(3), 1–51 (2023)
35. Zhang, Y., et al.: QVIP: an ILP-based formal verification approach for quantized neural networks. In: Proceedings of the 37th IEEE/ACM International Conference on Automated Software Engineering, pp. 1–13 (2022)
36. Zhao, Z., Chen, G., Wang, J., Yang, Y., Song, F., Sun, J.: Attack as defense: characterizing adversarial examples using robustness. In: Proceedings of the 30th ACM SIGSOFT International Symposium on Software Testing and Analysis (ISSTA), pp. 42–55 (2021)
37. Zhao, Z., Zhang, Y., Chen, G., Song, F., Chen, T., Liu, J.: CLEVEREST: accelerating CEGAR-based neural network verification via adversarial attacks. In: Singh, G., Urban, C. (eds.) SAS 2022. LNCS, vol. 13790, pp. 449–473. Springer, Cham (2022). https://doi.org/10.1007/978-3-031-22308-2_20
38. Zheng, H., et al.: NeuronFair: interpretable white-box fairness testing through biased neuron identification. In: Proceedings of the 44th International Conference on Software Engineering, pp. 1519–1531 (2022)

Syntactic vs Semantic Linear Abstraction and Refinement of Neural Networks

Calvin Chau[1], Jan Křetínský[2,3], and Stefanie Mohr[2]

[1] Technische Universität Dresden, Dresden, Germany
calvin.chau@tu-dresden.de
[2] Technical University of Munich, Munich, Germany
{kretinsky,mohr}@in.tum.de
[3] Masaryk University, Brno, Czech Republic

Abstract. Abstraction is a key verification technique to improve scalability. However, its use for neural networks is so far extremely limited. Previous approaches for abstracting classification networks replace several neurons with one of them that is similar enough. We can classify the similarity as defined either syntactically (using quantities on the connections between neurons) or semantically (on the activation values of neurons for various inputs). Unfortunately, the previous approaches only achieve moderate reductions, when implemented at all. In this work, we provide a more flexible framework, where a neuron can be replaced with a *linear combination* of other neurons, improving the reduction. We apply this approach both on syntactic and semantic abstractions, and implement and evaluate them experimentally. Further, we introduce a refinement method for our abstractions, allowing for finding a better balance between reduction and precision.

Keywords: Neural network · Abstraction · Machine learning

1 Introduction

Neural Network Abstractions. Abstraction is a key instrument for understanding complex systems and analyzing complex problems across all disciplines, including computer science. Abstraction of complex systems, such as neural networks (NN), results in smaller systems, which are not only producing equivalent outputs (such as in distillation [13]), but additionally can be mapped to the original system, providing a strong link between the individual parts of the two systems. Consequently, abstraction find various applications. For instance, the smaller (abstract) networks are more understandable and the strong link between the behaviours of the abstract and the original network allows for better explainability of the original behaviour, too; smaller networks are more efficient

This research was funded in part by the German Research Foundation (DFG) project 427755713 *GoPro*, the German Federal Ministry of Education and Research (BMBF) within the project *SEMECO Q1* (03ZU1210AG), and the DFG research training group *ConVeY* (GRK 2428).

É. André and J. Sun (Eds.): ATVA 2023, LNCS 14215, pp. 401–421, 2023.
https://doi.org/10.1007/978-3-031-45329-8_19

in resource usage during runtime; smaller networks are easier to verify. Again, with no formal link between the original network and, say, a distilled or pruned one, verifying the smaller one is of no use to verifying the original one. In contrast, for abstractions, the verification guarantee can be in principle transfered to the original network, be it via lifting a counterexample or a proof of correctness.

Altogether, abstractions of neural networks are a key concept worth investigating *eo ipso*, subsequently offering various applications. However, currently it is still very under-developed. For defining an abstraction, we need a transformation linking the original neurons to those in the abstraction. Equivalently, we need a notion of the *similarity of neurons*, to identify a good representative of a group of neurons. The difficulty in contrast to, e.g., predicate abstraction of programs is that neurons have no inner structure such as values of variables stored in a state. On the one hand, approaches based on bisimilarity [22] offer a solution focusing on the *"syntax"* of neurons: the weights of the incoming connections. The quantities give rise to an equivalence akin to probabilistic bisimulation. On the other hand, in search of a stronger tool, approaches such as [2] try to identify *"semantics"* of the neurons. For instance, given a vector of inputs to the network, the *I/O semantics* of a neuron [2] is the vector of activation values of this neuron obtained on these inputs. This represents a finite-dimensional approximation of the actual semantics of a neuron as a computational device. Either way, replacing several neurons with one that is very similar yields only moderate savings on size if the abstract network is supposed to be similar, i.e., yield mostly the same predictions and ensure a tight connection between the similar neurons.

Our Contribution. We focus on studying abstraction irrespective of the use case (verification, smaller networks, explainability), to establish a better principal understanding of this crucial, yet in this context underdeveloped technique. First, we explore a richer abstraction scheme, where a group of neurons can be represented not only by a chosen neuron but also by a *linear combination of neurons*. Thus instead of keeping exactly one representative per group, we can "reuse" the chosen representatives in many linear combinations; in other words, the representatives can attain many roles, partially representing many groups, which reduces their required count. We provide several algorithms to do so, ranging from resource-intensive algorithms aiming to show the limits of the approach to efficient heuristics approximating the former ones quite closely. We apply these algorithms to the semantic approach of [2] as well as to the syntactic, bisimulation-like approach similar to [22] not implemented previously. Experimental results confirm the *greater power of this linear-combination* approach; further, they provide insight into the *advantages of semantic similarity over the syntactic* one, pointing out the more advantageous future research directions.

Further, we provide a formal link between the concrete and abstract neurons by proving an error bound induced by the abstraction, showing the abstraction is valid and (approximately) simulates the original network. We show the bound is better than the one based on bisimulation. While still not very practical, the experiments show that even on unseen data, the error is always closely bounded by the error on the data used for generating the abstraction, and mostly even a lot smaller. This empirical version of the concept of error could thus enable the transfer of reasoning about the abstraction to the original network in a yet much tighter way.

In addition, we suggest *abstraction-refinement* procedures to better fine-tune the trade-off between the precision and the size of the abstraction. The experiments reveal that a more aggressive abstraction followed by a refinement provides better results than a direct, moderate abstraction. Hence involving our refinement in the abstraction process improves the resulting quality, opening new lines of attack on efficient neural network abstractions.

Summary. Our contribution can be summarized as follows:

- We define abstractions of neural networks with (approximate) equivalences being linear equations over semantics of neurons. We provide a theoretical bound on the induced error, see Theorem 1. We reflect this idea also on the syntactic, bisimulation-based abstraction.
- We implement both approaches and compare them mutually as well as to their previous, special cases with equivalences being (approximate) identities. We perform the experiments on a number of standard benchmarks, such as MNIST, CIFAR, or FashionMNIST, concluding advantages of semantic over syntactic approaches and of linear over identity-based ones.
- We introduce an abstraction-refinement procedure and also evaluate its benefits experimentally.

Related Work. There are various approaches for verification of NN, however, we are **not** presenting another verifier. Instead, we introduce an approach that is **orthogonal to verification** and could be integrated with an existing verifier. Therefore, we do not compare our approach to any verification tool and refer the interested reader to the Verification of Neural Networks Competition [4] for an overview of existing approaches [16,26,31,33].

Network compression techniques share many similarities with abstraction [7] and either focus on reducing the memory footprint [14,15] or computation time of the model [12], but in contrast, do not provide any formal relation to the original network, rendering them inappropriate for understanding redundancies or verification. Knowledge distillation is a prominent technique, which can reduce networks by a significant amount, but completely loses any connection to the original network [13], and can thus not be used in verification. There is some progress in using abstract domains for scalable verification, like [26,27,29], but they do not produce an abstracted NN for verification. Instead, they apply abstraction only tightly entangled together with the verification algorithm. These approaches also try to generate a more scalable verification, however, the key difference is that they do not return an actual abstracted network that could be reused or manually inspected. Katz et al. [8] introduce an abstraction scheme for NN, in which they decompose neurons into several parts, before merging them again to obtain an over-approximation of the original network. However, their approach is limited to networks with one output neuron. For networks with more output neurons, the property to be verified needs to be baked into the network, making the approach significantly less flexible. Additionally, this tight entanglement of specification and neural network does not allow for retrieving the abstraction later and reusing it for anything else than to verify that specific property. This strongly contrasts our generic and usage-agnostic abstraction and their property-restricted abstractions.

Some other works use abstraction after representing a neural network as an interval neural network [23], or more generally, by using more complex abstract domains [28]. While theoretically interesting, the practicality of these works has not been investigated. There are two approaches that we consider to be the closest to our work: a bisimulation-based approach [22], and *DeepAbstract* [2], which we will more closely introduce in the preliminaries, and compare to in the experiments.

2   Preliminaries

In this work, we focus on classification feedforward neural networks. Such a neural network N consists of several layers $1, 2, \ldots, L$, with 1 being the *input layer*, L being the *output layer* and $2, \ldots, L-1$ being the *hidden layers*. Each layer ℓ contains n_ℓ neurons. Neurons of one layer are connected to neurons of the previous and next layers by means of weighted connections. Associated with every layer ℓ that is not an output layer is a *weight matrix* $W^{(\ell)} = (w^{(\ell)}(i,j)) \in \mathbb{R}^{n_{\ell+1} \times n_\ell}$ where $w^{(\ell)}(i,j)$ gives the weights of the connections to the ith neuron in layer $\ell+1$ from the jth neuron in layer ℓ. We use the notation $W^{(\ell)}_{i,*} = [w^{(\ell)}(i,1), \ldots, w^{(\ell)}(i, n_\ell)]$ to denote the incoming weights of neuron i in layer $\ell+1$ and $W^{(\ell)}_{*,j} = [w^{(\ell)}(1,j), \ldots, w^{(\ell)}(n_{\ell+1}, j)]^\mathsf{T}$ to denote the outgoing weights of neuron j in layer ℓ. Note that $W^{(\ell)}_{i,*}$ and $W^{(\ell)}_{*,j}$ correspond to the ith row and j^{th} column of $W^{(\ell)}$ respectively. A vector $\mathbf{b}^{(\ell)} = [b^{(\ell)}_1, \ldots, b^{(\ell)}_{n_\ell}] \in \mathbb{R}^{n_\ell}$ called *bias* is also associated with each hidden layer ℓ. The input and output of a neuron i in layer ℓ is denoted by $h^{(\ell)}_i$ and $z^{(\ell)}_i$ respectively. We call $\mathbf{h}^\ell = [h^{(\ell)}_1, \ldots, h^{(\ell)}_{n_\ell}]^\mathsf{T}$ the vector of *pre-activations* and $\mathbf{z}^\ell = [z^{(\ell)}_1, \ldots, z^{(\ell)}_{n_\ell}]^\mathsf{T}$ the vector of *activations* of layer ℓ. The neuron takes the input $\mathbf{h}^\ell$, and applies an *activation function* $\phi : \mathbb{R} \to \mathbb{R}$ element-wise on it. The output is then calculated as $\mathbf{z}^\ell = \phi(\mathbf{h}^\ell)$, where standard activation functions include tanh, sigmoid, or ReLU [21]. We assume that the activation function is Lipschitz continuous, which in particular holds for the aforementioned functions [30]. In a feedforward neural network, information flows strictly in one direction: from layer ℓ_m to layer ℓ_n where $\ell_m < \ell_n$. For an n_1-dimensional input $\mathbf{x} \in \mathcal{X}$ from some input space $\mathcal{X} \subseteq \mathbb{R}^{n_1}$, the output $\mathbf{y} \in \mathbb{R}^{n_L}$ of the neural network N, also written as $\mathbf{y} = N(\mathbf{x})$ is iteratively computed as:

$$\mathbf{h}^{(0)} = \mathbf{z}^{(0)} = \mathbf{x}$$

$$\mathbf{h}^{(\ell+1)} = W^{(\ell)}\mathbf{z}^{(\ell)} + \mathbf{b}^{(\ell+1)} \tag{1}$$

$$\mathbf{z}^{(\ell+1)} = \phi(\mathbf{h}^{(\ell+1)}) \tag{2}$$

$$\mathbf{y} = \mathbf{z}^{(L)}$$

where $\phi(\mathbf{x})$ is the column vector obtained by applying ϕ component-wise to $\mathbf{x}$. We abuse the notation and write $\mathbf{z}^{(\ell)}(\mathbf{x})$, when we want to specify that the output of layer ℓ is computed by starting with $\mathbf{x}$ as input to the network.

2.1 Syntactic and Semantic Abstractions

We are interested in a general abstraction scheme that is not only useful for verification, but also for revealing redundancies, while keeping a formal link to the original network. We distinguish between two types of abstraction: semantic and syntactic. Syntactic abstraction makes use of the weights of the network, the syntactic information, and allows for overapproximation guarantees that are not restricted to specific inputs. However, as we shall see in the experiments, the semantic abstraction can capture the behavior of the original network on typical input data much more accurately than its syntactic counterpart. This comes at the cost of a more challenging error analysis.

Semantic Information. In line with *DeepAbstract* [2], we will create the semantic information based on a set of inputs, the *I/O set*, $X = \{\mathbf{x}_1, \ldots, \mathbf{x}_n\} \subseteq \mathcal{X}$, which is typically a subset of the training dataset. We use the inputs $\mathbf{x}_j \in X$, feed them to the network and store the output values $\{\mathbf{z}^{(\ell)}(\mathbf{x}_j)\}_{\mathbf{x}_j \in X}$ of a layer ℓ in a matrix $\mathbf{Z}^{(\ell)} = (z_i^{(\ell)}(\mathbf{x}_j))_{i,j}$. Note that the columns are the $\mathbf{z}^{(\ell)}(\mathbf{x}_j)$ and the rows, denoted as $\mathbf{Z}_{i,*}^{(\ell)}$, correspond to the values one neuron i produces for all inputs $\mathbf{x}_j$. We refer to the vector $\mathbf{Z}_{j,*}^{(\ell)}$ as the *semantics* of neuron i. This collection of matrices $\mathbf{Z}^{(\ell)}$ for all layers contains the semantic information of the network.

DeepAbstract. Since we will compare our approach to *DeepAbstract* [2], we will give a concise description of the idea of their work. First, it generates the semantic information $\mathbf{Z}$. For one layer ℓ, it clusters the rows of the matrix by using standard clustering techniques, e.g. k-means clustering [3]. Each cluster is considered to be a group of neurons that have similar semantics and similar behavior. Thus, only one group representative is chosen to remain and the rest is replaced by the representatives.

Bisimulation. The idea of [22] is to apply the notion of bisimulation to NN. A bisimulation declares two neurons as equivalent if they agree on their incoming weights, biases, and activation functions. Additionally, the paper introduces a δ-bisimulation that allows neurons to be equivalent only up to δ, i.e. two neurons i, j of layer ℓ with the same activation function are considered to be δ-bisimilar, if for all k : $|w^{(\ell-1)}(i,k) - w^{(\ell-1)}(j,k)| \leq \delta$ and $|b_i^{(\ell)} - b_j^{(\ell)}| \leq \delta$.

3 Linear Abstraction

Our abstraction of a NN is based on the idea that huge NN in their practical application are usually trained with more neurons than necessary. Since there

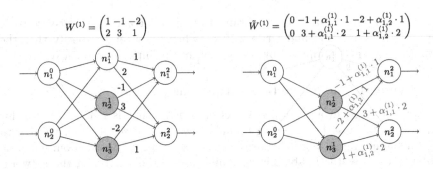

Fig. 1. Linear Abstraction - On the left, the original network with the basis B in blue. On the right, the abstracted network with the removed neuron n_1^1 and the changed output weights of the basis neurons n_2^1, n_3^1, where we assume that n_1^1 can be simulated by $\alpha_{1,1}^{(1)} \cdot n_2^1 + \alpha_{1,2}^{(1)} \cdot n_3^1$. (Color figure online)

are techniques to avoid "overfitting", users of machine learning tend to use NN that are bigger than necessary for their task [19]. Intuitively, such networks thus contain redundancies. We want to remove these redundancies to decrease the size of the network and make it more scalable for verification.

Existing approaches group together similar neurons, and then choose a representative. Instead, we propose to replace a neuron with a linear combination of other neurons. More specifically, we want to replace a neuron i of layer ℓ, not by one single neuron j, but rather by a clever combination of several neurons, called the *basis*, $B^{(\ell)} \subset \{1, \ldots, n_\ell\} \setminus \{i\}$, which is a subset of all neurons of this layer and in this case given as their indices. We assume that the behavior of a neuron can be simulated by a linear combination of the behavior of the basis neurons, i.e. by $\sum_{j \in B^{(\ell)}} \alpha_{i,j}^{(\ell)} \cdot \mathbf{Z}_{j,*}^{(\ell)}$ for some $\alpha_{i,j}^{(\ell)} \in \mathbb{R}$.

Example. Consider the neural network in Fig. 1. It has an input layer with two neurons n_1^0, n_2^0, one hidden layer with three neurons n_1^1, n_2^1, n_3^1, and an output layer with two neurons n_1^2, n_2^2. We assume that we are given the basis $B^{(1)} = \{n_2^1, n_3^1\}$, marked with blue color in the figure, and the linear coefficients $\alpha_{1,1}^{(1)}, \alpha_{1,2}^{(1)}$. That is, we assume that n_1^1 can be simulated by the linear combination $\alpha_{1,1}^{(1)} \cdot n_2^1 + \alpha_{1,2}^{(1)} \cdot n_3^1$. We can remove neuron n_1^1 and its outgoing weights $[1, 2]^\mathsf{T}$, and add the outgoing weights scaled by the linear coefficients to the basis neurons instead. We add $\alpha_{1,1}^{(1)} \cdot [1, 2]^\mathsf{T}$ to the outgoing weights of neuron n_2^1, so we get $[-1, 3]^\mathsf{T} + \alpha_{1,1}^{(1)} \cdot [1, 2]^\mathsf{T} = [-1 + \alpha_{1,1}^{(1)} \cdot 1, 3 + \alpha_{1,1}^{(1)} \cdot 2]^\mathsf{T}$, and respectively, we get $[-2 + \alpha_{1,2}^{(1)} \cdot 1, 1 + \alpha_{1,2}^{(1)} \cdot 2]^\mathsf{T}$ as the outgoing weights of neuron n_3^1.

The computational overhead to compute a linear combination compared to finding a representative is negligible, as we will see in our experiments (see Sect. 5.2). On the other hand, they provide more expressive power, subsuming the aforementioned clustering-based approach [2]. In particular, we can detect scaled weights that previous approaches failed to identify.

Please note that although it is possible to replace a neuron with a linear combination of any other neurons in the network, we will only use neurons from the same layer due to more efficient support by modern neural network frameworks.

In the following sections, we will answer three questions: How can one find a set of neurons that serves as a basis (Sect. 3.1)? How to find the coefficients for the linear combination (Sect. 3.2)? How to replace a neuron, once its representation as a linear combination is given (Sect. 3.3)?

3.1   Finding the Basis

Our approach is meant to find a sufficient smaller subset of neurons in one layer, which is enough to represent the behavior of the whole layer. We will make use of the semantic information of a layer ℓ, given as $\mathbf{Z}^{(\ell)} = (z_i^{(\ell)}(\mathbf{x}_j))_{i,j}$ (see Sect. 2.1). Based on this, we try to find a basis of neurons, i.e. a set of indices for neurons in this layer $\{j_1, \dots j_{k_\ell}\} = B^{(\ell)} \subset \{1, \dots, n_\ell\}$, which can represent the whole space as well as possible. To this end we want to find a subset of size $k = |B^{(\ell)}|$ such that $\| \sum_{j \in B^{(\ell)}} \alpha_{i,j}^{(\ell)} \cdot \mathbf{Z}_{j,*}^{(\ell)} - \mathbf{Z}_{i,*} \|$ is minimized. We denote with

$$
A_B = \begin{bmatrix} | & & | \\ \mathbf{Z}_{j_1,*}^{(\ell)} & \dots & \mathbf{Z}_{j_{k_\ell},*}^{(\ell)} \\ | & & | \end{bmatrix} \tag{3}
$$

the matrix containing the activations $\mathbf{Z}_{j,*}^{(\ell)}$ of the neurons in the basis as columns.

Greedy Algorithm. The problem of finding an optimal basis of size k w.r.t. L_2 distance can be seen as a variation of the *column subset selection problem* which is known to be NP-complete [25]. As a consequence, we use a variant of a greedy algorithm [1]. While it does not always yield the optimal solution, it has been observed to work reasonably well in practice [9,10].

It has already been observed that layers closer to the output usually contain more condensed information and more redundancies, and can, thus, be compressed more aggressively [2]. We present a greedy algorithm that chooses which layer contains more information and needs a larger basis instead of decreasing the basis sizes equally fast in each layer.

In Algorithm 1, we see that the procedure iteratively removes neurons from the basis. To this end, it iterates over all layers $l \in \{1, \dots, L\}$ in the network. It tries to remove one neuron at a time from the basis. Then it computes the projection error of the smaller basis, which is defined as $\| \mathbf{Z}^{(\ell)\top} - \Pi_{A_B} \mathbf{Z}^{(\ell)\top} \|$, where Π_{A_B} is the matrix that projects the columns of $\mathbf{Z}^{(\ell)\top}$ onto the column space of A_B. The columns of A_B are the rows of $\mathbf{Z}^{(\ell)}$ whose neurons belong to B. It greedily evaluates all neurons in all layers and selects the best neuron of the best layer to be removed. After checking every layer, the algorithm decides on the best layer and neuron to be removed, i.e. the one with the smallest error.

Since the approach thoroughly evaluates all possibilities, its runtime depends on both the number of layers and neurons. A natural alternative would be a heuristic that guides us similarly well through the search space. We provide our choice of heuristic below.

Algorithm 1. Greedy algorithm over all layers

1: Given: k neurons to be removed
2: $\forall l \in \{1, \ldots, L\} : B^{(\ell)} \leftarrow \{1, \ldots, n_l\}$
3: $error_{min} \leftarrow \infty$, $l_{best} \leftarrow -1$, $n_{best} \leftarrow -1$
4: **for** $i \in 1, \ldots, k$ **do**
5:     **for** $l \in 1, \ldots, L$ **do**
6:         **for** $j \in 0, \ldots, n_l$ **do**
7:             Compute the projection error $error_j$ of $A_{B^{(\ell)} \setminus \{j\}}$
8:             **if** $error_j < error_{min}$ **then**
9:                 $l_{best} \leftarrow l$
10:                $n_{best} \leftarrow j$
11:                $error_{min} \leftarrow error_j$
12:    $B^{l_{best}} \leftarrow B^{l_{best}} \setminus \{n_{best}\}$
13: **return** $B^1, \ldots, B^L$

Variance-Based Heuristic. Instead of a step-wise decision that takes a lot of computation time, we propose to use a variance-based heuristic. We define the variance of a vector $\mathbf{v} \in \mathbb{R}^n$ in the usual way by $\text{Var}(\mathbf{v}) = \sum_{i=0}^{n} (v_i - \text{Mean}(\mathbf{v}))^2$ where $\text{Mean}(\mathbf{v})$ is the mean of the vector values. W.l.o.g. let the neurons be numbered in such a way that $\text{Var}(\mathbf{z}_1^{(\ell)}) \geq \cdots \geq \text{Var}(\mathbf{z}_{n_\ell}^{(\ell)})$. We then choose the basis to contain the neurons with the k_ℓ largest variances, i.e. $B = \{1, \ldots, k\}$. We assume that neurons with a higher variance in their output values carry more information, and are, therefore, more relevant. Indeed, we can see in our experiments, i.e. Fig. 2, that the heuristic-based approach can achieve similar results, but in far less time.

3.2   Finding the Coefficients

Given a basis $B^{(\ell)}$ for some layer ℓ, computed with the before-mentioned approach, we want to find the coefficients that can be used to replace the remaining neurons which are not part of the basis. We fix a neuron i in layer ℓ that we want to replace and whose values are stored in $\mathbf{Z}_{i,*}^{(\ell)}$, and we want to minimize $\| \sum_{j \in B^{(\ell)}} \alpha_{i,j}^{(\ell)} \cdot \mathbf{Z}_{j,*}^{(\ell)} - \mathbf{Z}_{i,*} \|$ for $\alpha_{i,j}^{(\ell)}$.

Since we want to find a linear combination of vectors, a natural choice is **linear programming**. The linear program is straightforward and can be found in [6, Appendix C]. Note that with the linear program, we are minimizing the L_1-distance between the neuron's values and its replacement, i.e. $\| \sum_{j \in B^{(\ell)}} \alpha_{i,j}^{(\ell)} \cdot \mathbf{Z}_{j,*}^{(\ell)} - \mathbf{Z}_{i,*} \|_1$.

In a different way, we can also consider the vectors $\mathbf{Z}_{j,*}^{(\ell)}$ for $j \in B^{(\ell)}$ to span a vector space. If we are given a subset $\{\mathbf{Z}_{j,*}^{(\ell)} | j \in B^{(\ell)} \subset \{1, \ldots, n_\ell\}\}$ that forms a basis for this space, i.e. $\text{span}((\mathbf{Z}_{j,*}^{(\ell)})_{j \in B^{(\ell)}}) = \text{span}((\mathbf{Z}_{j,*}^{(\ell)})_{j \in \{1, \ldots, n_\ell\}})$, we can represent any other vector $\mathbf{z}_i^{(\ell)}$ in terms of this basis. However, we usually cannot represent one neuron perfectly by a linear combination of other neurons. **Orthogo-**

nal projection gives us the closest point in the subspace $\text{span}((\mathbf{Z}^{(\ell)}_{j,*})_{j\in B^{(\ell)}})$
for any vector, in terms of L$_2$-distance. Then, $\boldsymbol{\alpha} = [\alpha^{(\ell)}_{i,j_1},\dots,\alpha^{(\ell)}_{i,j_{k_\ell}}]^\mathsf{T} :=$
$(A_B^\mathsf{T} A_B)^{-1} A_B^\mathsf{T} \mathbf{Z}^{(\ell)}_{i,*}$ gives us the coefficients for the orthogonal projection of $\mathbf{Z}^{(\ell)}_{i,*}$
on the linear space spanned by the columns of A_B. For a more detailed description of orthogonal projection see e.g. [17, Chapter 6.8]. Note that we assume
that the columns of A_B are linearly independent. If not we can simply replace
the respective neurons directly.

3.3   Replacement

Assuming, we have a basis $B^{(\ell)}$ of this layer and we already know the coefficients
$\alpha^{(\ell)}_{i,j} \in \mathbb{R}$ for $j \in B^{(\ell)}$ that we need to simulate the behavior of neuron i. This
means, we have a linear combination $\sum_{j\in B^{(\ell)}} \alpha^{(\ell)}_{i,j} \cdot \mathbf{Z}^{(\ell)}_{j,*}$, which we want to use
instead of neuron i itself. We will replace the outgoing weights $W^{(\ell)}$ of this layer,
such that for all $j \in B^{(\ell)}$

$$\tilde{W}^{(\ell)}_{*,j} = [w^{(\ell)}(1,j)+\alpha^{(\ell)}_{i,j}w^{(\ell)}(1,i),\dots,w^{(\ell)}(n_{\ell+1},j)+\alpha^{(\ell)}_{i,j}w^{(\ell)}(n_{\ell+1},i)]^\mathsf{T} \quad (4)$$
$$= W^{(\ell)}_{*,j} + \alpha^{(\ell)}_{i,j}W^{(\ell)}_{*,i} \quad (5)$$

Furthermore, we set $\tilde{W}^{(\ell)}_{*,i} = [0,\dots,0]^\mathsf{T}$, and $\tilde{W}^{(\ell)}_{i,*} = [0,\dots,0]^\mathsf{T}$. This means that
we will not use the output of neuron i anymore, but rather a weighted sum of
the outputs of neurons in $B^{(\ell)}$, and that we will not even compute the value of i.
Additionally, we keep track of the changes we apply to the different neurons with
a matrix $D^{(\ell)} = (d^{(\ell)}_{j,i}) \in \mathbb{R}^{n_\ell \times n_{\ell+1}}$. Initially, $D^{(\ell)}$ is 0 and after each replacement,
we add $\alpha^{(\ell)}_{i,j} \cdot w^{(\ell)}(i,i')$ to $d^{(\ell)}_{j,i'}$ for $j \in B^{(\ell)}$ and $i' \in \{1,\dots,n_{\ell+1}\}$. This is necessary
for restoring neurons at a later point.

In the optimal case, the replacement will not change the overall behavior of
the neural network. We can derive a the same semantic equivalence from [22]
incorporated into our setting:

Proposition 1 (Semantic Equivalence). *Let N be a neural network with L
layers, ℓ a layer of N, i a neuron of this layer, and $B^{(\ell)} \subset \{1,\dots,n_\ell\}\backslash\{i\}$ a
chosen basis. Let $\tilde{N}$ be the NN after replacing neuron i by a linear combination
of basis vectors with coefficients $\alpha^{(\ell)}_{i,j}$, with the procedure as described above.*

*If for all inputs $\mathbf{x} \in X \subset \mathcal{X}$, $z^{(\ell)}_i(\mathbf{x}) = \sum_{j\in B^{(\ell)}} \alpha^{(\ell)}_{i,j} z^{(\ell)}_j(\mathbf{x})$, then N and $\tilde{N}$
are semantically equal, i.e. for all inputs $\mathbf{x} \in X$, $\tilde{N}(\mathbf{x}) = N(\mathbf{x})$.*

It is easy to see that this proposition is true, for a full proof see [6, Appendix A].
However, the proposition assumes equality of $z^{(\ell)}_i(\mathbf{x})$ and $\sum_{j\in B^{(\ell)}} \alpha^{(\ell)}_{i,j} z^{(\ell)}_j(\mathbf{x})$ for
$\mathbf{x} \in X$, which virtually never holds for real-world neural networks. Therefore,
we want to minimize the difference $|z^{(\ell)}_i(\mathbf{x}) - \sum_{j\in B^{(\ell)}} \alpha^{(\ell)}_{i,j} z^{(\ell)}_j(\mathbf{x})|$, which will not
yield a semantically equivalent abstraction, but an abstraction with very similar
behavior. We can then **quantify the difference** between the output of the

original network and the abstraction, i.e. the *induced error* with the following Theorem.

Theorem 1 (Over-approximation Guarantee). *Let N be an NN with L layers. For each layer ℓ, we have a basis of neurons $B^{(\ell)}$, and a set of replaced neurons $I^{(\ell)}$. Then, let $\tilde{N}$ be the network after replacing neurons in $I^{(\ell)}$ as described above.*

We can over-approximate the error *between the output of the original network N^L and the output of the abstraction $\tilde{N}^L$ for $\mathbf{x} \in X \subset \mathcal{X}$ by*

$$\|\tilde{N}^L(\mathbf{x}) - N^L(\mathbf{x})\| \le b(1 - a^{L-1})/(1 - a)$$

with $a = \lambda(\|W\| + \eta)$, $b = \lambda\|W\|\epsilon$, with $\lambda^{(\ell)}$ being the Lipschitz-constant of the activation function in layer ℓ, $\lambda = \max_\ell \lambda^{(\ell)}$, $\|W\| = \max_\ell \|W^{(\ell)}\|_1$, $\eta = \max_\ell \eta^{(\ell)}$, and $\epsilon = \max_\ell \epsilon^{(\ell)}$, assuming that for all layers $\ell \in \{1, \ldots, L\}$ and for all inputs $\mathbf{x} \in X$, we have

- *for $i \in I^{(\ell)}$: $|z_i^{(\ell)}(\mathbf{x}) - \sum_{j \in B^{(\ell)}} \alpha_{i,j}^{(\ell)} z_j^{(\ell)}(\mathbf{x})| \le \epsilon^{(\ell)}$*
- *$|\sum_{i \in I^{(\ell)}} W_{*,i}^{(\ell)} \sum_{t \in B^{(\ell)}} \alpha_{i,t}^{(\ell)}| \le \eta^{(\ell)}$*

In other words, we can over-approximate the difference in the output of the original and the abstracted network by a value that depends on the weight matrices, the activation function and the tightness of the abstracted neurons to their replacements. The proof can be found in [6, Appendix B]. This Theorem provides us with the **theoretical guarantee** that, given our abstraction, we can provide a valid over-approximation of the output of the original network.

Comparison to the δ-Bisimulation. Let us recap the error definition from [22]. The difference of the bisimulation and the original network is bounded by $[(2a)^k - 1]b/(2a - 1)$, where $a = \lambda|S|\|W\|$ and $b = \lambda(|P|L(\mathcal{N})\|x\| + 1)\delta^1$. In this notation, $|S|$ is the maximum number of neurons per layer in the whole network, $|P|$ the maximum number of neurons in the bisimulation (can be understood as the number of neurons in an abstraction), $L(\mathcal{N})$ is the maximum Lipschitz-constant of all layers, and δ is the maximum absolute difference of the bias and sum of the incoming weights.

The drawbacks of that approach are twofold: (i) the error is based on one specific input, and (ii) it makes use of the Lipschitz-constant of the whole network. Calculating the Lipschitz constant of an NN is still part of ongoing research [11] and not a trivial problem. In contrast, we improve on both. Our error calculation generalizes over a set of inputs. Additionally, we use local information, stored in the weight-matrices, to circumvent using the Lipschitz-constant of the NN.

4   Refinement

For certain inputs the abstraction might not reflect the behavior of the original network. For these inputs, so-called *counterexamples*, we may want to *refine* the

---

[1] Please note that this statement is slightly different from the paper ($(2a)^k$ instead of $(2/a)^k$), which we believe to be a typo in the paper.

abstraction, as opposed to starting the abstraction from the original network again. We consider an input to be a counterexample whenever the abstraction assigns it a different label than the original network. However, a counterexample can be any input that does not align with the specifications.

We propose to refine the abstraction by restoring some of the replaced neurons. To do this, we need to know which neurons should be replaced and how. We first briefly mention three heuristics to choose a neuron for restoration. Afterward, we explain how to restore a neuron. Note that the refinement offers more than a "roll-back" of the most recent step of the abstraction since it picks the step-to-be-rolled-back in retrospect reflecting all other steps, leading to a more informed choice. This could in principle be done directly in the abstraction phase, but at an infeasible cost of a huge look-ahead.

Refinement Heuristics. We propose three different heuristics: difference-guided, gradient-guided, and look-ahead.

- The *difference-guided* refinement looks at the difference of a neuron in the original and its representation as a linear combination in the abstraction. It replaces the neuron with the largest difference.
- The *gradient-guided* refinement additionally takes the gradient of the NN into account, that is computed as in the training phase of the NN. This takes into account how the whole network would need to change to fix the counterexample.
- The *look-ahead* is the most greedy method and would try out every replaced neuron. It would check how much the network would improve if the neuron was replaced and then chooses the neuron with the highest improvement.

More details on the approaches can be found in [6, Appendix D].

Restoration of a Neuron. The restoration principle can be seen as the counterpart of the replacement. Let $\tilde{N}$ be the network obtained by replacing several neurons in the original network N, where we want to restore a deleted neuron i of layer ℓ. To do this, we need not only to get the original neuron back, including its incoming and outgoing weights but also to remove the additional outgoing weights from the basis neurons. Intuitively, the restoration removes the linear combination, ensures that the original outgoing weights for the neuron are used, and adjusts the incoming weights of the neuron. We may have changed layer $\ell - 1$, and thus we cannot restore the original incoming weights of neuron i, but we have to adapt it to changes in the basis $B^{(\ell-1)}$. This can be done with the following changes:

- $\forall j \in B^{(\ell)}: \tilde{W}^{(\ell)}_{*,j} = \tilde{\tilde{W}}^{(\ell)}_{*,j} - \alpha_j W^{(\ell)}_{*,j}$
- $\tilde{W}^{(\ell)}_{*,i} = W^{(\ell)}_{*,i}$
- $\forall j \in B^{(\ell-1)}: \tilde{w}^{(\ell-1)}(i,j) = w^{(\ell-1)}(i,j) + d^{(\ell-1)}_{j,i}$

Afterward, we subtract $\alpha_j \cdot w^{(\ell)}(i,i')$ from $d^{(\ell)}_{j,i'}$ for $i' \in \{1,\ldots,n_{\ell+1}\}$ and $j \in B^{(\ell)}$.

5   Experimental Results

Our experimental section is divided into several parts: The first one covers how the different methods for finding a basis and the coefficients compare, as described in Sect. 3.2 and Sect. 3.1. The second part shows experiments on our approach in comparison to existing works, namely *DeepAbstract* [2] and our implementation of bisimulation [22] (which was not implemented before). The third part contains the comparison between the abstraction based on syntactic and semantic information. The fourth part describes our experiments on abstraction refinement. Finally, the last part contains experiments on the error induced by our abstraction. Note that supplemental experiments can be found in the Appendix.

Lastly, the work of Katz et al. [8] tightly couples the abstraction with the subsequent particular verification, by integrating the specification as layers into the network. It is, thus, not clear how an abstraction from [8] could be extracted from the tool and reused for another purpose. Additionally, our abstraction would have to be connected with some verification algorithm (DeepPoly, as done by DeepAbstract, or some other) to compare. *Any comparison of the two works would then mostly compare the different verification tools, not really the abstractions.* Although a comparison of different verifiers linked to our LiNNA is an interesting next step into one of the possible applications, it is out of the scope of this paper, which examines the abstraction itself (see Introduction).

Implementation. We implemented the approach in our tool *LiNNA* (*Li*near *N*eural *N*etwork *A*bstraction)[2]. We used networks that were trained on MNIST [20], CIFAR-10 [18], and FashionMNIST [32] for our experiments. In the following, we refer to the corresponding trained networks with "$L \times n$", where L denotes the number of hidden layers and n is the number of neurons in these hidden layers. All experiments were conducted on a computer with Ubuntu 22.04 LTS with 2.6 GHz Intel© Core™ i7 processors, and 32 GB of RAM.

Performance Measures. We will compare the approaches mostly on (i) the reduction rate and (ii) the accuracy on a test set. Intuitively, the *reduction rate* describes how much the NN was reduced by abstraction. If an NN N has in total n neurons, but after reduction, there are m neurons left, then the reduction rate is then defined as $RR(N) = 1 - \frac{m}{n}$. The *accuracy* of a NN on a test set is defined as the ratio of how many inputs are predicted with the correct label. This is the key performance indicator in machine learning and shows how well a network generalizes to unseen data. In evaluating our abstraction, we follow the same principle since we want to know how well the NN generalizes after abstraction. Note that this test set was not used for training or computing the abstraction.

5.1   Abstraction

Finding the Basis. We have given two different methods in Sect. 3.1 to find a good basis B. While the orthogonal projection yields an equally good abstraction

---

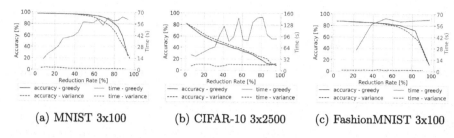

(a) MNIST 3x100   (b) CIFAR-10 3x2500   (c) FashionMNIST 3x100

Fig. 2. *Finding the basis for replacement* - Evaluation on different datasets. The plots contain a comparison of LiNNA while using the greedy variant (solid) and the variance-based heuristic (dashed) for finding a basis with orthogonal projection. Comparison of accuracy (blue) in percent and computation time (red) in seconds. (Color figure online)

compared to linear programming, it outperforms the latter in terms of runtime by magnitudes. Hence, we conducted the rest of the experiments with orthogonal projection. The full comparison between orthogonal projection and linear programming can be found in [6, Fig. 14, Appendix E].

When we compare the greedy and the heuristic-based approach, shown in Fig. 2, we see that the former outperforms the latter in terms of accuracy on MNIST and FashionMNIST. On CIFAR-10, the variance-based approach is slightly better. However, the variance-based approach is always faster than the greedy approach and scales better, as can be seen for all datasets. Unsurprisingly, the greedy approach takes more time for higher reduction rates, because it needs to evaluate many candidates. The variance-based approach just takes the best neurons according to their variance, which has to be calculated only once. Therefore, the calculation is constant in terms of removed neurons.

The plots show one more difference in the behavior: On MNIST and Fashion-MNIST, we see a quite stable accuracy until a reduction rate of 60%. We cannot see the same behavior on CIFAR-10. We believe this is due to the accuracy and size of the networks. Whereas it is fairly easy to train a feedforward network for MNIST and FashionMNIST on a regular computer, this is more challenging for CIFAR-10. We plan to include more extensive experiments including more involved NN architectures in future work. Finally, our abstraction relies on the assumption that NNs contain a lot of redundant information.

We want to emphasize, that in machine learning, it is common to train a huge network that contains many more neurons than necessary to solve the task [34]. After the introduction of regularization techniques (e.g. [24]), the problem of over-fitting (e.g. [5]) has become often negligible. Therefore, the automatic response to a bad neural network is often to increase its size, either in depth or in width. Our approach can detect these cases and abstract away the redundant information.

Finding the Coefficients. We have in total four different approaches to finding the coefficients: greedy or heuristic-based linear programming, and greedy or heuristic-based orthogonal projection. All four have similar accuracies for the

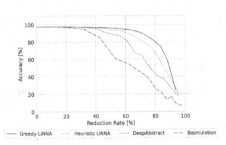

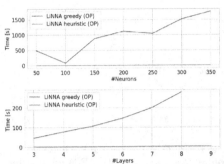

Fig. 3. *Comparison of LiNNA to related work* - LiNNA (greedy and heuristic-based variant), *DeepAbstract* [2], and our implementation of the bisimulation [22] is evaluated in terms of accuracy on the test set for a certain reduction rate. The experiment was conducted on an MNIST 3×100 network.

Fig. 4. *Scalability of LiNNA* - Average runtime for 20 different reduction rates on one network. The plot at the top depicts the runtime for MNIST networks with 4 layers, w.r.t. number of neurons. The plot at the bottom shows the runtime for MNIST networks with 100 neurons per layer, w.r.t. number of layers.

same reduction rate, whereas the heuristic ones are mostly just slightly worse than the greedy ones. For a more detailed evaluation, please refer to [6, Appendix G]. The runtimes of the four approaches, however, differ a lot. Take for example an MNIST 3×100 network. We assume that the abstraction is performed by starting with the full network and reducing up to a certain reduction rate. Thus, we have runtimes for each of the approaches for each reduction rate. We take the average over all the reductions and get 47 s for the greedy orthogonal projection, 5130 s for the greedy linear programming, 1 s for the heuristic orthogonal projection, and 2 s for the heuristic linear programming. Linear programming takes a lot more time than orthogonal projection, and, as already seen before, the heuristic approaches are much faster than the greedy ones. Please refer to [6, Appendix J] for more experiments on the runtime. Therefore, we propose to use the heuristic approach and the orthogonal projection.

Scalability. We evaluate how our approach scales to networks of different sizes. We evaluate (1) how our approach scales with an increasing number of layers, and (2) how it scales with a fixed number of layers but an increasing number of neurons. We show our experiments in Fig. 4. The runtime is the average runtime over 20 different reduction rates on the same network. One can imagine this as averaging the runtimes shown in Fig. 2. We can see that the variance-based approach has almost constant runtime, whereas the runtime of the greedy approach is increasing for both a higher number of layers and neurons.

Final Assessment. We have four possibilities on how to abstract an NN: greedy orthogonal projection, greedy linear programming, heuristic-based orthogonal

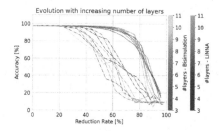
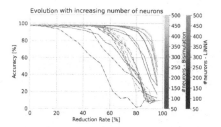

Fig. 5. *Evolution of the accuracy* on the test set for different reduction rates, for an increasing number of layers, or neurons. We show LiNNA (blue-green) for semantic abstraction, and for syntactic abstraction, bisimulation (red-yellow). The networks were trained on MNIST and have a fixed number of neurons (100) on the left, and a fixed number of layers (4) on the right.

projection, and heuristic-based linear programming. Given that the orthogonal projection outperforms linear programming in terms of accuracy and computation time, we propose to use orthogonal projection. We believe that it is sufficient to use the heuristic-based approach, thereby gaining faster runtimes and only barely sacrificing any accuracy. Whenever we refer to *LiNNA* from now on without any additions, it will be the heuristic-based orthogonal projection.

5.2   Comparison to Existing Work

We want to show how our approach compares to existing works, i.e. *DeepAbstract* and the *bisimulation*. Since there is no implementation available for the latter, we implemented it ourselves. Please refer to [6, Appendix F] for the details. The results of the comparison are shown in Fig. 3. It is evident that DeepAbstract achieves higher accuracies than the bisimulation, but LiNNA outperforms DeepAbstract and the bisimulation in terms of accuracy for all reduction rates.

   Concerning the runtime, we measure the runtime of each approach for a certain reduction rate, starting from the full network. We find that (in the median) LiNNA (greedy) needs 55 s up to 199 s, LiNNA (heuristic) 2 s up to 3 s, DeepAbstract 187 s up to 2420 s, and the bisimulation 1 s up to 2 s, on MNIST networks of different sizes (starting from 4 × 50 up to 11 × 100). The details can be found in [6, Appendix J]. The bisimulation performs best, however just slightly ahead of the heuristic-based LiNNA. The greedy LiNNA, as well as DeepAbstract both have a much higher computation time.

   However, in terms of accuracy, greedy LiNNA seems to be the best-performing approach, given sufficient time. Due to efficiency, we suggest using heuristic-based LiNNA, as it is as fast as the bisimulation, but its accuracy is a lot better and even close to greedy LiNNA.

   Since we are interested in the general behavior of the abstraction, we want to see how the methods work for varying sizes of networks, but not only in terms of scalability. In Fig. 5, we show the trend for bisimulation and LiNNA for an increasing number of layers resp. neurons per layer. On the left, we fix the

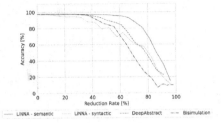
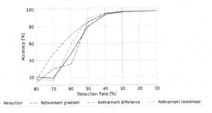

Fig. 6. *Syntactic VS. Semantic* - This plot shows the difference between using semantic resp. syntactic information for the abstraction on an MNIST 5 × 100 network. Semantic: LiNNA (semantic) and DeepAbstract. Syntactic: LiNNA (syntactic) and the bisimulation.

Fig. 7. *Refinement* - This plot shows the accuracy of an MNIST 5 × 100 network that was abstracted and refined to a certain reduction rate R. There is also a plot for an abstraction to the same reduction rate as after the refinement but without refining.

number of neurons per layer to 100 and incrementally increase the number of layers. On the right, we fix the number of layers to four and increase the number of neurons.

We can see that the performance of the networks from the bisimulation varies a lot and gets slightly worse when there are more layers, whereas LiNNA has a very small variation and the performance of the abstractions increases slightly for more layers. Both approaches compute abstractions that perform better the more neurons are in a layer, but LiNNA converges to a much steeper curve at high reduction rates.

For NNs with 400 or more neurons, LiNNA can reduce 80% of the neurons without a significant loss in accuracy, whereas the bisimulation can do the same only for up to a reduction rate of 55%.

5.3   Semantic vs Syntactic

In the following, we want to show the differences between semantic and syntactic abstractions. Recall that syntactic abstraction makes use of the weights of the network, the syntactic information, with no consideration of the actual behavior of the NN on the inputs. Semantic abstraction, on the other hand, focuses on the values of the neurons on an input dataset, which also incorporates information about the weights. DeepAbstract and LiNNA, both use semantic information, whereas bisimulation uses syntactic information. We additionally evaluate the performance of LiNNA on syntactic information.

Which type of information is better for abstraction: semantic or syntactic? Note that both DeepAbstract and the bisimulation represent a group of neurons by one single representative, whereas LiNNA makes use of a linear combination.

We summarize our results in Fig. 6. For smaller reduction rates, the bisimulation performs better than LiNNA on syntactic information; for higher reduction rates it is reversed. In general, the approaches based on semantics (DeepAbstract

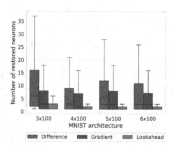
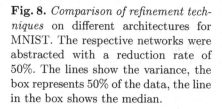

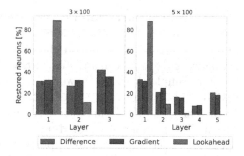

Fig. 8. *Comparison of refinement techniques* on different architectures for MNIST. The respective networks were abstracted with a reduction rate of 50%. The lines show the variance, the box represents 50% of the data, the line in the box shows the median.

Fig. 9. *Refinement on different layers* - We considered abstractions that were obtained with a 50% reduction rate and fixed 1000 counterexamples. The plots depict the percentage of restored neurons in the layers of the different MNIST networks.

and LiNNA - semantic) outperform the other two approaches w.r.t. accuracy. While abstraction based on syntactic information can provide global guarantees for any input, abstraction based on semantic information relies on the fact that its inputs during abstraction are similar to the ones it will be evaluated on later. However, we see that still the semantic information is more appropriate for preserving accuracy because it combines the knowledge about possible inputs with the knowledge about the weights.

5.4   Refining the Network

We propose refinement of the abstraction in cases where it does not capture all the behavior anymore, instead of restarting the abstraction process. We consider networks that are abstracted up to certain reduction rates, i.e. 20%, 30%, ..., 90%, and use the refinement to regain 10% of the neurons. For example, we reduce the network by 90% and then use refinement to get back to a reduction rate of 80%. We evaluate this refined network on the test dataset and plot its accuracy. Additionally, we show the accuracy of the same NN which is directly reduced to an 80% reduction rate, without refinement. This plot is shown in Fig. 7 for a 5 × 100 network, trained on MNIST.

The gradient and look-ahead refinement have a similar performance. However, the difference-based approach even outperforms the direct reduction itself. This behavior can be explained by the fact that the refinement and the abstraction look at different metrics for removing/restoring neurons. The refinement can focus directly on optimizing for the inputs at hand, whereas the abstraction was generated on the training set. In conclusion, the refinement can even improve the abstraction and it is beneficial to abstract slightly more than required, and refine for the relevant inputs, rather than having a finer abstraction directly.

Comparison of the Different Approaches. We collect images that are labeled differently by the abstraction and observe the number of neurons that are restored in order to fix the classification of each image. We ran the experiment on different networks that were abstracted with a 50% reduction rate and considered 1000 counterexamples for each network. The results are summarized in Fig. 8, where we have boxplots for each refinement method on four different network architectures. The look-ahead approach is the most effective technique since it requires the smallest number of restored neurons. In the median, it only requires 1 to 2 operations. The gradient-based approach performs noticeably worse but outperforms the difference-based approach on all networks. The computation time, however, gives a different perspective: Repairing one counterexample takes on average <1 s for the difference-based approach, 1 s for the gradient-based, but the look-ahead approach takes on average 4 s. Interestingly, the look-ahead approach restores fewer neurons but performs worse in accuracy. The difference-based performs better in terms of accuracy while restoring more neurons.

Insight on the Relevance of Layers. We also investigated in which layers the different refinement techniques tend to restore the neurons. The plots in Fig. 9 illustrate the percentage of restored neurons in each layer. Notably, the look-ahead approach restores most neurons in the first layer, and very few or none in the later layers, whereas the other approaches have a more uniform behavior. However, the more layers the network has, the more the gradient- and difference-based approaches tend to restore more neurons in the first layer. As reported already by [2], the first layers seem to have a larger influence on the network's output and hence should be focused on during refinement. It is even more interesting that the difference-based approach does not focus on the first layers as much as the look-ahead approach, but it is better in terms of accuracy.

5.5   Error Calculation

We want to show how the abstraction simulates the original network on unseen data not only w.r.t. the output but on every single neuron. In other words, is the discrepancy between the concrete and abstract network higher on the *test* data than on the *training* data that generate the abstraction, or does the link between the neuron and its linear abstraction generalize well?

In Fig. 10, we look at this ratio ("relative error of the abstraction"), i.e. the absolute difference of (activation values of) a simulated abstract neuron to the original neuron, once on the test dataset divided by the maximum value on the training dataset. We can see that there are cases where the error can be greater than one (meaning "larger than on the training set"), see the first row of the plot. However, the geometric mean, defined as $\left(\Pi_{i=1}^{N} a_i\right)^{\frac{1}{N}}$, calculated over all images is very small. Note that more experiments can be found in [6, Appendix L]. In conclusion, we can say that our abstraction is close to the original also on the test dataset, although the theoretical error calculation does not guarantee so tight a simulation. Future work should reveal how to further utilize the empirical proximity in transferring the reasoning from the abstraction to the original.

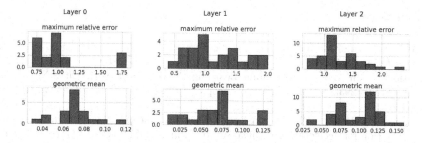

Fig. 10. *Histograms of the relative error* of the values of the neurons in an MNIST 3×100 network and its abstraction (reduced by 30%). The first row shows the maximum relative error of each neuron in the NN, that occurred for some input from the test set. The second row shows the geometric mean of the relative error of each neuron over 100 images of the test set.

6 Conclusions

The focus of this work was to examine abstraction not as a part of a verification procedure, but rather as a stand-alone transformation, which can later be used in different ways: as a preprocessing step for verification, as means of obtaining an equivalent smaller network, or to gain insights about the network and its training, such as identifying where redundancies arise in trained neural networks. (This is analogous to the situation of bisimulation, which has been largely investigated on its own not necessarily as a part of a verification procedure, and its use in verification is only one of the applications.)

We have introduced *LiNNA*, which abstracts a network by replacing neurons with *linear combinations* of other neurons and also equip it with a *refinement* method. We bound the error and thus the difference between the abstraction and the original network in Theorem 1. The theorem yields a lower and an upper bound on the network's output, thereby providing its over-approximation.

We showed that the linear extension provides better performance than existing work on abstraction for classification networks, both DeepAbstract, and the bisimulation-based approach. We focused our experimental evaluation on *accuracy*, since the aim of the abstraction is to faithfully mimic the *whole classification process* in the smaller, abstract network, not just one concrete property to be verified, which describes only a very specific aspect of the network. Interestingly, the practical error is dramatically smaller than the worst-case bounds. We hope this first, experimental step will stimulate interest in research that could utilize this actual advantage, which is currently not supported by any respective theory.

Furthermore, we show that the use of *semantic information should be preferred* over syntactic information because it allows for higher reductions while preserving similar behavior and being cheap since the I/O sets can be quite small. Bringing back semantics could take us closer to the efficiency of classical software abstraction, where the semantics of states is the very key, going way beyond bisimulation.

References

1. Altschuler, J., et al.: Greedy column subset selection: new bounds and distributed algorithms. In: Balcan, M., Weinberger, K.Q. (eds.) Proceedings of the 33nd International Conference on Machine Learning, ICML, New York City, NY, USA, vol. 48, pp. 2539–2548. JMLR Workshop and Conference Proceedings. JMLR.org (2016)

2. Ashok, P., Hashemi, V., Křetínský, J., Mohr, S.: DeepAbstract: neural network abstraction for accelerating verification. In: Hung, D.V., Sokolsky, O. (eds.) ATVA 2020. LNCS, vol. 12302, pp. 92–107. Springer, Cham (2020). https://doi.org/10.1007/978-3-030-59152-6_5

3. Bishop, C.M.: Pattern Recognition and Machine Learning. Information Science and Statistics, 5th edn. Springer, Cham (2007)

4. Brix, C., et al.: First three years of the international verification of neural networks competition (VNN-COMP). Int. J. Softw. Tools Technol. Transfer 1–11 (2023). https://doi.org/10.1007/s10009-023-00703-4

5. Caruana, R., Lawrence, S., Giles, C.: Overfitting in neural nets: backpropagation, conjugate gradient, and early stopping. In: Leen, T., Dietterich, T., Tresp, V. (eds.) Advances in Neural Information Processing Systems, vol. 13. MIT Press (2000)

6. Chau, C., Křetínský, J., Mohr, S.: Syntactic vs semantic linear abstraction and refinement of neural networks (2023)

7. Cheng, Y., Wang, D., Zhou, P., Zhang, T.: A survey of model compression and acceleration for deep neural networks. Preprint arXiv:1710.09282 (2017)

8. Elboher, Y.Y., Gottschlich, J., Katz, G.: An abstraction-based framework for neural network verification. In: Lahiri, S.K., Wang, C. (eds.) CAV 2020. LNCS, vol. 12224, pp. 43–65. Springer, Cham (2020). https://doi.org/10.1007/978-3-030-53288-8_3

9. Farahat, A.K., Ghodsi, A., Kamel, M.S.: A fast greedy algorithm for generalized column subset selection. Preprint arXiv:1312.6820 (2013)

10. Farahat, A.K., Ghodsi, A., Kamel, M.S.: An efficient greedy method for unsupervised feature selection. In: 11th International Conference on Data Mining, Vancouver, BC, Canada, pp. 161–170. IEEE (2011)

11. Fazlyab, M., et al.: Efficient and accurate estimation of Lipschitz constants for deep neural networks. In: Wallach, H., et al. (eds.) Advances in Neural Information Processing Systems, vol. 32. Curran Associates Inc. (2019)

12. Gong, Y., Liu, L., Yang, M., Bourdev, L.: Compressing deep convolutional networks using vector quantization. Preprint arXiv:1412.6115 (2014)

13. Hinton, G., Vinyals, O., Dean, J., et al.: Distilling the knowledge in a neural network. In: NeurIPS Deep Learning Workshop (2014)

14. Huang, G., Liu, Z., van der Maaten, L., Weinberger, K.Q.: Densely connected convolutional networks. In: Proceedings of the IEEE Conference on Computer Vision and Pattern Recognition (CVPR), pp. 4700–4708 (2017)

15. Jian, X., Jinyu, L., Yifan, G.: Restructuring of deep neural network acoustic models with singular value decomposition. In: Interspeech, pp. 2365–2369 (2013). https://doi.org/10.21437/interspeech.2013-552

16. Katz, G., et al.: The marabou framework for verification and analysis of deep neural networks. In: Dillig, I., Tasiran, S. (eds.) CAV 2019. LNCS, vol. 11561, pp. 443–452. Springer, Cham (2019). https://doi.org/10.1007/978-3-030-25540-4_26

17. Kirkwood, J.R., Kirkwood, B.H.: Elementary Linear Algebra. Chapman and Hall/CRC (2017)

18. Krizhevsky, A., Hinton, G., et al.: Learning multiple layers of features from tiny images (2009)
19. Lawrence, S., Giles, C., Tsoi, A.: Lessons in neural network training: overfitting may be harder than expected. In: Anon (ed.) Proceedings of the National Conference on Artificial Intelligence, pp. 540–545. AAAI (1997)
20. LeCun, Y.: The MNIST database of handwritten digits (1998). http://yann.lecun.com/exdb/mnist/
21. Maas, A.L., Hannun, A.Y., Ng, A.Y.: Rectifier nonlinearities improve neural network acoustic models. http://robotics.stanford.edu/~amaas/papers/relu_hybrid_icml2013_final.pdf
22. Prabhakar, P.: Bisimulations for neural network reduction. In: Finkbeiner, B., Wies, T. (eds.) VMCAI 2022. LNCS, vol. 13182, pp. 285–300. Springer, Cham (2022). https://doi.org/10.1007/978-3-030-94583-1_14
23. Prabhakar, P., Rahimi Afzal, Z.: Abstraction based output range analysis for neural networks. In: Wallach, H., et al. (eds.) Advances in Neural Information Processing Systems, vol. 32. Curran Associates Inc. (2019)
24. Schmidhuber, J.: Deep learning in neural networks: an overview. Neural Netw. **61**, 85–117 (2015). https://doi.org/10.1016/j.neunet.2014.09.003
25. Shitov, Y.: Column subset selection is NP-complete. Linear Algebra Appl. **610**, 52–58 (2021). https://doi.org/10.1016/j.laa.2020.09.015
26. Singh, G., Gehr, T., Püschel, M., Vechev, M.: An abstract domain for certifying neural networks. Proc. ACM Program. Lang. **3**(POPL) (2019). https://doi.org/10.1145/3290354
27. Singh, G., Gehr, T., Püschel, M., Vechev, M.T.: Boosting robustness certification of neural networks. In: 7th International Conference on Learning Representations, ICLR, New Orleans, LA, USA. OpenReview.net (2019)
28. Sotoudeh, M., Thakur, A.V.: Abstract neural networks. In: Pichardie, D., Sighireanu, M. (eds.) SAS 2020. LNCS, vol. 12389, pp. 65–88. Springer, Cham (2020). https://doi.org/10.1007/978-3-030-65474-0_4
29. Tran, H.-D., et al.: Robustness verification of semantic segmentation neural networks using relaxed reachability. In: Silva, A., Leino, K.R.M. (eds.) CAV 2021. LNCS, vol. 12759, pp. 263–286. Springer, Cham (2021). https://doi.org/10.1007/978-3-030-81685-8_12
30. Virmaux, A., Scaman, K.: Lipschitz regularity of deep neural networks: analysis and efficient estimation. In: Bengio, S., et al. (eds.) Advances in Neural Information Processing Systems 31: Annual Conference on Neural Information Processing Systems, NeurIPS, Montréal, Canada, pp. 3839–3848 (2018)
31. Wang, S., et al.: Beta-CROWN: efficient bound propagation with per-neuron split constraints for neural network robustness verification. In: Ranzato, M., et al. (eds.) Advances in Neural Information Processing Systems, vol. 34, pp. 29909–29921. Curran Associates Inc. (2021)
32. Xiao, H., Rasul, K., Vollgraf, R.: Fashion-MNIST: a novel image dataset for benchmarking machine learning algorithms. Preprint arXiv:1708.07747 (2017)
33. Xu, K., et al.: Fast and complete: enabling complete neural network verification with rapid and massively parallel incomplete verifiers. In: International Conference on Learning Representations (2021)
34. Zhang, C., et al.: Understanding deep learning requires rethinking generalization. CoRR, abs/1611.03530 (2016). http://arxiv.org/abs/1611.03530

Using Counterexamples to Improve Robustness Verification in Neural Networks

Mohammad Afzal$^{1,2(\boxtimes)}$ (iD), Ashutosh Gupta^1 (iD), and S. Akshay^1 (iD)

^{1} Indian Institute of Technology Bombay, Mumbai, India
^{2} TCS Research, Pune, India
afzal.2@tcs.com

Abstract. Given the pervasive use of neural networks in safety-critical systems it is important to ensure that they are robust. Recent research has focused on the question of verifying whether networks do not alter their behavior under small perturbations in inputs. Most successful methods are based on the paradigm of branch-and-bound, an abstraction-refinement technique. However, despite tremendous improvements in the last five years, there are still several benchmarks where these methods fail. One reason for this is that many methods use off-the-shelf methods to find the cause of imprecisions.

In this paper, our goal is to develop an approach to identify the precise source of imprecision during abstraction. We present a *novel* counterexample guided approach that can be applied alongside many abstraction techniques. As a specific case, we implement our technique on top of a basic abstraction framework provided by the tool DEEPPOLY and demonstrate how we can remove imprecisions in a targetted manner. This allows us to go past DEEPPOLY's performance as well as outperform other refinement approaches in literature. Surprisingly, we are also able to verify several benchmark instances on which all leading tools fail.

Keywords: Neural Networks · Abstraction Refinement · Robustness verification · Counterexample guided approaches

1 Introduction

Neural networks are being increasingly used in safety-critical systems such as autonomous vehicles, medical diagnosis, and speech recognition [1–3]. It is important not only that such systems behave correctly in theory but also that they are robust in practice. Unfortunately, it is often the case (see e.g., Goodfellow [4]) that a slight change/perturbation in the input can often fool the neural networks into an error. Such errors can be hard to find/analyze/debug as these neural networks contain hundreds of thousands of non-linear nodes.

To address this problem, an entire line of research has emerged focussing on automatically proving (or disproving) the robustness of such networks. Since automatic verification of neural networks is NP-hard [5], researchers use approximations in their methods. Classically, we may divide the methods into two

É. André and J. Sun (Eds.): ATVA 2023, LNCS 14215, pp. 422–443, 2023.
https://doi.org/10.1007/978-3-031-45329-8_20

classes, namely complete and incomplete. The methods [6–16] are complete. Since complete methods explore exact state space, they suffer from scalability issues on large-scale networks. On the other hand, abstraction based methods e.g., [17–23] are sound and incomplete, because they over-approximate the state space, but they scale extremely well to large benchmarks. A representative method DEEPPOLY [24] maintains and propagates upper and lower bound constraints using the so-called triangle approximation (also see Sect. 3.1). This is also sometimes called bound-propagation. Unsurprisingly, DEEPPOLY and other abstraction based methods suffer from imprecision. Hence, the methods [25–29] refine the over-approximated state space to achieve completeness. In [25,26,29] the authors eliminate the spurious information (i.e., imprecision introduced by abstraction) by bisecting the input space on the guided dimension. In [28], which also works on top of DEEPPOLY [24], the authors remove the spurious region by conjuncting each neuron's constraints with the negation of the robustness property and using an MILP (mixed integer linear programming) optimizer Gurobi [30] to refine the bounds of neurons. Another work that refines DEEP-POLY is κPOLY [31] which considers a group of neurons at once to generate the constraints and compute the bounds of neurons. One issue with all these approaches is that refinement is not guided by previous information/runs and hence they suffer from scalability issues.

In this paper, we consider the basic abstraction framework provided by DEEP-POLY and develop a novel refinement technique that is *counterexample guided*, i.e., we use counterexamples generated from imprecisions during abstraction to guide the refinement process. Our main contributions are the following:

- We introduce a new *maxsat-based* technique to find the cause of imprecision and spuriousness. Starting with an input where the abstraction does not get verified (we use a MILP solver to obtain this), we check whether the input generates a real counterexample of falsification of the property or if it is spurious, by executing the neural net. If it is a spurious counterexample, we identify the neuron or the set of neurons that caused it.
- We use these specially identified or *marked* neurons to split and refine. This ensures that, unlike earlier refinement methods, our method progresses at each iteration and eliminates spurious counterexamples.
- We adapt the existing refinement framework built on ideas from MILP-methods and implement this as a counterexample guided abstraction refinement algorithm on top of DEEPPOLY.
- We show that our technique outperforms to-the-best-of-our-knowledge all existing refinement strategies based on DEEPPOLY.
- We also identify a class of benchmarks coming from adversarially trained networks, where these state-of-the-art tools do not work well, because of the ineffectiveness of certain preprocessing steps (e.g., PGD attack [32])
- Incorporating such preprocessing techniques in our tool allows us to obtain a significant improvement in the overall performance of our tool. Our implementation is able to verify several benchmarks that are beyond the reach of state-of-the-art tools such as $\alpha\beta$-CROWN [33] and OVAL [34].

Related Work. A different but very successful line of research has been to revisit the branching heuristics for refinement and use ideas from convex optimization instead of linear or mixed integer linear programming. Starting from a slightly different abstraction/bound propagation method CROWN [23], the work in [14] adopts this approach. This is amenable to parallelizing and hence good for GPU implementations [15]. Recently, techniques based on cutting planes have been used to further improve the refinement analysis, solving more benchmarks at the cost of speed [16]. The success of this line of research can be seen by the fact that the state-of-the-art tool $\alpha\beta$-CROWN [33] (a highly optimized solver that uses a collection of different parametrized algorithms) has won the 2nd and 3rd international Verification of Neural Networks Competition (VNNCOMP'21, '22) in a field of leading tools for robustness verification. OVAL [34], another leading tool, uses multiple optimized techniques, which at its core perform an effective branch and bound on the RELU activation function. They attempt to compute the rough estimate on the improvement on objective function by splitting a particular neuron, and split neurons with the highest estimated improvement. Finally, in MARABOU [11], another leading complete tool, the authors search for an assignment that satisfies the constraints. They treat the non-linear constraints lazily with the hope that some non-linear constraints will not be needed to satisfy. Despite the enormous progress made by these tools in just the last 2–3 years, there still many benchmarks that are out of their reach. Our focus in this paper is orthogonal to these approaches, as we use counterexamples to guide the identification the source of imprecision. In our experiments in Sect. 5, we show that this allows us to solve many benchmarks which these cannot. Integrating our counterexample guided approach for imprecision-identification with these optimized tools (e.g., $\alpha\beta$-CROWN's branch and bound strategy) would be the next step towards wider coverage and performance. The constraints solved by $\alpha\beta$-CROWN, which also uses branch-and-bound, are from a dual space, and it is a priori unclear how to derive our maxSAT query from the failure of a run.

As mentioned earlier, DEEPSRGR [28] and KPOLY [31] use refinement of DEEPPOLY, but they are not counterexample guided. Elboher et al. [27] does perform counterexample guided abstraction refinement, but their abstraction technique is orthogonal to DEEPPOLY. They reduce the network size by merging similar neurons with over-approximation, while DEEPPOLY maintains the linear constraints for each neuron without changing the structure of the network. These approaches also suffer from scalability issues on large-scale networks.

Structure of the Paper. We start with a motivating example in the next Sect. 2. We define the notions and definitions in Sect. 3. Section 4 contains the algorithmic procedure of our approach as well as proofs of progress and termination. Section 5 contains our experimental results and we conclude in Sect. 6.

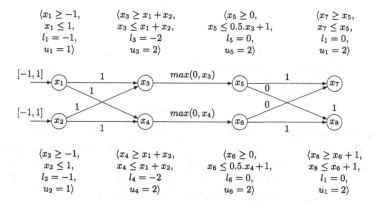

$$\langle x_1 \geq -1, \qquad \langle x_3 \geq x_1 + x_2, \qquad \langle x_5 \geq 0, \qquad \langle x_7 \geq x_5,$$
$$x_1 \leq 1, \qquad x_3 \leq x_1 + x_2, \qquad x_5 \leq 0.5.x_3 + 1, \qquad x_7 \leq x_5,$$
$$l_1 = -1, \qquad l_3 = -2 \qquad l_5 = 0, \qquad l_1 = 0,$$
$$u_1 = 1 \rangle \qquad u_3 = 2 \rangle \qquad u_5 = 2 \rangle \qquad u_1 = 2 \rangle$$

$$\langle x_2 \geq -1, \qquad \langle x_4 \geq x_1 + x_2, \qquad \langle x_6 \geq 0, \qquad \langle x_8 \geq x_6 + 1,$$
$$x_2 \leq 1, \qquad x_4 \leq x_1 + x_2, \qquad x_6 \leq 0.5.x_4 + 1, \qquad x_8 \leq x_6 + 1,$$
$$l_2 = -1, \qquad l_4 = -2 \qquad l_6 = 0, \qquad l_1 = 0,$$
$$u_2 = 1 \rangle \qquad u_4 = 2 \rangle \qquad u_6 = 2 \rangle \qquad u_1 = 2 \rangle$$

Fig. 1. Hypothetical example of neural network

2   A Motivating Example

Consider the neural network depicted in Fig. 1, which comprises one input layer, one hidden layer, and one output layer. The hidden layer is divided into two sub-layers: AFFINE and RELU, resulting in a total of four layers shown in Fig. 1. Every layer contains two neurons. The neuron x_8 has a bias of 1, and all the other neurons have a bias of 0. Our goal is to verify for all input $x_1, x_2 \in [-1, 1]$ the outputs satisfy $x_7 \leq x_8$. Our approach extends DEEPPOLY [24]. DEEPPOLY maintains one upper and one lower constraint and an upper and lower bound for each neuron. For a neuron of the affine layer, the upper and lower constraint is the same, which is the weighted sum of the input neurons i.e. x_3's upper and lower constraint is $x_1 + x_2$. For an activation neuron, the upper and lower expression is computed using triangle approximation [24], which is briefly explained in Sect. 3.1. To verify the property $x_7 \leq x_8$, DEEPPOLY creates a new expression $x_9 = x_7 - x_8$ and computes the upper bound of x_9. The upper bound of x_9 should not be greater than 0. DEEPPOLY computes the upper bound of x_9 by back substituting the expression of x_7 and x_8 from the previous layer. They continue back substituting until only input layer variables are left. The process of back substitution is shown in Eq. 1. After back substitution, the upper bound of x_9 is computed as 1, which is greater than 0, hence, the DEEPPOLY fails to verify the property.

$$x_9 \leq x_7 - x_8$$
$$x_9 \leq x_5 - x_6 - 1$$
$$x_9 \leq 0.5x_3 + 1 - 1 \qquad (1)$$
$$x_9 \leq 0.5(x_1 + x_2)$$
$$x_9 \leq 1$$

$$-1 \leq x_1 \leq 1 \qquad\qquad -1 \leq x_2 \leq 1$$
$$x_1 + x_2 \leq x_3 \leq x_1 + x_2 \qquad x_1 + x_2 \leq x_4 \leq x_1 + x_2$$
$$0 \leq x_5 \leq 0.5x_3 + 1 \qquad 0 \leq x_6 \leq 0.5x_4 + 1 \qquad (2)$$
$$x_5 \leq x_7 \leq x_5 \qquad\qquad x_6 + 1 \leq x_8 \leq x_6 + 1$$
$$x_7 > x_8 \ \text{(negation of property)}$$

There are two main reasons for the failure of DEEPPOLY. First, it cannot maintain the complete correlation between the neurons. In this example, neurons x_3 and x_4 have the same expression $x_1 + x_2$, so they always get the same value. However, in the DEEPPOLY analysis process, it may fail to get the same value. Second, it uses triangle approximation on RELU neurons. We take the conjunction of upper and lower expressions of each neuron with the negation of the property as shown in Eq. 2, and use the MILP solver to check satisfiability, thus addressing the first issue. The second issue can be resolved either by splitting the bound at zero of the affine node or by using the exact encoding (Eq. 6) instead of triangle approximation. But both solutions increase the problem size exponentially in terms of RELU neurons and this results in a huge blowup if we repair every neuron of the network.

So, the main hurdle toward efficiency is to find the set of important neurons (we call these *marked neurons*), and only repair these. For this, we crucially use the satisfying assignment obtained from the MILP solver. For instance, a possible satisfying assignment of Eq. 2 is in Eq. 3. We execute the neural network with the inputs $x_1 = 1, x_2 = 1$ and get the values on each neuron as shown in Eq. 4. Then we observe that the output values $x_7' = 2, x_8' = 3$ satisfy the property, so, the input $x_1 = 1, x_2 = 1$ is a spurious counterexample. The question is to identify the neuron whose abstraction lead to this imprecision.

$$x_1 = 1, x_2 = 1, x_3 = 2, x_4 = 2, x_5 = 2, x_6 = 0, x_7 = 2, x_8 = 1 \qquad (3)$$
$$x_1' = 1, x_2' = 1, x_3' = 2, x_4' = 2, x_5' = 2, x_6' = 2, x_7' = 2, x_8' = 3 \qquad (4)$$

Maxsat Based Approach to Identify Marked Neurons

To identify the neurons whose abstraction leads to imprecision, let us refer to Fig. 2. In the figure, p_i represents the abstract constraint space in layer l_i, while the solid black line denotes the spurious counterexample depicted in Eq. 3. On the other hand, the dashed green line represents the exact execution of the input point of the spurious counterexample, as denoted by Eq. 4.

The objective is to make the solid black line as close as possible to the dashed green line from the first layer to the last layer while keeping the first and last points the same, i.e., $x_1 = 1$, $x_2 = 1$, and $x_7 = 2$, $x_8 = 1$. The closest line to achieving this goal is represented by the dotted blue line, which is also the abstract execution but exhibits the highest closeness to the exact execution of the spurious counterexample. In this context, v_i refers to the vector of values of neurons in layer l_i of the solid black line, while v_i' and v_i'' represent the vectors of the dashed green and dotted blue lines, respectively.

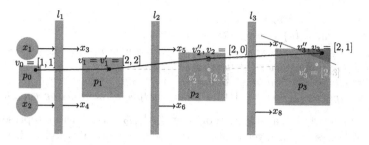

Fig. 2. Pictorial representation of our approach on example in Fig. 1 (Color figure online)

The green and black points are the same for the input layer, i.e., $[1, 1]$. On the first affine layer, l_1 also, the black point v_1 is the same as the green point v'_1 since the affine layer does not introduce any spurious information. For l_2, we try to make v''_2 close to v'_2, such that v''_2 reaches to the v_3. We do that by encoding them as soft constraints (i.e., $\{x_5 = 2, x_6 = 2\}$) while maintaining that the rest of the hard constraints are satisfied (see Eq. 5) e.g., input points $v_0 = v''_0$ and output points $v_3 = v''_3$ remain same. We mark the neurons of the layer where the dotted blue line starts diverging from the dashed green line, i.e., l_2. The divergence we find by the MAXSAT query. If MAXSAT returns all the soft constraints as satisfied, it means the blue point becomes equal to the green point. If MAXSAT returns partial soft constraints as satisfied, we mark the neurons whose soft constraints are not satisfied. In our example, MAXSAT returns soft constraints $\{x_5 = 2\}$ as satisfied, it means soft constraint of x_6 could not satisfied, so, we mark x_6. The dotted blue and solid black lines are the same for our motivating example since it contains only one ReLU layer. However, in general, it may or may not be the same. We optimize the dotted blue line to be close to the dashed green line while also resulting in as few marked neurons as possible.

$$x_1 = 1 \wedge x_2 = 1$$
$$x_3 = x_1 + x_2 \wedge x_4 = x_1 + x_2$$
$$0 \leq x_5 = 0.5x_3 + 1 \wedge 0 \leq x_6 \leq 0.5x_4 + 1$$
$$x_7 = x_5 \wedge x_8 = x_6 + 1$$
$$x_7 = 2 \wedge x_8 = 1$$
$$(5)$$

Once we have x_6 as the marked neuron, we use an *MILP based approach*, and add the exact encoding of the marked neuron (x_6) in addition to the constraints in Equation (2) and check the satisfiability, now it becomes UNSAT, hence, the property verified (see Eq. 6 for more details).

3   Preliminaries

In this section, we present some basic definitions, starting with a neural network.

Definition 1. *A neural network $N = (Neurons, Layers, Edges, W, B, Type)$ is a 6-tuple, where*

- *Neurons is the set of neurons in N,*
- *Layers = $\{l_0, ..., l_k\}$ is an indexed partition of Neurons,*
- *Edges $\subseteq \bigcup_{i=1}^{k} l_{i-1} \times l_i$ is a set of edges linking neurons on consecutive layers,*
- *$W : Edges \mapsto \mathbb{R}$ is a weight function on edges,*
- *$B : Neurons \mapsto \mathbb{R}$ is a bias function on neurons,*
- *$Type : Layers \mapsto \{\text{AFFINE}, \text{RELU}\}$ defines type of neurons on each layer.*

A neural network is a collection of layers $l_0, l_1, l_2, ...l_k$, where k represents the number of layers. Each layer contains neurons that are also indexed, with n_{ij} denoting the jth neuron of layer l_i. We call l_0 and l_k the *input* and *output layers* respectively, and all other layers as *hidden layers*. In our presentation, we assume separate layers for the activation functions. Though there are different kinds of activations, we focus only on RELU, hence each layer can either be AFFINE or RELU layer. The definition of W and B applies only to the AFFINE layer. Without loss of generality, we assume that the output layer is an AFFINE layer (we can always append an identity AFFINE layer), and layers $l_1, l_3, l_5, ..., l_k$ to be the AFFINE layers, layers $l_2, l_4, l_6, ..., l_{k-1}$ to be the RELU layers. If $Type_i = $ RELU, then $|l_{i-1}| = |l_i|$. We extend the weight function from edges to layers using matrix $W_i \in \mathbb{R}^{|l_i| \times |l_{i-1}|}$ that represents the weight for layer l_i, s.t.,

$$W_i[t_1, t_2] = \begin{cases} W(e) & e = (n_{(i-1)t_2}, n_{it_1}) \in Edges, \\ 0 & \text{otherwise.} \end{cases}$$

We also write matrix $B_i \in \mathbb{R}^{|l_i| \times 1}$ to denote the bias matrix for layer l_i. The entry $B_i[t, 0] = B(n_{it})$, where $n_{it} \in Neurons$.

To define the semantics of N, we will use vectors $val_i = [val_{i1}, val_{i2}, ...val_{i|l_i|}]$ that represent the values of each neuron in the layer l_i. Let f_i be a function that computes the output vector of values at layer i using the values at layer $i-1$ as $val_i = f_i(val_{i-1})$. For each type the layer the functions are defined as follows: if $Type_i = $ AFFINE, then $f_i(val_{i-1}) = W_i * val_{i-1} + B_i$; if $Type_i = $ RELU, then $f_i(val_{i-1})_j = max(val_{(i-1)j}, 0)$. Then, the semantics of a neural network N is a function (we abuse notation and also denote this function as N) which takes an input, an $|l_0|$-dimensional vector of reals and gives as output an $|l_k|$-dimensional vector of reals, as a composition of functions $f_k \circ ... \circ f_1$. Thus, for an input $v \in \mathbb{R}^{|l_0|}$, we write its value computed by N at layer i as $val_i^v = f_i \circ ... \circ f_1(v)$.

Let us define $LinExpr = \{w_0 + \sum_i w_i x_i | w_i \in \mathbb{R}$ and x_i is a real variable$\}$ and $LinConstr = \{expr$ op $0|expr \in LinExpr \wedge op \in \{\leq, =\}\}$. A *predicate* is a Boolean combination of $LinConstr$. We use real variable x_{ij} to represent values of n_{ij} in the predicates. Let P and Q be predicates over input and output layers respectively. A *verification query* is a triple $\langle N, P, Q \rangle$. We need to prove that for each input v, if $v \models P$, $N(v) \models Q$. We assume P has the form $\bigwedge_{i=1}^{|l_0|} lb_{0i} \leq x_{0i} \leq ub_{0i}$, where lb_{0i}, ub_{0i} are lower and upper bounds respectively for a neuron n_{0i}.

3.1 DeepPoly

We develop our abstract refinement approaches on top of abstraction based method DEEPPOLY [24], which uses a combination of well-understood polyhedra [35] and box [36] abstract domain. The abstraction maintains upper and lower linear expressions as well as upper and lower bounds for each neuron. The variables appearing in upper and lower expressions are only from the predecessor layer. Formally, we define the abstraction as follows.

Definition 2. *For a neuron n, an abstract constraint $A(n) = (lb, ub, lexpr, uexpr)$ is a tuple, where $lb \in \mathbb{R}$ is lower bound on the value of n, $ub \in \mathbb{R}$ is the upper bound on the value of n, $lexpr \in LinExpr$ is the expression for the lower bound, and $uexpr \in LinExpr$ is the expression for the upper bound.*

In DEEPPOLY, we compute the abstraction A as follows.

- If $Type_i = $ AFFINE, we set $A(x_{ij}).lexpr := A(x_{ij}).uexpr := \sum_{t=1}^{|l_{i-1}|} W_i[j,t] * x_{(i-1)t} + B_i[j,0]$. We compute $A(x_{ij}).lb$ and $A(x_{ij}).ub$ by back substituting the variables in $A(x_{ij}).lexpr$ and $A(x_{ij}).uexpr$ respectively up to input layer. Since P of the verification query has lower and upper bounds of the input layer, we can compute the bounds for x_{ij}. Consider the neuron x_3 in Fig. 1. Both its upper and lower constraints are same, represented by the expression $x_1 + x_2$. To compute the upper bound of x_3, we substitute the upper bounds of x_1 and x_2, which are both 1. Consequently, the upper bound is calculated as $2(1 + 1)$. Similarly, for the lower bound of x_3, we substitute the lower bounds of x_1 and x_2, which are both -1. Thus, the lower bound is computed as $-2(-1 + -1)$.

- If $Type_i = $ RELU and $y = $ RELU(x), where x is a neuron in l_{i-1} and y is a neuron in l_i, we consider the following three cases:
  1. If $A(x).lb \geq 0$ then RELU is in active phase and $A(y).lexpr := A(y).uexpr := x$, and $A(y).lb := A(x).lb$ and $A(y).ub := A(x).ub$
  2. If $A(x).ub \leq 0$ then RELU is in passive phase and $A(y).lexpr := A(y).uexpr := 0$, and $A(y).lb := A(y).ub := 0$.
  3. If $A(x).lb < 0$ and $A(x).ub > 0$, the behavior of RELU is uncertain, and we need to apply over-approximation. We set $A(y).uexpr := u(x - l)/(u - l)$, where $u = A(x).ub$ and $l = A(x).lb$. And $A(y).lexpr := \lambda.x$, where $\lambda \in \{0, 1\}$. We can choose any value of λ dynamically. We compute $A(y).lb$ and $A(y).ub$ by doing the back-subtitution similar to the AFFINE layer's neuron. Consider the neuron x_5 in Fig. 1, whose input is x_3. Since x_3's upper bound is positive and lower bound is negative, the behavior of x_5 becomes uncertain. The upper expression of x_5 is computed using the above method as $0.5 * x_3 + 1$. By backsubstituting the upper expression of x_3, it becomes $0.5(x_1 + x_2) + 1$. Using the upper bounds of x_1 and x_2, x_5's upper bound is computed as 2. On the other hand, the lower expression of x_5 remains 0, by taking the value of λ as 0.

The constraints for an AFFINE neuron are exact because it is just an AFFINE transformation of input neurons. The constraints for a RELU neuron are also exact if the RELU is either in the active or passive phase. The constraints for RELU are over-approximated if the behavior of RELU is uncertain. Although we may compute exact constraints for this case, but the constraints will be arbitrary polyhedron, which are expensive to compute. The DEEPPOLY abstraction finds a balance between precision and efficiency.

For the verification query $\langle N, P, Q \rangle$, we check if $\neg Q \wedge \bigwedge_{j=1}^{|l_k|} lb_{kj} \leq x_{kj} \leq ub_{kj}$ are satisfiable. If the formula is unsatisfied then we have proven the query successfully. Otherwise, DEEPPOLY fails to prove the query.

3.2 Solver

In our algorithms, we use two major calls CHECKSAT and MAXSAT. The function CHECKSAT in Algorithm 2, takes a quantifier-free formula as input and returns SAT or UNSAT. The function MAXSAT in the Algorithm 3 takes two arguments as input HARDCONSTR and SOFTCONSTR. The HARDCONSTR is a Boolean formula of constraints, and SOFTCONSTR is a set of constraints. The function MAXSAT satisfies the maximum number of constraints in SOFTCONSTR while satisfying the HARDCONSTR. The function MAXSAT returns SAT with the set of constraints satisfied in SOFTCONSTR, or returns UNSAT if HARDCONSTR fails to satisfy. We are using Gurobi(v9.1) [30] to implement both CHECKSAT and MAXSAT functions. Furthermore, Algorithm 2 includes a function called GETMODEL, which serves as a mapping from variables to satisfying values. The GETMODEL function is utilized in cases where CHECKSAT returns SAT to retrieve the satisfying assignment for the variables.

4   Algorithm

In this section, we present our method to refine DEEPPOLY. DEEPPOLY is a sound and incomplete technique because it does over-approximations. If DEEP-POLY verifies the property then the property is guaranteed to be verified, otherwise, its result is unknown. We overcome this limitation by using a CEGAR-like technique, which is complete. In our refinement approach, we mark some RELU neurons to have exact behavior on top of DEEPPOLY constraints, similar to the strategy of refinement in the most complete state-of-the-art techniques [14,15]. We add the encoding of the exact behavior to the DEEPPOLY constraints and use an MILP solver on the extended constraints to check if the extra constraints rule out all spurious counterexamples. The calls to MILP solvers are expensive, therefore we use the spurious counterexamples discovered to identify as small as possible set of marked neurons which suffice to be repaired.

4.1 The Top Level Algorithm

We start by describing Algorithm 1, where we present the top-level flow of our approach. The algorithm takes a verification query $\langle N, P, Q \rangle$ as input, where N is a neural network and P, Q are predicates over input and output layers respectively, and returns success if the verification is successful. Otherwise it returns a counterexample to the query. The algorithm uses supporting algorithms

---

Algorithm 1. A CEGAR based approach of neural network verification

---

Input: A verification problem $\langle N, P, Q \rangle$
Output: Verified or Counterexample

1: $\mathsf{cex}, bounds = preprocessing(N, P, Q)$
2: **if** cex is not None **then**
3:      **return** Failed(cex)   ▷ cex is a counter example
4: $A := \text{DEEPPOLY}(N, P, bounds)$ ▷ use DEEPPOLY to generate abstract constraints.
5: $marked := \{\}$
6: **while** True **do**
7:      result $=$ ISVERIFIED($\langle N, P, Q \rangle, A, marked$)
8:      **if** result $=$ CEX($v_0, v_1...v_k$) **then**
9:          **if** $N(v_0) \models \neg Q$ **then**
10:              **return** Failed(v_0)   ▷ v_0 is a counter example
11:          **else**
12:              $markedNt := \text{GETMARKEDNEURONS}(N, A, marked, v_0, v_1...v_k)$
13:              $marked := marked \cup markedNt$
14:      **else**
15:          **return** verified

GETMARKEDNEURONS and ISVERIFIED (described subsequently) to get more marked neurons to refine and check the validity of the verification query after refinement.

The first line of the algorithm performs preprocessing steps similar to state-of-the-art tools (e.g. $\alpha\beta$-CROWN). These preprocessing steps are optional and are explained in more detail in Sect. 5, where they are used to compare our results with those of state-of-the-art tools. The fourth line of Algorithm 1 generates all the abstract constraints by using DEEPPOLY, as described in Sect. 3.1. For a node $n_{ij} \in N.neurons$, the abstract constraints consist of the lower and upper constraints as well as the lower and upper bounds. Let $A.lc_i = \bigwedge_{j=1}^{|l_i|} A(n_{ij}).lexpr \leq x_{ij} \leq A(n_{ij}).uexpr$, which is a conjunction of upper and lower constraints of each neuron of layer l_i with respect to abstract constraint A. The $lexpr$ and $uexpr$ for any neuron of a layer contain variables only from the previous layer's neurons, hence $A.lc_i$ contains the variables from layers l_{i-1} and l_i. If the preprocessing steps in line 1 are applied, then DEEPPOLY generates the $lexpr$ and $uexpr$ for RELU neurons as per the triangle approximation. In this case, we may return a counter-example and stop or use these bounds without performing any back-substitution.

At line 5, we initialize the variable $marked$ to the empty set of neurons. At the next line, we iterate in a while loop until either we verify the query or find a counterexample. At line 7, we call ISVERIFIED with the verification query, abstraction A, and the set of marked neurons. In this verification step, the behavior of the marked neurons is encoded exactly, as detailed in Sect. 4.2. The call either returns that the query is verified or returns an abstract counterexample, which is defined as follows.

Algorithm 2. Verify $\langle N, P, Q \rangle$ with abstraction A

Name: IsVERIFIED
Input: Verification query $\langle N, P, Q \rangle$, abstract constraints A, $marked \subseteq N.neurons$
Output: verified or an abstract counterexample.

1: $constr := P \wedge (\bigwedge_{i=1}^{k} A.lc_i) \wedge \neg Q$
2: $constr := constr \wedge (\bigwedge_{n \in marked} exactConstr(n))$ ▷ as in Equation 6
3: $isSat = checkSat(constr)$
4: **if** isSat **then**
5:      $m := getModel(constr)$
6:      **return** $CEX(m(x_0), ..., m(x_k))$ ▷ Abstract counter example where x_i is a vector of variables in layer l_i
7: **else**
8:      **return** verified

Definition 3. *A sequence of value vectors* $v_0, v_1, ..., v_k$ *is an* abstract execution *of abstract constraint* A *if* $v_0 \models lc_0$ *and* $v_{i-1}, v_i \models A.lc_i$ *for each* $i \in [1, k]$. *An abstract execution* $v_0, ..., v_k$ *is an* abstract counterexample *if* $v_k \models \neg Q$.

If these algorithms return verified, we are done, otherwise we analyze the abstract counterexample $CEX(v_0, ..., v_k)$. The abstract counterexample $CEX(v_0, ..., v_k)$ may or may not be a real counterexample, so, we first check at line 8, if executing the neural network N on input v_0 violates the predicate Q. If yes, we report input v_0 as a counterexample, for which the verification query is not true. Otherwise, we declare the abstract counterexample to be spurious. We call GETMARKEDNEURONS to analyze the counterexample and return the cause of spuriousness, which is a set of neurons $markedNt$. We add the new set $markedNt$ to the old set $marked$ and iterate our loop with the new set of marked neurons. Now let us present IsVERIFIED and GETMARKEDNEURONS in detail.

4.2 Verifying Query Under Marked Neurons

In Algorithm 2, we present the implementation of IsVERIFIED, which takes the verification query, the DEEPPOLY abstraction A, and a set of marked neurons as input. At line 1, we construct constraints $contr$ that encodes the executions that satisfy abstraction A at every step. At line 2, we also include constraints in $constr$ that encodes the exact behavior of the marked neurons. The following is the encoding of the exact behavior [37] of neuron n_{ij}.

$$exactConstr(n_{ij}) := x_{(i-1)j} \leq x_{ij} \leq x_{(i-1)j} - A(n_{(i-1)j}).lb * (1 - a) \wedge \atop 0 \leq x_{ij} \leq A(n_{(i-1)j}).ub * a \wedge a \in \{0, 1\} \tag{6}$$

where a is a fresh variable for each neuron.

At line 3, we call a solver to find a satisfying assignment of the constraints. If $constr$ is satisfiable, we get a model m. From the model m, we extract an abstract counterexample and return it. If $constr$ is unsatisfiable, we return that the query is verified.

Algorithm 3. Marked neurons from counterexample

Name: GETMARKEDNEURONS
Input: Neural network N, DEEPPOLY abstraction A, $marked \subseteq N.neurons$, and abstract counterexample $(v_0, v_1...v_k)$
Output: New marked neurons.

1: Let $val_{ij}^{v_0}$ be the value of n_{ij}, when v_0 is input of N.
2: **for** $i = 1$ to k **do**   ▷ inputLayer excluded
3:    **if** l_i is RELU layer **then**
4:        $constr := \bigwedge_{t=i}^{k} A.lc_t$
5:        $constr := constr \wedge (\bigwedge_{n \in marked} exactConstr(n))$ ▷ as in Equation 6
6:        $constr := constr \wedge \bigwedge_{j=1}^{|l_{i-1}|} (x_{(i-1)j} = val_{(i-1)j}^{v_0})$
7:        $constr := constr \wedge \bigwedge_{j=1}^{|l_k|} (x_{kj} = v_{kj})$
8:        $softConstrs := \bigcup_{j=1}^{|l_i|} (x_{ij} = val_{ij}^{v_0})$
9:        $res, softsatSet := $ MAXSAT$(constr, softConstrs)$ ▷ res always SAT
10:       $newMarked := \{n_{ij} | 1 \leq j \leq |l_i| \wedge (x_{ij} = val_i(j)) \notin softsatSet\}$
11:       **if** $newMarked$ is empty **then**
12:           continue
13:       **else**
14:           **return** $newMarked$

4.3 Maxsat Based Approach to Find the Marked Neurons

In Algorithm 3, we present GETMARKEDNEURONS which analyzes an abstract spurious counterexample. In our abstract constraints, we encode AFFINE neurons exactly, but over-approximate RELU neurons. We identify a set of marked neurons whose exact encoding will eliminate the counterexample in the future analysis. As we defined earlier, let $val_i^{v_0}$ represent the value vector on layer l_i, if we execute the neural network on input v_0. Let us say $v_0, v_1, ..., v_k$ is an abstract spurious counterexample. We iteratively modify the counterexample such that its values coincides with $val_i^{v_0}$. Initially, $val_0^{v_0}$ is equal to v_0. Since we encode the affine layer exactly in $A.lc_i$, the following theorem follows.

Theorem 1. Let $v_0, v_1, ...v_k$ be an abstract execution. For all $1 \leq i \leq k$, if $Type_i = $ AFFINE and $val_{i-1}^{v_0} = v_{i-1}$, then $val_i^{v_0} = v_i$.

By the above theorem, v_1 and $val_1^{v_1}$ are also equal. The core idea of our algorithm is to find v_2' as close as possible to $val_2^{v_0}$, such that $v_0, v_1, v_2', ...v_{k-1}', v_k$ becomes an abstract spurious counterexample. We measure closeness by the number of elements of v_2' are equal to the corresponding element of vector $val_2^{v_0}$.

1. If v_2' is equal to $val_2^{v_0}$ then v_3' will also become equal to $val_3^{v_0}$ due to Theorem 1. Now we move on to the next RELU layer l_4 and try to find the similar point v_4', such that $v_0, v_1, v_2, v_3, v_4''...v_{k-1}'', v_k$ is an abstract spurious counterexample. We repeat this process until the following case occurs.
2. If at some i, we can not make v_i' equal to $val_i^{v_0}$ then we collect the neurons whose values are different in v_i' and $val_i^{v_0}$. We call them marked neurons.

In the algorithm, the above description is implemented using MAXSAT solver. The loop at line 2 iterates over RELU layers. Line 4 builds the abstract constraints generated by DEEPPOLY from layer i onwards. Line 5 encodes the exact encoding of marked neurons, i.e. x_6 is identified as a marked neuron in our motivating example. Line 6 and 7 ensure layer l_{i-1}'s neurons have value equal to $val_{i-1}^{v_0}$, and the execution finishes at v_k. The first and last line of Eq. 5 represents the constrains of line 6 and line 7, in our motivating example. At Line 8, we construct soft constraints, which encodes x_{ij} is equal to $val_i^{v_0}$. In our motivating example, the set $\{x_5 = 2, x_6 = 2\}$ represents the soft constraints. At line 9, we call MAXSAT solver. This call to MAXSAT solver will always find a satisfying assignment because our hard constraints are always satisfiable. The solver will also return a subset $softsatSet$ of the soft constraints. At line 10, we check which soft constraints are missing in $softsatSet$. The corresponding neurons are added in $newMarked$. If $newMarked$ is empty, we have managed to find a spurious abstract counterexample from $val_i^{v_0}$ and we go to the next layer. Otherwise, we return the new set of marked neurons.

4.4   Proofs of Progress and Termination

Our refinement strategy ensures progress, i.e., the spurious counterexample does not repeat in the future iterations of Algorithm 1. Let us suppose the algorithm GETMARKEDNEURONS gets the abstract spurious counterexample $v_0, v_1, ...v_k$ and returns marked neurons in some iteration of the while loop, say i^{th}-iteration. The call to MAXSAT at line 10 declares that $constr \wedge softsatSet$ is satisfiable. We can extract an abstract spurious counterexample from a model of $constr \wedge softsatSet$. Let m be the model. Let the abstract spurious counterexample be $cex = val_0^{v_0}, ..., val_{i-1}^{v_0}, v_i', ..., v_{k-1}', v_k$. Before the iteration i, cex follows the execution of N on input v_0. After the iteration i, we use the model to construct cex, i.e., $m(x_i) = v_i'$.

Lemma 1. *In the rest of run of Algorithm 1, i.e., future iterations of the while loop, ISVERIFIED will not return the abstract spurious counterexample cex again.*

Proof. For $n_{ij} \in newMarked$, the MAXSAT query ensures that $val_{ij}^{v_0} \neq v_{ij}'$. If we have the same counterexample again in the future then input of n_{ij} will be $val_{(i-1)j}^{v_0}$. Since we will have exact encoding for n_{ij}, the output will be $val_{ij}^{v_0}$, which contradicts the earlier inequality.

Next, we turn to termination of the algorithm. We have two lemmmas.

Lemma 2. *In every refinement iteration GETMARKEDNEURONS returns a non-empty set of marked neurons.*

Proof. By the definition of abstract spurious counterexample, $v_k \models \neg Q$. By the check at line 6 of Algorithm 1 $val_k^{v_0} \models Q$. If the set of returned new marked neurons is empty, $newMarked = \emptyset$ for each layer. Therefore, all the neurons in any layer l_i become equal to $val_i^{v_0}$, which implies v_k equals to $val_k^{v_0}$, but $v_k \models \neg Q$ and $val_k^{v_0} \models Q$, which is a contradiction.

Lemma 3. *In every refinement iteration* GETMARKEDNEURONS *returns marked neurons, which were not marked in previous iterations.*

Proof. We will show that if a neuron n_{ij} got marked in t^{th} iteration then n_{ij} will not be marked again in any iteration greater than t. Consider an iteration $t' > t$, if we get the marked neurons from layer other than l_i then n_{ij} can not be part of it because n_{ij} is in layer l_i. Consider the case where marked neurons are from the layer l_i in t'^{th} iteration. Since we have made n_{ij} exact in line 6 of Algorithm 3, its behavior while optimizing constraints will be same as the exact RELU. Moreover, $v'_{ij} = val^{v_0}_{ij}$, which implies the soft constraint for neuron n_{ij} will always be satisfied. Hence it will not occur as a marked neuron as per the criteria of new marked neurons in line 10 of Algorithm 3.

Lemmas 2 and 3 imply that in every iteration GETMARKEDNEURONS returns a nonempty set of unmarked neurons, which will now be marked. In worst case, the algorithm will mark all the neurons of the network, and encode them in the exact behavior. Thus, we conclude,

Theorem 2. *Algorithm 1 always terminates.*

5   Experiments

We have implemented our approach in a prototype and compared it to three types of approaches (i) DEEPPOLY [24] and its refinements KPOLY [31], DEEP-SRGR [28], (ii) other cegar based approaches, and (iii) state-of-the-art tools $\alpha\beta$-CROWN [14,15,23,37,38], OVAL [34,39–43], and MARABOU [11]. Furthermore, we conducted a comparison of performance across different epsilon values for all the tools employed. We extended this analysis to focus specifically on adversarially trained networks and observed a significant improvement in performance. Moreover, we conducted a detailed comparison with $\alpha\beta$-CROWN, utilizing the same preprocessing steps employed by the $\alpha\beta$-CROWN tool.

The tools $\alpha\beta$-CROWN and OVAL use a set/portfolio of different algorithms and optimizations. $\alpha\beta$-CROWN achieved the first rank consistently in both VNN-COMP'21 and VNN-COMP'22 (International Verification of Neural Networks Competitions)[1]. We use the same configuration to run $\alpha\beta$-CROWN and OVAL, which these tools used in VNN-COMP.

Implementation. We have implemented our techniques in a tool, which we call DREFINE, in C++ programming language. The tool DREFINE is available at https://github.com/afzalmohd/VeriNN/tree/atva2023. Our approach relies on DEEPPOLY, so we also have implemented DEEPPOLY in C++. We are using a

---

[1] We could not compare with VERINET, which is the 2nd and 3rd of VNNCOMP 2021 and VNNCOMP 2022 respectively, as we had difficulties with its external solver's (XPRESS) license. We also could not compare with MN-BaB since it required GPU to run. Also, since we are comparing with DEEPPOLY and KPOLY, and ERAN uses these techniques internally, we skipped a direct comparison with ERAN.

Neural Network	#hidden layers	#activation units	Defensive training
3×50	2	110	None
3×100	2	210	None
5×100	4	410	None
6×100	5	510	DiffAI
9×100	8	810	None
6×200	5	1010	None
9×200	8	1610	None
6×500	6	3000	None
6×500	6	3000	PGD, $\epsilon = 0.1$
6×500	6	3000	PGD, $\epsilon = 0.3$
4×1024	3	3072	None

(a)

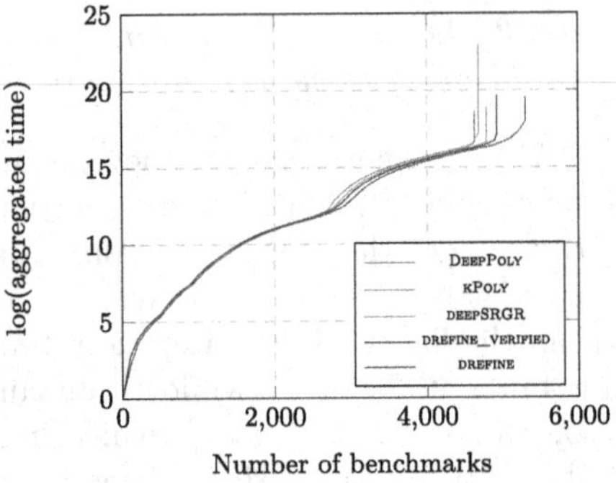

(b)

Fig. 3. (a) Neural networks details (b) Cactus plot [46] with related techniques: The x-axis represents the number of benchmarks solved, sorted in increasing order based on the time taken to solve them. The y-axis represents the cumulative sum of the time taken to solve the benchmarks up to a certain point on the x-axis.

C++ interface of the tool Gurobi [30] to check the satisfiability as well as solve MAXSAT queries.

Benchmarks. We use the MNIST [44] dataset to check the effectiveness of our tool and comparisons. We use 11 different fully connected feedforward neural networks with RELU activation, as shown in Fig. 3(a). These benchmarks are taken from the DEEPPOLY's paper [24]. The input and output dimensions of each network are 784 and 10, respectively. The authors of DEEPPOLY used projected gradient descent (PGD) [32] and DiffAI [45] for adversarial training. Figure 3(a) contains the defended network i.e. trained with adversarial training, as well as the undefended network. The last column of Fig. 3(a) shows how the defended networks were trained.

The predicate P on the input layer is created using the input image im and user-defined parameter ϵ. We first normalize each pixel of im between 0 and 1, then create $P = \bigwedge_{i=1}^{|l_0|} im(i) - \epsilon \leq x_{0i} \leq im(i) + \epsilon$, such that the lower and upper bound of each pixel should not exceed 0 and 1, respectively. The predicate Q on the output layer is created using the network's output. Suppose the predicted label of im on network N is y, then $Q = \bigwedge_{i=1}^{|l_k|} x_{ki} < y$, where $i \neq y$. One query instance $\langle N, P, Q \rangle$ is created for one network, one image, and one epsilon value. In our evaluation, we took 11 different networks, 8 different epsilons, and 100 different images. The total number of instances is 8800. However, there are 304 instances for which the network's predicted label differs from the image's actual label. We avoided such instances and consider a total of 8496 benchmark instances.

5.1 Results

We conducted the experiments on a machine with 64 GB RAM, 2.20 GHz INTEL(R) XEON(R) CPU E5-2660 v2 processor with CentOS Linux 7 operating system. To make a fair comparison between the tools, we provide only a single CPU, and 2000 seconds timeout for each instance for each tool. We use vanilla DEEPPOLY (i.e., DEEPPOLY without preprocessing in line 1 of Algorithm 1) to generate the abstract constraints of benchmarks instances. Figure 3(b) represents the cactus plot of (log of) time taken vs the number of benchmarks solved for the most related techniques. Table 1 and 2 represent a pairwise comparison of the number of instances that a tool could solve which another couldn't (more precisely, the (i, j)-entry of the table is the number of instances which could be verified by tool i but not by tool j), and Fig. 4, compares wrt epsilon, the robustness parameter.

Comparison with the Most Related Techniques: In this subsection, we consider the techniques DEEPPOLY, KPOLY, and DEEPSRGR to compare with ours. We consider DEEPPOLY because it is at the base of our technique, and the techniques KPOLY and DEEPSRGR refine DEEPPOLY just as we do. These tools only report VERIFIED instances, while our tool can report VERIFIED and counter-example. Hence, we compare these techniques with only VERIFIED instances of our technique in the line of DREFINE_VERIFIED in cactus plot Fig. 3(b).

Our technique outperforms the others in terms of the verified number of instances. One can also see that when they do verify, DEEPPOLY and KPOLY are often more efficient, which is not surprising, while our tool is more efficient than DEEPSRGR. From Table 1, we also see that our tool solves all the benchmark instances which are solved by these three techniques (and in fact around ∼700 more), except 14 instances where KPOLY succeeds and our tool times out.

Comparison with Cegar Based Techniques: CEGAR_NN [27] is a tool that also uses counter example guided refinement. But the abstraction used is quite different from DEEPPOLY. This tool reduces the size of the network by merging similar neurons, such that they maintain the overapproximation and split back in the refinement process. We can conclude from Table 1 that CEGAR_NN verified only 18.88%, while our tool verified 61.42% of the total number of benchmark instances. Although, in total CEGAR_NN solves significantly fewer benchmarks, it is pertinent to note that this technique solves many unique benchmark instances as can be inferred from Table 1.

Comparison with State-of-the-Art Solvers: The tools $\alpha\beta$-CROWN and OVAL use several algorithms that are highly optimized and use several techniques. The authors of $\alpha\beta$-CROWN implement the techniques [14,15,23,37,38], and the authors of OVAL implement [34,39–43]. The authors of MARABOU implement the technique [11]. Table 1 shows that all three tools indeed solve about

Table 1. Pairwise comparison of tools, e.g. entry on row KPOLY and column DEEPPOLY represents 156 benchmark instances on which KPOLY verified but DEEPPOLY fails. The green row highlights the number of solved benchmark instances by DREFINE and not others while the red column is the opposite.

Unverified / Verified	DEEPPOLY	KPOLY	DEEPSRGR	CEGAR_NN	αβ-CROWN	OVAL	MARABOU	DREFINE	TOTAL
DEEPPOLY	0	0	0	3708	63	66	383	0	4633
KPOLY	156	0	114	3760	63	66	389	14	4789
DEEPSRGR	54	2	0	3736	63	66	401	0	4687
CEGAR_NN	713	609	687	0	217	238	87	417	1624
αβ-CROWN	1672	1516	1618	4821	0	84	944	1095	6242
OVAL	1622	1466	1568	4789	31	0	902	1052	6189
MARABOU	2042	1892	2006	4741	994	1005	0	1624	6292
DREFINE	694	552	640	4106	180	190	655	0	5327

1000 (out of 8496) more than we do[2]. However, we found around 180 benchmarks instances where $\alpha\beta$-CROWN fails, and our tool works, and around 190 benchmarks on which OVAL fails and our tool works. Also, around 655 benchmarks where MARABOU fails and our tool works; see Table 1 for more details. In total, we are solving 59 unique benchmarks where all three tools fail to solve. Thus we believe that these tools are truly orthogonal in their strengths and could potentially be combined.

Epsilon vs. Performance: As a sanity check, we analyzed the effect of perturbation size and the performance of the tools. In Fig. 4, we present the comparison of fractional success rate of tools as epsilon grows from 0.005 to 0.05. At $\epsilon = 0.005$, the performance of all the tools is almost the same except CEGAR_NN and MARABOU. As epsilon increases, the success rate of tools drops consistently except CEGAR_NN and MARABOU. Here also, we perform better than DEEPPOLY, KPOLY, DEEPSRGR, and CEGAR_NN, while $\alpha\beta$-CROWN and OVAL perform better. We are performing better compared to MARABOU only when ϵ is less than 0.015.

Comparison with Adversarially Trained Networks: The networks considered for evaluation in this study are the ones corresponding to the 4st, 9th, and 10th rows of Fig. 3(a). These networks have been trained using adversarial techniques, where adversarial examples were generated using standard methods such as PGD/DiffAI, and the network was subsequently trained on these adversarial examples to enhance its robustness. Table 2 presents a pairwise comparison of verifiers on these adversarially trained networks, encompassing a total of 2223 benchmark instances. Our approach demonstrates significant superiority over DEEPPOLY, KPOLY, and DEEPSRGR in terms of performance on these benchmarks. While $\alpha\beta$-CROWN and OVAL outperform our approach by approximately 135 benchmarks, we are still able to solve 75 unique benchmarks that

---

[2] $\alpha\beta$-CROWN outperforms MARABOU in VNN-COMP'22, while in our experiments MARABOU performs better; potential reasons could be difference in benchmarks and that $\alpha\beta$-CROWN uses GPU, while MARABOU uses CPU in VNN-COMP'22.

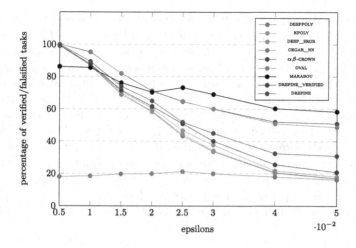

Fig. 4. Size of input perturbation (epsilon) vs. percentage of solved instances

Table 2. Pairwise comparison of tools on adversarially trained networks

Verified \ Unverified	DEEPPOLY	KPOLY	DEEPSRGR	$\alpha\beta$-CROWN	OVAL	DREFINE	TOTAL
DEEPPOLY	0	0	0	3	3	0	1626
KPOLY	9	0	9	5	4	2	1635
DEEPSRGR	2	2	0	3	3	0	1628
$\alpha\beta$-CROWN	302	295	302	0	1	205	1925
OVAL	312	304	310	11	0	214	1935
DREFINE	170	163	168	76	75	0	1796

remain unsolved by both of these tools. Considering the total number of benchmarks is 2223, this indicates a notable number of benchmarks that our approach successfully addresses.

Detailed Comparison with $\alpha\beta$-CROWN with Same Preprocessing: To evaluate the effectiveness of our approach, we conducted a benchmark analysis on the instances where refinement was applied. We applied the same preprocessing steps used by $\alpha\beta$-CROWN to filter the benchmarks.

The preprocessing steps include the so-called PGD (Projected Gradient Descent) attack, followed by CROWN [23] which is an incomplete technique. The PGD attack is a method that can generate counter examples. It works by iteratively updating the perturbation in the direction of the gradient of the loss function with respect to the input data, while constraining the magnitude of the perturbation to be within a predefined limit. If PGD fails, then CROWN runs to generate the over-approximated bounds.

After preprocessing, the total number of benchmarks was reduced to 2362, which were the benchmarks that were not solved by preprocessing steps. *Out of these benchmarks, $\alpha\beta$-CROWN was able to verify 626, while our approach verified 570 benchmarks. Notably, our approach was able to solve 311 benchmarks* that were not solved by $\alpha\beta$-CROWN, while $\alpha\beta$-CROWN solved 366 benchmarks that were not solved by our approach. All 311 benchmarks solved by our approach were from adversarially trained networks, while not a single benchmark out of 366 solved by $\alpha\beta$-CROWN were from adversarially trained networks, suggesting that our approach performs well for such networks, as PGD attack is not very effective on these benchmarks. These results indicate that the majority of the benchmarks (1095) solved by $\alpha\beta$-CROWN and not by our approach, as shown in Table 1, are likely solved by preprocessing steps rather than the refinement procedure. Further, the union of benchmarks solved by both tools results in a total of 937 benchmarks, demonstrating a clear improvement over the number of benchmarks solved by $\alpha\beta$-CROWN alone. This highlights the significant contribution of our technique in the context of portfolio verifiers, as it complements and enhances the overall performance when integrated with other verification tools.

Subroutine Time: We also conducted measurements to determine the average time required by the GETMARKNEURON subroutine and the REFINEMENT subroutine. The GETMARKNEURON subroutine exhibited an average execution time of 15.66 seconds, whereas the REFINEMENT subroutine took 89.69 seconds on average. In comparison, the GETMARKNEURON subroutine accounted for only 14.86% of the total time, which represents a small proportion. Furthermore, we measured the average number of marked neurons, which amounted to 14.81, and the average refinement iteration count, which stood at 3.19. These values also indicate a relatively small magnitude. These findings suggest that integrating our GETMARKNEURON method with an efficient refinement procedure could yield further improvements in overall performance.

6 Conclusion

We have presented a novel cegar-based approach. Our approach comprises two parts. One part finds the causes of spuriousness, while the other part refine the information found in the first part. Experimental evaluation shows that we outperform related refinement techniques, in terms of efficiency and effectivity. We also are able to verify several benchmarks that are beyond state of the art solvers, highly optimized solvers. Our experiments indicate when our technique can be useful and valuable as part of the portfolio of techniques for scalability of robustness verification. As futurework, we plan to extend our technique/tool to make it independent of DEEPPOLY and applicable with other abstraction based techniques and tools.

References

1. Bojarski, M., et al.: End to end learning for self-driving cars. Volume abs/1604.07316 (2016)
2. Amato, F., López, A., Peña-Méndez, E.M., Vaňhara, P., Hampl, A., Havel, J.: Artificial neural networks in medical diagnosis. J. Appl. Biomed. **11**, 47–58 (2013)
3. Hinton, G., et al.: Deep neural networks for acoustic modeling in speech recognition: the shared views of four research groups. IEEE Sig. Process. Mag. **29**(6), 82–97 (2012)
4. Goodfellow, I.J., Shlens, J., Szegedy, C.: Explaining and harnessing adversarial examples. In: Bengio, Y., LeCun, Y. (eds.) 3rd International Conference on Learning Representations, ICLR 2015, San Diego, CA, USA, 7–9 May 2015, Conference Track Proceedings (2015)
5. Katz, G., Barrett, C., Dill, D.L., Julian, K., Kochenderfer, M.J.: Reluplex: a calculus for reasoning about deep neural networks. Formal Methods Syst. Des. **60**, 87–116 (2021). https://doi.org/10.1007/s10703-021-00363-7
6. Lomuscio, A., Maganti, L.: An approach to reachability analysis for feed-forward ReLU neural networks. CoRR, abs/1706.07351 (2017)
7. Fischetti, M., Jo, J.: Deep neural networks and mixed integer linear optimization. Constraints Int. J. **23**(3), 296–309 (2018). https://doi.org/10.1007/s10601-018-9285-6
8. Dutta, S., Jha, S., Sankaranarayanan, S., Tiwari, A.: Output range analysis for deep feedforward neural networks. In: Dutle, A., Muñoz, C., Narkawicz, A. (eds.) NFM 2018. LNCS, vol. 10811, pp. 121–138. Springer, Cham (2018). https://doi.org/10.1007/978-3-319-77935-5_9
9. Cheng, C.-H., Nührenberg, G., Ruess, H.: Maximum resilience of artificial neural networks. In: D'Souza, D., Narayan Kumar, K. (eds.) ATVA 2017. LNCS, vol. 10482, pp. 251–268. Springer, Cham (2017). https://doi.org/10.1007/978-3-319-68167-2_18
10. Katz, G., Barrett, C., Dill, D.L., Julian, K., Kochenderfer, M.J.: Reluplex: an efficient SMT solver for verifying deep neural networks. In: Majumdar, R., Kunčak, V. (eds.) CAV 2017. LNCS, vol. 10426, pp. 97–117. Springer, Cham (2017). https://doi.org/10.1007/978-3-319-63387-9_5
11. Katz, G., et al.: The marabou framework for verification and analysis of deep neural networks. In: Dillig, I., Tasiran, S. (eds.) CAV 2019. LNCS, vol. 11561, pp. 443–452. Springer, Cham (2019). https://doi.org/10.1007/978-3-030-25540-4_26
12. Ehlers, R.: Formal verification of piece-wise linear feed-forward neural networks. In: D'Souza, D., Narayan Kumar, K. (eds.) ATVA 2017. LNCS, vol. 10482, pp. 269–286. Springer, Cham (2017). https://doi.org/10.1007/978-3-319-68167-2_19
13. Huang, X., Kwiatkowska, M., Wang, S., Wu, M.: Safety verification of deep neural networks. In: Majumdar, R., Kunčak, V. (eds.) CAV 2017. LNCS, vol. 10426, pp. 3–29. Springer, Cham (2017). https://doi.org/10.1007/978-3-319-63387-9_1
14. Wang, S., et al.: Beta-CROWN: efficient bound propagation with per-neuron split constraints for neural network robustness verification. In: Advances in Neural Information Processing Systems, vol. 34, pp. 29909–29921 (2021)
15. Xu, K., et al.: Fast and complete: enabling complete neural network verification with rapid and massively parallel incomplete verifiers. CoRR, abs/2011.13824 (2020)
16. Zhang, H., et al.: General cutting planes for bound-propagation-based neural network verification. CoRR, abs/2208.05740 (2022)

17. Dvijotham, K., Stanforth, R., Gowal, S., Mann, T.A., Kohli, P.: A dual approach to scalable verification of deep networks. In: UAI, vol. 1, p. 3 (2018)
18. Gehr, T., Mirman, M., Drachsler-Cohen, D., Tsankov, P., Chaudhuri, S., Vechev, M.T.: AI2: safety and robustness certification of neural networks with abstract interpretation. In: 2018 IEEE Symposium on Security and Privacy, SP 2018, Proceedings, San Francisco, California, USA, 21–23 May 2018, pp. 3–18. IEEE Computer Society (2018)
19. Singh, G., Gehr, T., Mirman, M., Püschel, M., Vechev, M.T.: Fast and effective robustness certification. In: Bengio, S., Wallach, H.M., Larochelle, H., Grauman, K., Cesa-Bianchi, N., Garnett, R. (eds.) Advances in Neural Information Processing Systems 31: Annual Conference on Neural Information Processing Systems 2018, NeurIPS 2018, Montréal, Canada, 3–8 December 2018, pp. 10825–10836 (2018)
20. Singh, G., Gehr, T., Püschel, M., Vechev, M.T.: Boosting robustness certification of neural networks. In: 7th International Conference on Learning Representations, ICLR 2019, New Orleans, LA, USA, May 6–9 2019. OpenReview.net (2019)
21. Weng, L., et al.: Towards fast computation of certified robustness for ReLU networks. In: International Conference on Machine Learning, pp. 5276–5285. PMLR (2018)
22. Wong, E., Kolter, Z.: Provable defenses against adversarial examples via the convex outer adversarial polytope. In: International Conference on Machine Learning, pp. 5286–5295. PMLR (2018)
23. Zhang, H., Weng, T.-W., Chen, P.-Y., Hsieh, C.-J., Daniel, L.: Efficient neural network robustness certification with general activation functions. In: Advances in Neural Information Processing Systems, vol. 31 (2018)
24. Singh, G., Gehr, T., Püschel, M., Vechev, M.: An abstract domain for certifying neural networks. Proc. ACM Program. Lang. 3(POPL), 1–30 (2019)
25. Wang, S., Pei, K., Whitehouse, J., Yang, J., Jana, S.: Formal security analysis of neural networks using symbolic intervals. In: 27th USENIX Security Symposium (USENIX Security 2018), pp. 1599–1614 (2018)
26. Wang, S., Pei, K., Whitehouse, J., Yang, J., Jana, S.: Efficient formal safety analysis of neural networks. In: Advances in Neural Information Processing Systems, pp. 6367–6377 (2018)
27. Elboher, Y.Y., Gottschlich, J., Katz, G.: An abstraction-based framework for neural network verification. In: Lahiri, S.K., Wang, C. (eds.) CAV 2020. LNCS, vol. 12224, pp. 43–65. Springer, Cham (2020). https://doi.org/10.1007/978-3-030-53288-8_3
28. Yang, P., et al.: Improving neural network verification through spurious region guided refinement. In: Groote, J.F., Larsen, K.G. (eds.) TACAS 2021. LNCS, vol. 12651, pp. 389–408. Springer, Cham (2021). https://doi.org/10.1007/978-3-030-72016-2_21
29. Lin, X., Zhu, H., Samanta, R., Jagannathan, S.: ART: abstraction refinement-guided training for provably correct neural networks. In: 2020 Formal Methods in Computer Aided Design, FMCAD 2020, Haifa, Israel, 21–24 September 2020, pp. 148–157. IEEE (2020)
30. Bixby, B.: The gurobi optimizer. Transp. Res. Part B 41(2), 159–178 (2007)
31. Singh, G., Ganvir, R., Püschel, M., Vechev, M.: Beyond the single neuron convex barrier for neural network certification. In: Advances in Neural Information Processing Systems, vol. 32 (2019)
32. Dong, Y., et al.: Boosting adversarial attacks with momentum. In: Proceedings of the IEEE Conference on Computer Vision and Pattern Recognition, pp. 9185–9193 (2018)

33. $\alpha\beta$-CROWN (2021). https://github.com/huanzhang12/alpha-beta-CROWN
34. Bunel, R., Mudigonda, P., Turkaslan, I., Torr, P., Lu, J., Kohli, P.: Branch and bound for piecewise linear neural network verification. J. Mach. Learn. Res. **21**, 1–39 (2020)
35. Cousot, P., Halbwachs, N.: Automatic discovery of linear restraints among variables of a program. In: Proceedings of the 5th ACM SIGACT-SIGPLAN Symposium on Principles of Programming Languages, pp. 84–96 (1978)
36. Cousot, P., Cousot, R.: Abstract interpretation: a unified lattice model for static analysis of programs by construction or approximation of fixpoints. In: Proceedings of the 4th ACM SIGACT-SIGPLAN Symposium on Principles of Programming Languages, pp. 238–252 (1977)
37. Tjeng, V., Xiao, K.Y., Tedrake, R.: Evaluating robustness of neural networks with mixed integer programming. In: 7th International Conference on Learning Representations, ICLR 2019, New Orleans, LA, USA, 6–9 May 2019. OpenReview.net (2019)
38. Zhang, H., et al.: A branch and bound framework for stronger adversarial attacks of ReLU networks. In: International Conference on Machine Learning, pp. 26591–26604. PMLR (2022)
39. Bunel, R.R., Turkaslan, I., Torr, P., Kohli, P., Mudigonda, P.K.: A unified view of piecewise linear neural network verification. In: Advances in Neural Information Processing Systems, vol. 31 (2018)
40. Bunel, R., et al.: Lagrangian decomposition for neural network verification. In: Conference on Uncertainty in Artificial Intelligence, pp. 370–379. PMLR (2020)
41. De Palma, A., Behl, H.S., Bunel, R., Torr, P., Kumar, M.P.: Scaling the convex barrier with active sets. In: Proceedings of the ICLR 2021 Conference. Open Review (2021)
42. De Palma, A., Behl, H.S., Bunel, R., Torr, P.H.S., Kumar, M.P.: Scaling the convex barrier with sparse dual algorithms. CoRR, abs/2101.05844 (2021)
43. De Palma, A., et al.: Improved branch and bound for neural network verification via lagrangian decomposition. CoRR, abs/2104.06718 (2021)
44. Deng, L.: The MNIST database of handwritten digit images for machine learning research [best of the web]. IEEE Sig. Process. Mag. **29**(6), 141–142 (2012)
45. Mirman, M., Gehr, T., Vechev, M.: Differentiable abstract interpretation for provably robust neural networks. In: International Conference on Machine Learning, pp. 3578–3586. PMLR (2018)
46. Brain, M., Davenport, J.H., Griggio, A.: Benchmarking solvers, SAT-style. In: SC^2@ ISSAC (2017)

Author Index

Printed in the United States
by Baker & Taylor Publisher Services